Praise for *George Eliot*

"Convincing."

—*London Review of Books*

"Fresh, graceful, and erudite."

—*Observer* (U.K.)

"[Hughes's approach] brings a sense of close familiarity with this private, inward woman....[A] refreshingly intimate portrait."

—*Kirkus Reviews*

"This excellent, extremely readable biography shows that neither George Eliot nor the Victorians were what we sometimes lazily think them....Hughes is supremely sympathetic toward her subject. Instead of debunking or psychoanalyzing, Hughes simply explains Eliot's motivations, showing how the pressures of her public role took a toll on her happiness and emotional security. And Hughes' treatment of the novels is assured, showing how each grew out of the changing circumstances of Eliot's life, a life that was and remains an inspiration."

—*Newsday*

"Masterly....This exhaustively researched biography, relying on primary texts, reveals Hughes's impressive storytelling ability. She portrays Eliot as a woman of depth and intelligence, one who gave voice to the uncertainties of a tumultuous era. Highly recommended."

—*Library Journal*

"George Eliot cut a controversial yet popular figure in her day....[This] absorbing, exhaustively researched biography befits a subject who, according to the author, was among the most intellectually rigorous writers the nineteenth century produced."

—*Biography Magazine*

"[A] triumph, intelligent, persuasive, and beautifully written."—*London Sunday Times*

"Eliot's emotional and intellectual development and freewheeling complexity are explored with a wonderfully fresh insight and authority....Most praiseworthy, though, is Hughes's ability to relate Eliot's controversial love life with the paradoxical stance of social conservatism that pervades her fiction."

—*Independent on Sunday* (U.K.)

"[An] immensely readable, clear-sighted account of this remarkable novelist's freewheeling life. The intelligent gusto with which [Hughes] performs her task is refreshing and delightful."

—*Independent* (U.K.)

By the same author:

The Victorian Governess

GEORGE ELIOT

The LAST VICTORIAN

KATHRYN HUGHES

Cooper Square Press

First Cooper Square Press Edition 2001

This Cooper Square Press paperback edition of *George Eliot* is an unabridged republication of the edition published in New York in 1999. It is reprinted by arrangement with Farrar, Straus and Giroux, LLC.

Published by Cooper Square Press
An Imprint of the Rowman & Littlefield Publishing Group
150 Fifth Avenue, Suite 817
New York, New York 10011

Distributed by National Book Network

Library of Congress Cataloging-in-Publication Data

Hughes, Kathryn, 1959–
   George Eliot : the last Victorian / George Eliot.
      p. cm.
   Originally published: London : Fourth Estate, 1998.
   Includes bibliographical references (p.) and index.
   ISBN 0-8154-1121-9 (pbk. : alk. paper)
      1. Eliot, George, 1819–1880. 2. Novelists, English—19th century—Biography. I. Title.

PR4681.H84 2001
823'.8—dc21
[B]   2001028024

For my parents
Anne and John Hughes
again

Contents

Illustrations

15. Self-portrait by François D'Albert Durade, courtesy of the Bibliothèque Publique et Universitaire, Geneva.

16. Portrait of John Chapman, courtesy of City of Nottingham Museums: Castle Museum and Art Gallery.

17. Portrait of Herbert Spencer, courtesy of the National Portrait Gallery.

18. George Eliot, from a drawing by Samuel Laurence, 1860 (misdated 1957), courtesy of the Mistress and Fellows of Girton College, Cambridge.

19. Portrait of George Eliot by Frederic Burton (1865), courtesy of the National Portrait Gallery.

20. Photograph of George Eliot by Mayall of Regent Street (1858), courtesy of Hulton Getty Picture Library.

21. Sketch of George Henry Lewes, Agnes Lewes and Thornton Hunt by William Thackeray, courtesy of the National Portrait Gallery.

22. Photograph of George Henry Lewes with Pug (1859), courtesy of the National Portrait Gallery.

23. Photograph of Holly Lodge, Wandsworth, courtesy of the Hulton Getty Picture Library.

24. The old mill at Arbury, watercolour, courtesy of the Mary Evans Picture Library.

25. Portrait of John Blackwood, courtesy of the George Eliot Fellowship.

26. G. H. Lewes, engraving from the *Illustrated London News*, courtesy of the Mary Evans Picture Library.

27. Photograph of the Priory, Regent's Park, courtesy of the Hulton Getty Picture Library.

28. The drawing room at the Priory, engraving from J. W. Cross's *George Eliot's Life*.

29. Barbara Leigh Smith as Bodichon, drawing by Samuel Lawrence (1861), courtesy of the Mistress and Fellows of Girton College, Cambridge.

30. Romola, illustration for the first edition by Frederic Leighton, courtesy of Time, Inc./Mansell/Katz.

Acknowledgements

Several times during the writing of this book I feared that I had turned into Edward Casaubon, the fastidious blocked cleric from *Middlemarch* who has been working for far too long on the 'Key to All Mythologies'. But unlike Casaubon, I did eventually start – and finish – writing and need to thank the many people and institutions who helped me along the way.

Anyone working on George Eliot bears a huge debt to Gordon Haight, the Yale academic who spent his life collecting her letters into nine immaculately edited volumes, as well as producing the excellent biography of 1968. Other Eliot scholars whose work has been particularly helpful include Rosemary Ashton and Ruby Redinger.

The Beinecke Rare Book and Manuscript Library at Yale University, the Warwickshire County Record Office and the Nuneaton Library all allowed me generous access to their manuscript holdings, from which I am very grateful to be permitted to quote. Thanks especially to Jonathan Ouvry, George Henry Lewes's great-great-grandson, for allowing me to cite the unpublished journals of Eliot and Lewes held at Yale. I am also grateful for the help I received from the British Library, the London Library and London University Library.

George Eliot called John Blackwood 'the best of publishers'. I could say the same of Christopher Potter at Fourth Estate, to whom I am very grateful for commissioning this book. My editor Katie Owen provided exactly that blend of insight and enthusiasm which authors fantasise about during the long, dark days of composition. Thanks go too to Ilsa Yardley for her immaculate copy-editing and to Leo Hollis for taking on the picture research. And, of course, I am indebted to Rachel Calder at the Tessa Sayle Agency for first putting me and Eliot together. More personally, I'd like to thank Karen Merrin for her friendship and my brother, Dr Michael Hughes of Brunel University, for hours of phone support, not to mention a crash course in German philosophy. But my greatest debt is to my parents who have never, in all the years I have spent writing about the nineteenth century, hinted that there might be easier ways to make a living.

Kathryn Hughes
London, June 1998

CHAPTER I

'Dear Old Griff'

Early Years
1819–28

IN THE EARLY hours of 22 November 1819 a baby girl was born in a small stone farmhouse, tucked away in the woodiest part of Warwickshire, about four miles from Nuneaton. It was not an important event. Mary Anne was the fifth child and third daughter of Robert Evans, and the terse note Evans made in his diary of her arrival suggests that he had other things to think about that day.[1] As land agent to the Newdigate family of Arbury Hall, the forty-six-year-old Evans was in charge of 7000 acres of mixed arable and dairy farmland, a coal-mine, a canal and, his particular love, miles of ancient deciduous forest, the remnants of Shakespeare's Arden. A new baby, a female too, was not something for which a man like Robert Evans had time to stop.

Six months earlier another little girl, equally obscure in her own way, had been born in a corner of Kensington Palace. Princess Alexandrina Victoria was also the child of a middle-aged man, the fifty-two-year-old Prince Edward of Kent, himself the fourth son of Mad King George III. None of George's surviving twelve children had so far managed to produce a viable heir to succeed the Prince Regent, who was about to take over as king in his own right. It had been made brutally clear to the four elderly remaining bachelors, Edward among them, that the patriotic moment had come to give up their mistresses, acquire legal wives and produce a crop of lusty boys. But despite three sketchy, resentful marriages, the desired heir had yet to appear. Still, at this point it was too soon to give up hope completely. Princess Alexandrina Victoria, born on 24 May 1819, was promisingly robust and her mother, while past thirty, was young enough to try again for a son. If anyone bothered to think ahead for the little girl, the most they might imagine was that she would one day become the elder sister of a great king.

Officially the futures of these two little girls, Mary Anne and Alexandrina Victoria, were not promising. As for every other female child born that year, the worlds of commerce, industry and the professions were closed to them. As adults they would not be able to speak in the House of Commons, or vote for someone to do so on their behalf. They would not be eligible to take a degree at one of the ancient universities, become a lawyer, or manage the economic processes which were turning Britain into the most powerful nation on earth. Instead, their duties would be assumed to lie exclusively at home, whether palace or farmhouse, as companions and carers of husbands, children and ageing parents.

Yet that, as we know, is not what happened. Neither girl lived the life that the circumstances of her birth had seemed to decree. Instead, each emerged from obscurity to define the tone and temper of the age. Princess Alexandrina Victoria, pushed further up the line of succession by her father's early death, even gave her name to it. 'Victorian' became the brand name for a confident, expansive hegemony which was extended absent-mindedly beyond her own lifetime. 'Victorian' was the sound of unassailable depth, stretch and solidity. It meant money in the bank and ships steaming the earth, factories that clattered all night and buildings that stretched for the sky. Its shape was the odd little figure of Victoria herself, sweet and girlish in the early years, fat and biddyish at the end. Wherever 'Victorian' energy and bustle made themselves felt, you could be sure to find that distinctive image, stamped into coins and erected in stone, woven into table-cloths and framed in cheap wood. In its ordinary femininity the figure of Victoria offered the moral counterpoise to all that striving and getting. The solid husband, puffy bosom and string of children represented the kind of good woman for whom Britain was busy getting rich.

George Eliot's image, by contrast, was rarely seen by anyone. Indeed, it was whispered that she was so hideous that, Medusa-like, you only had to look upon her to be turned to stone. And her name, during its early years of fame, suggested the very opposite of Victorianism. Her avowed agnosticism, sexual freedom, commercial success and childlessness were troubling reminders of everything that had been repressed from the public version of life under the great little Queen. By 1860 Victoria and Eliot had come to stand for the twin poles of female behaviour, respectability and disgrace. One gave her name to virtuous repression, a rigid channelling of desire into the safe haven of marriage and family. The other, made wickeder by male disguise, became a symbol of the 'Fallen Woman', banished to the edges of society or, in Eliot's actual case, to a series of dreary suburban exiles.

That was the bluster. In real life – that messy matter which refuses to run along official lines – the Queen and Eliot shared more than distracted, greying fathers. Their emotional inheritance was uncannily similar and pressed their lives into matching moulds. Both had mothers who were intrusive yet remote, a tension which left them edgy for affection until the end of their days. Victoria slept in the Duchess of Kent's room right up to her coronation, while Eliot spent her first thirty years looking for comfortable middle-aged women whom she could call 'Mother'. When it came to men, both clung with the hunger of children rather than the secure attachment of grown women. Prince Albert and George Henry Lewes not only negotiated the public world for their partners, but lavished them with the intense and symbiotic affection usually associated with maternally minded wives. And when both men died before them, their widows fell into an extended stupor which recalled the despair of an abandoned baby.

What roused them in the end were intense connections with new and unsuitable men. The Queen found John Brown, then the Munshi, both servants, one black. Eliot, meanwhile, married John Cross, a banker twenty years younger and with nothing more than a gentleman's education. Menopausal randiness was sniggeringly invoked as the reason for these ludicrous liaisons. Victoria was called 'Mrs Brown' behind her back. And when John Cross had to be fished out of Venice's Grand Canal during his honeymoon, the whisper went round the London clubs that he had preferred to drown rather than make love to the hideous old George Eliot.

Because of Eliot's 'scandalous' private life, which actually the Queen did not think so very bad, there was no possibility of the two women meeting. Yet recognising their twinship, they stalked each other obliquely down the years. Eliot first mentions Victoria in 1848 when, having briefly caught the revolutionary mood, she speaks slangily in a letter of 'our little humbug of a queen'.[2] Ironically, only eleven years later, Victoria had fallen in love with Eliot's first full-length novel, *Adam Bede*, because of what she saw as its social conservatism, its warm endorsement of the *status quo*. The villagers of Hayslope, headed by Adam himself, reminded her of her beloved Highland servants, and in 1861 she commissioned paintings of two of the book's central scenes by the artist Edward Henry Corbould.

George Eliot noticed how hard the Queen took the loss of Prince Albert in 1861 and, aware of the similarities in their age and temperament, wondered how she would manage the dreadful moment when it came to her. The Queen, in turn, was touched by the delicate letter of condolence that Eliot and Lewes wrote to one of her courtier's children on his death and asked whether she might tear off their double signature as a memento.[3]

The Queen's daughters went even further. By the 1870s Eliot's increasing celebrity and the evident stability of her relationship with Lewes meant that she was no longer a total social exile. Among the great and the good who pressed for an introduction were two of the royal princesses. Brisk and bright, Vicky and Louise lobbied behind the scenes for a meeting and then, in Louise's case at least, dispensed with royal protocol by coming up to speak to George Eliot first.[4]

The princesses were among the thousands of ordinary Victorians, neither especially clever nor brave, who ignored the early grim warnings of clergymen and critics about the 'immorality' of George Eliot's life and work. By the 1860s working-class men and middle-class mothers, New Englanders (that most puritan of constituencies) and Jews, Italians and Australians were all reading her. Cheap editions and foreign translations carried George Eliot into every kind of home. Even lending libraries, those most skittishly respectable of 'family' institutions, bowed to consumer demand and grudgingly increased their stock of *Adam Bede* and *The Mill on the Floss*.

What is more, all these Victorians read the damnable George Eliot with an intensity and engagement that was never the case with Dickens or Trollope.

While readers of *Bleak House* might sniff over the death of Jo and even stir themselves to wonder whether something might not be done for crossing-sweepers in general, they did not bombard Dickens with letters asking how they should live. That intimate engagement was reserved for Eliot, who alone seemed to understand the pain and difficulty of being alive in the nineteenth century. From around the world, men and women wrote to her begging for advice about the most personal matters, from marriage through God to their own poetry. Or else, like Princess Louise, they stalked her at concert halls, hoping for a word or a glance.

The worries which Eliot's troubled readers laid before her concerned the dislocations of a social and moral world that was changing at the speed of light. Here were the doubts and disorientations that had been displaced from that triumphant version of Victorianism. An exploding urban population, for instance, might well suggest bustling productivity, but it could also mean a growing sense of social anomie. Rural communities were indeed invigorated by their new proximity to big towns, but they were also losing their fittest sons and daughters to factories and, later, to offices and shops. Meanwhile the suburbs, conceived as a *rus in urbe*, pleased no one, least of all George Eliot, who spent five years hating Richmond and Wandsworth for their odd mix of nosy neighbours and lack of real green.

For if in one way Victorians felt more separate from each other, in others they were being offered opportunities to come together as never before. It was not just the railway that was changing the psycho-geography of the country, bringing friends, enemies and business partners into constant contact. The postal service, democratised in 1840 by the introduction of the Penny Post, allowed letters to fly from one end of the country to the other at a pace that makes our own mail service look like a slowcoach. Then there was the telephone which, at the end of her life, George Eliot was invited to try. As a result of these changes Victorians found themselves pulled in two directions. Scattering from their original communities, they spent the rest of their lives trying to reconstitute these earlier networks in imaginary forms.

Science, too, was taking away the old certainties and replacing them with new and sometimes painful ones. It would not be until 1859 that Darwin would publish *Origin of Species*, but plenty of other geologists and biologists were already embracing the possibility that the world was older than Genesis suggested, in which case the Bible was perhaps not the Last Word on God's Word. Perhaps, indeed, it was not God's Word at all, but rather the product of man's need to believe in something other than himself. This certainly was the double conclusion that Eliot came to during the early anonymous years of her career when she translated those seminal German texts, Strauss's *The Life of Jesus* (1835–6) and Feuerbach's *The Essence of Christianity* (1841). Her readers likewise wrestled with the awful possibility that there was no moral authority except the one which was to be found by digging deep within themselves. Not only did a godless universe lay terrifying burdens of responsibility upon the individual, but it unsettled the idea of an afterlife. To a culture which had always believed that, no matter how dismal earthly life might be, there was a reward waiting in heaven, this was a horrifying blow beside which the possibility that one was an ape paled into insignificance.

That much-vaunted prosperity turned out to be a tricky business too. For every Victorian who felt rich, there were two who felt very poor indeed, especially during the volatile 1840s and again in the late 1860s. During Eliot's early years in the Midlands she saw the effect of trade slumps on the lives of working families. As a schoolgirl in Nuneaton she had watched while idle weavers queued for free soup; at home, during the holidays, she sorted out second-hand clothing for unemployed miners' families. Even her own sister, married promisingly to a gentlemanly doctor, found herself as a widow fighting to stay out of the workhouse.

To middle-class Victorians these sights and stories added to a growing sense that they were not, after all, in control of the economic and social revolution being carried out in their name. Getting the vote in 1832 had initially seemed to give them the power to reshape the world in their own image: the repeal of the Corn Laws in 1846 had represented a real triumph of urban needs over the agricultural interest. But it soon became clear that early fears that 1832 would be the first step towards a raggle-taggle democracy were justified. On three occasions during the 'hungry forties' working-class men and women rallied themselves around the Charter, a frightening document demanding universal suffrage and annual parliaments. By the mid-1860s, with the economy newly unsettled, urban working men were once again agitating violently for the vote.

These were worrying times. The fat little figure of the Queen was not enough to soothe Victorians' fears that the blustery world in which they lived might not one day blow apart completely. In fear and hope they turned to the woman whose name they were initially only supposed to whisper and whose image they were seldom allowed to see. George Eliot's novels offered Victorians the chance to understand their edginess in its wider intellectual setting and to rehearse responses by identifying with characters who looked and sounded like themselves. Thanks to her immense erudition in everything from theology to biology, anthropology to psychology, Eliot was able to give current doubts their proper historic context. Dorothea's ardent desire to do great deeds, for instance, is set alongside St Teresa's matching passion in the sixteenth century and their contrasting destinies explained. In the same way Tom Tulliver's battles with his sister Maggie are understood not just in terms of their individual personalities, but as the meeting point of several arcs of genetic, cultural, and family conditioning at a particular moment in human history.

While disenchantment with Victorianism led readers to George Eliot, George Eliot's advice to them was that they should remain Victorians. Despite the ruptures of the speedy present, Eliot believed that it was possible, indeed essential, that her readers stay within the parameters of the 'working-day world' – a phrase that would stand at the heart of her philosophy. She would not champion an oppositional culture, in which people put themselves outside the ordinary social and human networks which both nurtured and frustrated them. From Darwin she took not just the radical implications (we are all monkeys, there is probably no God), but the conservative ones too. Societies evolve over thousands of years; change – if it is to work – must come gradually and from within. Opting out into political, religious or feminist Utopias will not do. Eliot's novels show people how they can deal with the pain of being a Victorian by remaining one. Hence all those low-key endings which have embarrassed feminists and radicals for over a century. Dorothea's ardent nature is pressed into small and localised service as an MP's wife, Romola's phenomenal erudition is set aside for her duties as a sick-nurse, Dinah gives up her lay preaching to become a mother.

Eliot's insistence on making her characters stay inside the community, acknowledge the *status quo*, give up fantasies about the ballot, behave as if there is a God (even if there isn't) bewildered her peers. Feminist and radical friends assumed that a woman who lived with a married man, who had broken with her family over religion, who was one of the highest-earning women in Britain, must surely be encouraging others to do the same. And when they found that she did not want the vote for women, that she felt remote from Girton and that she sometimes even went to church, they felt baffled and betrayed.

What Eliot's critics missed was that she was no reactionary, desperately trying to hold back the moment when High Victorianism would crumble. Right from her earliest fictions, from the days of *Adam Bede* in 1859, she had understood her culture's fragility, as well as its enduring strengths. None the less, she believed in the Victorian project, that it was possible for mankind to move forward towards a place or time that was in some way better. This would only happen by a slow process of development during which men and women embraced their doubts, accepted that there would be loss as well as gain, and took their enlarged vision and diminished expectations back into the everyday struggle. In *Daniel Deronda*, Eliot's penultimate book and last proper novel, she shows how this new Victorianism, projected on to a Palestinian Jewish homeland, might look and sound. Although it will cohere around a particular social, geographic and religious culture, it will acknowledge other centres and identities. It will know and honour its own past, while anticipating a future which is radically different. By being sure of its own voice, it will be able to listen attentively to those of others.

It was Eliot's adult reading of Wordsworth and Scott that instilled in her the conviction that 'A human life, I think, should be well rooted in some spot of a native land . . . a spot where the definiteness of early memories may be inwrought with affection'.[5] But it was during her earliest years, as she accompanied her father around the Arbury estate in his pony trap, that she fell deeply in love with the Midlands countryside. Her 'spot' was Warwickshire, the midmost county of England. Uniquely, the landscape was neither agricultural nor industrial, but a patchwork of both. In a stunning Introduction to *Felix Holt, The Radical*, George Eliot used the device of a stagecoach thundering across the Midlands on the eve of the 1832 Reform Act to describe a countryside where the old and new sit companionably side by side.

In these midland districts the traveller passed rapidly from one phase of English life to another: after looking down on a village dingy with coal-dust, noisy with the shaking of looms, he might skirt a parish all of fields, high hedges, and deep-rutted lanes; after the coach had rattled over the pavement of a manufacturing town, the scene of riots and trades-union meetings, it would take him in another ten minutes into a rural region, where the neighbourhood of the town was only felt in the advantages of a near market for corn, cheese, and hay.[6]

Mary Anne's early life, contained within the four walls of Griff farmhouse, where her family moved early in 1820, still belonged securely to the agricultural 'phase of English life' and was pegged to the daily and seasonal demands of a mixed dairy and arable farm. Although there were male labourers to do the heavy work and female servants to help in the house, much of the responsibility was shouldered by the Evans family itself. Like many of the farmers' wives who appear in Eliot's books, Mrs Evans took particular pride in her dairy, running it as carefully as Mrs Poyser in *Adam Bede*, who continually frets about low milk yields and late churnings. Like the wealthy but practical Nancy Lammeter in *Silas Marner*, too, Mrs Evans and her two daughters had bulky, well-developed hands which 'bore the traces of butter-making, cheese-crushing, and even still coarser work'.[7] Some years after George Eliot's death, a rumour circulated in literary London that one of her hands was bigger than the other, thanks to years of turning the churn. It was a story which her brother Isaac, now gentrified by a fancy education, good marriage and several decades of high agricultural prices, hated to hear repeated.

The rhythms of agricultural life made themselves felt right through Mary Anne's young adulthood. As a prickly, bookish seventeen-year-old left to run the farmhouse after her mother's death, she railed against the fuss and bother of harvest supper and the hiring of new servants each Michaelmas. And yet the very depth of her adolescent alienation from this repetitive, witless way of life reveals how deeply it remained embedded in her. Thirty years on and established in a villa in London's Regent's Park, her first thought about the weather was always how it would affect the crops.

But life on the Arbury estate was no bucolic idyll. The Newdigate lands contained some of the richest coal deposits in the county. As she grew older, the fields in which Mary Anne played had names like Engine Close and Coal-pit Field. Lumps of coal lay casually amid the grass. At night the girl was kept awake by the chug-chug of the Newcomen engine pumping water out of the mine less than a mile from her home. The canal in which she and Isaac fished was busy with barges taking the coal to Coventry. And when Mary Anne accompanied her father on his regular visits to Mr Newdigate at Arbury Hall, she would have noticed the huge crack which cut across the gold-and-white ceiling of the magnificent great hall. Subsidence caused by the mine-working had dramatically marked a building whose elaborate refashioning only a generation before had come to stand for everything that was elegantly Arcadian about aristocratic life.

Nor did Mary Anne have to look very far to fit the uneven textures of the Arbury estate into the wider landscape. Most of the people in the scrappy hamlet of Griff were not farm labourers but miners. In the nearby villages people were mainly employed in cottage industries like nail making, ribbon weaving and framework knitting. The pale faces and twisted bodies of the handloom weavers struck Mary Anne as absolutely different from the Arbury farmers, a contrast she was to use later in suggesting the weaver Silas Marner's alienation from his ruddy Raveloe neighbours.

Only a few miles along the road was Nuneaton, the market town where Mary Anne was soon to go to school. In her very first piece of fiction she describes the town – renamed Milby – as a place where intensive homeworking had already left its grimy mark: 'The roads are black with coal-dust, the brick houses dingy with smoke; and at that time – the time of handloom weavers – every other cottage had a loom at its window, where you might see a pale, sickly-looking man or woman pressing a narrow chest against a board, and doing a sort of treadmill work with legs and arms.'[8]

As Eliot's description of hard labour and pinched surroundings suggests, these were not prosperous times for the Midlands. Victory over Napoleon in 1815 had meant an end to protection against imports of French and Swiss ribbon. A couple of months before Mary Anne's birth, a cut in the rate paid to silk weavers brought an angry crowd out on to the street. There was jeering and jostling, and a man accused of working under-price was tied backwards on a donkey and led through the streets.[9] Later, as a schoolgirl in Nuneaton, she was to see hunger-fuelled rioting at first hand.

As Mary Anne followed her father from miner's cottage to farmhouse to Arbury Hall itself, she learned to place herself within this complex social landscape. She noted that while tenant farmers might nod respectfully at her, when she got to Arbury Hall, she was left in the housekeeper's room while her father went to speak to the great man. She observed a whole range of accents, dress, customs and manners against which her own must be measured and adjusted. In this way she built up a library of visual and aural references to which she could return in her imagination when she was sitting, years later, in Richmond trying to recapture the way a gardener or a clergyman spoke. It was this faithfulness to the actual past, rather than a greetings-card version of it, which was to become a plank in her demand for a new kind of realism in fiction. In *Adam Bede* she breaks off in the middle of describing the young squire's coming-of-age party to ask her sentimental, suburban reader: 'Have you ever seen a real English rustic perform a solo dance? Perhaps you have only seen a ballet rustic, smiling like a merry countryman in crockery, with graceful turns of the haunch and insinuating movements of the head. That is as much like the real thing as the "Bird Waltz" is like the song of the birds.'[10] Mary Anne Evans had not only seen labourers dancing, she had watched them getting drunk, making love, milking and shearing. She had been patronised by the gentry and petted by their servants. And while these pictures were neither charming nor quaint, they sustained her sense of being rooted in a community which was to carry her through the long years of urban exile. She knew every field, every hedgerow and every clump of trees. In later life, she had only to close her eyes and she could conjure up the smell of cows' breath, hay and fresh rain. But she also knew the way the muddy canal absorbed the sunlight and the noise the looms made as the weavers worked into the night. Looking at the world through her father's expert eyes, she learned to see that these two strands of life were not conflicting, but that they represented a particular moment in the development of English life. The rural community had not been destroyed, but it was being radically regeared towards technology, profit and the power of the individual to manage his own life. And no one had benefited more from these changes than Robert Evans.

Evans had been born in Roston Common, Derbyshire, in 1773, one of eight children. There were the usual family romances about gentry stock, but by the time Robert arrived any grand connections were nothing more than stories. His father, George, was a carpenter and his mother was called Mary Leech. The five Evans boys were determined to ride the wave of social and economic expansion unleashed by the first phase of industrialisation. Second son William rose to be a wealthy builder, while Thomas overcame a shaky start to become county surveyor for Dorset. Even dreamy Samuel, who turned Methodist and kept his eye on the future world, ran a ribbon factory. Only the eldest boy, George, was unsteady. He boycotted the family's carpentry business and there was talk of heavy drinking. When he died, the Evans clan turned its collective and implacable back on his young children.

Mary Anne was to experience both sides of this Evans legacy. Like her father and his brothers, she rose out of the class into which she was born by dint of hard work and talent. She left behind the farm, the dairy and the brown canal, and fashioned herself into one of the leading intellectual and literary artists of the day. But just like her uncle George – was it coincidence that she took his name as the first half of her writing pseudonym? – she learned what it was like to belong to a family which regularly excluded those of whom it did not approve. When, at the age of twenty-two, she announced that she did not believe in God, her father sent her away from home. Fifteen years later, when she was living with a man to whom she was not married, her brother Isaac instructed her sisters never to speak or write to her again. The Evanses, like thousands of other ambitious families at that time, demanded that its members forge their individual destinies while skirting nonconformity.

In the case of the Evans boys, those destinies were forged in the workshop rather than the classroom. When they did attend school – run by Bartle Massey, a name which would crop up in *Adam Bede* – it was to learn accounting, 'mechanics' and 'to write a plain hand'. Robert's hand did indeed remain plain all his adult life, but despite almost daily entries in his journal and a constant correspondence with his employers, he was never to become comfortable with the pen. Reading his papers remains a tricky business, thanks to patchy punctuation, haphazard spelling and a whimsical use of capitals and italics. 'Balance' becomes 'ballance', 'laughed' is 'laph'd', while 'their' and 'there' are constantly confused. Despite a career of forty years spent note-taking and report-making, Robert Evans remained uneasy with the written word, finding, like Mr Tulliver in *The Mill on the Floss*, 'the relation between spoken and written language, briefly known as spelling, one of the most puzzling things in this puzzling world'.[11]

Evans preferred to dwell in the stable and particular. As a young carpenter he had learned how to turn the elms and ash of Derbyshire and Staffordshire into windows, tables and doors. And as he walked through the forest on his way to the farmhouses where he was employed, he looked around at the trees that ended up on his work-bench. He took note of the conditions under which the best wood flourished. He saw when a stand was ready to be cut and when it should be left for a few weeks more. Later in his career it was said that he had only to look at a tree to know exactly how much timber it would yield.

To any landed proprietor, intent not simply on gazing at his parkland but increasing its profit, a man like Evans could be useful. It was now that he came to the attention of Francis Parker, a shrewd young gentleman of about the same age, who spotted the carpenter's potential to be more than a maker of cottage doors and fancy cabinets. Parker persuaded his father – another Francis Parker – to put Evans to work managing Kirk Hallam, their Derbyshire estate. So began Evans's career as a self-made man. Reworked in fiction as the ruptured rivalrous bond between Adam Bede and Arthur Donnithorne, the real-life Parker and Evans remained cordial, but always mindful of their vastly different stations. Over the next forty years they offered each other – often by letter, since Parker lived much of the time in Blackheath, Kent – cautious encouragement and condolence as the trials of their parallel lives unfolded.[12]

In 1806, by a cat's cradle of a will, Francis Parker senior inherited a life interest in the magnificent Warwickshire estate of Arbury Hall from his cousin Sir Roger Newdigate. Parker, now renamed Newdigate, moved to Arbury and brought Evans with him as his agent. Evans, by now thirty-three and a father of two, was installed at South Farm, from where he could manage the 7000-acre estate while running his own farm.

The Evans family and the Parker-Newdigate clan had attached themselves to one another in a mutually beneficial arrangement which was to last right down the nineteenth century. While the Newdigates spent many years and much money pursuing pointless lawsuits about who was responsible for what under the terms of Roger Newdigate's eccentric will, the Evans brothers quietly consolidated their own empire. With Robert now moved to Warwickshire, Thomas and William stayed behind to manage the Newdigates' Derbyshire and Staffordshire estates. The moment Robert's eldest boy was old enough, he was sent back to Derbyshire to learn the family trade. And when occasionally something did go wrong, Robert Evans stepped in quickly to make sure that there was no blip in the steady arc of the family's influence. In 1835 brother Thomas went bankrupt. This was a potential disaster, since if Thomas left his farm at Kirk Hallam he would also have to give up as estate manager. Robert immediately proposed a solution to his employer whereby he would become the official tenant of the farm, allowing Thomas and his son to continue to work the land and stay in place.[13] In the Evanses' world, business relationships always took precedence over family ones. Although during Mary Anne's childhood Robert made regular trips northwards, on only a couple of occasions did he take her with him to meet her uncles and aunts. Their odd-sounding dialect struck her as strange, but years later she found good use for it when she came to create the North Midlands accents in *Adam Bede*.[14]

Evans applied the same canny caution to his personal life. While working in Staffordshire he had noticed a local girl called Harriet Poynton. She was a servant, but a superior one. Since her teens she had been lady's maid to the second Mrs Parker-Newdigate senior and occupied a position of unparalleled trust. Her duties would have involved looking after the wardrobe and toilet of her mistress, buttoning her up in the morning and brushing out her hair at night. Constantly in her mistress's presence, the lady's maid frequently became the recipient of cast-off clothes, gossip and affection. All the signs suggest that Mrs Parker-Newdigate looked on Harriet as something like a daughter. Marriage to Harriet Poynton cemented Robert Evans's ties to his employers. The Parker-Newdigates were presumably delighted that two of their favourite servants had forged an alliance. At the very least it meant that their own comforts and conveniences would not be disturbed. In an unusual arrangement, Mrs Parker-Newdigate, now moved to Arbury Hall, insisted that Harriet continue to work after her marriage.

We know nothing of the courtship. It is hard to imagine Robert Evans divulging much beyond the current cost of elm or the need to drain the top field. But this was not about romance. Evans offered the thirty-one-year-old Harriet the respectability of marriage without the need to leave her beloved mistress. In return, her ladylike manner promised usefully to soften his blunt ways and flat vowels. They married in 1801 and children followed quickly. Robert was born in 1802, Frances Lucy, shrewdly named for Mrs Parker-Newdigate, in 1805.

In the end, it was Harriet's attachment to her mistress that killed her. In 1809 Mrs Parker-Newdigate went down with a fatal illness to which the heavily pregnant Harriet also succumbed. A baby girl, also Harriet, was born, but died shortly afterwards and was buried with her mother. In acknowledgement of her unique relation to them in both life and death, the Parker-Newdigates took the unusual step of adding Harriet's name – 'faithful friend and servant' – to the family memorial stone in nearby Astley Church.

Like all widowers with children, Robert Evans needed to marry again and quickly. We do not know who looked after the babies during the four years before he took his second wife. Perhaps Harriet's family rallied round. Maybe one of his sisters from Derbyshire came to help at South Farm. The next thing known for certain, however, is that he made another smart match. Christiana Pearson was the youngest daughter of Isaac Pearson, a yeoman who farmed at Astley. Yeoman farmers were freeholders and so harder to place socially than those who rented their farms, a point which was to unsettle the snobbish Mrs Cadwallader in *Middlemarch*.[15] The Pearsons were certainly not gentry, but they were prosperous, active sort of people, used to serving as church wardens and parish constables. If Evans's first marriage confirmed his allegiance to the Newdigates, his second proclaimed a growing independence from them.

The Pearson daughters – there were four of them – embodied a particular kind of rigid rural respectability which would be reworked by their niece to such powerful and funny effect in the Dodson sisters in *The Mill on the Floss*. Literary detectives have matched up the Dodsons to the Pearsons exactly. Ann Pearson, who married George Garner of Astley, became the model for Aunt Deane; Elizabeth was second wife of Richard Johnson of Marston Jabbett and formed the basis for rich, pretentious Aunt Pullet; while Mary, second wife of John Evarard of Attleborough, was transformed into thrifty, superstitious Aunt Glegg. The overriding characteristic of the Dodson sisters (and hence the Pearsons) is their sense of superiority on every imaginable topic and an assumed right to comment on those who do not match their exacting standards. 'There were particular ways of doing everything in that family: particular ways of bleaching the linen, of making the cowslip wine, curing the hams and keeping the bottled gooseberries, so that no daughter of that house could be indifferent to the privilege of having been born a Dodson, rather than a Gibson or a Watson.'[16]

Christiana was the youngest of the Pearson girls – there was a brother, too – and perhaps here lies the clue to why she agreed to become Robert Evans's second wife. Still unmarried in her late twenties, she may have wanted to flee the role of companion and nurse to ageing parents. Perhaps she also wanted protection from her overbearing sisters. At forty-one, Robert Evans was a vigorous man whose reputation as the cleverest agent in the area was growing all the time. No longer a servant exactly, he was a 'rising man'. South Farm needed a mistress, someone who could run a dairy, organise a household, feed the workmen and supervise the servants. Christiana Pearson could do worse than become the second Mrs Evans.

The marriage, in 1813, produced five children, three of whom survived. First came Christiana, always known as Chrissey, in 1814. Next, in 1816, was Isaac and two and a half years later came Mary Anne. The fact that these were all Pearson names suggests that Mrs Evans's nearby family continued to take what seemed to them a natural precedence and influence in the children's lives. That the last baby was a girl – Robert Evans's third – was probably a disappointment, especially since boy twins born in 1821 did not survive more than a few days. For a man who was still busy building a business dynasty, girls were not especially useful. They could run a farmhouse, but they could not trade, build or farm. Until they married – when they had to be provided with a dowry – they remained a drain on their family's resources.

Four months after Mary Anne's birth the family moved to Griff House, the Georgian farmhouse on the Coventry–Nuneaton road which was to be home for the next twenty-one years. It was far more impressive than the boxy South Farm and, together with the attached 280 acres of farmland, represented the high noon of Robert Evans's status and influence. There were eight bedrooms, three attics and four ground-floor living-rooms. A cobbled courtyard was surrounded by a dairy (which was to become the model for the richly seductive

Poyser dairy in *Adam Bede*), a dovecote and a labourer's cottage. The four acres of garden were picture-book perfect, with roses, cabbages, raspberry bushes, currant trees and, best of all, a round pond. During her adult years spent in boarding-houses, hotel rooms and ugly suburban villas, Mary Anne's imagination would return repeatedly to the Eden that was Griff. When, in 1874, Isaac's daughter Edith sent her some recent photographs of the house, Mary Anne found herself spinning back in time: 'Dear old Griff still smiles at me with a face which is more like than unlike its former self, and I seem to feel the air through the window of the attic above the drawing room, from which when a little girl, I often looked towards the distant view of the Coton "College" [the workhouse] – thinking the view rather sublime.'[17]

Although as a mature novelist George Eliot referred repeatedly to memory and childhood as the bedrock of the adult self, she actually left very little direct information about her own early years. Even John Cross, the man she married eight months before her death, wrestled with large gaps as he attempted to recall his wife's childhood for the readers of his three-volume *George Eliot's Life as Related in Her Letters and Journals*, published in 1885. To bulk out his first chapter he leaned heavily on the account of Maggie Tulliver's early years in *The Mill on the Floss*, introducing distortions which biographers spent the next hundred years consolidating into 'fact'.

Drawing on the relationship between Mr Tulliver and Maggie, Cross has Robert Evans clucking in wonder at the cleverness of his 'little wench' and making her a special pet. In fact, there is no evidence that Evans had a particular fondness for Mary Anne, although plenty to suggest that she worshipped him. By the time his youngest child was born, Evans was forty-six years old and established in both his career and family life. A head-and-shoulders portrait from 1842 shows him massive and impassive as a piece of great oak.[18] A high, wide forehead gives way to a long nose and broad lips – features that were repeated less harmoniously in Mary Anne. Evans radiated physical strength – one anecdote has him jauntily picking up a heavy ladder, which two labourers were unable to manage between them. But it was his moral authority that made him a figure to be reckoned with. Once, when travelling on the top of a coach in Kent, a female passenger complained that the sailor sitting next to her was being offensive. Mr Evans changed places with the woman and forced the sailor under the seat, holding him down for the rest of the journey.[19]

It was this reputation for integrity that meant that Evans was increasingly asked to play a part in the burgeoning network of charitable and public institutions, which were becoming part of the rural landscape during the 1820s and 1830s. His meticulous bookkeeping and surveying skills were an asset to church, workhouse and hospital. In a blend of self-interest and social responsibility, he was able to take advantage of this move towards a professional bureaucracy by charging fees for services rendered. Less officially he also became known as someone who would discreetly lend money to embarrassed professional men, including the clergy. By charging a fair interest, the frugal carpenter's son was able to make a profit out of those gentlemen who had been less successful than himself at negotiating the violent swings of the post-war economy.

But the heart of Evans's empire would always remain his work as a land agent. This was what he understood and where he excelled. Since the middle of the previous century English agriculture had been developing along capitalist lines. The careless old ways of farming were giving way to scientific methods, which promised to yield bigger crops and profits. Landowners now employed professional agents to oversee the efficient running of their estates. It was Robert Evans's job to ensure that the Newdigate tenant farmers kept their land properly fenced, drained and fertilised.[20] Livestock was carefully chosen according to its suitability for particular pasture. Farm buildings were to be light, airy and dry. Evans was an excellent draughtsman, and one of his letters to his employer includes a meticulous scale drawing of a proposed farm cottage, complete with threshing floor, corn bay, straw bay, cowshed, kitchen and dairy. Dorothea Brooke would have been delighted.[21]

Evans's expertise encompassed every aspect and activity of the Arbury estate. He regularly inspected the coal-mine, arranged for roads to be built and kept a watchful eye on the quarries, which were only a few yards from the gates of Griff House. As his reputation grew throughout the region, Evans came to be seen less as a clever servant of the Newdigates and increasingly as a professional man in his own right. Several other local landowners, including Lord Aylesford at Packington, now asked him to manage their land. Evans's relationship with the Newdigates became subtly different as he started to carry himself with more authority. Francis Parker-Newdigate senior was, according to local sources, 'a despisable character – a bad unfeeling Landlord'.[22] Evans was not prepared to carry out policies which he felt to be unfair. In 1834 he suggested to Newdigate that a particularly bad wheat harvest obliged him to return a percentage of the rent to the tenants. The old man was typically reluctant, so Evans wrote directly to his son, now Colonel Newdigate, in Blackheath. Permission to refund came back immediately.[23]

Years later, as interest in George Eliot's social origins reached fever pitch, a rumour arose that her father had been nothing more than a tenant farmer. According to this reading, Eliot's literary achievement became heroic, the stuff of fairy-tales, instead of the continuation of a trajectory which had started long before she was born. Indignantly, Eliot intervened to explain her father's status as a man of accomplishment and skill, in the process putting her own achievement into a more realistic context.

My father did not raise himself from being an artizan to be a farmer: he raised himself from being an artizan to be a man whose extensive knowledge in very varied practical departments made his services valued through several counties. He had large knowledge of building, of mines, of plantation, of various branches of valuation and measurement – of all that is essential to the management of large estates. He was held by those competent to judge as *unique* amongst land agents for his manifold knowledge and experience, which enabled him to save the special fees usually paid by landowners for special opinions on the different questions incident to the proprietorship of land.[24]

For all his modernity, Robert Evans remained a staunch conservative. Like many children who had gone to bed hearing stories of Madame Guillotine, he fetishised the need for strong government. And government, for him, must always be rooted in the power and prestige of land. It was not to Westminster he looked for leadership, but to the alliance of squire and clergy serving together on the magistrates' bench. Evans believed in keeping corn prices high by means of artificial protection even if that meant townsmen having to pay more for their bread. The notorious 'Peterloo' incident, a few months before Mary Anne's birth, in which the cavalry cut a murderous swathe through thousands of people gathered in Manchester to protest against the Corn Laws, would have drawn from Evans a shiver of fear followed by a glow of approbation. Closer to home, the violent hustings at Nuneaton in December 1832 would have confirmed his suspicion that extending the franchise to men with no stake in the land could result only in a permanent breakdown of precious law and order.[25]

Even if Robert Evans had not been a natural conservative, ties of deference and duty to the Newdigates meant that he was obliged to follow them in supporting the Tory party. He attended local meetings on the family's behalf and in 1837 made sure the tenants turned up to the poll by 'treating' them to a hearty breakfast. At times his support for the Tories against the reforming Whigs took on the flavour of a religious battle. Describing his efforts at the 1837 election in a letter to Colonel Newdigate, he urged 'we must not loose a Vote if we can help it'.[26]

We know less about Mrs Evans. Eliot mentions her only twice in her surviving letters, and Isaac and Fanny seem to have been unable to recall a single thing about her for John Cross when he interviewed them after his wife's death. Cross's solution was to take the generalised and evasive line, followed by many biographers since, that Mary Anne's mother was 'a woman with an unusual amount of natural force – a shrewd practical person, with a considerable dash of the Mrs Poyser vein in her',[27] referring to the bustling farmer's wife in *Adam Bede*. But what evidence there is suggests that Christiana Evans was actually more like Mrs Tulliver in *The Mill on the Floss*, a kind of Mrs Poyser minus the energy and wit, but with a similar stream of angry complaints issuing from her thin lips. Anecdotal sources indicate that from the time of her last two confinements Mrs Evans was in continual ill-health. She had, after all, lost twin boys eighteen months after Mary Anne's birth. For a woman who had already produced two girls, losing two sons, especially towards the end of her fertile years, must have been a blow. Whether this was the lassitude of bereavement, depression or physical exhaustion is not clear, but the impression that emerges is of a woman straining to cope with the demands of her family.

Raising stepchildren is never easy, but Christiana seems to have found it intolerable, especially once she had three babies of her own to look after.

Around the time of Mary Anne's birth, seventeen-year-old Robert was dispatched to Derbyshire to manage the Kirk Hallam estate, with fourteen-year-old Fanny accompanying him as his housekeeper and, later, as governess to a branch of the Newdigate family. It may not have been a formal banishment, but the effect was to stretch the elder children's relationship with their father and his second family to the point where on their occasional visits home they were greeted as stiffly as strangers.[28]

Chrissey, too, was rarely seen at Griff. According to John Cross, 'shortly after her last child's birth ... [Mrs Evans] became ailing in health, and consequently her eldest girl, Christiana, was sent to school at a very early age, to Miss Lathom's at Attleboro'.[29] Even during the holidays Chrissey rarely appeared at home: her biddable personality made her a favourite with the Pearson aunts who were happy to take her off their youngest sister's hands. Only Isaac was allowed to stay at Griff to the more reasonable age of eight or nine. Even at the end of her life, Eliot had no doubts that Isaac had been their mother's favourite. In part this was due to temperamental similarity. The boy's subsequent development suggests that he was a Pearson through and through – rigid, respectable, intolerant of different ways of doing things. But it may also be the case that Christiana was a woman who found it easier to love her sons – both living and dead.

Critics have long noted the lack of warm, easy mother–child relationships in Eliot's novels. Mothers are often dead and if they survive, then, like Mrs Bede, Mrs Holt and Mrs Tulliver, they are both intrusive and rejecting, swamping and fretful. Mrs Bede and Mrs Holt both demand constant attention from their sons by complaining about them. Mrs Tulliver, likewise, cannot leave Maggie alone. She worries away at the child's grubby pinafores, stubborn hair and 'brown skin as makes her look like a mulatter ... it seems hard as I should have but one gell, an' her so comical'.[30]

Throughout her career George Eliot repeatedly explored what it is like to be the child of such a mother, one who both pulls you towards her and pushes you away. In a late poem, 'Self and Life', she describes the lingering desolation of being put down too suddenly from a warm maternal lap.[31] Speaking in the more accessible prose of *The Mill on the Floss*, she shows the way in which a child in this situation responds with an infuriating mix of attention-seeking and self-punishing behaviour. In angry reply to Aunt Pullet's insensitive suggestion that her untidy hair should be cropped, Maggie Tulliver seizes the scissors and does the job herself.[32] In another incident she retreats to the worm-eaten cobwebby rafters, surely based on the attic at Griff, where she keeps a crude wooden doll or 'fetish' and, concentrating this time on the image of hated Aunt Glegg, drives a nail hard into its head. When her rage is exhausted, she bursts into tears and cradles the doll in a passion of remorse and tenderness.[33] Maggie's swoops from showy self-display to brutal self-punishment were rooted in the violent swings of Mary Anne's own childhood. An anecdote from around the age of four has her thumping the piano noisily in an attempt to impress the servant with her mastery of the instrument. Five years later she is cutting off her hair, just like Maggie. This sense that her childhood had been a time of uneasy longing remained with the adult Mary Anne. In 1844, at the age of twenty-five, she wrote to her friend Sara Hennell: 'Childhood is only the beautiful and happy time in contemplation and retrospect – to the child it is full of deep sorrows, the meaning of which is unknown.'[34]

Rejection by her mother forced Mary Anne to look elsewhere for a passionate, intimate connection. At the age of three she fell violently in love with her elder brother Isaac. She trotted behind him wherever he went, following him as he climbed trees, fished or busied himself with imaginary adventures down by the quarry. The Eden that was Griff now had its own tiny Adam and Eve. Eliot's 'Brother and Sister' sonnets, written in 1869, open with a description of the children as romantic soulmates, twins, each other's missing half.

> I cannot choose but think upon the time
> When our two lives grew like two buds that kiss
> At lightest thrill from the bee's swinging chime,
> Because the one so near the other is.[35]

But while they may be deeply attached to one another, there is still division and difference in this Eden. The boy in the sonnets and Tom in *The Mill on the Floss* are older, bigger and more powerful than the little sisters who dote on them. The girl in the sonnets watches, admiring, while her brother plays marbles or spins tops; Maggie idolises Tom as the fount of all practical knowledge. And to cope with this power imbalance, Maggie likes to fantasise that the positions are reversed. In a cancelled passage from *The Mill on the Floss*, she imagines that

> Tom never went to school, and liked no one to play with him but Maggie; they went out together somewhere every day, and carried either hot buttered cakes with them because it was baking day, or apple puffs well sugared; Tom was never angry with her for forgetting things, and liked her to tell him tales; . . . Above all, Tom loved her – oh, so much, – more, even than she loved him, so that he would always want to have her with him and be afraid of vexing her; and he as well as everyone else, thought her very clever.[36]

The split, when it comes, is awful. Tom comes home from school to find that Maggie has forgotten to feed his rabbits. His anger is swift and terrible, but it is his gradual pulling away into the realm of boydom which hurts even more. He begins to find Maggie's adoration tiresome, her chatter silly and her superior cleverness embarrassing. Gradually he turns into the stern, conventional patriarch who scolds, criticises and eventually ignores his wayward sister.

The separation of the boy and girl in the 'Brother and Sister' sonnets seems, at first, to be less traumatic. 'School parted us,' the narrator tells us, rather than some fierce falling-out. For several years 'the twin habit of that early time' is enough to let the children come together easily on their subsequent meetings. But as time goes by their lives carry them in opposite directions, to the point where, although 'still yearning in divorce', they are unable to find their way back to that shared language which once held them together.[37]

The fact that the brother–sister divided was a drama that Eliot treated twice, once in prose, then in poetry, suggests that it had deep roots in her own life. Certainly Mary Anne's early attachment to Isaac is on record as greedy and rapacious. After her death, Isaac Evans recalled for John Cross that on his return from boarding-school for the holidays he was greeted with rapture by his little sister, who demanded an account of everything he had been doing.[38] The scene is a charming one, but it hints at a distress which cannot be explained simply by sibling love. Behind the little girl's urgent questioning there lurked a deep need to possess and control Isaac for fear he might abandon her. But it was already too late. When the boy was about nine he had acquired a pony and could no longer be bothered with his little sister. Mary Anne responded by plunging into a deep, intense grief, which was to echo down the years. 'Very jealous in her affections and easily moved to smiles or tears,' Cross explained to his readers, 'she was of a nature capable of the keenest enjoyment and the keenest suffering, knowing "all the wealth and all the woe" of a pre-eminently exclusive disposition. She was affectionate, proud and sensitive in the highest degree.'[39]

Observing his wife's temperament in later life, John Cross believed that the pony incident provided the key to understanding George Eliot's personality. 'In her moral development she showed, from the earliest years, the trait that was most marked in her all through life – namely, the absolute need of some one person who should be all in all to her, and to whom she should be all in all.'[40] Later biographers have been quick to point out how this passage has become the cornerstone for a character reading of Eliot as needy, dependent and leaning heavily on male lovers and women friends for approval. Yet Eliot's later comments on her own personality, together with the pattern of her subsequent relationships, suggest that Cross was doing no more than telling it how it was. The early withdrawal of her mother's affection had left her with a vulnerability to rejection that would last a lifetime.

So when Mary Anne was sent away to boarding-school at the age of five, it was inevitable that she would take it hard. Even this was not the child's first time away from home. For the previous two years she and Isaac had spent every day at a little dame school at the bottom of the drive. In her two-up–two-down cottage, Mrs Moore looked after a handful of local children and attempted to teach them their letters in an arrangement that went little beyond cheap baby-sitting. But now Mary Anne was to join Chrissey at Miss Lathom's school three miles away in Attleborough, while Isaac was sent to a boys' establishment in Coventry: hence the reference to 'school divided us' in the 'Brother and Sister' sonnets. Boarding-school was not unusual for farmers' daughters, but five was an exceptionally early age to start. After only eleven years of marriage Christiana Evans had managed to clear Griff House of the five young people who were supposed to be living there.[41]

School did not turn out to be an emotional second start for Mary Anne. Although she sometimes came home on Saturdays, and saw her nearby Aunt

Evarard more often, she felt utterly abandoned. At the end of her life she told John Cross that her chief memory of Miss Lathom's was of trying to push her way towards the fireplace through a semicircle of bigger girls. Faced with a wall of implacable backs, she resigned herself to living in a state of permanent chill. The scene stuck in her memory because it reinforced her feelings of being excluded from the warmth of her mother's lap. No wonder, then, that her childhood nights were filled with dreadful dreams during which, reported Cross, 'all her soul ... [became] a quivering fear'.[42] It was a terror which stayed with her throughout her life, edging into consciousness during those times when she was most stressed, depressed or alone. Even in late middle age she had not forgotten that churning sickness, working it brilliantly into the pathology of Gwendolen Harleth, the neurotic heroine of her last novel, *Daniel Deronda*.

Children who are separated from their parents often imagine that their bad behaviour is to blame. Mary Anne was no exception. She interpreted her banishment from Griff as a sign that she had been naughty and adopted the classic strategy of becoming very good. The older girls at Miss Lathom's nicknamed her, with unconscious irony, 'Little Mama' and were careful not to upset her by messing up her clothes.[43] The toddler who had once loved to play mud pies with Isaac grew into a grave child who found other little girls silly. When, at the age of nine or ten, she was asked why she was sitting on the sidelines at a party, she replied stiffly, 'I don't like to play with children; I like to talk to grown-up people.'[44]

As part of her plunge into goodness, Mary Anne buried herself in books. Her half-sister Fanny, who had once worked as a governess, recalled for John Cross the surprising fact that the child had been initially slow to read, preferring to play out of doors with her brother. But once Isaac withdrew his companionship Mary Anne was left, like so many lonely children, to construct an imaginary world of her own. In 1839 she told her old schoolmistress Maria Lewis how as a little girl 'I was constantly living in a world of my own creation, and was quite contented to have no companions that I might be left to my own musings and imagine scenes in which I was chief actress. Conceive what a character novels would give to these Utopias. I was early supplied with them by those who kindly sought to gratify my appetite for reading and of course I made use of the materials they supplied for building my castles in the air.'[45] Quite who 'supplied' these novels is unclear. At the age of seven or so Mary Anne would have found very few books lying around Griff. The Evanses were literate but not literary and the little girl was obliged to read nursery standards like Aesop's *Fables* and *Pilgrim's Progress* over and over. Her father's gift of a picture book, *The Linnet's Life*, was special enough to make Mary Anne cherish it until the end of her life, handing it over to John Cross with a warm dedication.[46] Joe Miller's *Jest Book* was learned by heart and repeated *ad nauseam* to whoever would listen. In middle age Eliot recalled that an unnamed 'old gentleman' used to bring her reading material, but no more is known.[47] For the girl who was to grow up to be the best-read woman of the century, it was an oddly unbookish start.

CHAPTER 2

'On Being Called a Saint'

An Evangelical Girlhood
1828–40

AT THE AGE of eight Mary Anne took a step towards a new world, urban and refined. In 1828 she followed Chrissey to school in Nuneaton. Miss Lathom's had been only three miles from Griff and was attended by farmers' daughters with thick Warwickshire tongues, broad butter-making hands and little hope of going much beyond the three Rs. The Elms, run by Mrs Wallington, was a different proposition altogether. The lady herself was a genteel, hard-up widow from Cork. She had followed one of the few options available to her by opening a school and advertising for boarders whom she taught alongside her own daughters. There were hundreds of these 'ladies' seminaries' struggling to survive in the first half of the nineteenth century and most of them were dreadful. What marked out The Elms was its excellent teaching: by the time Mary Anne arrived, the school was reckoned to be one of the best in Nuneaton. Responsibility for the thirty pupils was shared between Mrs Wallington, her daughter Nancy, now twenty-five, and another Irishwoman, Maria Lewis, who was about twenty-eight.

The change of environment did nothing to help Mary Anne shed her shyness. Adults and children still steered clear, assuming they had nothing to offer the little girl whom they privately described as 'uncanny'.[1] Only the assistant governess Miss Lewis, with her ugly squint and her Irishness, recognised in Mary Anne something of her own isolation. Looking beyond the smooth, hard shell of perfection, she saw a deeply unhappy child 'given to great bursts of weeping'. Within months of her arrival at Nuneaton Mary Anne had formed an attachment to Miss Lewis, which was to be the pivot of both women's lives for the next ten years. Miss Lewis became 'like an elder sister' to the Evans girls, often staying at Griff during the holidays.[2]

Mr and Mrs Evans were delighted with Mrs Wallington's in general and Maria Lewis in particular. In their different ways they both set great store by their youngest girl getting an education. Shrewdly practical, Robert Evans had already schooled his eldest daughter, Fanny, to a standard that had enabled her to work as a governess to the Newdigates before her marriage to a prosperous farmer, Henry Houghton. Anticipating that the quiet, odd-looking Mary Anne might remain a spinster all her life, Evans was determined that she would not be reduced to relying on her brothers for support. A life as a governess was not, as Miss Lewis's example was increasingly to show, either secure or cheerful. Still, it was the one bit of independence open to middle-class women and Robert Evans was determined that it should be Mary Anne's if she needed it.

Christiana's hopes for her daughter were altogether fancier.[3] Like many a prosperous farmer's wife, she expected a stint at boarding-school to soften her child's rough corners and round out her flat vowels. A smattering of indifferent French and basic piano were the icing on the cake of an education designed to prepare the girl for marriage to a prosperous farmer or local professional man. In the case of young Chrissey the investment was soon to pay off handsomely. A few years after leaving Mrs Wallington's she married a local doctor, the gentlemanly Edward Clarke. Still, husbands were a long way off for little Mary Anne. All Mrs Evans hoped for at this stage was that her odd little girl would become near enough a lady. Maria Lewis may not have been pretty, but her careful manners and measured diction were held up to Mary Anne – who still looked and sounded like a farm girl – as the model to which she should aspire.

It did no harm, either, that Miss Lewis was 'serious' in her religion, belonging to the Evangelical wing of the Church of England. From the end of the previous century the Evangelicals had worked to revitalise an Established Church that had become lethargic and indifferent to the needs of a changing social landscape. A population which was increasingly urban and mobile found nothing of relevance in the tepid rituals of weekly parish worship. During the 1760s and 1770s, the charismatic clergyman John Wesley had taken the gospel out to the people, preaching with passion about a Saviour who might be personally and intimately known. For Wesley ritual, liturgy and the sacrament were less important than a first-hand knowledge of God's word as revealed through the Bible and private prayer. When it came to deciding questions of right and wrong, the authority of the priest ceded to individual conscience. This made Methodism, as Wesley's brand of Anglicanism became known, a particularly democratic faith. Mill workers, apothecaries and, until 1803, women, were all encouraged to preach the word of the Lord as and when the spirit moved them.

This challenge of Methodism, together with the continuing vitality of other dissenting sects such as the Baptists and the Independents, had forced the Established Church to put its house in order. The result was Evangelicalism – a brand of Anglicanism which held out the possibility of knowing Christ as a personal redeemer. In order to attain this state of grace an individual was to prepare her soul by renouncing all manner of leisure and pleasure. A constant diet of prayer, bible study and self-scrutiny was required to stamp out temptation. Yet at the same time as renouncing the world, the Evangelical Anglican was to be busily present within it. Visiting the poor, leading prayer meetings and worrying about the state of other people's souls were part of the programme by which the 'serious' Christian would reach heaven. Uninviting though this dour programme might seem, Evangelicalism swept right through the middle classes and even lapped the gentry during the first decades of the century. Its combination of self-consciousness, sentimentality and pious bustle went a long way to defining the temper of domestic and public life in early nineteenth-century England. In 'Janet's Repentance', one of her first pieces of fiction, George Eliot showed how Evangelical Anglicanism had worked a little revolution in the petty hearts and minds of female Milby, a barely disguised Nuneaton: 'Whatever might be the weaknesses of the ladies who pruned the luxuriance of their lace and ribbons, cut out garments for the poor, distributed tracts, quoted Scripture, and defined the true Gospel, they had learned this – that there was a divine work to be done in life, a rule of goodness higher than the opinion of their neighbours.'[4]

Even Robert Evans, not known for his susceptibility to passing trends, was affected by Evangelical fervour. During the late 1820s he went to hear the Reverend John Jones give a series of passionate evening sermons in Nuneaton. Jones's fundamentalist style was credited with inspiring a religious revival in Nuneaton and with provoking a reaction from more orthodox church members – events which Eliot portrayed in 'Janet's Repentance'. But Evans was too much of a conservative to do more than dip into this new moral and political force. As the Newdigates' representative, he was expected to uphold the tradition of Broad Church Anglicanism. The parish church of Chilvers Coton stood at the heart of village life and it was here the Evanses came to be christened – as Mary Anne was a week after her birth – married and buried. Labourers, farmers and neighbouring artisans gathered every Sunday to affirm not so much that Christ was Risen but that the community endured.

At a time when many country people still could not read, it was the familiar cadences of the Prayer Book rather than the precise doctrine it conveyed which brought comfort, a point Eliot was to put into the mouth of the illiterate Dolly Winthrop as she urged the isolated weaver Silas Marner to attend Raveloe's Christmas service: 'If you was to . . . go to church, and see the holly and the yew, and hear the anthim, and then take the sacramen', you'd be a deal the better, and you'd know which end you stood on, and you could put your trust i' Them as knows better nor we do, seein' you'd ha' done what it lies on us all to do.'[5]

While this was exactly the kind of hazy, casual observance which the Evangelical teenage Mary Anne abhorred, as a mature woman she came to value the way it strengthened social relations. Mr Ebdell, who had christened her, turns up in fiction as Mr Gilfil of 'Mr Gilfil's Love Story'. Schooled in his own suffering, Gilfil is a much-loved figure in the community, with an instinctive understanding of his parishioners' needs. He pulls sugar plums out of his pockets for the village children and sends an old lady a flitch of bacon so that she will not have to kill her beloved pet pig. Yet when it comes to preaching, that key activity for a new generation of zealous church-goers, Mr Gilfil is sadly lacking: 'He had a large heap of short sermons, rather yellow and worn at the edges, from which he took two every Sunday, securing perfect impartiality in the selection by taking them as they came, without reference to topics.'[6]

Gilfil begins a long line of theologically lax, but emotionally generous, Anglican clergy in Eliot's fiction which includes Mr Irwine of *Adam Bede* and Mr Farebrother in *Middlemarch*. Irwine may hunt and Farebrother play cards, much to the horror of their dissenting and Evangelical neighbours, but both extend a charity and understanding to their fellow men which was to become the corner-stone of Eliot's adult moral philosophy.

Ironically, it was just this kind of loving acceptance which drew Mary Anne away from her family's middle-of-the-road Anglicanism towards the Evangelicalism of Miss Lewis. At nine years old she was hardly able to comprehend the doctrinal differences between the two ways of worship, but she was easily able to register that Maria Lewis gave her the kind of sustained attention which her own mother could not. If loving God was what it took to keep Miss Lewis loving her, Mary Anne was happy to oblige. With the insecure child's eager need to please, she adopted her teacher's serious piety with relish. After her death, when family and friends were busy offering commentaries on Eliot's early influences, the idea grew that it was Maria Lewis's indoctrination that had provoked Mary Anne into the flamboyant gesture of abandoning God at the age of twenty-two. In fact Miss Lewis's observance, though rigorous, was always sweet and sentimental. She was hardly a hell-fire preacher, more a gentle woman who talked earnestly of God's tender mercies. But she was not so gentle, however, that she was not prepared to push the blame in the direction where she believed it lay. Reminiscing after Eliot's death, she maintained that it was Mary Anne's next teachers, the Baptist Franklin sisters, who were to blame for the girl's 'fall into infidelity'.[7]

The Franklins, whose establishment was in the smartest part of Coventry, ran the best girls' school in the Midlands. The ambitious curriculum and pious ambience attracted girls from as far away as New York. Too rarified for Chrissey Evans, who returned home to Griff after her stint at Mrs Wallington's, it was none the less the perfect place for twelve-year-old Mary Anne.

The Franklin sisters, Mary, thirty, and Rebecca, twenty-eight, were the daughters of a local Baptist minister who preached at a chapel in Cow Lane. Despite these stern-sounding origins, they were generally agreed to be the last word in female charm and culture. In what was becoming a classic pattern for the early nineteenth-century schoolmistress, Miss Rebecca had spent time in Paris perfecting her French before coming home to pass on her elegant accent to her pupils. Indeed, her combination of refinement and learning had given the younger Miss Franklin a personal reputation as one of the cleverest women in the county.

In such an exquisite atmosphere Mary Anne could hardly fail to flourish. Her French improved by leaps and bounds, and she won a copy of Pascal's *Pensées* for her efforts, a triumph which still gave her pleasure at the very end of her life. Her English compositions were immaculate, read with admiration by Miss Franklin 'who rarely found anything to correct'.[8] As the best pianist in the school, she was sometimes asked to play for visitors, even if she often fled from the parlour in 'an agony of tears' at her failure to excel.[9]

Mary Anne's educational progress went hand in hand with her social transformation. She had already lost her accent by listening carefully to Miss Lewis's pedantic, old-fashioned diction. Now she took Miss Rebecca as her model, developing the low, musical voice which in later life continued to hint at the effort it had taken to acquire. These were the years when the question of who or what was 'genteel' pressed hard upon the provincial middle classes. Women of the previous generation – like her brisk Pearson aunts – rooted their self-worth in keeping a spotless home and helping their husbands run a thriving business. They felt no shame in being spotted up to their elbows in whey or poring over an account book. But from the 1820s middle-class women were increasingly required to behave in ways which showed that they were 'ladies'. Ladies did not involve themselves in profit making and they employed domestic servants to do the rougher housework. Instead of curing bacon they spent their time in a series of highly ornamental activities – painting, music and fine needlework – which advertised the fact that their husbands and fathers could afford to keep them in leisure. Evangelicalism went some way towards curbing the worst excesses of this faux-gentility, but even a serious Christian like Mary Anne Evans was expected to drop the ways of speaking and behaving which she had learned in her parents' farmhouse.

The Franklins' brand of Baptism was mild, but still they believed in the conversion experience, that moment when an individual realises his sinfulness and asks to be born again in Christ. It is not clear if Mary Anne underwent a sharply defined crisis in her mid-teens, but it is certainly the case that she became more ponderously religious than ever before. She was always first to lead her schoolmates in spontaneous prayer, a habit that aroused in them feelings of queasy awe. One of the daughters of these unfortunate girls recalled years later that Mary Anne's schoolfellows 'loved her as much as they could venture to love one whom they felt to be so immeasurably superior to themselves'.[10]

Delighted with her growing reputation for perfection, Mary Anne's response was to compose a poem entitled 'On Being Called a Saint' in which she tortured herself deliciously with the possibility that she was not quite as perfect as everyone believed. Her opening stanza sighs,

> A Saint! Oh would that I could claim
> The privileg'd, the honor'd name
> And confidently take my stand
> Though lowest in the saintly band![11]

Saints, of course, are not supposed to worry about what they look like. At a time when even her most pious classmates were becoming interested in their looks and the things that went with them – flirtation, courtship, marriage – Mary Anne was increasingly aware that she was unlikely to attract many admirers. Her big nose, long upper lip and lank hair were really not so very ugly, especially at a time when many a teenage girl had to worry about black teeth and smallpox scars, but her mother's early lessons about her unacceptability had been well learned. Believing herself a fright, she became one.

Evangelical and dissenting Protestantism had always warned against the pleasures of the flesh, identifying vanity as a particularly besetting sin. Mary

Anne seized on this licence with enthusiasm, deliberately playing up her plain-ness by looking unkempt and adopting a severe style of dress, including an unflattering Quaker-type cap.[12] If being pretty was the one thing at which she did not excel, she would turn the situation on its head and become expert at looking plain. In a plodding essay on 'Affectation and Conceit' written at this time, she upbraids pretty, vapid women who 'study no graces of mind or intellect. Their whole thoughts are how they shall best maintain their empire over their surrounding inferiors, and the right fit of a dress or bonnet will occupy their minds for hours together.'[13] At fifteen Mary Anne was a long way from the realisation that she was just as guilty of manipulating her appearance in order to maintain superiority over her peers.

Throughout her adult life, other people made periodic attempts to get Mary Anne interested in her appearance. But her sense of hopelessness in this area was so embedded that nothing made much difference. While she was staying in a boarding-house in Geneva in 1849 a fellow guest – a marquise no less – insisted on giving her a more up-to-date hairstyle. Mary Anne felt ridiculous: 'All the world says I look infinitely better so I comply, though to myself I seem uglier than ever – if possible.'[14]

Years later, in 1863, when she and Lewes held a house-warming party at their new home off Regent's Park, their interior designer Owen Jones gave Mary Anne a talking-to about 'her general neglect of personal adornment' and insisted on shoehorning her into a splendid moiré dress bought especially for the occasion.[15]

Mary Anne reported these two incidents to her correspondents with amused disbelief. She was so convinced of her own ugliness, other people's kind atten-tions were always suspected as possible teases. As a result she never acquired the confidence which would have allowed her to make the best of herself. In middle age, when she was seen regularly at the theatre and in concert halls, she became well known for the awful mishmash of her outfits, part high fashion, part provincial dowdiness. At the end of her life, and married to the much younger John Cross, her attempts to put together a flattering new image earned her sniggers from the effortlessly elegant.

Yet behind the poker-faced demeanour which sometimes confused visitors into thinking she was a third Miss Franklin, Mary Anne's emotions worked as violently as ever. One schoolmate recalled her shock at finding a passionate demand for love scribbled in the back of the paragon's German dictionary.[16] The tearful exits which usually followed her piano recitals in the Franklins' drawing-room suggest the intensity with which she lived. Performance of all kinds was to remain a tricky business throughout her life. She longed for the praise, acclaim and love that went with setting her fiction before the public, but could not bear the criticism and gossip that naturally accompanied them. Her need to be right and perfect went beyond vanity and became a matter of survival, to the point where Lewes realised he had better suppress all but the most flattering reviews if she were not to plunge into a paralysing despair. The teenage Mary Anne was, if anything, even more thin-skinned. Performing for the Misses Franklin and their visitors offered the possibility of reaching an instant of perfection and, better still, having it witnessed by others. When that moment of transcendence failed to appear – because, in her own eyes, she had failed to reach the required standard – it was as if she had blown her last chance at love.

Mary Anne's surviving exercise book, too, reveals a deep interest in the whole drama of rejection. In her neat hand she copied out a trashy poem called 'The Forsaken' in which a young woman is jilted by a casual, arrogant man. Melodramatic though this might have been, it explores Mary Anne's experience of her brother's early coldness. The man in the poem behaves much as Isaac had done – leaving his sweetheart–sister bereft, while he sets out to explore a wider world, returning in this case not with a pony but with another woman. By way of a fantasy revenge, one of the last poems Mary Anne copied out in her notebook is 'To a Sister' in which a far-away brother begs his sister to remember him.[17] These verses and the trauma behind her choice of them laid the basis for Mary Anne's pessimistic expectations about adult sexuality: women are doomed to love men who will not love them back. The future she imagined for herself was the one which came to pass. Until the age of thirty-four she was to endure one romantic rejection after another.

In 1835 Christiana Evans fell ill with breast cancer, and at Christmas Mary Anne was called home from school to nurse her. All the French prizes and piano performances in the world could not rescue the cleverest girl in the school from the expectations which the nineteenth-century family placed on its unmarried daughters. Any hopes Mary Anne might have harboured about moving on from the Franklins to an even more prestigious school, perhaps on the Continent, were dashed by the summons home to Griff.

Mary Anne's entire education had been shaped by the demands of her mother's health. At five she had been sent away because Christiana was too frail to manage her and at sixteen she was being called back because she was dying. Characteristically, any grievance Mary Anne felt was kept well buried. The one surviving letter of this time, written to Maria Lewis, uses the conventional pieties of the sickroom, 'We dare not hope that there will be a permanent improvement.'[18] There wasn't. In the early hours of 3 February 1836 Christiana Evans died.

In a letter to his employer a few weeks later Robert Evans appeared to accept the situation stoically: 'I have gone through a great deal of pain and Greif, but it is the work of God therefore I submit to it chearfully as far as Human Nature will *permit*.'[19] In fact, he was far from resigned. When it became apparent in late December that Christiana was about to die, Evans had fallen violently and suddenly ill with a kidney complaint. The man who had always seemed as solid as an oak crumpled at the prospect of losing a wife for the second time. For a while it looked as if he too might die. But tender nursing and ferocious bleeding with leeches had their effect, and by mid-January he was shakily mobile. For a difficult few weeks it had seemed as if the Evans family – always a more fragile structure than it seemed – might collapse completely.

For the first time, almost, since Mary Anne's birth the three children of

Robert Evans's second marriage were living under one roof. Chrissey was the housekeeper, Isaac the apprentice and Mary Anne her father's surrogate wife. It was she who accompanied the old man on shopping trips to Coventry, mended his clothes and read from Walter Scott, the author whom they both loved. There is no evidence that the placid Chrissey resented her younger sister's place in their father's affections. Always her mother's favourite daughter, the elder girl was released by Mrs Evans's death into forming an attachment outside the family. A little over a year later she was married and her housekeeping duties devolved on Mary Anne.

With Isaac, the situation was not so easy. This could have been a time of reconciliation, with brother and sister moving beyond their childhood estrangement to build a new, adult relationship. But a single surviving anecdote which Cross tells from their intervening boarding-school years suggests that the tensions between them were as alive as ever. 'On coming home for their holidays the sister and brother began . . . the habit of acting charades together before the Griff household and the aunts, who were greatly impressed with the cleverness of the performance; and the girl was now recognised in the family circle as no ordinary child.'[20] No teenage boy enjoys being outshone by his younger sister, especially in front of those family members who had previously placed him first. Between the lines of an anecdote anxiously repeated by John Cross to emphasise the harmony between Isaac and Mary Anne, there lurked a rivalry which was to re-emerge now that the two were once more under the same roof.

On the surface theirs was an argument about religion. Isaac was a High Anglican, at the very opposite end of the spectrum from Mary Anne. At its most intellectually sophisticated, the Anglo-Catholic movement was rigorous and ascetic, favouring a return to the liturgy and monastic practices of the pre-Reform church. But Isaac had imbibed, probably from the tutor in Birmingham where he had finished his education, a more comfortable version, which celebrated the pleasures of the material world. While Mary Anne's transformation from village girl to young lady had been modelled on Evangelical ideals of genteel behaviour, Isaac's parallel metamorphosis into a gentleman – and that, indeed, is how he described himself in 1844 when he acted as executor to Aunt Evarard's will – had been along decidedly High Church lines. His was a faith which allowed a man to hunt, drink and dine, before absolving himself from sin through the sacrament. It would be hard to imagine a greater contrast with Mary Anne's conscience-scourging, Bible-reading puritanism.

Brother and sister were on a collision course and the crash came in August 1838. They spent a few days together in London, during which Mary Anne was picky about everything. The choir at St Paul's was frivolous and silly. Going to the theatre was sinful and she preferred to spend the evening reading. The only time she cheered up was on a visit to Greenwich Hospital. Finally, brother and sister went to a bookshop where he bought a couple of hunting sketches, while she pounced triumphantly on a copy of Josephus's *History of the Jews*.[21]

Here was a return to the power struggle of a decade earlier. Isaac's rejection of his little sister in favour of a pony had been the catalyst for her plunge into books and religion. Now she was using the intellectual muscle developed as a result to try and regain control of him. No longer sufficiently undefended to ask openly for love, she insisted that he bend down and do her will instead. The fact that he did not, that he constantly eluded her with his sociability and worldliness, only made her angrier. Her response was to become even more censorious, sniping at what she admitted later were his perfectly 'lawful amuse-ments'[22] and adopting a superior, critical tone whenever talking about him. 'Isaac is determinately busy, and altogether improving,' she wrote smugly to Maria Lewis on 13 March 1840, as if discussing an annoying child.[23]

There had been a brief rapprochement fifteen months before the trip to London when, on 30 May 1837, Chrissey married Edward Clarke at Chilvers Coton. On that occasion brother and sister broke down and had 'a good cry' at the realisation that life at Griff was moving into a new and unknown phase.[24] It was now that Mary Ann – newly elevated to 'Miss Evans' and minus the final 'e' of her Christian name – became the official housekeeper. Quite possibly her father offered to hire someone to do the job, leaving her free to study full-time at home. That she did not accept this tempting proposal suggests that she had a great deal at stake in becoming the mistress of Griff. John Cross, always anxious to absolve his late wife of anything that might hint at oddness or masculinity, emphasised the pleasure she took in 'the soothing, strengthening, sacred influences of the home life, the home loves, the home duties'.[25]

A mix of motives is more likely. Running a working farmhouse was one of the few opportunities for a middle-class woman to exercise her energy and organisational skills, and Mary Ann certainly enjoyed being 'an important personage at home'.[26] When the aunts came to dinner they could not fail to have noticed the gleaming tiles, polished furniture and well-stocked cupboards. The awkward, bookish little girl whom none of them had really cared for turned out to be a Pearson after all.

Keeping house for her father was also a way for Mary Ann to bind him closer to her. With her mother and elder sister out of the way, she was finally able to occupy the position of wife to Robert Evans. Over sixty and in indiffer-ent health, Evans was devolving more and more responsibility for the estate business on to Isaac. In time-honoured tradition, he expected his youngest daughter to be the comforter of his declining years, filling his evenings with companionship, reading and music, before nursing him to his grave. It was a dull, heavy burden, but one which allowed Mary Ann to monopolise the member of her family who, she maintained on the eve of his death a decade later, was 'the one deep strong love I have ever known'.[27]

But it would be wrong to imagine something gloomy and gothic for Mary Ann Evans. Chilvers Coton was not Haworth; Robert Evans was not Patrick Brontë; and the girl herself was certainly not running mad over the moors. Griff was a working farmhouse, Robert Evans was still active and Isaac had a sociable, busy life. Mary Ann found herself playing hostess to a steady stream of visitors. The Pearson aunts and her married sisters all lived near enough to make frequent appearances at Griff. Then there were the Derbyshire Evanses,

Samuel and his wife Elizabeth, who visited in early 1839. Mary Ann's former schoolteachers, Miss Lewis and the Misses Franklin, came to stay several times. Old family friends put up at Griff, sometimes for days at a stretch.

Nor was she entirely confined to home. In November 1839 she stayed with her old school friend Jessie Barclay in London, making her first train journey to get there. The following year her father took her to visit his brothers' families in Derbyshire and Staffordshire, making a detour on the way home to sightsee in Lincoln. Still, long-distance travel was neither easy nor cheap and the mail remained the chief way in which middle-class girls living at home continued their school friendships. Indeed, Hannah More, whose pious books Mary Ann much admired, referred to these post-school, pre-marriage years as the 'epistolary period of life'. Many of Mary Ann's letters from these years have not survived, but luckily forty-five remain, the majority written to Maria Lewis and Martha Jackson, an old classmate.

Evangelicalism, with its roots in the Puritan doctrines of the seventeenth century, had always placed the well-tended home at the heart of Christian life. Becoming mistress of Griff gave Mary Ann a larger sphere for her religious activities than she had hitherto known. Making jam and churning butter were not simply routine domestic tasks, but crucial ways of worshipping God. Determined to give up all worldly pleasures since 'I find, as Dr. Johnson said respecting his wine, total abstinence much easier than moderation',[28] she was in the powerful position of being able to make sure that everyone else at Griff did too – or else endure her smouldering disapproval. Every Michaelmas she sulked at having to organise a harvest festival supper. The pagan overtones of the feasting and drunkenness made the event 'nauseating' to her. Equally unpleasant was having to give up a day to the 'disagreeable bustle' of preparing for Isaac's twenty-third birthday, on 19 May 1839, which was to be marked by a crow-shooting party.[29] The one saving grace was that since the birthday itself fell on the Sabbath, the celebrations were held over until the next day. By the time she came to write *Adam Bede* twenty years later, Eliot's mature vision had transformed both the harvest supper and the coming-of-age party into occasions which celebrated the cohesion of village ties and the enduring nature of community life. At this point, though, they seemed witless and wanton.

That same crucial shift in perception is apparent in another incident which occurred around now. In early 1839 Mary Ann's Methodist aunt and uncle were visiting from Derbyshire. Elizabeth Evans was a devout Methodist and a one-time preacher. Her vocation and a few details about her career notoriously formed the basis of Eliot's portrayal of Dinah in *Adam Bede*. A genuinely good woman, Elizabeth Evans radiated the kind of generous fellow feeling which was anathema to her sour-minded niece. During the course of the visit Mrs Evans spoke joyfully about a minister she knew who had recently died. Undeterred by the fact that he was a drinker – a quality not likely to endear him to the abstinent Evangelical and dissenting conscience – she spoke enthusiastically about the man's good qualities and concluded that he was now surely in heaven. 'This was at the time an offence to my stern, ascetic hard views,' explained the middle-aged Mary Ann, 'how beautiful it is to me now!'[30]

Despite disapproving of her aunt's reluctance to condemn, Mary Ann seized upon Elizabeth Evans as the one person within the extended family network with whom she could share the daily experience of her faith. Sadly, most of this experience was a kind of torture. In a letter written just after the 1839 visit, Mary Ann pours out her despair at her failure to reach God. Even at this point, two and a half years before she gave up going to church, she was battling with the realisation that her gloomy and self-denying faith had little to do with the divine and a great deal to do with her own internal dramas.

> Instead of putting my light under a bushel, I am in danger of ostenta-tiously displaying a false one. You have much too high an opinion my dear Aunt, of my spiritual condition and of my personal and circumstantial advantages . . . I feel that my besetting sin is the one of all others most destroying, as it is the fruitful parent of them all, Ambition, a desire insatiable for the esteem of my fellow creatures. This seems the centre whence all my actions proceed.[31]

Certainly it was ambition rather than fellow feeling which powered Mary Ann's drive to become one of the most important figures in the parish. During these years she started a clothing club, organised bazaars, ran a Sunday School and visited the local workhouse, Coton College. 'We shall never have another Mary Ann Evans' was the ambiguous lament of those on the receiving end of her charity when she left for Coventry in 1841.[32] Spiritual and social yearnings dovetailed nicely when this pious busyness brought Mary Ann to the attention of Mrs Newdegate (who used the older spelling of the family name), the new mistress of Arbury Hall. Old Francis Parker-Newdigate had died in 1835 and the inheritance had passed to his cousin's wife, Maria Newdegate, and her son Charles. While Francis Parker-Newdigate had been indifferent to the welfare of his tenants, his successor was irritatingly involved. Devoutly Evangelical, Mrs Newdegate insisted that all the farmers should attend church at least once on Sunday. This new regime at Arbury Hall exactly suited Mary Ann, who soon became a pet of her father's new employer.

At the end of 1839 Mary Ann decided to start work on a chart laying out the history of the Church from the birth of Christ to the Reformation. If all went well it would be published and some of the profits would go towards building a new church at Attleborough. To help her with the vast research, she reported proudly to Maria Lewis that Mrs Newdegate 'permits me to visit her library when I please in search of any books that may assist me'.[33]

Only a few years previously Mary Ann had been made to wait in the house-keeper's room, while her father talked business with old Mr Newdigate. Now here she was, taking possession of the library, that symbol of culture, achieve-ment and learning. Her father's professional success and her own genteel education had eased her transformation from near-servant to near-lady. Instead of the awkward little girl with the thick Warwickshire accent of only a few years ago, there was an intense young woman with a well-modulated voice and an abundance of learning, as well as the required string of genteel accomplishments. Of course, no amount of round vowels and fancy arpeggios were ever going to give Mary Ann a smooth passage into the gentry. Mrs Newdegate might allow her agent's daughter to borrow her books and run her clothing club, but she was not going to invite her to dinner or allow her to marry her son. These distinctions of rank, so subtle and yet so rigid, grated on Mary Ann, as a passage from *Felix Holt*, perceptively quoted by John Cross suggests: 'No one who has not a strong natural prompting and susceptibility towards such things [the signs and luxuries of ladyhood], and has, at the same time, suffered from the presence of opposite conditions, can understand how power-fully those minor accidents of rank which please the fastidious sense can preoccupy the imagination.'[34]

Like many upwardly mobile men and women of the Victorian period, Mary Ann's transformation into a member of the genteel middle class remained open to scrutiny all her life. Eliza Lynn, a minor novelist of about the same age who met Mary Ann when she was in her early thirties and bore her a strange lifelong grudge, maintained that 'there was something underbred and provincial [about Marian Evans] . . . She held her hands and arms kangaroo fashion; was badly dressed; had an unwashed, unbrushed, unkempt look altogether.'[35] Even when George Eliot was at the height of her reputation and had acquired sufficient money to buy herself some new clothes and a hairbrush there were still those ready to snipe at her lack of breeding. In an increasingly secular age, her irregular relationship with G. H. Lewes was linked less often to the fact that she did not attend church than that she was, more pertinently, 'not quite a lady'.

Mary Ann's confidence about putting together an ecclesiastical chart reflects the scope of her reading during these Griff years. Although she had refused her father's offer of a housekeeper, she allowed him to fund her continuing education in other ways. Twice a week Signor Joseph Brezzi arrived from Leamington to teach her Italian and German – the language which was to play such an important part in her personal and professional life. Robert Evans also happily settled her bills at Short's, the Nuneaton bookseller who did his best to keep up with her often obscure demands. It was now that she embarked on a habit of private reading which was to form the foundation for one of the greatest self-educations of the century. During these gloomy Evangelical years of 1837–40 the books she chose were inevitably religious. None the less, her practice of careful study, shrewd analysis and clear summary writing (in the form of letters to Maria Lewis and Martha Jackson) laid the basis for the critical skills which she was to apply across the huge range of subject matter which she tackled during her working life.

Her letters to Maria Lewis, who was now installed unhappily as a governess in a clergyman's family near Wellingborough, set out a formidable list of titles during the years 1838 to 1839. The core text remained the Bible, which she read every day. To this was added a series of commentaries and theological works, which helped define her position on the doctrinal controversies that were close to tearing apart the Established Church. The *Tracts for the Times*, with their yearnings for an Anglican Church reconciled with Rome, predictably repelled her. She looked more favourably on Joseph Milner's *History of the Church of Christ* (1794-7) with its mild Evangelicalism and cautious tolerance towards dissenters. Another book she liked was John Hoppus's *Schism as Opposed to Unity of the Church* (1839), which attacked the assumption of Roman Catholics and Anglicans that the structure of their Church rested on the direct authority of God. Years later it was this ability to empathise with intellectual and psychological positions far from her own that would mark George Eliot's mature art. At the age of twenty, however, open-mindedness simply muddled her. 'I am powerfully attracted in a certain direction but when I am about to settle there, counter assertions shake me from my position.'[36]

Mary Ann's Evangelical conscience did not allow her to read for pleasure. Works of fiction, which took the reader away from the stern business of soul-saving and into a compensatory world of fantasy, were, she believed, particularly harmful. In an essay disguised as a letter to Maria Lewis on 16 March 1839 she set out her objection to novels: 'For my part I am ready to sit down and weep at the impossibility of my understanding or barely knowing even a fraction of the sum of objects that present themselves for our contemplation in books and in life. Have I then any time to spend on things that never existed?' With the convenient exception of her beloved Scott, plus a few individual works such as *Don Quixote* and *Robinson Crusoe*, Mary Ann sternly outlawed all novels in favour of religious and historical texts. Even fiction on religious themes, of which there was a huge outpouring at this time, 'should be destroyed for the public good as soon as born'.[37]

Instead Mary Ann filled up her tiny amounts of free time by plunging into biographies of the good and the great, identifying with their struggles while going out of her way to deny any hubris. The experiences of William Wilberforce, the Evangelical reformer who campaigned against slavery, struck an immediate chord: 'There is a similarity, if I may compare myself with such a man, between his temptations or rather besetments and my own that makes his experience very interesting to me. O that I might be made as useful in my lowly and obscure station as he was in the exalted one assigned to him.'[38] Other model lives devoured included John Williams, an obscure dissenting South Seas missionary, and the sentimental Hannah More whose Evangelical pieties were immensely popular in middle-class households. Favoured poets included those twins of religious verse, Cowper and Young.

Although piety was the cloak Mary Ann threw over her intellectual energy, at times the full scope of her ambition peeps through the learned references and pious quotations with which she peppers her letters to Maria Lewis. Her early drive did not dissipate just because she was now at home making cheese. If anything, frustrations about the limitations on her time intensified it. Her letters to Maria Lewis are didactic and pedagogic, anxious to display their superior knowledge. She lectures her former teacher on German pronunciation, recommends books, and generally acts like the older woman's spiritual and intellectual adviser.

But Mary Ann remained painfully aware that this desire to show off was the result of Ambition, her besetting sin. As a good Evangelical Christian, she should stamp on any impulse to push herself forward – these early letters are full of apologies for egotism, for talking too much about herself, for 'the frequent use of the personal pronoun'.[39] At twenty she was not able to integrate these two sides of her personality – the desire for attention and the wish to surrender the self – and the result is a series of emotionally and tonally uneven letters. A demand for attention from Maria is followed by a humble withdrawal, in which Mary Ann imagines Miss Lewis thinking critically of her and rushes to apologise.

> You will think me interminably loquacious, and still worse you will be ready to compare my scribbled sheet to the walls of an Egyptian tomb for mystery, and determine not to imitate certain wise antiquaries or antiquarian wiseacres who 'waste their precious years, how soon to fail?' in deciphering information which has only the lichen and moss of age to make it more valuable than the facts graphically conveyed by an upholsterer's pattern book.[40]

Ironically, the end point of this dance between advance and withdrawal was a dazzling display of learning and verbal dexterity, seen here in the elaborate comparison of her handwriting with Egyptian hieroglyphics. In these bursts of words we begin to see Mary Ann flushed with pleasure as she realises what she is capable of. For if literature was forbidden as sinful, language was some-how another matter. In May 1840 she sings to Maria, 'I am beguiled by the fascinations that the study of languages has for my capricious mind, and could e'en give myself up to making discoveries in the world of words.'[41] Eighteen months later she crows, 'I love words; they are the quoits, the bows, the staves that furnish the gymnasium of the mind.'[42]

These early letters, with their see-sawing between assertion and self-denial, were the crucible in which Eliot's mature prose style was formed. At this point Mary Ann had very little real sense of her correspondent as a real and separate person with problems of her own. There are a few sympathetic noises when Maria describes a particularly unpleasant row with her employers, but the focus quickly shifts back to Mary Ann. Maria Lewis functioned as a kind of imaginary audience, whose reactions were to be anticipated and described by Mary Ann herself, with no reference to what was really felt or thought.[43] This inventing of Miss Lewis's response to her loquacity is the embryo of a stylistic practice which Eliot was to employ heavily at the beginning of her novel-writing career. In *Scenes of Clerical Life*, for instance, she often breaks off her narrative to deal with an imaginary reader's response. Of Mr Gilfil, for instance, 'You already suspect that the Vicar did not shine in the more spiritual functions of his office.'[44]

The letters to Martha Jackson are different. Martha had attended the Franklin school where she was a pale imitation of Mary Ann, being both clever and 'serious' in her religion. Now back at home with her parents, Martha continued to be edgy about Mary Ann's intellectual superiority. In January

1840 Mary Ann, perhaps anticipating slow progress on the ecclesiastical chart, sent a warning shot to Martha not to tread too closely on her patch. 'I am right glad to read of your enjoyments . . . and of your determination to study, though, by the bye, it is hardly fair of you to trench on my field; I shall have you publishing metaphysics before my work is ready, a result of the superior development of a certain region of your brain over that of my poor snailship.'[45]

Even this was not sufficient to deter the thick-skinned Martha, who wrote back demanding a list of every book that Mary Ann was currently reading. Clearly the time had come to sort out questions of pre-eminence once and for all. In her next letter Mary Ann suggested that they should organise their correspondence around a series of set topics, turning their letters into virtual essays. At this point Martha sensibly withdrew from the fray. The next time we hear from her she has taken up the girlish hobby of flower names, rechristening her friends according to their particular characteristics. Mary Ann has been assigned 'Clematis' which means 'mental beauty'. Martha, meanwhile, has become 'Ivy' which refers to 'constancy' but which, as Mary Ann quickly points out in a letter of 30 July 1840, is also a creeping parasite.[46]

In these letters to Martha, Mary Ann was careful to stress how little time she had for study and so, by implication, how wonderfully she was doing in the circumstances. 'Pity the sorrows of a poor young housekeeper,' she intoned on 6 April 1840, 'and determine to make the very best use of your present freedom *therefrom.*' Later, in case Martha had missed the point, she continued, 'I am conscious of having straitened myself by the adoption of a too varied and laborious set of studies, having so many social duties; otherwise circumstanced I might easily compass them all.'[47]

Competitiveness with Martha aside, Mary Ann's frustration about the small amount of time available to her was pressing and real. The ecclesiastical chart never got off the ground. Before she was even near to finishing it, another appeared on the market in May 1840. Pretending not to mind, she declared it 'far superior in conception to mine' and made a show of recommending it to friends.[48] The combined duties of housekeeper, hostess, companion and charity worker were so time-consuming that even personal letters could rarely be written at one sitting. 'I am obliged to take up my letter at any odd moment,' she wrote to Maria Lewis on 7 November 1838, 'so you must excuse its being rather a patchwork, or to try to appear learned, a tessellated or mosaic affair.'[49] And even when she did manage to write, her other life often inscribed itself on the paper: 'I write with a very tremulous hand as you will perceive; both this and many other defects in my letter are attributable to a very mighty cause – no other than the boiling of currant jelly.'[50]

This rigorous schedule of early mornings and late evenings crammed with private study was by no means unique to Mary Ann Evans. Florence Nightingale was doing the same thing in nearby Lea Hurst. So was Elizabeth Barrett in Wimpole Street. So were hundreds of other nameless middle-class girls who yearned for a life which went beyond the trivialities of the parlour and the store cupboard. What made Mary Ann Evans special was not simply her energy and determination, but also her ability to master a range of subjects far beyond the curriculum of even the best ladies' seminary. A letter written to Maria Lewis on 4 September 1839 demonstrates both the strengths and limitations of this kind of self-education. Mary Ann's use of the geological metaphor not only indicates that her reading was now straying beyond the strictly religious, but that she was acquainted with the new scientific discoveries which would soon shake orthodoxy to its core. More immediately, it articulates her secret terror that, without the advantages of a formal education, her reading might lack fruitful cohesion, amounting in the end to nothing more than accumulated junk.

> I have lately led so unsettled a life and have been so desultory in my employments, that my mind, never of the most highly organized genus, is more than usually chaotic, or rather it is like stratum of conglomerated fragments that shews here a jaw and rib of some ponderous quadruped, there a delicate alto-relievo of some fernlike plant, tiny shells, and mysterious nondescripts, encrusted and united with some unvaried and uninteresting but useful stone. My mind presents just such an assemblage of disjointed specimens of history, ancient and modern, scraps of poetry picked up from Shakspeare, Cowper, Wordsworth and Milton, newspaper topics, morsels of Addison and Bacon, Latin verbs, geometry entomology and chemistry, reviews and metaphysics, all arrested and petrified and smothered by the fast thickening every day accession of actual events, relative anxieties, and household cares and vexations.[51]

Life at Griff may have been tense between 1838 and 1840, but not enough to explain the constant depressions and headaches which dogged Mary Ann. In her letters to Maria Lewis, who was in the genuinely stressful position of working and living with people who did not value her, she complains constantly of 'low' spirits and whole days lost in generalised unwellness. This was the beginning of a set of symptoms that was to plague her for the next forty years, becoming particularly acute whenever she was wrestling with her writing. Whole years of her life – 1862 and 1865 stand out especially – were lost to misery and migraine as she battled with *Romola, The Spanish Gypsy* and *Felix Holt, The Radical.*

At the age of twenty Mary Ann Evans was not to embark on her novel writing for another decade and a half. But the sickness and despair suggest that she was already engaged in a bitter struggle with a part of herself which insisted on expression. During these dull, miserable years she fought to overcome an overwhelming and ill-defined sense of destiny which she placed under that pejorative umbrella 'Ambition'. The letter to Elizabeth Evans in March 1839 shows that she already had some inkling that much of her religiosity was nothing more than the desire to stand well in the world. But when she turned to the possibility of a more active kind of achievement, of the sort represented in the biographies she loved to read, she was brought up short by the lack of possibilities open to her. When in 1841 she moved to Coventry with her father, the delighted Misses Franklin introduced her to their accomplished friends 'not only as a marvel of mental power, but also as a person "sure to get something up very soon in the way of a clothing-club or other charitable undertaking" '.[52] This, baldly put, was the full scope of activity open to the prosperous, accomplished middle-class girl. Unlike the Franklins themselves, Mary Ann could not even find a vocation in teaching. The universities and professions were not open to her. Surely the cleverest, saintliest girl in the school could not be expected to spend her life getting up a clothing club?

Writing was one possibility. In the previous generation respectable women like Jane Austen and Hannah More had found success. No particular qualification was needed, and there was the great advantage that you could write at home, well away from the market-place in which no lady could be seen to participate. From her earliest years Mary Ann had toyed with the idea that her destiny might be literary. An anecdote from her childhood has her so entranced by Scott's *Waverley* that she commits a large chunk of it to heart.[53] Her surviving school notebook from around the age of fifteen contains the beginnings of a novel, 'Edward Neville', clumsily modelled on the work of G. P. R. James, who produced a series of poor-man's-Scott historical fictions during the 1830s.[54] The abandoned ecclesiastical chart, no matter how pious its origins, also suggests a pull towards publication. And in January 1840 Mary Ann finally achieved her dream of seeing her work in print. 'As o'er the fields', a poetic leave-taking of the earth and its pleasures as the speaker prepares for heaven, was accepted by the *Christian Observer*.

The novel, the chart and the poem all represent different kinds of writing which Mary Ann was trying on for size. Her attempts at the last two were easier for her conscience to accommodate, being mandated by her strict faith. The idea of writing fiction was still too dangerous. It involved dissolving into the imaginative state which she had identified as so perilous to the serious Christian searching for salvation. In the celebrated letter of 16 March 1839 which posterity has always found so wry Mary Ann tells Maria Lewis that her early and undisciplined passion for novels has 'contaminated' her with 'mental diseases' which 'I shall carry to my grave'.

The same see-sawing between desire and repression, joy and rage, was apparent in her ambivalent relationship with music during these years. Although she continued to have private piano lessons and to play for her father, opportunities for performing in front of others were few. Now Mary Ann adopted a censorious attitude towards those who allowed themselves the pleasure of demonstrating *their* talent. In another pompous letter to Maria Lewis, written 6–8 November 1838, she reports that she recently attended an oratorio at Coventry and hated every minute of it. 'I am a tasteless person but it would not cost me any regrets if the only music heard in our land were that of strict worship, nor can I think a pleasure that involves the devotion of all the time and powers of an immortal being to the acquirement of an expertness in so useless (at least in ninety nine cases out of a hundred) an accomplishment can be quite pure or elevating in its tendency.'[55] This reads strangely from a girl who in later life was to derive such pleasure from music and who would explore the nature of performance and artistry, especially for women, in *Daniel Deronda*. The ludicrous insistence that she has no ear for music and takes no pleasure in its secular uses suggests that exactly the opposite is the case. Just as in the earlier letter she fought against the recognition that she would like to write a novel and had already tried to do so, here she struggles with her desire to return to the days when she dominated the Franklins' drawing-room with her piano playing.

At times this battle against love, beauty and imagination became too much. When, in March 1840, desire threatened to press in on Mary Ann from all sides, she broke down completely. Shortly after arriving at a party given by an old family friend she realised that 'I was not in a situation to maintain the *Protestant* character of the true Christian' and decided to distance herself. Standing sternly in the corner, she looked on from the sidelines while the other guests danced, chatted and flirted. Battling with an urge to surrender to the rhythm of the music and also, perhaps, to be the centre of attention, she took refuge first in a headache, then in an attack of screaming hysterics 'so that I regularly disgraced myself'.[56]

The fact that Mary Ann repeated the story in a letter to Maria Lewis suggests that, far from feeling embarrassed by the incident, she was secretly delighted. As she saw it, her shouting and weeping attested to her holiness. For her hostess, the 'extremely kind' Mrs Bull, it probably suggested something quite different. Here, clearly, was a young woman in deep distress. As Mary Ann was no longer able to hold together the two parts of herself, the saint and the ambitious dreamer, something would surely have to give.

CHAPTER 3

'The Holy War'

Coventry
1840–1

FROM THE END of 1839 there were signs that Evangelicalism was losing its constricting grip on Mary Ann. Her reading, which for so many years had been pegged exclusively to God, now began to range over areas which she had previously outlawed. Where once she had warned darkly of Shakespeare 'we have need of as nice a power of distillation as the bee to suck nothing but honey from his pages',[1] now she quoted him with unselfconscious ease. She also used her increasing facility in German to read the decidedly secular Goethe and Schiller.

More crucially, she returned to the Romantic poets, whom she had not touched since her faith intensified in her mid-teens. She mentions both Shelley and Byron, men whose scandalous private lives would have disqualified them from her reading list only a couple of years previously. Through them, she entered a realm where the self dissolved luxuriously into feeling and imagination – the very process she had struggled to resist through her hysterical resistance to novel reading and musical performance. She also learned about the authority of individual experience in determining personal morality, even if that meant rebelling against social convention. It was, however, the more sober Wordsworth who particularly impressed her. Investing in a six-volume edition of his work to mark her twentieth birthday on 22 November 1839, she declared, 'I never before met with so many of my own feelings, expressed just as I could . . . like them.'[2] It was an admiration which was to grow to become one of the most enduring influences on her life and work. Wordsworth's insistence, particularly in 'The Prelude', on the importance of landscape and childhood in shaping the adult self gave an external validation to the connections she was now making between her own past and the emerging conflicts of the present.

Those conflicts concerned the what and how of daily faith. As she continued her careful comparison of the different denominations, Mary Ann's sympathies began to shift and broaden. By March 1840, she could read a book by the Anglo-Catholic William Gresley and find herself 'pleased with the spirit of piety that breathes throughout'. In the same letter she mentions with approval three of the most celebrated texts of the High Church Oxford Movement – *Oxford Tracts*, *Lyra Apostolica* and *The Christian Year*. The last of these became a particular favourite, and several of her letters now quoted the 'sweet poetry' of its author John Keble, the kind of thing which only eight months earlier she would have characterised as the work of Satan.[3]

Mary Ann was also reading widely in the natural sciences. The elaborate geological metaphor she had used despairingly to Maria Lewis to describe the random contents of her mind suggests that she was well acquainted with Charles Lyell's *Principles of Geology*, the work which paved the way for Darwin's implicit questioning of Genesis. Now, when she came across a book like *The Doctrine of The Deluge*, which attempted to sustain the scriptural account of the beginning of the world, she found it 'allusive and elliptical' where once she would have treated it as Gospel.[4]

Maria Lewis could hardly fail to pick up the clues that Mary Ann was moving away from the Evangelicalism which had sustained their friendship during the past ten years. If she had not taken account of the drift in her former pupil's reading matter, she surely noticed a new tone in her letters. Although not necessarily less pious, they were shorter, lighter and not so inclined to quote from the Bible. A few months earlier Martha Jackson had signified her secession from intellectual competition with Mary Ann by assigning them both flower names and retreating into the language of conventional letter writing. Now Mary Ann, armed with her own flower name dictionary, dubbed Maria Lewis 'Veronica', meaning 'fidelity in friendship', and showered her with sugary declarations of love. Instead of the sober and stilted greetings with which she had used to open her letters, she employed the kind of arch flourish associated with young ladies' correspondence: 'Your letter this morning, my Veronica, was sweet to me as the early incense of the Jasmine, and sent a thrill from my heart to my finger ends that impels them at the risk of indigestion, to employ the half hour after dinner, being the only one at liberty, to thank you for the affection that same letter breathes.'[5]

But the fulsomeness of the tone calls attention to the lack of real feeling it is trying to conceal. Interspersed with these overblown protestations of love were alarming, and surely intentional, hints that Maria was no longer the emotional centre of her life. By May 1841 Mary Ann had moved from Griff to the outskirts of Coventry, and was keen to let Maria know that she was busy making new and exciting contacts. In a letter of the 21st she mentions 'my neighbour who is growing into the more precious character of a friend.'[6] This teasingly unnamed acquaintance was, in fact, Elizabeth Pears, the woman who was to introduce Mary Ann to the circle of people who would replace Maria as her confidante. For Miss Lewis, now middle-aged and soon to be out of a job, it must have felt as if every anchor in her life was being pulled away.

As the power balance between the two women shifted, their roles polarised. Maria became the junior member of the partnership, asking Mary Ann for advice about where she should look for work next. Mary Ann, in return, slipped easily into the role of advice-giver, discouraging Maria from running a school of her own by citing a whole string of horrors including 'rent, taxes, bad debts, servants untrustworthy, scarlet fever, panic of parents, imposing tradesmen'.[7] Instead, she promised she would look out for a position in a private household for Maria, and even asked Signor Brezzi if he knew of a family that needed a governess. But when a possible situation did present itself in May 1841, Mary Ann took the opportunity to drop hints to Maria about the change in her own religious opinions.

> Of course in Mr. W's family perfect freedom of thought and action in religious matters would be understood as an unquestioned right, but as education, to be such, implies aggression on supposed error of every kind and incubation of truth it is probable you would not choose to put yourself in a position apparently requiring the anomalous conditions of neutrality and command. It is folly to talk of educating children without giving their opinions a bias. This is always given whether weak or strong, not always nor perhaps in a large proportion of cases, a permanent one, but one instrumental in determining their point of repose.[8]

The message is coded, though easily unpicked. In matters of religious faith, Mary Ann supports the principle of 'perfect freedom of thought and action' in preference to Maria's assumed desire to stamp out 'supposed error of every kind'. She finishes with an oblique warning that while Maria may have used her authority as a governess to shape Mary Ann's early religious views, her former pupil is now beginning to think for herself.

Throughout the summer of 1841 Mary Ann's letters to Maria continue in this contradictory fashion. Elaborate pledges of affection are followed by hurtful snubs. On 12 August she declared, 'How should I love to join you at Margate now that you are alone!' before bewailing the fact that 'I have no one who enters into my pleasures or my griefs, no one with whom I can pour out my soul, no one with the same yearnings the same temptations the same delights as myself.'[9] How wounding to the woman who had spent the last decade as Mary Ann's chief confidante. How could the girl claim that she had no one who understood her? What were these 'yearnings' and 'temptations' which separated them? Once again, Mary Ann realised she had gone too far, adding disingenuously, 'Pray regard all I have written as cancelled in my own mind.'[10] But Maria could not. She wrote back anxiously demanding reassurances that nothing had changed. The response she got was inflatedly insincere, declaring, 'Yes, I firmly believe our love is of a nature not to be changed by place or time.'[11] Maria, by now rattled, countered with 'a very ambiguous reply' and suggested that it might not be a good idea for her to visit at Christmas. Mary Ann did her best to sound reassuring in her next letter, but actually came across as evasive, skidding off into a description of the glorious autumn weather.[12] Then, on 16 October 1841, she gave the clearest indication yet that something was different, if not actually wrong. In an abrupt postscript on that day she writes, 'May I call you Maria? I feel our friendship too serious a thing to endure even an artificial name. And restore to me Mary Ann.'[13] Despite her reasoning that a return to their real names reinstated the dignity of the friendship, it sounded more as if Mary Ann wanted to withdraw from a correspondence which had become a bore.

But turning Veronica back into Maria did not have the desired effect. Far from easing up on her demands for reassurance, Maria redoubled her anxious enquiries to know exactly what was going on. Exasperated by her growing revulsion for the older woman, on 23 October Mary Ann let loose with a brutal letter, conspicuously lacking the respect due to a former teacher.

> You are veritably an overreaching friend, my dear Maria, not content with my scribbling a couple of sheets to every quarter of the moon, you even insist on dictating the subjects of the same, and the one you now impose on me is at once so sterile, so incomprehensible and so unfascinating that I should be quite justified in refusing to descant *thereon*. If you complain that my letters become increasingly illegible, just take into consideration the necessary effect of having to write a few pages almost daily. This has been the case with me of late, and I am likely to be more and more busy, if I succeed in a project that is just now occupying my thoughts and feelings.[14]

Maria, unsurprisingly, did not reply and Mary Ann realised that this time she was in danger of losing her only intimate friend: despite her boastful teasing, her new contacts in Coventry had not yet yielded the kind of emotional intimacy she craved. In a continuation of that earlier pattern of assertion followed by withdrawal, she wrote a few days later with muffled apology – 'tell me that you forgive my – something between brusquerie and confusion in my last letter.'[15]

Somewhat mollified, Maria responded by again raising the vexed subject of her Christmas visit. After a delay of a week and a half, Mary Ann wrote back with the strongest hint yet that something profound had happened to her which Maria might not like. She mentions that her 'whole soul has been engrossed in the most interesting of all enquiries for the last few days, and to what result my thoughts may lead I know not – possibly to one that will startle you, but my only desire is to know the truth, my only fear to cling to error'. Then she continues urgently, 'Think – is there any *conceivable* alteration in me that would prevent your coming to me at Christmas? I long to have a friend such as you are I think I may say alone to me, to unburthen every thought and difficulty – for I am still a solitary, though near a city.'[16]

Maria evidently wrote back reassuring Mary Ann that there could be no 'conceivable alteration' in her friend that would make her not want to spend Christmas with her. Word of Mary Ann's religious crisis may have already reached Maria Lewis through their network of mutual acquaintances. Or perhaps she put Mary Ann's restlessness down to the fact that the Evans family was going through one of its periodic crises.

Isaac was about to be married. Some time previously, probably when he was living with his tutor in Birmingham, he had met a woman called Sarah Rawlins. A large dowry from her leather-merchant father sweetened the fact that she was ten years older than the prospective groom. The two families had long been acquainted and Mr Rawlins had been a pallbearer at Christiana's funeral. And with a son in the church, the whole family was clearly working its passage away from Trade. Like his father before him, Isaac was shrewdly cautious when it came to choosing a bride. Sarah, as with Christiana in the generation before, appeared to have most of the qualities required in the wife of a young man determined to consolidate his position as a gentleman.

Isaac was a ditherer in emotional matters, especially when their ramifications reached so far. If he and Sarah married, the obvious move was for them to become the new master and mistress of Griff, especially now that Isaac was already running much of the business. But in that case, where would Robert and Mary Ann live? Doubtless Sarah would be quite happy to look after the old man, but whether she really wanted her young sister-in-law watching her every move was quite another matter. Mary Ann might not have relished every aspect of housekeeping, but she depended on it for her sense of identity and was not about to relinquish it easily. 'I will only hint', she writes to Maria Lewis in May 1840, 'that there seems a probability of my being ... severed from all the ties that have hitherto given my existence the semblance of a usefulness beyond that of making up the requisite quantum of animal matter in the universe.'[17] Toppled from her throne, she was unlikely to become an easy and serene deputy to Sarah. Her role henceforth would be marginal and ambiguous, involving a great deal of routine needlework and, in time, childcare. More specifically, it would mean taking instructions from the woman who had usurped her in Isaac's life.

Such a potentially unhappy arrangement might well have caused Isaac to think twice about marrying Sarah at all. In July 1840 Mary Ann reports that her brother has gone to Paris and that the marriage is uncertain 'so I know not what will be our situation'.[18] Two months later the couple are re-engaged, although this time Mary Ann is cautiously optimistic that Isaac and Sarah will set up home elsewhere, so that 'I am not to be dislodged from my present pedestal or resign my sceptre'.[19] A few weeks further on the situation has changed again, although this time a workable solution emerges. Isaac and Sarah are to take possession of Griff, while Robert and Mary Ann will move to a new home in Coventry.

Mary Ann's letters to Maria are loyally reticent about the anxiety to which she was being subjected during these ten agonising months. However, she was clearly at breaking-point. In September, possibly to celebrate the fact that the engagement was back on, Mary Ann travelled to Birmingham with Isaac for the annual festival. Together with Sarah they attended a concert of oratorios by Handel and Haydn, during which Mary Ann did her usual party piece of breaking down in hysterical tears, attracting embarrassed glances from her neighbours.[20]

Some of Mary Ann's upset can be explained by her continuing battle to resist the pull towards musical performance. She had displayed the same panicky defensiveness two years earlier during the oratorio at Coventry and again at Mrs Bull's dancing party. This time, though, there was an added pressure.

Sarah's presence at the concert was a reminder to Mary Ann that she was on the point of losing the three things which gave her life ballast: Griff and its landscape, her authority as housekeeper and tireless parish worker, and the constant attention, albeit antagonistic, of her brother Isaac.

None of this would have been so bad if Mary Ann had felt that it would not be long before she too would be getting married and moving to a new home of her own. Her gradual release from Evangelicalism meant that she no longer necessarily believed that marriage was a worldly snare and by 1840 there are signs that she was beginning to notice attractive men when they crossed her path. In March she fell for a nameless young man whom she felt obliged to give up because of his lack of serious religion, or indeed any religion at all. Her one comfort from this short, intense attachment was that she was probably the first person to have said any prayers on his behalf.[21]

A couple of months later she was describing Signor Brezzi, her language tutor, as 'all external grace and mental power', even though she told herself (via a letter to Maria Lewis), '"Cease ye from man" is engraven on my amulet.'[22] This was the first of many infatuations with men who stood in the role of teacher. Until the age of thirty-four Mary Ann was to be involved in a series of unhappily one-sided love affairs, in which she confused a man's delight in her intellect as a declaration of his sexual involvement. Luckily in this case there was no embarrassing moment of reckoning and the bachelor Brezzi seems to have been unaware of the feelings he had aroused in his eager pupil. Their lessons continued smoothly on her arrival in Coventry.

Although neither of these crushes had been very important, still Isaac's engagement a few months later triggered Mary Ann's sense of abandonment and her terror that she would be alone for ever. Even at this late stage she retreated into the language of Evangelicalism to explain to Martha Jackson – with whom she found it easier to talk about these things than the spinsterish Maria Lewis – about why she felt obliged to renounce her desperate need for love. 'Every day's experience seems to deepen the voice of foreboding that has long been telling me, "The bliss of reciprocated affection is not allotted to you under any form. Your heart must be widowed in this manner from the world, or you will never seek a better portion; a consciousness of possessing the fervent love of any human being would soon become your heaven, therefore it would be your curse."'[23] But if Mary Ann had decided to give up on marriage, her family had not. The reasoning behind the move to Coventry was that it would give her the chance to move in the social circles which might yield a husband. At twenty-one she was of a suitable age to embark on courtship and, although not pretty, she was clever, prosperous and good. A man might do worse than marry Miss Evans.

Coventry made Nuneaton look dingy and parochial. With its population of 30,000 and its fast railway to London, it crackled with purpose. Instead of the poky cottages with their clanking handlooms, there were steam-powered factories to which the workers walked every morning. And although the local ribbon trade fluctuated wildly, dependent on the vagaries of fashion and cheap foreign imports, it was still sufficiently sound to support a wealthy middle-class élite of manufacturers. Linked through a cat's cradle of business partnerships and marriage, these families managed to combine a handy knack of making a profit with a busy social conscience. Educated, progressive and earnest, they favoured a broad range of social and municipal reform designed to improve the living conditions of the people who worked for them. It was men like these, rather than the old alliance of gentleman and parson, who increasingly dominated the city council.

If Coventry seemed to offer the perfect environment for Mary Ann, then the house Robert Evans took on the outskirts of the city showed her off to best advantage. Bird Grove was an impressive Georgian semi-detached building, set back from the Foleshill road in its own woody grounds. It was large enough for both Mary Ann and Robert to have their own studies. Flanked by similar properties owned by the city's worthies, Bird Grove was a testimony to its new tenant's social standing. Although Robert Evans was not well known in Coventry, his choice of house announced that here was a man who, even in retirement, regarded himself as a pillar of the community. On hearing that Evans was about to move into the new house, his former employer Lord Aylesford 'Laphd and said they would make me Mayor'.[24]

Although it was a relief to Mary Ann finally to move to Coventry in the middle of March 1840, leaving Griff was a wrench: 'it is like dying to one stage of existence,' she told Martha Jackson.[25] The strong feelings she had developed for the countryside, its buildings and people, as she drove around the Arbury estate with her father, had not dissolved over the intervening years of bookishness. Griff farmhouse would always remain the shape and colour of her childhood, the scene of those fierce loves which Wordsworth told her were the root of the adult self. Translated to Foleshill she found herself experiencing 'a considerable disturbance of the usual flow of thought and feeling on being severed from the objects so long accustomed to call it forth'.[26]

Moving to Coventry in order to give Mary Ann a stab at courtship sounded like a good idea, but it soon became clear that neither she nor her father knew where to start. Evans's contacts were all based in Griff, which was five miles away, or the even more distant Nuneaton. Chrissey and Fanny were both nearby, but neither was in a position to launch her younger sister into Coventry society. Ever energetic, despite his increasing frailty, Evans decided to make church attendance the starting point of their new life. The obvious place to go was Trinity, in the centre of Coventry, since its vicar had previously owned the lease on Bird Grove. Within a month of moving to Foleshill, Evans was acting as sidesman. Father and daughter frequently made trips to other churches in the area to hear a particular clergyman preach. Ironically, just as Mary Ann was beginning to have serious, though still secret, doubts about her faith, her father was becoming more intense and discriminating in his church attendance.

During these first few months in Coventry, there was no outward change in Mary Ann to suggest that she was anything other than a devout Evangelical

Anglican. Her dour, censorious manner continued to repel those who made tentative approaches towards her. A family called Stephenson, friends of Maria Lewis, talked to her at church and said that they looked forward to seeing her soon. Yet neither Mrs Stephenson nor her two young daughters called at Bird Grove, not sure if their friendship was really wanted. With the hypersensitivity of the very shy, Mary Ann felt the snub keenly and hit back with lofty disdain, declaring in a letter to Maria that the two Stephenson girls 'possess the minimum of attraction for me'.[27]

All the same, there is a hint that she was beginning to wonder whether other people – just like the silly Misses Stephenson – did not sometimes have the right idea. On one occasion she found herself shocked by the bright clothes of one local congregation, before going on to ponder 'how much easier life would be to her, and how much better she should stand in the estimation of her neighbours, if only she could take things as they did, be satisfied with outside pleasures, and conform to popular beliefs without any reflection or examination'.[28] As it dawned upon her that her search for spiritual truth might mean that her current social isolation would soon be replaced by total ostracism, Mary Ann longed for the easy life which came with a numb conscience.

Still, she was not completely solitary during these first months in the city. The Misses Franklin tried to be helpful, singing her praises to their extensive circle of cultured, nonconformist friends. One important introduction was to the Sibree family, who lived not far away. Mr Sibree was minister of the local Independent Chapel, John junior was preparing to follow him into the ministry and sixteen-year-old Mary was a clever, lively girl who would become the first of the many ardent younger female admirers who clung to Mary Ann throughout her life.

An even more crucial contact was Elizabeth Pears, the neighbour who Mary Ann had hinted to Maria was 'growing into the more precious character of friend'.[29] Mr and Mrs Abijah Hill Pears, to give them their magnificent full name, lived in the house adjoining Bird Grove. Mr Pears, a ribbon manufacturer, was a leading Liberal in the city and about to be made mayor. He was in partnership with one of the Misses Franklin's brothers and it was through them that Mary Ann came to meet his Evangelical wife. The Franklins, as we have seen, introduced their distinguished former pupil with the oddly textured compliment that not only was she a 'marvel of mental power' but also 'sure to get up something in the way of a clothing-club'. Sure enough, within a few weeks of moving into the area Mary Ann had set up just such a scheme for unemployed miners and had organised the older and more established Mrs Pears into helping her.[30]

Although on the surface Mary Ann continued to behave with her usual pious busyness, her private reading during these first months in Coventry was taking her deeper into unorthodoxy. The frequent starting points for her speculations were books which had been written to bolster literal interpretations of the Bible, but which raised more questions than they could answer. Books like Isaac Taylor's *Physical Theory of Another Life* (1836) and John Pye Smith's *Relation between the Holy Scriptures and Some Parts of Geological Science* (1839) attempted to respond to the onslaught made on orthodox Christianity by the new discoveries in physical science about the material origins of the earth. Both, however, failed to deal with these counter-proposals and ended up weakening their case. Other authors whom Mary Ann now encountered had already made the journey from orthodoxy and were able to present their material in a more open manner. John Pringle Nichol, who wrote *The Phenomena and Order of the Solar System* and *View of the Architecture of the Heavens* (1839), both of which gave Mary Ann great pleasure, had felt obliged to give up Holy Orders because of the change in his religious beliefs.

But by far and away the most single influential book Mary Ann came across during these months was Charles Hennell's *An Inquiry Concerning the Origin of Christianity*. It had first been published in 1838, and a second edition – the one which Mary Ann bought – appeared in August 1841. Exactly when she read *An Inquiry* is unclear, but it is certainly the case that she was aware of the book's existence and general argument by the autumn of 1841, not least because all the major participants in its remarkable genesis were related to her friend and neighbour Elizabeth Pears.

Charles Hennell was a London merchant who, along with his tribe of adoring sisters, had been brought up as a Unitarian. Unitarianism was the most tolerant, rational and forward-thinking of the many Protestant sects which flourished during the first part of the nineteenth century. The novelist Elizabeth Gaskell, the writer Harriet Martineau and Florence Nightingale were all brought up within its generous and humane parameters. Unitarians rejected any kind of mysticism, including the doctrine of the Trinity and the divinity of Christ. Jesus was a great teacher, philosopher and living example, but not the Son of God. Although Unitarianism had developed outside the Anglican Church and within the dissenting tradition, it excluded much of the apparatus associated with nonconformity. There was no original sin, no doctrine of atonement and certainly no elect of chosen souls destined for heaven.

The Unitarians more than made up for their tiny numbers by their bustling, active presence in public life. With their intellectual roots in the Enlightenment philosophers Locke and Hartley, they placed a great deal of emphasis on the influence of education and environment in determining adult personality. Less concerned with the hereafter than the here and now, they worked hard to make certain that the best conditions prevailed for both individuals and societies to reach their full potential. This meant welcoming scientific progress, intellectual debate and the practical reforms that would naturally follow. In London, Coventry, Liverpool, Norwich and Manchester Unitarians were associated with a whole range of progressive causes from non-denominational education to the abolition of slavery. It was this social radicalism, combined with their rejection of Christ's divinity, which made them highly suspect to the Anglican Establishment and even other dissenters, to whom they seemed little more than atheists and revolutionaries.

In 1836 Charles Hennell's youngest sister Caroline, always known as Cara, had married a prosperous twenty-five-year-old Coventry ribbon manufacturer, Charles Bray. Since his adolescence Bray had moved in and out of faith.

During his apprenticeship in London he had taken the same path as Mary Ann into dour, self-denying Evangelicalism. Since then he had enjoyed sufficient income and leisure to follow up a whole range of alternative ways of looking at the nature of man and his relationship to God.

Bray was particularly influenced by a strand in the Unitarian philosophy known by the awkward name of Necessitarianism. This had its roots in the work of the eighteenth-century philosopher Joseph Priestley, who maintained that the moral and physical universe was governed by unchanging laws authored by God. It was the duty of man to discover these rules and then follow them, in effect working with God to promote an ever-improving world. Bray's reading of Necessitarianism resulted in a personal creed that was cheerful and vague, but productive of social change. He believed in a God who did not need to be formally worshipped since 'God will always do what is right *without asking* and not *the more for asking*'.[31] Instead of wasting time in prayer, Bray threw himself into a whole range of progressive causes designed to improve the quality of life for the people he employed in his flourishing ribbon business. His quirky, optimistic philosophy was summarised in his two-volume *The Philosophy of Necessity*, which was published in October 1841, just before he met Mary Ann Evans.

Given his puppyish lack of tact, it is surprising that Charles Bray managed to conceal his views from Cara until their honeymoon in Wales. It was then that he started his intellectual onslaught, believing that he 'had only to lay my new views on religious matters before my wife for her to accept them at once. But . . . I only succeeded in making my wife exceedingly uncomfortable.'[32] Uncomfortable she may have been, but as a woman of principle and integrity, Cara was not about to brush her new husband's objections to Christianity under the table. One of the central tenets of Unitarianism was the individual's duty to question every new piece of information, knowledge or experience, even if it implied an error in the *status quo*. Although deeply attached to her faith, Cara felt obliged to consider her husband's proposition that there was no firm evidence for the divine authorities of the scriptures.

Cara asked her brother, Charles Hennell, to undertake a rigorous assessment of Bray's claims on her behalf. Hennell had only just completed his own very thorough investigation of these matters, concluding that the spare creed of Unitarianism did indeed rest on incontrovertible Biblical evidence. But being a man of moral energy, he agreed to his sister's request to re-evaluate his work. The result was *An Inquiry Concerning the Origin of Christianity*, which scrupulously separated the known historical facts of Jesus's life from the later accretions of myth, fantasy and desire. Hennell took each Gospel in turn, explored the personal slant of the author and teased out those points at which objectivity gave way to invention. There is, Hennell argues, insufficient evidence to support the view that Christ was divinely born, worked miracles, was resurrected from the dead or ascended into heaven. Everything that happened to Him was explicable within 'the known laws of nature'. Out of this exhaustive study Jesus emerges as 'a noble-minded reformer and sage, martyred by crafty priests and brutal soldiers'. In a conclusion that echoes his brother-in-law

Charles Bray, Hennell argues that there is no point in concentrating on a future life because it is impossible to know whether it exists. Man's focus should be on the present, both in terms of the pleasures he can derive from 'this beautiful planet' and also in the improvements he can make in the lives of himself and others.[33]

Once Cara Bray had absorbed her brother's findings, she stopped going to church and suggested her husband do likewise. Her strict regard for conscience and horror of hypocrisy meant that she could not bear the idea of attending a service in whose teachings she did not believe. That did not imply, however, that she now considered herself an atheist. On the contrary, she pursued God as earnestly as ever – Mary Ann was to maintain that Cara was 'the most religious person I know'[34] – through private reading, careful thought and selective attendance at a variety of sermons, meetings and even services. She believed, as Mary Ann was to come to believe, that it was the duty of each individual to follow the truth wherever it might lead, without fear of social disgrace or superstitious terror.

Ironically, Elizabeth Pears first took Mary Ann with her on a visit to the Brays because she hoped, according to her brother Charles Bray, 'that the influence of this superior young lady of Evangelical principles might be beneficial to our heretical minds'.[35] In fact, after nine lonely months in Coventry, Mary Ann doubted that she was about to have much of an effect on anyone. 'I am going I hope to-day to effect a breach in the thick wall of indifference behind which the denizens of Coventry seem inclined to entrench themselves,' she wrote to Maria Lewis on 2 November, 'but I fear I shall fail.'[36] She did not, although Charles Bray's recollection of their first meeting, written up in the autobiography he produced at the end of his life, may well have been embellished by hindsight. 'I can well recollect her appearance and modest demeanour as she sat down on a low ottoman by the window, and I had a sort of surprised feeling when she first spoke, at the measured, highly cultivated mode of expression, so different from the usual tones of young persons from the country. We became friends at once.'[37]

Either at this meeting, or a subsequent one, Mary Ann and the Brays started to talk about religion. The young woman who had been introduced to them as a strict Evangelical turned out to be almost as advanced a free-thinker as they were themselves. The point was a crucial one to Cara Bray who resented the implication, which hung around for years, that she and her husband were responsible for converting Mary Ann from deep piety to unbelief. For this reason, too, Charles Bray stressed in his autobiography that Mary Ann had already bought Hennell's *Inquiry* by the time he and his wife met her in November 1841. However, the flyleaf of her copy is inscribed with the date 1 January 1842. Two explanations are possible. The first is that Mary Ann did not actually read the book until several months after meeting the Brays, which seems unlikely. The second, and more feasible, is that she had already tackled the book once before meeting the Brays and reread it subsequently during December, enthused by her acquaintance with the author's sister and brother-in-law. Writing '1st of Jany' on the flyleaf was her way of marking the moment when she formally renounced orthodox Christianity. For it was on the very next day, 2 January 1842, that she refused to go to church.

Christmas Day 1841 passed off unremarkably at Bird Grove. Fanny and Henry Houghton, Chrissey and Edward Clarke, Isaac and Sarah Evans, all came to dine at Foleshill. Two days later Robert Evans left on a business trip to Kirk Hallam, while Maria Lewis went to Nuneaton to look over a school she was hoping to run. Both of them had returned by Sunday, 2 January, the day on which Mary Ann refused to go to Trinity church.[38] She may have waited to make her stand until Maria was there because she wanted a buffer between herself and her father. Or perhaps she needed the woman who had shaped her earliest beliefs to witness their rejection. Either way, this was no momentary faltering of faith. A fortnight later, with Maria Lewis now gone, she was still refusing to accompany her father to church.

Robert Evans's response was to withdraw into a cold and sullen rage. It was not the state of Mary Ann's soul that troubled him so much as the social disgrace that came from having a daughter who refused to go to church. He had gone to considerable trouble and expense to ensure that she was given the best possible chance of marriage and here she was, undermining his efforts. He would, in truth, probably have been delighted if she had eased up on the fanatical religiosity which was in danger of repelling all but the most pious suitor. But to swing violently the other way and reject church worship altogether was to put herself outside respectable society. By refusing to accompany him to Trinity Mary Ann was condemning herself to spinsterhood.

In this 'holy war', as Mary Ann was to dub the difficult weeks that followed, God, housing and marriage were all tangled up together. The roots of the crisis went back to those ten uncertain months during which it was unclear whether Isaac would marry and take over Griff. Although Mary Ann's letters to Maria during that time cast Isaac obliquely in the role of prevaricator, it is unlikely that a young man of twenty-five was powerful enough to hold the whole family to ransom. It was the old man himself, Robert Evans, who could not decide whether this was the time to hand over the business and, if so, where he and Mary Ann would now live. Staying at Griff, moving in with Chrissey at Meriden, going to a cottage on Lord Aylesford's Packington estate, or opting for a smart town house in Coventry were all possibilities over which Evans pondered. And it was during this stop-start, yes-no period that Mary Ann was brought up sharp against the realisation that as an unmarried woman she had no power to shape her own life. It was her job to endure while Evans dithered, delayed and distracted himself from giving her a clear indication about the future.

When Mary Ann refused to go to Trinity with Robert Evans, she was rejecting not just her Heavenly Father but her earthly one too. The God who had tied her in self-denying, guilt-ridden knots for so many years had become identified with the patriarchal Evans, who remained indifferent to her emotional security and peace of mind. Rejecting an orthodox God was not simply about being up to date with theological and scientific debate. Nor was it concerned solely with asserting the primacy of individual conscience. It was, for Mary Ann, a refusal to be tied into a nexus of obligations that required her to attend church in order to get herself married and so relieve her father of the cost of her support.

As a result, the holy war was fought on two distinct levels. Evangelical and dissenting friends like the Sibrees, the Franklins and Mrs Pears fielded their most persuasive and sophisticated acquaintances in an attempt to argue Mary Ann out of her doubts. Within the Evans family itself, however, the struggle concerned more practical issues like daughterly duty, bricks and mortar, money and marriage. Robert Evans's first response was to treat Mary Ann with 'blank silence and cold reserve' – a literal sending to Coventry – followed by '*cooled glances, and exhortations to the suppression of self-conceit*'.[39] When this didn't work, Evans called upon his other children to persuade their younger sister to change her mind. Fanny Houghton, a well-read woman who also had doubts about orthodox Christianity, urged Mary Ann to keep her thoughts to herself and continue with outward observance.[40] Chrissey had no particular argument to make, but was requested to keep Mary Ann out of Robert's way by having her to stay at Meriden. It was during these few days that Isaac rode over from Griff to 'school' Mary Ann about where her duty lay. According to Isaac the expensive house at Foleshill had been taken in order to find Mary Ann a husband. Wilfully to put herself outside the marriage market by refusing to go to church was an act of great financial selfishness. Cara Bray, reporting the whole saga to her sister Sara Hennell, explained:

> It seems that brother Isaac with real fraternal kindness thinks that his sister has no chance of getting the one thing needful – ie a husband and a settlement, unless she mixes more in society, and complains that since she has known us she has hardly been anywhere else; that Mr Bray, being only a leader of mobs, can only introduce her to Chartists and Radicals, and that such only will ever fall in love with her if she does not belong to the Church.[41]

As if to confirm the truth of this pounds-shillings-and-pence argument, Robert Evans arranged to give up the lease of Bird Grove and set about preparing to move to a small cottage on Lord Aylesford's estate. True to form, he would not make it clear whether or not he expected Mary Ann to come with him. This frustrating silence continued even once she had returned from Meriden to Foleshill at the end of February.

In a desperate attempt to provoke her father into communication, Mary Ann wrote him a letter, the only one to him which survives. It is an extraordinary document for a girl of twenty-two to write – intellectually cogent, emotionally powerful. She starts by making clear the grounds for her rebellion. She assures him that she has not, contrary to his fears, become a Unitarian. Nor is she rejecting God, simply claiming the right to seek Him without the clutter of man-made dogma and doctrine. As far as the Bible is concerned, 'I regard these writings as histories consisting of mingled truth and fiction, and while I admire and cherish much of what I believe to have been the moral teaching of Jesus himself,

I consider the system of doctrines built upon the facts of his life . . . to be most dishonourable to God and most pernicious in its influence on individual and social happiness.' For this reason, continues Mary Ann, it would be impossible for her 'to join in worship which I wholly disapprove' simply for the sake of social appearance. She then proceeds to discuss the vexed issue of 'my supposed interests' and the financial aspects of the case. She understands that now she has put herself beyond the reach of respectable society, it is unfair to expect her father to maintain the expensive Coventry house. The last thing she wants is to syphon off capital which will eventually be divided among all five Evans children. Then she turns to the question of where she is to go next.

> I should be just as happy living with you at your cottage at Packington or any where else if I can thereby minister in the least to your comfort – of course unless that were the case I must prefer to rely on my own energies and resources feeble as they are – I fear nothing but voluntarily leaving you. I can cheerfully do it if you desire it and shall go with deep gratitude for all the tenderness and rich kindness you have never been tired of shewing me. So far from complaining I shall joyfully submit if as a proper punishment for the pain I have most unintentionally given you, you determine to appropriate any provision you may have intended to make for my future support to your other children whom you may consider more deserving.

She ends the letter with a resounding fanfare of self-justification. If Robert had any doubts about the fundamental shift in Mary Ann's beliefs, he had only to notice the absence of the usual Evangelical references – to God, to Heaven, to the Scriptures – and the substitution of language borrowing from (though not necessarily endorsing) Charles Bray's Necessitarianism and Cara Bray's Unitarianism. 'As a last vindication of herself from one who has no one to speak for her I may be permitted to say that if ever I loved you I do so now, if ever I sought to obey the laws of my Creator and to follow duty wherever it may lead me I have that determination now and the consciousness of this will support me though every being on earth were to frown upon me.'[42]

Robert Evans was unmoved. A few days later he told Lord Aylesford that he would soon be going back to the cottage at Packington and a week after that he put the lease of Bird Grove with an agent. In response, Mary Ann decided to go into lodgings in Leamington and look for a job as a governess. Mrs Pears promised to go with her to help her settle in. With Mary Ann's obvious erudition it might seem as though any family would be delighted to employ her. But her unorthodox religious views were not obvious recommendations for a post in a provincial middle-class home. And even if she did manage to find one, the unhappy example of Maria Lewis meant that she was under no illusions about the hardship of a governess's life, with its 'doleful lodgings, scanty meals'. Still, anything was better than the current 'wretched suspense'.[43]

In the end Mary Ann never got to Leamington. By the middle of March Isaac had given up 'schooling' and started mediating and the situation looked as though it might be resolved. Cara Bray reported the whole sequence of events in a letter written to her sister Mary. She tells how she had met Mary Ann in the street and had noticed 'a face very different from the long dismal one she has lately worn'.[44] The reason for the change of mood was that Isaac had sent a conciliatory reply to the letter she had written to her father explaining her motives. In this, Isaac accepted that Mary Ann had no wish to upset the family and acknowledged that she had been treated 'very harshly' simply for wanting to act according to her principles. He stressed that 'the sending her away' was entirely Robert's idea and had nothing to do with money, but arose simply because 'he could not bear the place after what had happened'. Isaac then finished the letter by 'begging' Mary Ann not to go into lodgings, but to come to stay at Griff instead, 'not doubting but that Mr Evans would send for her back again very soon'. In the meanwhile, explains Cara, Mr Evans has taken Bird Grove off the market and will stay there until Michaelmas, 'and before that time we quite expect that his daughter will be reinstated and all right again'.[45]

But Cara was jumping ahead, perhaps because, despite what she publicly protested, she felt responsible for Mary Ann's religious rebellion and wanted to reassure herself that no great harm had been done. Certainly Griff provided a welcome and welcoming interlude for Mary Ann, who was delighted not only with Isaac's new friendliness towards her, but also with the way in which old acquaintances greeted her cheerfully, despite knowing all about her unfortunate position. However, according to a letter she wrote from there on 31 March, nothing had really changed: Robert Evans was pushing ahead with improvements on the Packington cottage, where he presumably intended to live alone. Agonised by the lack of clarity about her own future, Mary Ann swung between defiant assertion and indirect pleading, declaring vehemently to Mrs Pears that she did 'not intend to remain here longer than three weeks, or at the very farthest, a month, and if I am not then recalled, I shall write for definite directions. I must have a *home*, not a visiting place. I wish you would learn something from my Father, and send me word how he seems disposed.'[46]

With the three weeks up, there was a small amount of progress to report. After an unexpected intervention from Isaac's wife Sarah, Mr Evans had agreed that Mary Ann should return to live with him. The young Mrs Evans had explained to the old man that making Mary Ann's material comfort dependent on a change of heart was the best way of ensuring she would never compromise. Doubtless Sarah had no intention of sharing or giving up Griff now that she was happily settled, and was keen to argue for reconciliation and a continuation of the *status quo*. But although Mr Evans had softened sufficiently to agree to take his daughter back, he still could not decide where they were to make their home. In Coventry she had become 'the town gazing-stock' and Evans was not certain whether he could bear the embarrassment of continuing to live there. His latest idea was to move to what Mary Ann described gloomily as 'a most lugubrious looking' house in the parish of Fillongley, where Lord Aylesford was one of the chief landowners. This constant change of plan was sending Mary Ann to the brink: 'I must have a settled home if my mind is to become healthy and composed, and I shall therefore write to my Father in a week and request his decision. It is important, I know, for him as well as myself that I should return to him without delay, and unless I draw a circle round him and require an answer within it, he will go on hesitating and hoping for weeks and weeks.'[47] Presumably Mary Ann drew that circle and got a satisfactory reply. By 30 April she was back at Foleshill with her father. A bargain had been struck: she would accompany him to church while he would let her think whatever she liked during the services.

While the Evanses were sulking, conferring and writing letters to one another about money, Mary Ann's Evangelical and dissenting friends stood by, ready to do what they could. Elizabeth Pears, Rebecca Franklin and the Sibree family displayed tact and sensitivity in their dealings with both Mary Ann and her father. Although disappointed that their clever young friend had turned her back on the faith which personally sustained them, they did not rush to condemn her. As people who set great store by the authority of individual conscience in deciding outward behaviour, they would never have urged her towards hypocrisy. At the same time, they were aware that much of the crisis was due to the inability of either Mary Ann, Robert or Isaac Evans to inhabit a world of uncertainty, tolerance and compromise. Their duty, as they saw it, was to hold the family together long enough for a workable solution to emerge.

In the middle of March Robert Evans called on the Franklin sisters and, bewildered and exasperated, complained that Cara Bray had badgered his daughter into becoming a Unitarian. Miss Rebecca quickly responded that 'she did not think Mrs. B. had shown any disposition to proselytize'. Along with Elizabeth Pears she impressed upon the old man that disowning Mary Ann was wrong and that 'the world would condemn him'.[48]

In the meantime the energetic Miss Franklin tried everything she could to reconvert her star pupil. She asked a clever, well-read Baptist minister friend to talk to the girl. He returned from their encounter insisting, 'That young lady must have had the devil at her elbow to suggest her doubts, for there was not a book that I recommended to her in support of Christian evidences that she had not read.'[49]

Next the Sibrees tried. In the small space of time she had known them Mary Ann had become attached to these pious, educated people who represented a family culture so different from her own. Mrs Sibree, an Evangelical Anglican, believed that 'argument and expostulation might do much' to bring Mary Ann back into the fold. For this reason she was careful to maintain a friendly welcome to the young neighbour. Mary Ann, for her part, was pathetically keen not to be rejected. 'Now, Mrs Sibree, you won't care to have anything more to do with me,' she teased anxiously. 'On the contrary,' replied the older woman, 'I shall feel more interested in you than ever.'[50]

First Mr Sibree himself tried to convince Mary Ann of the literal truth of the Gospels in a series of encounters so intense that Mary Ann was left shaking.[51] Next Mrs Sibree asked Reverend Francis Watts, a professor of theology from Birmingham, to try. Watts was a highly educated man with a formidable grounding in the German Biblical criticism that had done so much to cast doubt on the divine authority of the Scriptures. But he too confessed himself beaten, murmuring only, '*She* has gone into the question.'[52]

Despite the fact that the most subtle and clever men in the Midlands could not persuade Mary Ann to change her mind, on 15 May 1842 Robert Evans was able to record the end of the holy war: 'Went to Trinity Church. Mary Ann went with me to day.'[53] On the surface it seemed as if Mary Ann had done the very thing she had declared she would not – compromised her convictions for the sake of social respectability. But it was, as she began to see for the first time in her life, more complicated than that. Agreeing to attend church while keeping her own counsel involved giving up the glamour and notoriety of the past few months. At the height of the holy war she had written a letter to Maria Lewis in which she spoke of her realisation that the martyr is motivated by the same egotistical impulse as the court sycophant.[54] It was gradually dawning on her that her high-minded rebellion had been fuelled by her old enemy, Ambition.

A month or so later there was another suggestion, this time in a letter written to Mrs Pears from Griff, that Mary Ann no longer believed herself fully justified in the actions she had taken: 'on a retrospection of the past month, I regret nothing so much as my own impetuosity both of feeling and judging.'[55] It was a conclusion which was to stay with her for the rest of her life, for decades later she told John Cross that 'although she did not think she had been to blame, few things had occasioned her more regret than this temporary collision with her father, which might, she thought, have been avoided by a little management'.[56]

It was not that she believed her commitment to seek God outside a formal structure was mistaken, simply that she began to realise that she had other obligations no less important. Her needs as an individual had to be balanced against her duties as a daughter. Ultimately, what sustained humanity was not adhering blindly to a theory, political belief or religious practice, but the ties of feeling which bound one imperfect person to another. She would not give up her new beliefs for the sake of respectability, but she would forgo the glamour of shouting them from the roof-tops. She would endure people thinking that she had fudged her integrity if it meant that she could stay with the beloved father whom she had so deeply hurt. Far from giving up the authority of private conscience, she was stripping it of all its worldly rewards, including the glamour of being thought a martyr.

Eighteen months later, in October 1843, Mary Ann wrote out her fullest statement on the matter in the form of a letter to Sara Hennell, Cara's elder sister, who had since become her best friend. By now she had had time to absorb and reflect upon the turbulence and pain of the holy war. Her personal feelings of regret had been broadened into the kind of generalised observation on human nature which would come to typify the wise, tolerant narrative voice of her novels. 'The first impulse of a young and ingenuous mind is to withhold the slightest sanction from all that contains even a mixture of supposed error. When the soul is just liberated from the wretched giant's bed of dogmas on which it has been racked and stretched ever since it began to think there is a feeling of exultation and strong hope.' This soul, continues Mary Ann, believes that its new state of spiritual awareness more than compensates for the old world of error and confusion left behind. What's more, it is determined to spread the good news by proselytising to all and sundry. A year or two on, however, and the situation appears quite different. 'Speculative truth begins to appear but a shadow of individual minds, agreement between intellects seems unattainable, and we turn to the *truth of feeling* as the only universal bond of union. We find that the intellectual errors which we once fancied were a mere incrustation have grown into the living body and that we cannot in the majority of causes, wrench them away without destroying vitality.' Finally she broadens her argument, linking her own experience within the Evans family to a model of the world at large.

> The results of non-conformity in a family are just an epitome of what happens on a larger scale in the world. An influential member chooses to omit an observance which in the minds of all the rest is associated with what is highest and most venerable. He cannot make his reasons intelligible, and so his conduct is regarded as a relaxation of the hold that moral ties had on him previously. The rest are infected with the disease they imagine in him; all the screws by which order was maintained are loosened, and in more than one case a person's happiness may be ruined by the confusion of ideas which took the form of principles.[57]

The conclusions Mary Ann drew from the holy war prepared the way for her response to the difficult situation, fifteen years later, of being the unmarried 'wife' of George Henry Lewes. Living outside the law, she was socially ostracised in the same way Robert Evans feared would result from her non-attendance at church. However, much to the chagrin of her feminist friends, she refused to be known by her single name and insisted on being called 'Mrs Lewes'. She steered clear of giving support to a whole cluster of causes, including female suffrage, which might be supposed to be dear to the heart of a woman who had shocked convention by living with a man outside wedlock. This fundamental separation of private conscience from public behaviour was the founding point of Eliot's social conservatism. The fact that she loved a married man might authorise her own decision to live with him, but it could never justify a wider reorganisation of public morality. Family and community remained the best place for nurturing the individual moral self. Social change must come gradually and only after a thousand individuals had slightly widened their perceptions of how to live, bending the shape of public life to suit its new will. Revolution, liberation and upheaval were to have no place in Mary Ann's moral world.

Nor did they have any in her fiction. George Eliot's heroes and heroines may struggle against their small-minded communities, but in the course of their lives they learn that true heroism entails giving up the glory of conflict. Reconciliation with what previously seemed petty is the way that leads to moral growth. Romola, fleeing from her unfaithful husband Tito, is turned around in the road by Savonarola and sent back to achieve some kind of reconciliation.

Maggie, too, returns to St Ogg's after she has fled with Stephen and submits to the censure of the prurient townspeople. Dorothea's fantasies of greatness end up in the low-key usefulness of becoming an MP's wife.

The holy war cast a long spell not only over the fictions Mary Ann was to write, but over the intimate details of her daily life. None of her relationships would ever be quite the same again. On the surface, her friendship with Maria Lewis continued much as before. The first few letters of 1842 are lighter because more truthful. However, soon the correspondence starts to fail, spluttering on fitfully until Robert Evans's death in 1849, but with a notable lack of candour on Mary Ann's part. In a letter of 27 May she politely declares herself 'anxious' about whether Maria plans to visit, but prepares herself for the fact that Maria may be too 'busy' to reply immediately.[58] What Mary Ann had perhaps not fully recognised was that Maria was lonely and reluctant to give up her friendship with a family which had so often provided her with a home during the holidays. In fact, Maria continued to visit Foleshill over the next few years, but there was an increasing sense that she was visiting the whole family (she had, after all, taught Chrissey too) and not just Mary Ann. And there are signs that Mary Ann found these visits an increasing chore. In a letter of 3 January 1847 Cara wrote to her sister Sara, '[Mary Ann] is going to have a stupid Miss Lewis visitor for a fortnight, which will keep her at home.'[59] The nastiness of the tone is a surprise – Cara was a sweet-natured woman not inclined to hand out easy snubs. More than likely she was repeating what she had heard Mary Ann say of the squinting, pious, middle-aged schoolmistress who refused to realise that she was no longer wanted.

The exact end of the relationship is not clear. Reminiscing after Eliot's death, her friend Sara Hennell recalled that the estrangement had been 'gradual, incompatibility of opinions, etc, that Miss Lewis had been finding fault, governess fashion, with what was imprudent or unusual in Marian's manners and that Marian always resented this'. Certainly Maria had made a sharp comment about the unsuitability of Mary Ann hanging on to Charles Bray's arm 'like lovers'.[60] Still, it was Mary Ann who made the decisive break when she demanded that Maria return all the letters she had written her. Understandably hurt, Maria said that 'she would lend them her, but must have them returned'.[61] But once she had them in her possession Mary Ann reneged, citing the authority of a friend (probably Charles Bray) who told her that letters belonged to the writer to do with as she pleased. It is not entirely clear why Mary Ann wanted them. It may be that she felt the correspondence with Maria represented a part of her that had not so much been left behind as absorbed into a larger and more tolerant present. Gathering the letters may have been a way of recouping and qualifying the energy of the Evangelical years. Or perhaps Mary Ann still felt guilty about her less than straight dealing with Maria during the year running up to the holy war and wanted to regain control of the evidence of her hypocrisy. Or possibly she had simply outgrown this first important relationship with a person outside her family and wanted to mark its end. Significantly, she did not keep the letters but handed them over to Sara Hennell, the woman who had replaced Maria as her most intimate friend.

Mary Ann had no further contact with Maria Lewis until 1874, when she learned through Cara where she was living (in Leamington) and sent her a warm letter together with ten pounds – a practice she continued regularly until her death. Maria responded to the renewed contact with affection and admiration: 'As "George Eliot" I have traced you as far as possible and with an interest which few could feel; not many knew you as intimately as I once did, though we have been necessarily separated for so long. My heart has ever yearned after you, and pleasant it is truly in the evening of life to find the old love still existing.'[62]

Maria was quite right about knowing Eliot better than anyone. After the author's death she found herself eagerly courted by biographers keen for recollections of those early years. Although she was happy to talk to Edith Simcox when she came calling in 1885, she was understandably more cautious about giving away more tangible pieces of the past. Although on the best of terms with John Cross and delighted with his *Life*, still she refused to let him publish the letter which Eliot had sent with that first ten pounds. Having been robbed of the correspondence that had meant so much to her, she was determined to keep this tiny scrap of her star pupil to herself.

Mary Ann's other friendship from those schoolgirl Evangelical years – with Martha Jackson – also did not survive the change in her religious beliefs. Martha's mother, noting a change in the tone of Mary Ann's letters and also hearing rumours of what had happened, 'expressed a wish that the correspondence should close', fearing that her daughter might be led into infidelity. In fact, there was little chance of that. Martha remained defiantly orthodox until the end of her life, refusing to let John Cross use extracts from her correspondence with Mary Ann on the strange grounds that, since he was probably not a Christian, he could not be trusted with the material.[63]

From the beginning of 1840 Mary Ann's relationship with her Methodist aunt and uncle had also been cooling. As her Evangelicalism waned her letters to Derbyshire became sporadic and more inclined to talk about family matters – moving houses, marriages, births. A visit to Wirksworth in June 1840 had dragged, partly, she said later, because 'I was simply less devoted to religious ideas'.[64] A final extant letter to Samuel Evans, written by Mary Ann three months before her refusal to attend church, uses echoes of the old language of orthodox faith to hint at her new independence from it. 'I am often, very often stumbling, but I have been encouraged to believe that the mode of action most acceptable to God, is not to sit still desponding, but to rise and pursue my way.'[65]

Her growing certainty of her own beliefs and her corresponding tolerance of other people's meant that in the years that followed Mary Ann rediscovered her affection for her aunt and uncle. Mary Sibree recalled for John Cross how Mary Ann told her 'of a visit from one of her uncles in Derbyshire, a Wesleyan, and how much she had enjoyed talking with him, finding she could enter into his feelings so much better than she had done in past times, when her views seemed more in accordance with his own'.[66] Certainly by the time she came to write *Adam Bede* her antagonism towards orthodox ways of worship, particularly Methodism, had softened into an intuitive understanding of its value and meaning for people whose culture was now so very different from her own.

Unfortunately, Elizabeth and Samuel Evans never managed to extend that same understanding to their niece. Stories of her infamy became worked into the family inheritance. Their granddaughter remembered as a child being told by her mother that Mary Ann Evans was 'an example of all that was wicked'. The Staffordshire branch of the family felt the same way. Well into the twentieth century, Mary Ann was still whispered about as a cousin 'whose delinquency was an aggravated kind'.[67]

In the immediate aftermath of the holy war, Mary Ann had not yet developed the tolerance which would allow her to appreciate the value of views which were not her own. Nor did she have the social poise that would permit her to express that empathy gracefully. Thus it was awkward to discover on her return from Griff to Foleshill on 30 April 1841 that Elizabeth and Samuel Evans, together with William Evans, were making a visit. The next day was a Sunday and, keen to avoid conflict, Mary Ann took refuge at Rosehill, the Brays' home. There, much to her delight, Cara let her look at the letters which her brother Charles Hennell had written to her while writing *An Inquiry*. At Rosehill, Mary Ann had found the spiritual and intellectual home that was to sustain her for the next eight years.

CHAPTER 4

'I Fall Not In Love With Everyone'

The Rosehill Years
1841–9

FROM NOW ON Mary Ann spent every free moment with the Brays. Although Rosehill was less than a mile from Bird Grove, the contrast could hardly have been greater. While the Evans household was conservative, conventional and nominally devout, the Brays' was radical, avant-garde and truth-seeking. Here was the perfect atmosphere for Mary Ann to explore her new beliefs and the emotional release that came with them.

At the time Mary Ann first went to Rosehill Charles Bray was at the height of his reforming zeal. Prosperous, young and boundlessly energetic, he pursued a bundle of good and forward-thinking causes in the city and beyond. A passionate advocate of non-sectarian education, he built a school for children from dissenting families who had been excluded from Anglican institutions. He campaigned for sanitary reform and set up a public dispensary. He ran an anti-Corn Law campaign. Other projects were more visionary than feasible. He built a teetotal Working Men's Club to lure labourers away from pubs, set up an allotment scheme so that they could produce their own food and established a co-operative store to undercut local shop prices. Unfortunately, the working classes of Coventry did not share Bray's ideas about how they should live. Both the club and the gardening scheme failed through lack of support, while the store was forced to close by local shopkeepers determined to retain their monopoly.

Bray's generosity and intellectual open-mindedness – many called it sloppiness – meant that he attracted friends easily. Rosehill had quickly become established as the place where any visiting reformer, philosopher or thinker could be assured of a warm welcome. Indeed, said Bray in the puffed-up autobiography he wrote at the end of his life, anyone who 'was supposed to be a "little cracked", was sent up to Rosehill'.[1] During these years Mary Ann met virtually everyone who was anyone in free-thinking, progressive society. The socialist Robert Owen, the American poet Ralph Waldo Emerson and the mental health reformer Dr John Conolly were just a few of the people who took their turn sitting on the bear rug which the Brays spread out in the garden every summer. Here, under a favourite acacia tree, they spent long afternoons in vigorous debate, intellectual gossip and various degrees of flirtation.

For just as the Brays challenged conventional thinking in every area of life, so their attitudes to marriage and sexual love were markedly unorthodox. Nor was this openness confined to daring chat. As people who thought deep and hard about how to live, they had come to the conclusion that the monogamy demanded by the marriage vows did not suit human nature, or at least did not suit theirs. Although enduringly attached to one another, both had taken long-term lovers.

Just how this arrangement had come about, and how openly it was acknowledged by others, is obscured by the reticence which the couple was obliged to observe in order to remain active in Coventry public life. Indeed, the main account of their irregular marriage was written down in code and not untangled until the 1970s. The stenographer was the phrenologist George Combe, who examined Bray's head for lumps and bumps in 1851 and concluded that his 'animal' qualities were impressively predominant. Probing further, Combe extracted the following confession from his friend: 'At twelve years of age he was seduced by his father's Cook and indulged extensively in illicit intercourse with women. He abstained from 18 to 22 but suffered in health. He married and his wife has no children. He consoled himself with another woman by whom he had a daughter. He adopted his child with his wife's consent and she now lives with him. He still keeps the mother of the child and has another by her.'[2]

This makes sense of some odd references in Mary Ann's letters to Cara Bray during May 1845. Writing from Coventry to her friend on holiday in Hastings, Mary Ann says reassuringly, 'Of Baby you shall hear to-morrow, but do not be alarmed.'[3] A couple of days later she writes, 'The Baby is quite well and not at all triste on account of the absence of Papa and Mamma.'[4] Whoever this baby was, it did not last long at Rosehill. A month later an entry in Cara's diary suggests that the baby was removed from the household. Clearly this first attempt at adoption had not worked out. Baby's real mother may have wanted her back or perhaps Cara, while dedicated to young children through her teaching and writing, did not take to this particular infant. An attempt the following year with another baby, sister of the first, was successful and this time the Brays adopted Elinor, known as Nelly. Over the years Mary Ann became attached to the girl and when news of her early death came in 1865 it touched her deeply.

The fact that the first baby had been returned to its mother suggests that the Brays' family life did not run as rationally or smoothly as Charles liked to believe. Although the details are sketchy, it appears that for a time he tried to get the children's mother, Hannah Steane, to live at Rosehill as nursemaid. One version has Cara accepting this, but changing her mind when Hannah produced an illegitimate son, named Charles after his father. Henceforth Hannah, now reincarnated as Mrs Charles Gray, wife of a conveniently absent travelling salesman, was established in a nearby house – into which Bray could slip discreetly – with her growing family, five excluding Nelly.[5]

Cara's answering love affair was more circumspect. According to a gossipy report from her sister-in-law in 1851, 'Mrs Bray is and has been for years decidedly in love with Mr Noel, and . . . Mr Bray promotes her wish that Mr Noel should visit Rosehill as much as possible.' Edward Noel was an illegitimate cousin of Byron's wife, a poet, translator and owner of an estate on a Greek island. He was also married with a family. Whether he and Cara became physically intimate is not clear: one version maintains this was an unreciprocated passion. All the same, once Noel's wife died from consumption in 1845, the way was clear for him to become a familiar fixture on the edge of Rosehill life.[6]

The Brays' was the first of three sexually unconventional households which had a great impact on the young Mary Ann, whose romantic experience at this point was confined to a crush on her language teacher. Later she would find herself in a curious *ménage à quatre* with John Chapman, the publisher with whom she boarded in London during the early 1850s. And her subsequent dilemma over whether to live with George Henry Lewes was the result of his inability to divorce on the grounds that he had condoned his wife's affair with another man.

It would be good to think that these open marriages were founded on a principled rejection of the ownership of one person by another, and in particular of women by men, of the kind which John Stuart Mill would set out in *The Subjection of Women* in 1869. But in fact there was more than a whiff of male sexual opportunism and hypocrisy about the various set-ups. Charles Bray, after all, maintained in public that 'Matrimony is the law of our being, and it is in that state that Amativeness comes into its proper use and action, and is the least likely to be indulged in excess';[7] yet he did not confine himself to adultery with Hannah. There were rumours that 'the Don Juan of Coventry' had previously enjoyed an affair with Mary Hennell, one of Cara's elder sisters. And there was even a suggestion that he and Mary Ann became lovers at some point. Certainly Maria Lewis objected to the way the two clung together and Sara Hennell admitted after Mary Ann's death that she had always disapproved of the girl depending too much on male affection – perhaps specifically on the affection of her brother-in-law.[8] Bessie Rayner Parkes, who was later to become one of Mary Ann's best friends in London, certainly always believed that Mary Ann and Charles Bray had been lovers.[9]

Cara Bray, too, was inconsistent on the question of marital fidelity. Although she allowed her husband to have affairs and was herself at least emotionally intimate with Edward Noel, she reacted with Mrs Grundy-ish horror when Mary Ann went to live with George Henry Lewes in 1854. For five years she refused to communicate properly with her friend, let alone to see her. That a woman as progressive and principled as Cara should display such embarrassed confusion over sex outside marriage is a reminder of how deeply entrenched were codes of respectable behaviour – especially female behaviour – in even the most liberal Victorian circles.

Although the Brays' attitude could seem contradictory, in other lights it was subtle and realistic. Just as Mary Ann had learned during the holy war that spectacular rebellion is often the result of wilful egotism, so the Brays realised that there was little to be gained by publicly embracing the open relationships advocated by their friend the socialist Utopian Robert Owen. They preferred to remain within society and work for its improvement, rather than withdraw to an isolated and principled position on its margins. Whether the world thought them scandalous or hypocritical did not concern them. It was this example of adherence to a complex inner necessity, regardless of how one's behaviour might be interpreted, which Mary Ann now absorbed. It would stand her in good stead in the years to come when she lived with Lewes and, on his death, went through an Anglican marriage service with John Cross. Her apparent inconsistency bewildered family and friends. Isaac Evans was scandalised by the union with Lewes, but appeased by the marriage to Cross. Her old friend Maria Congreve, on the other hand, was serene about Lewes, but disappointed by what she perceived to be the hypocrisy of the 1880 wedding service. In these apparent switches of principle Mary Ann demonstrated her determination to live flexibly according to the fluctuations of her own inner life rather than in observance of other people's needs and rules.

Whether Mary Ann actually had a physical relationship with Charles Bray remains frustratingly unclear. The fact that all her letters to him prior to 1848 have disappeared suggests that they were at least emotionally intimate and that someone wanted the evidence destroyed. But even if they were lovers, it was more than a sexual affair that was responsible for the blossoming of Mary Ann's personality during these Rosehill years. The loving acceptance of Cara Bray and the intellectual companionship of Sara Hennell gave her a sense of being wanted – the first she had experienced since those early days with Isaac. Her young neighbour, Mary Sibree, recalled that 'Mr and Mrs Bray and Miss Hennell, with their friends, were *her* world, and on my saying to her once, as we closed the garden door [at Rosehill] together, that we seemed to be entering a Paradise, she said, "I do indeed feel that I shut the world out when I shut that door." '[10]

This new happiness permeated every part of Mary Ann's being. Now she played the piano and sang in front of other people without bursting into tears. Instead of refusing to read novels, she argued for them on the grounds that 'they perform an office for the mind which nothing else can'.[11] She relaxed sufficiently about her appearance to allow Cara to paint her portrait – a sweet, flattering water-colour which fooled no one and now hangs in the National Portrait Gallery.[12] She accompanied the Brays on holidays to other parts of the country and became a favourite with the friends and family they visited on the way.

With Mary Ann soaking up every new subject which the Brays pushed her way, it was inevitable that she should become interested in phrenology. The practice of bump-reading might seem like so much mumbo-jumbo now, but during the mid-nineteenth century it held considerable appeal for those who were trying to make connections between man's physical constitution and his psychological processes. During a trip to London in July 1844 Charles Bray persuaded Mary Ann to have a cast made of her head – luckily it was no longer necessary to have one's hair shaved off – and set about analysing its shape. Writing at the end of his life, and after hers, Bray naturally relied on *post hoc* knowledge to give his findings extra bite. In the following extract from his autobiography he creeps from phrenological 'fact' to interpretations of Mary Ann's subsequent behaviour.

> In the Feelings, the Animal and Moral regions are about equal; the moral being quite sufficient to keep the animal in order and in due subservience, but would not be spontaneously active. The social feelings were very active, particularly the adhesiveness. She was of a most affectionate disposition, always requiring some one to lean upon, preferring what has hitherto been considered the stronger sex to the other and more impressible. She was not fitted to stand alone.[13]

As Mary Ann's willingness to contemplate phrenology suggests, her intellectual relationship with others softened during this period. During the high drama of the holy war, the competitive Evangelical had given way to the combative free-thinker. Now, during the 1840s, Mary Ann began the long journey towards empathy and tolerance which was to mark the mature narrative voice of George Eliot. A passage from Bray's autobiography describes her at the very beginning of this bumpy process.

> I consider her the most delightful companion I have ever known; she knew everything. She had little self-assertion; her aim was always to show her friends off to the best advantage – not herself. She would polish up their witticisms, and give them the *full* credit of them. But there were two sides; hers was the temperament of genius which has always its sunny and shady side. She was frequently very depressed – and often very provoking, as much so as she could be agreeable – and we had violent quarrels; but the next day, or whenever we met, they were quite forgotten, and no allusions made to them.[14]

Increasingly Mary Ann was able to move beyond these violent reactions and come to rest in a position of disciplined tolerance towards others. This was particularly true in matters of faith. In the immediate aftermath of the holy war Mrs Sibree had been doubtful about letting Mary Sibree take German lessons from Mary Ann in case the older girl should unsettle her daughter's religious beliefs. Mr Sibree, however, did not 'see any danger' and the lessons began on Saturday afternoons. During these Mary Ann was always careful to steer clear of theological discussion, to the disappointment of Mary who tried to provoke the infamous Miss Evans into saying something controversial. Every time Mary tried to steer the conversation round to a dangerous topic, Mary Ann countered with a gentle reminder of 'the positive immorality of frittering ... [time] away in ill-natured or in poor profitless talk'. On one occasion the sixteen-year-old girl announced provocatively 'how sure I was that there could be no true morality without evangelical belief. "Oh, it is so, is it?" she [Mary Ann] said, with the kindest smile, and nothing further passed.'[15]

Mary Ann's deflective comments concealed the kernel of her argument with organised religion. In a letter of 3 August 1842 she told the Revd Francis Watts, one of the men who had tried to argue her out of infidelity, that feeling obliged to serve humanity out of a sense of duty and fear of punishment worked against 'that choice of the good for its own sake, that answers my ideal'.[16] Now that she was no longer burdened with having to save her soul through conspicuous good works, Mary Ann was able to concentrate on what really needed to be done. Finding that she was unsuited to some kinds of philanthropy – an attempt to help Cara at the infants' school had not been a success – she thought carefully about how she could be most useful. Often this turned out to be as inglorious as making a direct financial contribution. When one of the Sibrees' servants became burdened with the responsibility for newly orphaned nephews and nieces, she offered to pay for the care and education of 'a chubby-faced little girl four or five years of age'.[17] Again, she contributed two guineas to the Industrial Home for young women for which Mrs Sibree was collecting funds. 'I tell of this', says Mary Sibree, writing after Mary Ann's death, 'as one among many indications of Miss Evans's ever-growing zeal to serve humanity in a broader way, motivated as *she* felt by a higher aim than what she termed "desire to save one's soul by making up coarse flannel for the poor".'[18]

Other people sensed this expansion in Mary Ann's inner life and responded accordingly. No longer a chilly saint to be revered and avoided, she was approached by friends and servants who now came to her with their problems, 'to an extent', remembered Mary Sibree, 'that quite oppressed her'.[19] It was a phenomenon which was to last the rest of her life. Seven years later, when she was staying alone in a Geneva pension, she found herself a magnet for every lonely or anxious guest who needed someone to talk to. Twenty years on she was regularly besieged in letter and in person by men and women from around the world who were convinced that she, and she alone, could understand their story.

Thanks to growing family pressure, Mary Sibree had little contact with Mary Ann over the next few decades. But in 1873, as Mrs John Cash, wife of a prosperous manufacturer and the new mistress of Rosehill, she visited the woman who was now known as Marian Lewes in London. 'It touched me deeply to find how much she had retained of her kind interest in all that concerned me and mine, and I remarked on this to Mr Lewes, who came to the door with my daughter and myself at parting. "Wonderful sympathy," I said. "Is it not?" said he; and when I added, inquiringly, "The power lies there?" "Unquestionably it does," was his answer.'[20]

Mary Ann spent her first day home after the holy war at Rosehill reading letters which Charles Hennell had written to his sister Cara while working on *An Inquiry*. It was not just intellectual curiosity that made the experience so delightful. The fact that Hennell had responded to his sister's religious doubts by devoting two years of his hard-pressed time to produce this magnificent piece of work resonated deep within Mary Ann. Her own brother Isaac had met his sister's crisis of conscience with coldness, calculation and a complete lack of understanding. Charles Hennell, by contrast, seemed to have all the qualities desirable in an ideal brother–lover.

So it was painful to learn that he was already in love with someone else. Elizabeth Rebecca Brabant was the talented daughter of an intellectually minded doctor whose patients had included Thomas Moore and Samuel Taylor Coleridge. Indeed, she got her nickname – 'Rufa' – from some verses the latter had written about her striking red hair. Dr Robert Brabant had taught himself German in order to study the work of eminent theologians such as David Friedrich Strauss, who had done so much to reveal the man-made origins of the Bible. In 1839 Dr Brabant was an inevitable early reader of Charles Hennell's *An Inquiry*, which reached many of the same conclusions as Strauss. Delighted by the book, Brabant invited its author to his home in Devizes. Hennell, in turn, was enchanted by Rufa Brabant, to whom he quickly proposed. The good doctor, however, opposed the match when he examined the young man and found him to be consumptive. It is hard, now, to conceive the terror that tuberculosis generated a hundred and fifty years ago: the nearest analogy might be to finding that one has a slow-growing malignant tumour. The young couple agreed not to see each other but, by way of continuing their relationship, Rufa undertook to translate Strauss's most important book, *Das Leben Jesu* (1835–6), for her suitor. Remarkably, Hennell, who did not know German, had written *An Inquiry* without detailed knowledge of its contents.

When Rufa arrived in Coventry to visit the Brays in October 1842 it was inevitable that Mary Ann would not like her. All the more so when Charles Hennell turned up the next day, presumably against Dr Brabant's wishes. Rufa not only had the kind of hair which inspired poets, she read German theology in the original and enjoyed the love of a kind, clever man. However, during the next three weeks Mary Ann was able to draw on the emotional discipline which was eventually to become an integrated part of her personality. Writing to Sara Hennell on 3 November, she admits that her first impression of Rufa 'was unfavourable and unjust, for in spite of what some caustic people may say, I fall not in love with everyone'. On further acquaintance, she is happy to report: 'I admire your friend exceedingly; there is a tender seriousness about her that is very much to my taste, and thorough amiability and retiredness, all which qualities make her almost worthy of Mr Hennell.'[21]

There followed a tricky nine months during which events conspired to push Mary Ann and the officially unengaged Charles Hennell together. In March 1843 he turned up at Rosehill for a fortnight. In May he accompanied her and the Brays on a visit to Malvern. In July things came to a painful head when the same party, this time supplemented by Rufa, took a longer trip to Wales. During a ten-day stay in Tenby, Rufa badgered Mary Ann into attending a ball at the pavilion. Excruciatingly, no one asked her to dance. Doubtless Rufa was trying to be kind, but the news that she had resumed her engagement to Charles Hennell, this time with her father's approval, only pointed up the differences between the two young women. Both were clever and serious. But one was pretty and well connected and the other was not. And it was Rufa, with her magnificent hair and a pedigree rooted in the intellectual middle classes, who had bagged Charles Hennell.

There was a consolation prize of sorts. Mary Ann was to be a bridesmaid at the wedding, which took place on 1 November in London. The service was conducted by the country's leading Unitarian minister, William Johnson Fox, at the Finsbury Chapel. Escorted by Charles Bray, Mary Ann spent a week in London, staying with Sara Hennell, who lived with her mother in Hackney. The last time she had visited the city had been in 1838 with Isaac, during the height of her Evangelical phase. The gloomy teenager who had glowered at the suggestion of a trip to the theatre had been replaced by a young woman eager to pack as many cultural experiences as possible into the time available. But despite the fun and bustle, Mary Ann was still feeling left out and left behind by the Brabant–Hennell marriage. This was her third time as a bridesmaid and it was hard to imagine that it would ever be her turn to enjoy the loving attention which other women seemed to claim by right. So in these dispiriting circumstances it was delightful to receive an invitation from Rufa's father, asking her to accompany him home to Devizes for a holiday. She had first met the sixty-two-year-old Dr Brabant when he had joined the Brays' party in Wales and, persuaded by the fact that Rufa had come into some money, had given permission for the young couple to marry. If she could not have Charles Hennell as a brother–lover, then perhaps she might claim Robert Brabant as a more congenial substitute for the still disapproving and distant Robert Evans.

Luckily, Dr Brabant was ripe for the role in which he had been cast. He begged Mary Ann to consider Devizes *her* home for as long as she was deprived of a permanent arrangement in Warwickshire. Even now, eighteen months after the holy war, Isaac and Robert Evans were still making noises about moving Mary Ann back to the country. To have a charming, educated older man telling her that she must consider his library as her particular domain must have been intoxicating. She responded eagerly to his attentions, rapturously boasting in a letter to Cara that her host had christened her 'Deutera, which *means* second and *sounds* a little like daughter'.[22] Her next letter, on 20 November, continues in the same breathless vein. 'I am in a little heaven here, Dr. Brabant being its archangel . . . time would fail me to tell of all his charming qualities. We read, walk and talk together, and I am never weary of his company.'[23] She wrote to her father asking him if she could extend her stay to 13 December.

Not everyone in the Devizes household shared Mary Ann's view of paradise, especially Dr Brabant's wife and her sister. The latter, Miss Susan Hughes, had alerted Mrs Brabant, who was blind, to the fact that Miss Evans was permanently entwined with the doctor. Mrs Brabant immediately wrote to Rufa to ask her to tear herself away from her new husband and come down to Devizes to see if she could calm her over-ardent friend. Rufa in turn told her sister-in-law Cara what was going on and begged her to caution Mary

Ann by letter about her behaviour. Miss Hughes, meanwhile, took the most direct path by advising Mary Ann on the train times home, three weeks before her proposed departure.

Mary Ann was too enraptured to take the hint. She insisted on extending her stay and when Cara wrote warning her to beware of Dr Brabant, she snapped back, 'He really is a finer character than you think.'[24] The time had come for Mrs Brabant, whom Mary Ann had previously described as 'perfectly polite', to put her foot down. She demanded that Mary Ann depart immediately, a fortnight early, and swore that if she were ever to return then she, Mrs Brabant, would leave at once. It would be nice to report that the 'archangel' intervened and stood up for his 'Deutera'. In fact, according to John Chapman paraphrasing Rufa in 1851, Dr Brabant 'acted ungenerously and worse, towards Miss E. for though he was the chief cause of all that passed, he acted towards her as though . . . the fault lay with her alone'.[25]

The roots of the Devizes crisis went deeper than the emotional topsoil turned over by the wedding. Mary Ann was probably not the first, and certainly would not be the last, young woman towards whom Brabant was over-familiar. In 1885 her cattiest literary rival, Eliza Lynn, told Herbert Spencer that she too had received advances from Dr Brabant during a visit to Devizes in 1847. Never missing an opportunity to snipe, Lynn expressed amazement that Miss Evans could bear to encourage Dr Brabant, who she declared was 'more antipathetic than any man I have ever known . . . his love-making purely disgusting'.[26]

Nor was this the first time that Mary Ann had let an intellectual rapport with an older man overstep the mark. Revd Francis Watts, a friend of the Sibrees, had been one of the subtle thinkers enlisted to persuade Mary Ann back into the fold during the holy war. Although unsuccessful, he admitted to Mrs Sibree that Miss Evans had 'awakened deep interest in his own mind, as much by the earnestness which characterised her inquiries as by her exceptional attainments'.[27] Mary Ann was equally taken with the Revd Watts. In a pattern which was to be repeated several times over the next decade, she used her intellect to keep a clever, unavailable man interested in her. While still in exile at Griff she had written to Watts suggesting that he oversee her translation of Vinet's *Mémoire en faveur de la Liberté des Cultes*. With its proposition that man's capacity for goodness is not dependent on his belief in an afterlife, Vinet's book lay at the heart of her new beliefs. Enclosing a sample of her translation, she courted Watts in language which set abject humility alongside flirtatious presumption: 'I venture to send you an échantillon that you may judge whether I should be in danger of wofully travestying Vinet's style, and if you approve of my project I shall be delighted if you will become foster-father to the work, and arrange for its publication.'[28]

A second letter, nearly three months later, makes it clear that it is Watts's interest in her, rather than hers in Vinet, which makes the project meaningful to her. 'I shall proceed *con amore* now that you encourage me to hope for the publication of the memoir. I confess my spirits were flagging at the idea of translating four hundred pages to no purpose.' And then in a curiously oblique manner she continues: 'A friend has given some admonitions that led me to fear I have misrepresented myself by my manner . . . It gives me much pain to think that you should have received such an impression, and I entreat you to believe that the remembrance of you, your words and looks calls up, I will not say humble, but self-depreciating reflections and lively gratitude.'[29]

Watts must have been sufficiently reassured by Mary Ann's acknowledgement of her over-familiarity to continue his involvement in the project throughout the autumn of 1842. However, a letter received in December sounded warning bells again. Writing to acknowledge the receipt of some books he had lent her, Mary Ann gushed, 'I beg you to understand that I consider myself *your* translator and the publication as yours, and that my compensation will be any good that may be effected by the work, and the pleasure of being linked to your remembrance.'[30]

Now Watts had no choice but to acknowledge that Mary Ann's interest in Vinet arose out of her deep feelings for him. Panicked by the implications, he withdrew from the project and the correspondence, claiming busyness and possibly family illness as an excuse. The next thing we hear is that Mary Ann is returning his books and has given up on Vinet with the strange explanation that she has started translating 'a part of Spinoza's works for a friend'.[31] In fact, the friend was Cara and, far from begging Mary Ann to start work on it, Cara had wanted to do it herself, telling her sister Sara: 'I grieved to let Mary Ann carry it off, for I am sure I could understand his [Spinoza's] Latin better than her English; but it would disappoint her.'[32]

In truth, Mary Ann had embarked on Spinoza as a face-saving device, a way of rejecting Watts as surely as he had rejected her. It was a tactic she was to use in the even more embarrassing case of Dr Brabant, at whose suggestion the Spinoza translation was being done. Her last letter written from Devizes on 30 November 1843, a couple of days before her departure, gives the impression to Cara, who knew otherwise, that she is leaving on her own terms. She talks of her 'grief at parting with my precious friends', but makes no specific reference to the man who had previously been the epicentre of her correspondence.[33]

From the moment she returned to Coventry Mary Ann adopted an attitude of studied condescension about Dr Brabant, referring to him in public as if he were a ridiculous pest. Yet she could never quite bear to bring the relationship to a decisive close. Following the Devizes débâcle the archangel and his Deutera did not communicate for three years. However, when in 1846 Mary Ann finished the translation of Strauss, which she had taken over from Rufa, she could not resist sending Brabant a bound copy. Perhaps she wanted to show him that his second daughter could manage a piece of work which exceeded anything his first might have managed. The appearance of Miss Evans's parcel ruffled a few feathers in Devizes, and Sara Hennell was immediately asked to find out exactly what was going on. Mary Ann responded to her enquiry with defensive loftiness: 'Pray convince her [Rufa] and every one concerned . . . that I am too inflatedly conceited to think it worth my while to run after Dr. Brabant or his correspondence.' It is true, she admits, that she has initiated contact with him, but 'as a favour *conferred* by me rather than *received*'. And in case this should seem too obviously at odds with known history, she qualifies this with, 'If I ever offered incense to him it was because there was no other deity at hand and because I wanted some kind of worship pour passer le temps.'[34]

Over the next few years Mary Ann kept up this slighting tone towards the doctor. In February 1847 when she wanted to return his copy of Spinoza to him – the one she had started translating instead of Vinet – she imagined hurling it towards Devizes so that it would leave 'its mark somewhere above Dr. B's ear'.[35]

Brabant, by contrast, was unencumbered by embarrassed feelings and continued to display jaunty self-possession in his dealings with Mary Ann. In August of that year Sara reported that Mary Ann had received 'a most affectionate invitation from Dr. B. a few days ago to go to Germany with him!'[36] Although there would have been others in the party, Mary Ann refused. Starting up a correspondence with the archangel was one thing, reliving the embarrassment of the Devizes episode quite another.

Still, the good doctor refused to disappear completely. Whenever he was in town he stayed at 142 The Strand, the Chapmans' boarding-house where Mary Ann lodged during the early 1850s. On one such occasion when their paths crossed Mary Ann informed Cara that the 'house is only just exorcised of Dr. Brabant', as if he were a nasty smell.[37] Yet the very next day she wrote appreciatively of the doctor's visit to Charles Bray, mentioning that he had taken her 'very politely' on an excursion to Crystal Palace, as well as the theatre.[38]

Brabant's most celebrated reappearance in Mary Ann's life was in the shape of Edward Casaubon, the pedantic, ineffectual scholar of *Middlemarch*. For all Brabant's bustling endeavour, he never actually managed to sustain any piece of intellectual work. According to Eliza Lynn, Brabant 'used up his literary energies in thought and desire to do rather than in actual doing, and [his] fastidiousness made his work something like Penelope's web. Ever writing and rewriting, correcting and destroying, he never got farther than the introductory chapter of a book which he intended to be epoch-making, and the final destroyer of superstition and theological dogma.'[39]

Mary Ann saw for herself just how ineffectual Brabant really was when, at the beginning of 1844, she took over Rufa's translation of Strauss's *Das Leben Jesu*. The new Mrs Hennell had found the work too onerous to combine with married life and suggested to her sister-in-law Sara that Mary Ann might like to step in. This was a delicate situation. Having watched Rufa carry off Charles Hennell, was Mary Ann being offered her cast-off translation as some kind of compensation? If this suspicion did go through her mind, Cara and Sara surely pressed her to set it to one side. They were both aware of how desperately she needed a substantial piece of work to stretch and exhaust a mind prone to pull itself to pieces. Mary Ann's previous attempts at sustained intellectual work – the ecclesiastical chart, the translation of Vinet – had faltered through her own failure to get started. At the end of her life she told John Cross of her 'absolute despair' at this point of achieving anything.[40] The big attraction of the Strauss was that the translation was already commissioned – by the Radical MP Joseph Parkes – so there would be an external authority driving her to complete the project.

On taking up Strauss, Mary Ann asked Dr Brabant, via Sara Hennell, for some work he was rumoured to have done already on the concluding section. When the translation finally arrived it turned out, true to form, to be scrappy and incomplete. In any case, Mary Ann soon realised that trying to follow someone else's translation was 'like hearing another piano going just a note before you in the same tune you are playing'.[41] Putting aside the doctor's jottings, she started again from scratch.

Translating Strauss was to dominate her life for the next two years. Unable to concentrate for more than four hours a day, she evolved the method she was to follow when writing fiction of working from 9 a.m. to 1 p.m. This meant that she managed to cover about six pages of Strauss a day. Sara, who had turned down the translation before it had been offered to Rufa, agreed to act as Mary Ann's editor. Letters went back and forth between London and Coventry discussing various points of translation as they arose. When a section of the work was completed, Mary Ann mailed it to Sara to read through and check against the original. This reliance on the post caused constant worries about late and non-arriving packages. 'I sent a parcel of MS to you on Friday. Have you received it? I thought I should have heard that it had arrived safely when you sent the proof,' was a typically anxious communication between Mary Ann and Sara during a particularly difficult stretch.[42]

The translation was a remarkably difficult piece of work, which would have taxed the most scholarly, university-educated brain. There were fifteen hundred pages of what Mary Ann described despairingly as 'leathery' German, with many quotations in Latin, Greek and Hebrew. At times it was only Sara's brisk enthusiasm that kept her going: 'Thank you for the encouragement you sent me – I only need it when my head is weak and I am unable to do much.'[43] Even more tricky than finding literal meaning was the teasing out of nuance. Was it 'Sacrament' or 'The Sacrament'? Was 'Dogmatism' quite what Strauss meant by '*das Dogma*'?[44] And then there were pedantic, Rebecca Franklin-ish bickerings about English. Was 'as though' as good as 'as if'? Was it 'finally' or 'lastly'?[45]

Although the title of the work was *The Life of Jesus*, it is the subtitle – *Critically Examined* – which provides the key to Strauss's methodology. He takes each episode in the life of Jesus, as told in the four Gospels, and shows how it 'may be considered not as the expression of a fact, but as the product of an idea of his earliest followers'.[46] Steeped in the Jewish tradition of the returning Messiah, Jesus's disciples shaped their understanding of their master's life to fit inherited expectations. Strauss's aim was to unpick that process and show how the 'historical' Jesus had been created out of a series of Evangelical 'mythi'.

There was nothing in Strauss that was new or strange to Mary Ann. She had long since come to the conclusion that Jesus was a gifted human teacher and not the Son of God. However, she did worry about the theologian's relentlessly totalitarianising approach, which insisted on subsuming inconvenient exceptions into the arc of his narrative. 'I am never pained when I think Strauss right,' she wrote in the autumn of 1845, 'but in many cases I think him wrong, as every man must be in working out into detail an idea which has general truth, but is only one element in a perfect theory, not a perfect theory in itself.'[47] The crucifixion was a case in point. Strauss had to concede that the Jews' expectations of the Messiah did not include one who was to suffer and die, let alone rise again. So where did this part of the Gospel narrative come from? Strauss was obliged to conclude weakly that 'Jesus Himself may have reached the conclusion of the necessity of his death . . . or the whole idea might have been added *after* his death.'[48]

It was this stripping away of all that was 'miraculous and highly improbable' from the Gospels which oppressed Mary Ann the deeper she went into *Das Leben Jesu*. All her life she had read the Bible not simply as the revelation of God, but as the metaphorical language of her own experience. The quotations in her letters to Maria Lewis were not just for pious show, but a way of describing complex inner states. To be robbed of that language – for that is what she experienced Strauss as doing – was to be deprived of a vital part of herself. Her disillusionment with *Das Leben Jesu* became particularly acute at the beginning of 1846, when she tackled the detailed analysis of the crucifixion and resurrection. Describing herself as 'Strauss-sick', she fled to Rosehill, avoiding the first-floor study at Bird Grove, where she was supposed to be getting on with her work. She was, reported Cara in a letter to Sara, deathly pale and suffering from dreadful headaches.[49] To pull herself through this Slough of Despond she placed a cast of the Risen Christ together with an engraving in a prominent place by her desk. This was her way of reasserting the mystery and hopeful joy of the New Testament narratives which continued to sustain her long after she had given up orthodox Christianity.

Once the work was finished, except for routine worries over proofs, Mary Ann's spirits began to rise. At the end of May 1846 she headed off to see Sara in London with the promise that 'we will be merry and sad, wise and nonsensical, devout and wicked together!'[50] It was not simply liberation from the daily grind of translation that gave her such a delightful feeling of relief. The fact that the book was coming out at all was reason for celebration. Only a year earlier it had looked as though Strauss might go the same way as the ecclesiastical chart and Vinet – into oblivion. In May 1845 Joseph Parkes's assurance that he would finance the publication started to look shaky and Mary Ann began 'utterly to despair that Strauss will ever be published unless I . . . print it myself. I have no confidence in Mr Parkes and shall not be surprized if he fail in his engagement altogether.'[51]

In the end, the book did come out, published by John Chapman of Newgate Street. Mary Ann received only twenty pounds for her two years' work and her name does not appear on the title page – or indeed anywhere else. None the less, its impact on her life was huge. *Das Leben Jesu* was a supremely important book and the name of its translator could not fail to circulate among well-informed people. Mary Ann's meeting with the publisher John Chapman, while staying with Sara in summer 1846, was the catalyst for her move to London three years later and the start of her journalistic career. And, of course, the translation brought her to the notice of Strauss himself, who provided a preface in which he described her work as 'accurata et perspicua'.[52] In 1854 they finally met, thanks to the fussy ministrations of none other than Dr Brabant. Whether by chance or not, the good doctor popped up on the train on which Mary Ann and G. H. Lewes were travelling to Germany to start their life together, having fled gossiping London. Brabant insisted on introducing her to Strauss, whom he claimed as a kind of friend. The meeting, which took place over breakfast in a hotel in Cologne, turned out dismally. Strauss spoke little English and Mary Ann not much German. For this reason, or perhaps the buzzing presence of the insufferable Dr Brabant, Strauss appeared 'strange and cast-down' and the encounter drew to an embarrassed close.[53]

Once the exhilaration of being released from her task had settled, Mary Ann was in a position to assess the Strauss experience. Despite her dedication, a strain of ambivalence runs through her comments about the whole business of translation. It was, when all was said and done, not original or creative work, but 'trifling' stuff. She resented having had to worry about whether or not Parkes would come through with the money for something which was 'not important enough to demand the sacrifice of one's whole soul'.[54] Even at this stage Mary Ann knew that she wanted to be something more than a mediator of other people's words, although in later life she told a correspondent that at this point she stayed with translation because she felt that it was all she could do well.[55] Although she had completed three substantial translations by the time she started to write fiction, she never drew attention to the fact and would have been quite happy for her involvement in them to have remained little known.

Yet in the immediate aftermath of Strauss her loftiness concealed considerable pride in her achievement. She was pleased with Charles Wicksteed's review in the *Prospective Review* praising the 'faithful, elegant, and scholarlike translation'.[56] And when an old school friend approached her for advice about how she might earn her living as a translator, Mary Ann was quick to defend her own patch. Although she conceded that Miss Bradley Jenkins was clever, she poured scorn on her assumption that 'she could sit from morn till noon, from noon till dewy eve, translating German or French without feeling the least fatigue'.[57] It was one thing for Mary Ann Evans to think translation beneath her, quite another for an old classmate to assume she could do the same thing just as well.

One important legacy of the Strauss years was the deepening of Mary Ann's friendship with Sara Hennell. They had first met by proxy, during those difficult months of the holy war in the spring of 1842. From Cara, Mary Ann had heard all about her clever elder sister who had worked as a governess to the Bonham Carter family. Sara, meanwhile, followed the trials of Cara's interesting young neighbour through the letters she regularly received from

Rosehill. The two women were finally introduced that summer, when Sara spent one of her many holidays in Coventry. Six weeks of music and talk laid the foundations of a friendship which would become the most important of both women's lives for the next few years.

In many ways Sara Hennell was a clever, sophisticated version of that first governess in Mary Ann's life, Maria Lewis. While Miss Lewis worked in the house of a Midlands clergyman, Miss Hennell had taught the daughters of a wealthy, cultured Unitarian Liberal MP. Instead of a relationship with her employers marked by resentment and insecurity, Sara Hennell was treated respectfully, enjoying the friendship of her eldest pupil long after she had ceased to teach her. While Maria Lewis's notions of good behaviour were provincial and old-fashioned, Sara Hennell was used to fitting gracefully into life in the best circles. Most significantly, while Miss Lewis remained narrowly Evangelical, Sara Hennell set out from the Unitarianism of her childhood to explore and expand her faith through careful study of the new Biblical criticism. She followed her brother Charles into print, publishing several books on theology throughout her long life.

When Mary Ann handed the letters she had so abruptly demanded back from Maria Lewis to Sara, she was signposting the similarities in the position the two women occupied in her life. Like Maria, Sara was located at a convenient distance, available for holiday visits and intense correspondence, but not the tedium and messiness of everyday contact. Mary Ann's letters to Sara are less self-enclosed than those to Maria, but still there is a sense that she uses them as a way of exploring her own thoughts rather than as a means of exchanging ideas and feelings. One of the first letters she writes to Sara is the important reassessment of the lesson learned during the holy war, in which she elevates the community of feeling over the hair-splitting of intellectual debate. Throughout the correspondence it is Sara's job to provide an informed listening ear rather than a provocative intervention in her young friend's flow of thought. It is the idea of Sara, rather than Sara herself, which becomes the enabling force.

Mary Ann was guiltily aware of the narcissism running through her correspondence and indeed, the first few letters to Sara recall the early ones to Maria Lewis in their anxiety about appearing egotistical. 'An unfortunate lady wrote a note, one page of which contained thirty I's. I dare not count mine lest they should equal hers in number.'[58] However, after a tentative start in which Mary Ann struggled to find a voice to speak to the Sara whom she held in her mind's eye, the correspondence started to flow. Within a year, Mary Ann was addressing Sara as *'Liebe Gemahlinn'*, *'Cara Sposa'* and 'Beloved Achates' – all terms which claimed her as something more than a friend.

Eliot's early biographers, from her husband John Cross right down to Gordon Haight in the 1960s, felt uncomfortable with the language of sexual affection the two women used to one another. Cross simply left out the offending passages, while Haight anxiously explained them away in terms of contemporary conventions of female friendship. In fact, the language in the letters exceeds that used by even the closest women friends during the period. 'This letter is only to tell you how sweet the genuine words of love in your letter to Cara have been to my soul. That you should really wish for me is a thought which I keep by me as a little cud to chew now and then,' writes Mary Ann on 15 November 1847.[59] Eighteen months later Mary Ann is teasing Sara with the idea that she may have been unfaithful. 'I have given you a sad excuse for flirtation, but I have not been beyond seas long enough to make it lawful for you to take a new husband – therefore I come back to you with all a husband's privileges and command you to love me ... I sometimes talk to you in my soul as lovingly as Solomon's Song.'[60]

By the autumn of 1842 it was already a joke in the Bray–Hennell circle that Mary Ann fell in love with everyone she met. At twenty-three she was still searching for that intense maternal love which her own mother had been unable to provide at the crucial stage in her development. Unfortunately, or perhaps not, neither Watts nor Brabant had been in a position to give her the kind of replacement mothering she craved. Both had backed off with differing degrees of grace. Sara Hennell, however, was in an altogether different position. Single and living with her mother, she was emotionally free to enter into an intense and absorbing relationship. Seven years older to the week than Mary Ann, she was young enough to seem a contemporary in the way that Maria Lewis never had, yet sufficiently mature to take on the role of mentor and nurturer.

The erotic language which Mary Ann used is a signal of the insecurity she felt about just how much Sara really loved her. By playing with ideas of possession, fidelity, flirtation and jealousy, she was both expressing and containing her fear that Sara might abandon her, just as Isaac Evans, Francis Watts, Robert Brabant and Robert Evans had all done. Yet by the time she was using analogies to Solomon's Song in 1849 – the most explicitly erotic section of the Old Testament – she was already less dependent on the relationship. This echoed the pattern with Maria Lewis: it was at the point when Mary Ann wanted to leave the friendship that her declarations of love became most extravagant.

The reasons for the drift apart were familiar too. If Mary Ann was the one who used the language of love, it was Sara whose feelings stood the test of time. Unattached to any man except her brother, Sara's devotion to Mary Ann did not wax and wane every time an interesting diversion appeared. Mary Ann, by contrast, used her relationship with Sara as a small child would her mother – as a secure emotional base from which to explore the world. Five years into the friendship the discrepancy in the amount the women needed one another started to show. Just like Maria Lewis, Sara expressed her insecurity about the strength of Mary Ann's attachment in governessy comments about the inappropriateness of her behaviour with the opposite sex. 'Poor little Miss Hennell', reported Edith Simcox in 1885, 'apparently always disapproved of Marian for depending so much on the arm of man.'[61]

Hand in hand with this emotional estrangement there went an intellectual one. In July 1848, during a season in which all Europe was in revolt against the old ways, Mary Ann wrote to Sara defending her new regard for the work of Jean-Jacques Rousseau and George Sand. From her tone it is clear that she felt or knew that Sara would disapprove of her reading authors whose names were synonymous with sexual freedom and political revolt. 'I wish you thoroughly to understand that the writers who have most profoundly influenced me ... are not in the least oracles to me ... For instance it would signify nothing to me if a very wise person were to stun me with proofs that Rousseau's view of life, religion, and government are miserably erroneous.' The point was, she maintained, that it was Rousseau's art which had made her look at the world in quite a different way, sending 'that electric thrill through my intellectual and moral frame which has awakened me to new perceptions'.[62]

George Sand had an even more wretched personal reputation than Rousseau in Britain. A woman who dressed as a man and lived apart from her husband stood out in comparison with Elizabeth Gaskell and even the eccentric Brontës. Mary Ann, who as a novelist would become known as 'the English George Sand', worked hard to reassure Sara that she was not about to take the original as her model. 'I should never dream of going to her writings as a moral code or text-book.' What excited her, she said, was that, like Rousseau, Sand was able 'to delineate human passion and its results'.[63] Both these French writers might lead irregular lives and be indifferent literary stylists, but their ability to see characters truly and whole moved her with a sense of what the novel might achieve.

During the height of her friendship with Sara Hennell – 1843 to 1848 – there was no room in Mary Ann's life for another significant emotional attachment. Not that that stopped her family trying to find her suitable suitors. The 'problem' of Mary Ann's singleness continued to rumble on, with Isaac always ready to hint that she was being selfish by remaining a drain on her family's resources. Even the sensible Fanny Houghton, her half-sister, was keen to introduce Mary Ann to potential partners. In March 1845 she told Mary Ann about a young picture restorer working on the big house at Baginton, who she thought might be suitable. A meeting was arranged and, true to form, within two days Mary Ann was bewitched, believing the boy to be 'the most interesting young man she had seen and superior to all the rest of mankind'. On the third day the young man made an informal proposal through Mr Houghton saying 'she was the most fascinating creature he had ever beheld, that if it were not too presumptuous to hope etc. etc., a person of such superior excellence and powers of mind'. Turning down a definite engagement, Mary Ann none the less gave permission for him to write. Cara describes the girl as 'brimful of happiness; – though she said she had not fallen in love with him yet, but admired his character so much that she was sure she should.'[64]

This was the first time that Mary Ann had been involved with a man who was available and who returned her feelings. The fact that both Francis Watts and Robert Brabant were older and married had allowed her to express intense longing, safe in the knowledge that no commitment would be required of her. With the young picture restorer it was different. Now that real emotional engagement was on offer, Mary Ann backed off. In the few days following her return from Baginton she was racked with dreadful headaches, which only leeches could relieve. By the time the young man appeared at Foleshill she had decided that he wouldn't do at all 'owing to his great agitation, from youth – or something or other', reported Cara vaguely to Sara. The next day Mary Ann 'made up her mind that she could never love or respect him enough to marry him and that it would involve too great a sacrifice of her mind and pursuits'.[65]

However, Mary Ann did not get any relief from giving the young man her decision, especially when her letter ending the affair crossed with his to Mr Evans asking for permission to marry her. All she felt was enormous guilt at having led him on. She toyed with the idea of starting the relationship up again. 'Not that she cares much for him,' reported Cara, 'but she is so grieved to have wounded his feelings.'[66]

But there may have been more to it than that. On 21 April, three weeks after what was supposed to be her final decision, Mary Ann is writing to Martha Jackson about the relationship as if it may continue. 'What should you say to my becoming a wife? . . . I did meditate an engagement, but I have determined, whether wisely or not I cannot tell, to defer it, at least for the present.'[67] Although Mary Ann had no real interest in this particular man, she was enjoying the experience of being the courted one, the adored. An offer of marriage, no matter how unsuitable, brought her into the fold of ordinary, lovable women.

To Sara, however, she gives a very different version of events. A letter written two weeks before the one to Martha Jackson speaks as though the relationship is well and truly a thing of the past. 'I have now dismissed it from my mind, and only keep it recorded in my book of reference, article "*Precipitancy, ill effects of*".' She ends by confirming that her first allegiance is to Sara whose 'true Gemahlinn' or husband she is, which 'means that I have no loves but those that you can share with me – intellectual and religious loves'.[68] At this relatively early stage in their friendship Mary Ann was anxious not to alienate Sara by any suggestion of 'infidelity'. At the age of twenty-five her emotional allegiance was still to an unavailable partner, a woman. It would be nearly another decade before she would risk falling in love – this time lastingly – with an almost available man.

It was not just the Evans clan who tried to matchmake Mary Ann. Although Robert and Isaac were convinced that the Brays were cavalierly indifferent to her marriage prospects, in fact, Cara was quietly working away behind the scenes. In July 1844, returning from a holiday in the Lake District, the Brays took Mary Ann to stay with Cara's young cousins in Manchester. The two young men, Philip and Frank, escorted the party round the city on a fact-finding mission to see whether Engels's recently published description of the slums was accurate. It was. Cara wrote in horror to her sister-in-law Rufa, 'The streets and houses where humans do actually live and breathe there are worse than a book can tell'.[69] But this was not her only disappointment. 'I wish friend Philip would fall in love with her [Mary Ann],' she wrote wistfully to her mother a few weeks later, 'but there certainly were no symptoms of it.'[70] But at the party's next stop, in Liverpool, romance seemed more likely.

One of the guests at dinner was William Ballantyne Hodgson, Principal of the Liverpool Mechanics Institute, who was interested in the increasingly popular subjects of mesmerism and clairvoyance. He put Mary Ann in a hypnotic trance, which terrified her, since she was unable to open her eyes 'and begged him most piteously to do it for her'.[71] Hodgson's concentration on Mary Ann during dinner suggests a definite romantic interest in her. Writing to a friend afterwards he described the evening as 'Altogether a delightful party' and admiringly listed the modern and classic languages which the extraordinary Miss Evans was able to read.[72]

Men like Hodgson, Watts, Brabant and Bray who expressed a fascination with Mary Ann's mind were used to mixing with clever women. Far from being comfortable with the simpering Angel in the House, the women in their lives were educated, well read and independent-thinking. So it is a clue to Mary Ann's outstanding intellectual and spiritual radiance that she was so consistently the object of male attention. Indeed, the American poet Emerson, who met her during a visit to Rosehill in July 1848, could only repeat over and over to Charles Bray, 'That young lady has a calm, serious soul.'[73]

Hodgson and Emerson came into contact with Mary Ann only briefly. Other men, equally swept up by the exhilaration of talking to a woman whose mind ranged as widely as their own, found their lives profoundly altered by contact with Mary Ann Evans. John Sibree, the elder brother of her pupil Mary, was studying to become an Independent minister at Spring Hill College, Birmingham. Like Sara Hennell, he had made Mary Ann's acquaintance by proxy, through letters which Mary had written to him while he was at Halle University, describing the drama of the holy war. During one of his holidays from Spring Hill, Sibree finally got to meet the woman about whom he had heard so much. Characteristically, they forged their friendship by reading Greek together and, once Sibree returned to college in Birmingham, the correspondence continued. The letters which Mary Ann wrote to Sibree during the first half of 1848 are unlike any others she was to write during her whole life. As performance-oriented as ever, she none the less imagines him as a very different audience from Sara Hennell or Maria Lewis. This time she is at pains to show herself as a fun, flirtatious and even daring woman. For instance, Hannah More, whose pious work she had used to recommend to all and sundry, is now dismissed as 'that most disagreeable of all monsters, a bluestocking – a monster that can only exist in a miserably false state of society, in which a woman with but a smattering of learning or philosophy is classed along with singing mice and card playing pigs'.[74] Doubtless Mary Ann was attempting to distance herself from the drab image of a bluestocking, all the while trying to impress Sibree with her references to Handel, Hegel and Disraeli.

The letters to Sibree are also unusual in discussing politics. Throughout her life Mary Ann seldom mentioned contemporary events. But in spring 1848, with much of Europe in turmoil, it was impossible not to be drawn in. To those who know her in her mature incarnation as a conservative thinker, Mary Ann's brash enthusiasm for sudden change comes as a shock. She starts off by using the language of the barricades: 'decayed monarchs should be pensioned off: we should have a hospital for them, or a sort of Zoological Garden, where these worn-out humbugs may be preserved.' Of Louis Philippe, who with his 'moustachioed sons' had recently escaped to Britain, 'for heaven's sake preserve me from sentimentalizing over a pampered old man when the earth has its millions of unfed souls and bodies.' Victoria, meanwhile, is 'our little humbug of a queen'. When it comes to predicting whether revolution will happen in Britain, Mary Ann has already identified her country's unique capacity for slow constitutional change which, as a mature writer, she would elevate over political solutions. Writing to Sibree, however, she sees this as second-best to the thrill of revolution: 'There is nothing in our constitution to obstruct the slow progress of *political* reform. This is all we are fit for at present. The social reform which may prepare us for great changes is more and more the object of effort both in Parliament and out of it. But we English are slow crawlers.'[75]

Whenever Mary Ann engaged with a man intellectually, her emotions were not far behind. The tone of the Sibree letters quickly turned personal. On 8 March 1848 she ticked him off for writing too formally and asked for some details about his innermost life. 'Every one talks of himself or herself to me,' she boastfully claims and demands that he write to her about his religious beliefs. 'I want you to write me a Confession of Faith – not merely *what* you believe but why you believe it.'[76] Sibree had already read Mary Ann's translation of Strauss and was starting to have his doubts about his calling. The act of marshalling an account of his faith seems to have been the final stage in resolving to abandon the ministry. This was, of course, a massive step for, as Mary Sibree explained decades later to John Cross, 'the giving up of the ministry to a young man without other resources was no light matter.'[77]

Just how influential Mary Ann was in Sibree's decision to give up his orthodox faith is not absolutely clear. Certainly she read the letters which Mrs Sibree and Mary wrote to John during the whole crisis, and she herself enclosed a letter with the former's correspondence. In this letter she says, 'You have my hearty and not inexperienced sympathy . . . I have gone through a trial of the same genus as yours . . . I sincerely rejoice in the step you have taken – it is an absolutely necessary condition for any true development of your nature.'[78]

While the Sibrees had been tolerant and understanding when Mary Ann had given up church-going, it was quite a different matter when their own son took a similar course. It is not clear how much they blamed Mary Ann for influencing him, but they certainly felt she played a significant part. From 1848 Mary Ann had fewer meetings with Mary and the German lessons seem to have stopped. When Mary Ann moved to Geneva for eight months in 1849, Mary Sibree asked her to write to her care of Rosehill, presumably because she did not want her parents to know that their friendship was continuing. Mary Ann refused, telling the Brays: 'Please to give my love to her [Mary] and tell her that I cannot carry on a correspondence with anyone who will not avow it.' Perhaps she was feeling particularly annoyed with all things Sibree because Mr Sibree senior had just turned up with his brother in Geneva, which Mary Ann thought 'a piece of impertinent curiosity', suspecting that they had come to spy on her.[79] In the same way that she had been scathing about Brabant, Mary Ann now declared that Mr Sibree, whom she had once wanted as a substitute father, looked 'silly' while his brother was 'vulgar-looking'.[80] She could not get over her hurt that the Sibrees had not given her the total understanding she craved. They were, she said in a later letter, benignly selfish, exhibiting 'the egotism that eats up all the bread and butter and is ready to die of confusion and distress after having done it'.[81]

As the John Sibree episode suggests, Mary Ann's relationships with men during this period were tinder-box affairs. She formed sudden bonds with dramatic results. Either she was thrown out of their house, or they were thrown out of a job. There were tears and headaches, and leeches and embarrassments, which in some cases lasted down the years. She began to despair that anyone would want a peaceful, sustained relationship with her. Often known as Polly, an old Warwickshire form of 'Mary', she allowed Sara to make an unflattering pun on her name by changing it again to 'Pollian', a play on Apollyon, the monster in Revelation who also makes an appearance in *Pilgrim's Progress*. It chimed with her growing sense of herself as repulsive and wrong. In October 1846 she wrote an extended fantasy for Charles Bray – surely influenced by her reading of Carlyle's *Sartor Resartus* – in which she pictures herself as an old, ugly translator whose only hope now is to form a rational marriage with a dusty old German theologian. 'The other day as I was sitting in my study, Mary [Sibree] came with a rather risible cast of expression to deliver to me a card, saying that a gentleman was below requesting to see me. The name on the card ran thus – Professor Bücherwurm, Moderig University [Professor Bookworm of Musty University] . . .' The professor then addresses Mary Ann:

> 'I am determined if possible to secure a translator in the person of a wife. I have made the most anxious and extensive inquiries in London after all female translators of German. I find them very abundant, but I require, besides ability to translate, a very decided ugliness of person. . . . After the most toilsome inquiries I have been referred to you, Madam, as presenting the required combination of attributes, and though I am rather disappointed to see that you have no beard, an attribute which I have ever regarded as the most unfailing indication of a strong-minded woman, I confess that in other respects your person at least comes up to my ideal.'

Mary Ann then describes herself as responding: 'I thought it possible we might come to terms, always provided he acceded to my irrevocable conditions. "For you must know, learned Professor," I said, "that I require nothing more in a husband than to save me from the horrific disgrace of spinster-hood and to take me out of England."'[82] Professor Bookworm is clearly based on that German professor of theology to whom Mary Ann had already given up two years of her life, D. F. Strauss. And although she could not have known it at the time, it was Strauss who would, by a twisted turn of events, rescue Mary Ann from spinsterhood. In the meantime, however, it was another crisis altogether that would take her out of England.

CHAPTER 5

'The Land of Duty and Affection'

Coventry, Geneva and London
1849–51

BY THE END of the 1840s, that most stormy of decades for Britain, life had been transformed for nearly everyone in Mary Ann's circle. Unsettled by the revolutions in Europe, John Sibree had rebelled against his family culture, thrown over the ministry and opted for the precarious teaching and translating career of the self-supporting intellectual. The Brays' silk business was under pressure from cheap foreign imports and Rosehill would never again be run with such expansive ease. Meanwhile Chrissey, the meek and mild Evans girl who had left little impression on anyone, had been quietly sinking into chronic poverty and ill-health. Unlike her canny businessmen brothers, the gentlemanly Dr Clarke was not good with money. During the middle decades of the century medicine was busy pulling away from its roots in the apothecary shop and fashioning itself into a profession. Improved training and practice was one way of doing it. Living like a gentleman was another. No longer content to be seen as a clever servant, the physician–doctor now ran an 'establishment', which rivalled that of his well-heeled patients. His front door was opened by a maid, his dinner served on fine china and his rounds made on a good horse. In practice, however, the cost of maintaining a conspicuously prosperous estab- lishment often proved too much for an income that was far from secure. Just as Lydgate in *Middlemarch* discovers that his natural inclination to live well cannot be supported from the fees he receives as a doctor newly arrived in the area, so Edward Clarke was increasingly unable to balance the books.

By 1842 the situation was so grim that Dr Clarke was forced to raise money by selling a house which had been left to his wife by her uncle Evarard. Robert Evans, still playing his role as money lender to the feckless gentry, gave his son-in-law £250 for the Attleborough property and, a few months later, advanced him another £800 on loan to help move the whole family to Barford, near Warwick, for a new start.[1] But still it was not enough. Within three years Clarke was bankrupt and the whole family decamped in panic to Bird Grove.

From this low point it recovered neither its health nor prosperity. Dr Clarke died in 1852, leaving six surviving children. Chrissey was left to do her ineffectual best, scrabbling around for cheap schooling and apprenticeships, and at one point even considering moving the household out to Australia.[2] In 1859, worn out by her own fertility and bad luck, Chrissey died at the age of forty-five.

Although Mary Ann continued to hunger for romantic love, her elder sister's example offered a stern warning about its consequences. Gritty Moss, Mr Tulliver's sister in *The Mill on the Floss*, is surely based on Chrissey. Described as 'a patient, loosely-hung, child-producing woman',[3] Mrs Moss has the hopeless look of someone defeated by too many babies and a husband who never manages to get into profit. As a married woman Chrissey had no rights to her own property – it was Edward Clarke, after all, who sold her house back to her father. If she was unfaithful, her husband could divorce her. If he had a lover, she was obliged to stay put. Whatever the reasons for a legal separation – and there were only a handful each year, among those wealthy and smart enough not to care what other people thought – the children automatically belonged to their father. Chrissey, as far as anyone knows, had no desire to end her marriage to Edward Clarke. But she had probably never wanted to give birth to nine children, a financial and physical strain that almost certainly hastened her death: her childless sister lived to sixty-one, her brother to seventy-four. Despite being married to a doctor, Chrissey seems to have had no access to the contraceptive knowledge that, only ten years later, would allow Mary Ann and Lewes to make the decision not to bring illegitimate children into the world.

Chrissey's marriage was one of several which Mary Ann scrutinised as she approached her late twenties, those last-chance courtship years for a woman in the mid-nineteenth century. There were the Brays, with their advanced attitudes to sexual arrangements and sufficient money to support Mrs Gray and her brood of bastards. There was married, childless Fanny, who had time and energy to read the new higher criticism, but felt obliged to keep her opinions to herself. There were Isaac and Sarah, conventionally married and busy bringing up their four children to take their place among the professional classes. None of these were agonisingly miserable matches, but they were all compromised by wavering sexual attraction, intellectual incompatibility, or force of habit. Certainly none matched Mary Ann's ideal of a true meeting of hearts and minds.

The fault, she concluded like many before and since, lay not with individual human failing, but with the institution of marriage itself. While marriages in Britain were not arranged in the literal sense, young middle-class people were often pressured by their families into engagements with people they barely knew. 'How terrible it must be', Mary Sibree remembered Mary Ann saying, 'to find one's self tied to a being whose limitations you could see and must know were such as to prevent your ever being understood!' Far happier, Mary Ann concluded, was the Continental arrangement of dissolving marriages once affection had died.[4]

These remarks, recalled in hindsight by Mary Sibree for John Cross, are suspiciously prophetic. Within fifteen years of making them, Mary Ann Evans was to become a notorious victim of Britain's stringent divorce laws. But although Sibree probably polished up her tale for posterity, the 'problem' of marriage was a subject which engaged Mary Ann from the moment she first became aware of the competing pressures of family, personal and religious law. Her impulsive courtship of the picture restorer in the spring of 1845 had shown her how easy it was to rush into a marriage that would suit no one except the people who had arranged it, in this case her half-sister Fanny Houghton. During the holy war she had learned painfully that obedience and revolt in relation to an external law mattered far less than adherence to a complex inner truth.

In June 1848, during a dismal holiday with her failing father in St Leonards-on-Sea, Mary Ann clawed out a few hours to read the just-published *Jane Eyre*. As she sat huddled in a cold hotel, the book threw a sharp beam of light on to her own situation. Speaking of Rochester's commitment to care for his mad wife, Mary Ann declared in a letter to Charles Bray: 'All self-sacrifice is good – but one would like it to be in a somewhat nobler cause than that of a diabolical law which chains a man's soul and body to a putrefying carcase.'[5] She was quite aware that she, too, was chained soul and body to a putrefying carcass. But the difference between her situation and Rochester's was that her chains were made not of an abstract law but the living, loving ties of human affection.

If conventional marriage looked increasingly unappealing and unlikely, the problem still remained of how Mary Ann was to live once her father died. Isaac's continuing grumblings about the 'selfishness' of her single state suggested that he was never going to want her at Griff. The Clarkes could not support themselves, let alone an extra mouth. The last time the subject had come up, during the holy war, governessing in Leamington had emerged as a grim possibility. Fortunately, since then new and more appealing options had presented themselves. In April 1845 Mary Ann met Harriet Martineau, whose sister-in-law was a cousin of Cara's.[6] Martineau belonged to a tiny band of early-Victorian women who supported themselves through high-quality journalism and authorship. Born into the thriving nexus of Norwich Unitarianism she had received a good education by the standards of the day. Too deaf to follow her sisters into governessing when the family business failed, she started in print by writing the hugely successful *Tales of Political Economy*, moral fables that explained the virtues of free trade in simple terms, which the uncertainly literate would understand. From there she was to expand her range to include, by the time of her death in 1876, autobiography, fiction and an embarrassingly emphatic endorsement of mesmerism (hypnosis) as a cure for all kinds of ills. Although as a jobbing journalist Martineau's work appeared all over the place, she was most closely linked with the *Westminster Review*, the periodical founded by James Mill and Jeremy Bentham in 1824 to espouse the hard, happiness-driven philosophy of utilitarianism.

In some ways Martineau was not an attractive role model for Mary Ann, being plain, gauche and gossipy. Her deafness required her to carry a large ear trumpet which she used to control and inhibit others. If she grew bored with a conversation, she withdrew the trumpet and started to shout over the top of the unfortunate speaker. Hans Christian Andersen, who once met her at a garden party in London, was so exhausted by the experience that he had to go and lie down afterwards. Her old-maidish respectability ran alongside a prurient interest in other people's doings, creating a nasty tendency to bad-mouth. Years later, at the height of the scandal over Mary Ann's elopement with Lewes, Martineau whipped herself up into a frenzy of disapproval. She even started a strange, self-aggrandising rumour that Mary Ann had written her an insulting letter prior to leaving for the Continent.[7] That Mary Ann did not expose Martineau as a meddling fantasist in 1854 and continued to express admiration and even affection for her until her death twenty years later says a great deal about the debt she believed she owed her. More than any other woman in early-Victorian Britain, Martineau's example pointed the way out of dependent provincial spinsterhood.

It was with Martineau's example in mind that Mary Ann started to write articles for the *Coventry Herald* in October 1846. Charles Bray had bought the radical paper during the previous summer as a platform in his continuing battle with the city's ruling Tories. Mary Ann's laboured and lame pieces did not contribute much to the struggle. The most interesting thing about the series of loose, rambling essays entitled 'Poetry and Prose from the Notebook of An Eccentric'[8] which appeared from December is her use of the form to which she was to return only at the very end of her life. Like *Impressions of Theophrastus Such*, published in 1879, 'Poetry and Prose' purports to be the jottings of a middle-aged man and, in this first attempt, comes over as implausible and dull. The reviews she wrote for the paper were much more successful, building on real interests and knowledge. The first, which appeared in October 1846, was a cogent commentary on three books by the French historians Jules Michelet and Edgar Quinet.[9]

Mary Ann's journalism, and the reading which informed the best of it, had to be fitted around her increasingly heavy duties as a sick-nurse. Just as her mother had used her ill-health to send Mary Ann away from the family home, her father now used his frailty to bind her to it. Evans still loathed the Brays for their hijacking of his clever, respectable little girl into unorthodoxy. Jealous and resentful of Mary Ann's continued attachment to Rosehill, he tried everything in his power to turn her attention back towards him. The most spectacular skirmish came in October 1845, when Mary Ann was due to accompany the Brays and Sara Hennell to Scotland. This promised to be a particularly exciting trip, since the plan was to tour Scott country, exploring the landscape long branded into her imagination from repeated readings of the Waverley novels. But from the start Robert was determined that she should not go. He put forward the desperate argument that Chrissey and Edward's arrival at Bird Grove, following their final bankruptcy, required her presence. In the end Charles Bray intervened, stressing how much Mary Ann needed a change of scene to lift her health and spirits.[10] Reluctantly, Evans agreed, but on the evening following her departure he fell from his horse and broke a leg. Isaac dispatched a letter to Glasgow telling Mary Ann to come home immediately.

Luckily it missed her and the party toured Greenock, Glasgow, Loch Lomond and Stirling, blithely unaware of the drama unfolding in Warwickshire. When the letter finally caught up with Mary Ann in Edinburgh, she wanted to set out immediately and alone. Bray talked her into staying another day and the whole party went to visit Scott's grand castle home in Abbotsford. The next day, 28 October, they all set out for home, travelling via Birmingham.

Robert Evans lived on for another grim three and a half years. At times, Mary Ann feared she was going mad with the strain of looking after him. He was not a man who said thank you, believing that his youngest daughter's care and attention was his natural due. He was often grumpy and always demanding, wanting her to read or play the piano or just talk. During the ghastly visit to St Leonards-on-Sea in May–June 1848, Mary Ann reported to the Brays that her father made 'not the slightest attempt to amuse himself, so that I scarcely feel easy in following my own bent even for an hour'.[11] Trapped on the out-of-season south coast, she tried to stretch out the days with 'very trivial doings . . . spread over a large space', to the point where one featureless day merged drearily into the next.[12]

The result was the kind of depression she had not experienced since the years of intense isolation at Griff. Spoofing Scott, she wrote to Charles Bray from the dismal guest-house that 'my present address is Grief Castle, on the river of Gloom, in the valley of Dolour'.[13] Without other people to reflect her back to herself – Robert Evans's hungry demands only made her feel invisible – she felt herself on the brink of a terrifying disintegration. In a desperate letter to Sara, she cried out, 'I feel a sort of madness growing upon me.'[14]

But throughout this slow pounding of her spirits Mary Ann's devotion to her father never wavered. Mr Bury, the surgeon who attended Evans during these last years, declared that 'he never saw a patient more admirably and thoroughly cared for'.[15] Still deeply regretful of the pain she had caused him during the holy war, Mary Ann took her father's nursing upon her as an absolute charge. And while the limits that her sick-room duties imposed upon her time and freedom often irked, they also satisfied her need for a vocation. Just as giving up two years of her life to the tortuous Strauss had calmed her fears that she was achieving nothing in her life, so the burden of caring for her father left neither time nor energy to agonise over her ultimate lack of direction. While others, especially Cara, marvelled at her sacrifice and patience, Mary Ann understood that it was her devotion to her father which made life possible. Without this 'poetry of duty' she feared herself 'nothing more than miserable agglomerations of atoms'.[16] Frightened about relaxing for a second, she had even begun translating Spinoza's *Tractatus Theologico-Politicus* in her spare time: 'she says it is such a rest to her mind,' reported Cara Bray wonderingly.[17]

This makes sense of the puzzle that it was in the final few months of Robert Evans's life that Mary Ann found her greatest ease. She was with him all the time now, worrying about the effect of the cold on his health, tying a mustard bag between his shoulders to get him to sleep, sending written bulletins to Fanny and Robert about his worsening condition. There are no surviving letters to Isaac and Chrissey, and no evidence that they shared the load with her. It was Mary Ann's half-brother Robert who spent the last night of their father's life with her, a fact she remembered with gratitude all her life. Yet although she declared that her life during these months was 'a perpetual night-mare – always haunted by something to be done which I have never the time or rather the energy to do',[18] she accepted that she would have it no other way. To Charles Bray she reported that 'strange to say I feel that these will ever be the happiest days of life to me. The one deep strong love I have ever known has now its highest exercise and fullest reward.'[19] To some extent this was because Evans was finally able to unbend a little and say 'kind things' to Mary Ann. 'It shows how rare they are', said Cara tartly, 'by the gratitude with which she repeats the commonest expressions of kindness.'[20] But it was not just that. As the abyss of life without home, family or purpose loomed, Mary Ann clung to her exhausting duties as a way of keeping terror at bay.

It could not be held off for ever. When the final hours came, on the night of 30–31 May, disintegration threatened once again. In panic, Mary Ann sat down and scribbled an anguished note to Cara and Charles: 'What shall I be without my Father? It will seem as if a part of my moral nature were gone. I had a horrid vision of myself last night becoming earthly sensual and devilish for want of that purifying restraining influence.'[21]

But, of course, it had never been her father who had protected Mary Ann from herself. It was her attachment to him, her elevation of his care into an absolute duty, which had disciplined the warring parts of herself into working together. For this reason Evans's deliberate snubbing of her in his will may not have hurt her as much as it has outraged her biographers. There was nothing odd about his leaving the valuable Derbyshire and Warwickshire properties to Robert and Isaac respectively, while his three daughters received relatively small amounts of cash. Fanny and Chrissey had both been given a thousand pounds on their marriage and now got another thousand. Mary Ann received two thousand pounds in trust, the income to be administered by her brother, half-brother and the family solicitor. But it was in the tiny details that Evans's will stung. The novels of Walter Scott, from which Mary Ann had read so tirelessly during the last few years of his life, were given to Fanny who, as far as we know, had no particular attachment to them. It was a small, cutting gesture, the only way Robert Evans knew to show Mary Ann that he had still not forgiven her for the holy war.

Robert Evans was buried next to his second wife in Chilvers Coton churchyard on 6 June 1849. Only six days later the Brays and Mary Ann set off for the Continent. Even in the midst of this double upheaval, Mary Ann's old, impul-sive ways reasserted themselves. Three months earlier she had reviewed James Anthony Froude's novel *The Nemesis of Faith* for the *Coventry Herald*. The book was a particularly shocking example of 'the crisis of faith' novel and instantly became a *cause célèbre*. The tale of a clergyman who loses his faith and falls in love with a friend's wife was sufficiently scandalous to get the book burned at Exeter College, Oxford, where Froude was, though not for much longer, a Fellow. Its publisher, John Chapman, who had also brought out the Strauss translation, sent a copy of *The Nemesis of Faith* to Mary Ann, who reviewed it rapturously in the *Herald*. Writing anonymously, as was usual at that time, she thrilled that 'the books which carry this magic in them are the true products of genius'.[22] She also wrote a complimentary note to Froude, coyly signing it 'the translator of Strauss'. In an uncharacteristic burst of discretion, Chapman refused to divulge Mary Ann's identity, so Froude was obliged to respond via the publisher. Guessing that the translator of Strauss had also written the *Herald* review in which he was described as a 'fallen star', Froude suggested flirtatiously that 'she might help him to rise'. Receiving the letter in 'high glee', Mary Ann ran to Rosehill to show it to Cara, who reported herself 'so pleased she should have this little episode in her dull life.'[23] Mary Ann was in love again. It was now that she wrote to Sara teasingly representing herself as an unfaithful and aloof husband, giving her intoxication with Froude as the reason for her distraction. By this time she had read his previous book, *Shadows of the Clouds*, and declared herself in the grip of 'a sort of palpitation that one hardly knows whether to call wretched or delightful'.[24]

The fallen star and the translator of Strauss finally met when Froude came to visit Rosehill in early June. The timing could not have been worse. Robert Evans had been buried the day before and Mary Ann was beside herself with grief. The burden of the past months and years had left her thin and pale. Still, when Bray suggested that Froude might like to join them on the Continental trip, he enthusiastically agreed. But then a strange thing happened. Four days later Charles, Cara and Mary Ann were in London, about to board the train to Folkestone, when John Chapman dashed up at the last minute with the decidedly odd message that Froude could not accompany them after all because he was about to be married.[25]

The most likely explanation behind this clumsy little drama is that Froude, despite finding Mary Ann less appealing in person than print, had decided that he would like to go abroad with the Brays. At this stage it looked as though the party would be larger, perhaps including Edward Noel and another old friend called Dawson. Over the next few days, when all the extra travellers had dropped out, Froude realised that he was being matchmade with Mary Ann.

Cara Bray might be in an unconventional marriage herself, but she was as keen as any of the Evanses to find Mary Ann a partner, especially now she was released from daughterly duties. Apart from anything, it would absolve the Brays from having her to live with them. It was one thing to have Mary Ann as a stimulating neighbour, quite another to live with her as a depressed and demanding member of the household. The only hitch in Cara's scheme was that Froude did not have the slightest desire to marry Mary Ann. Panicked by the thought of spending the next few weeks pushed together with an over-ardent ageing spinster, he took the coward's way out and sent his friend Chapman with the last-minute message. The fact that he chose to emphasise his engagement as the reason he could not travel is tellingly strange. Presumably he had been aware of it – he married Charlotte Grenfell only four months later – when he agreed to the trip. We do not know what passed between Mary Ann and Froude at their meeting a few days earlier, but it is clear that she had spent the previous dreary months building him up in her imagination. Did her pent-up need push her into reckless declarations of affection, just as it had with Dr Brabant? Did Froude find himself repelled by a clingy, ugly woman when he had been expecting a pretty girl with whom he might flirt for a few weeks on the way to the altar? Whatever the exact reason, the party which left for Folkestone consisted of only three.

As it turned out, it was probably just as well that Froude decided not to catch the train. Over the following weeks, as the party made its way through Calais, Paris, Avignon, Marseilles, Genoa and finally on to Geneva, Mary Ann emerged as a weepy and demanding travelling companion. Still laid low by grief, on several occasions during a fraught horseback journey through the Alps she was seized by hysterics, convinced that a broken side-saddle was about to pitch her into oblivion. Over a decade later, remembering with mortification just how tiresome she had been, she thanked Cara for her patience. 'How wretched I was then – how peevish, how utterly morbid! And how kind and forbearing you were under the oppression of my company!'[26]

The year before, John Sibree's decision to spend a year in Geneva after giving up the ministry had prompted Mary Ann into envious raptures: 'O the bliss of having a very high attic in a romantic continental town, such as Geneva.'[27] Now she decided to follow his example. For the first time in her life she had the time and just enough money to live how and where she pleased. Her father was dead and her siblings did not need her. She had been left £100 cash in her father's will in lieu of some household items given to Chrissey and Fanny. If she was careful, she had enough to last the year. On 23 July she wrote to tell her half-sister Fanny of her plans: 'The day after tomorrow I part from my friends and take up my abode at Geneva where I hope that rest and regular occupation will do more for my health and spirits than travelling has proved able to do.'[28] Two days later, and quite probably breathing a sigh of relief, the Brays returned to Coventry, Mary Ann having been installed in a respectable pension in the centre of the town.

It is too easy to write up these Geneva months as a kind of heroic turning point in Mary Ann's life, a breaking out of provincial spinsterhood into something brave and independent. John Cross certainly saw it like this, declaring that Geneva represented 'a delightful, soothing change after . . . the monotonous dullness . . . of an English provincial town like Coventry, where there is little beauty of any sort to gladden the soul.'[29] It would be good to imagine Mary Ann expanding in the bracing atmosphere of this most liberal of cities, transforming herself from provincial bluestocking into European intellectual. But much of the time she spent in Geneva was marked by loneliness, disappointment and the familiar frustrated longing for intimacy. She spent a lot of time holed up in her pension. And although she had French and German, this was not a passport to Swiss culture, which anyway turned out to be more stodgily bourgeois than anything she had experienced among the avant-garde of Coventry.

Friendships formed with other tourists were fleeting and shallow, something which always unsettled her. Unable to stick it out for a year, she returned home after only eight months.

None the less, Geneva did represent a particular stage in Mary Ann's creative development. It was now that her potential as a novelist emerged. Previously her published work consisted of erudite translation, workmanlike reviews and heavy-handed attempts at humorous essays. The letters she had written in Coventry had been lively and acute, but it was in the ones she sent from Geneva that the scope of her observant eye became clear. It was now, too, that she first started to write a journal, though unfortunately the first part of it, covering 1849–54, was destroyed by John Cross, anxious to eliminate evidence of her bumpy emotional life before she settled into unwedded commitment with G. H. Lewes. But if there is no journal account of her time in Geneva, we do still have a clutch of long, vivid letters describing the shabby genteel atmosphere of life in a Swiss boarding-house.

The recent revolutions in France and Italy had resulted in a flow of well-heeled refugees into tolerant Geneva. Not yet permanently exiled, they hovered within striking distance of their homes, waiting to see how the political dust would settle. The Campagne Plongeon, where Mary Ann was staying, contained some of these stateless gentlefolk, including the Marquis de St Germain and his extended family, who were temporarily unable to return to their native Piedmont because of their association with the discredited regime.

It was not just the politically dispossessed who found refuge at Campagne Plongeon. There were two sad Englishwomen in residence, both cut off from their family and cultural roots. The Baronne de Ludwigsdorf was a refined woman who spoke perfect French and German, and reminded Mary Ann of Cara. She also had minimal self-esteem, declaring that, while she would like to be Mary Ann's friend, 'she does not mean to attach herself to me, because I shall never like her long'.[30]

The reasons for the other Englishwoman's dislocation were more straightforward. Mrs Lock 'has had very bitter trials which seem to be driving her more and more aloof from society,'[31] reported Mary Ann. In the gossipy atmosphere of the pension, the details soon emerged. Apparently Mrs Lock's daughter had married a French aristocrat by whom she had two daughters. But the previous year the young woman had run off with her husband's cousin. Mrs Lock was so ashamed that she felt obliged to stay away from her old life in England. 'No one likes her here,' explained Mary Ann bluntly, 'simply because her manners are brusque and her French incomprehensible.'[32]

The third category comprised tourists. There were an American mother and daughter. The former was 'kind but silly – the daughter silly, but not kind, and they both of them chatter the most execrable French with amazing volubility and self-complacency.'[33] European visitors tended to be more cultured. Mary Ann was mildly pleased to meet Wilhelm von Herder, grandson of the philosopher, who took her boating and from whom she purloined a copy of Louis Blanc's *Histoire de dix ans, 1830–1840*.

Hurt by the lack of letters from home, Mary Ann turned to this ragbag crew for comfort. Recently orphaned, her need for surrogate parenting was more intense than ever and she worked hard to turn each of the middle-aged female guests into a surrogate mother. Of course, her letters to Cara and Charles were designed to let them know just how well she was doing without them. None the less, she does genuinely seem to have become a favourite in the Campagne Plongeon community. The Marquise de St Germain, for instance, declared that she loved her and fiddled with her hair, making 'two things stick out on each side of my head like those on the head of the Sphinx'.[34] The Baronne de Ludwigsdorf was 'a charming creature – so anxious to see me comfortably settled – petting me in all sorts of ways. She sends me tea when I wake in the morning, orangeflower water when I go to bed, grapes, and her maid to wait on me.'[35] Madame de Vallière, who ran the pension and was herself a political exile, is described as 'quite a sufficient mother'.[36] Even the brusque and unpopular Mrs Lock turns out, in that insistently repeated word, to be 'quite a mother',[37] fussing over Mary Ann and making sure she had people to talk to at dinner.

In return Mary Ann offered these women something which was unique in the disappointed, self-absorbed atmosphere of the pension – an empathic listening ear. Charles Bray had been the first to identify the girl's ability to set her own concerns temporarily on one side, while she absorbed the truth of another. Now she developed the capacity even further, drawing confidences out of people who were long used to hugging their unhappiness to themselves. Baronne de Ludwigsdorf, for instance, 'has told me her troubles and her feelings, she says, in spite of herself – for she has never been able before in her life to say so much even to her old friends.'[38] Mary Ann's long journey out of the narcissistic self-enclosure of the Maria Lewis letters towards an understanding of other people's separateness, and hence their likeness, was one which her fictional characters from Hetty Sorrel to Gwendolen Harleth would be obliged to make again and again.

But despite her letters to Coventry stressing how many new friends she was making, life in a Geneva boarding-house was not the romantic idyll Mary Ann had rapturously imagined for John Sibree. The idea of her striding unselfconsciously about the birthplace of her beloved Jean-Jacques Rousseau was quickly dispelled by oppressive Continental ideas of propriety. The constraints on a young woman were far greater than they were for a man. She was expected to dress with more care than she did back home, a demand which bored and worried her. And there was the problem of a chaperon. In Britain a single woman of thirty was assumed to have passed from nubile girlhood to settled spinsterhood and her good name was no longer at risk if she went out in public alone. In Geneva, explained Mary Ann in a letter to Rosehill, there was less latitude: 'people do not seem to think me quite old enough yet to ramble about at will . . . I confess I am more sensitive than I thought I should be to the idea that my being alone is odd. I thought my old appearance would have been a sufficient sanction and that the very idea of impropriety was ridiculous . . . As long as people carry a Mademoiselle before their name, there is far less liberty for them on the Continent than in England.'[39]

In other ways, however, Geneva came up to its reputation as a free-thinkers' haven. In the pension itself, Mary Ann's lack of orthodox faith made her immediately conspicuous among the pious residents. The Catholic Marquise worried, with an obliquely prophetic quality, that without a formal religion any marriage vows Mary Ann might make in the future would be meaningless. There was some embarrassment, too, when it came to her dealings with a devout British father-and-daughter pair, the Forbeses. Miss Forbes made friendly advances – lending Mary Ann a book, inviting her on a walk, turning up in her room 'till I began to be uncomfortable under the idea that they fancied I was evangelical and that I was gaining their affection under false pretenses – so I told Miss Forbes that I was going to sacrifice her good opinion and confess my heresies.'

She need not have worried. The Forbeses' response to the news of Mary Ann's unorthodoxy was gratifyingly mild. 'I quite expected from their manner and character that they would forsake me in horror, but they are as kind as ever.'[40] The same thing happened a few weeks later when Mary Ann moved out of the pension and into the home of a Swiss couple, the D'Albert Durades. 'They appear to be evangelical and conservative, b[ut] one finds these views in company with more breadth of cultu[re] here than one can ever augur from them in England,' she reported in a jibe at the narrowness of nonconformist Coventry culture.[41]

Doubtless this relaxed acceptance of other people's faith, or lack of it, was partly due to the city's atmosphere of religious tolerance and partly to the emotional constitution of the Forbeses and the D'Albert Durades themselves. But it was also the result of a significant interior shift in Mary Ann from the rigidly self-righteous days of the holy war. Now able to acknowledge the beauties and benefits of orthodox faith, she no longer felt the need to hold herself rigidly apart from conventional worship. On Sunday mornings she went to church, taking pleasure in clever sermons and congregational piety without feeling that she was compromising her own deeply held views.[42] She was no longer interested in setting herself up against Christianity, and the tension that hung over her Coventry days melted away.

But behind this façade of happy busyness, Mary Ann often felt low. These weeks following her father's death revealed just how fragile were the ties holding the Evans family together. By late July she had not heard from any of her siblings, despite having written to all of them twice. In a letter of the 23rd she begged Fanny, 'I am very, very anxious to hear of you, but I am discouraged to write by post until I have some intimation that you care about me enough to write.'[43] A month later she learned through the Brays the reason for her half-sister's silence: apparently Fanny felt that Isaac's letters absolved her from having to write. But there had never been any letters from Isaac. The only correspondence Mary Ann had received from Griff was a brief note from Isaac's wife, Sarah, informing her of the death of her eight-year-old niece Clara Clarke. This would explain why Chrissey had not written, but was no excuse for anyone else. Mary Ann was beside herself. Abandoning her decision to do nothing until she had heard something, she sent Fanny a beseeching letter.

'Have I confided too much in your generosity in supposing that you would write to me first? or is there some other reason for your silence? I suffer greatly from it. . . . I have not spirit to write of myself until I have heard from you, and have an assurance from yourself that you yet care about me.'[44]

This was enough, finally, to rouse Fanny to put pen to paper, whereupon Mary Ann punished her by making her wait several weeks for a reply. Fanny, quick enough to spot the power play, did not write for another five months, forcing Mary Ann once again to write another letter on 4 February, begging for 'only half a dozen lines'.[45]

It was not just family who were disappointing. The Coventry trio was proving unable, or unwilling, to keep up with Mary Ann's demands for news, gossip, attention. When deprived of contact with people who could reflect her back to herself, Mary Ann was always in danger of falling into the terrifying belief that she did not exist. 'I shall lose all my identity unless you keep nourishing the old self with letters,' she threatened, 'so pray write as much and as often as you can.'[46] Perhaps Cara, Sara and Charles were repelled by a hunger which arose so clearly out of her own need rather than a genuine concern for how her friends were faring as the family silk business started to go under. Or maybe they felt exasperated by Mary Ann's drizzle of complaints – a bilious stomach, a trunk which arrived disordered, a lack of warm clothes. The first real sign that the Brays were losing patience with Mary Ann came in response to her floating the idea that she might sell off her *Encyclopaedia Britannica* and her globes in order to raise cash for a piano and instruction in a variety of subjects. These items were stored at Rosehill so, in effect, Mary Ann was asking Cara and Charles to arrange for their sale. Perhaps she was even hinting that they might like to buy them themselves. This time she had gone too far. It was left to Sara to explain to Mary Ann that her constant dissatisfaction and covert demands for sympathy had a wearying effect on those who were forced to listen. Her letter has been lost, but Mary Ann's reply – pointedly sent to the Brays rather than Sara – contains clues to its gist.

> I am quite timid about writing to you because Sara tells me that Mr Hennell says 'there is much that is morbid in your character (his observations were upon your letters only) with a dwelling on yourself and a loving to think yourself unhappy'. Nothing can be truer than the observation, but I am distressed and surprized that this is so very evident from letters in which I have really tried to avoid everything which could give you pain and have imagined that I have only told you of agreeables except the last, which I hope you understood to be playful in its grumbling. I am ashamed to fill sheets about myself, but I imagined that this was precisely what you wished. Pray correct my mistake, if it be one.[47]

Mary Ann felt doubly snubbed. She knew she had a tendency to talk about herself and to dwell on all that was wrong. Her letters to Maria Lewis had been full of apologies for just those faults. But during the Rosehill years she had felt sufficiently accepted to risk being herself, without constantly apologising for her egotism. Cara and Sara had always seemed genuinely sympathetic to the difficulties of her situation. Now here she was, being told that she was a whiny bore. In effect, she had been encouraged to lower her guard, only to be told how awful she was when she did. What made it even worse was that Sara had annexed the authority of her brother Charles Hennell, knowing full well that he was a man whom Mary Ann had once loved, and quite possibly still did.

Despite the seeming humility of her response, Mary Ann was sufficiently affronted to hit back. In a letter of 26 October she suggested that while she greatly respected Charles Hennell, she thought Sara and Cara relied far too much on his opinion and had turned him into 'a *vox Dei*'.[48] Perhaps she could not help contrasting the close loving bond between Hennell and his sisters and the cold indifference with which her own brother treated her. None the less, from now on she took care to exclude anything that sounded like a moan from her letters. The tone became resolutely upbeat, with an emphasis on just how well she was getting on with her new life. References to her misery were neutralised with defensive humour: 'I am determined to give you no pretext for sending me either blue pill or bitters. You shall not know whether I am well or ill, contented or discontented, warm or cold, fat or thin.'[49] Actually, she was not doing so well at all. About three weeks after receiving the critical letter from Sara, Mary Ann had quit the pension and moved into private lodgings. After the first excitement of finding herself a favourite among the ladies of Campagne Plongeon, she was beginning to realise she had little in common with them. Kind though they might be, their gossipy, snobbish conversation could be oppressive when one wasn't in the mood. It had got to the point where she was avoiding going down to the communal salon in the evening. Brusque Mrs Lock had turned out to be surprisingly perceptive after all when she warned: 'You won't find any kindred spirits at Plongeon, my dear.'[50]

Cut off from the intense intimacy which was as necessary to her as oxygen, Mary Ann began to wilt. Even her hair started to fall out. The only way to avoid the depression which had overtaken her the last time she had stayed in a guest-house, at dreary St Leonards-on-Sea, was to find another Rosehill – and quickly. On 9 October she moved out of the pension to become a paying guest in the home of Monsieur and Madame D'Albert Durade, a cultured middle-aged couple with two sons. 'I feel they are my *friends*,' she wrote with barbed emphasis to Fanny, 'Without entering into or even knowing the greater part of my views, they understand my character, and have a real interest in me'.[51] Significantly, it was time for another name change: the D'Alberts gave Mary Ann the diminutive name of 'Minie' and she responded by turning them into surrogate parents. Madame D'Albert Durade, in particular, became yet another mother. It was this 'Maman's' liberality with candles which particularly thrilled her. Christiana Evans had been angry with young Mary Anne for wasting candle power by reading in bed, whereas Madame D'Albert Durade 'scolds me when she comes in and sees me reading by a single bougie'.[52] Was it her own family's niggardliness Mary Ann was thinking of when she wrote pointedly to the critical Brays: 'You will think me childish to talk of such things, but to me it is so blessed to find any departure from the rule of giving as little as possible for as much as possible'.[53]

Every letter thrills with some new piece of kindness bestowed by Madame D'Albert Durade. On 24 October Mary Ann describes her making 'a spoiled child of me'.[54] On 4 December she reports how 'She kisses me like a mother, and I am baby enough to find that a great addition to my happiness'. Even the housemaid Jeanie is more nurturer than servant: she 'says to me every morning, in the prettiest voice "Madame a-t-elle bien dormi cette nuit?"'[55]

But Mary Ann's need for mothering was not the only old emotional claim which reasserted itself just now. Madame might have turned out to be a perfect mother, but it was her artist husband who was to fulfil the role of soulmate. After only a fortnight's acquaintance, Mary Ann was already in raptures with Monsieur D'Albert. Her letter of 24 October must have caused consternation at Rosehill, with its ominous echoes of the sorry Brabant business.

> For M. D'Albert I love him already as if he were father and brother both. You must know he is not more than 4 feet high with a deformed spine – the result of an accident in his boyhood – but on this little body is placed a finely formed head, full in every direction. The face is plain with small features, and rather haggard looking, but all the lines and the wavy grey hair indicate the temperament of the artist. I have not heard a word or seen a gesture of his yet that was not perfectly in harmony with an exquisite moral refinement – indeed one feels a better person always when he is present ... His conversation is charming. I learn something every dinner-time.[56]

The Brays knew Mary Ann too well to take much comfort from her deliberate emphasis on Monsieur D'Albert's physical infirmities. Reading between the lines it was quite clear that the middle-aged painter and the young English tourist were busy forming an exclusive bond. Further on in the same letter, Mary Ann lets drop that Monsieur D'Albert has been reading poetry to her. Two days later she tells Charles Bray that Monsieur D'Albert is going to escort her up a nearby mountain. On 15 February she says with self-conscious nonchalance, 'You will be amused to hear that I am sitting for my portrait – at M. D'Albert's request – not mine.'[57] The fact that Mary Ann continued to mention Madame with great affection in her letters was no reassurance to the Brays. They would have recalled that she had gushed over Mrs Brabant even while in the process of being thrown out by her.

But if Mary Ann's presence caused tension in the D'Albert Durade household, it cannot have been too great, at least at first. November, December and January passed without obvious disruption. On 9 February Mary Ann wrote to Fanny, with whom she was now in contact, telling her that she planned to be home 'as soon as the Jura is passable without sledges – probably the end of March or beginning of April'.[58] A few days later she told the Brays: 'Something has been said of M. D'Albert's accompanying me to Paris, but I am afraid he cannot afford the journey – and alas! I cannot afford to pay for him.'[59] So it comes as a surprise to learn that as early as 18 March she set out

– on sledge – with Monsieur D'Albert as her escort all the way to London.

What had happened to trigger such a sudden change in Mary Ann's plans? Had Madame D'Albert, irritated by the idea of Monsieur squandering money accompanying their young guest to Paris, declared that, for all she cared, he could leave immediately and go all the way to England with the girl? Or perhaps, less sensationally, money was squeezed from the household budget to allow Monsieur D'Albert to take a longed-for trip to visit the London art galleries. Certainly, he made the most of his opportunities in town before joining Mary Ann at Rosehill for a few days of local sightseeing.

There is mystery, too, hanging over their subsequent correspondence. After Mary Ann's death Monsieur D'Albert Durade explained to John Cross that he destroyed all the letters she had written to him on his return to Geneva because he feared that posterity would misconstrue her use of the familiar '*tu*' over the more formal '*vous*'.[60] He was probably right to be cautious, not so much because the world could not be expected to know that Madame had given permission for this verbal intimacy, but because a whiff of scandal invariably surrounded Mary Ann's dealings with men. In part this was because of the infamous relationship with Lewes, through which all her other friend-ships were retrospectively viewed, but also because there was always a dis-turbing intensity to the way in which she attached herself to other women's men. Mathilde Blind, who wrote the first biography of Eliot in 1883 and got most of her information from Cara Bray, said of Monsieur D'Albert, 'it is whispered that he suggested some of the traits in the character of the delicate-minded Philip Wakem in the "Mill on the Floss"'.[61] 'Whispered', an odd choice, suggests that there was something about the intensity of Mary Ann's relationship with the middle-aged hunchback dwarf which struck even the generous-minded Cara as strange.

By the time Mary Ann was a successful writer and happily settled with Lewes, any lingering awkwardness towards the D'Albert Durade household had disappeared. Monsieur D'Albert translated five of her novels into French and, together with Madame, welcomed the couple warmly when they made a trip to Geneva in the summer of 1860. Over twenty years later, with Madame and Mary Ann both dead, John Cross made a final pilgrimage to Geneva and found the physically fragile Monsieur D'Albert 'carrying well the weight of eighty winters'.[62]

The move from the Campagne Plongeon to the D'Albert household had brought Mary Ann nearer to the kind of life she had imagined for herself in Geneva, a kind of glamorised Rosehill existence. Her hosts were touchingly eager to integrate her into their social circle, which was composed of cultured, serious people. There were trips to the theatre and private dramatic readings at home. The regular Monday musical evenings were, she took care to tell the Brays, as good as the ones in Coventry.

In her newfound contentment, Mary Ann let go her usually rigorous pro-gramme of reading and study. She had long since abandoned the translation of Spinoza's *Tractatus*, which she had taken up to cram her mind during the last months of her father's life. Instead, she told the Brays in a letter of

4 December, 'I take walks, play on the piano, read Voltaire, talk to my friends, and just take a dose of mathematics every day to prevent my brain from becoming quite soft.'[63] Actually, being Mary Ann, she did quite a lot more than that. On Wednesdays and Saturdays she attended a course of lectures on Experimental Physics by Professor Arthur de la Rive.

While all this was pleasantly diverting, the problem of what she was to do with the rest of her life was no nearer a solution. She did not look forward to returning to England, but recognised it as the place where she had her roots. It was becoming increasingly clear to her that landscape was the seedbed of the moral self. Just as Hetty Sorrel in *Adam Bede* fails to develop an ethical sense because she has been yanked out of her native soil, so Mary Ann believed that if she stayed abroad she would be cut off from those old associations and relationships out of which an authentic vocation would emerge. Her inheritance from her father would yield ninety pounds a year and she may also have had a tiny bit of income from her aunt Evarard who had died in 1844. The total sum was a useful cushion, but not enough for true independence. Significantly, in a letter to the Brays on 4 December, Mary Ann imagines her future role not in terms of the public identity of a writer or teacher, but as 'some woman's duty' involving the care of others or, as we might expect from Mary Ann, a single other: 'I can only think with a shudder of returning to England. It looks to me like a land of gloom, of ennui, of platitude, but in the midst of all this it is the land of duty and affection, and the only ardent hope I have for my future life is to have given to me some woman's duty, some possibility of devoting myself where I may see a daily result of pure calm blessedness in the life of another.'[64]

For all Mary Ann's romantic talk about roots, the return to her native landscape was a miserable business. The disappointing behaviour of her family during her stay in Geneva should have warned her about the kind of welcome she could expect. After parting from Monsieur D'Albert in London, she visited Rosehill for a few days, before embarking on a tour of her brothers and sisters. Less than a fortnight at Griff with Isaac and Sarah was enough to make her wonder why she had travelled all the way from Switzerland 'to come and see people who don't want me'.[65] The visit to Meriden went better, with Mary Ann allowing that 'Dear Chrissey is much kinder than any one else in the family and I am happiest with her. She is generous and sympathizing and really cares for my happiness.'[66]

Absorbed in their own routines of family and business life, none of her siblings had time to give their younger sister the kind of sustained concentration she craved. She was probably in a particularly demanding mood, miserable that no vocation had emerged from her renewed contact with the Warwickshire soil. She had always been ready to admit that looking after her father absolved her from having to think about what to do with her life. Now, just as she had always suspected, the prospect of being free to choose how and where to live had her longing for the certainties of the constricting past. What made her situation bearable was that she was beginning to perceive that her unhappiness was not just the result of her own inadequacy, but was an experience shared by many. It was this growing ability to link individual experience with the broader human condition that was to carry her eventually into writing fiction.

In a letter of 4 April 1850 to her old school friend Martha Jackson with whom she was still in sporadic contact, she moves from the particular to the general in what would become one of the defining characteristics of her narrative voice. 'My return to England is anything but joyous to me, for old associations are rather painful than otherwise to me. We are apt to complain of the weight of duty, but when it is taken from us, and we are left at liberty to choose for ourselves, we find that the old life was the easier one.'[67] In fact, she was not entirely without ideas for the future. Elsewhere in the letter she sketches two possibilities. Either she will return to Geneva, or she will stay in Britain, but move to London. A week later she asks Sara to find out about the rates for the boarding-house run in The Strand in London by the publisher John Chapman. 'I am not asking you merely for the sake of giving you trouble,' she says, still raw from Sara's accusations of pushiness, 'I am really anxious to know.'[68]

Sara Hennell had first met John Chapman in 1846 when both were living in Clapton, an elegant suburb to the north-east of London. Clapton and adjacent Hackney had long been home to the liberal-minded lawyers, bankers, merchants and manufacturers who made their living in the commercial district of the city. Street after street of symmetrical Georgian town houses shaped a culture which was learned and pious, but also radical and acute. The inhabitants of Clapton were not establishment people. The men had not been to Oxford or Cambridge, the women were independent and clever, and the boys were just as likely destined for the warehouse as the high court. There were several thriving Unitarian congregations and a string of good girls' schools. Once the day's business was done – and Clapton people worked hard for their living – they visited their neighbours to make music, discuss science and philosophy, and fall cautiously in love. It was at just such a gathering that Sara Hennell had first met John Chapman, the publisher responsible for so many of the esoteric and radical books around which this progressive culture coalesced.

In the end, Clapton turned out to be too quiet for John Chapman, who was never happy unless he was living in the midst of mayhem. In 1847 he took the lease on a large house in central London and set about creating the layers of chaos he craved. The bottom floor of number 142 The Strand was given over to his publishing and bookselling business, while the rest of the house was occupied by his family, together with the string of lodgers who followed him wherever he went. The overall effect was to create an avant-garde guesthouse where out-of-town writers, intellectuals and scholars could stay in congenial surroundings while visiting friends, meeting publishers or going to libraries. According to its printed blurb, 142 The Strand offered guests 'the advantages of an Hotel, combined with the quiet and comfort of a Private Residence'.[69] First-class rooms were £2 10s a week and a fire in the bedroom cost an extra 3s 6d. Breakfast was at 8.30, lunch at one and dinner at six. Any man and the occasional woman of letters visiting London during the late forties and fifties was sure at some point to sample Mrs Chapman's slapdash housekeeping. It was not unusual for twenty people to sit down to dinner. Emerson stayed at 142 and so, from the sublime to the ridiculous, did Dr Brabant. The regular evening parties which had begun in Clapton continued, now swollen by those literary stars who had been too grand to make the journey out to the suburbs.

The Strand also provided something like a permanent home for young people from the provinces trying to make their way in that ramshackle, part-fantasy construction known as literary London. William Hale White, later famous as the novelist Mark Rutherford, lodged there, while Eliza Lynn, the young novelist who had already published two novels, had been a paying guest at Clapton. Just as Rosehill never shook off its reputation for loose living, so the whiff of immorality always clung to the Chapmans' various households. Perhaps in a defensive recognition that John Chapman and her husband shared more than a love of progress, Cara Bray commented to Sara that it was 'very peculiar' of Eliza Lynn to take lodgings in Clapton: 'how many more young ladies is . . . [Mr Chapman] going to have?' she asked tartly.[70]

It is not clear whether John Chapman did actually ever 'have' Eliza Lynn. What is certain is that irregular sexuality played as large a part in his life as it had in Charles Bray's: not for nothing were both men known as 'Don Juan'. The similarities between them were striking. Both came from outside the public school and university-educated élite. Enthusiastically self-taught, they moved lightly from subject to subject, unhampered by the specialist's reverence for subject boundaries. More interested in the modern world than the ancient, they looked to French and German philosophy to make sense of the godless universe unfolding around them. Physical science, still largely excluded from the official syllabus and confined to the studies of butterfly-collecting clergy, seemed to them to hold the clues to man's past and his future. Facilitators rather than original talents, their knack lay in publicising the ideas of those who had the temperament and intellect to go deeply into these matters. Presided over by Chapman, 142 The Strand became the metropolitan equivalent of Rosehill, an unofficial headquarters of the progressive élite.

Chapman's origins were, like Bray's, provincial and commercial.[71] He was born in Nottingham in 1821 and apprenticed to a watchmaker in Worksop. Quick to latch on to any new idea from phrenology to the co-operative movement, he soon fell out with his master and ran away to Edinburgh, where his brother was studying medicine. From there, Chapman went to Adelaide where, in a typical boast, he claimed to have made a fortune as a watchseller. Whatever capital he had amassed was – his story – wiped out in a homecoming shipwreck. Unbowed, he nonchalantly declared his intention to try doctoring instead. Some training at St Bartholomew's and possibly in Paris followed, but it came to a sudden end in 1843. Although he had not been lucky enough to inherit family money, the twenty-two-year-old Chapman was clever enough to marry it: Susanna Brewitt came with a large fortune, thanks to her father's Nottingham lace business. No longer obliged to pursue the tedium of a training,

Chapman moved with his new wife to London, where he used her fortune to buy a small publishing house devoted to the production of radical and progressive titles.

One of the books Chapman published was Mary Ann Evans's translation of Strauss. Although there is no record of their first meeting, it must have been during one of her stays in Clapton with Sara during 1846. Her anxiety about whether the Strauss would ever get published probably skewed her first impression of Chapman. Still, he clearly made an impact. She had a plain woman's defensiveness when it came to talking about desirable men. Expecting rejection, she was always quick to disclaim any attraction on her part. 'Mr Chapman . . . was always too much of the *interesting* gentleman to please me,' she wrote in a letter to Sara in February 1847 and, aware how unconvincing it sounded, immediately crossed it out.[72]

Their next meeting took place in the summer of 1850 when Chapman appeared at Rosehill where Mary Ann was staying after her return from Geneva. He came again in October 1850, this time bringing Robert Mackay, whose *The Progress of the Intellect* he had just published. Mackay's work was a sure synthesis of Strauss's Biblical demythologising, Hennell's residual piety and Bray's optimistic Necessitarianism. God still had a notional place as Prime Cause, but the emphasis was on man's obligation to discern the moral laws which underpinned the universe as surely as physical ones. Chapman had already arranged that a critique of the book would appear in the *Westminster Review* and now he asked Mary Ann to write the piece. Although the *Review* could no longer claim the prestige it had enjoyed in its heyday, still it had great symbolic currency among liberal intellectuals. There was hardly anyone whose work had not appeared in its pages. Carlyle, Mill and Martineau were all contributors. For Mary Ann Evans, whose critical work had hitherto appeared only in the uneven and provincial *Coventry Herald*, it was a great chance.

Although completely unknown outside her immediate circle, Mary Ann was probably the person most qualified in Britain to assess Mackay's book. Without any conscious manoeuvring on her part, she had found herself at the heart of the busy network of influences which had produced *The Progress of the Intellect*. Not only had she brought Strauss before an English audience, she also lodged with Charles Bray and was friends with his brother-in-law, Charles Hennell. She understood the intellectual trajectories of each man – if Bray can be said to have had any such thing – and saw how Mackay was situated in relation to each of them. Nor did she make the mistake of so many reviewers, then as now, of simply describing and amplifying the author's arguments. She was confident enough to argue with Mackay's interpretation of Greek myths and also to point out a few repetitions. The voice she employs is that of an embryonic George Eliot narrator – vast in scope, dizzyingly well-informed, able to show the connections between the tiniest details and the large frame.[73]

The Mackay review was Mary Ann's calling-card to a different kind of life. She delivered it to Chapman in person in November and stayed on for two weeks to see whether lodging at The Strand might suit her permanently. The experiment went well. She had long passed her adolescent shyness and was by now used to fitting into other people's groups. Musical evenings and literary chat were where she excelled. On the last Friday of her stay she met Eliza Lynn, Chapman's former lodger. Lynn, secure in the achievement of already being a published novelist, was very happy to patronise the slightly older girl from the provinces. She chirruped that Mary Ann was 'such a lovable person' and maintained that she was 'never so attracted to a woman before'.[74] Mary Ann, in return, was impressed with Eliza Lynn's intellectual-looking spectacles and the fact that she had the appearance of a bona fide 'literary lady'. But Mary Ann was not all uncritical gush. She was sharp enough to notice that Eliza Lynn, for all her stodgily paraded learning, was not a great or original intellect. If Miss Lynn could support herself in London by her pen, then so surely could she.

The two weeks Mary Ann spent at The Strand before returning temporarily to Coventry for Christmas gave her the chance to familiarise herself with the strange dramas and intrigues of this unhappy household. The Chapmans' marriage was not a good one. Susanna's useful fortune did not offset her fourteen years' seniority to her husband. Although she had been able to give him two fine children, Beatrice and Ernest, there was also a deformed, backward boy who was boarded out with relatives. Never a pretty woman, by the time of the move to The Strand she was already over forty to her husband's handsome twenty-eight and beginning to slow down. On 10 August 1851 Chapman wrote in his diary, 'Susanna's incapability of walking far or fast, and general debility presses upon me how much she has aged latterly, and makes the future look sad.'[75]

Perhaps what depressed Chapman most was that Susanna's physical stodginess reflected her mental capacity. She was conventional, stubborn and sloppy, instinctively opposed to the new ideas which gripped Chapman like a fever. She took it personally if people held opinions that were different from her own and her idea of intellectual debate was to repeat her point more loudly than before. 'Her chief reading is novels,'[76] Chapman told his diary sadly in July 1860, revealing just how low was the status of fiction until George Eliot had started to elevate it the previous year with the publication of *Adam Bede*.

One can hardly blame Susanna for not finding the time to improve herself physically or mentally. She ran the ramshackle enterprise which was 142 The Strand with only the minimum of domestic help. Chapman's finances were generally in a muddle and he expected his wife to perform miracles on a shoestring. In many marriages one partner develops skills and qualities to compensate for the other's lack of them. This was not the case with the Chapmans. Susanna was just as chaotic and histrionic as her husband, which allowed him to spend a great deal of time criticising her for the very qualities which many of his clients and friends found so exasperating in himself. In 1860, a particularly bad year for their marriage, he noted: 'while the fuss and bustle of . . . [Susanna's] management is a continual disturbance, all is orderly and quiet in her absence.'[77] Many would have said exactly the same of him.

In any case, some of Susanna's intrusive bluster was surely due to her resentment that Chapman had installed his mistress in the house bought with her money. Technically, thirty-year-old Elisabeth Tilley was governess to young Beatrice and Ernest. But her patchy education and general unsuitability for the job signposted to anyone who cared to think about it that she was actually Chapman's lover. Eliot's biographers have long differed over whether Susanna Chapman was aware of what was going on between her husband and Elisabeth Tilley. Chapman's diary – never the most reliable witness to anything but his own internal fantasies – suggests that an unstable and largely unspoken arrangement operated whereby Susanna tolerated Chapman's relationship with Elisabeth, but insisted on a continuing precedence in the social organisation of the household. This was hardly a recipe for a tranquil life, which was probably just as well since all the participants in this triangle loved kicking up a fuss. On 30 July 1851 Chapman recorded a typical incident:

> Susanna and I had a serious altercation about going [out] on Sundays – an old subject: – She said how much she should like to spend the whole of the Sundays out, I said 'yes, so should I, but you prevented it,' meaning that she would not recognize my right to take her or E. as I might think best something like alternately. Her remarks were one tissue of exaggeration misrepresentation prevarication and passion I bore it calmly, with one or two exceptions, when I could not help stopping her by saying she was a liar, for which I afterwards apologized.[78]

What further heightened the drama was that Chapman's and Elisabeth's relationship was by no means a secure shadow marriage. Chapman spent a lot of time wondering out loud whether he loved her quite as much as he used to, to which Elisabeth responded hysterically by giving notice. The news that the clever Miss Evans from Coventry would be coming back permanently after Christmas was enough to make Elisabeth doubly jumpy about her position. She fired off a couple of letters to Rosehill over the holidays, in which she probably warned Mary Ann not to get too close to her lover. As a consequence, when Mary Ann turned up at Euston Square station on the afternoon of 8 January her manner was 'formal and studied' towards Chapman, who had come to meet her.[79] Elisabeth's attitude, by contrast, was anything but restrained. The very next day she laid into Chapman about bringing Miss Evans to The Strand. In a diary entry which he later deleted Chapman recorded: 'Had a very painful altercation with Elisabeth the result of her groundless suspicions hence I have been in a state of unhealthy excitement all day. – She gave notice at the dinner table that she intended to leave in the Autumn.'[80]

Far from groundless, Elisabeth's suspicions about her lover's intentions towards the plain, clever lodger from the Midlands were spot on. It was Chapman, after all, who had encouraged Mary Ann to come to London, by setting her up with her first bit of prestigious journalism. During his two meetings with her at Rosehill the previous year he had also told her what a help she could be to him in his publishing business. While he had the contacts and the enthusiasm to keep the business expanding, he needed someone with her deep, scholarly knowledge to guide him away from the false trails and spectacular blunders which happened whenever he got out of his intellectual depth. Neither Susanna nor Elisabeth was suitable soulmate material, although Susanna did occasionally help with proof-reading. Miss Evans, with her extraordinary gifts, was exactly the person Chapman needed both to stir up and sustain the regime at 142 The Strand.

For Mary Ann, becoming John Chapman's right-hand woman represented the kind of vocation which had seemed so out of reach when she wrote her last despairing letter to the Brays from Geneva. Now, within weeks of returning to dull, indifferent Coventry, here was a handsome man asking her to join with him in a glorious project to change the world. What is more, he had promised to help her break into free-lance journalism and, as earnest of his good faith, had placed her first piece in the *Westminster Review*. The fact that Chapman was not only married but had a mistress would not have deterred her, just as it had made no difference with Dr Brabant, M. D'Albert and, in the early days, Charles Bray. It was not that she was cruel, exactly, or indifferent to other women's situations, but her own deep needs for intellectual and emotional intensity were still incapable of being schooled. Or almost. For Chapman's observation that she was 'formal and studied' at Euston Square suggests that this time Mary Ann was determined at least to try to avoid the turmoil which had followed in her wake at Devizes and Geneva.

As a signal that this was to be a new phase in her life, Miss Evans announced to the Strand-dwellers that from now on she would like to be known as 'Marian'. She had played with the idea ever since she was a schoolgirl learning French, trying out 'Marianne' in her exercise book. But now the time felt right for a radical change. 'Mary Anns' were two-a-penny in rural Warwickshire. 'Marian' sounded much more suitable for a woman who intended to take London by storm.

CHAPTER 6

'The Most Important Means of Enlightenment'

Life at *The Westminster Review* 1851–2

JOHN CHAPMAN LOVED and needed women as much as they loved and needed him. Unlike so many progressive middle-class men of the mid-century who espoused a programme of political, social and legal reform, Chapman actually believed that all women were his equals and some his superiors. He acknowledged and celebrated Marian's intellect without the least condescension, humbly seeking and following her advice about the editorial side of his business. In private he asked her to teach him German and submitted his own half-baked attempts at essay-writing to her critical scrutiny. Dazzled by Marian's mind, he felt not the slightest need to control or diminish it. Brabant, Bray and D'Albert Durade had all displayed similar intellectual generosity, and Chapman was to be the next link in a chain which was to lead Marian finally and happily to George Henry Lewes.

It was not only women's minds which fascinated Chapman. When he eventually qualified as a medical doctor in 1857 he specialised in gynaecology, treating certain diseases of women by means of heat and cold applied along the spine.[1] Every time his mistress Elisabeth Tilley had a period he marked the event in his diary, although this was not so much a signal to fuss around with hot-water bottles as to return to his wife's bed. A few years later he courted Marian's friend Barbara Leigh Smith with the peculiar suggestion that having sex with him, and perhaps even a baby, would sort out her menstrual cycle. Once again, the clinical noting down of the physical intimacies between them, this time in a series of explicit letters to Leigh Smith, seems to have been the crucial ingredient in Chapman's enjoyment of their affair.[2]

Amongst the people who bought his books, there was nothing unusual about Chapman's disregard for conventional sexual morality. The right of both sexes to form relationships unsanctioned by marriage had been part of the Utopian programme from the days of William Godwin at the end of the previous century. The Brays practised a version of polygamy whereby both were free to take other lovers. Their friends the Thornton Hunts lived with another couple in Bayswater, where it was rumoured they shared more than domestic expenses. But Chapman's need for multiple partners had less to do with intellectual conviction and more with a craving for the excitement and chaos inevitably engendered. The slammed doors, tearful scenes and angry words made him feel alive in a way that the deep calm of monogamy never could. Whenever his personal life looked in danger of settling, he whipped up a storm by showing one lover a letter written by another. His habit of candour, so different from Brabant's evasiveness, allowed him to pass on information, encourage confrontations and generally keep the drama at fever pitch. Then, when it seemed as though there was nothing more to savour, he lived the experience again in a series of anguished diary entries.[3]

The discovery of Chapman's 1851 diary on a Nottingham bookstall in 1913 meant that John Cross's official version of Marian's life at The Strand had to be completely rewritten. Cross had always been extremely sensitive about the rumours which clung to his wife's association with Chapman even years after her death. The worst of these, for which no evidence has ever been found, was that Marian had given birth to a son by Chapman and that the child had been smuggled away to Edinburgh. No wonder, then, that Cross felt it prudent virtually to exclude Chapman from *George Eliot's Life*. Marian's letters to Chapman are barely quoted and the good doctor was never asked for his recollections, perhaps because Cross was well aware that the appalling old man loved to boast that George Eliot had once been in love with him. Anyone reading Cross's account of Marian's years at the *Westminster* would assume that Chapman was a professional acquaintance of hers rather than her lover and the man who mediated her transition from provincial bluestocking to metropolitan intellectual.

Mindful of the letters she had received from Elisabeth Tilley over Christmas, Marian arrived at The Strand in January with every intention of steering clear of sexual involvement with Chapman. But he was a difficult man to resist, being engagingly naked in his desires. On the very morning of her arrival, in a gesture whose significance surely cannot entirely have escaped him, he searched the dawn skies with his telescope for a sighting of the planet Venus.[4] A few days later he helped Marian choose a piano for her room and spent the morning listening to her play Mozart,[5] much to the fury of Susanna, who immediately suggested getting a piano for the drawing-room. But the new instrument did not arrive in time and by the following weekend Chapman and Marian had become lovers. Chapman always took care to note in his diary whenever he had sex with Elisabeth, and over 18–19 January he used a similar code to suggest two sessions of love-making with Marian.[6] That something beyond flirtation had occurred is suggested by the fact that Elisabeth and Susanna immediately responded by collapsing with bad pains in the head and leg respectively. By the following Wednesday the tension had become unbearable and a showdown inevitable. With pleasurable relish Chapman recorded the details in his diary.

January 22nd

Invited Miss Evans to go out after breakfast, did not get a decisive answer, E. afterwards said if I did go, she should be glad to go, – I then invited Miss Evans again telling her E. would go whereupon she declined rather rudely, Susanna being willing to go out, and neither E. nor S. wishing to walk far I proposed they should go a short distance without me, which E. considered an insult from me and reproached me in no measured terms accordingly, and heaped upon me suspicions and accusations I do not in any way deserve. I was very severe and harsh, said things I was sorry for afterwards, and we became reconciled in the Park.

Miss Evans apologized for her rudeness tonight, which roused all E's jealousy again, and consequent bitterness. S. E. and Miss Evans are gone to spend the evening with Mr and Mrs Holland.[7]

Having a sexual interloper in the house at least had the effect of drawing Susanna and Elisabeth closer together. All it took was a little stirring on Elisabeth's part for wife and mistress to reach the joint conclusion that Miss Evans and Chapman were, in the latter's complacent phrase, 'completely in love with each other'.[8] This recognition laid the ground for some new and exciting scenes, in which the four main players spent their time flouncing out of rooms, having headaches and suing for uneasy peace.

It was ironic that this sexual melodrama was played out against Chapman's increasing prissiness about his personal reputation. He had agreed to publish Eliza Lynn's third novel, *Realities*, typically without having bothered to read it all the way through. Keen to break away from her reputation as a writer of turgid academic prose, Lynn had included a love scene which Susanna, who had done some preliminary editing of the book, considered *risqué*. Chapman, with his knack of mixing up his personal and public life to dire effect, now gave responsibility for the Lynn manuscript to Marian, a gesture that naturally succeeded in making Susanna even more jealous than before.

Eliza Lynn was also annoyed that her manuscript had been assigned to the new favourite. It is not certain whether she had ever been Chapman's lover, but as a clever, free-thinking woman she had certainly enjoyed his attention during her time as his lodger in Clapton. Although she had taken care to gush affectionately to Marian at their first meeting, privately Eliza had her marked down as pretentious and provincial. To be asked to submit to her editorial judgement was the final insult. Before Marian had a chance to start work on the manuscript, Eliza Lynn appeared dramatically at The Strand and announced that she would agree to only one of the suggested changes.

There followed just the kind of titillating situation which Chapman loved. Eliza Lynn's stubbornness in sticking by what he described as 'a love scene which is warmly and vividly depicted, with a tone and tendency which I entirely disapprove',[9] gave him the chance to talk about sex with four women, setting one up against the other. In the course of the next few weeks he sided with Marian against Eliza, and with Eliza against Susanna. He got Elisabeth to read the dubious passage and was pleased when she agreed with Susanna that it should not be published. He then proceeded to get Marian to go with him to see Eliza, to whom he declaimed pompously that 'as I am the publisher of works notable for the[ir] intellectual freedom it behoves me to be exceedingly careful of the *moral* tendency of all I issue'.[10] As with most of the dramas which Chapman whipped up, events did not so much come to a head as trail off in embarrassment. In the end, and only after a lawyer had been called in, *Realities* was published elsewhere.

It was against this chaotic background of comings and goings, tears and reconciliations, that Marian tried hard to establish the kind of life for which she had come to London. She dutifully took advantage of the cultural opportunities available to her, hearing Francis Newman lecture on geometry and Faraday on magnetism. At The Strand she continued to dine, debate and sing with the stream of clever men who passed through Mrs Chapman's dining-room. But as she was painfully aware, intellectual hobbies and new friendships were no substitute for solid achievement. Getting the review of Mackay into the January edition of the *Westminster* was starting to look like a fluke. Her offer to do a follow-up piece and waive the fee was disappointingly turned down. Chapman fared no better when he tried to get the *Edinburgh Review* to commission her, even though he was careful to refer to her as a man throughout the negotiations.[11] However, a newish weekly periodical called the *Leader* did accept a couple of pieces on Harriet Martineau's and Henry Atkinson's *Letters on the Laws of Man's Nature and Development*.[12]

It was not the slow start to her literary career, however, which drove Marian from The Strand. By the end of February the tension between herself, Susanna and Elisabeth was so great that every encounter became an excuse for a row. On the 21st Marian went to Chapman's room to borrow a dictionary, found Elisabeth there, and the result was a confrontation that 'increased [the] bitterness in both their minds'.[13] The pages of Chapman's diary for the next few days have been torn out, suggesting that the histrionics were reaching a pitch which was too painful, even for him. During this unrecorded week Susanna and Elisabeth appear to have combined forces to get Marian out of the house. When the diary entries resume they show Chapman taking Marian on a last, hectic round of visits to the theatre, opera and art galleries, before escorting her to Euston Square station on 24 March.[14]

In less than three months Marian's launch into a life which was supposed to be financially independent and intellectually fulfilling had ground humiliatingly to a halt. To make matters even more painful, she was leaving behind a man for whom she felt deeply, a man with whom she had made physical love. In his usual complacent way Chapman recorded their anguished platform conversation in his diary:

She was very sad, and hence made me feel so. – She pressed me for some intimation of the state of my feelings – <I told her that I felt great affection for her, but that I loved E. and S. also, though each in a different way.> At this avowal she burst into tears. I tried to comfort her, and reminded [her] of the dear friends and pleasant home she was returning to, – but the train whirled her away very very sad.[15]

By now the Brays must have become used to Marian's embarrassingly sudden departures from other people's houses. They were probably too tactful to question her closely, although they would have been aware that letters still continued to travel regularly between Rosehill and The Strand. Marian had agreed to undertake two projects from Coventry for Chapman. The first was an analytical catalogue of his publications – in effect a list of all the titles and a summary of their contents. The second was an abridgement of Strauss, for which she was promised £100. In theory all should now have been quiet, with Marian at least a hundred miles from Elisabeth Tilley and even further from Susanna Chapman, who was on a family visit to the West Country. But quiet was the one thing Chapman could never stand: on his first night back in The Strand with only Elisabeth for company he found himself overwhelmed by 'a sense of extreme loneliness'.[16] So he cranked up the pitch by sending Marian a couple of spiteful letters which Susanna had written about her from Truro. Marian's response – immediately forwarded to Susanna – was to declare angrily that she would continue with the catalogue only 'on condition that you state or rather, I should hope re-state to Mrs. C. the fact that I am doing it, not because I "like" it, but in compliance with your request'.[17]

Over the next couple of weeks Marian's mood softened, partly because she was removed from the scene, but also because the work she was doing for Chapman genuinely engaged her. In an attempt at reconciliation with Susanna she wrote 'an able and excellent' letter which Chapman forwarded to Truro.[18] This seems to have done the trick, although Elisabeth Tilley remained implacable. A note which Marian sent to Chapman on 28 April made the governess fly into a frenzy and beg her lover never to speak to Miss Evans again.[19]

But Chapman was incapable of living without the painful complications of Marian's presence. Within days of Elisabeth's tearful request he was busy contriving a situation which would require Miss Evans to return to The Strand. Just as Bray had bought the *Coventry Herald* as a platform for his views, so Chapman had long dreamed of owning and editing a liberal journal in which the ideas that he and his business stood for might be more widely circulated. A few months previously he had talked about buying the ailing *Westminster Review*, but was unsure whether he could raise the money – a dilemma which was to dog his career. Now Edward Lombe, a wealthy and liberal eccentric who was already subsidising the *Westminster*, wrote to Chapman offering to help him set up a quarterly journal. With Lombe's financial support, Chapman quickly agreed on a price for the magazine with the proprietor, W. E. Hickson.

Although he had long had fantasies about editing the *Westminster*, Chapman was just about realistic enough to know that he was not up to the job. If he were not to look ridiculous then he needed to find a right-hand man who had the intellectual scope and depth to shape a publication that only a decade previously had been put together by J. S. Mill. Luckily he already knew that man, who was living in Coventry and called Marian Evans. On 27 May he visited Marian at Rosehill to discuss her future involvement with the *Westminster*. He found her 'shy calm and affectionate',[20] although this did not last when over the next few days he spelled out the terms of her return to The

Strand. He made it clear that his first priority was to keep Elisabeth living with him, even if this meant giving up his sexual relationship with Marian. A couple of days later, during an excursion to Kenilworth Castle, he tried to expand on the way he felt about her. Clumsily, he moved the conversation round to 'the wonderful and mysterious embodiment of all the elements characteristics and beauties of nature which man and woman jointly present. I dwelt also on the incomprehensible mystery and witchery of beauty.' Quick to take the hint, Marian burst into tears and 'wept bitterly'.[21] In the gentlest way he knew, Chapman was telling Marian that she was not pretty enough to make him risk losing Elisabeth by continuing their affair.

Why did Marian agree to return to The Strand on such demeaning terms? There could be no question of her becoming the official assistant editor of the magazine. Advanced thinkers were not so advanced at mid-century that they were able to accept a woman at the head of a distinguished publication like the *Westminster*. Potential benefactors and contributors would shy away if they knew who was really in charge. In time, Marian's identity was bound to leak out, but by then it was hoped that the reputation of the new *Westminster Review* would be sufficiently secure to withstand the gossip. At this delicate stage in the proceedings it was essential to be discreet. Which is why when Chapman went to see Thomas Carlyle on 10 October to persuade him to write a piece for the first issue, his assistant editor was obliged to walk up and down on the pavement outside.[22]

Odd though it might seem to anyone who saw Marian hovering outside Carlyle's Chelsea home on that day, it felt quite natural to her. From the moment she had first taken up Vinet to translate under the direction of Francis Watts, she had been in training for just this kind of transparency. As the *Westminster*'s uncredited assistant editor she would once again become the medium through which a man might deliver his important message to the world. When she wrote to the Brays from Geneva about needing to find a vocation, she had talked about sweetening and easing the life of another. By agreeing to help Chapman she would be doing just that. The fact that she would receive neither his sexual love nor public acknowledgement nor any pay beyond her board and lodging appealed to Marian's growing pleasure in resignation. Just as Maggie returns to face the censure of the townspeople after her apparent elopement with Stephen, so Marian embraced the opportunity to return to 142 The Strand and face Susanna's and Elisabeth's continuing suspicions. This time, noted Chapman in his ever-open diary, she was determined to come not as a combatant but as a penitent.

But there were more practical considerations pulling Marian back to The Strand. As an educated single woman of modest means she was no different from the 20,000 or so who worked as governesses, trading educational 'accomplishments' for a roof over their heads. She could not live with the Brays for ever and Chapman was offering board and lodgings in return for her editorial and administrative help. There would also be the chance to make extra money by contributing articles to the magazine.

Shortly after that miserable day at Kenilworth, Marian dried her tears and agreed to become Chapman's 'active co-operator' in the *Westminster*.[23] A couple of nights later, with a theatricality which had become the signature of this whole exhausting business, she and Chapman 'made a solemn and holy vow which henceforth will bind us to the right'.[24] Their affair, if it could be called that, was over. The mood of delicious sacrifice continued throughout Chapman's stay at Rosehill. On her return from Kenilworth, Marian took up Thomas à Kempis's *De Imitatione Christi*, which had been a comfort during her father's last days, and recommended it to Chapman who scribbled down an extract about resignation in his diary.[25] She was careful not to let anyone see her unhappiness, singing especially well during a musical evening with the Brays' other guests, the Thornton Hunts, whose destiny was so strangely tangled with her own. The next night, 2 June, she went without dinner so that she might get on with the prospectus, a document that was part mission statement and part fund-raiser, aimed at potential benefactors of the new *Westminster Review*.

Over the next few weeks Marian stayed in Coventry, while Chapman negotiated her return to The Strand with Elisabeth and Susanna. The distance and stability afforded by Rosehill allowed Marian to come to terms with the changed nature of her relationship with Chapman. As she disengaged from him sexually, she found a new detachment and authority in her professional dealings with him. Her letters over the next weeks are restrained and practical, concerned mainly with *Westminster* business. Chapman, by contrast, had plunged straight back into the emotional maelstrom of 142 The Strand. On 15 June 1851 a row with Susanna about whether she could use three drawers in his desk ended up with her setting fire to her letters.[26] The following day, Chapman's birthday, was 'made wretched by Elisabeth's positive assurance that she will not live in The Strand after Miss Evans comes to London'.[27] In the midst of this hysterical flap, Marian started to seem like a distant and cool oasis. A very ordinary letter she sent him on 20 June had him dizzy with rapture: 'Miss Evans' little note is inexpressibly charming, so quick, intelligent and overflowing with love and sweetness!' And then, because he could never just enjoy things the way they were, 'I feel her to be the living torment to my soul.'[28]

In a carefully stage-managed rapprochement with the ladies of The Strand, Marian arrived in London with the Brays in the middle of August. On the 15th Chapman spent the day with them at the Great Exhibition before bringing Marian home to 'make a call' on Susanna. From Chapman's point of view it all went splendidly: after dinner he and Marian got through a great deal of *Review* business. Elisabeth and Susanna were less happy, predictably dissolving into headache and tears respectively.[29] None the less, during that evening an emotional and social Rubicon was crossed. By the end of it, without anything specific being said, the way had been cleared for Miss Evans to return to The Strand.

The Prospectus for which Marian had gone without dinner on 2 June mapped out a brave future for the once great *Westminster Review*.[30] Ever since the high water mark of John Stuart Mill's editorship in the 1830s, the magazine's performance and prestige had been in decline. Now Marian, writing as 'the Editors', promised a journal which would once again engage fully with the transforming intellectual landscape of mid-Victorian Britain. The guiding philosophy would be both gradualist and radical, advocating change, but insisting on its organic nature. Sharp scrutiny of 'established creeds and systems' would, it was maintained, lead not to their destruction but to their re-emergence in a stronger, refined form. For instance, although the implications of the new Biblical criticism would be pursued to their logical conclusion, the editors promised to 'bear in mind the pre-eminent importance of a constructive religious philosophy, as connected with the development and activity of the moral nature'. Fearless and unsentimental assessment of the *status quo* would, it was hoped, reveal the wondrous connectedness of all things: 'opposing systems may in the end prove complements of each other.' And although they had no doubt that the best change was snail slow, the editors had no objections to helping things along. They were, announced the Prospectus, in favour of extending the suffrage, reforming the judiciary, ending religious discrimination and, in a restatement of the *Westminster*'s most hallowed principle, freeing trade from every kind of restriction.

Marian's growing emotional detachment from Chapman allowed her to see clearly that if people thought he was the active editor of the *Westminster* they would dismiss it out of hand. But if it became known that he was relying on a woman to do the work, even if it was the clever lady translator of Strauss, then there would be even greater unease. Rightly convinced that Chapman was not fully aware of the delicacy of their situation, Marian nudged him towards discretion, suggesting a formula if anyone pressed for details: 'With regard to the secret of the Editorship, it will perhaps be the best plan for you to state, that for the present *you* are to be regarded as the responsible person, but that you employ an Editor in whose literary and general ability you confide.'[31]

But even with the public relations sorted out, the Prospectus pleased no one. John Stuart Mill thought it too conservative. James Martineau, Harriet's brother, Unitarian minister and long-time contributor, sneered that it was too low-brow and worried about its atheism – a charge which had dogged the magazine since the days of Bentham.[32] And Hickson, who at this point still owned the *Westminster*, was naturally annoyed by Chapman publicising the coming changes so far in advance.[33] It was left to Marian, still in exile in Coventry, to guide Chapman through the squalls that the Prospectus had created. With brisk authority, she substantially corrected the draft of his response to Mill, changing the punctuation and altering the phraseology. The fearsome James Martineau needed even more careful handling. Despite his grudging remarks about the Prospectus, Martineau had agreed to write a piece for the first issue on 'Christian Ethics and Modern Civilisation' and now wrote to Chapman asking for guidelines. Unable to respond confidently, Chapman went all the way to Coventry on 23 August to get Marian's advice.[34] She drafted a letter for him to send to Martineau in which she explained exactly what was wanted.

If Marian had not realised it before, the experience of supervising Chapman's responses to Mill and Martineau made her see just how shaky was his grasp of intellectual detail. Chapman, however, seems still to have been labouring under the delightful illusion that his work was capable of standing alongside that of his most distinguished contributors. In September he started to make worrying noises about writing a piece on national representation for the first issue. Using blatant flattery, Marian persuaded him to stick to what he did best, which was being a figurehead. He was vain enough to swallow her argument, writing complacently in his diary on 21 September: 'Miss Evans thinks I should lose power and influence by becoming a writer in the Westminster Review, and could not then maintain that dignified relation with the various contributors that she thinks I may do otherwise.'[35]

All the while that Marian was in charge of the *Westminster* she managed to keep Chapman out of its pages. But by 1855 he was once again chafing at the bit. One evening, after dining with her and Lewes, he produced an article which he said was intended for the July issue. Although the *Westminster* was no longer her responsibility, Marian found it hard to sound encouraging. The next day, 25 June 1855, having read his article, she wrote a careful letter in which she pointed out the continuing weaknesses in his writing style: 'whenever you pass from narrative to dissertation, certain old faults reappear – inexactness of expression, triads and duads of verbs and adjectives, mixed metaphors and a sort of watery volume that requires to be reduced by evaporation.'[36] As always, Chapman took Marian's comments to heart. He dejectedly withdrew the article from the magazine and begged for general reassurance about his writing. She wrote back in the nicest way she knew how: 'There is no reason for you to be desponding about your writing. You have made immense progress during the last few years, and you have so much force of mind and sincerity of purpose that you may work your way to a style which is free from vices, though perhaps you will never attain felicity – indeed, that is a free gift of Nature rather than a reward of labour.'[37] Chapman revised the article along the lines she suggested and finally put it in the October 1855 issue of the *Westminster*.

After spending the summer of 1851 rearranging Chapman's tangled thoughts and bad prose, it must have been exhilarating for Marian to see a piece of her own work in print. A late-September edition of the *Leader* carried her review of William Rathbone Greg's *The Creed of Christendom*, which ironically had been turned down by the *Westminster* earlier in the year. She was broadly sympathetic to Greg's work, which displayed exactly that kind of robust common sense she so admired. Chapman noted in his diary on 23 September that the *Leader*'s co-editor, George Henry Lewes, 'called in the afternoon to express his high opinion of Miss Evans' Article'.[38]

Lewes, who always seemed to be everywhere in literary London, was also a contributor to the January 1852 issue of the *Westminster*, the first for which Marian and Chapman were responsible. He was in excellent company. Although Mill and Carlyle had turned Chapman down, there was the Unitarian cleric William Johnson Fox on 'Representative Reform', Edward Forbes of

King's College on shellfish, Greg on labour relations, Francis Newman on suffrage, Froude on Mary Stuart and, of course, James Martineau on 'The Ethics of Christendom'. Marian's particular responsibility was the lengthy book review section for which the *Westminster* became celebrated. Every month she sifted through the huge number of books newly published in Britain, America, Germany and France, and selected about a hundred for review – a process which kept her keenly up to date with the latest developments in philosophy, literature and history. The review essays are composite efforts and although she occasionally contributed some copy herself – in the first issue she covered Carlyle's *The Life of John Sterling* – Marian's hand is seen mainly in the passages which link one contributor's work to another's. Anyone scouring the *Westminster Review* of 1852–4 for examples of George Eliot's early writing will find only a handful of pieces and they, according to current practice, are anonymous. At this stage the bulk of Marian's responsibilities consisted of coaxing and pruning the work of others. She came up with the topics, advised Chapman which writer to commission, proof-read the copy and followed its progress safely through the press.

The weeks leading up to the first issue were fraught. Writing to Cara, Marian describes her bedroom table groaning with books 'all to be digested by the editorial maw' and predicts 'terribly hard work for the next 6 weeks'.[39] A few weeks on, with publication looming, she is racked with headaches 'just when I ought to have been working the hardest.'[40] Three days later, on 23 December, she reports to the Brays that work is 'so heavy just for the next three days – all the revises being yet to come in and the proof of my own article – and Mr. Chapman is so overwhelmed with matters of detail that he has earnestly requested me to stay till Saturday'.[41] In the event she agreed, staying in London over Christmas Day, before returning to Rosehill on 27 December.

Although the first issue received a mixed response, within nine months the *Westminster Review* had re-established itself as the leading intellectual quarterly of the day. The phrenologist George Combe, admittedly a huge fan of Marian's at this point, praised her to the skies. Marian delightedly repeated to the Brays: 'he says, he thinks the *Westminster*, under *my* management the most important means of enlightenment of a literary nature in existence – the Edinburgh, under Jeffrey, nothing to it etc. etc.!!!'[42] Lewes, not yet Marian's lover, also told the readers of his periodical the *Leader* that 'It is now a Review that people talk about, ask for at the clubs, and read with respect. The variety and general excellence of its articles are not surpassed by any Review.'[43] To read the ten issues for which Marian Evans was responsible is to be presented with a snapshot of the best progressive thought at mid-century. The way forward in education, industry and penal reform is mapped out. Science is well covered, especially those pathways which lead inexorably towards Darwin – geology, botany, biology. Herbert Spencer introduces his theory of evolution over four issues. Theology, philosophy and history provide the heart of the magazine, the most notable success, with hindsight, being a piece on the hitherto unknown Schopenhauer. Apart from the long review section, there are articles on Shelley, Thackeray, Balzac and many others. Foreign affairs are covered with pieces on British policy in Europe and Russia. The difficult problem of Ireland, currently in the grip of a famine, is returned to again and again.

As the stature of the magazine grew, so did Marian's confidence in her ability to run it. Although her role was still formally unacknowledged, it was increasingly clear that she was the driving force. The dowdy woman from Nuneaton was now in her element, picking and choosing between some of Britain's and Europe's finest minds who offered their work to the *Westminster*. William Hale White, who worked as a sub-editor, remembered a woman in her absolute element: 'I can see her now, with her hair over her shoulders, the easy chair half sideways to the fire, her feet over the arms, and a proof in her hands, in that dark room at the back of No 142.'[44] A letter Marian wrote to Chapman during a holiday in Broadstairs in August 1852 shows just how familiar she had become with the foibles of different contributors and how confident she was in dealing with their squabbles, demands and small vanities. Briefing Chapman on the October 1852 issue, she briskly instructs him to give Froude twenty-six pages, warns that Mill and Martineau will inevitably clash and suggests he forward a note to Charlotte Brontë. Then she turns her attention to future issues, throwing out comments which would not sound out of place from a magazine editor today. 'Don't suggest "Fashion" as a subject to any one else – I should like to keep it.' And, again, 'I have noticed the advertisement of the British Q[uarterl]y this morning. Its list of subjects is excellent. I wish you could contrive to let me see the number when it comes out. They have one subject of which I am jealous – "Pre-Raphaelism in Painting and Literature". We have no good writer on such subjects on our staff. Ought we not, too, to try and enlist David Masson, who is one of the Br[itish] Q[uarterly] set?' She then adds a few funny remarks about James Martineau's endless complaint about the *Westminster* not toeing the Unitarian party line, before going on to make the serious point that it is precisely this heterodoxy which is the magazine's greatest strength.

> Martineau writes much that we can agree with and admire. Newman ditto, JS Mill still more, Froude a little less and so on. These men can write more openly in the Westminster than anywhere else. They are amongst the world's vanguard, though not all in the foremost line; it is good for the world, therefore, that they should have every facility for speaking out. Ergo, since each can't have a periodical to himself, it is good that there should be one which is common to them – id est, the Westminster.[45]

But it was not simply the editorial content of the *Westminster* which concerned Marian. At many points it looked as if the magazine was about to fold. In part, this was because Chapman was a hopeless financial manager, mixing up the accounts of his various different businesses into a giant tangle. But even an immaculate administrator would have found it hard to make the figures add up. The *Westminster* sold only 650 copies every quarter, which did not bring in nearly enough to cover the £250 contributors' bill. To make matters worse, Lombe, the chief backer, had died in March 1852, while Dr Brabant had been forced to call in a loan to Chapman of £800. The magazine continued thanks only to Chapman's uncanny luck in getting other people to bail him out. The *Westminster Review* still had a symbolic presence in the nation's intellectual landscape and men of a progressive persuasion felt uneasy about letting it fade away without making some kind of effort. Donations dribbled in, topped up by substantial loans from the Unitarian brewer Flower and the wealthy manufacturer Samuel Courtauld.

Chapman did not help himself by the combative approach he adopted towards the rest of the publishing industry. In 1852 he protested against the Booksellers Association's right to fix book prices and found himself outlawed as a result. The majority of publishers now refused to supply him with their books. Loving every minute of his notoriety, Chapman ran a piece in the April issue on the whole sorry business, and organised a meeting of well-known authors to gather at The Strand on 4 May. Dickens was in the chair, and intellectual stars like Wilkie Collins, F. W. Newman, Lewes, Spencer, Henry Crabb Robinson and Richard Owen were there to hear the excellent speeches. Letters from Mill, Cobden and Carlyle were read out. The meeting went off splendidly and at midnight Marian struck up 'See the Conquering Hero Comes' on the piano to acknowledge Chapman's genius at having turned the difficult situation into some kind of triumph. But the greatest achievement of all that night belonged to her. For in a room containing the cleverest, most influential people in Britain, she was the only person wearing a dress.[46]

No amount of intellectual excitement and professional fulfilment could make up for the fact that, for the first time since spring 1851, Marian's life was devoid of sexual affection. Her short infatuation with Froude had been followed by six months with D'Albert Durade over the winter of 1849–50, which in turn had been succeeded by the exhausting Chapman affair. Now there was no one. Terrified of provoking a situation whereby his assistant editor would once again be sent to Coventry, Chapman had been scrupulous in sticking to the terms of their 'holy vow'. Although Marian did nothing to try to make him change his mind, she could not help feeling flat, plain, loveless. Was this how the life of a professional woman had to be? As she established herself at the *Westminster,* she realised that the chance of achieving the satisfactions of ordinary womanhood – a husband, a family – were becoming increasingly remote. Her anxiety about how her life might be continued in overwrought identifications with other women in similar situations. For instance, after reading a memoir of Margaret Fuller, an American feminist who came late to family life, she wrote to a friend, 'You know how sad one feels when a great procession has swept by one, and the last notes of its music have died away, leaving one alone with the fields and sky. I feel so about life sometimes. It is a help to read such a life as Margaret Fuller's. How inexpressibly touching that passage from her journal – "I shall always reign through the intellect, but the life! the life! O my God! shall that never be sweet?"'[47]

On various occasions these identifications with other professional women provoked angry denials. Thus, when the distinguished fifty-year-old Swedish novelist and feminist Frederika Bremer turned up at The Strand, Marian recognised her as a possible future model for her life and lashed out in dismay. Bremer was, according to Marian, 'extremely ugly, and deformed. . . . Her eyes are sore – her teeth horrid . . . She is to me a repulsive person, equally unprepossessing to eye and ear.'[48] Harriet Martineau, whom she had met before and who had been the catalyst for this move to London, was also taken to task for the 'vulgarity' of her looks and gestures.[49]

But if it was hard to draw inspiration from the handful of older women who lived by their wits, Marian found herself increasingly becoming a role model to a new generation of younger girls. Bessie Rayner Parkes was a member of the Rosehill–Strand circuit by virtue of her father, the Radical Midlands MP Joseph Parkes who had bankrolled Marian's Strauss translation. Hugely cosseted yet ardently feminist, Bessie developed a crush on the clever, independent Miss Evans, who thrillingly answered to neither husband nor father. Marian, in turn, seems to have been less taken with Bessie, who was ten years younger than her, especially when she pestered for advice on her competent but derivative poetry. Marian responded as she increasingly would when forced to read someone's work – refusing easy praise and insisting that Bessie practise, practise, practise: 'Work on and on and do better things still'.[50] Chapman proved a softer, more politic touch: later that year he published Bessie's poems to tepid reviews.

Marian was reluctant to encourage Bessie's ardent friendship because she knew perfectly well that the Parkeses worried about the amount of time their daughter was spending at The Strand. A reputation for godlessness would not harm a girl who moved in Bessie's circles, but a hint of sexual scandal could. Marian was known not just for being clever, and 'advanced' in her religious views, but also for quite possibly having slept with Bray, Brabant and Chapman. And while all this doubtless only added to her glamour in Bessie's eyes, Marian was anxious that she should not be accused of leading anyone astray. Adopting the tone she had once used in similar circumstances to Mary Sibree, she admonished Bessie, 'Now, dear child, don't be playing pranks and shocking people, because I am told they lay it all to me and my bad influence over you.'[51] She understood better than Bessie that while no one cared if Joseph Parkes lived a sexually irregular life – and he did – it was quite another thing for his daughter to be suspected of doing the same. Her experience of seeing how avant-garde households like the Brays, the Chapmans and now the Parkeses organised these matters provided a vital foretaste of how she would herself be treated once she went to live with Lewes. While male writers, intellectuals, academics, doctors and politicians were increasingly happy to visit the unofficial 'Mrs Lewes', they felt quite differently about allowing their wives and daughters to do the same. Even at the end of her life, conventional matrons stayed away.

Marian no longer felt the need to match Bessie's anxious ardour. The days of leaning heavily on another woman as if she were a kindred spirit, a husband, were gone for good. From now on a different pattern emerged in her relation-

George Eliot's father, Robert Evans: 'the one deep strong love I have ever known.'

'He was the elder and a little man,' explains Eliot in the 'Brother and Sister' sonnets, written in 1869, in which she recalled her close childhood attachment to her brother Isaac.

South Farm, Arbury, where George Eliot was born on 22 November 1819.

Griff House, the farmhouse to which George Eliot and her family moved when she was four months old. Set in 280 acres, Griff represented the high noon of Robert Evans's status and influence.

Left: Cara Bray, Eliot's Coventry neighbour, gave her young friend a blend of sympathy and intellectual rigour that was lacking in the Evans household. *Right:* 'My beloved spouse' was how Eliot frequently addressed Sara Hennell, Cara's sister, during the height of their passionate friendship in the 1840s.

'Everyone who was supposed to be a "little cracked" was sent up to Rosehill,' said Charles Bray, Cara's husband. The Brays' Coventry home became an essential stopping-off place for any liberal intellectual passing through Coventry.

Charles Bray, 'The Don Juan of Coventry', had six children by his mistress and affairs with several other women, including his wife's sister and possibly George Eliot.

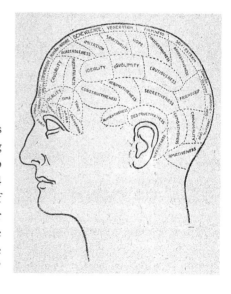

A phrenological bust. Many serious mid-Victorians believed that reading head bumps was the key to understanding personality. In 1844 Charles Bray had a cast made of George Eliot's skull and later analysed it. 'The social feelings were very active, particularly the adhesiveness.'

Top left: George Eliot wrote of this portrait of her by Cara Bray (1842): 'Her benevolence extends to the hiding of faults in my visage.' *Top right:* George Eliot by François D'Albert Durade. 'You will be amused to hear that I am sitting for my portrait – at M. D'Albert's request – not mine,' wrote Eliot to the Brays in February 1850. *Above:* An early photograph of Eliot, precise date unknown.

Left: Charles Christian Hennell, the beloved brother of Sara Hennell and Cara Bray. Eliot greatly admired his ground-breaking investigation into the origins of the New Testament and may have had hopes of marrying him.
Right: 'I am in a little heaven here, Dr Brabant being its archangel,' wrote Eliot when she went to stay with Dr Robert Brabant in 1843. The sixty-two-year-old man and the twenty-four-year-old girl read German together and went for long walks.

'He is not more than four feet high with a deformed spine...but on this little body is placed a finely formed head,' explained Eliot of François D'Albert Durade, with whom she lodged during her stay in Geneva in 1849–50.

John Chapman, editor of the *Westminster Review*, was another mid-Victorian liberal intellectual known as 'Don Juan'. As well as employing her, Chapman had a brief affair with Eliot.

Eliot fell in love with Herbert Spencer in 1852 and hoped that they would marry. When he rejected her on the grounds that she was too ugly, she mourned: 'If you become attached to someone else, then I must die.'

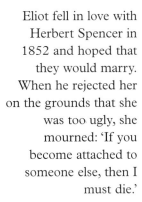

Top left: Samuel Laurence's sketch for his portrait of Eliot (misdated 1857, actually 1860). Lewes hated this portrait of Eliot at forty, believing it made her look miserable. *Top right:* Lewes was 'in raptures' with this painting by Frederic Burton (1865) which Eliot herself declared would be 'positively' the last time she would be painted. *Above:* To those correspondents who wrote asking for a picture, Eliot always pretended she had 'no photograph of myself, having always avoided having one taken'. This one of 1858, by Mayall of Regent Street, explains why.

ships. It would be she who decided how close to allow a younger, admiring woman to come. A letter Bessie wrote to her friend, Barbara Leigh Smith, on 12 February 1853 shows the kind of reverential awe which Marian's reputation for moral wisdom was already capable of inspiring in others.

> Do you know, Marian Evans has changed to me lately, has seemed to have finally made up her mind to love me ... She said the other day, having made me sit close to her, and looking full into my eyes: 'I thought when I first knew you, you had a great deal of self-esteem in the sense of putting forth your own opinions, but I have quite lost the impression. I suppose when we love people, we lose the sense of their faults.' I was inexpressibly touched. I nearly cried. The odd mixture of truth and fondness in Marian is so great. She never spares, but expresses every opinion, good and bad, with the most unflinching plainness, and yet she seems able to see faults without losing tenderness.[52]

Barbara Leigh Smith was to become an even greater friend of Marian's, and perhaps the only one whom she looked upon as her intellectual and moral equal. Her background was as sophisticated and progressive as Marian's was provincial and conventional. Like Bessie, Barbara came from a distinguished family of Unitarian reformers, men and women who had been at the forefront of virtually every progressive campaign and good cause since the beginning of the century. What made her odd was her illegitimacy. Her father, Benjamin Leigh Smith, a Radical MP, felt unable to marry her mother because she was a milliner. None the less he looked after her, and the five children they had together, with generous tenderness. Although the Leigh Smith tribe would always be tainted with illegitimacy – even their progressive Bonham Carter and Nightingale cousins steered clear – they were furnished with a privileged, enlightened childhood. Following her father's and grandfather's great interest in art, Barbara had taken lessons from William Henry Hunt. Unlike many another 'young lady painter' of her generation, she was not a dabbler, but persevered to become a fine artist. When she came of age in 1848 she was provided with £300 a year which, unlike Marian's ninety pounds, was enough to release her from having to earn a living. She spent her time and money usefully, continuing her artistic training and, together with Bessie, working energetically to open up educational and job opportunities to women.[53]

These friendships with Barbara and Bessie opened up a new kind of social life to Marian. For the past ten years she had been used to sitting down to supper with clever men, but the atmosphere had always been informal, bohemian, even chaotic. Susanna Chapman was usually in such a muddle that it was not unusual for the dinner to arrive an hour late. The conversation at the Leigh Smiths and the Parkeses was no less intellectual, but it was set on an entirely different scale. At the Parkes mansion in Savile Row and the Leigh Smiths' establishment in Blandford Square there were huge rooms, fine china and a flock of servants. The Parkes mansion was big enough to hold huge balls, to which Marian was twice invited. On these occasions she refused, knowing that this was not an environment in which she did well. The dancing, the flirtation, the quick repartee made her feel like the plain teenager who had brought the party to a stop with her hysterics all those years ago in Warwickshire. She made her scrappy wardrobe the excuse for not going. 'It would be a crucifixion of my own taste as well as other people's to appear like a withered cabbage in a flower garden.' What she liked and where she shone was in the intimacy of a dinner party where 'people think only of conversation, [and] one doesn't mind being a dowdy'.[54] She dined regularly at both the Parkeses' and the Leigh Smiths', becoming a particular favourite of Joseph Parkes. Writing years later, Bessie remembered how

> from 1851 to 1855, she used to wear black velvet, then seldom adopted by unmarried ladies. I can see her descending the great staircase of our house in Savile Row (afterwards the Stafford Club), on my father's arm, the only lady, except my mother, among the group of remarkable men, politicians, and authors of the first literary rank. She would talk and laugh softly, and look up into my father's face respectfully, while the light of the great hall-lamp shone on the waving masses of her hair, and the black velvet fell in folds about her feet.[55]

Here was Marian in her element. Released from the need to compete with other women on grounds of dress or beauty, she used her intellect and her intensity to captivate whichever man she had set her heart on.

One of those men was Herbert Spencer, to whom she had been introduced during her visit to London in the August of 1851. As sub-editor of *The Economist*, Spencer lived and worked just over the road from the *Westminster*. The previous year Chapman had published Spencer's *Social Statics*, a hugely influential book, which applied the concept of evolution and adaptation to questions of social organisation. Spencer believed that the human race was moving slowly towards political freedom, which he defined as the right of every man 'to do whatsoever he wills provided he does not infringe the equal freedom of any other man'. Despite the excluding pronoun, Spencer believed that both sexes should share in this freedom, since 'no woman of truly noble mind will submit to be dictated to'. However, he was sufficiently a man of his time to balk at giving the vote to women, no matter how noble-minded they might be.[56]

Like so many other significant people in her life – Chapman and Bessie especially – Spencer also came from the Midlands, in this case Derby. He was the only child of an intelligent, energetic Wesleyan couple. His uncle, the Reverend Thomas Spencer, was a clergyman who used the pulpit to campaign for the abolition of the Corn Laws and the ending of slavery. The Revd Spencer also believed that the English working class would never be free from their masters while they stayed muddle-headed with drink. In 1845, during a visit to Coventry, he had spoken so passionately for teetotalism that Marian had to be restrained by Cara from running up to the front of the hall and adding her name to the pledge.

Despite coaching from his Cambridge-educated uncle, Herbert Spencer did not shine at classics, taking more naturally to mathematics and science. At seventeen he joined the railways as a civil engineer, before gravitating to

London where he fiddled with mechanical inventions and tried his hand at periodical writing. Gradually his interest broadened from technical subjects to social ones, or rather he applied his 'scientific' discipline to the study of man's social organisation, out of which emerged the new discipline of sociology. By the time Marian met him, the thirty-one-year-old Spencer was recognised as one of the cleverest men in London, a genuinely original mind among the synthesisers. Over the next fifty-two years of his long life there was hardly a subject which he did not colonise, including philosophy, biology, statistics and ethics. He was, as *Social Statics* demonstrated, an enthusiastic believer in evolution well before *Origin of Species* appeared in 1859, and it was he rather than Darwin who coined the phrase 'survival of the fittest'.

Although his modern, non-university education was typical of the men with whom Marian was involved throughout her life, Spencer's emotional make-up could not have been more different from Bray's, Chapman's or Lewes's. Celibate where they were sexual, cold where they were warm, detailed where they were broad, he had a rigid, chilly personality. Perhaps it was the result of being the only surviving child of a brood of nine, but Spencer saw danger in everything. Emotional attachment spelled chaos, and whenever a love affair threatened the loss of his carefully composed self, he scuttled back into the intricate theoretical world, which was the shape and content of his working life. Rather than pursuing relationships with real women, he postulated endlessly about the conditions necessary for an ideal love. Although he worried about his bachelor status, whenever a suitable partner presented herself he came up with perfectly good reasons why it would never work. Either he did not have enough money to marry, or he was too busy, or the woman in question was unsuitable. The fact was that although Herbert Spencer loved to study humanity, his self-engrossment made any kind of real contact with another human being impossible.

But if he was incapable of emotional closeness, there was nothing Spencer liked more than intellectual contact. Miss Evans was a delightful person with whom to spend time, being not only cleverer than many of his friends, but female to boot. Spencer's preoccupation with his bachelorhood meant that he was keen to be seen around town with a woman. The possibility of having a lover, and having others witness that possibility, was enough to take the edge off his fearful recognition that he would never marry. As arts critic for *The Economist* he received free press tickets for the theatre and the opera, and he often invited Marian to accompany him to Covent Garden. As the evenings lengthened, their friendship moved from the semi-professional to something which passed for intimacy. By April they were meeting regularly for long, sunshiny chats on the terrace of Somerset House, to which Chapman had a private key.

But if Marian was busy falling in love, Spencer was already retreating into cold calculation. On 23 April he wrote to his friend Edward Lott, carefully setting out the terms of his new attachment: 'Miss Evans, whom you have heard me mention as the translatress of Strauss and as the most admirable woman, mentally, I ever met. We have been for some time past on very intimate terms. I am frequently at Chapman's, and the greatness of her intellect conjoined with her womanly qualities and manner, generally keep me at her side most of the evening.'[57]

Marian's affection for Spencer was characteristically ardent. For the first time in her life she was involved with a man who, on the face of it, was entirely suitable. Not only was he free to marry, but his background was close to hers. Like her, he was an original thinker in areas where Bray, Chapman and Brabant were second-rate. She was perceptive enough to know that his intellectual rigidity – trimming empirical evidence to fit prearranged theories – would clash with her growing respect for the integrity of the specific and individual. But her need for a soulmate, never deeply buried, had resurfaced with a vengeance, leading her to sexualise this most unsexual of men. Old emotional patterns were reanimated as she rushed into love with a man who could not return her affection.

By the time Spencer wrote to Lott praising Marian's virtues, he had already told her that there could be no question of romance between them. In a letter to another friend, written after her death, he reported what happened next.

> After a time I began to have qualms as to what might result from this constant companionship. Great as was my admiration for her, considered both morally and intellectually, and decided as was my feeling of friend-ship, I could not perceive in myself any indications of a warmer feeling, and it occurred to me that mischief would possibly follow if our relations continued. Those qualms led me to take a strange step – an absurd step in one sense. I wrote to her indicating, as delicately as I could, my fears. Then afterwards, perceiving how insulting to her was the suggestion that while I felt in no danger of falling in love with her, she was in danger of falling in love with me, I wrote a second letter, apologising for my unin-tended insult. She took it all smilingly, quite understanding my motive and forgiving my rudeness. The consequence was that our intimacy continued as before. And then, by and by, just that which I had feared might take place, did take place. Her feelings became involved and mine did not. The lack of physical attraction was fatal. Strongly as my judge-ment prompted, my instincts would not respond.[58]

When Marian received her first rejection from Spencer in April she did indeed take it 'smilingly' – at least on the surface. Her reply to him, on the 21st, makes a self-deprecating joke about how it had never crossed her mind that his intentions might be other than platonic. 'I felt disappointed rather than "hurt"', she wrote with forced lightness, 'that you should not have sufficiently divined my character to perceive how remote it is from my habitual state of mind to imagine that any one is falling in love with me.'[59] Nothing could be further from the truth. On 30 March, just before Spencer declared himself, Marian had revealed in a heavy-handed joke to Cara just where her hopes were heading: 'I had two offers last night – not of marriage, but of music – which I find it impossible to resist.'[60]

Once Spencer's intentions became clear, Marian back-pedalled with the

Brays to hide her humiliation. On 27 April she wrote a dishonest letter to Coventry in which she made out that Spencer's desire to keep the friendship platonic was a joint one: 'We have agreed that we are not in love with each other, and that there is no reason why we should not have as much of each other's society as we like.'[61] By agreeing to be friends with the man whom she wanted as her lover, Marian was ensuring that their daily intimacy continued. In time, once the pressure of the situation had eased, she hoped that the jumpy Spencer might move slowly towards her. And indeed, over the late spring, they did continue to meet regularly. More trips to Covent Garden and roof-top chats were followed, in June, by a trip to Kew to examine the flowers for signs of evolutionary adaptation.[62]

The Brays knew well by now that the more studiedly casual Marian's tone when talking about a man, the more deeply she was involved with him. As keen as ever to foster a romance which might lead to an offer of marriage, they suggested inviting Spencer up to Rosehill when she was there, hoping that the bear rug under the acacia tree might do the trick. Marian's response to the suggestion was a tangle of denied desire and defensive posturing.

> I told Herbert Spencer of your invitation, Mr Bray, not mentioning that you asked him *with me*. He said he should like to accept it – but I think it would be better for him to go down when I am with you. We certainly could not go together, for all the world is setting us down as engaged – a most disagreeable thing if one chose to make oneself uncomfortable. 'Tell it not in Gath' however – that is to say, please to avoid mentioning our names together, and pray burn this note, that it may not lie on the chimney piece for general inspection.[63]

While she clearly loved the fact that literary London had her down as almost married, Marian was careful to feign irritation. The last thing she wanted now was for Spencer to think that she was anything but loftily disinterested in his friendship. Yet as the summer progressed it became clear that no amount of behind-the-scenes manoeuvring and tight-lipped discretion was ever going to bring Herbert Spencer to the altar. By the time he did spend a while with Marian at Rosehill in late October, the possibility of romance had long since passed.

If only Marian had realised that Spencer was never going to marry anyone – he died a bachelor at eighty-three – she would have been spared a summer of humiliation and despair. In order to avoid the painful recognition that he could not be close to anyone, Spencer rationalised his rejection of Marian on the cruel grounds that she was too ugly to marry. Cruel because not only did he give this reason to her, but also circulated it publicly. In his autobiography, published posthumously in 1904, he hinted heavily: 'Physical beauty is a *sine qua non* with me; as was once unhappily proved where the intellectual traits and the emotional traits were of the highest.'[64] But this was clearly rubbish, since he was on record as having rejected two other women who were perfectly pretty but who, naturally, failed in some other respect. In 1854, around the time that Marian eloped with Lewes, Spencer wrote two articles on 'Personal

Beauty' for the *Leader* in which he cited examples of ugliness that are suspiciously reminiscent of Marian's physiognomy – heavy jaw, large mouth, big nose.[65] Her failure to display conventional female characteristics did not, as one might imagine, delight and liberate him, an effeminate man himself. Rather, it threatened his own precarious sense of masculinity. The timing of these nasty articles is particularly telling, appearing just as Marian was beginning a loving and fulfilling relationship with George Henry Lewes. Hating himself for not being able to respond to her love, Spencer kicked out and punished Marian instead.

The question of George Eliot's ugliness has always embarrassed her biographers who at times seem almost unable to bear the truth. In this they are no different from many of Marian's friends at the time whose solution was to rewrite or redraw the heavy, horsy features. Bessie Rayner Parkes, writing in 1894, typically maintained that 'In daily life the brow, the blue eyes, and the upper part of the face had a great charm. The lower half was disproportionately long. Abundant brown hair framed a countenance which was certainly not in any sense unpleasing, noble in its general outline, and very sweet and kind in expression. Her height was good, her figure remarkably supple; at moments it had an almost serpentine grace.'[66]

D'Albert Durade, meanwhile, did the equivalent in paint, his portrait of Marian in 1850 showing her with neat, inoffensive features, which bore no relation to the photograph taken only a few years later. While there can be no doubt that charisma goes a long way to offsetting a big nose, there is a danger that downplaying Marian's plainness obscures the quality of her relationships with men and other women. To be pretty was not simply a delightful bonus for the middle-class Victorian woman, but an integral part of her social and sexual status. A bewitching face could go a long way towards making a bachelor overlook a lack of fortune or even education in his prospective bride. Of course, in the circles in which Marian moved one might expect that wit, erudition and wisdom would offset the need for regular features. But Charles Hennell, John Chapman and Herbert Spencer were sufficiently men of their time to want their women to be both beautiful and accomplished. By the time she was thirty-five Marian had been obliged to watch on several occasions while pretty women like Rufa Brabant and Elisabeth Tilley claimed the men she wanted for herself.

Spencer's rejection of Marian on the grounds of ugliness, following so soon after Chapman's little speech on beauty at Kenilworth Castle, plunged her into a pit of self-loathing. Even at the beginning of the friendship she had been telling the Brays, 'See what a fine thing it is to pick up people who are short-sighted enough to like one.'[67] By the end of April the self-accusations had become vicious: she describes herself as 'a hideous hag, sad and wizened', 'an old witch' and even a jellyfish.[68] At thirty-three she feared that she was a Frederika Bremer in the making, destined to become an ugly old bluestocking seeking intimacy in a commercial boarding-house.

Once Marian had wrapped up the July 1852 issue of the *Westminster*, she fled the sultry heat of London's summer – one of the hottest for years – and headed for the seaside town of Broadstairs, where she took a cottage for two months. Her life as an independent yet respectable woman required an intricate negotiation of the social proprieties of a small provincial town. It was highly unusual for a woman to take a holiday on her own and the Chapmans felt it important that they should both escort her down to Broadstairs and see her settled. Perhaps in this way they hoped to make it clear to the landlady of Chandos Cottage that while Miss Evans might be eccentric, she was not immoral. This was the first of many occasions in which worrying about what landladies thought became a major preoccupation.

The first letter Marian wrote to Spencer from Broadstairs, on 8 July, is tentative with desire and doubt. She wants him to come and visit her, but is ruefully aware that her need does not match his.

> Dear Friend
>
> No credit to me for my virtues as a refrigerant. I owe them all to a few lumps of ice which I carried away with me from that tremendous glacier of yours. I am glad that Nemesis, lame as she is, has already made you feel a little uneasy in my absence, whether from the state of the thermometer or aught else. We will not inquire too curiously whether you long most for my society or for the sea-breezes. If you decided that I was not worth coming to see, it would only be of a piece with that generally exasperating perspicacity of yours which will not allow one to humbug you.[69]

So she was thrilled when Spencer booked into a local hotel on 10 July, boasting coyly in a letter to Charles Bray, 'I am obliged to write very hurriedly, as I am not alone.'[70] In between sea-shore walks and shared meals she pressed for a resolution to their ambiguous situation. Miserably cornered, Spencer had no choice but to make it clear for a second and definitive time that he was not in love. In that painful moment Marian was forced to give up the fantasy that his aloofness was a nervous prelude to deeper commitment. In the anguished hours which followed his departure she panicked at the possibility that her boldness had lost Spencer not only as a husband, but also as a friend. The thought of resuming the drudgery of life at The Strand unleavened by his companionship was bleak beyond belief. In despair she sat down and wrote, pleading to be allowed to claw back some of what she believed she had lost.

> I know this letter will make you very angry with me, but wait a little, and don't say anything to me while you are angry. I promise not to sin any more in the same way.
>
> My ill health is caused by the hopeless wretchedness which weighs upon me. I do not say this to pain you, but because it is the simple truth which you must know in order to understand why I am obliged to seek relief.
>
> I want to know if you can assure me that you will not forsake me, and that you will always be with me as much as you can and share your thoughts and feelings with me. If you become attached to some one else,

then I must die, but until then I could gather courage to work and make life valuable, if only I had you near me. I do not ask you to sacrifice anything – I would be very good and cheerful and never annoy you. But I find it impossible to contemplate life under any other conditions . . . Those who have known me best have always said, that if ever I loved any one thoroughly my whole life must turn upon that feeling, and I find they said truly. You curse the destiny which has made the feeling concentrate itself on you – but if you will only have patience with me you shall not curse it long. You will find that I can be satisfied with very little, if I am delivered from the dread of losing it.

I suppose no woman ever before wrote such a letter as this – but I am not ashamed of it, for I am conscious that in the light of reason and true refinement I am worthy of your respect and tenderness, whatever gross men or vulgar-minded women might think of me.[71]

This was the last and most desperate time in her life that Marian would beg for affection. The longing of the past ten years, of loving men who loved other women, climaxed in the agony of these few paragraphs. She was prepared to settle, as she had settled before, for a love which was partial, conditional, shared. What she had not fully realised, nor would for many years, was that Spencer needed her as much as she needed him. Far from wanting to break off contact, nothing suited him more than continuing to enjoy the companionship of the cleverest woman in London without the burden of commitment. He responded to her desperate letter with a cautious offer of friendship, to which she immediately and gratefully agreed, writing this time more formally to 'Mr Spencer':

It would be ungenerous in me to allow you to suffer even a slight uneasiness on my account which I am able to remove . . . The fact is, all sorrows sink into insignificance before the one great sorrow – my own miserable imperfections, and any outward hap is welcome if it will only serve to rouse my energies and make me less unworthy of my better self . . .

If, as you intimated in your last letter, you feel that my friendship is of value to you for its own sake – mind on no other ground – it is yours. Let us, if you will, forget the past, except in so far as it may have brought us to trust in and feel for each other, and let us help to make life beautiful to each other as far as fate and the world will permit us. Whenever you like to come to me again, to see the golden corn before it is reaped, I can promise you such companionship as there is in me, untroubled by painful emotions.[72]

It is not clear whether Spencer did come down again to Broadstairs towards the end of August. Certainly he and Marian spent some time together at Rosehill in October. But from this low point of summer 1852 their lives took different paths. For while at this point it was Marian who was racked with psychosomatic headaches and the agonies of opportunities lost, it was Spencer whose life was to be taken over and destroyed by them. In January 1853 the

Revd Spencer died, leaving his nephew a legacy of £500. Spencer immediately gave up *The Economist* and set out on his first trip to Europe. What should have been an exquisite experience turned into a flat, debilitating one. The landscape of the Rhine and the Alps failed to impress, and at Frankfurt he was laid low with toothache. When he returned to London in the autumn his general malaise combined with odd panicky pains was diagnosed as a weak heart. Whether this weakness was a literal or metaphorical one is not clear. Spencer's symptoms seem to have been more nervous than physical. He wandered around town unable to sleep, getting progressively seedier. A few months recuperating at home in Derby set him up for a trip to Wales, where he intended to finish the book he was writing called *Psychology*. Symbolically, he had just completed the chapter on Feelings and was on to Reason when he suffered an emotional and physical collapse, which took the form of a 'sensation in the head – not pain nor heat nor fulness nor tension, but simply a sensation, bearable enough but abnormal'.[73] He never fully recovered, becoming a semi-invalid and a permanent hypochondriac. For the rest of his life he fussed over his pulse rate, plugged his ears when the outside world got too exciting, and dealt with insomnia by wrapping his head in a towel soaked in salt water and topped it with a ludicrous rubber cap.

It is no coincidence that around the time of this nervous collapse, Marian was becoming intimate with George Henry Lewes who was, ironically, Spencer's best friend. As he watched Marian strike out into a sexually and emotionally fulfilling relationship, Spencer was obliged to confront the fact that there would be no similar happy ending for him. He became even more obsessed with his failure to marry, constantly initiating conversations on the subject with friends and then rejecting the proposed solutions. When one female acquaintance suggested acutely that getting married might relieve some of his neurotic symptoms, he argued: 'I labour under the double difficulty that my choice is very limited and that I am not easy to please. Moral and intellectual beauties do not by themselves suffice to attract me; and owing to the stupidity of our educational system it is rare to find them united to a good physique. Moreover there is the pecuniary difficulty.'[74]

It is hard to believe that there were no beautiful, clever and good women available to marry (although perhaps there were none who wanted to marry him). Likewise, the old excuse about money no longer applied, thanks to his uncle's legacy. Later on, as he moved into middle age, Spencer used the excuse of his work as the reason why he could not sustain a relationship. 'Habitually before I have yet finished rejoicing over my emancipation from a work which has long played the tyrant over me, I make myself the slave of another. The truth is, I suppose, that in the absence of wife and children to care for, the carrying out of my undertakings is the one thing that makes life worth living – even though, by it, life is continually perturbed.'[75]

As Spencer became increasingly wedded to his work, the narcissistic tendencies which had been apparent in his affair with Marian hardened into an impenetrable armour. The rigidity which had insisted during their trip to Kew that if the flowers didn't fit in with his theories of evolution then there must be something wrong with the flowers now extended to every part of Spencer's life and work. He was obsessed with establishing the priority of his ideas in an area where many were moving towards the same conclusions, or, as Gordon Haight, Eliot's first modern biographer, puts it succinctly, 'he believed in the evolution of everything except his own theories'. He started his autobiography years before he died, sending out drafts to friends, and rewriting furiously to take account of their comments. He wanted to create a perfect version of himself, in which he stood at the centre of every important intellectual movement of the mid and late nineteenth century. For instance, he claimed to have been the first person to suggest to Marian that she should write fiction – 'I thought I saw in her many, if not all, of the needful qualifications in high degrees' – despite the fact that she had been playing with the idea years earlier and that it was Lewes who was to push her into action.[76] Naturally, he liked to stress the fact that it was he who had first brought her together with Lewes, overlooking the fact that it was Chapman who had made the introduction.

In the circumstances it is ironic that for all Spencer's attention to what posterity might think of him, it was Marian's reputation rather than his which lasted. Spencer's desperation to prove the originality of his ideas is strangely prescient. Many of them were overshadowed by those of Darwin and later by Freud so that, in the late twentieth century, it is hard to isolate anything that belongs absolutely to him save for that famous phrase 'the survival of the fittest'. Marian, however, turned a similar interest in the relationship between the mind and the body, and the organisation of society, into work whose originality and creativity still resonate today.

But it was not only his professional image which Spencer fretted over. If anything, he was even more concerned about how people viewed his private life and, in particular, his failure to marry. During the retrospective gossip which followed Marian's death in 1880, he was horrified to discover that there was a long-standing rumour to the effect that he had fallen in love with her during 1852 and that she had thrown him over in favour of Lewes. For a man who could not bear to be seen to need other people it would be hard to think of a more humiliating story. He thought about issuing a formal denial, but was dissuaded by sensible friends. Next he asked John Cross to put the matter right when Cross came to write his late wife's biography. Three years later, with the *Life* nearing completion, Spencer again wrote to Cross and expressed his worry over the we-are-not-in-love letter of 27 April. He suggested Cross add a gloss along the lines of 'The intimacy naturally led to rumours. It was said that Mr Spencer was in love with her. This however was not true. I have the best possible warrant for saying that his feeling did not pass the limits of friendship.' Cross was not keen, believing that it simply stirred up matters. Spencer tried again with another wording, which again Cross rejected, suggesting a formula of his own. Spencer snapped back: 'Much better no note at all than the one you propose.' Cross took him at his literal word, but out of deference to his feelings deleted the 'we are not in love' sentence, leaving it at, 'We have agreed that there is no reason why we should not have as much of each other's society as we like.' Even this would not do for Spencer, who wrote huffily to Cross on publication: 'As the account now stands it is not only consistent with the report that I was jilted for Lewes, but tends to confirm it. Such a fact as that I was anxious to visit the Brays when she was there, and such a fact as that my name quietly drops out as a companion while Lewes' comes in, gives colour to the statement, and there is nothing I can see to negative it. I cannot say that I have been fairly used.'[77]

In Spencer's support, it should be pointed out that he could, if he had wished, have made public the two desperate Broadstairs letters, which proved conclusively that he was the jilter and not the jilted. Instead, he sealed them up, together with a few others, and instructed that they should not be opened until 1985. For a man so vain about his public image it was a generous gesture. In effect he was allowing George Eliot's reputation as a wise, self-contained sibyl to continue at the cost of his own cherished sense of inviolability. It was the closest Herbert Spencer ever came to love.

CHAPTER 7

'A Man of Heart and Conscience'

Meeting Mr Lewes
1852–4

THE STRAND HAD never seemed so dismal as it did on Marian's return from Broadstairs in late August 1852. The magnificent weather of a seaside summer had given way to the thick wetness of a London autumn. Yet one more stab at love had gone wrong and there was nothing to look forward to except work, which was no longer new or exciting. The pile of review books had got higher in her absence, the contributors were as childishly demanding as ever and John Chapman's finances seemed to get more perilous, if such a thing were possible. It was Marian's dreary job to keep the whole precarious structure steady. It was not the editorial routine, which was necessarily frustrating, so much as the tangled business and social relationships which ran in tandem. There were famous contributors to keep sweet and would-be ones to be held at bay. Rich men had to be courted for their cash, then dissuaded from contributing long and boring articles on their hobby-horses. At times it felt as if, far from being the leading intellectual publication of the day, the *Westminster Review* was a kind of vanity publishing venture with Marian adjudicating between competing egos. The sky got darker, the fog thicker, the schedule more impossible. In a letter to Sara Marian described a state of mind reminiscent of those dreadful weeks at St Leonards with her dying father. 'I have felt something like the madness which imagines that the four walls are contracting and going to crush one.'[1]

Just in time she decided on another break. It was a measure of Marian's autonomy that, by this point, it was she and not John Chapman who decided when and for how long she could be spared from The Strand. With the October issue safely out, she headed north to stay with two old friends. The trip was significant because it was the last she would take as an anonymous woman. At this point her cleverness and independence made her unusual, but she was not yet notorious. In the next couple of years her life would undergo a convulsion that would leave the two people whom she was visiting – George Combe and Harriet Martineau – feeling deeply betrayed and determined not only never to see her again, but to make sure that no one else did either.

Both Combe and Martineau displayed that curious mixture of liberalism and narrowness, permissiveness and prudery which was a feature of the mid-Victorian avant-garde. Each had developed ways of understanding the material world – phrenology in the case of George Combe, Positivism and mesmerism (a variation of hypnosis) in the case of Martineau – which most people thought crackpot. Like John Chapman, both Combe and Martineau believed that to protect the integrity of their beliefs they had to be seen to lead conventionally moral lives. But unlike Chapman they more or less managed it, which is why when Marian Evans, princess of the progressive avant-garde, went off with a married man in 1854, they took it personally. Not only had she acted on the desires which they themselves found troublesome – Combe had married at forty-five a woman whose fortune bankrolled his business, while Martineau was currently making a fool of herself with a man twenty years younger – but she had given every Tory, every churchman, every pious lady tract writer, a good reason to damn the whole basket of liberal causes, from electoral reform to vegetarianism, as seditious and evil nonsense.

At this stage, though, George Combe was still delighted with Miss Evans. Examining her scalp during a visit to Rosehill in August 1851 he had come to the conclusion that she was, with the possible exception of the US abolitionist Lucretia Mott, 'the ablest woman whom I have seen', and paid special homage to her 'very large brain' and her big organ of Concentrativeness.[2] During his subsequent stays at The Strand he was shrewd enough to notice that it was Marian who was responsible for the upturn in the *Westminster*'s reputation, and he used the language of phrenology to hint to Chapman that he should take her advice wherever possible: 'She has certain organs large in her brain which are not so fully developed in yours, and she will judge more correctly of the influence upon other persons of what you write and do, than you will do yourself.'[3]

Marian arrived in Edinburgh on 5 October 1852. Although she had spent the previous month feeling that her life was going nowhere, it was a kind of comfort to remember that the last time she had been in the city, seven years before, things had been even more dismal. It was on that occasion that she had been summoned home 'with a heavy heart' by her father's broken leg. Life might seem limited now, but it was far removed from the hopelessness of that dreary time. What is more, the Combes' household in elegant Melville Street turned out to be just the place to rest, recuperate, and 'nourish sleek optimism'.[4] There were good fires and attractive views, even if her host did have a tendency to talk endlessly about himself, leaving Marian nothing to do but nod and grunt in agreement. If she seemed bored, Combe certainly didn't notice. He was more delighted than ever with Miss Evans, noting approvingly in his diary that she was 'thoroughly feminine, refined, and lady-like'.[5]

Meanwhile, Harriet Martineau, ensconced in the Lake District, was getting deafer, shouting more than ever and increasingly entranced with her own thoughts, schemes and habits. Long since absent from London and surrounded by adoring acolytes, she was isolated from the rough and tumble of intellectual debate, which would have kept her flexible, sharp and open to other ways of thinking. Those who dared to disagree with her – especially her brother James – increasingly found themselves dragged into feuds, which snaked poisonously down the years.

On 20 October Marian left Edinburgh for Martineau's lakeside cottage at Ambleside. As usual, she had long since revised her initially harsh assessment of the veteran writer and now found the older woman 'quite handsome from her animation and intelligence. She came behind me, put her hands round me, and kissed me in the prettiest way this evening.'[6] With Martineau's constant and much younger companion Henry Atkinson in tow, the two women walked and drove around the spectacular Windermere landscape, stopping to inspect the model cottages which were Martineau's latest passion.

Fresh air, good scenery and the charm of being made a fuss of did Marian a deal of good. The holiday was rounded off with ten days at Rosehill, from where she announced in a letter to Bessie Rayner Parkes that she now felt 'brave for anything that is to come after'.[7] And what came after was indeed grim. Barely had Marian taken up the reins again at The Strand than the news came that Chrissey's husband, Edward Clarke, was dead. Never robust, he had been ground down by having to support too many children and a medical practice that failed to flourish. Succumbing finally to the TB which had already killed his brother, the gentlemanly Clarke left Chrissey with six children under fifteen and an income, once everything was sold up, of £100 a year – about the same as Marian scraped by on in London.

Passive as ever, and now made helpless by grief, Chrissey invited her younger brother and sister to arrange her future as they thought best. Isaac grudgingly suggested Chrissey move back to live rent free in the house at Attleborough that had once belonged to her, before Clarke had sold it to Robert Evans to raise cash. Increasingly recognisable as Tom Tulliver in *The Mill on the Floss*, whose hard brand of charity had been learned from his Dodson aunts, Isaac was not prepared to do more for Chrissey than he absolutely had to. She would not be allowed to starve, but nor would she be rescued from the consequences of her disastrous marriage choice.

Marian, meanwhile, had dropped the January proofs to be at Meriden over Christmas. But there were limits, too, to what she was able to give. After only a few days cooped up with the six young Clarkes she came to the unsurprising conclusion that she would be more help back in London, 'the dear creatures here will be a constant motive for work and economy'.[8] But she had not counted on Isaac's reaction to her failure to consult him first. The scars from the holy war had never fully healed. Isaac still deeply resented his younger sister for acting in ways which affected the internal economy of the family. Now here she was again, putting her own eccentric needs over those of the Evans clan. Maiden aunts with small legacies were expected to come home to support their widowed sisters, not to continue their self-indulgent ways in London. Furious that his wilful sister had once again evaded his control, the increasingly patriarchal Isaac shouted at her never to ask him for a favour in the future, 'which, seeing that I never have done so,' pointed out Marian wryly in a letter to the Brays, 'was almost as superfluous as if I had said I would never receive a kindness from him.'[9]

At the beginning of February Marian was back in Warwickshire trying to decide what to do next. Crammed into the tiny Attleborough house the children had become noisy and out-of-hand. No amount of 'romping and doll dressing' with 'Aunt Pollie' was going to solve the problem of their long-term future.[10] Concerned friends had suggested putting some of them in the orphanage, a reminder of the grim fate that even the most respectable of families could face in the economically volatile early 1850s. Another suggestion came from an old patient of Clarke's who offered to fund the eldest boy's passage to Australia. Although these were the kind of practical, unsentimental solutions which appealed to Isaac, Chrissey would not hear of splitting up the family. Still, the idea of emigrating had caught Marian's imagination. 'What do you think of my going to Australia with Chrissey and all her family? – to settle them and then come back?' she asked the Brays in a letter of 11 April 1853.[11] The Brays' response is unrecorded, but the bizarre notion of George Eliot in the Antipodes came to nothing.

Although Marian was prepared to brave a three-month sea journey for the sake of her sister, she was not, however, going to give up the independent life which had been so painfully won over the last four years. The idea of going home to 'that hideous neighbourhood amongst ignorant bigots is impossible to me'. She would rather commit suicide and 'leave my money, perhaps more acceptable than my labour and affection'. Nor was she prepared to take responsibility for moving Chrissey out of the house while staying on herself in London. The curiously oblique explanation she offered in her letter to Cara was: 'My health might fail and other things might happen to make her, as well as me, regret the change.'[12] Was this a hint at her growing hope that she might one day live with Lewes? In the circumstances the only feasible solution was for Chrissey to carry on living in Attleborough under Isaac's grudging protection, while Marian sent her what extra money she could manage from London.

Unfortunately, this was not likely to amount to much. The financial affairs of the *Westminster Review* were now in such a dire state that it was difficult to pay the contributors. Over the last few years Chapman had managed to hobble on, but by the spring of 1854 his usual tactic of borrowing money to pay off existing loans was catching up with him. His total debt was now a massive £9000. 'The way he [Chapman] is behaving is, between ourselves, generally the prelude to bankruptcy,' Joseph Parkes confided to his daughter Bessie.[13] But this time there was a new, and saving, twist to the crisis. One of Chapman's largest creditors, James Martineau, now saw his chance to carry out what he had been itching to do for ages: take over the godless *Westminster* and turn it into a platform for his particular brand of Unitarianism. But he had reckoned without the slow, cold spite of his sister Harriet. Following a savage review he had given her dreadful *Letters on the Laws of Man's Nature and Development* of 1851, Harriet Martineau was looking for revenge. Saving the *Westminster* from bankruptcy would allow her the delightful possibility of stopping her brother from getting what he wanted. In June 1854 she lent Chapman £500 which, along with other loans, was enough to pull him out of his current hole.[14] Yet again he had wriggled away from disaster.

But Marian had other reasons for wanting to move away from The Strand. Now that it was clear that Chapman would never be able to pay her a salary, she needed to work towards becoming a free-lance writer, independent of the *Westminster*. The first step was to find accommodation elsewhere. Although the arrangement would bring practical difficulties – for as long as she was involved in editing the *Westminster* there would be much to-ing and fro-ing – it was a way of flagging the fact that she had intentions, hopes and interests which lay beyond John Chapman's tottering empire. In January 1853 she wrote to Charles Bray declaring, 'At last I have determined to leave this house and get another home for myself.'[15] Chapman, however, seems to have bribed her to stay, for by March she was telling Bray, 'Instead of changing my street, I have changed my room only, and am now installed in Mr. Chapman's. It is very light and pleasant, and I suppose I must be content for a few months longer.'[16] But over the next few months her growing intimacy with Lewes shook her out of her apathy and compelled her to change her situation. Although the Chapmans would probably have been delighted to welcome Lewes as a nightly visitor to Miss Evans's room, Marian did not want to conduct her new relationship under their over-interested gaze. Chapman was a notorious blabber-mouth who was bound to spread news of this intriguing situation. By the middle of October Marian was installed in rooms at 21 Cambridge Street, Hyde Park, made homey by some pictures lent by Barbara Leigh Smith. Five months earlier Lewes had left his family home and was living in a borrowed flat off Piccadilly. The two addresses were a convenient fifteen minutes apart and far enough away from The Strand to minimise the chances of bumping into any loose-tongued *Westminster* contributors.

Not long after the move Marian told Chapman that she also wanted to quit her editorial duties at the *Review*, whereupon he flew into a characteristic panic and begged her 'to continue the present state of things until April.'[17] Even after all this time, he was still incapable of managing the magazine's most basic routine on his own. When Edward Clarke died just before Christmas 1852 Marian had left for Meriden without finishing the proofs of the January issue. As a result the magazine appeared full of careless mistakes. Marian had also had enough of trying to mediate between self-important contributors and the exasperatingly vague Chapman. At the end of 1853 she found herself caught in the middle of a particularly nasty scrap. George Combe had written an article on prison reform, maintaining that prison discipline should be based on phrenological principles. The piece was waffly, vague and not nearly good enough for the *Westminster*. Yet Combe was one of its main financial supporters and not to be offended. Chapman dithered, Combe got high-horsish and Marian, now semi-detached from the *Review*, begged Combe not to make her 'a referee in any matters relating to Mr. Chapman, as I have nothing whatever to do with his affairs'.[18] Still, she could not escape having to edit Combe's article twice over, first as an independent pamphlet, then as a much reduced, though no less boring, article for the April issue.

Giving up editorial work at the *Westminster* did not mean that Marian was finally free of Chapman's chaotic embrace. As she moved into the next phase of her working life she became even more dependent on the work he was able to put her way. In June 1853, Marian had made an arrangement with Chapman to produce two books for his new Quarterly Series. The original advertisement for the series – which promised works 'by learned and profound thinkers, embracing the subjects of theology, philosophy, Biblical criticism, and the history of opinion' – mentioned two forthcoming titles by 'the translator of Strauss's *Life of Jesus*'. These were a translation of Feuerbach's *The Essence of Christianity*, as well as an original work, 'The Idea of a Future Life'.[19] So Marian was appalled when she learned that Chapman, scuppered by the lack of subscriptions to the series, had more or less decided not to publish either book. It was not the money which bothered her – profits were likely to be minimal – but the familiar embarrassment of the whole thing. On 2 December 1853 she wrote a stern letter to Chapman in which one senses the influence of that seasoned and tough negotiator, George Henry Lewes. Marian tells Chapman fiercely: 'I bitterly regret that I allowed myself to be associated with your Series, but since I have done so, I am very anxious to fulfil my engagements both to you and the public.' She explains that she is not bothered about the money, but 'I don't think you are sufficiently alive to the ignominy of advertising things, especially as part of a subscription series, which never appear'. She ends by pressing him for a definitive answer on Feuerbach and reminds him that their combined honours are at stake.[20] In the event, Chapman was shamed into going ahead with Feuerbach, although 'The Idea of a Future Life' never appeared. By June 1854, and with bankruptcy looming, the Chapman family, minus Elisabeth Tilley, had moved to Blandford Square and the publishing business to King William Street. The strange community at 142 The Strand was broken up for good.

When Chapman first introduced Marian to George Henry Lewes on 6 October 1851 at Jeff's bookshop in Piccadilly, the omens were not good.[21] Marian, as always when meeting new people, was defensive and critical. Only a few months earlier Chapman had delivered the appalling news that she was too ugly to love, so instinctively she was ready to kick out at other people's homeliness. Lewes was one of the few people in London who was demonstrably plainer than herself. He was famously ugly, with wispy light-brown hair, a straggly moustache, pitted skin, a red, wet mouth and a head that looked too large for his small body. 'A sort of miniature Mirabeau' was how Marian described him soon afterwards, alluding to the notoriously plain French statesman.[22] Most people were much ruder. Monkeys and dogs were what usually came to mind.

Lewes and Marian already knew each other by reputation. Only a few weeks earlier Lewes had mentioned to Chapman that he liked Miss Evans's piece on Greg's *The Creed of Christendom*, which had just appeared in the *Leader*, the weekly magazine he co-edited. The compliment, however, was not returned. Marian was in the process of thinking carefully about which writers she wanted to use in the re-launched *Westminster* and Lewes was not one of them. His journalistic versatility, fuelled by the need to provide for a tribe of children, meant that his articles appeared everywhere: he once boasted that there wasn't a periodical in London he didn't have access to except the *Quarterly*. He had a journeyman's ability to get quickly to the heart of any subject from philosophy to theatre, opera to zoology, and turn in the required number of words tailored exactly to his audience. In addition he translated plays for the stage, sometimes acted in them himself and had written a couple of novels. In an age which increasingly valued the work of the specialist, Lewes's facility across a range of media seemed not only old-fashioned but superficial. Marian wanted the best people writing in the *Westminster*, and she did not consider Lewes to be up there with Mill, Froude and Carlyle. Backed by Chapman, who sneeringly referred to Lewes as 'a bread scholar', she used his work grudgingly and only when she absolutely had to: 'Defective as his articles are, they are the best we can get *of the kind*.'[23]

But Lewes's dubious reputation was built on more than his slapdash working methods. Over the past few years his name had become synonymous with a long-running sex scandal which intrigued literary London. Since 1849, and possibly well before, his wife Agnes had been conducting an affair with his friend and co-editor at the *Leader*, Thornton Hunt. At least four of the nine children Agnes was to bear were actually little Hunts and had their natural father's distinctively dark skin to prove it.

Lewes, in the meantime, was rumoured to have taken comfort with many different women. The details are vague, pieced together from retrospective gossip, but one persistent story had him getting a young girl pregnant, then asking Mrs Gaskell to find a foster-mother for the child. Another garbled source, a heavy-handed *roman-à-clef* published as late as 1945, had him seducing a maidservant on his honeymoon and fathering a bastard.[24] None of these revelations was any more shocking than those that circulated about other free-thinking couples, but the point was that Lewes made no attempt to hide who he was or what he was doing. Unlike Charles Bray and John Chapman, he did not bother to negotiate with conventional sensibilities by constructing a respectable façade. Thanks to a childhood spent partly abroad, he felt and acted like a man of the world. His dress was dandyish, his conversation knowing, his manner familiar. A letter written to a close male friend in 1853 gives the flavour of the man. He talks, nudgingly, of his friend's 'private adventures', implies that his own news is too sexy to put in a letter and drops into French to describe the progress of his affair with Marian:

Of all your public doings in Labassecour I have heard. Your private adventures I hope to hear over snug cigarettes in Cork St. Profitez en, mon ami! . . .

Of news I dont know that there is any – at least not *writable* . . . May one ask when is Ward coming back? & Brussels answers When?

For myself I have been furiously occupied dissecting Fishes and carrying a torch into unexplored regions of Biology tant bien que mal. I must now set to work & write a play to get some money. L'amour va son train.[25]

Marian was too much the provincial puritan to have been impressed or titillated by Lewes when she met him at Jeff's. In any case, her heart and mind were about to be taken over by the painful Spencer business. Lewes, by contrast, was sufficiently detached to notice Miss Evans. Over the next few weeks he made certain that he bumped into her again. It was hardly difficult. He was a close friend of Herbert Spencer's; the *Leader*'s office was just over the road from The Strand; and, of course, he was interested in working for Chapman's re-launched *Westminster*. In his retrospective tweaking of events Spencer maintained to Cross in 1884 that it was not until nearly a year later that Lewes started to visit Miss Evans of his own accord, without needing Spencer's presence as an excuse. But in fact as little as six weeks after the introduction in Jeff's Lewes seems to have been calling unchaperoned at the *Westminster*.

As it became increasingly clear throughout the summer of 1852 that Herbert Spencer would never be able to offer her a fulfilling relationship, Marian allowed his friend Lewes to come further and further into her awareness. It might seem strange that at the very time she was writing anguished letters to Spencer begging for his love she was contemplating a relationship with his friend. But more than any other novelist then or now, Marian Evans was able to understand the ambivalence that allows one to love two people at once: it is the dilemma that Dorothea, Gwendolen and Maggie all face. By the middle of September Marian was mentioning Lewes in her letters in a way that suggests he was becoming an integral part of her life, rather than an occasional feature. On 22 November, her thirty-third birthday, she casually tells Charles Bray how she had settled down to work in the late afternoon, 'thinking that I had two clear hours before dinner [when] – rap at the door – Mr. Lewes – who of course sits talking till the second bell rings'.[26]

Spencer was hurt by this shift in Marian's attention from himself to his friend, which is why he later became obsessed with proving to the world that she had not thrown him over for Lewes. Seeing Lewes build the kind of relationship with her which he had been unable to manage himself, he took refuge not only in psychosomatic illness but also in a nasty carping, which continued down the years. Both Marian and Lewes eventually developed the insight to understand and neutralise the effect of his behaviour on them. Marian dealt with his hypochondria by making a joke of it, while Lewes came to recognise that Spencer 'always tells us the disagreeable things he hears or reads of us and never the agreeable things', although he put it down to professional rather than personal jealousy.[27] To be fair, this remark was made during a tense time, when Marian held Spencer responsible for leaking the truth about her authorship of *Adam Bede*. It is a testimony to all three players that the friendship eventually settled and endured. Spencer became a regular at the Priory, introduced the Leweses to John Cross and was Marian's final visitor a few days before her death in 1880.

Marian was slow to let the Brays know about her changing emotional allegiances. During the first half of 1852, Lewes appears in her letters in the guise of Spencer's shadow. Yoking Lewes to Spencer was a way for Marian to mention a man who increasingly interested her without upsetting the sensibilities of Rosehill. The Brays' own living arrangements may have been unorthodox, and they were certainly good friends with the Thornton Hunts, but they were unlikely to be enthusiastic about Marian's new attachment. The fact that Lewes was married, combined with his reputation as a womaniser, were exactly the factors which always made Marian's love affairs so traumatic. Although it was years since she had taken conventional opinion into account, she still looked to the Brays, Cara especially, to be her guiding conscience. She wanted their approval of the jaunty, naughty little man and knew she was not likely to get it.

But despite herself, Marian could not resist dropping delighted hints to the Brays about her growing happiness. In March 1853 she tells Sara that the 'genial and amusing' Lewes 'has quite won my liking, in spite of myself'.[28] The following month she casually mentions to the Brays that 'Lewes has been quite a pleasant friend to me lately' – and then immediately crosses it out.[29] That same month she took care to write to Cara that she had discovered that Lewes was 'a man of heart and conscience wearing a mask of flippancy'.[30] By now the two were probably lovers and it was during these quiet, dark months of early 1853 that Marian began to learn the true story behind one of London's most talked-about men.

George Henry Lewes had been born in April 1817, the son of John Lee Lewes and Elizabeth Ashweek.[31] He did not know – and never found out – that he was illegitimate. Setting an uncanny precedent, John Lee Lewes was already married, to a woman called Elizabeth Pownall, by whom he had four children. In 1811 John Lee Lewes left his first family in Liverpool to set up home with Elizabeth Ashweek in London. Together they had three boys, of whom George was the youngest.

The Lewes family was steeped in unorthodoxy. John Lee Lewes's father had been the middlingly well-known comic actor Charles Lee Lewes, who managed to get married three times. Something less than a gentleman and thoroughly provocative in his beliefs, Lewes *grandpère* loved to shock. During a run in Aberdeen of an adaptation of Molière's *Tartuffe*, he clashed pens with a local Methodist minister who had denounced him from the pulpit. Other literary productions included those typical eighteenth-century forms – memoirs, sketches, satirical bits and pieces, all thoroughly knock-about in tone. John Lee Lewes followed his father into print, but anaemically. He edited the great man's work as well as producing some plodding patriotic poetry. Shortly before George's birth he disappeared to Bermuda, never to be seen again. Elizabeth told the boys their father was dead.

The next five or so years must have been bleak for the family. It is unclear how Elizabeth Lewes, as she styled herself, survived in something approaching respectability. It was probably desperation which drove her in November 1823 to marry Captain John Willim. A former captain in the East India Company, the forty-six-year-old Willim was now retired on half-pay. While this was better than nothing, it was hardly a fortune. In any case, Willim and his wife got on badly, and the boys seem to have regarded him as a tetchy nuisance. It is quite possible that for periods of the marriage the Captain actually lived apart from his ready-made and probably unwanted family. Even towards the end of his life he was causing trouble, refusing to let anyone into the London home, which he was again sharing with his wife. Lewes, by now the only surviving son, knew enough of the Captain to take his mother's complaints seriously. 'I told her to tell him that unless he could treat her better she should come and live with us,' he recorded in his journal.[32] When Willim died in 1864 Lewes dutifully sorted out the estate but confided to the publisher Blackwood that he was hardly sad about the removal of the man who had made his mother's life a misery.[33]

So Lewes's childhood was edgy and restless. The family circled southern England and northern France looking for somewhere cheap to live. From Stroud in Gloucestershire they moved to Southampton and by 1827 they were in Plymouth, staying with Mrs Willim's sister. The following year the Lewes–Willim household was on the move again, this time crossing the channel for a stay in Nantes. Living economically and anonymously in France was a popular option for impoverished middle-class British families who found it impossible to keep up standards at home. It was now that George began to learn the French language and manners which were to become such a remarked-on part of his adult persona. When the American feminist Margaret Fuller met him at the Carlyles' she reported that he was a 'witty, French, flippant sort of man'.[34] Henry James recalled another dinner party, in the last year of Lewes's life, where the little man told a string of funny stories in colloquial French. James was unusual in approving of Lewes's gay cosmopolitanism.[35] Most commentators followed Margaret Fuller in inferring that there was a 'sparkling shallowness' in Lewes's ability to straddle cultures and sensibilities. This suspicion was part of a more general xenophobia, which looked upon foreigners, Frenchmen particularly, as upstarts and bounders. It was a prejudice that was to dog Lewes all his life.

Yet Lewes's unusual familiarity with French culture – deepened when the family moved the following year to the Channel Isles – had more important results than an ability to wave his hands around and tell *risqué* jokes. As Marian had begun to discover, beneath the jauntiness was a man of passionate intellectual engagement. He may have written for money – and who did not? – but he also had a genuine desire to introduce his English readers to the best of French thought, writing and philosophy. Without George Henry Lewes, the work of Auguste Comte and George Sand would have taken far longer to become known outside a tiny privileged circle.

What made this achievement so extraordinary was that Lewes's formal education had been patchy and short. Returning to England from Jersey, he attended Dr Charles Parr Burney's seminary in Greenwich, which had a fine academic reputation, but was as cold and cruel as any attended by English boys during this period before public school reform. There was no money for university and so, just like all the other men in Marian's life, Lewes left school before he was sixteen and set to work, reading voraciously in his spare time. Unencumbered by the traditional syllabus, the young Lewes had the freedom to roam through the 'new' subjects, which were currently transforming the

intellectual landscape. He believed that the living languages were more important than dead ones, science more relevant than the classics, literature more
revealing than history. In only a few years the curricula at the great public
schools and ancient universities would be reformed in line with this kind of
thinking, but in the 1830s it was young men from humble backgrounds like
Lewes, Bray, Spencer and even Chapman who built and disseminated the
knowledge that would transform the way people understood their world.
Mostly Lewes delighted in his intellectual modernism, but occasionally the
taunts of Oxford men like Froude hit home. Once Lewes was freed from the
need to write for the market by Marian's growing wealth, his lingering sense
of insecurity meant that he was always in danger of weighing down his light,
pliable text with too many footnotes.

After a stint in a lawyer's office Lewes moved to a Russian merchant's before
deciding that he wanted to be a doctor. He attended lectures, probably at
University College, but was turned off clinical work because he could not bear
to witness the patients' pain. This might sound like a face-saving formula for
a young man who lacked the ability or sticking-power to finish a long training,
but in Lewes's case it may have been true. Certainly, he remained fascinated
by physiology all his life. In the 1860s he settled down to concentrate his work
on the connection between the mind and the body, puzzling away at those
areas from which psychoanalysis would emerge at the end of the century. The
result was his monumental book *Problems of Life and Mind*, which Marian
completed from his notes after his death.

Unlike Marian, Lewes had no orthodoxy from which to rebel, no belief
system against which to struggle. The mid-Victorian story of agonised doubt,
Orders abandoned, and fellowships discarded had no place in his life. His
rackety, atheistic upbringing had inclined him from the start to the new rational
ideas which were coming off the Continent. As a nineteen-year-old it was quite
natural for him to gravitate to a group of 'students' which met in Red Lion
Square 'whose sole object was the amiable collision of contending views, on
subjects which, at one time or another, perplex and stimulate all reflecting
minds'.[36] One of the members, a Jewish watchmaker named Cohn, introduced
Lewes to the ideas of Spinoza, whose work was almost unknown in Britain.
With characteristic enthusiasm, Lewes set about translating Spinoza's *Ethics*
from the Latin and with equally characteristic impatience he gave it up. But
he never abandoned his interest in the philosopher, writing an article on him
for the *Westminster* in May 1843, at around the time when Marian started
translating an unspecified text of Spinoza's in an attempt to distract herself
from the stormy aftermath of the Brabant affair. This was just one of the
uncanny coincidences in their early lives which, in knowing hindsight, seem
to have made it inevitable that they would be drawn together in early middle
age. As Marian and Lewes moved closer during 1852 and 1853 they surely
talked about this outcast philosopher from two centuries before who had played
such an important part in both their intellectual lives. Spinoza had called upon
man to dismantle the elaborate frameworks through which he viewed the world
and to accept things clear-sightedly as they are. This meant giving up the

fantasy of a Divine presence and concentrating on smaller, closer truths. For instance, the philosopher suggested that man must author his own morality, using healthy self-regard as the foundation for loving others. Feuerbach had developed these ideas in *The Essence of Christianity*, where Marian, naturally, would have spotted them during her work on its translation. Lewes, in the meantime, found himself in sympathy with Spinoza's insistence that the mind constructs its own meaning and was to develop this point over five volumes in *Problems of Life and Mind.*

Having abandoned medicine, Lewes decided with characteristic nerve to become a 'philosopher and poet'.[37] Given his unorthodox background and constitutional irreverence, it was inevitable that he would be drawn towards the raggle-taggle end of literary society. And in the context of the 1830s that meant becoming a member of the circle which surrounded the bohemian poet Leigh Hunt. Hunt, by now in his fifties, had been a member of the Byron–Shelley set, imbibing with them a kind of romantic communism, which he tried to live out even in the depths of Chelsea. He affected a saintly innocence, which concealed a cunning, pragmatic side. Charles Dickens quickly got the measure of the man, caricaturing him in *Bleak House* as Harold Skimpole, a guileful romantic poet who declares himself too daft to understand the workings of the world, but canny enough to accept the gift of a sovereign. Leigh Hunt's chief attraction for Lewes was that he had been an intimate of Shelley's. For Lewes, like every other young man of restless disposition and romantic spirit, worshipped the poet. To 'right-minded' people 'Shelley' was a word to be whispered quietly, a dark synonym for the worst kind of atheistic loose-living. But to Lewes and his like the man was a visionary who preached a life of absolute integrity. 'If one quality might be supposed to distinguish him pre-eminently,' he declared in an early essay in the *Westminster* in 1840, 'it was that highest of all qualities – truthfulness, an unyielding worship of truth.'[38]

Ostensibly Lewes wanted to get close to Hunt because he knew the silly grand old man had contacts, memories and papers which would help in his cherished scheme of writing a biography of Shelley. But he was also shrewd enough to have spotted that Hunt had gathered around himself an interesting group of young men who might prove useful. Lewes cultivated them nakedly. He wrote to one of them, the artist William Bell Scott, describing himself as 'a student living a quiet life, but have a great gusto for intellectual acquaint-ance'.[39] Scott agreed to be his friend and his later recollections of Lewes are the only ones we have from this time. According to Scott, young Lewes was 'an exuberant but not very reliable or exact talker, a promising man of parts, a mixture of the man of the world and the boy'.[40] He was also, Scott hinted, sexually promiscuous. Certainly, Lewes's letters from this time suggest a like-able, cocky, restless young man, desperate to get himself noticed by all the right people – especially female ones. From Germany, where he stayed for nine months in 1838 to learn the language, literature and philosophy, he trumpeted to Leigh Hunt, 'I am intimate here with a great many of the first families and am considerably petted, especially by my best friends ever, the ladies.'[41]

Lewes was too clever not to marry well. On his return from Germany he met Agnes Jervis, the nineteen-year-old daughter of Swynfen Jervis, a Radical MP for Bridport in Dorset. Jervis was a fussy, grubby little man with a genuine love of literature and the classics. Lewes, now armed with fluent German, may have been been employed to tutor Agnes's brothers at Darlaston Hall, the family's house near Stoke-on-Trent. Alternatively, he may have been working as Jervis's secretary. Another theory has him meeting Agnes in London through the Hunt circle. In light of the way the marriage turned out, there was later gossip about Lewes eloping with the under-age Agnes, pursued by her infuriated father. But in fact Jervis was far from being a heavy-handed Victorian papa. A devotee of Godwin and Shelley, he shared with his future son-in-law the view that emotional attachments could not be trammelled by legal forms. If the young couple were in love, he was certainly not going to interfere. He gave written permission for Agnes to marry and on 18 February 1841 stood witness at her wedding to the twenty-three-year-old George Henry Lewes.

Nor was Agnes the unwitting victim of two men's libidinous conniving. Well educated and clever, she was clear-eyed about her own future. All the evidence suggests that, young as she was, Agnes understood and approved of what she was going into. Throughout her long life – she died in 1902 – she never once complained about Lewes or begrudged his relationship with Marian. True, she was careless and demanding about money, expecting her husband to support her tribe of children by another man, but she never gave the slightest suggestion that she considered herself the victim of the piece.

But in 1841 these marital post-mortems were a long way off. Agnes was a strikingly pretty girl and Lewes, everyone agreed, was a lucky man. W. B. Scott described Agnes as 'one of the loveliest creatures in the world', while Jane Carlyle, who along with her husband took a strangely proprietorial interest in the Leweses' marriage, called her a 'charming little wife'.[42] Agnes was clever, too, a good enough linguist to take on some translating work to boost their meagre funds. Despite being the great-niece of an earl, Agnes does not seem to have brought much of a dowry with her and the young couple were obliged to live in a series of rooms in Kensington, more often than not with his mother. Still, they were happy. Thomas Carlyle remembered how 'They used to come down of an evening to us [in Chelsea] through the lanes from Kensington, and were as merry as two birds'.[43] There may have been some casual infidelity on Lewes's part, but nothing serious. In time, four baby boys appeared: Charles Lee (1842), Thornton Arnott (1844) (named after Hunt), Herbert Arthur (1846) and St Vincent Arthy (1848).

Domestic happiness did not so much mellow Lewes as make him more determined to succeed. While his pushiness annoyed some, others were charmed in spite of themselves. Macvey Napier, editor of the stuffily prestigious *Edinburgh Review*, dismissed him as a 'coxcomb' although the chilly John Stuart Mill, still influential at the *Westminster*, put up a defence for the young man on the grounds that 'he is confident but not at all conceited, for he will bear to be told anything however unflattering about what he writes'.[44] Napier, however, took a lot of convincing and it was not until October 1843 that he accepted one of the articles with which Lewes had been pestering him for the last three years. Mill, however, made sure that his protégé's pieces appeared regularly in the *Westminster*, including the article on Shelley, all that remained of the original project of publishing a biography of the great man. He also gave Lewes detailed notes on articles that were intended for publication elsewhere. Whenever he wrote about his favourite subject of German philosophy Lewes had a habit of trying to out-Carlyle Carlyle, slipping into the ranting, rhetorical style that had burst into print in *Sartor Resartus*. Mill sensibly and gently steered Lewes towards a more authentic voice for the pieces he was now contributing regularly to the *British and Foreign Review*, the *Foreign Quarterly Review* and the *Monthly Magazine*.

In 1845–6 snide comments about Lewes's showy versatility escalated with the publication of his *Biographical History of Philosophy*. Aimed at the layman, the history consisted of four little volumes, tracing the development of Western philosophy from the Greeks to Auguste Comte. Lewes, undeniably biased, emphasised the contribution of empiricists like Aristotle, Locke and Hume over the metaphysicians Plato, Descartes and Leibnitz. He saw philosophy culminating in the near-contemporary work of Auguste Comte, whom he designated 'the Bacon of the nineteenth century' and on whom he would write in more detail later. Academic critics sneered at the way the *Biographical History* cantered through the centuries on a sightseeing tour of esoteric thought. None the less, its brisk, clear tone made it a best-seller among the people for whom it was intended and even those for whom it was not. In 1853 Marian reported proudly to Sara that Lewes had visited Cambridge and discovered 'a knot of devotees there who make his history of Philosophy a private text-book'.[45] As late as the 1930s the book was still popular among London University students who used it as a crib.[46]

During the first nine years of the marriage domestic happiness seems to have fuelled Lewes's astonishing productivity. But by 1849 it was becoming clear that growing disillusionment lay behind his increasingly hectic and fragmented schedule. The roots of the distress went back to the free-living culture in which the marriage had been contracted. Right from the start, Lewes and Agnes had agreed that monogamy was an unnatural obligation and one which, in all conscience, they could not follow. As rational free-thinkers they gave each other permission to follow their sexual desire wherever it might lead. But what neither had ever considered was what would happen if one of them fell in love with someone else.

Thornton Hunt was Leigh Hunt's eldest son and had known Lewes from before his marriage. The two young men had knocked around London together, edited a magazine and sent each other crude, slangy letters which were not as funny as they thought. Hunt took after his father, being careless, grasping and a free-thinker. Inspired not only by Shelley, but also by the French socialist Fourier, Hunt and his wife Kate were enthused by the idea of communal living. Together with two other couples – Hunt's sister, who was conveniently married to Kate's brother, and the painter Samuel Laurence who was married to Kate's cousin – they set up home together in Bayswater. In addition they were joined by some single women, probably relatives. Officially, the inhabitants of the house in Queen's Road were pooling material resources. In time, it became apparent that they were sharing sexual partners too.

Despite much retrospective gossip, it is fairly clear that Agnes and Lewes never lived in Queen's Road, although they were frequent visitors during the time when the 'phalanstery' was at its most notorious. Sly references to the community pop up again and again in disguised – and distorted – recollections of the period, often written decades later. Eliza Lynn, speaking through the male narrator of her autobiographical novel *Christopher Kirkland*, remembered how, arriving as a youngster in London, 'I fell in with that notorious group of Free-lovers, whose ultimate transaction was the most notable example of matrimony void of contract of our day.'

Exactly what Lynn meant by this is not clear. Much of the gossip surrounding the community in Queen's Road was fuelled by the fantasies of fascinated onlookers. Were the Hunts engaged in wife-swapping? And could that perhaps, by extension, include group sex? In actual fact, the Hunts' domestic arrangements seem to have involved nothing more titillating than an agreement that they need not be faithful to one another. Although Lynn was keen to point out that Lewes was 'the most pronounced Free-lover of the group, and openly took for himself the liberty he expressly sanctioned in his wife', there is no suggestion that Lewes completed the symmetry by becoming sexually involved with Kate Hunt.[47] Instead, he seems to have confined himself to short-term liaisons far beyond the confines of the commune.

The only firm bit of evidence we have specifically about the emerging relationship between Hunt and Agnes is a pencil sketch done by the novelist Thackeray in 1848. It shows Agnes sitting at the piano with Lewes standing by her, either singing or ready to turn the pages. A few feet behind, watching them intently, is Thornton Hunt. He is more lightly sketched than the other figures, but his presence dominates the group.[48] By now it was clear that Thornton Hunt had become a ghostly third party in the Leweses' marriage.

The situation was not helped by the fact that Lewes had never given up his bachelor habit of spending a great deal of time on the Continent, gathering research for his articles and books. In 1842, armed with letters of introduction from J. S. Mill, he went to Paris to seek out Comte, de Tocqueville and Michelet. Three years later he was in Berlin, looking for Friedrich Schelling, August Boeckh and Ludwig Tieck. In 1846 he returned to Paris to force an introduction to George Sand, the scandalous novelist whom he admired most in the world and about whom he wrote with passionate conviction. It was, coincidentally, just at this time that Marian Evans was having to defend her admiration for George Sand to a disapproving Sara Hennell.

Even back home in Britain Lewes could not sit still. At the beginning of 1849 he lectured at the Liverpool Mechanics Institute on the history of philosophy, before moving on to Manchester where he not only reprised the lectures but also appeared at the theatre as Shylock in the *The Merchant of Venice*. He found time, too, to take the leading role in his own play, *The Noble Heart*. Lewes had greasepaint in his blood and had always toyed with the idea of a stage career. He had spent the 1840s performing in various companies, including Dickens's celebrated amateur troupe. But the experience of playing Shylock again late in 1849, this time in Edinburgh, finally convinced him that he was never going to succeed as a professional actor. His bright sparkle and facile wit might dominate any drawing-room, but on a cavernous stage his small body and light voice were easily swamped. From now on Lewes confined himself to writing for and about the theatre. Under the name of 'Slingsby Lawrence' he continued to translate so-so French farces for money. More important, he became a theatre critic in the form of 'Vivian', the loud, louche bachelor-ish persona which he adopted for his review work at the *Leader*.

It is impossible to know whether Lewes's continual absences were the cause or the result of the marriage breakdown. Certainly his habit of raving to Agnes about the beautiful women whom he had met on the road cannot have helped. Either way, by April 1849 sharp-eyed Jane Carlyle had noticed a definite change in Agnes towards her husband. 'I used to think these Leweses a perfect pair of love-birds, always cuddling together on the same perch – to speak figuratively,' she told her cousin in a letter, 'but the female love-bird appears to have hopped off to some distance and to be now taking a somewhat critical view of her little shaggy mate!'[49] We cannot know, either, why Hunt appealed to Agnes. He was not as funny or as clever as Lewes and he was almost as ugly. Perhaps it simply came down to the fact that he was there. Only three months later Agnes became pregnant by her lover. Edmund Alfred was born on 16 April 1850, just a fortnight after the first issue of the *Leader*, co-edited by Hunt and Lewes, appeared.

Although Lewes had sanctioned Agnes's affair with Thornton on condition that no child was born from the liaison, he still took the fateful step of registering the child as his own. As the law stood, by giving Hunt's child his name Lewes was condoning Agnes's adultery and relinquishing the right to sue at any point for divorce. By this one administrative act he would condemn Marian Evans to a life as a sexual and social outcast. Although it would be eighteen months before he would meet her, the puzzle remains as to why at the age of thirty-three he closed off so many options for his future life. A clue may lie in the fact that only two weeks previously his youngest son St Vincent Arthy had died of whooping cough. In the midst of despair it may have been that the joy of a new child, even another man's, went some of the way towards filling the void. Then again, the *Leader* had just been launched after months of agonised fund-raising, and it might have seemed pointlessly destructive to create tension between the two co-editors at their moment of triumph. But perhaps, after all, the real explanation is that, despite the façade of moral flippancy which offended so many, Lewes was a man of integrity. Having agreed with Agnes on the rules of their relationship, he was not about go back on them just because his pride had been hurt. He accepted that this situation, publicly humiliating though it might be, was the result of an agreement into which he had entered willingly.

Agnes's feelings for Hunt turned out to be deep and lasting. Eighteen months later, on 21 October 1851, she gave birth to another of his children, this time a girl called Rose Agnes. By now Lewes ceased to think of himself as her husband and had moved out of Bedford Place. Throughout the upheaval Thornton Hunt remained his usual complacent self. Around this time he intoned sententiously in the *Leader* that 'Human beings are born with passions; you will not discipline those passions by ignoring them' and continued to argue for a reform of the marriage and divorce laws.[50] True to his word, Hunt generously went on sleeping with his wife right through his affair with Agnes. Kate Hunt had ten children in all, two of them born within weeks of two produced by Agnes. Hunt's liaison with Agnes produced another two babies and continued at least until 1857, when Mildred Jane Lewes was born.

No matter how amicable their feelings for one another and how rational their personal choices, it was inevitable that the Lewes–Hunt friendship would eventually buckle under the strain. For a time the excitement of producing a new and highly regarded weekly magazine carried them through their differences. Their responsibilities, in any case, were distinct: Hunt was in charge of the political coverage, Lewes the arts and cultural side. But over the following months odd hints and nudges in the magazine suggest that Lewes was finding it increasingly hard to work alongside the man who was publicly cuckolding him. Shortly after the birth of Agnes's daughter Ethel Isabel in October 1853 Lewes used his Vivian persona to reveal his unhappy situation. Reviewing a farce called *How to Make Home Happy*, he heavy-handedly informed his readers, 'As I have *no* home, and that home is not happy, I really stand in need of [the author's] secret.'[51]

But on this occasion the normally nimble Vivian was lagging behind events. By the time he made the remark his alter ego Lewes had already moved out of the family home and was well into his relationship with Marian Evans, with whom he would spend the rest of his life. At first glance it might not seem clear why this affair should last any longer than the countless others Lewes had already enjoyed: this, indeed, was the substance of the Brays' objections to him as a partner for Marian. But at thirty-five, homeless and alone, Lewes had had enough of the free love that had brought him to what he later called this 'dreary, wasted period of my life'.[52] Despair had burned away his ideological certainties and prepared him to try something, anything, to bring stability into his life.

Whether he was always faithful to Marian is not clear. Their odd situation meant that throughout most of their life together he continued to receive invitations, while she did not. In effect, this left him free to play the merry bachelor, sauntering around clubland, turning up at the theatre, attending dinner parties. But by then his careful pose as a ladies' man was just that, a bit of play-acting. He might flirt and tell *risqué* stories in French, but mostly he came home to her as soon as he could. There is a story that after Lewes's death Marian discovered from reading his papers that he had been unfaithful to her. According to this account her hurt and anger turned to loathing, and shortly afterwards she accepted John Cross's unlikely proposal.[53] Sober-minded biographers have been quick to point out that the evidence is malign and slight.

Yet, it is hard to believe that a man who from his earliest adult years had been a parallel lover should, merely by an effort of will, change himself into an uncompromising monogamist.

But the possibility of Lewes's occasional infidelity should not be taken as a comment on the quality of his love for Marian. In a brief journal entry of January 1859 he recalled with great tenderness the moment when they were first introduced: 'to know her was to love her, and since then my life has been a new birth.'[54] Although he had always been sexually involved with women, Lewes's interest in them extended far beyond their bodies. He liked clever women. Indeed, he had married one. His articles on female novelists are, save for a few stray conventionalities, full of admiration for their particular skills and sensibilities. At a time when many thought Charlotte Brontë's work scandalous, he wrote publicly and privately of his admiration for her. Back in the late 1840s he had published two bad novels and was quick to spot when others, whatever their sex, could do things which he could not. It was he, not Spencer, who first suggested that Marian should write fiction and he was characteristically generous when she succeeded. He recognised that she was cleverer and more talented than he, and never felt the need to punish her for it. As for the fact that Marian was plain – well, he had already married a pretty girl and it had not brought him happiness.

Marian, for her part, responded to Lewes's breadth of intellect. Initially she had assumed that his versatility was a cynical ploy to exploit the periodical market, but gradually she came to realise that his interest in these subjects – and in the many more that would follow – was genuine and, when given an opportunity, deep. As for his womanising, she had several times been drawn to men who were polygamists. One explanation might be that she felt that she did not deserve a man of her own and so continually found herself forced to share. But another possibility was that these men – Bray, Chapman, even Brabant and now Lewes – were unusual in being able to relate to women in an easy, intimate way. As gender codes formalised during the first decades of Victoria's reign, men and women found themselves leading increasingly segregated lives. Marian Evans, unusual in spending her working life among men, was drawn to partners who could match her ability to transcend limited ideas about what it meant to be a man or a woman.

As the uncanny similarities between Lewes's intellectual history and her own became clear during the winter of 1852–3, Marian must have felt as if she had found her soulmate. Her family history, in particular her abbreviated relationship with her mother, left her always hungry for that rapt merging. At first she found it with Isaac, and later in her intense friendships with Maria Lewis and Sara Hennell. Her early relationships with men outside the family were likewise marked by this intensity: losing Chapman and Spencer had sent her into a numb slump from which only this new attachment roused her. But with Lewes she finally found a man who was able to give her the kind of reassurance, attention, support – in fact, the mothering – which she craved. Far from frustrating her, their isolated life provided the exclusivity and intensity which she desired so badly and which had evaded her for so long. When she talked of herself and Lewes as 'Siamese twins', it was with pride and complacency in her voice.

There were sufficient contrasts, too, in Marian's and Lewes's backgrounds to ensure that tedium did not set in. Friends noticed how Marian listened with rapt attention to Lewes's funny, unlikely tales of theatrical life. Tom Trollope, a close friend of both, suggested: 'It must have offered so piquant a contrast with the middle-class surroundings of her early life.'[55] Lewes's sparkling gaiety had a well-attested capacity to enchant those who found it hard to be light-hearted. The solemn Herbert Spencer described Lewes as 'full of various anecdote; and an admirable mimic; it was impossible to be dull in his company'.[56] Even Eliza Lynn, who bore Lewes and Eliot a strange, pointless grudge, acknowledged that 'wherever he went there was a patch of intellectual sunshine in the room'.[57] Now Marian Evans, that intense and serious woman, had also fallen under the spell of the man who would famously be described as 'the mercurial little showman'.

By the summer of 1853 Lewes was, for those in the know, a highly visible fixture in Marian's life. Coventry still got the coded version, but nevertheless it is possible to work out from Marian's letters to Rosehill that Lewes visited her during her six-week holiday on the south coast. Marian's mood in St Leonards could not have been more different from the one in Broadstairs the previous year. On that earlier occasion Herbert Spencer had been a reluctant and chilly visitor, bringing final confirmation of his lack of sexual feeling for her. Her letters to him had been beseeching, to Coventry watchful and resigned. But twelve months on there has been a transformation. Her happiness spills out of her letters to the Brays. There are the usual little hints and nudges that Lewes has come down from town to see her. But the main evidence comes in her warm descriptions of her surroundings. From her cottage at St Leonards she describes 'a vast expanse of sea and sky for my only view . . . The bright weather and genial air – so different from what I have had for a year before – make me feel as happy and stupid as a well-conditioned cow. I sit looking at the sea and the sleepy ships with a purely animal *bien-être*.'[58]

Away from London's prying eyes and blessed with weather that was almost Continental, it was quite possibly now that Marian and Lewes began to discuss the possibility that one day they might live together. It would be hard to overestimate the seriousness of this decision. The Fallen Woman was a figure which haunted the mid-Victorian imagination. Not a prostitute exactly, she was conceived as a woman who had allowed herself to become sexually intimate with a man who could not or would not marry her. Cast out from society, her only way of living was quietly and anonymously. Either she could become the man's common-law wife, take his name, and hope that no one found out about the true nature of her situation. Or she could move to a new neighbourhood and start again, claiming either to be a widow (if there was a child) or else a spinster of the parish. But none of these options was open to Marian. She and Lewes needed to live in London for their work, and they were too notorious to be able simply to disappear to a new part of town. If they decided to cohabit, the price they would pay would be utter notoriety and the effective ending of any public life for Marian.

For this reason it made sense to have a trial run abroad where they – and their status – were either not known or not bothered about. Germany was an obvious destination, since Marian had already translated two of its most important theological works and Lewes was preparing a biography of its greatest intellectual figure, Goethe. In addition, Germany had the practical advantage of being cheap – an important consideration, as Lewes would still be responsible for supporting Agnes and her family financially.

Viewed retrospectively, it looks as if Marian and G. H. Lewes were destined to be together. But such a happy ending was hardly certain as they lived through these first eighteen months of their relationship. Although he was separated from his wife, Lewes did not yet consider the arrangement permanent. Indeed, it was not until the autumn of 1854 that it seems to have become quite clear that Agnes did not want him back. In a letter to Charles Bray from Weimar Marian wrote mysteriously, 'Circumstances, with which I am not concerned, and *which have arisen since . . . [Mr Lewes] left England* [my italics], have led him to determine on a separation from Mrs Lewes.'[59] We do not know what these circumstances were, nor why their timing was so significant. But it is a shock to realise that it was only at this late stage that Marian considered herself able to make permanent plans to be with Lewes.

Although it would always be crucially important to Marian's self-image that she had not carried off another woman's husband, this odd letter to Bray makes it clear that when she left for Germany Lewes did not yet know if he would at some point return to his wife. Far from being an informal honeymoon to confirm the new 'marriage', this Continental holiday appears more in the light of a trial cohabitation. The fact that it went well pushed Lewes into making a final and decisive break from his wife. Although in the years that followed Agnes would never accuse Marian of breaking up her marriage, there would be plenty who would do just that. Marian Evans became known not just as the woman who lived with a man without being his wife, but as one who took another woman's husband.

Given that Lewes did not make a final commitment to the relationship until they were already in Weimar, Marian's decision to travel with him to Germany was extremely brave. Agnes might change her mind and want Lewes back, or the relationship might simply run its course. While Marian did not doubt Lewes's sincerity, she knew that those who had her best interests at heart worried that he would tire of her as he had of so many before. Since the holy war she had learned to live with the censure of conventional society, but it was one thing to do so with the man she loved beside her and quite another to live the rest of her life as a jilted, untouchable woman. Once the news was out that she had spent the summer living as Lewes's 'wife', she would never be allowed to return to her status as an unusual but respectable woman. 'Spent Christmas Day alone at Cambridge St,' she wrote in her journal in December 1853,[60] the only entry from this time to survive Cross's savage pruning. It was a glimpse of what life might be like if the coming gamble did not pay off.

During the months when Marian was deciding whether to risk making her relationship with Lewes public she was sustained by her work on Feuerbach, which Chapman was finally committed to publishing. Feuerbach's *Das Wesen des Christentums* (*The Essence of Christianity*) (1841) was an attempt to salvage the spirit of Christianity in an intellectual landscape for ever changed by Strauss. If the Bible was no longer a literal account of faith, then what was left? Feuerbach suggested that religion was a psychological necessity for man, who projected the best of himself upon God and then proceeded to worship his own magnificence. Far from resulting in an arid solipsism, Feuerbach's Christianity was a warm and generous humanism, which saw acts of love between men as the building blocks of faith: 'Love is God himself, and apart from it there is no God'.[61] Most relevantly for Marian, Feuerbach included sexual love in his definition of the sacred. What mattered was not the legal forms which contained that love, but the quality of the attachment. According to Feuerbach the only 'religious' marriage was one which was 'spontaneously concluded, spontaneously willed, self-sufficing.' A marriage 'the bond of which is merely an external restriction . . . is not a true marriage, and therefore not a truly moral marriage.'[62] It was the clearest theological justification Marian would find for her coming decision to live with Lewes.

Marian followed the same system with Feuerbach as she had used with Strauss. As soon as she had finished a passage she sent it to Sara in Coventry, who checked her work against the original. The process was less painful this time, partly because the German was easier and partly because she was in greater sympathy with Feuerbach than she had been with Strauss. This time there were no letters about her being 'Feuerbach-sick'. The translation was published in mid-July and for the first and only time in her career she allowed her real name 'Marian Evans' to appear on the flyleaf. In this way she publicly identified the moral basis of the extraordinary step she was about to take of starting her own 'marriage' to G. H. Lewes.

There were other less esoteric sources to which Marian turned in an attempt to find justification for the pandemonium she was about to create. On 10 July she wrote to Sara to prepare her for her departure, declaring, 'I shall soon send you a good bye, for I am preparing to go to "Labassecour".'[63] Labassecour was Charlotte Brontë's name for Brussels, the country to which Lucy Snowe travels in *Villette* in an attempt to find a richer, more authentic life. She also finds Paul Emanuel, the difficult and unsuitable man with whom she falls in love. The unconventional passion of Brontë's third book was far more to Marian's taste than *Jane Eyre*, which she had read in 1847 during the ghastly holiday at St Leonards. In *Villette*, equally admired by Lewes, Marian found the endorsement she had been looking for. She would have been even more intrigued to learn that Lucy Snowe's highly charged relationship with M. Emanuel was based on Brontë's own love for a married man, her employer Constantin Heger.

As the time approached when they would have to reach a decision about whether to make the relationship public or abandon it as impossible, both Marian's and Lewes's health gave way. The strain of keeping her intentions secret from Cara and Sara, not to mention the prospect of losing their friend-ship, brought Marian the usual cycle of nervous and physical symptoms. In a letter written to Sara she touched directly on the isolation she was feeling and the even greater isolation which she feared was to come: 'I am terribly out of spirits just now and the pleasantest thought I have is that whatever I may feel affects no one else – happens in a little "island cut off from other lands".'[64] These remarks rang warning bells with Sara, who thought she sensed a return to the intense morbidity of the Geneva letters. She alerted her sister, who immediately wrote to Marian asking how on earth she could consider herself an island when she had so many good friends. In replying carefully to Cara, Marian moved from her own circumstances to a consideration of the general human condition in a way which prefigures the wise narrator of her novels.

> When I spoke of myself as an island, I did not mean that I was so exceptionally. We are all islands . . . and this seclusion is sometimes the most intensely felt at the very moment your friend is caressing you or consoling you. But this gradually becomes a source of satisfaction instead of repining. When we are young we think our troubles a mighty business – that the world is spread out expressly as a stage for the particular drama of our lives and that we have a right to rant and foam at the mouth if we are crossed. I have done enough of that in my time. But we begin at last to understand that these things are important only to one's own consciousness, which is but as a globule of dew on a rose-leaf that at mid-day there will be no trace of. This is no high-flown sentimentality, but a simple reflection which I find useful to me every day.[65]

Lewes was in an even worse state. In April he had collapsed with dizziness, headaches and ringing in the ears. It might seem as if he had less to lose than Marian, having no good name to impugn. None the less, it was a huge step for him to separate publicly from Agnes and the children whom he loved. The responsibility of providing for them would not stop and it was hard to see how he could afford to set up a separate home with a new partner. And careless though he often was about these things, he was aware that he was asking Marian to give up a great deal by coming with him to Germany. At some point they would be obliged to return to London and face the fact that she was now a social exile. If his feelings for her faded after a year or two then he would be forced to bear the hideous knowledge that the world held him respon-sible for ruining the reputation of London's cleverest woman. Under the strain of these considerations, Lewes eventually ground to a halt and was ordered to the country for a month by his doctor. This, however, did not do the trick because, explained Marian, 'His poor head – his only fortune – is not well yet.'[66] He was soon sent off again, this time to try the famous water cure at Malvern.

While Lewes languished in the country, Marian undertook to do his *Leader* work for him. Several of the pieces which appeared in the magazine during these weeks have her stamp on them. Given that she was still struggling with the Feuerbach proofs, it confirms that by now she thought of herself and

Lewes as a unit. Six months earlier she had sprung to his defence like a terrier when Chapman proposed to publish a review by T. H. Huxley of Lewes's translation of Comte's *Philosophy of the Sciences* and Harriet Martineau's abridged translation of *Positivist Philosophy*. Comte's attempt to study mankind by taking God out of the picture and seeing what was left was guaranteed to appeal to those two stringent atheists George Henry Lewes and Harriet Martineau. Positivism, as Comte's philosophy was called, concerned itself with classifying and describing the social organisation of human life along lines which Herbert Spencer had already found highly suggestive when writing his *Social Statics*. In other words, Positivism was an embryonic sociology which promised to reveal the new, secular secrets of Man's existence.

While Huxley was complimentary about Martineau's treatment of Comte, which was published by Chapman, he dismissed Lewes as having 'mere book-knowledge' of science. Here was the same old accusation about Lewes being nothing more than a hack, dressed up in a slightly different way. Still at this point acting as editor of the *Westminster*, Marian did everything she could to make sure that the review was pulled. First she pointed out to Chapman that it would look ridiculous for a book published by him to be so obviously puffed in the *Westminster*. When this tactic failed she wrote him a letter marked 'Private' in which she defended Lewes's right to make a serious contribution to scientific debate. She warns Chapman 'that the editors of the Review will disgrace themselves by inserting an utterly worthless & unworthy notice of a work by one of their own writers' and goes on to describe Lewes as Huxley's superior in intellect and fame.[67]

But Chapman for once refused to take her advice and the review appeared in the January 1854 edition. Was he punishing Marian because she was about to leave him to run the magazine on his own? Or was he punishing Lewes for taking away a woman whom he had loved and whom he still needed? If Marian was aware that there was something more than editorial impartiality behind Chapman's decision to run the review, she did not hold a grudge. As her resolve to go to Germany with Lewes strengthened, she was keen that the Chapmans would not be inconvenienced. Now that they had moved to new accommodation they were making noises about having Miss Evans as their boarder once again, but 'I could not feel at liberty to leave them after causing them to make arrangements on my account, and it is quite possible that I may wish to go to the continent or twenty other things'.[68]

Pressure was coming from the Combes, too, who were pushing Marian to spend her summer with them on the Continent. Everyone, it seemed, wanted a piece of Miss Evans. She would not be able to hold them off much longer.

On 11 June Charles Bray came to visit Marian in London and she told him of her intention to live with Lewes. Perhaps it was then that they agreed she would not tell Cara and Sara of her plans when she came to visit them at Rosehill a week later. She had always taken pains to keep the nature of her relationship with Lewes secret from Cara – on one occasion putting her off coming to visit her at her lodgings in Cambridge Street in case there might be some sign of Lewes's habitual presence.

With her London friends Barbara and Bessie she may have been more confiding. According to Bessie's daughter, Marian 'asked my mother to walk round Hyde Park with her, and in the course of that walk she told her what she meant to do. My mother reminded her that she, Marian, had not liked Lewes at all when she first met him, and she told her the infinitely more serious fact that Mrs Gaskell knew a girl whom he had seduced, but that made no difference. She had quite made up her mind.'[69]

She had indeed. During her mid-June holiday in Coventry Marian spent three weeks sitting on the bear rug under the acacia tree and keeping her counsel. The next the Brays heard of her was when they received a breathless note dated 19 July:

Dear Friends – all three
    I have only time to say good bye and God bless you. Poste Restante, Weimar for the next six weeks, and afterwards Berlin.
Ever your loving and grateful
Marian.[70]

CHAPTER 8

'I Don't Think She Is Mad'

Exile

1854–6

ON 20 JULY 1854 Marian Evans left her lodgings in Cambridge Street and set off on a journey from which there could be no return. She got to St Katharine's Dock, in the shadow of the Tower of London, at about eleven o'clock and 'found myself on board the Ravensbourne, bound for Antwerp'. The way Marian records this momentous sequence in her journal – only the second entry to have survived John Cross's censorship – is revealing. She describes herself involuntarily drifting on to the *Ravensbourne*, as if her conscious mind is unable to cope with the implications of what she is doing. It is exactly the state in which Maggie Tulliver in *The Mill on the Floss* allows Stephen Guest to lead her on to the boat that will carry her away to a new and irreversible phase of her life.

Nerves had made Marian arrive early 'and in consequence I had 20 minutes of terrible fear lest something should have delayed G'. Underneath her anxieties about missed cabs and botched arrangements was the terror that her well-meaning friends had been right after all and that Lewes would abandon her just at the point when she had given up everything to be with him. But she need not have worried: 'before long I saw his welcome face looking for me over the porter's shoulder and all was well.'[1]

Too excited to sleep, Lewes and Marian sat up on deck all night, watching the red-black sky gradually lift over the Belgian coast. Over the following weeks their decision to come away together would attract the kind of quivering disgust that greeted Maggie Tulliver on her return to St Ogg's. But while Maggie was away for just a few days, it would be eight months before Marian returned to London to face the chorus of disapproval. For now she could sit on deck with the man she loved and watch the far-away streaks of lightning show up the outlines of passing fishing boats. No one who glanced at the shabby middle-aged couple talking over their travel plans could have guessed they had stumbled on a scandal that would soon have the best and brightest of British tongues wagging in fascinated dismay.

The first person to spot them, still on board ship, was Robert Noel, brother of Cara's lover Edward.[2] Noel conducted his marriage to a German baroness on 'Continental' lines and was rumoured to have had many lovers. He lived, appropriately enough, in Bohemia, where he was heading after a fortnight's visit to Rosehill. The encounter passed without embarrassment. Robert Noel was the last man to raise a disapproving finger at the unmarried couple, although he may have found it impossible not to gossip about them when he wrote to his large circle of friends in Britain.

The next old friend to pop up was Dr Brabant. After arriving in Belgium, Marian and Lewes had spent a few days sightseeing in Antwerp, Brussels and Liège, before catching a train to Germany. The good doctor materialised on the platform, invited himself into their carriage and talked solidly all the way to Cologne. On arrival he bustled around, setting up the stilted meeting between Marian and Strauss.[3] Was it coincidence that Brabant reappeared in Marian's life just as she was making an irrevocable commitment to another man? And did his insistence on producing Strauss like a rabbit out of a hat constitute a competitive and aggressive act towards Lewes? Marian's letters and journal do not speculate.

Another familiar face was Arthur Helps, Lewes's old friend, who made a detour to Weimar on his way home from Spain. He had known about Lewes's plan to live with Marian in Germany and the fact that he had gone out of his way to visit was mentioned pointedly by Marian in her letters.[4] Helps was a courtier and favourite of Queen Victoria, and his acceptance of the situation seemed significant. But this was Labassecour, not London. Back in Britain, Lewes continued to spend his Christmas holidays at Vernon Hill, Helps's country house, to which Marian was pointedly not invited.

Meeting with the occasional kind face could not have prepared Marian and Lewes for the storm which was blowing up at home. Indeed, it sometimes seemed as if literary Britain put its pen down in the late summer of 1854 and spent the next few weeks gossiping about the liaison between its crown princess and court jester. Those who knew Marian and Lewes well, and others who thought they did, exchanged angry, eager judgements on the runaway couple. Letters flew between London, Coventry and Edinburgh. Speculation turned into rumour and rumour hardened into 'fact' in a process which Marian would describe in her accounts of parish pump chatter at both St Ogg's and Middlemarch. And as summer gave way to autumn, word trickled back to Weimar that some of those people closest to Marian and Lewes considered themselves irrevocably betrayed.

Marian's first letter to Rosehill was written on 16 August, a good month after she had arrived on the Continent. The tone is guarded, as if she is not sure what response she will receive. Addressed pointedly to Charles Bray alone, the closing 'much love to all' avoids mentioning Sara and Cara by name.[5] The sisters wrote back separately and Sara subsequently maintained that these letters (now lost) were 'full of affection', despite the fact that she and her sister 'strongly disapproved' of Marian's decision to live with Lewes.[6] So it was tactless of Marian to continue to address her next letter, of 23 October, to Charles Bray alone. A clue to her insensitivity lies in its content, which is a spirited defence of Lewes's behaviour towards his family, a subject to which she would return obsessively. As far as Marian was concerned, these were matters she had always discussed with Charles – a point she made to defend herself against Sara's accusations that she had deliberately excluded her closest women friends from her correspondence. But it was the concluding paragraph of Marian's letter which caused most offence:

> I am ignorant how far Cara and Sara may be acquainted with the state of things, and how they may feel towards me. I am quite prepared to accept the consequences of a step which I have deliberately taken and to accept them without irritation or bitterness. The most painful conse-quence will, I know, be the loss of friends. If I do not write, therefore, understand that it is because I desire not to obtrude myself.[7]

'Not to *obtrude* yourself,' stormed Sara in reply, 'when if you ever thought our friendship good for any thing, you must know how anxious we have been to hear from you!'[8] For ten years Sara and Cara had been surrogate mothers to Marian. At a time when their own lives had not always been easy the Hennell sisters had guided their awkward young neighbour from morbid late adolescence, through the traumas of the holy war and the pain of various bad love affairs, to the watershed of her father's death and something approaching maturity. They had presided over Marian's transformation from a priggish schoolgirl into the cleverest woman in the land. The bear rug under Rosehill's acacia tree had been the setting for one of the greatest intellectual and social educations of the century. And now she was telling them that they had probably never been very interested in her anyway.

Just as the holy war was the result of nearly a year of simmering family tension about power, precedence and accommodation, so the split from Rosehill, which never really healed, had been brewing for a couple of years. Soon after Marian arrived at the *Westminster*, Charles Bray had taken it upon himself to tell Sara that Marian's feelings towards her had changed. Sara, deeply hurt, wrote demanding to know whether it was true, which in turn prompted a strangely ambiguous response from Marian. The letter starts, reassuringly enough, by declaring that, as far as Mary Ann is concerned, Charles Bray 'was never more completely in error. If there is any change in my affection for you, it is that I love you more than ever, not less.' Then the tone becomes heavy with hints. 'I have admitted to Mr Bray that I perceived what it was in you that frequently repelled him and chilled his affection for you.' Having planted seeds of doubt, Mary Ann then scampers back into declarations of continued affection along the lines of 'I do believe in my love for you and that it will remain as long as I have my senses'.[9] This crazy swing between snub and sugar exactly recalled Mary Ann's letters to Maria Lewis, just at the point when she was suffocating under the older woman's plea for reassurance. Now the newly named Marian, busy making friends and lovers in London, no longer felt that Sara understood her life or had any real place in it.

After another exchange of proud, clumsy letters between Weimar and Cov-entry in the autumn of 1854, Cara stopped writing. Sara, however, continued to try to make sense of their changed relationship. 'I have a strange sort of feeling that I am writing to some one in a book and not the Marian that we have known and loved so many years', she wrote in the 'birthday' letter of 15 November which she always sent around the time of their joint anniversaries. 'Do not mistake me, I mean nothing unkind.'[10] As a symbol of what had been lost, she stitched a small Ax into the letter, a tiny reminder that for so many years Marian had delighted to call her 'Achates', after the best friend of Virgil's hero Aeneas.

While the Rosehill women quietly tried to come to terms with Marian's changed allegiances, Charles Bray was busy attempting to defend her reputation at large. As one of the two men to whom Marian had confided her plans – Chapman was the other – he was left explaining her behaviour to a spluttering George Combe. Bray's first tactic was to suggest that Marian and Lewes were merely platonic travelling companions, and when this started to look thin he hastened to reassure Combe that 'my wife and Miss Hennell are sadly troubled about all this and wish me to say that Miss E's going had not their sanction, because they knew nothing at all about it'.[11] Self-involved as ever, Combe was mortified to think that the woman whose skull he had pronounced perfect turned out to have a character which made a monkey out of phrenology, not to mention his own reputation. Desperate to reclaim the high ground for the practice of bump reading he asked Bray in an anguished letter whether there was 'insanity in Miss Evans's family; for her conduct, with *her* brain, seems to me to be like . . . morbid mental aberration'. Complacently sweeping aside Bray's own irregular sexual life, which he knew included an illegitimate second family, Combe proceeded to quiz him about what would happen if Marian tried to return to Rosehill. 'If you receive her into your family circle, while present appearances are unexplained,' he wheedled, 'pray consider whether you will do justice to your own female domestic circle, and how other ladies may feel about going into a circle which makes no distinction between those who act thus, and those who preserve their honour unspotted'.[12]

Bray's response was a carefully judged attempt to distance himself from Marian's behaviour, while preserving the integrity of phrenology as an accurate tool for predicting behaviour. 'Mind I have no wish to defend the part she is taking – only I do not judge her,' he told Combe hypocritically. 'I don't think she is *mad*. She had organically, all the intellectual strength of a man and . . . in feeling all the peculiar weaknesses of woman.'[13]

At the same time as she was writing to Charles Bray defending Lewes's character and her decision to be with him, Marian was conducting a parallel correspondence with John Chapman. Her letter of 15 October starts with a rejection of the rumour that Lewes has abandoned his family before launching into the kind of martyrish set piece which had so offended the Coventry women: 'I have counted the cost of the step that I have taken and am prepared to bear, without irritation or bitterness, renunciation by all my friends. I am not mistaken in the person to whom I have attached myself. He is worthy of the sacrifice I have incurred, and my only anxiety is that he should be rightly judged.'[14]

Luckily, Chapman was unoffendable. In any case, he was thoroughly enjoying being at the heart of the biggest scandal to hit London for years. Although, with the *Westminster* under so much pressure from the high-minded Unitarian lobby, it would have made sense to put distance between himself and Marian, he could not resist drawing attention to their earlier love affair. He frantically boasted to Robert Chambers that, far from being an innocent, Miss Evans had once thrown herself sexually at him. When this rumour spread too quickly and too fast, Chapman was left trying to backtrack, panicking to Chambers: 'A word about Miss E[vans]. – I am very anxious that what I *said* to you about *her especially*, should be regarded as strictly confidential . . . I should be sorry . . . to be thought disposed to disparage her. I only dropped the word I did because I felt that Lewes was not as you imagined almost alone to blame.' Then he continued with extraordinary hypocrisy, 'Now I can only pray, against hope, that . . . [Lewes] may prove constant to her; otherwise she is *utterly* lost.'[15]

. Those who spluttered loudest at Marian's and Lewes's departure for the Continent were defending their own personal and professional interests. Combe, for instance, had long disliked Lewes because of his rejection of phrenology as so much bunk. And he was as twitchy as ever about the bad publicity which would stick to the progressive cause in general. 'T. Hunt, Lewes, and Miss Evans have, in my opinion, by their practical conduct, inflicted a great injury on the cause of religious freedom,' he thundered to Charles Bray.[16] And to make his point he gave up his subscription to the *Leader*. Joseph Parkes, too, received the news 'in a white rage, as if on the verge of a paralytic stroke', believing that the behaviour of his one-time favourite had put back the progressive cause by a hundred years.[17] The fact that Parkes ran a mistress in tandem with a wife was apparently not the same thing at all.

Likewise, Harriet Martineau's reaction to Marian's 'elopement' was fuelled by her rivalry with Lewes over who was the greater authority on Auguste Comte. Stirred up by a flabby intervention from John Chapman, Martineau retreated into paranoid fantasy. She put around the story that Marian had written her an 'insulting' letter from Weimar, presumably crowing about her life with Lewes. Unlikely though this was, in London's overheated atmosphere this scrap was sufficiently plausible to get repeated at the Reform Club. Martineau had always been pathologically jealous of women who acted on their sexuality: she fell out with Elizabeth Barrett when she went off with Browning and thought that her good friend Charlotte Brontë had spoiled *Villette* by going on too much about love. Now she became apoplectic at the thought that Miss Evans was enjoying sexual happiness with that little mountebank Lewes. Seldom nice about anyone, Martineau specialized in the long-held grudge. Her autobiography, written fifteen or so years before her death but published posthumously, was full of jibes, spites and rages against all those who had crossed her, particularly her brother James. Marian hated its score-keeping, but was perhaps relieved to find that she was not mentioned. So it was lucky that she never saw a letter which Martineau wrote to a friend during Lewes's long decline: 'Do you know that Lewes is likely to die? . . . What will . . . [Miss Evans] do? Take a successor, I shd expect.'[18]

News of the Harriet Martineau complication arrived in Weimar on 11 October in the form of 'a painful letter from London [which] caused us both a bad night'.[19] It had come from Thomas Carlyle, the veteran writer and Germanist who had been one of Lewes's mentors ever since his arrival in London almost twenty years ago. In his letter Carlyle raised the more general accusation that Marian had taken Lewes away from his wife and family. Lewes's response has been lost, but it seems to have done the trick, because Carlyle's next letter is much more sympathetic. This in turn prompted Lewes to explode in a baroque expression of relieved thanks. 'I sat at your feet when my mind was first awakening; I have honoured and loved you ever since both as teacher and friend, and *now* to find that you judge me rightly, and are not estranged by what has estranged so many from me, gives me strength to bear what yet must be borne!' He then goes on to reassure Carlyle that 'there is no foundation for the scandal as it runs. My separation was in nowise caused by the lady named, nor by any other lady.' As for the whole Martineau business, he promises Carlyle that Marian 'has *not* written to Miss Martineau at all – has had no communication with her for twelvemonths – has sent no message to her, or any one else – in short this letter is a pure, or impure, fabrication – the letter, the purport, the language, all fiction'.[20]

Although Carlyle was apparently appeased by this explanation – he knew just how odd Miss Martineau could be – a note which he added on the bottom of Lewes's second letter suggests that he continued to disapprove of Marian, whom he sniggeringly dubbed 'the strong-minded woman'. This was not out of any loyalty to Agnes – indeed, he had urged Lewes to part from her. But the idea that Miss Evans was now in Weimar working with Lewes on Goethe unsettled him. More than anyone, Carlyle had been responsible for introducing the great man's life and work to Britain. He looked upon Lewes as his natural heir and was happy for him to write the first biography of Goethe in English. But it was quite a different matter to contemplate an interloper – albeit a supremely well-qualified one – admitted to the sacred cause. Having the Goethe biography dedicated to him may have gone a long way towards reconciling Carlyle to Lewes, but he never learned to like – or approve of – his strong-minded companion.

Painful though all this gossip was, it may have provided the necessary spur for Lewes to separate formally from Agnes. For it was on 23 October that Marian wrote her oblique letter to Bray in which she hinted that 'circumstances with which I am not concerned, and which have arisen since he left England, have led him to determine on a separation from Mrs Lewes'.[21] Could it be that those 'circumstances' were the surprising severity of London's reaction to Lewes's and Marian's departure, including some nasty speculation that this might be a temporary arrangement? Was it at this point that Lewes realised that his strategy of acting with tact and discretion towards the two women in his life had only increased the scope for vicious rumours about them? Whatever the exact reasoning, it was now that George Henry Lewes told Marian Evans that his future lay with her alone.

★ ★ ★

Lewes was welcomed in Weimar with a respect and affection that would have surprised and annoyed literary London. His interest in German philosophy and literature went back to 1838 when he had spent nine months in Berlin and Vienna learning the language. Armed on that occasion with a letter of introduction from Carlyle, the young Lewes adopted his usual strategy of making contacts, flirting with women and reading frantically. With the Shelley biography abandoned, he had turned to Germany's greatest poet and literary figure instead. Over the next ten years Lewes fitted bits and pieces of research on Goethe into his crazy schedule, but never managed to go beyond secondary sources. Now, finally, he was returning to Germany in an attempt to fill out and finish a book that lay close to his heart.

Marian recorded her impression of Weimar in three separate and overlapping accounts. As was to become her habit, she wrote up her journal retrospectively, organising 'Recollections of Weimar 1854' at a distance of a few weeks in Berlin, the city to which she and Lewes travelled next. From this seedbed she wrote two money-spinning articles about Weimar which appeared in *Fraser's Magazine* in June and July 1855.[22] The result is an unusually detailed account of the first three months of her full-time life with Lewes.

Marian's first reaction to Weimar when she arrived on 2 August was: 'how could Goethe live here in this dull, lifeless village?' Although the sleepy atmosphere and old-fashioned buildings reminded her of an English market town, there was none of the plump prosperity she was used to in Warwickshire. The local sheep were 'as dingy as London sheep and far more skinny'. Still, the lodgings which she and Lewes quickly found were comfortable, even if the landlady and her maid had the freakish features of pantomime peasants.[23]

Lewes, the accomplished networker, started making calls immediately. Armed with a letter of introduction from Strauss he contacted Gustav Scholl, director of the Art Institute, who had edited Goethe's letters and essays. Scholl was at the heart of Weimarian society and through him Lewes and Marian met the resident intellectual community. No one, not even the two Englishmen who lived permanently in Weimar and almost certainly knew that Marian was not married, cared about her unusual situation. She was included in every invitation issued to Lewes and was soon absorbed in the kind of semi-public social life which was now closed to her in London.

But it was Lewes who came up with the introduction that meant most. During his 1839 stay in Vienna he had met Franz Liszt. Now the composer had been reincarnated as the Duke of Weimar's kapellmeister, a post which had once been held by Bach. Marian approached the maestro with something approaching rapture. To Charles Bray she confided that Liszt was 'the first really inspired man I ever saw', while to Bessie Rayner Parkes she gushed, 'he is a glorious creature in every way.'[24]

While Marian was partly responding to Liszt's musicianship – 'for the first time I heard the true tones of the piano' – it was the parallels between the great man and her own dear Lewes which fired her imagination.[25] Liszt was a plain man in whose 'divine ugliness' she insisted on seeing a great soul breaking through. This, she claimed unsurprisingly, 'is my favourite kind of physique' and went on to use it as a model for the musician Klesmer in *Daniel Deronda*.[26] The similarities between Liszt and Lewes went further: the composer was living with a woman to whom he was not married. Princess Carolyne Sayn-Wittgenstein had recently left her husband and, although in Russia her infidelity was punished by the confiscation of her estates, in Weimar she was treated with common sense and courtesy. Although Marian responded to the Princess with her usual defensiveness – 'she is short and unbecomingly endowed with embonpoint' – not to mention the 'blackish' teeth and 'barbarian' profile, the likeness in their situation soon softened her.[27] Before long, Lewes and Marian were meeting Liszt and his princess every couple of days and through them were introduced to Clara Schumann and Anton Rubinstein, as well as to the work of Wagner. The first two they found interesting, the third – billed as 'the music of the future' – puzzling.

What shines through Marian's accounts of this first month in Germany is her intense pleasure at finally being openly and fully close to the man she loved: 'I am happier every day and find my domesticity more and more delightful and beneficial to me,' she sang to John Chapman.[28] For the first time since she had met Lewes she was enjoying the everyday intimacies of married life: waking up together, taking a picnic in the park, wandering to nowhere in particular. They even carved their initials in the little wooden hut where Goethe spent his summers. Lewes, his health better than at any time in the previous year, was back to his usual buoyant self, entertaining her with his impressions of Edmund Kean, recounting a dreadful night spent trying to lecture the working class of Hackney on *Othello*. Under the spell of their emotional and sexual compatibility, what had first seemed charmless and provincial about Weimarian culture now revealed itself as unpretentiously joyful. Marian noted with pleasure how the people flocked to the park in the evenings to take coffee and how they attended the nearby theatre without any fuss as to dress or etiquette. When she wrote up her recollections retrospectively, the park at Weimar became a symbol of the new freedom in her relationship with Lewes: 'Dear Park of Weimar! In 1854, two loving, happy human beings spent many a delicious hour in wandering under your shade and in your sunshine, and to one of them at least you will be a "joy for ever" through all the sorrows that are to come.'[29]

But by the time she came to write these words these sorrows were more than distant phantoms. Marian and Lewes arrived in Berlin on 3 November in search of good libraries and new Goethe contacts. Under the charm of their love for one another the unpromising Duchy of Weimar had been turned into a little paradise full of kind-hearted friends and simple goodness.[30] Their Weimarian friends had given them a touching send-off. Liszt had turned up the night before with a bag of sweets for the journey, Scholl had insisted on 'kissing G again and again on the lips'. Even Lora, the ugly little maid, appeared on the station platform with a bouquet for Marian clutched in her grimy hand.

Berlin could not have been more different, with its modern buildings, expensive lodgings, bad beds and streets clogged with overdressed tourists. The season was on the turn and soon heavy snow would blast through the city, making even the short walk from their lodgings to the hotel where they took dinner a chilly ordeal. By this time the painful news from London had trickled in and Marian and Lewes were in the middle of their highly charged correspondences with Thomas Carlyle, John Chapman and Charles Bray. As the reality of their situation broke in upon their dreamy happiness, even the surrounding buildings and streets started to seem oppressive. Hordes of soldiers – '300,000 puppets in uniform' – marched menacingly through the streets.[31]

Still, with George Henry Lewes around it was impossible to be gloomy for long. 'The day seems too short for our happiness, and we both of us feel that we have begun life afresh – with new ambition and new powers,' insisted Marian to John Chapman.[32] On their first morning – a Sunday – they were walking along Unter den Linden when Lewes was accosted by Karl August Varnhagen von Ense, the Goethe scholar whom he had met on his first trip to Germany sixteen years ago. Varnhagen, though elderly, was still a key player in Berlin's intelligentsia and through him Marian and Lewes found themselves with a ready-made social life. At a party which Varnhagen threw for them four days later Marian met Henriette von Solmar, a distinguished hostess who invited the couple to attend one of her near-nightly salons where intellectually minded Berlin gathered for conversation.

No one was bothered by the fact that Marian and Lewes were not married, not even Varnhagen, who had always taken an avuncular interest in Agnes. Likewise Fraülein von Solmar who, as Marian was quick to point out to Charles Bray, moved in 'the best society of Berlin'.[33] Painters, sculptors and scientists, both bachelors and family men, happily welcomed the couple without comment into their homes.

One of these homes, which particularly charmed Marian, belonged to Professor Otto Friedrich Gruppe, a man even more versatile than Lewes, who had written on everything from Greek drama to contemporary politics. In the short piece she wrote on Gruppe for the *Leader* in July 1855 Marian, clearly thinking of Lewes, took the opportunity to point out the advantages of this kind of easy facility. 'Those who decry versatility ... seem to forget the immense service rendered by the *suggestiveness* of versatile men, who come to the subject with fresh, unstrained minds.'[34] But Marian also responded well to Gruppe the specialist, writing favourably of his latest book, *The Future of German Philosophy*, which rejected metaphysics in favour of solid empiricism. Yet more than anything else it was Gruppe's domestic life which caught her imagination. He had married a woman thirty years younger than himself by whom he had two children, and his humble flat at the top of several flights of stairs seemed a perfect tableau of domestic contentment. By this time Marian and Lewes had probably reached the decision not to have children, which may account for Marian's sometimes sentimental accounts of happy German families in her journal entries of these weeks.

Equally interesting was the relationship of Adolf Stahr, a scholar who specialised in Spinoza and Goethe. For the last nine years the still-married Stahr had been living with Fanny Lewald, a feminist and novelist whom Lewes had met during a second trip to Germany in 1845. Although Lewes and Marian had reservations about the pretentious, gossipy couple, they embarked on a cautious friendship with them. One day – 6 February – they arrived at the home they shared only to find that Stahr's divorce had come through and he and Lewald had 'gone to be married at last'.[35] Was it with some wistfulness that Marian later noted that they 'seemed the happier for it'?

Germany was never meant to be a holiday. Lewes and Marian were there to work. Agnes and her expanding brood gobbled up money, and Thornton was following in the Hunt family tradition of flagrant irresponsibility: his financial contributions were sketchy in the extreme. Despite having come to Germany to finish his book, Lewes still needed to generate short-term income. During these months he knocked off two translations of French farce and managed to keep his regular column on the *Leader* ticking over, arranging for his twenty-pound fee to be sent directly to Agnes.

But the main project was Goethe. Surprisingly, there was no good biography in either German or English. Lewes quickly set about gathering the primary material – mainly recollections from people who had known the poet – which would distinguish his book from the lacklustre versions that had gone before. He interviewed two frail old men who had worked as Goethe's secretary before his death, as well as a woman who had been at the court when Goethe first came to Weimar. In Berlin he spoke to the sculptor Christian Rauch, who emphasised just how lovable the great man had been. In Weimar Goethe's daughter-in-law Ottilie arranged for Lewes to see the poet's study and bedroom. Together Marian and Lewes made day trips to the Duke's summer residence, where Goethe had masterminded chamber-scale theatricals, and to Ilmenau, where his small wooden house was set in idyllic surroundings.[36]

Marian's Dorothea-like wish to help a man with his work had at last been granted. Although when she had first met Lewes she was far from thinking anything about him great, observing him work at close quarters had changed her mind. His enthusiasm for Goethe was raw and real, with nothing of the 'bread scholar's' careful calculation. Of course, identification played a part. The German writer's ability to move elegantly between poetry and science helped Lewes find an authority for his own much-mocked versatility. And in Lewes's account of why Goethe broke off his engagement to Frederika Brion – 'he was perfectly right to draw back from an engagement which he felt his love was not strong enough to fulfil' – one hears a coded justification of his ending of the marriage to Agnes.[37]

Although Marian was not instinctively drawn to Goethe, she naturally considered it her duty to become interested. Her insight into his two great novels, *Wilhelm Meister* and *Elective Affinities* – often dismissed as immoral and boring to boot – enriched Lewes's treatment of them and became the basis of an important article she would write for the *Leader* on their return home.[38] In addition she supplied the English translation for the passages that Lewes wanted to extract, as well as for the complicated genealogical tables that appear in the book. For all this she received a credit in the final footnotes as an 'accomplished German translator'.

While Lewes was welcomed in Germany as an old friend and distinguished scholar, Marian was (barely) known as the English translator of Feuerbach and Strauss. Their relative positions in London, with Miss Evans as the highly respected editor of the *Westminster Review* and Lewes as the pushy hack, had been reversed. On the surface this did not bother her. Love had made her temporarily content and happy to take dictation when Lewes's headache stopped him from writing his regular pieces for the *Leader*. Yet only a few months earlier, while in the depths of her own headache, she had written to Cara from London of her 'despair of achieving anything worth the doing'.[39] How long would it be before that restless ambition, part of her nature since her very first day at school, would insist on making itself known once again?

The tensions in Marian's position spilled out in a piece she wrote for the *Westminster Review* from Germany on Victor Cousin's book on Madame de Sablé and other literary women of seventeenth-century France. It is an odd, uneven article, less a review than an essay which uses the three books it is supposed to be noticing as a peg on which to hang a bigger argument. Writing, as always, anonymously, Marian starts with the bold assertion that 'our own feminine literature is made up of books which could have been better written by men.'[40] The only country where this is not the case is France, where 'if the writings of women were swept away, a serious gap would be made in the national history'.

What makes Frenchwomen so different from everyone else? Marian embarks on a strange (to us) physiological argument that the Frenchwoman's 'small brain and vivacious temperament' is better for the business of literature than the English and German woman's more 'dreamy and passive' constitution. She then shifts to ground that sounds familiar, which seems, in fact, like a defence of her own unusual experience of living and working among men. In seventeenth-century France, Marian explains, women ran salons into which they invited the cleverest men of art and science, and so gained a unique access 'to a common fund of ideas, to common objects of interest with men'. The result was not simply beneficial to the women themselves, but allowed them to develop relations with men formed 'in the maturity of thought and feeling, and grounded only on inherent fitness and mutual attraction'. This in turn had an enriching effect on the culture, allowing both men and women to develop their highest potential and write novels out of a sense of their own gendered fullness. Marian ends with a barely disguised plea for her kind of female, one who has used her access to high culture to turn herself into a woman whose intellectual and emotional difference delights the best kind of man. 'Then we shall have that marriage of minds which alone can blend all the hues of thought and feeling in one lovely rainbow of promise for the harvest of human happiness.'

Chapman did not like the article, annoyed by the way his former assistant editor had hijacked a routine commission and turned it into a manifesto for her own scandalous position. Her heavy-handed distancing device – 'heaven forbid that we should enter on a defence of French morals, most of all in relation to marriage!' – was, in the circumstances, plain embarrassing.[41] Chapman was currently under pressure from the high-minded Unitarians to distance himself from the scandalous atheism implied by Miss Evans's decision to live with a man outside marriage. Although he paid her the agreed fifteen pounds for it, he did not write to thank her, nor did he ask her to do any more – a serious blow at a time when she desperately needed to make money. Chapman may also have been piqued by her revelation that she had revised her final draft along lines suggested by Lewes. Even when he was her lover, Chapman would never have presumed to offer Marian advice on her writing, nor would she have accepted it.

During these months in Germany Marian's confidence as a writer fell in proportion as her personal happiness rose. At home the Feuerbach translation had been met either with stony silence or, from James Martineau writing in the *Westminster*, with sneering hostility. Now Marian was facing the realities of life as a free-lance writer, without the prestige of a leading publication behind her. She was dependent on Chapman for any commissions he put her way, a reverse of the previous power balance between them, which showed up in the gushing way she acknowledged his first letter to her at the beginning of August asking her to write the piece on Madame de Sablé. Chapman's cool response to the finished piece made her wary of suggesting other topics, even though, as she told Sara, there were 'plenty of subjects suggested by new German books which would be fresh and instructive in an English Review'.[42] In January she finally plucked up courage to suggest 'Ideals of Womanhood' for the *Westminster* and, when that failed to take, 'Woman in Germany'.[43] Chapman turned this down too, perhaps sensing another strident manifesto on the way, and grudgingly agreed only to a piece on Eduard Vehse's *Memoirs of the Court of Austria*, a cut-and-paste job which hardly stretched her, but did at least pay.

After six months in Germany, Marian had succeeded in producing only a handful of magazine articles. This was not going to be enough to keep her, let alone Lewes's family in London. So when Lewes told her that he had an outstanding contract with a London publisher to produce a translation of Spinoza's *Ethics* she leaped at the chance to do the work for him. 'I cannot bring myself to run the risk of a refusal from an editor,' she explained to Sara, 'so I am working at what will ultimately yield something which is secured by agreement with Bohn [the publisher].'[44] She started work on 8 November and although money was her prime motive, she was far from regarding this as routine work. She had long been interested in the philosopher's clear, logical thought, which had had such an obvious impact on both Feuerbach and Strauss, not to mention Goethe. Almost ten years previously she had started translating Spinoza during a particularly unsettled time in her life and later while she was waiting for her father to die. Now she was to take him up again at a time of great happiness. There was something satisfactory about having come full circle.

Although Marian produced little finished work during these months, still she was reading more than ever before, soaking up material that would feed a burst of creativity once she returned to London. At their lodgings in Dorotheenstrasse Marian and Lewes set up the routine which they would follow for most of their lives. They wrote and translated in the morning, walked in the afternoon and either visited friends or read in the evening, working through Shakespeare, Heine, Lesser, Macaulay and the inevitable Goethe.

By the time Marian came to record her recollections of these evenings in the lodgings, made cosy with coffee, gingerbread and rolls, she was already back in England. After a final hectic week of cultural tourism, she and Lewes had set out for Calais on 11 March 1855, travelling via Brussels and Cologne. This return journey could not have been more different from the one they had made eight months before. On that occasion the Channel had been as smooth and perfect as glass. Now it was sufficiently choppy to make them both sick. On 13 March they got to Dover and spent a queasy night in a hotel before finding lodgings the next day for Marian in Sydney Place. She stayed here alone working on Spinoza, while Lewes went up to London to sort out his family affairs and make arrangements for their future life together.

As Marian reworked her experience of the past few months in her journal she became increasingly aware of how much she had lost by coming home. The Germans might be a coarse, vulgar people who put their knives in their mouths, told unfunny jokes and said what they thought, but they were 'at least free from the bigotry and exclusiveness of their more refined cousins'.[45] Just how bigoted and exclusive those cousins could be she was about to find out.

The month in Dover went miserably. After nearly a year of sociable living with a merry man it was hard to be alone. Marian had not been so isolated since those early years at Griff keeping house for her father and brother. Now once again in exile, she filled her days writing, reading and taking blustery walks over the cliffs.

Working on her journal recollections of Berlin allowed her to revisit the past for a while. But the moment she finished, on 27 March, migraine overwhelmed her. Three solid weeks on Spinoza provided a kind of cure, allowing her to follow the thread back to a more certain time. She continued, too, with the ambitious reading plan begun in the Dorotheenstrasse. Still, it was not enough. She was hankering for Labassecour, for anywhere but this dreary boarding-house where, presumably, she had either to present herself as the spinster 'Miss Marian Evans' or as the married lady 'Mrs George Lewes', when in fact she was neither. Already she was planning a future far away from here, announcing to Bray that the moment Goethe and Spinoza were safely through the press, she and Lewes would take off on 'a new flight to the south of Germany and Italy, for which we both yearn'.[46]

The uncertainty of these few weeks pressed on old and aching bruises. Abandonment was the black thread which ran through Marian's life like a curse. First her mother, then Isaac, then Chapman, Brabant and Spencer had all rejected her demands for love. It was what she knew and what she dreaded. Only two and a half years earlier she had sat alone in a cottage in another south-coast town and begged Herbert Spencer to let her have a corner of his life. Over these recent months in Germany she had finally come to know the pleasure of a mutual love. It was exactly the kind of relationship which suited her: exclusive, isolated, rapt. Now that she was back in Britain, reality pressed down in the shape of other people and circumstances that she could not control. Had she known what London gossip was saying about her situation, she would have felt even greater despair. Speculation was mounting that Lewes would, in the words of Joseph Parkes, 'tire of & put way Miss Evans – as he has done others'.[47]

On 9 April Marian received a 'painful letter' which for the next week made her 'feverish and unable to fix my mind steadily on reading or writing'.[48] Since none of the correspondence between Marian and Lewes has survived, it is impossible to know what it contained. Was Lewes trying to withdraw from Marian? Surely not. Whatever else he might have been, he was a man of his word. Gordon Haight suggests that the problem may have been Agnes, from whom Marian had asked for a definite undertaking that the marriage was over. But years later Cara Bray told Edith Simcox that, far from being tricky, Agnes had sent a message saying that she 'would be very glad if he could marry Miss Evans'.[49] The last time Marian had used the word 'painful' to describe a letter it had been from Thomas Carlyle, repeating Harriet Martineau's wild babblings. Perhaps the April letter was not from Lewes at all, but from a third party repeating some hurtful gossip about her situation.

As a matter of pride Marian did not let her agony seep into her letters. To Sara she maintained that she was 'well and calmly happy' and to Bessie Rayner Parkes she said her mind was 'deliciously calm and untroubled so far as my own lot is concerned'. She repeated her warning to 'believe no one's represen-tations about me, for there is not a *single person* who is in a position to make a true representation'.[50] As ever, she told herself – and her correspondents – that she did not give a fig what they thought about her. Yet she remained acutely attuned to every nuance in their letters, getting pettish with Charles Bray when she thought she detected a cool note.[51]

In the end, Lewes did prove true and Agnes generously straightforward. By mid-April Marian had the undertaking she wanted and Lewes had made the best financial arrangements in the circumstances. On the 18th she went up to town and joined him at lodgings in Bayswater. This may not have been the first time they had described themselves as 'Mr and Mrs Lewes', but it was certainly the beginning of what they referred to as their marriage. It worried feminists, then and now, that when Marian Evans went to live with George Henry Lewes she insisted on being known as his 'wife' and calling herself 'Mrs Lewes'. It looked as if Marian Evans, that 'strong-minded woman', was cowering behind the formal conventions of suburban womanhood.

In a way she was. Landladies, those sharp-eyed Mrs Grundys who had loomed so large in her adult life, would almost certainly have turned away any couple who announced themselves as Mr Lewes and Miss Evans. But there was a principle at stake too, even if it was one which some found hard to understand. Marian had never been anything but a believer in marriage, a point which she made graphically when she married John Cross at the end of her life. Both through the voice of Feuerbach, and in her own words in the 'Woman in France' essay, she had written of the need for a true marriage, which brings a whole man and a whole woman together in voluntary association. What appalled her about legal marriage was its shackling of men and women who hardly knew one another in relationships that were almost bound to fail. Once love had died the two parties were condemned, like Rochester and Bertha, or Lewes and Agnes, or Goethe and Frederika, to a dreary wasteland where incompatibility turned to indifference or worse. For as long as Marian felt that she and Lewes had a truly moral marriage she would claim the right to be known as Mrs Lewes.

No matter how many times Marian explained her position, some friends continued to refer to her as 'Miss Evans'. Bessie Rayner Parkes was the worst culprit, her 'forgetfulness' a measure of the confusion she felt about her own future. Increasingly absorbed in campaigns to improve education and employment opportunities for single women, Bessie had by now embarked on her half-hearted ten-year engagement to Sam Blackwell. This was also the time when she was receiving bullying letters from her adulterous father warning her to stay away from Miss Evans and her 'vice'. In the circumstances it was hardly surprising that Bessie started to become anxious about what the institution of marriage meant for women and what it might have in store for her. Writing to her fiancé during the height of the gossip about Marian in the autumn of 1854, she declared with preachy nervousness, 'Now when we remember the men who form illegal connexions sub rosâ – who do vile & bad things, & keep up a white washed character, I feel more lenient to that little Weimar home than others do.'[52] Was this a hint to her fiancé that she would not countenance the kind of marriage which her mother had endured? In any event, the engagement with Blackwell was finally broken off in 1866. The following year, at the age of thirty-seven, she married Louis Belloc, by whom she had a son, Hilaire, and a daughter.

On 30 April Bessie defied her father's ban and called on the Leweses. The next day Marian wrote to her – by way of Barbara Leigh Smith – with a reminder to send any letters 'care of G. H. Lewes Esq'. But a year later Bessie was still addressing Marian by her maiden name, for which she received a sharp rebuke: 'Your address to me as *Miss Evans* was unfortunate, as I am not known under that name here. We find it indispensable to our comfort that I should bear Mr. Lewes's name while we occupy lodgings, and we are now with so excellent a woman that any cause of removal would be a misfortune. If you have occasion to write to me again, please to bear this in mind.'[53]

Part of Bessie's reluctance to acknowledge Marian's 'marriage' came from the scandalous things she had heard about Lewes from her father. It was not until her close friend Barbara Leigh Smith spent some time with the couple a year later that Bessie really began to accept the arrangement. In August 1856 Barbara joined Lewes and Marian for a few days at Tenby where they were on an extended holiday. She had come to see Marian and at this point merely tolerated Lewes, whom she considered in that snobbish way of which the Victorian avant-garde were quite capable to be not quite a 'gentleman'. She left Wales, however, with a completely different view, writing to Bessie, 'I do wish, my dear, that you would revise your view of Lewes. I have quite revised mine. Like you, I thought him an extremely sensual man. Marian tells me that in their intimate marital relationship he is unsensual, extremely considerate.

His manner to her is delightful. It is plain to me that he makes her extremely happy.'[54]

Although Bessie's and Barbara's visits went well, Marian was far from relaxed when the rest of her friends made that first symbolic call to see the new Mrs Lewes. For women like Rufa Hennell, widowed in 1850 and not to remarry until 1857, it was a bold decision. For the mid-Victorians sin, especially female sexual sin, was a contaminating mist, which could envelop bystanders who got too close. Marian was flummoxed to see Rufa on 28 April, but blamed her panic lamely on a lack of fresh air: 'I was so stupified and heated by having sat in-doors writing all day, that she must have carried away anything but a charming image of me.'[55]

Charles Bray's visit was even more tense. He did not come and see the Leweses until 10 July, by which time they had moved to accommodation in East Sheen, near Richmond. It was the first time that he had ever seen them together and he probably felt as odd about it as they did. Knowing how much Bray disliked Lewes, Marian was clearly terrified that he would try to make mischief. A short while before, she had written to him begging him not to repeat a cutting remark she had made about Lewes two or three years earlier.[56] Bray refrained from such obvious tactics during his visit, but when he found Marian taking her 'husband's' side in yet another argument about phrenology he dressed up his jealousy as high-minded disappointment. Lewes was down with a cold and a face abscess, and so unable to work his distracting magic on what sounds like a leaden evening. Writing a few days later to Bray, Marian excused 'the fact of my having been ill as some apology for the very imperfect companionship and entertainment I gave you'.[57]

When Sara Hennell came to visit in early September the fates were equally unhelpful. She called without warning and found the Leweses out on a river trip.[58] Perhaps this was part of a bridge-building exercise by the Hennell sisters, because around the same time as Sara's letter explaining about the aborted visit came one from Cara, framed as a query about what Marian wanted done with some bed linen stored at Rosehill. Cara was too conscientious a woman simply to drop her objections to Marian's relationship. This was the first Marian had heard from her since Weimar. But although she seems to have repeated her disapproval in her letter, there was something about it that made Marian sense she would be open to a reply. On 4 September Marian sat down and wrote the most cogent and considered statement of her actions to date. She reassures Cara that 'if there is any one action or relation of my life which is and always has been profoundly serious, it is my relation to Mr Lewes ... Light and easily broken ties are what I neither desire theoretically nor could live for practically. Women who are satisfied with such ties do *not* act as I have done – they obtain what they desire and are still invited to dinner.' The haughty, martyrish tone which had given so much offence over the past year is now gone. Instead, Marian dwells with gratitude on the love she has received from Cara: 'I think not one of the endless words and deeds of kindness and forbearance you have ever shewn me has vanished from my memory.'[59]

The letter – sweet, dignified – got Cara and Marian writing again, although it would be another four years before they met. Both sides remained jumpy. Only four months later, at New Year 1856, Marian wrote to Charles Bray to tell him how humiliated she felt by the fact that an invitation to visit Rosehill had been issued by him alone.

> I have never answered your note in which you invited me to call at your house on my way to my sister's [where she was staying over Christmas]. I am sure that note was written with the kindest intentions, but if you had thought twice you would have seen that I was not likely to take a journey twice as long as necessary and walk all through Coventry in order to make a call where I had only the invitation of the master of the house.[60]

The rudeness of the note suggests Marian's hypersensitivity about how she was treated and the roots of her growing social isolation. Ever attentive to the slightest snub, she made it a rule never to accept invitations from even her most well-meaning friends. There was a danger that she might visit their home only to find some fellow guest or high-minded servant taking offence. Even the most fleeting contact with an acquaintance in the street ran the risk of a cold shoulder. For that reason Marian barely went to London: during her first year in south-west London she made the journey only a couple of times, giving the awful smokiness as her reason for staying away. Any errands or business was done by Lewes, who made a weekly trip to see Agnes and the children at Bedford Place.

For the same reason Marian shunned her neighbours in Park Shot, Richmond, to which they had moved in October 1855. Her letters and journals never mention the kind of casual socialising that was supposed to be one of the great advantages of this new kind of semi-rural living. There was no bumping into a friendly face in the park, no gossiping in a shop. Terrified of the cut which would follow once rumour got around of her 'unfortunate position' Marian kept herself to herself, avoiding all but the most necessary and anonymous contact with others.

What started as a protective strategy became, over time, a preferred option. Once Marian became famous through her writing and her irregular relationship achieved some kind of respectability through its longevity, she began to receive an increasing number of invitations – to dinner, to the theatre, to parties. But still she refused, proudly insisting that people had to come to her. This reached its apogee with the Sunday afternoons at the Priory from the late 1860s, that salon-type arrangement which Marian had praised in her essay 'Woman in France'. By this time she had reached iconic status and every week twenty or more men – and it was mainly men – filed into the drawing-room for an audience. It was an arrangement which suited her psychologically. By controlling whom she came into contact with, Lewes ensured that no snigger, snub or critical remark ever reached her ears to upset her frail equilibrium.

Later there would be criticism that Marian's by now self-imposed isolation led her to become cut off from the feedback which would have disciplined her work, stopping her falling into the self-indulgence of *Romola* and *The Spanish Gypsy*. But at this stage in her career it had the opposite effect, allowing her to concentrate all her energies on her writing. The creative drought which had hit in Germany, perhaps as a result of too many invitations to dinner, disappeared. Now under pressure to earn money to support Agnes Lewes, Marian found a new energy for her work. Chapman had written to her at Dover, offering the 'Belles Lettres' section of the magazine. Although the twelve pounds a quarter were extremely welcome, the benefits were far more than financial. Over the next two years Marian read and reviewed 166 books, which amounted to an intensive course in contemporary literature, particularly fiction. In the process she noticed what worked and what did not, what she liked and what seemed stale and contrived. As her desire to write fiction pushed further to the front of her mind, she started to think seriously about the kind of novel she wanted to write. Thus when she read *Westward Ho!*, Charles Kingsley's Elizabethan romance, she warmed to the bold, vivid adventure, but hated the bossy, priggish narrator who sounded like a parson giving a sermon. Kingsley had a nasty habit of pulling at the reader's sleeve, telling her whom to like, and whom to reject as utterly awful: 'he can never trust to the impression that scene itself will make on you, but, true to his cloth, must always "improve the occasion",' wrote Marian in the review which appeared in the July 1855 edition.[61]

It was this nursery-rhyme morality which Marian also objected to in Geraldine Jewsbury's *Constance Herbert*. Here the three good-as-gold heroines renounce marriage because they fear passing on the strain of inherited madness which snakes through their family. But over time it becomes clear that in each case the fiancé they gave up was a bad lot anyway. In her review Marian railed against this 'notion that duty looks stern, but all the while has her hand full of sugar-plums, with which she will reward us by and by'.[62]

This plea for fiction which represented life as it is, not life as it ought to be, continued in the articles which Marian wrote for the *Leader*. In the eighteen months following her return from the Continent she wrote thirty-one articles for the weekly, for which she got about a guinea apiece. Control of the magazine had passed from Lewes and Hunt – who had left to edit the *Telegraph* – to Edward Pigott, a delightful man who visited the new couple on their holiday in Tenby and was one of the few friends of Lewes to write John Cross a letter of congratulation when he married Marian. Pigott was happy to let Marian write a piece on Goethe as a pre-publication puff for Lewes's forthcoming biography. She chose to write a piece defending the detached stance Goethe takes in *Wilhelm Meister* towards his characters, a practice which was customarily viewed as 'destitute of moral bias'. Unlike Kingsley and Jewsbury, Goethe lets his people work out their own destiny, rewarding them with neither torment nor bliss, but with a mixed bag of indifferent outcomes. And this, points out Marian, is not only because life has a way of dishing out deserts randomly but because it is impossible, truly, to know who is good or bad. 'Everywhere he [Goethe] brings us into the presence of living, generous humanity – mixed and erring, and self-deluding,' she explains with obvious approval, 'but saved from utter corruption by the salt of some noble impulse, some disinterested effort, some beam of good nature, even though grotesque or homely.'[63]

In the event, the Goethe biography needed no pre-publication push from

Marian. It was a magnificent book, showing Lewes at his best: lucid, humane, agile. It would be hard to think of anyone better able to follow Goethe through every aspect of his versatile life, from the stage to science, from poetry to philosophy. Lewes's *Goethe* did more than any other book of the century to bring German culture to the middling mass of Britons. A popular and critical success, it sold quickly and garnered admiring reviews from the quality press. It turned out to be a major money-spinner, too, bringing Lewes a significant income for the rest of his life. But this was not why Marian thought so highly of the book. 'I can't tell you how I value it', she wrote to Bray, 'as the best product of a mind which I have every day more reason to admire and love.'[64]

Goethe was one of those people whom the subject of Marian's next *Westminster* piece would have consigned to the everlasting flames. Dr John Cumming was a minister of the Scottish National Church whose hell-fire-and-brimstone sermons typified the rigid, ungenerous version of Protestant Christianity which Marian had embraced in her youth.[65] Cumming concentrated his attention lovingly on what hell would feel like, and little time on what a life dedicated to Christ would entail. He disregarded the small virtues of everyday life – a conjugal kindness, a voluntary honesty – in favour of an all-embracing duty to give one's life to the Lord. Instead of reaching the divine through loving her husband, a wife should be careful that she was not distracted from her love of God. It would be hard to imagine a greater antithesis to Feuerbach.

Cumming's hell was kept alight not only with Puseyites who had gone over to Rome but with the souls of doubters, those men and women like Marian who wanted to believe, but who wrestled daily with the implications of revealed religion. Instead of a helping hand, Cumming offered them only gleeful spite. 'Nowhere in his pages have we found a humble, candid, sympathetic attempt to meet the difficulties that may be felt by an ingenious mind,' reported Marian. 'Everywhere he supposes that the doubter is hardened, conceited, consciously shutting his eyes to the light.'[66]

The piece is confident, probably because Marian had only to think herself back into the 'dogmatic perversions' of her youth to experience the kind of mind which could have produced such an unlovely doctrine: small, hard, frightened. Lewes was stunned by its fluency, and during a walk in Richmond Park told her that he was convinced 'of the true genius in her writing'.[67] Others thought so too. Back in Coventry, Mary Sibree, now Mrs John Cash, whose life had been so profoundly touched by the holy war, read the piece out to the Brays, who all agreed that 'it must be yours . . . No one else *could* do it.'[68]

It was fortunate that Marian scored such a success so soon after coming back from Germany, because only five months later she experienced her first major publishing set-back. With Lewes's 'big book' now safely through the press, it was time to pay attention to Marian's. She finished translating Spinoza's *Ethics* in February 1856 and looked forward to her reward. 'You don't know what a severely practical person I am become, and what a sharp eye I have to the main chance,' she wrote to Bray. It was probably money matters which lay behind her request to him in the same letter to 'be so good as not to mention *my* name in connection with . . . [Spinoza]. I particularly wish not to be known as the translator of the Ethics.'[69] It was Lewes, after all, who had the contract with the publisher, not she. As far as we know, his plan was to fudge the issue of authorship when he presented the finished work to Bohn.

But it never got that far. Since 1854, when the arrangement had been made, Bohn senior had grown lukewarm about publishing Spinoza and used the fact that Lewes had made an oral contract with his son as a justification for renegotiating the price. Writing to Lewes, he asked him to come and see him with the manuscript 'and we will then enter into a proper agreement'. At this Lewes took great offence and dashed off an angry letter: 'I altogether decline to have transactions with a man who shows such wonderful facility in forgetting . . . I beg you will send back my m.s. and consider the whole business at an end between us.'[70] Punch-drunk on his success with Goethe, Lewes may have believed that he could afford to swagger. But despite approaching another publisher, he failed to get the *Ethics* published.

It was an extraordinary episode. In the *Westminster–Leader* circle, there were plenty of pompous men only too ready to huff and puff when they considered themselves insulted. But Lewes was not one of them. Nimble and pragmatic, he was used to dealing with publishers and editors who played it less than straight. So why did he fly off the handle at a little sharp practice? Guilt may have been part of it, the recognition that he himself was going to effect a sleight of hand by implying that Marian's work was his own. But he may also have taken offence at the implication that Bohn was not keen to publish a book about ethics from London's most notorious adulterer.

If it had been any other man in Marian's life who had sabotaged fifteen months' solid work it would be tempting to see envy at work. But in their twenty-five years together Lewes never said or did a nasty thing towards Marian. He honoured her talent as the greater, but refused to feel dwarfed by comparison. He had lived long and hard enough to be simply grateful when her work turned out to generate sufficient income to allow him to give up journalism and turn to the kind of serious scientific work he had so longed to do. Perhaps in these post-Germany months he had grown as touchy as Marian about imagined slights. Never in the least protective of his own reputation, he none the less felt responsible for hers. If he had the faintest suspicion that Bohn knew that the translation was by Marian and had rejected it because of her 'unfortunate' situation he would have rushed into the fray like the shaggy Skye terrier he physically resembled.

For Marian the Spinoza incident must have seemed like a bad omen for her new life with Lewes, which she had always envisaged as a blending of personal affection and shared intellectual endeavour. She had published two translations without the help of a 'husband', and must surely have wondered what lesson could be learned from Lewes's failure to complete on a deal which had seemed so certain.

The loss of income from fifteen months' worth of work could not have come at a worse time. While Marian and Lewes had been in Germany Agnes Lewes had run up a big debt. Her emotional generosity towards her husband and his new partner was part and parcel of an optimistic personality, which assumed that there would always be enough to go round – with some to spare. This contrasted sharply with Marian, who had grown up in a household where love and money were carefully measured out. Even at her wealthiest she kept a sharp eye on her accounts. Still, she never took refuge in the resentful carping of a second wife, nor in the farmer's daughter's disapproval of the feckless gentry. Even after Lewes's death she continued to pay Agnes an annual allowance.

In the circumstances it was easier for Marian and Lewes to focus their angry feelings on Thornton Hunt. Despite the fact that he now had a regular wage from his post at the *Telegraph*, Hunt showed little inclination to provide for the three children he had so far fathered by Agnes. Lewes remained legally responsible for the support of all the offspring who bore his name, as well as Agnes's outstanding debt. To tide him over he took out a loan, but continued to press Hunt to fulfil his responsibilities. Finally, on 16 December 1856 Hunt panicked, snapped and responded with a display of injured innocence and a challenge to a duel. It was a silly, flamboyant gesture, typical of the whole self-dramatising Hunt clan.

Concentrating his resentment on Hunt allowed Lewes to remain on cordial, if occasionally exasperated, terms with Agnes. He visited his three sons once a week and until 1859 kept some of his books at Bedford Place, a point which has sometimes puzzled biographers. Although the children were old enough, at thirteen, eleven and nine, to wonder why their father lived apart from their mother, they seem to have inherited his constitutional gaiety and determination never to be a drag on others. Lewes had not spoken about his new domestic situation to the boys and the occasional surviving letter to them makes no mention of Marian. When he took them to the beach at Margate for a week in 1855 she stayed behind in Richmond. As far as the boys were concerned, life went on much the same with Mama, their nurse Martha Baker ('Nursie'), a string of new babies and regular visits from Uncle Thornton and Papa.

It is a credit to Lewes that he remained an active, loving father to his sons. His letters to them are affectionate, playful and respectful, quite unlike anybody's idea of a remote Victorian papa. From Germany he wrote: 'Here I am in the capital of the Grand duchy of Weimar, about which you, Thornie, know something already, I have no doubt – or soon will. It is a very queer little place although called the "Athens of Germany" on account of the great poets who have lived here; one of them, the greatest of all, you know already by the portraits and little bust in our house – I mean *Goethe*.'[71]

But jolly letters from a glamorous father were not going to constitute a sufficient education for the Lewes boys. The problem of where to send them to school was looming. Charles and Thornie were presently at Bayswater Grammar, but Lewes did not think it would do for much longer. Marian was clearly involved in the discussion too, for in April 1856 she wrote to Charles Bray asking if he thought her old friend John Sibree would be prepared to tutor the boys.[72] Having given up the ministry, Sibree now made his living by that precarious mix of tutoring and translation. His free-thinking credentials were impeccable and his published work on Hegel well regarded. It would be hard to think of a more erudite, sceptical, authentic man in whom to place the education of the sons of G. H. Lewes.

But Sibree said no, perhaps out of a reluctance to become involved once more with the woman whom his parents blamed for ruining his life. Sara Hennell stepped in with details of Hofwyl, a Swiss school run along Pestalozzian lines which the Noel brothers had attended. It was perfect for the Lewes boys, offering the kind of liberal, wide-ranging and above all European education which had so distinctively shaped their father. It was also far enough away from London to keep them clear of painful gossip about their parents' situation. On 25 August 1855 Lewes picked up his sons at London Bridge station and took them via Paris to Berne. He stayed for three days to settle them in at the school, before returning to a toothachy Marian who always found separation from Lewes painful, especially when it was caused by his previous life.

Besides paying the school fees, Lewes gave Agnes an annual allowance which was never less than £250. In 1855, a good year thanks to Goethe, his income was only £430 13s. This meant that he and Marian had to live in an extremely modest way. The house at Richmond was small, and Marian later recalled how difficult it was to concentrate on her writing with Lewes's pen scratching away on the other side of the room. Their diet was meagre to the point where they often felt faint. Marian's early experience as a housekeeper enabled her to budget effectively and with a certain grim pleasure she told Bray, 'I keep the purse and dole out sovereigns with all the pangs of a miser.'[73] Holiday plans were often changed at the last minute because of a lack of funds. In Germany, for instance, the original idea had been to go to Dresden from Weimar, but the money would not stretch to it and they travelled straight to Berlin instead. Staying in Ilfracombe for seven weeks in early summer 1856, Marian rationed them to just two trips up the Tor, because the threepence-a-head charge was too expensive to allow for any more visits.[74]

Money and family were equally entwined in Marian's life, and had been ever since that day in 1841 when Isaac had shouted that her odd behaviour was draining her father's capital. As a woman she did not have direct access to her own income and depended on her brother to deliver her twice-yearly interest payments. Disapproving of what he knew of her life in London, Isaac did his best to make things difficult. Preparing to leave for Weimar, she had asked him to make sure that her next instalment was paid to Charles Bray promptly on the due date, 1 December. Isaac, reluctant to write letters, or at least to write them to Marian, sent a message via Chrissey that he would pay the interest when he received it and no sooner.[75] This put her in an awkward situation with Charles Bray, who was no longer wealthy enough to accommodate a shortfall, and who had already kindly advanced her December payment. So when some months later, now in anxious exile in Dover, Marian wrote to Isaac to ask him from now on to pay her income straight into the Coventry and Warwickshire Bank, she had little confidence that he would do as she asked since, as she told Bray, 'he is not precise in answering letters (mine at least) [so] it is difficult to know what he will do.'[76] This time, though, he seems to have done as she requested and the arrangement held for the next two years, until her momentous decision to tell him of her 'marriage' and consequent request to pay her money directly to Lewes.

Out of her late-arriving and thinly stretched income Marian sent occasional gifts of five or ten pounds to Chrissey, to help with the school fees for the eldest girl, Emily. They were much needed. The good news that the two eldest Clarke boys had been found 'situations' – as what we don't know – was spoiled by hearing later that the eldest, Robert, had proved 'so naughty that he has had to leave his situation and they are determined to send him to sea'.[77] Six months later, while they were preparing to leave Weimar, the sad news came that 'naughty' Robert had drowned.[78]

When Marian went to visit Chrissey over Christmas and New Year 1855–6, it looks as if neither Isaac nor Fanny made the short journey to see her. Although Marian had not told them that she was living with Lewes, it is impossible to believe that the news had not filtered back. Isaac and Fanny might not have been part of the Rosehill circle, but they were intelligent and sophisticated people. Marian's changing instructions about where to send her money must have alerted him to a shift in her circumstances. And, anyway, Charles Bray was incapable of keeping a secret. Something more than indifference had surely kept Isaac and Fanny away from Attleborough that Christmas. Either way, this was the last time that Marian would set foot in the place that she was about to bring so vividly alive in her novels.

Under the influence of Herbert Spencer, whom he had met back in 1851 during that 'dreary wasted time' of his life, Lewes rediscovered his early interest in biological science. Working on the multi-faceted Goethe had pushed him further along this path and he had begun to read seriously in areas not tackled since he was a medical student tramping the wards. The result of this renewed interest had been an article in the October 1852 issue of the *Westminster* on 'Goethe as a Man of Science', as well as a chapter on the same subject in the 1855 book.

But Huxley's 1854 sneer that Lewes was nothing but a 'book scientist' still stung. To remedy the situation Lewes borrowed a microscope from Arthur Helps, determined to turn himself into a practitioner. A near neighbour in Richmond was Professor Richard Owen, one of the country's leading academic scientists, who welcomed Lewes's friendship, as well as encouraging his interest. Instead of reading about other men's experiments, Lewes now began to do his own, albeit in a small way. During an expedition to see Goethe's little wooden house at Ilmenau in the summer of 1854, he had cut a caterpillar in two and watched, fascinated, while the head began to eat the tail. Marian had made a little box in order to carry the insect back to their lodgings and observe further. Believing, as always, that it was her duty to support a great man in his work, she naturally followed this new direction in Lewes's life with enthusiasm, helping him search for polyps during their week's holiday in Worthing in

September 1855. Back home in Richmond, science now played a part equal to literature in their lives and a typical day involved 'reading Homer and science and rearing tadpoles'[79], not to mention a stint with William Whewell's heavy-going *History of the Inductive Sciences*.

The Leweses' holiday at Ilfracombe in May 1856 continued this same fine-grained blend of science and art, vacation and work. Just as Goethe had been the *raison d'être* for the trip to Germany, so the focus for this trip was a series of articles Lewes had planned called 'Sea-Side Studies' which were to appear in *Blackwood's Magazine*. They were not heavy pieces – Huxley would not have approved – but they were hugely popular and reflected the new passion of Victorians for skimming rock pools, tapping away at fossils and scooping up bits of foliage. Marian and Lewes spent their first mornings in Devonshire scrambling over the rocks at low tide, looking for various kinds of anemones. It soon became clear that they were inexperienced and ill-equipped: the tall thin jars which they had brought all the way from London did not seem to agree with the anemones, which insisted on floating upside down. It was Marian's job to roll up her sleeve, plunge her arm into the jar and turn the stubborn creatures the right way up.[80]

To get some expert advice, Lewes made a call on the local curate George Tugwell, a small young man who was an experienced naturalist. Tugwell not only lent them the right sort of jar for their specimens, but joined them on their expeditions. Dressed in old coats and big hats, the trio spent their mornings chipping away at fossils and filling their jars with rock-pool finds. In the late afternoon and evening Lewes examined the day's takings under the microscope, before carefully classifying and recording them. Marian, who was meant to be absorbed in two big pieces for the *Westminster*, found herself becoming more and more interested and 'every day I gleaned some little bit of naturalistic experience'.[81] Once liberated from her journalism on 17 June, she gave her full attention to the range of beautiful seaweeds to be found in the local rock pools, reading up about them in the evening so that she could get 'a little more light on their structure and history'.[82]

This new experience of close observation, description and categorisation had a massive impact on Marian's writing. 'I never before longed so much to know the names of things as during this visit to Ilfracombe,' she wrote in her journal. 'The desire is part of the tendency that is now constantly growing in me to escape from all vagueness and inaccuracy into the daylight of distinct, vivid ideas.'[83] On the long walks she took with Lewes in the afternoons, Marian began to see the connections between the natural history of the landscape and that of man. 'When one sees a house stuck on the side of a great hill, and still more a number of houses looking like a few barnacles clustered on the side of a great rock,' she wrote, 'we begin to think of the strong family likeness between ourselves and all other building, burrowing house-appropriating and shell-secreting animals.'[84]

These Ilfracombe observations were, in part, an attempt by Marian to see whether she could do for the British countryside what Wilhelm Heinrich von Riehl had done for the German. One of the *Westminster* pieces she was currently working on concerned von Riehl's attempts to study German peasant life as if he were a naturalist looking at an animal species.[85] Drawing on her knowledge of evolutionary science – Darwin might not yet have published, but others like Herbert Spencer certainly had – Marian quotes with obvious approval von Riehl's conclusion that social change among the peasant classes must always be snail slow.

> What has grown up historically can only die out historically, by the gradual operation of necessary laws. The external conditions which society has inherited from the past are but the manifestation of inherited internal conditions in the human beings who compose it; the internal conditions and the external are related to each other as the organism and its medium, and development can take place only by the gradual consentaneous development of both.[86]

Von Riehl's conclusions exactly suited Marian's conservative temperament. Apart from her brief flirtation with radicalism in 1848, she had always discounted political solutions imposed from above in favour of slow, gradual change pushing up from below. Primed by her father's stories of the French Revolution and nourished by her own observations of the slow-changing Warwickshire countryside, she believed that 'a wise social policy must be based not simply on abstract social science, but on the Natural History of social bodies'.[87]

This plea for an acceptance of *things as they are* leads Marian into making a case for a new kind of realism in art. In the article, which appears in the July 1856 issue of the *Westminster*, Marian turns aside temporarily from von Riehl as she endorses Ruskin's complaint that all too often peasants are portrayed as straight out of a picture postcard or an opera chorus – all rosy-cheeked honesty. Instead, she asks for a new accuracy in painting, drama and literature that would show peasants as they are, neither touched up nor toned down. This request comes not from a pedantic desire for detail, but from a powerful belief that it is art's duty to make us aware of realities which are not our own: 'We want to be taught to feel, not for the heroic artisan or the sentimental peasant, but for the peasant in all his coarse apathy, and the artisan in all his suspicious selfishness.'[88]

Eager to practise what she preached, Marian now tried her hand at a couple of bits of description of local life in her journal. The first was a report of the celebrations which Ilfracombe put on to mark the end of the Crimean War. With minute attention to detail she described the yards of bunting, an unconvincing reconstruction of the allied armies, a half-hearted race for village boys and, after dark, a row of fires along the tors. The second piece of writing was a description of two local 'cockle women' whom she saw at Swansea, their next destination.

> One of them was the grandest woman I ever saw [wrote Marian in her journal] – six feet high, carrying herself like a Greek Warrior, and treading the earth with unconscious majesty. They wore large woollen shawls of

a rich brown, doubled lengthwise, with the end thrown back again over the left shoulder so as to fall behind in graceful folds. The grander of the two carried a great pitcher in her hand, and wore a quaint little bonnet set upright on her head. Her face was weather beaten and wizened, but her eyes were bright and piercing and the lines of her face, with its high cheek-bones strong and characteristic.[89]

From Swansea the Leweses moved to Tenby, a place to stir up memories for Marian. Sara Hennell was unpleasantly quick to remind her by letter of their visit there thirteen years ago. Unpleasant because it was then that Rufa Brabant had announced her engagement to Charles Hennell and, by way of painful compensation, had taken Marian to a dance at the assembly rooms to try and find her a man. It was strange for Marian to contrast that uncertain time with the security of the present. Now she had a partner she loved and a new best woman friend to take the place of envious Sara. On 12 July Barbara Leigh Smith joined the Leweses at Tenby. She was looking and feeling exhausted by the traumas of the previous year. John Chapman had been urging her to become his mistress and have his baby on the strange grounds that it would sort out her irregular periods. He even pointed to Marian and Lewes as a happy example of how well these things could work out.[90] Barbara's father, although he had not been married to her mother, was outraged by the proposition and had thundered that his elder daughter had better go to America if she wanted to go in for that sort of thing. In the end, Barbara had decided against setting up a liaison with Chapman and had come to Tenby to recover from the relationship. She arrived ready to pitch in and immediately set about using her skills as an artist to record various specimens for Lewes. Predisposed to dislike the little man, she left Tenby a few days later believing that he was a good, dear creature who made Marian happy. Fresh from her relationship with Chapman, Barbara was in the mood to discuss sex. During the long sandy days at Tenby she drew from Marian the confidence that Lewes was a considerate lover and that they practised birth control, having made the decision not to have children. If Marian went into details about her preferred method of contraception, Barbara did not pass them on to Bessie, who in turn reported the conversation to her daughter. Condoms, of a reusable variety, were available by now and the rhythm method was also practised in an *ad hoc* way by those who understood it. Lewes, as a one-time medical student and physiologist, may be assumed to have been one of the initiated few who had grasped the fact that pregnancy was most likely to happen in the middle of a woman's cycle.

On the surface, Marian was less productive in Tenby than she had been in Ilfracombe. Since finishing the piece on von Riehl she recorded that she had 'done no *visible* work' but added, 'I have absorbed many ideas and much bodily strength; indeed, I do not remember ever feeling so strong in mind and body as I feel at this moment.' Then she admitted to herself what had been brewing for ten years: 'I am anxious to begin my fiction writing.'[91]

It was a momentous psychological breakthrough. Until now Marian had approached the realisation that she wanted to be a novelist crab-like, from the side. There must have been a bit of talk about her ambitions back in Coventry because in 1846 Sara had spotted that, newly released from the dreary Strauss, Mary Ann was looking 'very brilliant just now – we fancy she must be writing her novel'.[92] This was perhaps the point at which Marian wrote the description of the Staffordshire farmhouse and its neighbours which, according to her journal entry of 6 December 1857, 'How I Came to Write Fiction', had come to nothing and, 'I lost any hope that I should ever be able to write a novel, just as I desponded about everything else in my future life.'[93] But one night during their stay in Berlin she had plucked up courage to show these yellowing pages to Lewes who, although liking them, confirmed her fears that 'he disbelieved in my possession of any dramatic power'.[94]

The words cut deep, seeming to confirm Marian's own low opinion of what she might achieve as a fiction writer. Even when Lewes managed to sell her journal recollections of Weimar in the form of two essays for *Fraser's* in the June and July 1855 issues, she was defensively aware that they too were almost wholly descriptive. Retreating to the high ground, she told Bray not to mention her name in connection with the essays 'for to people who do not enjoy description of scenery it will seem very tame and stupid, and I really think a taste for descriptive writing is the rarest of all tastes among ordinary people'.[95]

It was a shame. Lewes had not meant the comment nastily. He truly admired her descriptive writing, and scholars have been quick to spot the passages from her unpublished journals which he lifted – with her permission – and put straight into his own work. He was keen for her to write fiction, not least because it paid better than essay writing and they were, as always, looking for 'the main chance'. He had been genuinely impressed by the Cumming essay and kept up a gentle pressure that she should try to write fiction. Now, in Tenby, he suggested it again. 'You have wit, description and philosophy – those go a good way towards the production of a novel. It is worth while for you to try the experiment.'[96]

Marian takes up the story: 'one morning [in Tenby] as I was lying in bed, thinking what should be the subject of my first story, my thoughts merged themselves into a dreamy doze, and I imagined myself writing a story of which the title was – "The Sad Fortunes of the Reverend Amos Barton".' Excited, she woke herself properly and immediately told Lewes of her idea. 'He said "O, what a capital title!" and from that time I had settled in my mind that this should be my first story.'[97]

CHAPTER 9

'The Breath of Cows and the Scent of Hay'

Scenes of Clerical Life and Adam Bede
1856–9

HAVING WAITED FIFTEEN years to start writing fiction, it was excruciating to have to put it off for three weeks longer. But back home in Richmond there was a big pile of *Westminster Review* work waiting for Marian. In theory she should have been able to get through it quickly, since the house was empty, Lewes having left almost immediately for Switzerland with the boys. But as usual when she felt abandoned, especially in favour of Lewes's family, she fell ill. Agonising face-ache was first diagnosed as neuralgia, then as an impacted wisdom tooth which, with the help of two doses of chloroform, was eventually removed. Exhausted with pain, Marian begged Chapman to let her off the 'odious article' she had agreed to produce for the October 1856 issue on top of her usual 'Belles Lettres' commitment.[1] But Chapman was having none of it. In the past eighteen months his attitude to her contributions had changed tack from lukewarm to wildly enthusiastic. As the *Westminster* increasingly lost its way, Marian's articles were emerging as one of its most dependable features. Once again, John Chapman needed Marian Evans more than she needed him.

Far from being a pointless detour, the 'odious' piece turned out to be highly relevant. 'Silly Novels by Lady Novelists' is a cutting critique of the stream of trashy fiction written by women, which glutted the book market during the middle decades of the century.[2] Working through this material allowed Marian to think carefully about the kind of writing she wanted to avoid. By showing what a novel should *not* be, she was setting out a literary manifesto for her style of fiction.

She starts by considering what she calls 'the mind-and-millinery species' of novel. The heroine, usually an heiress if not a peeress, is always 'the ideal woman in feelings, faculties and flounces'.[3] Pretty, witty and wise, she dispenses good advice and *bons mots* to a circle of adoring men. Marian deftly takes apart *Compensation*, a recent addition to the genre, in which a four-year-old frames perfect pieties, while his mother tackles the Bible in Greek, Hebrew and Sanskrit. All this against a jumbled plot of Italian mistresses, deathbed conversions and poisoning attempts on old ladies.

Another kind of silly novel produced by lady novelists, mostly of High Church leanings, is the 'oracular species'.[4] Impatiently waving aside any obligation to depict real life, the writer of the oracular species prefers to tackle the big philosophical questions: 'the ability of a lady novelist to describe actual life and her fellow-men, is in inverse proportion to her confident eloquence about God and the other world.'[5] Knotty problems like the existence of evil are unravelled against a background of high melodrama, usually involving a long-lost brother, not to mention a mad gypsy. Once again, the heroine is sparklingly clever and given to spouting bad theology at the drop of a lace handkerchief.

But it was a third category of fiction, the 'white neck-cloth' species, which particularly annoyed Marian. These novels were infused with the Evangelical sensibility which she had espoused so earnestly as a girl. In effect, they were love stories for serious-minded Christians, 'in which the vicissitudes of the tender passion are sanctified by saving views of Regeneration and the Atonement'.[6] It was their patent inaccuracy which jarred – instead of setting the story among the lower and lower middle classes where Evangelicalism flourished, these novels contained as many baronets and fancy carriages as any High Church title. Marian's first and most urgent obligation as a novelist would be to restore Evangelicalism to where it properly belonged, among the shopkeepers and artisans of urban Britain.

The essay finishes with a clarification of Marian's position. She is not opposed to female novelists in principle. Harriet Martineau, Currer Bell aka Charlotte Brontë and Mrs Gaskell have all produced work which is far from 'silly'. But the fact that novel writing requires no formal qualifications has meant that women of little education and vast pretensions have been encouraged to try their hands, with dire results. As for that old chestnut about women being forced into writing fiction out of financial necessity, Marian will have none of it: 'Where there is one woman who writes from necessity, we believe there are three women who write from vanity.' Then, surely thinking of her own situation, she continues sternly: 'and besides, there is something so antiseptic in the mere healthy fact of working for one's bread, that the most trashy and rotten kind of feminine literature is not likely to have been produced under such circumstances.'[7]

Just as in her essay on Madame de Sablé, Marian is making a plea for her kind of writer. Fiction should be left to the handful of women who have been educated alongside men, yet who retain a particularly female capacity for observation and empathy. Their motivation is not the desire to show off or keep themselves busy, but the sober (and, in fact, hard to reconcile) combination of financial need and deeply held vocation. In short, fiction should be written by women like Marian Lewes.

'Silly Novels' went off to Chapman on 12 September. But even now Marian was not free to start on her fiction. It took another week before the 'Belles Lettres' contribution was finally dispatched. A crucial punctuation point had been reached, which Lewes acknowledged by taking Marian up to town on a rare trip to the theatre. It was on 23 September, according to her journal, that she finally 'Began to write "The Sad Fortunes of the Reverend Amos Barton", which I hope to make one of a series called "Scenes of Clerical Life"'.[8]

The way Marian framed her intentions is telling. Not sure if she could sustain the dramatic tension necessary for a full-blown novel, she opted for a piece of descriptive writing, something which she already knew she could do. If it turned out well she would extend the work by adding other self-contained 'Scenes' until she had a manuscript approaching the length of a full-length novel. The unity would come not through the plot but by planting references in the first story – 'The Sad Fortunes of the Reverend Amos Barton' – which would feature in subsequent tales, setting up threads of connection between the episodes.

Lewes was not surprised that the first part of 'Amos Barton' went well. He had always known that Marian could do description and he was delighted to discover that dialogue came easily to her too. Unlike the heroines of the 'Silly Novels', her characters spoke in rhythms that sounded real. Instead of long, unlikely monologues, there was authentic-sounding exchange in broad War-wickshire dialect. But it was still not clear whether she could do drama. The crunch point came after a couple of weeks when she reached the climax of her story, the point where Amos Barton collapses in anguish beside the deathbed of Milly, the meek wife whom he has taken for granted. Lewes went up to town to give Marian a chance to work undisturbed on the crucial scene. When he returned she read out what she had produced and, according to her journal, 'We both cried over it, and then he came up to me and kissed me, saying, "I think your pathos is better than your fun".'[9] George Eliot had been born.

The character of Amos Barton was based on John Gwyther, the local curate during Marian's Evangelical years at Griff. Shepperton church with its 'intelligent eye' of a clock is easily identified as Chilvers Coton church.[10] The 'College' where Barton visits the paupers was the workhouse which Marian could see from the attic window. Gwyther had just the right kind of clumsy earnestness to appeal to the teenage Mary Ann Evans. An enthusiastic Evangelical, he had set about purging the parish of its lax devotional habits. This entailed scrapping old hymn tunes in favour of the up-to-date versions favoured by nonconform-ists, opposing old country customs like the wakes and coming down hard on minor lapses of honesty among the local servant population. In short, Gwyther displayed all the disdain for the tenacity of local custom which the adult Marian had identified in her article on 'The Natural History of German Life' as the reason why political or social reform imposed from outside was bound to fail.

The switch in the young Mary Ann's attitude to Mr Gwyther and his reforming ways probably came during the holy war. Gwyther may have been one of the clergymen who was wheeled in to try and make her change her mind, and his third-rate brain – notwithstanding the fact that it had trundled through Cambridge – would have been no match for hers. But she may also have been disillusioned by the scandal circulating about his private life. Although the details are not clear, it seems that Gwyther had become over-friendly with a raffish newcomer to the parish who styled herself a 'Countess' and enjoyed a suspiciously close relationship with a man who was supposed to be her father, but whom gossiping tongues set down as a lover. The disillusioned Mary Ann may have found it hard to see how she was supposed to accept moral guidance – not to mention the eternal damnation which Evangelicals were so keen on handing out – from a man whose own conduct would not stand up to scrutiny.

The outline of Mr Gwyther's life, including the death of his wife in childbirth, was reworked by Marian and given to the character of Amos Barton. Barton is exactly the kind of clergyman who is absent from the 'white neck-cloth' species of high-toned Evangelical romance novel. He is middle-aged and shabby, with a nasty tendency to sniff. His spelling is bad, his punctuation worse. 'It was not in his nature to be superlative in anything; unless, indeed, he was superlatively middling, the quintessential extract of mediocrity.'[11] The narrator of the story understands that his readers might like a more conventionally attractive hero and is quick to point out that this, unfortunately, is not how life is. 'Depend upon it,' the (apparently) male narrator says to his lady reader, 'you would gain unspeakably if you would learn with me to see some of the poetry and the pathos, the tragedy and the comedy, lying in the experience of a human soul that looks out through dull grey eyes, and that speaks in a voice of quite ordinary tones.'[12] If this story is not to the reader's taste, the narrator suggests that she try one of the many new novels – the 'Silly Novels' of the *Westminster* essay – which are packed with 'ermine tippets, adultery, and murder'.[13]

In 'Amos Barton' Marian's recollections of the village culture of her childhood are brought into focus through the lens of current preoccupations. She hits off the tone of village gossip perfectly. The local farmer and his wife, Mr and Mrs Hackit, the doctor, Mr Pilgrim, and Mrs Patten, 'a childless old lady, who had got rich chiefly by the negative process of spending nothing', gather in the evening to chew the fat over Barton's odd modernising ideas and his put-upon wife Milly.[14] In what would be the first of many choric scenes in Eliot's novels written in broad Midlands dialect, Mrs Patten gets indignant at Barton's nosiness about the state of her soul: 'I've never been a sinner.'[15] Mrs Hackit, who some critics have suggested is based on Marian's mother, meanwhile, declares, 'How nice . . . [Mrs Barton] keeps her children! . . . – six children, and another a-coming. I don't know how they make both ends meet.'[16]

But what seems like a generally benign scrutiny of their spiritual leader quickly turns to something sharper once the widowed Countess moves into the parish with her brother Mr Bridmain. Glamorous, vain and self-publicising, Caroline Czerlaski plays the part of Evangelical gentlewoman to perfection. She pouts at the low church attendance, flatters Amos that he is a great preacher and hints that she has the power to advance his career. She patronises simple, kind-hearted Milly with lavish compliments, which she clearly doesn't mean. While Amos blushes and bridles at this unaccustomed attention, his colleagues and parishioners feel increasingly uneasy. The neighbouring clergy dislike the way Czerlaski fawns over Barton, while the village chorus is convinced that there must be something unsavoury about her relationship with her 'brother'.

Marian's description of the Shepperton rumour machine draws on her experience of being the subject of intense gossip in her own village, literary London. Within weeks of her leaving for the Continent with Lewes in July 1854, stories were circulating about how she had lured him away from his family, not to mention the peculiar invention of the 'insulting' letter which she was supposed to have written to Harriet Martineau.[17] In the same way, Shepperton gossips manage to construct a story about the Countess and her relationship with both her brother and Barton, which is far more lurid than the actual ordinary truth.

The Countess, as it turns out, really is a Countess – albeit one who began life as a governess. And her brother Mr Bridmain is indeed her half-brother who made his fortune doing nothing more disreputable than working his way up to a partnership in a silk business. Naturally, speculation reaches fever pitch when the Countess moves into the vicarage. Bridmain has decided to marry his half-sister's maid and Caroline Czerlaski declares herself too humiliated to remain under his roof. As is often the way in life, the story seems to say, it is petty vanity rather than grand passion which powers life's tragedies. For the Countess's arrival means extra strain for the already stretched Barton household with its six small children, one on the way and a harassed maid-of-all-work. The Countess lies in bed until ten and takes a separate breakfast at eleven. She monopolises the pregnant Milly's attention, diverting her from the daily round of household tasks. She insists on Nanny, the maid, running around after her small, greedy lapdog. It is this final imposition which proves to be the tinder box. Ordered to get some extra milk for the dog, Nanny explodes in a hail of home truths to which the Countess responds by flouncing out of the Bartons' life for ever.[18]

But relief comes too late. Milly, exhausted by the extra work that her thoughtless guest and complacent husband have created, gives birth prematurely and dies a few days later. Only now does Amos begin to grasp how hurtful his behaviour towards his uncomplaining wife has been. His parishioners, previously alienated by his tactless behaviour, set aside their disapproval and rally round the curate and his family. 'Cold faces looked kind again, and parishioners turned over in their minds what they could best do to help their pastor.'[19] The squire tucks a twenty-pound note into his letter of condolence and offers to find a place at school for the two eldest girls. Neighbouring clergy collect forty pounds between them. The previously disapproving Hackits invite Dickey, one of the Barton boys, to stay, while one of the other clergy families make 'particular pets' of Fred and Sophy.[20] The whole community demonstrates Feuerbach's doctrine of human love in action and in a bit of underlining Marian makes the point that Barton's 'recent troubles had called out their better sympathies, and that is always a source of love. Amos failed to touch the spring of goodness by his sermons, but he touched it effectually by his sorrows; and there was now a real bond between him and his flock.'[21]

Marian and Lewes had agreed that if the story seemed to work, they would send it to *Blackwood's Magazine*. Lewes picked on *Maga*, as it was familiarly known, because he had recently enjoyed a run of luck there with his own pieces and was on increasingly good terms with its editor, John Blackwood. As far as the history of English literature is concerned, it was a stroke of huge fortune that Marian's first work was entrusted to the one publisher in Britain whose tact, faith and patience were equal to the battering which Marian would inflict on her way to becoming the greatest novelist of the age.

John Blackwood was the sixth son of the Edinburgh publisher who had founded *Blackwood's Magazine* and the associated publishing house. He was not an obvious candidate to midwife Marian's career, being highly conventional in both his religious and political beliefs. This, after all, was the man who christened each of his successive pet dogs 'Tory'. But by the time publisher and author came together – and it was not until 1858 that Blackwood officially learned the identity of 'George Eliot' – they had both matured to a point where they were able to perceive and value the integrity of the other. Blackwood, who was only a year older than Marian, responded to her moral and intellectual seriousness, even while he deplored her 'unfortunate' situation: as late as 1861 he could be heard to mutter, 'I never can think of her situation without positive pain.'[22] Marian, meanwhile, was drawn to Blackwood's patent sincerity and to a conservative outlook which was not so very far from her own. He was a natural Anglican, but remained tolerant of other sects, honouring the social and psychological comfort which they offered to their followers. He would have been horrified to think himself a Feuerbachian but that, intuitively, is what he was.

If anyone was the odd one out in this relationship it was Lewes, whose hustling instincts sometimes threatened a relationship which lasted, more on than off, until Blackwood's death in 1879. At this stage, though, Lewes's clever salesmanship was exactly what was needed to get Marian into print. On 6 November he sent 'Amos' off to Blackwood, describing it as the manuscript of 'a friend who desired my good offices with you'.[23] His covering letter puffs the story by 'confessing' that he first had doubts about 'my friend's power as a writer of fiction'. This all changed, however, when he read the manuscript and developed a 'very high admiration . . . [for the] humour, pathos, vivid presentation and nice observation'.[24] He goes on to explain that the 'Scenes' – he manages to make it sound as if there are others already written – are intended to illustrate 'the actual life of our country clergy about a quarter of a century ago; but solely in its *human* and *not at all* in its *theological* aspect'. This, he believes, has not been done since the work of Jane Austen fifty years earlier. Despite the fact that his 'friend' is a new author, Lewes finishes with a brisk discussion of copyright details, which cleverly introduces the idea that if Blackwood does not wish to serialise the stories in the magazine, there are plenty of others who will.[25]

The first sentence of Blackwood's prompt reply must have filled Marian and Lewes with delight: 'I am happy to say that I think your friend's reminiscences of Clerical Life will do.' Practised editor that he was, though, Blackwood made it clear that he would need to see other 'Scenes' before he could make a definite offer. He then proceeded to put forward a few valid criticisms of the piece – there was a tendency to describe characters rather than showing them in action, the conclusion is 'the lamest part of the story', the Barton children are unnecessarily individualised. However, he finishes generously: 'If the author is a new writer I beg to congratulate him on being worthy of the honours of print and pay. I shall be very glad to hear from you or him soon.'[26]

With a touchiness that was increasingly to mark her professional relationships as well as her personal ones, Marian insisted on reading rejection into Blackwood's generally approving comments. On this occasion Lewes, too, seems to have thought the publisher disappointingly lukewarm and in his next letter he has another go at talking up 'Amos Barton': 'It struck me as being fresher than any story I have read for a long while, and as exhibiting in a high degree that faculty which I find to be the rarest of all, viz. the dramatic ventriloquism.'[27] Blackwood was too much his own man to be influenced by such blatant tactics, but a promised second look at 'Amos' did result in him agreeing to publish it without seeing any companion pieces.

This was lucky, since none were written. Moreover, Marian was now obliged to put down the 'Scenes' and return to a long *Westminster* article on the Evangelical poet Edward Young, which she had begun back in April.[28] Once again, her journalistic preoccupations paralleled and developed the ideas she was working on in her fiction. Young's stickily sententious poetry, especially his 'Night Thoughts', had been a favourite of hers in adolescence. Returning to it now she found herself repelled by its hazy grandiloquence, its inability to capture the concrete glory of either God or the natural world. Young, in short, is the eighteenth-century clerical male equivalent of the lady novelist, incapable of identifying a single authentic thought or feeling.

With the Young essay dispatched on 4 December, Marian stayed on in London over Christmas to write the second 'Scene of Clerical Life'. This was the first December that she had not gone home to Warwickshire, choosing instead to spend it alone at Richmond, while Lewes twinkled his way through two weeks at Vernon Hill, Arthur Helps's country residence. Apart from being the natural star of the house party, Lewes read 'Amos' out loud to the assembled company and was quick to pass on the favourable comments to Blackwood. If people guessed it was the work of the unofficial Mrs Lewes they were too polite to say so. Blackwood himself, meanwhile, was canvassing opinions among his own circle. One close friend, W. G. Hamley, with whom he usually found himself agreeing, came out 'dead against Amos', finding the true-to-life style depressing.[29] The novelist Thackeray was diplomatically non-committal, while the urbane Albert Smith reported that members of the Garrick 'generally seem to have mingled their tears with their tumblers over the death bed of Milly'.[30]

But while Blackwood was shrewd enough to take soundings from men whose judgement he trusted, he still did not fully understand what his new author – who had declared a wish to be known only by the pseudonym 'George Eliot' – was about. He was puzzled by Amos's unheroic life and nagged by the persistent worry that some slight on the clergy might be implied. Disappointed to discover that Blackwood did not empathise completely with the kind of fiction she wanted to write – or rather, that he was not the soulmate she had been looking for since her earliest days – Marian took the strangely sideways and snubbing step of sending a letter to his brother and colleague, Major William Blackwood, explaining her literary philosophy. Just as someone who does not like the Dutch school of realist art will never like a particular example of the genre, so, says Marian, readers who long for idealistic and unrealistic novels are not going to warm to her brand of slice-of-life fiction. The only kind of criticism she is interested in, she maintains with all the authority of an established writer of fiction, is the sort which assesses her writing in terms of what it has set out to do.[31]

In light of this letter the Blackwoods were probably dreading that the next 'Scene' would have even more drippy noses, cold houses and bad grammar. So 'Mr Gilfil's Love Story' must have come as a pleasant surprise. The setting and the plot were straight out of one of the 'Silly Novels', which Marian had so recently lampooned. The idea, if not the personality, of Mr Gilfil is based on Revd Bernard Gilpin Ebdell, who had been vicar of Chilvers Coton and Astley until his death in 1828. Ebdell was the protégé of Sir Roger Newdigate, who owned the magnificently modernised Arbury Hall where the young Mary Anne had accompanied her father on estate business. Ebdell had married Sally Chilton, a local collier's daughter whose beautiful singing voice had persuaded Lady Newdigate informally to adopt and educate the girl. In Marian's story the details have been changed. Sir Christopher Cheverel and his wife find little Caterina Sarti in Naples and take the orphaned baby back home to Cheverel Manor to be raised as something between a daughter, servant and pet. Although Caterina is expected to marry Gilfil, who openly adores her, she is actually in love with Captain Wybrow, the weak, shiftless heir to the Cheverel estate, who is a prototype of all those unsatisfactory young men in George Eliot's mature fiction: Arthur Donnithorne, Godfrey Cass, Tito Melema. Frenzied with jealousy when she discovers that Wybrow is to marry a woman from his own class, Caterina takes a dagger and plans to stab him. She is saved only by the fact that he dies before she can reach him, killed by a congenitally weak heart. The ever-devoted Gilfil hears Caterina's confession of murderous thoughts and absolves her of all guilt, believing that, when the moment came, she would not have been able to use the dagger. Soon after, he weds her but, unlike the real marriage between Ebdell and Sally which lasted twenty-three years, Gilfil's happiness is cut short when Caterina fails to flourish as a country clergyman's wife and dies soon after.

'Mr Gilfil's Love Story' does not work. The plot is melodramatic and fantastical – the climax has Caterina plucking a dagger from the gallery wall before rushing out into the gracious grounds to stab the philandering Wybrow. Blackwood hated this bit too, but not so much on the grounds of improbability as the fact that his readers were just as unlikely to warm to a Latin murderess as they were to a sniffing curate. He urged Marian – still in the guise of 'George Eliot' – to touch up the character of Caterina, 'giving a little more dignity to her character'.[32] Marian replied – grandly, given that this was only her second piece of fiction – that she was unable to alter anything 'as my stories always grow out of my psychological conception of the dramatis personae ... My artistic bent is directed not at all to the presentation of eminently irreproachable characters, but to the presentation of mixed human beings in such a way as to call forth tolerant judgement, pity, and sympathy.'[33] A month later, still not having got the point, Blackwood suggested obliquely to Lewes that the scene in which Caterina planned to stab Wybrow should be changed to a dream sequence.[34] 'George Eliot' wrote back sternly, 'it would be the death of my story to substitute a dream for the real scene. Dreams usually play an important part in fiction, but rarely, I think, in actual life.'[35]

If Blackwood was now wishing that he had stuck to his original and usual plan of not accepting a new writer's work without having seen the complete manuscript, he was good enough not to say so. Still, he was even more bemused when presented with the heroine of the next 'Scene', 'Janet's Repentance'. Janet Dempster is a middle-class woman, a battered wife and an alcoholic. The only thing which stops her leaving her brutal lawyer husband is a deep self-loathing which tells her that she is not good enough for anything else. Her one lifeline is her friendship with the local Evangelical clergyman Edmund Tryan, whose brand of energised Christianity has galvanised the religious life of Milby, a barely disguised Nuneaton. While the ladies of the parish have immersed themselves enthusiastically in a programme of private prayer and public good works, a faction led by Janet's husband supports orthodox Anglicanism. This leads to public rioting, as the anti-Tryanites campaign to keep the 'cant' of fashionable Evangelicalism out of their pulpits. As part of an overcrowded background, Marian sketches in the several nonconformist sects that also claim part of the Milby population as their congregation. Writing from what she emphasises to Blackwood is 'close observation ... [from] real life', she shows how these groups interact at the social as well as the theological level.[36] For instance, while it might appear as if the town were bitterly split on doctrinal issues such as infant baptism, nothing was going to stop the Anglican doctor Mr Pilgrim from treating dissenters or the local grocer from selling them candles. Likewise, it is not Mr Tryan's particular beliefs that save Janet, so much as the empathy he is able to extend to her as a result of his own tragic experiences. Feuerbach seeps into the narrator's voice when 'he' declares: 'Our subtlest analysis of schools and sects must miss the essential truth, unless it be lit up by the love that sees in all forms of human thought and work, the life and death struggles of separate human beings.'[37]

The character of Edmund Tryan was based on the Reverend John Jones, whose popular Sunday evening sermons on the outskirts of Nuneaton both Maria Lewis and Robert Evans had attended back in the late 1820s. Jones's particular brand of Evangelical fervour had brought him into conflict with the local lawyer James Buchanan, husband of the former Nancy Wallington whose mother was headmistress of the school Mary Anne attended. Inevitably called upon by Blackwood to 'soften' her story, Marian maintained that 'the real Dempster was far more disgusting than mine; the real Janet alas! had a far sadder end than mine'. Once again sounding like a seasoned novelist instead of a beginner, she maintained grandly, 'as an artist I should be utterly powerless if I departed from my own conceptions of life and character.'[38] She then tells Blackwood that she quite understands if he wishes not to print 'Janet's Repentance' in *Maga*. Blackwood did not know – how could he? – that 'George Eliot' was currently undergoing a painful and final divorce from her brother Isaac because of her adulterous relationship with Lewes. In her mind Blackwood's mild criticism of her work had become merged not only with the condemning choric voice of literary London, but also the specific rejection by Isaac, so that it seemed as if the whole world disapproved of her. In a hurt and self-righteous flounce, she threatened to withdraw from the game completely. Luckily Blackwood, coached by Lewes, responded with just the right emollient touch: 'I do not fall in with George Eliots every day and the idea of stopping the Series as suggested in your letter gave me "quite a turn" to use one of Thackeray's favourite phrases.' Most important, he made it clear that he believed there would be 'many years of happy friendly and literary intercourse before us'.[39] Marian caught the change of tone and replied with matching optimism, hinting that one day she might be able to step out from behind the pseudonym 'George Eliot' and reveal herself to him, hoping that in the process he would become 'a personal friend'.[40]

On 4 February 1857 Marian had written to Major William Blackwood:

> Whatever may be the success of my stories, I shall be resolute in preserving my incognito, having observed that a *nom de plume* secures all the advantages without the disagreeables of reputation. Perhaps, therefore, it will be well to give you my prospective name ... and accordingly I subscribe myself, best and most sympathizing of editors,
>   Yours very truly,
>   George Eliot[41]

Biographers have long speculated about how the baby girl christened Mary Anne Evans turned into George Eliot. At the end of her life Marian told her husband John Cross that she picked the name because 'George was Mr Lewes's Christian name, and Eliot was a good mouth-filling, easily-pronounced word'.[42] There are other, more fanciful, explanations, but this seems the most likely. More difficult to unravel are the complex psychological negotiations which lay behind Marian Evans clinging to her *nom de plume* for a full twenty years after her true identity became known.

When Lewes first approached Blackwood with the manuscript of 'Amos' it made sense for him to conceal the author's real name. Marian Evans Lewes was the most infamous woman in literary Britain and Blackwood was running a family magazine. The shock of who she was could well have coloured Blackwood's response to the story, especially given its frank tone about sexual matters. But there was another reason. Although her journalism appeared anonymously, everyone who mattered – editors, publishers, friends – knew who had written it. If Marian were to produce novels under her own name which went on to fail, there was a danger that she might damage her reputation as a writer of serious non-fiction. Using a *nom de plume* allowed her to protect her reputation as a journalist, a point she made obliquely to John Blackwood on 14 March 1857: 'if George Eliot turns out a dull dog and an ineffective writer – a mere flash in the pan – I, for one, am determined to cut him on the first intimation of that disagreeable fact.'[43]

The fact that Marian continued to author all her books under the name 'George Eliot' – a practice which continues to the present day – suggests that there were other, more enduring, reasons behind her adoption of a pseudonym. Morbidly sensitive to criticism, she would likely have been unable to continue to write if reviewers had been publicly assessing the work of Marian Evans Lewes. There was already more than enough opprobrium directed towards that particular name. As the years went by and her real identity became generally known, 'George Eliot' developed into a brand name, a 'logo', which allowed Marian to keep a crucial psychological distance from any criticism directed towards her work and, by extension, her person. And given that the response from reviewers and readers was not always good, it was often only this distance which allowed her to go on writing.

There remains, though, the question of why the pseudonym had to be male. Women like Elizabeth Gaskell and Harriet Martineau, who wrote under their own names and were far from 'silly', were having great success in both the full-length and periodical fiction markets. Marian may have been afraid that her fiction might not be included in this illustrious small band of women whose work was judged as 'cavalierly as if they had been men'.[44] Anxious to avoid having her fiction praised and patronised as the work of a woman, she followed the example of the Brontës in placing her work in the domain occupied by male, that is genderless, writing. But while there always seemed to be an odd and obvious disjuncture between the male *noms de plume* 'Acton, Currer and Ellis Bell' and the work which went out under them, in Marian's case there was something entirely fitting about the soubriquet 'George Eliot'. Her main complaint about lady novelists in her 'Silly Novels' essay had been that they wrote on subjects – from theology to tradesmen – about which they had no real knowledge. Spoonfed a scrappy education and confined to the drawing-room, their partial experience of the world showed up in books which were rooted in nothing but impoverished imagination. Marian had lived a different kind of life, earning her living among clever men. She had had access to the broadest and richest culture, and had mastered its influences and nuances. She understood why Amos's Cambridge education would have made him Low Church, why ribbon weavers had narrow chests, why it was Watteau who would best be able to capture the gothicised charms of Cheverel Manor. Taking a male pseudonym was not so much a request to be judged as a male writer as a recognition that she was writing from a unique perspective in English literature, neither wholly male nor female but transcending both.

At the most intimate levels of Marian's psyche a male identity fitted. Her phenomenal erudition placed her firmly within the mid-Victorian stereotype of the bluestocking, whose book-learning was supposed to have shrivelled her ovaries and turned her into a surrogate man. She fell foul, too, of that curious double-thinking which suggested that a woman who was sexually 'fallen' was also de-sexed, stripped of those feminine attractions that would make a decent man desire her. Whether Marian absorbed these images from her environment or the seeds were planted more deeply within her, it is certainly the case that she struck those who met her as masculine. When Blackwood first saw her, admittedly on the occasion of being introduced to 'George Eliot', he reported back to his wife, 'She is a most intelligent pleasant woman, with a face like a man.'[45] Years later, Edith Simcox recalled that her beloved's features were 'too large and rugged for womanly beauty'.[46] Physical comparisons were always being made with Dante, Locke, Savonarola. Just as Lewes had a strong female side, so Marian had a corresponding male part. While he nurtured and protected her, she assumed the role of paterfamilias, bringing in an income to support not only the two of them but also a string of hapless Lewes and Clarke relatives.

From the start, Lewes tried to throw Blackwood off the scent. On 15 November 1856 he described the author of 'Amos Barton' as 'my clerical friend' and, to further confuse matters, submitted a piece on biology by 'another friend', Revd George Tugwell – the naturalist curate from Ilfracombe.[47] Blackwood took the bait, for three days later he told Lewes, 'I am glad to hear that your friend is as I supposed a Clergyman.'[48] This explicit assertion left Lewes in a difficult position. To allow Blackwood to labour under such a misapprehension was straining the parameters of good conduct, even by Lewes's shaky standards. So in his next letter a few days later he tried to sound casual – and failed – when he said, 'Let me not forget to add that when I referred to "my clerical friend" I meant to designate the writer of the clerical stories, not that he was a clericus.' Then he made things worse by adding, 'I am not at liberty to remove the veil of anonymity – even as regards social position. Be pleased therefore to keep the whole secret – and not even mention *my* negotiation or in any way lead guessers – (should any one trouble himself with such a guess – *not* very likely) to jump from me to my friend.'[49]

In his nervousness Lewes had surely signposted to Blackwood exactly who 'George Eliot' was – none other than his most notorious and closest 'friend'. In any case, as early as 27 January Blackwood's London manager, Joseph Langford, was writing anxiously to his boss, 'Who wrote Amos Barton? Can you tell me? I have heard a hint that I dare not entertain and from no bad judge.'[50] It suited the Blackwoods to play along with the fiction that they did not have a clue who George Eliot might be. As a family firm they were taking a risk publishing work by the notorious Marian Evans Lewes, especially since this was turning out to be increasingly explicit about sexual matters. Just as Marian found it useful to keep a second persona going, so did the Blackwoods. Apart from enabling them to pretend to the rest of the world that they did not know whom they were publishing, it shielded them from the reality themselves. Even once the Blackwoods had been introduced to Marian Lewes they found it more comfortable to think of her as 'George Eliot', and continued to write to and about her under this name.

For eighteen months after receiving 'Amos Barton', the Blackwoods paid lip-service to the idea that George Eliot was a particularly shy friend of Lewes who wished to stay anonymous. They made out Eliot's cheques to Lewes and expressed no surprise when it turned out that he was accompanying Lewes on his holiday to the Scilly Isles in 1857. On 10 February John Blackwood pushed the joke even further by telling 'My Dear George Eliot' that he had been struck by the similarity between the handwriting of his newest author and an old contributor called 'Captain George Warburton'. However, said Blackwood, 'I found a remarkable resemblance but not identity, nor does Amos seem to me anything like what that good artillery man would or could write.'[51]

The fact that Marian and, more especially, Lewes really thought the Blackwoods believed their subterfuge suggests how their social isolation had cut them off from reality. In December 1857 when Major Blackwood, who ran the business side of things, called on them in Richmond Marian seems genuinely surprised to discover that 'it was evident to us when he had only been in the room a few minutes that he knew I was George Eliot'.[52] Still she did nothing, perhaps feeling that she should wait until she had a chance to reveal her identity to John Blackwood. The first opportunity came two months later. According to Marian's journal: 'On Sunday the 28th Mr. John Blackwood called on us, having come to London for a few days only. He talked a good deal about the "Clerical Scenes" and George Eliot, and at last asked, "Well, am I to see George Eliot this time?" G. said, "Do you wish to see him?" "As he likes – I wish it to be quite spontaneous." I left the room, and G. following me a moment, I told him he might reveal me. Blackwood was kind.'[53]

During the first few months of Marian's novel-writing career, the *nom de plume* came under no particular pressure. Criticism of the *Scenes of Clerical Life*, which was released as a two-volume book in January 1858, concentrated on the quality of the writing rather than the identity of the author. *The Times*'s notice was 'highly favourable' and got the point entirely. Samuel Lucas praised Eliot's 'pathos in depicting ordinary situations' and did not seem the least put off by the sniffy noses.[54] The *Saturday Review* notice also understood what Marian was trying to do and she must have been particularly pleased by the spontaneous reference to Ruskin, who was quoted as saying that a good book should bring one 'to love or reverence something with your whole heart'.[55]

Even more gratifying were the responses of Jane Carlyle and Charles Dickens, both of whom Marian had requested should be sent copies of the book by Blackwood. Dickens immediately guessed that, 'George Eliot' or no, this was clearly written by a woman. If not, 'I believe that no man ever before had the art of making himself, mentally, so like a woman, since the world began.'[56] Jane Carlyle, on the other hand, took 'George Eliot' at his face value, imagining for him 'a wife from whom he has got those beautiful *feminine* touches in his book'.[57] There is something disturbing about this often-quoted letter. The flirtatious, prattling tone which Mrs Carlyle uses to the middle-aged clergyman she has imagined as its recipient feels odd directed towards a woman whose partner and his first wife she had once known very well indeed.

★　　★　　★

On 15 March 1857 Marian and Lewes set out for the Scilly Isles. He needed to do more 'naturalising' for the second part of 'Sea-Side Studies', and her fiction work – she was just winding up 'Mr Gilfil' and about to begin 'Janet's Repentance' – was portable. Marian recorded a careful account of their journey in her journal. The coach trip from Plymouth to Truro gave her a chance to cast her increasingly disciplined naturalist's eye over her fellow travellers – a local lad who ate buns, an old sailor who was 'a natural gentleman', 'a pretentious, vulgar young man with smart clothes, dirty nails, and original information in physiology'. She noted, too, details of the social and geographic landscape, including the way the clay industry changed the colour of the water around St Austell and the precise history of a 'fine church tower'.[58]

For eight wet, windy days they were stuck in Penzance before travelling to St Mary's, Scilly, on 26 March 1857 where they took rooms at the Post Office. The creeky shoreline was a perfect hunting-ground for the zoophytes, molluscs and annelids which Lewes had come to study at close quarters. In between expeditions to the rock pools Marian worked on 'Mr Gilfil', finishing the Epilogue out of doors on a sunny April morning.

After a seven-week stay Marian and Lewes moved on to the second stage of their island holiday. On 11 May they left for Jersey, where Lewes had spent a short but significant part of his boyhood, learning French and spending evenings 'of perfect bliss' at the theatre.[59] Inevitably it all seemed smaller and tattier than he remembered. But it must have been interesting for Marian to see the place which was the nearest thing to 'home' for the rootless Lewes.

Childhood and family ties were in any case at the front of Marian's mind now. While in Scilly she had received a letter from Warwickshire telling her that Chrissey's family had been struck by typhus.[60] One little girl, Fanny, had died on 26 March and another, Katy, and Chrissey herself were seriously ill. The letter had actually been written by Sarah Evans, on behalf of her husband who hated putting pen to paper. By 16 April, having heard nothing for over a fortnight, Marian wrote to Isaac begging for more news. Assuming Chrissey was now out of danger, Marian asked him to advance fifteen pounds out of her six-monthly income to pay for a holiday so that her sister could get away from 'that fever-infected place'.[61] Isaac wrote back immediately saying that Chrissey had taken a turn for the worse and was now gravely ill. Unfortunately he does not seem to have bothered to let Marian know when the danger had passed. It was from Fanny that she eventually got the news a fortnight later that both Chrissey and Katy had pulled through.[62]

The fact that Marian had felt bold enough to ask Isaac to advance fifteen pounds from her income, when two years previously he had told her that he was unable to accommodate even her reasonable request that she be paid on time, suggests a new confidence in the circumstances of her own life. By the end of 1857 she would have earned £443 for *Scenes of Clerical Life* in both magazine and book form. In the last analysis, if Isaac insisted on retaining control over her life by refusing to arrange an advance, Marian was in a position to send Chrissey the fifteen pounds direct.

There were other reasons why Marian felt brave enough to tell her family about her personal situation. Her happiness with Lewes was deepening and becoming more secure. The unarticulated fear that he might one day leave had receded. The birth of another child to Agnes by Thornton Hunt on 21 May made it more unlikely than ever that the marriage would ever be mended. There was no one in the world, except perhaps the three teenage boys at Hofwyl, who was still unaware of their father's relationship with Marian. And even they would not be kept in the dark for much longer. Over the next year Lewes began to drop Miss Evans's name into the conversation when he visited the boys. By July 1858 he was bringing them presents from his mysterious new friend.

Five days after the arrival of Agnes's new and final baby, a girl called Mildred, Marian wrote to both Isaac and Fanny explaining her situation. Or rather, she hinted at it in language which, to the contemporary reader, seems coded and confusing. Indeed, in the letter to Isaac it sounds as if Marian is saying she is married in the ordinary, orthodox way. This suggests that, despite her disclaimer in the first sentence that Isaac would be 'surprized' to hear her news, she guessed that he was already aware of her general situation, even if he did not know all the details. She carefully avoids using the word 'marriage' in her letter, reporting instead that she has 'changed my name' and has 'someone to take care of me in the world'. She refers to Lewes as her 'husband' and describes him as being 'occupied entirely with scientific and learned pursuits.'[63]

In the same envelope Marian enclosed a letter to Fanny, explaining that she was not sure of her full address in Leamington. Written in a more intimate, sisterly tone, the contents are just as confusing.

> Next, let me ask you to open your eyes and look surprised, for I am going to tell you some very unexpected news. I am sure you retain enough friendship and sisterly affection for me to be glad that I should have a kind husband to love me and take care of me . . . My husband has been well known to me for years, and marriage is a very sober and serious thing when people are as old as we are, so that the future is as little of a problem to me, as it can be to any of us. He is older than I am, not at all full of wealth or beauty, but very full indeed of literature and physiology and zoology and other invisible endowments, which happily have their market value. Still better, he is a man of high honour and integrity and the kindest heart, of which, of course, I think all the better because it is devoted to me.[64]

It is hard to know what Fanny Houghton made of this. Her response has not survived, although we know that it was prompt. Marian gave her 'a thousand thanks' for it and seems to have been relieved by the content, for her next letter is full of tender concern. She advises on cheap places on the Continent that might be good for Henry Houghton's health and asks Fanny to put gentle pressure on Isaac to advance the fifteen pounds for Chrissey's holiday.[65] It is just possible that Fanny may have failed to understand that Marian was announcing a cohabitation rather than a formal marriage. On the other hand, this was the woman who back in the 1840s had read the Higher Criticism and confided to her half-sister that she shared her doubts about the literal interpretation of the Bible. It seems unlikely that such a shrewd, modern mind would not have put two and two together. But whatever the reason behind Fanny's initially generous reaction to her sister's news, it changed sharply once she had been spoken to by Isaac. Only a fortnight later Fanny wrote breaking off all contact with Marian.

Isaac's response was slower than Fanny's and when it eventually arrived, on 9 June, the reason for the delay became clear. The letter came not from Isaac himself but from Vincent Holbeche, the family solicitor, who lost no time in explaining the situation. 'I have had an interview with your Brother in consequence of your letter to him announcing your marriage. He is so much hurt at your not having previously made some communication to him as to your intention and prospects that he cannot make up his mind to write, feeling that he could not do so in a Brotherly Spirit.'[66] Holbeche then proceeds, ominously, 'Permit me to ask when and where you were married' before asking for details about Lewes's address so that the payment of her income to his bank account might go through smoothly.

Marian replied immediately to Holbeche. In a tone of proud disinterestedness she says that she quite understands Isaac's reasons for using an intermediary – if her feelings were equally hostile she would have had to do the same. Of her alliance with Lewes she explains that 'Our marriage is not a legal one, though it is regarded by us both as a sacred bond. He is at present unable to contract a legal marriage, because, though long deprived of his first wife by her misconduct, he is not legally divorced.' Marian then explains that although she has been Lewes's 'wife' for nearly three years, she has not told her family before because 'knowing that their views of life differ in many respects from my own, I wished not to give them unnecessary pain.' She then carefully makes the point that her decision to keep her relationship with Lewes secret had nothing to do with self-interest.

> It may be desirable to mention to you that I am not dependent on any one, the larger part of my income for several years having been derived from my own constant labour as a writer. You will perceive, therefore, that in my conduct towards my own family I have not been guided by any motives of self-interest, since I have been neither in the reception nor the expectation of the slightest favour from them.[67]

If her tone sounds hard and defensive, Marian makes it clear that her feelings towards Holbeche himself are warm. She finishes by telling him how grateful she has always been for the way he intervened when her father was making his will. Instead of being given household goods like her sisters, she received £100 cash, which helped tide her over that difficult first year. 'I daresay you have forgotten the circumstances, but I have always remembered gratefully that instance of thoughtfulness on my behalf, and am glad to have an opportunity of acknowledging it.'[68]

A month after sending off the momentous letter to Holbeche Marian wrote to Sara Hennell saying, 'I dare say I shall never have any further correspondence with my brother, which will be a great relief to me.'[69] She was right.

Although Holbeche forwarded the letter, Isaac never replied. Not until Marian lawfully married John Cross in 1880 did he break his silence by writing to congratulate her. Yet behind the scenes Isaac remained deeply engaged with his sister, instructing Fanny and Chrissey to have nothing more to do with her. Both women, although older than Isaac, immediately complied. Chrissey one can understand: she was dependent on Isaac's grudging patronage, if not his actual charity. But the response of brisk, clever Fanny, a prosperous married woman and only a half-sister, remains a disappointment to this day.

Chrissey's compliance with Isaac came as a shock to Marian, who only a few days earlier had confidently predicted to Sara Hennell: 'I do not think Chrissey will give up correspondence with me in any case, and that is the point I most care about, as I shall still be able to help her as far as my means will allow.' Chrissey stayed silent until two years later when she knew she was dying. In late February 1859 she wrote to Marian, expressing her regret for 'having ceased to write and neglected one who under all circumstances was kind to me and mine'.[70] Marian intimated that she was prepared to go to Warwickshire, but Chrissey responded in a few pencilled words that she did not think she was strong enough to bear the excitement of seeing her estranged sister. By 15 March she was dead. The whole scrappy coda upset Marian intensely. Lewes, normally the most generous of men, confided in his journal that he almost wished Chrissey had not made this last stab at contact, because it came just when Marian had more or less become resigned to the silence.

The split with Isaac was the final 'divorce' of the 'Brother and Sister' sonnets. The whole incident had been a reprise of the holy war, played out in the next generation down. Isaac Evans might not yet have the stature of Robert Evans but at the age of forty he had assumed the duty of upholding the law of the father. Fifteen years before, Isaac had accused Mary Ann of being a drain on her family because she refused to find a husband. Now she had found one and he was telling her it was the wrong sort. She had put off the confrontation for a long time because she knew the trouble it would bring. In early 1856, just before the departure to Ilfracombe and Tenby on the holiday that was to see her start her career as a fiction writer, she had written a short piece for the 29 March edition of the *Leader* on a new edition of Sophocles's *Antigone*.[71] Antigone is a strong woman who defies King Creon because she wants to give a proper burial to her brother Polynices who has been declared a traitor. The conflict is set up between the rules of the state and the necessity to honour private needs. Isaac had started as Polynices, the brother whom Antigone will die for, the brother of the early sonnets, the young Tom Tulliver whom Maggie trots after like a pony. But over time he had transmuted into Creon, the critical, conventional voice – of George Combe, of Harriet Martineau, of the adult Tom Tulliver.

The effect of this final divorce from her family was to bind Marian more closely than ever to Lewes. Strangely, she counted this time as one of her happiest. In her usual end-of-year journal assessment for 1857 she wrote:

My life has deepened unspeakably during the last year: I feel a greater capacity for moral and intellectual enjoyment, a more acute sense of my deficiencies in the past, a more solemn desire to be faithful to coming duties, than I remember at any former period of my life. And my happiness has deepened too: the blessedness of a perfect love and union grows daily . . . Few women, I fear, have had such reason as I have to think the long sad years of youth were worth living for the sake of middle age.[72]

★   ★   ★

The decision to reveal the true identity of 'George Eliot' to Blackwood in February 1858 came because Marian and Lewes were about to leave for a twelve-week trip to Germany. Until now, Blackwood's correspondence with his new author had been sent care of Lewes, even during the Islands holiday. But to suggest that Eliot also happened to be spending his summer in Germany with Lewes would be straining credibility to breaking point.

In any case, it was vital for publisher and author to be able to communicate freely without an intermediary, since Marian was by now six months into her new full-length novel. On the evening when she revealed her identity to Blackwood she had sweetened what was probably a bitter though expected pill by giving him the first thirteen chapters of *Adam Bede* which, she had already promised, would be 'a country story – full of the breath of cows and the scent of hay'.[73] Blackwood glanced at the first page, smiled, told her, 'This will do', then settled down to read as much as he could on his way back to Edinburgh, feeling 'very savage when the waning light stopped me as we neared the Scottish Border'.[74]

Logistically there was no reason why the second part of *Adam Bede* could not be written abroad. Lewes wanted to go to Munich, a place which, Marian told Sara, 'swarms with professors of all sorts'.[75] Buoyed up by the success of 'Sea-Side Studies', Lewes was determined to continue his transformation from a journalist who wrote about science into a professional scientist. He had already started work on *The Physiology of Common Life*, a serious and, as it turned out, hugely influential book which would be very different in tone from the chatty rock-pool amateurism of 'Sea-Side Studies'.

They left London on 7 April and the trip out, which included a two-day stop at Nürnberg, gave Marian new material for her 'naturalising' eye. 'Every house differed from its neighbour, and had a physiognomy of its own,' she told her journal, 'though a beautiful family likeness ran through them all, as if the burghers of that old city were of one heart and soul.' These careful descriptions of the professional observer were cut across by more urgent splashes. At Bamberg she noticed an elderly couple in the train who 'spoke to each other and looked so affectionately, that we said directly "Shall we be so when we are old?" '[76]

In many ways being in Munich was like a replay of the German trip of 1854. They even bumped into Strauss again, though this time the meeting flowed more smoothly. Once again, the weather was unsettled, which sent Marian into a grim cycle of headache and shivers. A stream of invitations – to dinner, the opera, the theatre – cut into the working day, slowing down progress on *Adam Bede*. Lewes's fantasies about being acknowledged as a professional intellectual rather than a pushy huckster were more than fulfilled. The Goethe book had made his name in Germany, and every scientist, historian and writer who clustered round the first-rate University of Munich was eager to make his acquaintance. Laboratories were thrown open, books lent, introductions made and a steady supply of live frogs provided for his experiments.

Just as during her previous stay in Germany, no one seemed to know, or care, that Marian was technically unmarried. But the pleasure of being able to go out and about with Lewes was soon spoiled by being obliged to play a role to which she was not accustomed – that of wife. Instead of being able to join in discussions with men of the calibre of the anatomist Karl von Siebold and the chemist Justus von Liebig, Marian was obliged to sit on the sofa at the other end of the room, listening to their wives spout what she contemptuously called 'stupidities'.[77] It was a timely reminder of how little she had lost by her exclusion from a conventional social life in England, a point she was to make often over the years.

Marian's response to orthodox gender roles would always be contradictory. For while she was happy to have escaped the usual duties assigned to women, she was keen to celebrate them in others. She needed and wanted women to be gentle, nurturing and domestic. She was still hungry for a mother, especially when Lewes departed for a week to Hofwyl on 18 June leaving her feeling edgy and abandoned. Frau von Siebold obligingly stepped into the role by bringing Marian flowers, taking her to the theatre and sweeping her off to meet her sister.[78] In her comments on German life and art Marian increasingly picked out the mundane – which for women meant the domestic – as worthy of attention. In her journal she notes with pleasure several little family scenes where the women are absorbed in domestic work, looking after children and keeping their cottages clean. Even professors' wives get more approval if they are doing homey things. And at the local art gallery it was Rubens's ability to capture the energy of the everyday which delighted her: 'What a grand, glowing, forceful thing life looks in his pictures – the men such grand bearded grappling beings fit to do the work of the world, the women such real mothers.'[79] In Dresden, where the Leweses travelled next, it was examples of the Dutch realist school by Dou and Terborch, complete with placid housewives and calm grandmothers, which enthralled her.

Here is the puzzle about Marian which bothered critics then and now. While in her most intimate and habitual life she flouted orthodox social roles, her politics and her novels dealt with the *status quo*, with life how it is rather than how it might be. At the very time that she was sneering at dumpy German Fraus who expected her to chat about women's things, she was writing that famous chapter 17 in *Adam Bede* – 'In Which the Story Pauses a Little' – which demands the reader celebrate a world of embedded custom and habit – a world which includes women in all their frumpy domesticity. In this chapter she – or perhaps it should be 'he' since the voice is that of Eliot's omniscient narrator – takes issue with the lady reader who wants pretty people and a romantic plot far removed from daily realities.

But, bless us, things may be lovable that are not altogether handsome, I hope? . . . Paint us an angel, if you can . . . paint us yet oftener a Madonna . . . but do not impose on us any aesthetic rules which shall banish from the region of Art those old women scraping carrots with their work-worn hands, those heavy clowns taking holiday in a dingy pot-house, those rounded backs and stupid weather-beaten faces that have bent over the spade and done the rough work of the world – those homes with their tin pans, their brown pitchers, their rough curs, and their clusters of onions.[80]

After six merry weeks in Munich, Marian and Lewes moved on to a rainy stay in the Tyrol, a nostalgic trip (for Lewes) to Vienna and an important stop (for Marian) in Prague. It was here that she saw the Jewish synagogue that would figure in her short story 'The Lifted Veil'. On 17 July they reached Dresden and settled for six hard-working weeks. By swearing off society – 'we live like Hermits here,' said Lewes – and getting up at six every morning, Marian managed almost to complete the second half of the second volume of *Adam Bede*.[81] It was only once they were on their way back home through Leipzig that they relaxed their regime to accept dinner invitations from the usual mix of publishers, professors and scientists. On 2 September they arrived home in Richmond.

Shortly afterwards, Marian completed volume two and sent Blackwood the next helping of *Adam Bede*. Writing to her as 'My Dear Sir' he had already commented favourably on the chapters he had taken away with him back in March. 'The story is altogether very novel and I cannot recollect anything at all like it. I find myself constantly thinking of the characters as real personages, which is a capital sign.' Of course, he had made the usual worried noises about those bits which seemed rude or *risqué*: the proverb describing one of the village girls seemed to imply more than it should and he hoped (in vain, as it turned out) that Arthur Donnithorne's secret meetings with Hetty 'will not come to the usual sad catastrophe!' He warmed to Dinah's relentless Methodist piety and hoped that the easygoing clergyman Mr Irwine might get more godly as the story went on. Having regretted accepting 'Mr Gilfil' and 'Janet's Repentance' for serialisation before he had been able to read them through, Blackwood was careful to ask this time for 'a sketch of the rest of the story'.[82] Marian refused, knowing perfectly well that if she told him about her plan for a plot which included premarital sex, an illegitimate baby and infanticide Blackwood was bound to panic. She explained that there was no point in her submitting a synopsis, believing that her story could not be 'judged apart from my *treatment*, which alone determines the moral quality of art'.[83] Her point was this: the most anodyne plot could turn out to be deeply immoral, a scandalous story might illustrate profound truths. What mattered was the way it was done. Sensing that *Adam Bede* probably contained strong stuff, Blackwood decided that it should go straight into book form, bypassing serialisation in *Maga*.

Even now Blackwood was nervous about just what it was he had on his hands. Despite his support for George Eliot, he never seems entirely to have understood the genius of what he was reading. Once again, he gave a muted response to the second part of *Adam Bede* and had to be nudged into enthusiasm by Lewes. On 4 October he wrote to congratulate Marian on Hetty Sorrel – 'One seems to *see* the little villain' – and confesses that he finds it hard to feel as sympathetic as he should for stern, unbending Adam when he discovers that Hetty has been having an affair with Arthur. He warns Marian that 'the degree of success will depend very much upon the third volume' and says that he will wait until he has seen it before he decides how many copies to print.[84] In the event, the third volume moved Blackwood to unusual superlatives. 'I am happy to tell you that I think it capital,' he wrote on 3 November and made immediate arrangements to start setting up the type.[85]

Blackwood's hostile (in Marian's eyes) response to 'Janet's Repentance' had effectively stopped *Scenes of Clerical Life* and made her determined to start over, this time taking a larger canvas. The story of *Adam Bede* is famously knitted together from two sources which date from her youth. First there is the anecdote her Methodist Aunt Elizabeth Evans had told her about the time, before her marriage, when she was a lay Methodist preacher. Elizabeth Tomlinson, as she was then, had befriended a young girl condemned to hang for murdering her illegitimate baby. In a state of extreme distress and denial, Mary Voce refused to admit her crime to either herself or the authorities. Elizabeth prayed with her overnight in her prison cell, finally obtaining a last-minute confession before accompanying her to the gallows. Lewes had been struck by the incident when Marian had mentioned it to him in December 1856, suggesting that it would make a good story. From this little seed Marian spun the story of Hetty Sorrel, a farmgirl who becomes pregnant by the young squire and tries to hide the evidence by murdering the baby. Condemned to hang, Hetty is comforted by her kinswoman Dinah Morris, a Methodist lay preacher, who stays with her in prison and finally coaxes a confession from her.

The second source for the novel was the stories Robert Evans had told Marian about his youth as a carpenter, forester and bailiff on the Newdigates' Derbyshire and Staffordshire estates at the turn of the century, the period in which *Adam Bede* is set. By the time Marian came to write her retrospective journal account of the 'History of *Adam Bede*' she was in the middle of an embarrassing crisis, which suggested that she had simply 'lifted' characters from real life and put them straight into print. In the circumstances she was defensively quick to maintain that 'Adam is not my father any more than Dinah is my aunt'.[86] None the less Adam's physical and moral uprightness, the sense of his having been hewn from a massive piece of English oak, recall everything that we know about Robert Evans.

We meet Adam in the opening scene, at the end of a long and hard day. He is the foreman in a carpentry business which serves the local farming community, building doors, windows and wainscoting. Already we are in the middle of the 'working-day world', familiar from the Dutch interior scenes which Marian admired so much. Adam, too, is described in a way which makes him sound as if he has come straight out of a Rubens painting. He is monumental yet precise, his brawny arm 'likely to win the prize for feats of strength; yet the long supple hand, with its broad finger-tips, looked ready for works of skill'.[87]

Adam's attitude to his work is informed by a reverence for his fellow man. Unlike his Methodist brother Seth – shades of Robert's younger brother Samuel – he is not interested in textual disputation or elaborate piety. Prompted by the workmen's talk about the girl preacher who is due to talk on the common that night, Adam argues for a worship more integrated with the everyday, affirming that 'there's the sperrit o' God in all things and all times – weekday as well as Sunday – and i' the great works and inventions, and i' the figuring and the mechanics'. Sounding like a Feuerbachian he argues: 'if a man does bits o' jobs out o' working hours – builds a oven for 's wife to save her from going to the bakehouse, or scrats at his bit o' garden and makes two potatoes grow istead o' one, he's doing more good, and he's just as near to God, as if he was running after some preacher and a-praying and a-groaning.'[88]

Adam's powerful integrity brings him to the notice of the gentry, towards whom he is naturally deferential. A long-time favourite of the squire's grandson, Arthur Donnithorne, he is appointed overseer of the estate's considerable woodland. Clearly Adam is destined to rise, just like Robert Evans, to a position of importance and influence in the local community. When the narrator pauses at the end of chapter 19 to deliver an oration on the quiet, honourable virtues of Adam Bede it is impossible not to hear also a tribute from Marian Evans to her father.

> He was not an average man. Yet such men as he are reared here and there in every generation of our peasant artisans – with an inheritance of affections nurtured by a simple family life of common need and common industry, and an inheritance of faculties trained in skilful courageous labour: they make their way upward, rarely as geniuses, most commonly as painstaking honest men, with the skill and conscience to do well the tasks that lie before them. Their lives have no discernible echo beyond the neighbourhood where they dwelt, but you are almost sure to find there some good piece of road, some building, some application of mineral produce, some improvement in farming practice, some reform of parish abuses, with which their names are associated by one or two generations after them.[89]

Other characters, too, seem drawn from Marian's earliest past. Mrs Poyser, the fretful, bustling farmer's wife, fits some of what we know of Marian's own mother, Christiana. The dairy, which is Mrs Poyser's pride and joy, was likewise the centre of Mrs Evans's prestige and influence at Griff House. The stream of pithy sayings which pour from Mrs. Poyser's mouth are not, as Marian was quickly indignant to point out to Blackwood, local and general turns of phrase: 'there is not one thing put into Mrs Poyser's mouth that is not fresh from my own mint.'[90] But while the specifics may have been her own, it is hard to imagine where else she could have got that voice except from sharp-tongued Christiana Evans and her trio of formidable Pearson sisters.

Still, Marian was right to be annoyed by the naïve assumption that her art consisted simply of transferring family members and recollections straight into print. In her journal she insisted: 'Indeed, there is not a single *portrait* in "Adam Bede"; only the suggestions of experience "wrought up into new combinations".'[91] It was from those scraps of experience that she built the people who walk through her books. Her characters have intricate psychologies, made up of the constant interplay between inherited personality and social environment, nature and nurture. 'Our deeds determine us, as much as we determine our deeds; and until we know what has been or will be the peculiar combination of outward with inward facts, which constitutes a man's critical actions, it will be better not to think ourselves wise about his character.'[92] The best example of Eliot's psychological sophistication comes with Mrs Poyser who, in the hands of Charles Dickens, would be reduced to a two-dimensional character memorable only for a series of catch-phrases. Eliot, by contrast, is able to extract the pithy humour from Mrs Poyser – one of her sayings was even quoted during a Commons debate in March 1859 – while still making her a fully rounded character capable of emotional growth. Eliot places the Poysers in a specific social context, among those hard-working tenant farmers who dread social disgrace as much as a curdled cheese. When her niece Hetty is exposed as sexually incontinent and a murderess, Mrs Poyser feels the shame acutely and personally. By the end of the book she has changed from a self-righteous scold into a reflective woman, demonstrating something approaching pity for the poor girl. In a Dickens novel she would simply be repeating her best one-liners.

Arthur Donnithorne, too, is a masterly study of 'mixed and erring humanity', to use Marian's favourite quotation from Goethe. The attractive young squire of Hayslope starts the story as fresh as a daisy, with a natural benevolence, which means that he does not have to work very hard to be good. He genuinely wants the best for his tenants, his family and his friends. Most of all he wants the best for himself. His ideas of right behaviour are hazy and lazy, and never involve any personal discomfort. When he does someone a wrong he is quick to make amends, but in a manner so self-serving that it fails to mean much: 'if he should unfortunately break a man's legs in his rash driving, [he] will be able to pension him handsomely; or if he should happen to spoil a woman's existence for her, will make it up to her with expensive *bon-bons*, packed up and directed by his own hand.'[93] Essentially narcissistic, Arthur never empathises sufficiently to wonder about his effect on others. He has his way – literally, with Hetty – then feels sorry for himself, and for her, when the liaison threatens to disrupt his life. Well-meaning and kind, he is also selfish, thoughtless and weak.

Hetty, too, is psychologically true, and the narrator's (and the reader's) response to her correspondingly complex. She is as beautiful as the kitten, baby and canary to which she is often compared, and her rosy charms hold everyone's attention. In chapter 7, 'The Dairy', Arthur, the narrator and the reader watch while the self-conscious cherub pats and moulds the butter in such a way as to show off her best side and her prettiest dimples. She is not a bad girl, we are told later, simply a 'trivial' one. But she commits one of the biggest sins possible in George Eliot's moral world, that of being discontented with the circumstances of her everyday life. She finds farmwork boring and hates looking after her small cousins. The local suitors who present themselves, including Adam Bede, seem dull and ploddy alongside the dashing figure of Arthur Donnithorne, who showers her with kisses and pearl ear-rings. She feels hot surges of frustration that her bonnet is faded, her shoes clumpy, her handkerchief unscented. All she thinks about is how marriage to Arthur will turn her into a lady.

Hetty's problem is that she has no real relationship with the physical or human landscape around her. 'There are some plants that have hardly any roots: you may tear them from their native nook of rock or wall, and just lay them over your ornamental flower-pot, and they blossom none the worse. Hetty could have cast all her past life behind her and never cared to be reminded of it again.'[94] Dinah Morris, by contrast, has 'grown deep' into her native county and cannot easily transplant herself to Hayslope from native Stonyshire. What keeps her properly attached to her birthplace is not so much the bleak, treeless uplands as the rough miners and factory workers whose lives she understands and to whose souls she ministers. Hetty, by contrast, hates the witless farmers, artisans and servants who make up her social world. In the end her crime is not that of having sex before marriage, or even murdering her baby, but of wanting to upend the social order by escaping from who and what she is.

It is the landscape, then, which is the major character in *Adam Bede*. Although Marian researched details of local flora from secondary sources, she based her portrait of the agricultural year on her own memories. In chapter 22, 'Going to the Birthday Feast', she describes the tail end of July as 'a time of leisure on the farm – that pause between hay and corn-harvest' – a point which would surely be missed by any town-born writer working in the library. The flowers are all over, the animals have lost their baby prettiness, the woods 'are all one dark monotonous green'.[95] The precision of the details owes a great deal to those 'naturalising' practice runs in Marian's journal.

Human life in Hayslope is plotted with equal precision. On Sunday mornings the farmers huddle outside the church door discussing business before rushing in to the service at the last minute. The tenants who sit down at Arthur's coming-of-age are ranked carefully according to the size of their land. When Wiry Ben dances at the party he does so earnestly and with none of the elegance of what the narrator calls 'a ballet rustic'.[96] This is the real countryside, where village girls get pregnant, cheeses curdle and local farmers can't help being pleased when the crops in a neighbouring county fail.

It is odd to see Marian celebrating the rituals of agricultural life as the social glue which binds individuals into complex moral relationships with one another. For just like Hetty, the teenage Mary Ann Evans had often found herself bored and repulsed by the coarseness of the people around her. The preparations for Isaac's twenty-third birthday party had made her grumpy; Michaelmas, with its servant hirings, were so 'nauseating' to her.[97] Her town-bred Evangelicalism had made the beery chat and loud laughter of farm life seem coarse and disgusting. But now she found in these old rituals and formulaic responses a consolidation of the ties which for centuries had bound men and women together in mutual obligation.

Religion is valued in *Adam Bede* for the way in which it supports humane values. The local clergyman is Revd Irwine, a cheerful Anglican who preaches poorly but loves the people among whom he lives. A gentleman and a scholar, he is also something of a pagan, preferring a quotation from Sophocles over one from Isaiah. He is not good at biblical disputation, but the names of the young men and women he christened twenty years ago remain as fresh as ever. Crucially, he perceives no threat from Dinah Morris, the young woman who preaches extempore from a cart on the common. Methodism had been set up by John Wesley to fill the void left by exactly that lax Anglicanism which Irwine represents. Dinah's mission is to reach those who feel themselves unmoved by the tepid rituals of Sunday church service. But just as she behaves gracefully towards Irwine, so he takes a keenly benign interest in her work. The young girl and the middle-aged man refuse to condemn one another, but instead seek the value in an approach so different from their own. Both Irwine's good-natured paternalism and Dinah's intense soul-searching manifest in the acts of practical charity of which the Feuerbachian narrator so obviously approves.

There had always been a question mark in Lewes's and Marian's minds, if not in Blackwood's, about her ability to 'do' drama. *Adam Bede* was not a 'Scene' but a novel, and no amount of delightful descriptions of butter-making or country dancing was going to sustain a story over 600 pages. In her journal account of the 'History of *Adam Bede*', Marian says that when she began to write the only elements she had decided on besides the character of Dinah were the character of Adam, his relation to Arthur and their mutual relation to Hetty. It was Lewes who provided the two key suggestions. From the earliest chapters he became convinced that Dinah would be a popular character – possibly true for contemporary readers, surely not for us – and suggested that ultimately she should marry Adam. More successfully, he suggested that Arthur and Adam should have a fight in the woods over their competing attentions for Hetty.[98]

While Marian did manage to sustain dramatic tension for three-quarters of the book, the last part is an anticlimax. For writers of realism, endings are always difficult, a point Marian made to Blackwood when he complained that the conclusions of 'Amos' and 'Gilfil' were too huddled up: 'Conclusions are the weak point of most authors, but some of the fault lies in the very nature of a conclusion, which is at best a negation.'[99] Hetty is not hung in the end, but gets a pardon, which Arthur delivers at the very last minute – a device taken from Scott's *Heart of Midlothian*. Next Marian has to devise a way for Adam and Dinah to come together, a tedious business. In particular, Marian has to work hard to get Dinah, who has previously turned down Seth on the grounds that she wants to devote herself to her ministry, to accept Adam. Marian's solution – a carefully researched one – is to use the 1803 ban on women remaining as Methodist preachers to have Dinah give up the ministry. Now the way is free for her to move to Hayslope and become a wife and mother.

Dinah's destiny has always attracted much criticism from feminist critics, who see it as the first in a line of compromised endings for Eliot heroines, those energetic girls like Esther and Dorothea who are given nothing more exciting to do than become some man's wife. What makes it all the more difficult in Dinah's case is that, historically, her fate could have been different. Just like Marian's Aunt Elizabeth, she could have joined another Methodist congregation and continued to preach, even combining her ministry with family life. But Marian was not writing campaigning, Utopian fiction. The fact was that around 1800 very few middle-class women – which is what Dinah becomes through her marriage to the upwardly mobile Adam – did work outside their husband's business.

What has bothered critics is not so much that Marian gave her heroines such low-key endings, but that she threw the moral weight of the book behind them. She seems to approve of the littleness of Dinah's destiny, just as she had delighted in all those paintings of Dutch matrons, visits to homely German professors' wives and Chrissey looking after her babies. Yet it was a life she had rejected for herself, often scathingly so. It is this tension between the sacredness of *things as they are* and her own trajectory as a self-made woman which confused Marian's contemporaries just as it continues to unsettle us.

CHAPTER 10

'A Companion Picture of Provincial Life'

The Mill on the Floss
1859–60

'TALKING OF GOOD books it is really gratifying to see our confidence in Adam Bede so confirmed,' Lewes chirruped to Blackwood on 21 April 1859. 'Two out of every three people I meet speak to me about it.'[1]

Only a few months earlier the mood had been very different. Although the book had been ready to go to press at the end of November 1858, Blackwood had dragged his feet. His excuse to the Leweses was that he was already committed to bringing out Bulwer-Lytton's novel *What Will He Do With It?* in January, and did not want to run the two books against each other. The fact that Bulwer-Lytton's dithering over the proofs had caused a backlog at the printers may have had more to do with it. But perhaps there was also a reluctance on Blackwood's part to take the plunge with a book whose subject matter and pseudonymous authorship were almost certainly bound to cause a storm.

The wait made Marian and Lewes jumpy. A few weeks earlier Herbert Spencer had told them over dinner that the notorious blab John Chapman had guessed the real identity of George Eliot. Rumours drifting in from Warwickshire suggested that Evans family members were also putting two and two together. If publication were delayed any longer there would be no chance of bringing out *Adam Bede* pseudonymously and, as Marian told Blackwood on 1 December 1858, 'I wish the book to be judged quite apart from its authorship.'[2] Fidgety with frustration, she put together a 'Remonstrance' which, she told Blackwood in a letter of 22 December, Mr Lewes had suggested should be attached to the beginning of *Adam Bede*.[3] The essay has been lost, but presumably it took nosy critics and readers to task for trying to break the author's incognito. Blackwood hated it and pulled Lewes up sharply for indulging Marian's dangerous fantasies: 'It is not like so knowing a party as you to suggest so dangerous a preface as that proposed for G.E.'[4]

The matter was quickly dropped and the Leweses were forced to sit on their hands for another five weeks until *Adam Bede* finally appeared. Fleeting though the crisis had been, it flagged many of the problems that were to make the following year such a harrowing one. Marian's ambivalence about being identified as the author of her work, Lewes's tendency to fly off the handle and Blackwood's instinctive dislike of confrontation all played a part in creating the difficulties to come.

When *Adam Bede* appeared in three volumes on 1 February 1859 it was not an instant hit. The all-important Charles Edward Mudie, who ran the biggest circulating library in the country and could make or break a new novel, agreed to take fifty copies, grudgingly increased to 500 under pressure. It was only when the notices began to appear, three weeks later, that everyone started discussing – and buying – the latest literary sensation, George Eliot's *Adam Bede*. Mostly the reviewers picked up on the same things as Blackwood. They were charmed by the pastoral, amused by Mrs Poyser and her pithy sayings, shocked by the obstetric details – which strike the modern reader as downright coy – of Hetty giving birth in a field. The high point was E. S. Dallas's review in *The Times* on 12 April which declared, 'There can be no mistake about *Adam Bede*. It is a first-rate novel, and its author takes rank at once among the masters of the art.'[5] The effect on sales was stunning. By the middle of March the first edition was sold out. By the summer the book was on its fifth print run. Gratifyingly, Mudie begged to be allowed to order extra. At the year's end it was calculated that a very healthy 15,000 copies of *Adam Bede* had gone.

Even more gratifying were the personal testimonies that found their way to Marian. 'Praise is so much less sweet than comprehension and sympathy,' she wrote to Charles Bray on 7 September 1859 and luckily she got plenty of both.[6] Jane Carlyle, still trying to decide whether George Eliot was a clergyman, gave the surest confirmation of success when she declared that the novel had put her 'in charity with the whole human race'.[7] J. A. Froude, perhaps unaware he was writing to the ardent Miss Evans from whom he had fled ten years previously, framed his praise in equally specific terms, declaring that *Adam Bede* 'gave no pleasure. It gave a palpitation of the heart. That was not pleasure; but it was a passionate interest.'[8]

In Edinburgh the reaction was equally discerning. A cabinet-making brother of the Blackwoods' clerk George Simpson responded with delight to the accuracy of the workshop scenes.[9] His testimony went a long way towards cancelling the later sneer of Thomas Carlyle: 'I found out in the first two pages that it was a woman's writing – she supposed that in making a door, you last of all put in the *panels*.'[10] It is lucky that Marian never heard this, for no one's approval mattered more than Thomas Carlyle's. Knowing that his youth had been spent 'among the furrowed fields and pious peasantry', the Sage of Chelsea had become identified in her mind with Robert Evans. If Carlyle liked the book then so, by her odd reckoning, would her father have done. In fact, Carlyle never could be persuaded to admire George Eliot, even before he knew she was that 'strong-minded woman' Marian Evans, and certainly not afterwards.

Even the fact that the Queen admired *Adam Bede* would not have made up for the disappointment over Carlyle. Victoria's recommendations had sped all over Europe, from Prussia, where her daughter was Crown Princess, to Belgium, where her uncle Leopold was King. Hayslope's rural rhythms and old-fashioned moral values reminded her of the Scottish Highlands. Adam Bede, with his strong back and straight talking, could almost have been one of her beloved gillies. It was now that Her Majesty commissioned two watercolours, one of Dinah preaching, the other of Hetty in the dairy.[11]

It felt sweet to Marian, ostracised for the past five years, to be fussed over, accepted (albeit as George Eliot) and placed at the very heart of the culture which had snubbed her. Yet as sales soared and reviewers gushed, she found herself overcome by a cold, sick dread. On 10 April she told Blackwood, 'few authors, I suppose, who have had a real success, have known less of the flush and the sensations of triumph that are talked of as the accompaniments of success.'[12]

What spoiled Marian's pleasure was her deep suspicion of popularity. Writing novels was, for her, a moral activity, more akin to producing philosophy than telling stories. While discerning comments from Jane Carlyle, Charles Dickens and J. A. Froude filled her with pleasure, she was gripped by the fear that if too many people liked her writing she must be doing something wrong. She even managed to communicate this to the normally pragmatic Lewes, whose response to the praise for *Adam Bede* became uncharacteristically tetchy. The opinion of the *Statesman*'s reviewer that the book was 'One of the best novels we have read for a long time' only succeeded in making Lewes snap, 'The nincompoop couldn't see the distinction between Adam and the mass of novels he had been reading.'[13] Behind the graceless comment lay Marian's contagious terror that *Adam Bede* had been mistaken by reviewers and readers alike as nothing more than an accomplished potboiler. For this reason she scrutinised Blackwood for signs that he was trying to market the book in the wrong way. On 25 February 1859 she wrote begging him not to extract from the reviews phrases like 'best novel of the season' or 'best novel we have read for a long while' in order to puff new editions of the book.[14] Yet, confusingly, only a few months earlier she had quizzed him sharply about why Mudie 'has almost always left the C[lerical] S[cenes] out of his advertised list, although he puts in very trashy and obscure books?'[15]

Luckily by now Blackwood recognised his new author's tricky, tortured nature. He also understood what he was required to do about it. In a tactful letter of 16 March 1859 he opens with 'I think I may now fairly congratulate you upon being a *popular* as well as a great author', before continuing carefully, 'The sale is nothing to the ring of applause that I hear in all directions. The only qualm that ever came across me as to the success of the book was that really to enjoy it I required to give my mind to it and I trembled for that large section of Novel readers who have little or no mind to give, but now I think the general applause is fairly enlisting even noodles.'[16]

The central contradiction about Marian which Blackwood grasped was that despite her proclaimed indifference to what the mass of people thought about her books, she remained morbidly dependent on their good opinion. She had never wanted to be an avant-garde writer, appealing only to the knowing few. By choosing to write novels, and by setting her stories among ordinary people, she was reaching for the broadest audience. And because that audience would, if it had known the details of Marian Evans's personal life, surely have rejected her, it became doubly important that George Eliot's novels should be accepted unconditionally. Any dip in sales was interpreted by Marian as a judgement not just of her artistic skill but of her decision to live with Lewes out of wedlock. Deep despair combined with lofty declarations of indifference usually followed quickly. It would not be long before Lewes decided to keep the sales figures to himself and begged Blackwood to do the same.

This violent swing between the need to be loved and the desire to stand above it all, between the thirst for acclaim and the suspicion of popularity, exhausted Marian in the months following the publication of *Adam Bede*. More crucially, it led her into a bewilderingly volatile position about money, which came close to destroying her relationship with the Blackwoods before it had hardly started.

It was the need to improve their joint finances which had first led Lewes to suggest that Marian try her hand at fiction. Initially Marian was able to rationalise this motivation by the curious suggestion that there was something 'antiseptic' about writing for money which guarded against the production of highly coloured trash. But with the huge success of *Adam Bede* came new temptations. It would be so easy to follow the example of a popular Blackwood novelist like Margaret Oliphant who paid her sons' Eton fees by churning out 200-odd novels which bore more than a family resemblance. Marian had even toyed with the idea of producing a sequel to *Adam Bede*, possibly focusing on the popular Poysers.[17] But to write derivative fiction in order to make certain money ran counter to her strong need to produce work which was socially and morally useful. 'I don't want the world to give me anything for my books', she declared at one point to Blackwood during the tense negotiations of 1859, 'except money to save me from the temptation to write *only* for money.'[18]

This pious wish the Blackwoods could easily have granted. The amount they had given her for the *Scenes* and *Adam Bede* was fine and fair. But Marian's wavering self-worth led her into aggressive demands over what she should be paid for her next book, at this point usually referred to simply as 'Maggie'. Add Lewes's love of intrigue to the mix and the stage was set for six months of embarrassment and hurt feelings.

The first Blackwood heard about Marian's new novel was in a letter of 31 March 1859, when she mentioned that it would be 'as long as *Adam Bede*, and a sort of companion picture of provincial life'.[19] Although this sounded promising, over the next few months several things happened to make Blackwood less sanguine. First there was the odd, gloomy short story called 'The Lifted Veil', which Marian had sent for interim publication in *Maga*. It is doubtful if he would have accepted it from anyone else and it must have made him reconsider whether George Eliot was going to turn out to be a one-book wonder.

Next, a series of embarrassing developments was making the Blackwoods uncomfortably aware that it would not be feasible to hide George Eliot's identity for ever. Before long, everyone would know that the exquisitely moral *Adam Bede* had been written by the woman famous for taking someone else's husband. Once that happened it was inevitable that sales of this and any subsequent novel would suffer. Indeed, once Mudie learned that George Eliot was Marian Evans, he threatened to boycott *The Mill on the Floss* completely. Blackwood, too, had received plenty of intelligence from his friends and from Joseph Langford, his London manager, that once the authorship was known the book was unlikely to sell well among the family audience.

The crisis which threatened to unmask Marian centred on a genteel down-and-out from Nuneaton called Joseph Liggins, whose supporters claimed he had written *Scenes* and *Adam Bede*. Liggins, a baker's son who had been spoiled for the world by a Cambridge education and hopes of a church career, cut so shambling a figure that it is hard to believe he thought up the fraud himself. Indeed, he may never actually have maintained that he was Eliot, but simply allowed others to think he was. Quite why so many local gentry and clergy jumped to his cause is not clear: one theory has enemies of Lewes from *Leader* days stirring up the fuss as a kind of revenge.[20] Whatever the origins of the deception, the result was to unleash a scandal that not only prematurely unmasked Marian, but raised doubts about her integrity and talent, which took years to die down.

When the Liggins rumour – or 'Liggers' as his name was scrambled in some press reports – first surfaced after the publication of the *Scenes* it all seemed light-hearted enough. Writing to Blackwood from Munich on 20 May 1858, where Marian was deep in *Adam Bede*, Lewes could even see it as a useful smokescreen: 'the more confidently such reports are spread, the more difficult will be the detection of the real culprit.'[21] Nearly a year later, with the rumour now taking hold in Warwickshire, Marian was still finding it funny. On 10 April 1859 she tells Blackwood that she has heard from 'an old friend' – actually Sara Hennell – that Joseph Liggins was now attracting sympathy on the grounds that he had not received a penny from the Blackwoods for his work. 'I hope you and Major Blackwood will enjoy the myth,' she teases.[22]

But within several days the mood had changed. Marian might have wanted to conceal her identity, but that was quite another matter from letting someone else 'bear his arms on my shield'. On 15 April George Eliot wrote to *The Times* denying a statement which had appeared there a few days earlier from a busybody Nuneaton cleric that Liggins had written *Scenes of Clerical Life* and *Adam Bede*. In a robust letter Eliot, who on grounds of gender and class could hardly be considered a gentleman, waxed indignant about how 'he' had been deprived of the usual courtesies extended to that breed. 'Allow me to ask whether the act of publishing a book deprives a man of all claim to the courtesies usual among gentlemen? If not, the attempt to pry into what is obviously meant to be withheld – my name – and to publish the rumours which such prying may give rise to, seems to me quite indefensible, still more so to state these rumours as ascertained truths.'[23] The Leweses had sent the letter to *The Times* without consulting the Blackwoods first, sensing that the publishers were a long way behind them. In truth, it suited the Blackwoods to let the Liggins rumour play for as long as possible. The more muddle there was, the longer it would be before George Eliot was definitively identified as Marian Evans Lewes.

Far from fading away, the crisis grew. By the middle of April a group of Warwickshire gentlemen were organising a subscription for Liggins to compensate him for the shabby treatment he was supposed to have received at the hands of the Blackwoods. Now that outright fraud was implied, the Leweses were moving towards the position that only a definitive statement that Marian was the author of *Scenes* and *Adam Bede* would refute the claims of the Liggins camp. Blackwood, more used to the rough and tumble of publishing, remained sanguine about being branded a cheat and in a letter of 18 May 1859 begged the Leweses to 'KEEP YOUR SECRET' until he had had a chance to meet them face to face. Nine days later he arrived at Wandsworth and, according to Lewes's journal, 'urged that the secret should stedfastly be kept, at least until after the next book'.[24]

In return for the Leweses' continuing silence, Blackwood agreed to get involved in scotching the rumour. On 6 June he endorsed another letter to *The Times* from George Eliot. As far as Marian and Lewes were concerned, it was too little too late. 'I am surprised at . . . the equanimity with which you have both sat down under the absurd imputation,' Lewes wrote coldly.[25] What stung was the realisation that the Blackwoods had been motivated by different concerns all along. The publishers' priority was less to spare Marian's feelings than to protect book sales. But what the Leweses found most hurtful of all was the implication that there was something tainted, embarrassing, wrong with the name Marian Evans Lewes.

By May the situation was out of hand. In Warwickshire a manuscript of Eliot's work in Liggins's writing was doing the rounds. Marian and Lewes constructed an angry letter to *The Times* denouncing Liggins as 'an imposter and a swindler'.[26] The editor of the newspaper, Delane, advised Blackwood to get the letter toned down. Marian sulkily agreed, but before she had a chance to go into print with the new version, a crucial communication arrived from Barbara Leigh Smith. Married in 1857 to an eccentric French doctor called Bodichon, Barbara spent half the year in Algeria and half in Britain. She was presently in London on one of her long summer sojourns. Barbara, who by now knew the secret of Marian's authorship, reported on the gossip she had picked up on her recent round of smart drawing-rooms: 'They assured me all the literary men were certain it was Marian Lewes . . . that they did not much like saying so because it would do so much harm . . . From their way of talking it was evident they thought you would do the book more harm than the book do you good in public opinion.'[27]

Finally Barbara had said what the Blackwoods had been hinting at all along: people thought that Marian Evans Lewes was ashamed to come out as the author of *Adam Bede* because of her unconventional private life. If this were not enough to make Marian righteously determined to break the secret, then a vicious article in the *Athenaeum* three days later did the trick. 'It is time to end this pother about the authorship of "Adam Bede",' ran a piece by William Dixon in the magazine's gossip column. 'The writer is in no sense a "great unknown"; the tale, if bright in parts, and such as a clever woman with an observant eye and unschooled moral nature might have written, has no great quality of any kind.'[28] Condensed into a few savage paragraphs were the two most hurtful accusations that had been made against Marian over the past few months. First, that she was a shameful woman pretending to be a respectable one. Second, that she had thought up the whole Liggins rigmarole as a gimmick to boost the sales of her books. On 2 July 1859 the Blackwood brothers attended a summit at Wandsworth, where the Leweses were now living, and it was agreed that the pseudonym would be given up. Although lunch went well, with John Blackwood struck by how happy Marian looked, by the end of the day she had crumpled under the delayed impact of the *Athenaeum* piece. A letter written to Barbara that evening breaks off abruptly with the shaky explanation: 'I [am] very poorly and trembling, and am only fit to sit in a heap with a warm water bottle at my feet. So no more now.'[29]

The whole miserable business had left Marian suspicious about John Blackwood's loyalty. Eighteen months earlier her brother had rejected her claim to be 'Mrs Lewes' and now her publisher was making it clear that 'Marian Evans Lewes' was a name with which his family could not afford to be associated. Just as resentment towards Isaac had so often been played out through money, so Marian now expressed her disappointment in Blackwood by testing the limits of his financial commitment to her.

The negotiations over *The Mill* started off pleasantly enough. After a long day at Wandsworth on 25 June, John Blackwood reported to his brother, in retrospect a touch complacently, that Marian 'honestly confesses to a most deep seated anxiety to get a large price for the new Tale and I think we will be well able to afford to give it. It should be a little fortune to her.'[30] Over the next few months there was nothing to suggest that anything was wrong. Blackwood continued to send good news about the sales of *Adam Bede* and to commiserate over the nastiness of the *Athenaeum* piece. He generously offered to bring forward one of the scheduled payments for *Adam Bede* if it would help with the Leweses' heavy moving costs to Wandsworth. He even picked up on an earlier hint that Marian wished some noble patron would send her a pug as a thank you for *Adam Bede*. After getting a sporting cousin to scour the country for the right sort of animal, in July Blackwood via Langford presented a delighted Marian with Pug. Despite the chill which was to set into their correspondence over the next few months, no letter from Marian or Lewes was complete without a mention of the new arrival's wagging tail and sneezing habits.

Although Blackwood liked what he had read of the manuscript of 'Maggie', he had dragged his feet over making a firm offer. On 13 September Marian tried to nudge him into action. Resentful that she had to expose herself like this, she compensated with a defensively bold tone. Reminding him that 'I have now so large and eager a public' that any new novel was bound to sell well, she expressed her concern that if the book was first serialised in the magazine, up to 40,000 readers would be lost for the subsequent book publication.[31] She wanted to know how Blackwood proposed to compensate her.

Blackwood picked up on the aggressive tone and consulted the Major before responding. But far from being a supple parry, his letter of 21 September was clumsy, oblique and, as it turned out, deeply damaging. Instead of addressing her arguments against serialisation, Blackwood plunged straight in with 'I wish to have your new novel for the Magazine as from what I read of the story I feel confident that it will be admirably adapted for publication there. Publishing in that form we will give you at least as much as we would for it to publish in any other way.'[32] He offered her £3000 for serialisation and book copyright for four years, without making it clear whether this included compensation for the loss of sales from readers who had seen the story in the magazine. He also, nastily, cut her down to size by reminding her that *Scenes* had actually been a poor seller until *Adam Bede* had arrived on the market as a retrospective tonic. Then, in an uncharacteristically insensitive conclusion, he added that he did not intend to attach the name 'George Eliot' to the magazine instalments of the new book, 'and it would be great fun to watch the speculation as to the author's life'.[33] Having been briefed about her anguish over the *Athenaeum* attack, it is odd that Blackwood should think that it would be remotely 'fun' for Marian to undergo yet more gossip about her private life.

The very next day Marian sent her icy response.

> Your letter confirms my presupposition that you would not find it worth your while to compensate me for the renunciation of the unquestionable advantages my book would derive from being presented to the public in three volumes with all its freshness upon it.
>
> It was an oversight of mine not to inform you that I do not intend to part with the copyright, but only with an edition. As, from the nature of your offer, I infer that you think my next book will be a speculation attended with risk, I prefer incurring that risk myself.[34]

This time Blackwood took three weeks to reply, having first consulted an outraged Major. In the circumstances, the letter was a model of restraint. John Blackwood sent good news of the flourishing sales of *Adam Bede* and *Scenes*, dealt tactfully with yet one more detour in the Liggins business, and said simply and generously, 'The Major and I are very sorry indeed that you cannot entertain our proposal for the new Tale. I hope Maggie gets on as gloriously as she promised.'[35]

Marian's response was ominous. For a start, she signed herself 'Marian Evans Lewes' rather than 'George Eliot', a switch which Major Blackwood was quick to spot – 'I am rather sorry to see the change of signature.' The name which bound publisher and author together, in secret and success, was being decisively withdrawn. 'George Eliot', Marian was reminding Blackwood, belonged to her alone. There were other signs, too, that she was angry. Avoiding any mention of current negotiations, she ticked him off about some proof-reading mistakes in a new edition of *Adam Bede* and dropped heavy hints about the book's continuing 'great success'.[36]

Blackwood must have had to bite his tongue when he replied on 27 October. He apologises for the printing blunders, delights in the progress of 'Maggie' 'in whom I shall always feel a very keen interest' and tells her that Blackwoods are going to give her an extra-contractual £400 as an acknowledgement of the huge success of *Adam Bede*.[37] Marian's response by return contains crisp thanks, spends a whole paragraph on how enduringly wonderful *Adam Bede* is, and harries Blackwoods for not taking action over the publisher Newby, who has advertised a bogus sequel to *Adam Bede*.[38]

This time the saintly Blackwood had been pushed too far. Marian's mean-mindedness threw him into a 'fit of disgust'.[39] He was perfectly aware that she was being courted by other publishers – indeed, she had made a point of telling him – and assumed that she was now playing a waiting game to see who would offer the best price for her new novel. His hurt feelings quickly became office gossip. Simpson, the clerk in Edinburgh, wrote to Langford, the London manager, saying: 'Mr. John and Major B are utterly disgusted and I do think would now decline the new book if it were offered them.' Usually the Black-wood people managed to use Lewes as the scapegoat for any little bits of bad behaviour from Marian, but this time Simpson maintained that it was Eliot who was 'inordinately greedy' and expected some 'wonderful price' from a rival firm.[40] By 16 November, in a flurry of mixed pronouns, he was denounc-ing George Eliot on the grounds that 'he was an avaricious soul' who had 'sold herself to the highest bidder'.[41]

On 18 November Lewes attempted to break the stand-off with a letter that only succeeded in making things worse. 'What days these are for furious speculation in the periodical world!' he crowed to Blackwood. 'My precious time is occupied with declining offers on all sides – every one imagining that he can seduce George Eliot, simply because he (the everyone, not G.E.) *wants* that result.'[42] Obvious though the tactic was – Simpson snorted to Langford that it was the sort of crass gambit that young ladies went in for – it happened to be true. The year before, an 'oily and fair-spoken' American literary agent had offered Marian an extraordinary £1200 for a short story while a Derby clergyman had suggested that she might like to contribute a piece to the *Parish Magazine* urging the clergy to elevate their notions of love and courtship.

Most of the overtures, however, were from altogether more orthodox quar-ters. None other than Lewes's old friend Charles Dickens had recently made contact after twenty-three years. He had liked *Scenes* and loved *Adam Bede*, maintaining that 'I cannot praise it enough'.[43] Now he was after a novel to serialise in his new periodical *All the Year Round*. When he came to dinner at Holly Lodge, the Wandsworth house to which they had moved in February 1859, the evening went well. Although Dickens was always careful to emphasise that he had not actively tried to poach Eliot from Blackwoods, he was happy to exploit the Leweses' dissatisfaction with the Edinburgh firm. He asked Lewes to write a piece for *All the Year Round* on the Newby business and the whole ethics of advertising bogus sequels. But it was Marian he was really after. The terms Dickens proposed for Eliot's work were flatteringly generous, allowing her to keep the copyright and reprint the novel in book form with whichever publisher she chose. But time was the problem. The Leweses never seem to have considered giving Dickens *The Mill* and Marian did not see how she could meet his deadline by having her next book ready to start serialisation in summer 1860.

Dickens was especially keen that *All the Year Round* should be a success because the previous year he had disbanded his previous magazine *Household Words*, after a quarrel with the publishers Bradbury and Evans. They, in turn, had set up *Once a Week* to rival Dickens's new project and were equally keen to court George Eliot. The editor, Samuel Lucas, laid siege to Marian during the spring of 1859, sending letters care of Blackwood asking her to contribute a serial. Marian asked Blackwood to respond with a refusal on her behalf, hoping that he would take note of how greatly she was in demand.[44] Bradbury and Evans's next strategy was to approach Eliot through Lewes, even resorting to asking him to write a novel for them. Lewes does not seem to have been offended by so blatant a tactic and even discussed with Marian whether he should take up their offer. In the end he decided – wisely, given the awfulness of his two early tries at fiction – that 'I should not swerve from Science'.[45]

Throughout these tense autumn months Marian continued to drop hints that despite having rejected Blackwood's offer she still expected that he would be the book's publisher. On 6 October she wrote to Langford, the London manager, and asked him to recommend a 'hard-headed lawyer' who could brief her on the legal background to Mr Tulliver's court case.[46] Lewes, too, was keenly aware that there was still no firm and viable agreement with any publishing house for the new book. In fact, Smith and Elder were soon to make an offer, a staggering £4500. But this reached Wandsworth on 1 December and four days earlier Marian had decided that she could not wait any longer. In desperation she had written to Blackwood:

> I am induced to ask you whether you still wish to remain my publishers, or whether the removal of my incognito has caused a change in your views on that point.
> I have never myself thought of putting an end to a connection which has hitherto not appeared inauspicious to either of us, and I have looked forward to your being my publishers as long as I produced books to be published; but various indications, which I may possibly have misinterpreted, have made me desire a clear understanding in the matter.[47]

Two days later Blackwood replied with what turned out to be the breakthrough letter. He is frank about being 'very much annoyed or rather, I should say, hurt at the tone in which my offer for the new novel was replied to.' He acknowledges that other publishing companies 'may offer a sum such as I would neither think it right nor prudent to give'.[48] He says that he would have quite understood if Marian had taken a higher offer 'but I think I should have been told so frankly instead of having my offer treated as if it were not worth consideration at all'.[49] But it was in his concluding paragraph that Blackwood showed himself once again to be attuned to her particular dilemma. He admits that he has always opposed the withdrawal of the incognito and recognised frankly that 'in the eyes of many' it will prove a disadvantage. However, 'my opinion of your genius and confidence in the truly good, honest, religious, and moral tone of all you have written or will write is such that I think you will overcome any possible detriment from the withdrawal of the mystery which has so far taken place.'[50]

Marian responded with equal candour, explaining that she had been hurt by Blackwood ignoring her queries about whether he would recompense her for the loss of book sales through serial publication. She also admitted: 'Your proposition at the same time to publish the story without the name of George Eliot seemed to me (rendered doubly sensitive by the recent withdrawal of my incognito) part of a depreciatory view that ran through your whole letter, in contrast with the usual delicacy and generosity of your tone.'[51] Then she explained how annoyed she had been by his refusal to take steps to stop Newby advertising the bogus sequel to *Adam Bede*.

Blackwood's final letter in this painful sequence was, uncannily, written from that 'fine quaint old place' Arbury Hall where he had gone as the guest of Charles Newdegate, Isaac Evans's employer. He said nothing new in his letter composed carefully over 2–4 December – merely repeating that he had always wanted to bring out 'Maggie', that he nearly always published anonymously in the magazine, and that he and his brother knew their business well enough to know whether to tackle Newby or whether to let him expose himself as a scoundrel. He proceeded to invite himself to lunch on the following Wednesday at Wandsworth so that he could make a binding arrangement over 'Maggie'. When Blackwood arrived on 7 December, the vexed issue of serialisation was dropped as well as Lewes's lingering hope of bringing the book out in monthly shilling instalments. It was agreed that Blackwood would give her £2000 for book publication. It was not a particularly generous offer, especially when compared with the magnificent sum of £4500 from Smith and Elder, which had come in a few days previously. But at least 'we may consider the publication of Maggie settled', Marian wrote with something approaching relief on 20 December.[52]

The relationship with the Blackwoods was not the only one which came near to breaking over the incognito business. Marian's closest friendships, already changed by her intimacy with Lewes, were further strained by the decision to keep her authorship secret. The Brays, Sara Hennell and John Chapman had all provided support during the difficult Coventry and Strand years, and were bound to feel hurt when they discovered that they had been shut out from Marian's growing happiness and success. Never keen on Lewes, they found it easy to blame the little man for pulling the girl they thought they knew into a shadowy world of fudge and equivocation.

The first pressure on the incognito had come from Warwickshire. In her chatty letter acknowledging Marian's 'marriage' in late May 1857 Fanny Houghton had mentioned that Joseph Liggins, a man remembered vaguely from the half-sisters' overlapping youth, was said to be the author of the new series in *Blackwood's Magazine*. If Fanny was angling for a confession, she was disappointed. Marian wrote back with a mixture of contrived vagueness – mis-calling the stories 'Clerical Sketches' – and inexplicable certainty, telling Fanny that no less an authority than Mr Blackwood had told Mr Lewes that the stories were by 'Mr. Eliot, a clergyman, I presume'.[53]

Fanny was not the only member of the Evans family to have suspicions. Isaac had also been reading *Blackwood's Magazine* and found his thoughts jumping to his sister. Later, when *Adam Bede* came out, he had been heard to mutter that 'No one but his Sister could write the book' and that 'there are things in it about his Father that she must have written'.[54] Although Isaac had resolved never to speak to Marian, he was proud enough to grumble about her.

Frustratingly, we do not know what Isaac thought about Marian's next book, *The Mill on the Floss*, which so obviously draws on their shared childhood. The next we hear of the Evanses is not until 1866 when Fanny wrote to Isaac about the up-coming *Felix Holt* – perhaps also with a hint of exasperated pride? – 'I am on the tip-toe of expectation to see the forthcoming novel by Mary Ann. It is too much to hope that no member of her own family will figure in it.'[55]

The Evanses were not the only Midlands people to have been reading George Eliot's work with interest. In May 1858 John Blackwood was watching the Derby at Epsom when he was hailed by Charles Newdegate with, 'Do you know that you have been publishing a capital series of stories in the Mag., the Clerical Scenes, all about my place and County?' Newdegate was certain the author was Liggins, but was so delighted with the tales' 'delicacy, good taste, and good feeling' that he appeared not to be in the least offended. Indeed, he seemed to relish the whole business enormously, boasting that he was sure he could provide a 'key' to the characters and their real-life counterparts.[56]

If Blackwood was unsettled by the revelation that his new author's refreshingly 'realistic' fiction might be nothing more than crude documentary, he disguised it in a lightly worded request to Marian that she should 'write me a line with a message' to Newdegate.[57] Marian was quick to sense the seriousness of the implications and her answer went far beyond 'a line'. As always when under pressure, she retreated to an Olympian position, declaring that 'it is invariably the case that when people discover certain points of coincidence in a fiction with facts that happen to have come to their knowledge, they believe themselves able to furnish a key to the whole'. She admits that 'certain vague traditions' about Sir Roger Newdigate were woven into the story of Sir Christopher Cheverel, but 'the rest of "Mr Gilfil's Love Story" is spun out of the subtlest web of minute observation and inward experience, from my first childish recollections up to recent years'.[58]

This was not the first time Blackwood had found himself accosted by people who claimed to have relatives who had stepped out of a George Eliot story. The previous August he had received a letter from the Revd W. P. Jones of Preston asking if he was planning any more 'Clerical Scenes'. According to Mr Jones, 'Janet's Repentance' was based on an episode in the life of his dead brother and he was 'utterly at a loss to conceive who could have written the statements or revived what should have been buried in oblivion'.[59] When gently pressed by Blackwood, Marian had, as always, taken refuge in a defensively superior attitude to the way in which ordinary mortals insist on misunderstanding the creative process. 'I suppose there is no perfect safeguard against erroneous impressions or a mistaken susceptibility.'[60]

But the third time it happened, Blackwood was getting worried. In June 1859 he received a badly constructed, uncertainly grammaticised letter from Revd John Gwyther, the curate at Chilvers Coton whose unlikely crush on a mysterious Countess had provided the raw material for 'The Sad Fortunes of the Reverend Amos Barton'. In laborious detail Gwyther explains how his 'Eldest Daughter' had been reading the 'Clerical Scenes' when she spotted the borrowing. With unexpected insight Gwyther says that he doesn't believe that Joseph Liggins had it in him to produce the 'Clerical Scenes'. He believes the author must be a Mr King, who was curate at Nuneaton during those crucial years.[61]

Perhaps because he was shocked by how Gwyther's meandering and ungrammatical communication was exactly the kind that Barton would have written, Blackwood thought it deserved a detailed response. Marian composed a letter in which she came the closest she would ever get to an admission – and perhaps a recognition? – that she had gone too far in using the details of other people's lives.

> The author of the 'Scenes of Clerical Life' and 'Adam Bede' begs me to inform you that he is not the Rev. W. H. King, but a much younger person, who wrote 'Amos Barton' under the impression that the clergyman whose long past trial suggested the groundwork of the story was no longer living, and that the incidents, not only through the licence and necessities of artistic writing, but in consequence of the writer's imperfect knowledge, must have been so varied from the actual facts, that any one who discerned the core of truth must also recognize the large amount of arbitrary, imaginative addition.
>
> But for any annoyance, even though it may have been brief and not well-founded, which the appearance of the story may have caused Mr. Gwyther, the writer is sincerely sorry.[62]

The worrying suggestion that Marian was some kind of plagiarist would not go away. The reluctant admission by the Liggins camp in November 1859 that their man had, after all, not written the *Scenes* and *Adam* only succeeded in clearing the ground for new and embarrassing rumours. The chief source of these was Charles Holte Bracebridge, a huffy-puffy magistrate with a genius for getting things wrong. Just like Mr Brooke of *Middlemarch*, Bracebridge had 'gone into everything', but with no obvious benefit to himself or anyone else. Genuinely moved by Liggins's broken-down home and outstanding grocery bills, the well-meaning meddler had been at the forefront of the campaign to raise funds for the literary genius so shamefully treated by Blackwoods.[63]

Even once Bracebridge had been forced to give up the idea of Liggins's authorship by a series of letters from Charles Bray, he clung to the odd theory that Liggins had 'collected' the material from which Marian, whom he remembered from a meeting during the Rosehill days, had written her fiction. This in turn led him to make his own blundering investigations into the models for the characters in her books. Most damagingly, he interviewed the garrulous daughter of the Methodist Elizabeth Evans, who claimed that her cousin Marian had often come to Wirksworth in her youth, pumped her mother for stories of the preaching life and had even copied down one of her sermons. As far as the gullible Bracebridge was concerned, this was all the proof needed to show that the tall, calm, fair Dinah Morris was an exact copy of the tiny, noisy, dark Elizabeth Evans.

After another exchange of letters Bracebridge mercifully began to splutter out of steam. On 9 October he wrote: 'I frankly accept your declaration as the truth, and I shall repeat it, if the contrary is again asserted to me.'[64] But the whole business had left Marian with an urgent need to defend her creative practice to the Brays and Sara Hennell. These, after all, were the people to whom she had on several occasions voiced her fear that she did not have a jot of creative talent. In the light of all the excited local gossip, were they now harbouring suspicions that she had indeed done nothing more than rifle through her earliest memories and change a few names?

Certainly Charles Bray had never seemed to grasp just how offensive Marian found Bracebridge, nor how serious were the implications of his claims. On 19 September Marian had written Bray a long letter trying to explain: 'I *am* seriously annoyed at Mr Bracebridge's conduct and letters.' She cedes that there are two portraits in 'Clerical Scenes' – Amos Barton and Buchanan – but that '*there is not a single portrait in Adam Bede*'. Determined to redeem herself as a creative artist rather than a journalistic hack, she ends, 'I do not think you would suspect me of telling falsehoods about my works: but you might imagine there was truth in these statements about *Adam Bede*.'[65]

Knowing Bray's leakiness, Marian made it clear that these comments were to go no further. But two weeks later she wrote to Sara explaining the extent to which Dinah Morris was modelled on Elizabeth Evans and this time she may have authorised Sara to use the information as she saw fit. For twenty years later, when Marian's death started up new chatter about the origins of her art, Sara felt free to send a copy of this 7 October letter to a newspaper. In what amounts to a miniature essay Marian carefully lays out the extent of her contact with her Methodist aunt. There were three meetings in all, during the late 1830s and early 1840s. During one of these Elizabeth Evans told her the story of her epic prison visit, the incident which formed the kernel for the Hetty Sorrel story. This is the extent of Marian's borrowing. 'How curious it seems to me that people should think Dinah's sermon, prayers, and speeches were *copied* – when they were written with hot tears, as they surged up in my own mind!'[66]

Even now the Brays could be forgiven for wondering if Marian was telling the truth about where her fiction came from. They had been kept in the dark for several months over her relationship with Lewes, as well as the fact that she was successfully writing fiction. And in the months leading up to a difficult evening in June 1859 when she finally revealed to them that she was George Eliot, her manner had been shifty. In October 1858 when Sara had asked which recent pieces in the *Westminster* belonged to her, she had teased, 'Do not guess at authorship – it is a bad speculation. I have *not written a word* in the Westminster'.[67] Only six months earlier Charles Bray had joked that she must be about to bring out a novel to which she parried by asking when his poem was going to appear, before concluding, 'Seriously, I wish you would not set false rumours, or any other rumours afloat about me. They are injurious.'[68] No one could blame the Brays for being confused. Marian had wanted them to guess that she was writing fiction, and had dropped heavy hints to that effect – a ploy she had also used with Bessie Rayner Parkes when explaining why she was not free to contribute a piece to her newly established *English Woman's Journal*. Yet when they followed her lead by asking questions about her work, she clammed up and accused them of nosiness.

The actual moment of revelation went horribly wrong. On 20 June the Leweses attended a performance of the *Messiah* at the Crystal Palace and afterwards dined with the Brays and Sara Hennell. A couple of years earlier the Brays had sold Rosehill to John Cash and his wife, the former Mary Sibree, and had joined Sara and her mother at Ivy Cottage, in the grounds of the big house. They had also, perhaps unwisely, bought a house in Sydenham for which they had constant problems finding tenants. On this occasion Sara had come down from Coventry clutching her latest work-in-progress, *Thoughts in Aid of Faith*, keen to get her old friend's reactions. Mary Ann, however, had her own plans for this meeting, the first she had had with Cara since she had left for Germany with Lewes. She was about to reveal that she was the mysterious author of the new literary hit, *Adam Bede*. In the excitement of the moment, Sara's dreary manuscript got pushed aside.

At the end of the visit, Lewes returned Sara's manuscript to her, together with negative comments about the 'decided disapprobation' which both he and Marian felt for its laborious attempt to extract a framework for faith in the context of unbelief.[69] Sara was hugely hurt, crying on the way home in the train because she had not had her much-anticipated chance to go through her work with Mary Ann herself. Charles Bray, who had never liked Sara very much anyway, wrote conspiratorially to Mary Ann the next day: 'I know you would not have grudged the half hour she wanted, although I am quite of opinion, no good could have come of it. *I don't believe she can do better* and if she likes to amuse herself and spend her money in publishing, she can afford it and she does no one any harm and it may attract some *half-doz* congenial minds.'[70]

But before she received this letter, Marian had already written to Sara apologising for the way in which her own exciting news had hijacked their meeting. She regretted 'that the blundering efforts we have made towards mutual understanding have only made a new veil between us'. Then she continues, 'Dear Sara, believe that I shall think of you and your work much, and that my ear and heart are more open for the future because I feel I have not done what a better spirit would have made me do in the past.'[71]

If Sara had been under the illusion that her friendship with Mary Ann was under pressure only from the geographical distance between them, she was now obliged to recognise that there were fundamental forces keeping them apart. The letter she wrote acknowledging that something had changed for ever was graceful, touching and sad: 'I have been fancying you, as ten years ago, still interested in what we then conversed together upon . . . I see now that I have lost the only reader in whom I felt confident in having secure sympathy with the *subject* (not with *me*) whom I most gratefully believe – believed in – that she has floated beyond me in another sphere, and I remain gazing at the glory into which she has departed, wistfully and very lonely.'[72]

With Herbert Spencer there was no need to fudge. On 12 October 1856 he had stopped off in London during one of those interminable health-boosting Continental trips. According to Spencer's version – designed, as always to give him the leading role – he had again suggested that Marian should try her hand at fiction, only to be told that she had already started on 'Amos Barton'. Although Marian's decision to confide in Spencer seems to have been spontaneous, it was judicious. A man who habitually gave so little of himself away could be trusted with other people's closest secrets. But after two years of absolute discretion Spencer found himself in a difficult position. During dinner with the Leweses on 5 November 1858 he revealed that the newly elevated 'Dr' John Chapman had asked him 'point blank' if Marian had written the *Scenes*.[73] Spencer's fastidiousness about not spreading the rumour also meant that he found it hard to lie to an old associate. In any case, as he later explained in his autobiography, 'I have so little control over my features that a vocal "No" would have been inevitably accompanied by a facial "Yes".'[74]

Lewes and Marian were furious at what they saw as Spencer's treachery. They waved away his scruples with their favourite precedent, that of Scott who had denied being the author of the Waverley novels and justified himself later by saying it was akin to claiming the right to stay silent in court. Years later Marian was to distance herself from such blatant dishonesty by claiming that she had no idea that Lewes had issued categoric denials on her behalf. In the highly strung state in which the Leweses now approached anything to do with the incognito issue, Spencer's inability to see things their way appeared as deliberate mischief-making. When Pug arrived from Blackwood, Marian theatrically declared that the creature had come 'to fill up the void left by false and narrow-hearted friends'.[75]

It would have been difficult for Spencer to give Chapman a categoric denial, since the good doctor was clearly confident about his hunch. Like the Coventry trio, he had noticed that Marian had done no journalism over the past eighteen months. Despite the fact that he had sent her an extra five pounds for her marvellous essay on Young, she had ceased to suggest new topics for the *Westminster*. Chapman was familiar enough with her finances to know that she needed to get money from somewhere and his mind naturally turned to fiction, especially the *Scenes of Clerical Life* with their Warwickshire settings around which she had guided him during that crucial visit to Rosehill during which they had agreed to abandon their affair. The moment Spencer had left after dropping his bombshell on 5 November, Marian sat down and wrote to her old lover:

> I have just learned that you have allowed yourself to speak carelessly of rumours concerning a supposed authorship of mine. A little reflection in my behalf would have suggested to you that were any such rumours true, my own abstinence from any communication concerning my own writing, except to my most intimate friends, was evidence that I regarded secrecy on such subjects as a matter of importance. Instead of exercising this friendly consideration, you carelessly, certainly, for no one's pleasure or interest, and to my serious injury, contribute to the circulation of idle rumours and gossip, entirely unwarranted by any evidence . . . Should you like to have unfounded reports of that kind circulated concerning yourself, still more should you like an old friend to speak idly of the merest hearsay on matters which you yourself had exhibited extreme aversion to disclose?[76]

This must have given Chapman an uncustomary pause for thought, since he did not reply for nearly two months. Although Marian had told her journal on 30 November that she did not intend to have anything more to do with him, she none the less responded to his letter when it eventually arrived, if only to give herself the pleasure of saying 'it does not seem likely that further letter-writing would advance our mutual understanding'.[77] Being elevated to the status of a professional man had not changed Chapman's most basic emotional responses. The idea that Marian was not available to him was hugely exciting, and he begged for the chance to come to Wandsworth and explain his behaviour. But she refused, saying coldly that she was far too busy moving house.

This was enough to whip up Chapman into a frenzy. By February he was writing again, this time hinting that he knew she was George Eliot. This was serious stuff and drew an immediate response from Lewes:

> My dear Chapman,
>   Not to notice your transparent allusion in your last, would be improperly to admit its truth. After the previous correspondence, your continuing to impute those works to Mrs Lewes may be *meant* as a compliment, but *is* an offence against delicacy and friendship. As you seem so very slow in appreciating her feelings on this point, she authorizes me to state, as distinctly as language can do so, that she is not the author of 'Adam Bede'.[78]

Now that there was no point in courting the Leweses, Chapman exploited his privileged information for all it was worth. Still involved with the *Westminster*, he inserted a paragraph at the end of a long review of *Adam Bede* in April 1859, which nudged and winked the reader towards the idea that George Eliot must surely be a woman.[79]

The fact that Lewes had done exactly the same thing in 1847 to Charlotte Brontë, virtually telling readers of his review of *Jane Eyre* that Currer Bell was a woman, did not mean that there was any mercy for Chapman. Henceforward he was *persona non grata*, although he was clumsy enough not to have realised the extent of his disgrace. Nine months later he wrote, with breath-taking cheek, to ask whether he could reprint Marian's five big *Westminster* essays in book form, sharing the profits with her. 'Squashed that idea,' Lewes reported briskly in his journal.[80]

In the Leweses' brooding state, Spencer's determination to stick to his principles seemed like a gleeful attempt to undermine them. An unhappy visit in March 1859 ended with Lewes telling his journal that 'jealousy, too patent, and too unequivocal, of our success, acting on his own bitterness at non-success, has of late cooled him visibly'.[81] Yet only six months later Spencer managed to redeem himself in the only way which worked with Marian, by writing a letter praising her work. He declared that he had read *Adam Bede* 'with laughter and tears and without criticism. Knowing as you do how constitutionally I am given to fault-finding, you will know what this means.'[82]

Barbara Bodichon, as always, was the only person to get it exactly right. She had not prodded and probed Marian during those eighteen months when the fiction was still a secret. Yet nor had she expressed unflattering disbelief when the authorship became clear. Gratifyingly, she claimed to have guessed Marian's identity when she came across an extract from *Adam Bede* in an Algerian newspaper, which made her exclaim, 'that is written by Marian Evans, there is her great big head and heart and her wise wide views.'[83] This was exactly the thing which both Marian and Lewes liked to hear. Except, of course, for the fact that Barbara had made the blunder of calling Marian by her 'maiden' name. In a postscript to the letter of thanks which Marian wrote on 5 May 1859 Lewes added, 'dear Barbara, you must not call her Marian Evans again: that individual is extinct, rolled up, mashed, absorbed in the Lewesian magnificence!'[84]

Barbara kept her secret even once she was back in London, becoming the Leweses' eyes and ears in the city's literary drawing-rooms. Her revelation in June that everyone assumed that Marian Lewes was too ashamed to admit to being George Eliot proved to be the spur that ended the incognito. On the 30th of that month Lewes wrote to tell Barbara that they had decided to break the secret. 'You may tell it openly to all who care to hear it that the object of anonymity was to get the book judged on its own merits, and not prejudged as the work of a woman, or of a particular woman.'[85]

It would be odd if this atmosphere of paranoia had not seeped into Marian's writing. At the height of the Liggins scandal, and before she had properly started on *The Mill*, she had sent what she called a '*jeu de melancolie*' to Blackwood.[86] 'The Lifted Veil' was part-way between short story and novella, and pleased no one. The tone was indeed melancholy, recalling the gothic doom of Mary Shelley and Edgar Allan Poe, and resembling the kind of thing which Mary Braddon was soon to do so well at. Written in the first person, it recounts the experience of a weak, wealthy young man called Latimer, who has the ability both to see into the future and to read others' minds. These odd gifts bring him to the edge of despair, as he finds himself assaulted by the rush of hostile, envious, degrading thoughts which proceed from the people around him. Latimer is also able to foresee the moment and method of his death, which he knows will be contrived by his wife Bertha, an evil woman whose attraction lies in the fact that she is the only person whose mind he cannot read.

Despite the weirdness of the piece, there are ingredients in the story which mark it as Marian's. The Continental settings of Geneva, Vienna and Prague clearly come from her memories stored up from the 1858 trip. The scientific details, which culminate in a ghoulish blood tranfusion in which Bertha's maid is temporarily raised from the dead, must have been inspired by Lewes's experiments on live frogs. But, more specifically, it is Latimer's experience of being assaulted by the unspoken envy, spite and hate of his immediate circle which echoes Marian's own situation. When she wrote to Blackwood to thank him for Pug, she had said, melodramatically, 'I see already that he is without envy, hatred, or malice – that he will betray no secrets, and feel neither pain at my success nor pleasure in my chagrin.'[87] In her isolated brooding, the hoo-ha over Liggins had turned from a bit of unpleasant gossip into a concerted effort by enemies to strip her of every happiness.

Blackwood was sufficiently acute to see where the darkness in 'The Lifted Veil' came from. He hated the story, but managed merely to say soothingly to Marian that he wished 'the author in a happier frame of mind and not thinking of unsympathising untrustworthy keepers of secrets'.[88] Still, he was too much the businessman to let sympathy interfere with profit. While he was prepared to publish the story in *Maga* and give her £37 10s for it, he was not going to fall in with Lewes's suggestion that he break his practice of anonymous publication and use George Eliot's name as a way of stopping the Liggins rumour, on the grounds that the Warwickshire homebody was hardly likely to produce a tale of pseudo-science set on the Continent.

Blackwood's refusal to 'fritter away the prestige' of George Eliot on a duff story prompted a new spasm of suspicion in Marian. She was less offended by his lukewarm response to her work than by the realisation that the Blackwood brothers must often have discussed her 'unfortunate position' between themselves. This feeling that she was being watched and whispered about seeped even into her feelings about her new home, Holly Lodge, in suburban Wandsworth, where she began to feel that she was constantly overlooked by 'houses full of eyes'.[89]

The Leweses had moved into the house at a propitious time, five days after the publication of *Adam Bede*. Holly Lodge, in Wimbledon Park Road, was bigger than anywhere they had lived before, and the expansion reflected their increased wealth and growing certainty in one another. Only a few weeks earlier Marian had written in her year's end journal entry: 'Our double life is more and more blessed, more and more complete', while Lewes told his journal that he felt 'a deepening of domestic happiness'.[90] The new house was intended as a family home, where the Lewes boys could base themselves when they had finished their schooling in Switzerland. Significantly, this was also the first time that Lewes would move all his books and belongings out of the marital home in Kensington and into the home he shared with Marian.

Convenience rather than lingering attachment to the marriage was the reason why he had taken so long to make a complete break. Dealings with the first Mrs Lewes continued to be reasonably warm, as long as the discussions steered clear of money. Agnes adored Pug when Lewes brought him for a visit, and Nursie dog-sat at Holly Lodge when the couple went on holiday to Wales in the September of 1859. Agnes had been an early reader of 'Amos Barton' in manuscript and loved it, although she did not know the identity of the author. The Leweses' increased affluence meant that the £250 which they gave Agnes each year was less of a strain to find. Only occasionally did Marian allow herself to criticise Agnes to others – probably the second wife's habitual complaint about her predecessor's extravagance – and she always sent out written retractions immediately afterwards.[91]

Marian's earnings from *Adam Bede* allowed the Leweses to house-hunt in the prosperous south-west London suburbs of Mortlake and Putney before settling on Wandsworth. After years of using landladies' sheets and plates, now was the time to invest in their own and they went up to town on several bulk-buying shopping trips. It was this sudden acquisition of the paraphernalia of middle-class prosperity after years of penny-pinching which alerted some sharp-eyed observers to the possibility that Marian Lewes might indeed be the author of this year's most successful new novel, *Adam Bede*.

Letters which Marian wrote during the early weeks at Holly Lodge remind one of the years she had spent running a working farmhouse. The perennial problem of finding a good servant has her putting adverts in *The Times*, making enquiries locally and even consulting Cara Bray about the possibility of importing various reliable Coventry girls down to London. But it was a measure of the unusually flexible way in which the Leweses divided their responsibilities that Lewes took over much of this routine domestic correspondence so that Marian could concentrate on her new novel.

Nor did moving into a suburban villa mean that the Leweses suddenly adopted the conventional life of a prosperous middle-aged couple. People still refused to come and see 'Mrs Lewes', regardless of whether they knew she was George Eliot. Barbara Bodichon had recently reported her failure to badger Mrs Owen Jones, wife of the designer, into visiting with the rather tactless declamation, 'Oh Marian, Marian, what cowards people are!'[92] In fact, Marian was probably relieved: with the Liggins gossip at its height she did not have the slightest desire to expose herself to the small-minded disapproval of 'respectable society'.

Despite having put the word around that they did not wish to get caught up in the tiresome business of social calling, shortly after their arrival the Leweses received a visit from their near neighbours the Congreves. Marian vaguely recalled Maria Congreve from Warwickshire. Her father, Dr Bury, had attended Robert Evans during his last illness and sung Miss Evans's praises as a devoted sick-nurse. Richard Congreve was a clergyman who had given up Orders so as to pursue and publicise the work of Auguste Comte. Maria was keen to know Marian: she claimed that the older woman had made such an impression on her during their one brief meeting at Foleshill that she had often continued to think about her during the intervening years.[93] In the meantime she had heard all the Coventry gossip about Marian going to live with Lewes and was struck by 'the unfairness with which a connection like theirs was visited by society – the man cut off from scarcely anything, the woman from all she most values'.[94]

The men were less predisposed to get on. Although Lewes had been an enthusiastic pioneer of Comte's early work, he had parted company with the philosopher over his attempts to turn Positivism into a religion, complete with saints, temples and a sort of pseudo-Madonna. Congreve, the one-time clergyman, remained enthusiastic about this development and had just translated Comte's *Catechisme Positive* (1852). He also retained an Oxford man's disdain for the garrulous little Lewes, who could never quite throw off the tag of journalist, despite his best endeavours. Privately, Congreve wished it were possible to see Marian without her jaunty Siamese twin.

Still, Lewes and Congreve were careful enough to make sure that their intellectual differences did not spoil the intense friendship which was developing between their women. Maria Congreve would be the first of a series of younger women – in this case there was a seventeen-year gap – who would offer Marian uncritical devotion until the end of her life. Marian, who was in a particularly fragile mood at the time, was highly susceptible to Maria's offer of undying loyalty. The Congreves had no sooner set off on a five-month trip to Europe in May than Maria was writing letters to Holly Lodge, promising that Marian was never out of her thoughts. Marian in turn walked Maria's dog and kept an eye on her garden. Already regretting the decision to move to claustrophobic Wandsworth, she none the less maintained extravagantly to her new friend that 'you are worth paying a price for'.[95]

Lewes had been due to make his annual visit to Hofwyl just when the storm over the *Athenaeum* piece and the decision to drop the incognito had blown up. He could hardly leave Marian in Wandsworth, surrounded by the houses with their unblinking eyes. Since the Congreves had by now reached Lucerne on their tour, it made sense for Marian to travel out with Lewes on 9 July and stay with their new friends while he went on to Hofwyl to see the boys. During these soft, golden days Marian revealed to Maria that she was George Eliot. Away from Lewes's sceptical presence, she may also have discussed the possibility of an afterlife. With Chrissey gone, the question of what survives of the soul after death pressed upon her. Although she could not allow herself the easy consolation of an orthodox view of heaven, the Positivists' idea that the essence of the departed person remains in the memories of those left behind became an increasing comfort to Marian. It was to form the main theme of her best-known poem 'O May I Join the Choir Invisible', which the Positivists adopted as their anthem.

This visit to Hofwyl was a special one, for it was now that Lewes told his sons about the full extent of his relationship with the woman whom they had previously known only as the mysterious 'Miss Evans' who sent good wishes and excellent presents. During a walk in the woods Lewes 'unburthened myself about Agnes to them. They were less distressed than I had anticipated and were delighted to hear about Marian.'[96] The emotional blow was softened by the discovery that their new stepmother was the author of *Adam Bede,* a book whose celebrity had reached even their isolated boarding-school community.

Lewes was not the only one with family responsibilities now. Later that summer, at the end of August, Marian and he broke their journey back from a few days' holiday in Wales at Lichfield, where Chrissey's two surviving daughters had been placed at school by their father's brother.[97] Just like the Lewes boys, the Clarke girls seem to have been delighted to learn about their new nearness to fame.[98] Marian stayed in touch, making sure there was enough money for clothes and books. Emily, the eldest, wrote regularly and it would be interesting to know if the teenage girl ever let slip to her Uncle Isaac any details about her glamorous, generous 'Aunt Pollie'.

After Lichfield the Leweses had headed for Dorset where Marian was keen to find a mill in which she could set her new novel. At the beginning of the year she had gone into town to the London Library to research 'cases of inundation' and found useful examples of widespread destruction in the north-east of England during the late eighteenth and early nineteenth centuries.[99] She knew that the climax of the book would involve a huge, destructive flood and it was important that she get the details straight in her own mind. There had been a mill at Arbury, but she needed to find something on a bigger scale. Although an obliging miller in Weymouth showed her over his property, it was not quite right, so in late September the Leweses tried Newark and Gainsborough in Lincolnshire. This time Marian found what she was looking for. The Trent and its tributary the Idle would do nicely for her fictional Floss and Ripple. By the time she returned to her writing that October she had a clear picture of the landscape which was to play such a major part in *The Mill on the Floss.*

It is that landscape, wide and flat, which opens the book. A nameless narrator, chilly in the weak February sun, wanders on the outskirts of the red-roofed town of St Ogg's. He – the confident tone seems to suggest the voice is male – describes the fields stretching into the distance, the hedgerows thickened with trees and the ships laden with coal, wood and seed which pass up the River Floss to unload their cargoes at the waiting wharves. Turning off to walk along the banks of the tributary Ripple, the narrator comes across Dorlcote Mill, familiar from many years before. The big wheel ceaselessly spurts out 'diamond jets of water', while the wagoner drives the grain-laden horses home over the bridge.[100] Meanwhile a little girl – who turns out to be Maggie Tulliver – is watching the scene intently, barely distracted by the 'queer white cur with the brown ear' who leaps and barks beside her.[101]

It soon becomes apparent that the narrator's description of the landscape goes beyond simple scene-setting. There is a Riehl-like understanding of the relationship between the natural world and the men and women who inhabit it. Maggie's fearsome Dodson aunts are as inevitable and integral a part of St Ogg's as the red roofs and twisty streets. The three women – inspired by Christiana Pearson's sisters – are described as examples of how peasant life has developed in provincial urban Britain by the end of the 1820s. There is Aunt Glegg, who hoards her stock of good linen and lace until the old stuff is worn out. Her clothes are so carefully conserved that by the time she gets to wear them they are spotted with mould and comically old-fashioned. Then there is Aunt Pullet whose marriage to a wealthy farmer allows her to indulge a passion for fancy medicine. She lovingly lines up her blue bottles and shudders at her elder sister Glegg's insistence on carrying a mutton bone in her pocket to ward off rheumatism.

As if to underline that it is Riehl and his *Natural History of German Life* which inspires this analysis, the narrator halts the story half-way through the book and takes us along the banks of the Rhône. We are shown the remains of deserted villages, long destroyed by catastrophic floods. Far from suggesting that a noble way of life has tragically disappeared, the narrator suggests that 'these dead-tinted, hollow-eyed, angular skeletons of villages on the Rhône, oppress me with the feeling that human life – very much of it – is a narrow, ugly, grovelling existence, which even calamity does not elevate, but rather tends to exhibit in all its bare vulgarity of conception; and I have a cruel conviction that the lives these ruins are the traces of were part of a gross sum of obscure vitality, that will be swept into the same oblivion with the generations of ants and beavers'.[102] The Tullivers and the Dodsons are likewise 'emmet-like', their respectable, ignorant lives devoid of the harsh necessity that makes the rural peasantry romantic or the intellectual capacity that nudges town dwellers to stretch beyond themselves for something 'beautiful, great, or noble'.[103]

The narrator tells us that it is important we should feel the 'oppressive narrowness' of Maggie's and Tom's existence if we are to understand the dilemmas of their lives. Using ideas of evolution drawn from the just-published *The Origin of Species* (1859), but long familiar to Marian from her wide reading in natural science, the narrator describes how Tom and Maggie are destined to rise above 'the mental level of the generation before them'. But their minute progress is not so much a glorious triumph as a painful struggle with the previous generation to which they are still bound with 'the strongest fibres of their hearts'.[104] Maggie's yearning for a life which exceeds that of her mother and aunts is thwarted not simply by the limitations of the society in which she lives, but by her own residual attachment to the traditional duties of a daughter. Like Marian, she spends years caring for her infirm father, waiting and watching while Tom claims the wider world as his arena. 'While Maggie's life-struggles had lain almost entirely within her own soul, one shadowy army fighting another, and the slain shadows for ever rising again, Tom was engaged in a dustier, noisier, warfare, grappling with more substantial obstacles, and gaining more definite conquests.'[105]

The frustration of Maggie's ambitions have bothered feminist critics for years. She stands in that line of George Eliot heroines from Dinah through Romola to Dorothea who are allowed to work towards a meaningful identity and even, temporarily, to find one, before being granted a diminished scope of action at the end of the book. Maggie, who has struggled with faith, longed for culture, and searched for education, is obliged by her family's reduced circumstances to become a schoolteacher. Her only access to polished living is as a guest in her cousin Lucy Deane's house. When she dares to defy convention by spending the night away from home in the company of a man to whom she is not married, she ends up ostracised. In the slow evolutionary crawl there is no place in St Ogg's for the female who refuses to be reconciled to her place in nature. Or, as her bewildered father puts it, 'an over 'cute woman's no better nor a long-tailed sheep'.[106]

This evolutionary plot is just one of the organising threads of *The Mill on the Floss*. Another is Greek tragedy, which is why Lewes favoured the title 'The House of Tulliver', with its echoes of 'The House of Atreus'. The Tullivers are brought low by a mixture of human failing and uncanny coincidence. Mr Tulliver becomes bankrupt after he overreaches himself by going to law. Dorlcote Mill ends up in the hands of his sworn enemy, lawyer Wakem, who then offers Tulliver employment as its manager. Wakem's eldest son, the hunchback Philip, happens to have been educated with Tom and so has met and fallen in love with Maggie. Thus the stage has been set for a fierce battle years later when Tom refuses to allow Maggie to continue her meetings with the son of the man he blames for his father's ill-fortune.

Greek tragedy, too, inspires the famous ending in which Maggie and Tom are joined together in death in a way they never managed in life. A freakish flood sweeps through the valley and Maggie goes to rescue Tom from the mill in a boat. As the brother and sister row towards St Ogg's huge fragments of industrial flotsam overwhelm them and they go down 'in an embrace never to be parted – living through again in one supreme moment, the days when they had clasped their little hands in love, and roamed the daisied fields together'.[107]

Strictly speaking, the ending breaks the rules of Greek tragedy because it has nothing to do with what has gone before. The flood is a terrible act of God, rather than the result of any action by Maggie, Tom or anyone else. The coming together of the estranged brother and sister arises not from any consequence of the plot, but from Marian's own deep desire to experience vicariously a reconciliation with the brother who now seemed lost to her for ever. The last few turbulent pages of the book were written in an emotional frenzy. 'Mrs Lewes is getting her eyes redder and *swollener* every morning as she lives through her tragic story,' Lewes reported to Blackwood with grim approval during the first week of March.[108] A month later, and now on holiday in Italy, Marian reported to Blackwood that Maggie and her sorrows still clung to her painfully.[109]

The puffy red eyes and lingering low spirits suggest that Marian was more closely attached to this material than she had been to any other. *Adam Bede* and *Scenes of Clerical Life* were based on stories and characters suggested from other people's pasts: *The Mill on the Floss* trawled her own. Just like little Maggie, she too had run away to join the gypsies, had cried away her unhappiness in the wormeaten attic, had felt her mother's disappointment in her plainness. Most crucially, she had known what it was to devote herself to an older brother who did not want her, who meted out stern punishments for minor mistakes, who preferred riding his pony to playing with a little girl.

No writer has ever given a better account of the relationship between brother and sister. Tom and Maggie bicker over jam puffs, fishing rods and pocket money. Maggie's spark and cleverness is constantly checked by Tom's need to rule and punish. Despite the final passage of the book, which suggests that in death they finally returned to a state of merged rapture, in fact we never see Maggie and Tom achieve more than fleeting harmony.

In her depiction of the young Tom Tulliver Marian excavated the origins of the beloved boy who had grown up to be the stern, unyielding Isaac Evans. Right from the start, Tom is described as having inherited the rigid righteousness of his Dodson relatives. By only thirteen, 'he was particularly clear and positive on one point, namely that he would punish everybody who deserved it: why, he wouldn't have minded being punished himself if he deserved it, but then, he never *did* deserve it.'[110] As he grows into a man Tom's 'saturnine sternness' enables him to graft year after year until he is able to pay back his father's debtors and reclaim the mill. But it is this very fixity that means he is unable to understand why Maggie should want to be friends with Philip Wakem, the son of their father's enemy. Despite the fact that he knows and likes Philip personally, Tom is unable to moderate his view of the world to allow Maggie to continue to meet the man with whom she is half in love. He is, in Eliot's famous phrase, a 'man of maxims' who applies clumsy moral generalisations to unique and delicate circumstances.[111]

If Tom is unable to accommodate the situation with Philip Wakem, how much less is he able to understand Maggie's brief infatuation with Stephen Guest. In the scene when she returns from her chaste night on the boat, he greets her with spitting rage. Marian had informed Isaac of her own elopement by letter and had never had to face his immediate reaction, only his settled contempt. In this encounter between Maggie and Tom she imaginatively worked out how that conversation might have gone between herself and Isaac. Tom, 'trembling and white with disgust and indignation', shouts at her, 'You will find no home with me . . . You have disgraced us all . . . I wash my hands of you forever. You don't belong to me.'[112] Maggie tries to explain that her relationship with Stephen is sexually innocent – something which Marian could not claim with Lewes – but Tom is unable to hear her. Instead, he rages at her in a way which Marian remembered from those endless rows during the holy war when Isaac accused her of consulting only her own wishes. 'You struggled with your feelings, you say. Yes! *I* have had feelings to struggle with – but I conquered them. I have had a harder life than you have had; but I have found *my* comfort in doing my duty. But *I* will sanction no such character as yours: the world shall know that *I* feel the difference between right and wrong.'[113]

Marian's intense involvement with her material meant that she lingered over it for longer than she should. She admitted to Blackwood that she had treated Tom's and Maggie's childhood years with such an 'epic breadth' that the rest of the story had become oddly squashed. It is not until the third volume that she fully introduces Stephen Guest, the man for whom Maggie will ruin her reputation. In the rush, Guest becomes little more than a quick sketch of a wealthy, careless young man and Maggie's 'elopement' with him – the relationship is not consummated – remains unlikely.

What is well handled, because once again it comes straight from Marian's own raw experience, is the community reaction to Maggie's 'sin'. Drifting down river on a boat with Stephen, Maggie has reminded herself just in time that he is engaged to her cousin Lucy. Despite Stephen's protestations of love for her, Maggie is determined to set aside her own desires in favour of duty and the couple return after a night on board ship together. St Ogg's is scandalised. 'The world's wife' would not have minded too much if they had come back married. It would even have found glamour and romance in the situation, despite the unhappiness caused to Lucy Deane and Philip Wakem, to whom Maggie was half-promised. But what the local gossips cannot forgive Maggie is her coming back a 'fallen woman', devoid of either virtue or husband. While in a young man of Stephen Guest's age and class such a lapse can be forgiven, Maggie Tulliver is nothing more than 'a designing bold girl'.[114] These chapters were written just at the time when the Liggins scandal was focusing attention on Marian's own irregular domestic situation. In her deft, sarcastic analysis of how the world's wife is quick to condemn behaviour that she neither knows nor understands, she was surely thinking of those women like Mrs Owen Jones who had refused Barbara Bodichon's invitation to get to know her. And it was to avoid the kind of speculation and scrutiny that had been stirred up by the publication of *Adam Bede* that four days after *The Mill* was finished Marian and Lewes set off for Rome.

CHAPTER 11

'Pure, Natural Human Relations'

Silas Marner and Romola
1860–3

THE FACT THAT *The Mill on the Floss* was still untitled as it went to press suggests a lingering confusion as to what it was actually about. As late as 4 January 1860 Lewes was writing to Blackwood with a short-list of suggestions. The first, 'Sister Maggie', with its emphasis on the relationship between Maggie and Tom, had always been Marian's working title. But Lewes thought it sounded like a children's story and preferred 'The House of Tulliver', which dignified the book by underscoring its links with Greek tragedy. The third option, 'Maggie Tulliver', gave too much weight to Maggie, just as 'The Tullivers' or 'The Tulliver Family' upset the balance by stressing one group of characters over the others. Two days later John Blackwood tentatively came up with an idea of his own, *The Mill on the Floss*.[1] Given that they had only recently patched up their quarrel, Marian was not about to fall in too easily with his suggestion. She could not resist pointing out that his version was 'of rather laborious utterance' and that, anyway, Dorlcote Mill was on the Ripple, not the Floss. Still, it would do.[2]

Blackwood's first complete reading of the manuscript as its official publisher brought the usual mix of fulsome compliment and hinted criticism. In a letter of 3 February he hailed Mrs Tulliver as 'a great creation', her husband as 'irresistible', and Maggie, Tom and Bob Jakin as 'delightful'. But despite this being the third George Eliot book he had published, Blackwood had still not got the hang of her particular brand of realism. Ever the family publisher, bits of description struck him as gratuitously coarse. He winced at 'lymphatic' Mrs Tulliver, and objected to Mrs Moss as 'a patient, loosely hung, child-producing woman'.[3] Marian bowed to pressure and changed both phrases in the final version, although the account of the unfortunate Mrs Sutton, whose swollen legs produced so much fluid 'they say you might ha' swum in the water as came from her', stayed in due to an oversight.[4]

Blackwood's childlike insistence on reading fiction as if it described real life and his commercially canny preference for happy endings meant that he was never going to admire *The Mill* as much as *Adam Bede*. In his opinion neither Stephen nor Philip was good enough for Maggie and, given the shame over her 'elopement' with Stephen, it was probably better that she should die: 'She could not have been happy here.' None the less he recognised the skill it had taken to draw him into such an intense identification. He revealed flatteringly to Marian that reading the last tragic chapters had made him 'start from my seat and walk to the Major's adjoining room exclaiming, "By God she is a *wonderful* woman"'.[5]

To other correspondents Blackwood was more muted about *The Mill*'s merits and chances. On 24 April 1860 he wrote to Lewes in Rome with the good news that Mudie had given up his threat to boycott the book on the grounds of its infamous authorship and was 'nibbling at a third thousand'.[6] However, the word from the Garrick, where Langford had been taking the temperature, was 'not so universally favourable'.[7] The gentlemen of clubland who had wept over the *Scenes* and warmed to *Adam Bede* were less taken with *The Mill*. Blackwood put this down to the fact that there was no longer any secret about Marian's authorship. Lewes thought so too, but also confided to his journal that *The Mill* was not 'so intrinsically interesting as "Adam". Neither the story nor the characters take so profound a hold of the sympathies. Mais nous verrons. It is early days yet.'[8]

The critics, as it turned out, did find *The Mill* interesting, even if they didn't entirely understand it. Dallas, who had always been such a champion of Marian's work in *The Times*, once again opened his review with a thundering ' "George Eliot" is as great as ever.' He delighted in the detailed depiction of Tom's and Maggie's childhood, and thought the Dodson aunts well done. But much to Marian's frustration he also damned the redoubtable Mrs Glegg, Pullet and Deane as narrow, ignorant and coarse. On 27 May 1860 Marian wrote to William Blackwood from Florence in genuine bewilderment, 'I have certainly fulfilled my intention very badly if I have made the Dodson honesty appear "mean and uninteresting", or made the payment of one's debts appear a contemptible virtue in comparison with any sort of "Bohemian" qualities.'[9]

A year later she got the same obtuse response from *Macmillan's*. The reviewer there took Eliot to task for lauding Maggie over Tom and gave the boy what amounted to a character reference, insisting: 'He alone has the self-denial to do what he does not like, for the sake of doing right.' Again, Marian was frustrated by this misunderstanding of the creative process: 'as if it were not *my* respect for Tom which infused itself into my reader – as if he would have respected Tom, if I had not painted him with respect.'[10]

But if the reviews were sometimes off the mark, at least they were free of the nosy spite which had made the publication of *Adam Bede* such an ordeal. By now 'George Eliot' was accepted by all but the most prissy readers as a phenomenon quite detached from the unfortunate circumstances of Marian Evans Lewes's life. And although *The Mill* might not have been as popular as *Adam Bede*, it made twice the profit. Soon after the Leweses arrived in Rome Blackwood wrote to say that the book had sold a gratifying 4600 copies during the first four days of publication. Three weeks later the figure had risen to 6000, with 500 more being printed.[11] Blackwood was genuinely delighted that Marian was assured of at least £3250, but couldn't resist pointing out that she had probably made as much by their hard-won arrangement as she would have with any of the publishers who had been tempting her with fantastic sums during 1859.[12]

The good news allowed the Leweses to relax their hold on the purse strings. After years of travelling on a budget, it was heady not to have to count the cost of anything. In Rome they splashed out on some expensive prints and in Venice they engaged a natty courier who showed them round the sights and shops, and serenaded them with love-songs. The decision to come away had been a good one. As each sybaritic week succeeded another, Marian's anxious enquiries to Blackwood about the financial and critical fate of *The Mill* began to tail off. Even her dank pessimism could not withstand the sunny pleasures of an Italian spring.

Following a few days in Paris, the Leweses had timed their arrival in Rome for Easter week. But they had not bargained for the crowds of pilgrims and tourists who poured into the Holy City, cramming every corner and filling all available beds. After one night in a pricey, sky-high hotel room, they found reasonable lodgings with a Frenchman and his local wife, on whom Marian could practise her rusty Italian. But still it was impossible to relax. The pushing crowds and pious mumbling pressed down heavily. Lewes found the whole phenomenon of popular Catholicism 'very odious; built on shams' and felt particularly queasy when a young priest who had arrived to bless their lodgings simply 'gabbled out some phrases with indifference and haste'.[13] Marian, too, found the ceremonies 'a melancholy, hollow business', despite having felt moved to kneel in St Peter's when the Pope passed by.[14]

The flatness of Marian's response to the surrounding spectacle worried her sufficiently to make a note of it in her journal 'Recollections of Italy 1860'. She despaired that when she stood in front of a work of art or religious icon 'I am not enjoying the actual vision enough'. This not only affected her pleasure in the moment but meant that when she tried to recall the image later it constantly eluded her. This terror of losing peak moments comes through in her account of the interior of St Peter's. Her first impression was of its magnificence, but on later visits the image was spoiled by the ugly red drapes which had been hung to obscure the beautiful marble.[15] It was this combination of ennui and disappointment, not to mention red curtains, which Marian gave to Dorothea Brooke during her disappointing honeymoon in Rome: 'in certain states of dull forlornness Dorothea all her life continued to see the vastness of St Peter's, the huge bronze canopy, the excited intention in the attitudes and garments of the prophets and evangelists in the mosaics above, and the red drapery which was being hung for Christmas spreading itself everywhere like a disease of the retina.'[16]

While Lewes's stomach lurched at the sight of thousands of genuflecting tourists, Marian was able to imagine, envy even, the comfort to be derived from regular religious practice. The news in March that her young niece Katy

Clarke had died had pressed painfully upon her continuing agnosticism and refusal to take easy comfort in the idea of an afterlife. Any remaining traces of her youthful hostility towards organised religion had long dissolved, as she had explained in a letter to M. D'Albert Durade the previous December. Now back in touch after a silence of many years, M. D'Albert had expressed surprise that his free-thinking 'Minie' could have written the passages of orthodox Christianity which he had found in *Adam Bede*. Marian explained that

> Ten years of experience have wrought great changes in that inward self: I have no longer any antagonism towards any faith in which human sorrow and human longing for purity have expressed themselves; on the contrary, I have a sympathy with it that predominates over all argumentative tendencies. I have not returned to dogmatic Christianity – to the acceptance of any set of doctrines as a creed, and a superhuman revelation of the Unseen – but I see in it the highest expression of the religious sentiment that has yet found its place in the history of mankind, and I have the profoundest interest in the inward life of sincere Christians in all ages.[17]

This tolerance shone through in Marian's discussions with Barbara Bodichon about the increasing leanings of her circle towards Catholicism. In December 1860 Barbara wrote explaining how her sister Nanny, coping with the recent death of her father and the illness of another sister, yearned for 'a religion with forms and ceremonies, something present, something of routine, and how many do want it! ... Now don't think I am going over with Bessie [Rayner Parkes, who eventually converted in 1864] to the C.C. but I do see that the "golden rule" and the matins and vespers she attends do her daily good, make her more cheerful and bright.'[18]

Here was exactly what Marian – through Feuerbach – had been saying for years. In her next novel, *Silas Marner*, she was to explore the power of even the most enervated Anglicanism to provide a form and focus for human longing. In the book, good-natured blacksmith's wife Dolly Winthrop has been pricking the letters IHS on her cakes ever since she can remember, under the vague impression that 'they're good letters, else they wouldn't be in the church'. It is her belief in these 'good letters' which impels her to offer the cakes to Silas in a gesture of fellow feeling which she can ill afford.[19] Likewise, she chivies the isolated weaver into going to church in the belief that he will gain a powerful sense of being linked to the wider community, both human and divine.

To Barbara's letter of December 1860 Marian replied sympathetically, admitting that she too found comfort in the rituals of liturgy. She had seen nothing wrong in kneeling for a blessing from the Pope and once she moved to central London in late 1860, she sometimes attended services at the Unitarian chapel in Little Portland Street, taking pot luck with the preachers. All the same, she told Barbara, 'I have faith in the working-out of higher possibilities than the Catholic or any other church has presented'.[20] For her the best and most difficult option was still to live one's life without what she called in an uncanny and unintentional echo of Marx's famous phrase the 'opium' of religion.

Going to Italy was not just about hiding from hostile reviews or distracting Marian from the tragic fate of 'poor Maggie'. The next three months were to be the last that the Leweses could count on being alone together for a long time. They were due to finish their holiday in Berne, from where they would take Lewes's eldest son back home to live with them in London. The 'dual solitude' of the past six years was about to be interrupted by a seventeen-year-old boy.

When Lewes had broken the news to his sons the previous summer about their parents' odd living arrangements they had seemed to take it well. The dislocations of the past ten years had taught them to be resilient, flexible and discreet. Apart from the occasional wistful comment, they accepted without fuss that they never came home for the holidays. Presumably Lewes worried that having them in London each summer would entail a premature explanation of his separation from Agnes. But he was also keen to protect Marian and her work from the impact of three puppyish young men. Despite being a loving and involved father, Lewes always put his relationship with Marian first. And if the boys felt angry about their abandonment they were sufficiently attuned to their parents' culture of silence not to say so. Instead, they filled their letters 'home' to Agnes's Kensington address with cheerful accounts of piano lessons and butterfly catching and messages of love to 'the babies' – the four children by Hunt whom they still thought of as their full siblings.

Although the Lewes boys had known about Marian's place in their father's life for the past year, the meeting at the Bernerhof Hotel in June 1860 was the first time they would meet her face to face. Deliberately casual and bright though they probably were on this occasion, they had clearly been rehearsing the thing in their minds for some time. Knowing that Marian and Lewes were due to pay a visit to the school, Thornie had written in advance asking for instructions about how to introduce their common-law stepmother to a classmate who had already met Agnes:

> as he has seen Mamma, and knows her, he will of course see that Mother is not she, so that we have agreed, viz: Charles and I, that we had better tell him, enjoining at the same time secrecy, as at any rate, he would know it three or four months later, when he goes home. Mother will have therefore when we present him to say 'How d'ye do!' etc etc. And we only wait for your permission to tell him . . . You have told Mamma, that you had told us, didn't you? In [your] her last letter there were one or two sentences from which Charles and I concluded you had.[21]

This last line suggests how adept Thornie and his eldest brother had become at decoding communications from their parents. Yet it also displays the jaunty swagger and self-assertion which were unmistakably his father's. Thornie's descriptions of schoolboy life are full of sound and fury, as if he were the hero of his own picaresque adventure. His natural linguistic ability, given free play at the multi-tongued Hofwyl, allowed him to hop delightedly between French, German and English in a way which recalls Lewes's letters as a young man. He also shared his father's interest in the natural world, collecting butterflies and small animals for enthusiastic stuffing. Touchingly, he had saved the best examples of his handiwork for his new stepmother.

Although Lewes and Agnes must have agreed that he would take responsibility for their three boys, leaving her to concentrate on her second family by Hunt, there never seems to have been any serious consideration that Thornie would come and live with his father and his new partner. This noisy lad was never going to fit easily into the Leweses' quiet and productive London schedule. Naturally he would be provided for, the next stage of his education funded out of Marian's growing wealth. But he would be kept as far away as possible from their London home, first in Edinburgh, then in Africa, from which he returned in 1869 only to die.

As a result of conversations with the headmaster, Dr Müller, during the June 1860 visit, Lewes decided that he would remove Thornie from Hofwyl along with Charlie. One idea was for the lad to go straight to Geneva where he would be tutored by M. D'Albert Durade, but this plan turned out to be too expensive. Next it was agreed that he would be steered towards the East India Office, in which case he would need to spend several years topping up his education at a British school. Oddly, Lewes decided that Edinburgh High School was the only place that would do, although he made a great fuss of asking Blackwood to find a kind family with whom Thornie could lodge.[22] That the boy might go to school in London and live with his father seems never to have been considered. Nor was there any chance of Thornie being allowed to disrupt the grown-ups' plans for the summer: although he officially left Hofwyl in June, he stayed there through the summer, spending only a grudging three days in London at the end of September before being whisked away to Edinburgh for the start of term.

Thornie's first year in Scotland went well. The Blackwood contingent, ever helpful beyond the call of duty, rallied round to keep a protective eye on the young man whom they had ominously dubbed 'Caliban'.[23] He was invited to stay on the Blackwoods' country estate, Mrs Blackwood cooked him dinner, George Simpson took him on rambles and young Willie, the Major's son, offered youthful companionship. Thornie's natural brightness kept him near the top of his class and still left enough energy over for general wickedness. On one occasion he got home late from the theatre and climbed into his room through a window. The next day his landlord and moral caretaker, the classics master Mr Robertson, threatened to report the boy to his father, whereupon Thornie answered cheekily:

'So you can!'
    This put him in an awful rage, so, calling me an insolent dog, he made his shoeleather acquainted with my posterity. You need not ask me what I did; I did what you would have done in my place – knocked him down.[24]

In the light of bulletins like these, it is hardly surprising that Marian did not look forward to Thornie breaking up for the first summer from Edinburgh. By now she was wrestling with the interminable *Romola*, and the clash and clatter which followed the boy wherever he went penetrated into the anguished quiet of her study. None the less, she found time to express her affection the best way she knew how, by coaching him for the first of his Civil Service exams which he passed easily before being shipped back to Hofwyl for the rest of the holiday. The interested, loving attention he continued to receive from the excellent Dr Müller and his wife, not to mention the presence of his younger brother Bertie, obscured the fact that the Lewes family used Hofwyl as a crèche for inconvenient adolescents.

At the end of his second year in Edinburgh Thornie took the examination for the Indian Service and managed to come a reasonable thirty-eighth out of 270. But things began to fall apart during his third and final year. Now that the prospect of India loomed, Thornie decided that he had never been interested anyway. Instead of cramming for his final exam, he devoted himself to his stamp collection, about which he had always been passionate. Unsurprisingly he failed, which, Marian explained in a letter to the D'Albert Durades, 'was a great grief and disappointment to us'.[25]

Thornie had displayed all the laziness and indecision of a rich man's son who could afford to squander an opportunity in the certainty that there would be another one along shortly. For Lewes and Marian, both self-made people who continued to work like Trojans through middle age, it must have been a bitter puzzle. Thornie refused his father's request to try the exam again and announced that he was going to Poland to fight the Russians. Before he could carry out his threat he was bundled back to Hofwyl, while his father pulled strings and consulted well-placed friends about what to do next.

Charles Lewes, a year Thornie's senior, was a very different proposition. His eldest-child seriousness, quiet manners and sense of responsibility marked him out as someone who could be assimilated into the Leweses' London regime without too much bother. He would make a reliable housekeeper in their absence and his excellent piano playing would be an asset in this most musical of households. Later his secretarial skills were put to good use keeping the 'office' running during the Leweses' extended trips abroad. All this while he managed to earn steady promotion at the Post Office, get married and raise a family.

Of course, at seventeen Charles represented nothing but potential: in 1860 the main advantage to the plodding boy was simply that he was gentle, loving and, unlike his younger brother, did what he was told. Anthony Trollope, the Post Office's most famously literary employee, kindly negotiated the complicated procedure which allowed Charles to take the entrance exam for the service. Coached by two of the finest brains in Britain, even the mediocre boy could hardly do anything but come an easy first. On 15 August 1860 he was appointed a supplementary clerk, second-class, at a salary of eighty pounds.

In order to ease Charlie's journey to work, as well as give him access to concert halls and theatres, Marian and Lewes agreed that they would find a house in central London. For Lewes this was not much of a hardship: it is difficult to imagine a man less suited to suburban living. But for Marian, the countrywoman who even in greenish Wandsworth continued to long for an orchard and rough pasture, it was a huge sacrifice. She had made enough money from *The Mill* to afford a second home in the country and here she was, obliged to spend it on an ugly rented house in Harewood Square, Marylebone. Three months of staring at its hideous yellow curtains were followed by a move to a house in nearby Blandford Square 'which we have taken for three years', Marian recorded in her journal: 'hoping by the end of that time to have so far done our duty by the boys as to be free to live where we list.'[26]

Although there can be no doubt that Marian genuinely suffered from being cooped up in town, she derived a compensatory psychological advantage from stressing the extent of her sacrifice: 'I languish sadly for the fields and the broad sky; but duties must be done, and Charles's moral education requires that he should have at once a home near to his business and the means of recreation easily within his reach' was a refrain which she repeated over and over.[27] As a woman still widely regarded as having deprived a family of its father, here was her chance to show that she was the antithesis of a home-wrecker. She presented herself as an 'angel in the house', hovering over the kind of chaste domestic environment in which a young man might shelter from the corrupting pressures of the outside world. To any female correspondent involved in bringing up a child she was quick to claim the sisterhood of shared experience, stressing always her anxiety about her own 'tall boys'.

So it was lucky that Charles was sufficiently biddable to slot into the part reserved for him in this highly staged reconstitution of Lewes's family life. Instructed by his father in July 1859 to write to 'Miss Evans' from Hofwyl as if she were his mother, he obligingly complied. His first letter sensibly concentrated on their shared love of music and finished: 'Give three kisses to Father, one for each of us, and tell him to give you the same for us. I remain, dear Mother, Yours affectionately, Charles Lewes.'[28] Marian, who had been referring to Lewes's sons as 'our boys' for over a year now, could not match Charles's fluent intimacy and her reply came back awkwardly signed 'your loving Mother, Marian Lewes'. It was not until her third letter in this sequence, written in November, that she found a voice which adequately represented her odd position as a common-law stepmother. This time she signed herself 'Your loving Mutter' – using the German in which all the boys had been educated to suggest her distance from conventional motherhood.[29]

Marian's anxiety to present herself as a proper mother led to some dull, preachy letters. Making Charlie a present of a watch, she is careful to remind him that it is a reward for the good use he has made of his time at Hofwyl. When he complains that he has lost an archery competition because of a duff bow, she is quick to tell him that a bad workman always blames his tools. Moral homilies and exhortations to do better are regularly interspersed with excruciating references to the physical signs of puberty. One wonders how many unfunny jokes about his slow-growing whiskers the lad was forced to endure.

Rehearsing their new family roles in letters was one thing, playing them for real was another. Acutely aware that they could not afford to flounder, Marian and Lewes plunged wholesale into family life – any family's life. Their first move after Hofwyl was to take Charles to Geneva where Marian saw her old 'family', M. D'Albert Durade and 'Maman', for the first time in twenty years. She had already renewed her ties with them by appointing M. D'Albert as the French translator of *Adam Bede* and now she authorised him to do *The Mill* as well. Lewes for his part was delighted to see how truly the D'Alberts 'loved and prized Polly' and, to strengthen the family connection, asked them to take Thornie into their household.[30]

From Venice Marian had written ahead to Nursie, currently house-sitting at Holly Lodge, asking her to make Charlie's bedroom as welcome as possible. Charles repaid this fussing admirably, spending his first few weeks in London cramming for his Post Office exam and immersing himself in an instantly intimate relationship with his '*Mutter*'. By May 1861 Lewes could report exultantly to Blackwood that 'it would interest you to see her with the eldest, who *worships* her, and thinks no treat equal to having her all to himself for an evening to make, and be made much of. Among the many blessings that have come to me late in life this of seeing the perfect love between her and the children is one of the greatest; perhaps because it was one of the rocks ahead.'[31]

Marian, too, was keen to stress how well this little family was doing under her moral guidance. Within two weeks of Charlie's arrival, she was writing to Charles Bray to tell him: 'I think we are quite peculiarly blest in the fact that this eldest lad seems the most entirely lovable human animal of seventeen and a half, that I ever met with or heard of: he has a sweetness of disposition which is saved from weakness by a remarkable sense of duty.'[32] Meditations on Charles's specialness were woven into her letters to both friends and acquaintances. Yet despite her insistence to M. D'Albert in August 1860 that Charles was 'improving constantly and applying himself with admirable resolution and good sense to the everyday work of life', the inconvenient truth was that the boy was not doing very well at all.[33] In May 1862 Anthony Trollope confided to Lewes that Charles's superiors at the Post Office had reported that he 'was careless, slow, and inefficient'.[34] The problem, Trollope generously suggested, might be that Charles wasn't very quick in English, having been educated mainly in German. Certainly his letters from Hofwyl are spotted with clumsy constructions. Whatever the root of the problem, Charles was doggedly persistent in putting it right. Within a year he was back on course, getting promoted steadily and eventually rising to the creditable post of Principal Clerk by 1880, the year of his *Mutter*'s death.

If Charles's and Thornie's double failure to excel was galling to Marian, it could at least be redeemed in her letters by stressing Charles's goodness and Thornie's likeness to his father. But the third boy, Bertie, offered no such compensation. He was slow and stupid, and not even very good. His letters from Hofwyl are near to illiterate and today he would be diagnosed as dyslexic. Overawed by his new stepmother's reputation for cleverness, Bertie's anxiety to impress only made it worse. On 24 August 1859 the fourteen-year-old began babyishly to his father, 'I take pains to write and to spell. I am writin a letter to Mother about the journey. I am very pleased with the journey indeed. The only big letter that I can not do well is D, it is very difficult to make. I hope Mother will be satsfyed with my letter.' Two days later, he started the dreadfully anticipated letter with 'Dear Mother! I hope you will be satisfied with my letter'.[35] She probably wasn't. There was little about Bertie which could be made to flatter a woman anxious to demonstrate her parenting skills to the world. In the circumstances it is hardly surprising that the boy was left to cool his heels at Hofwyl for another three years.

The strain of London living, of becoming a *Mutter* at the age of forty, gradually settled itself over Marian's face. In March 1860 the portrait painter Samuel Laurence, who had lived with the Hunts in the notorious 'phalanstery' all those years ago, asked if he might paint her. He had the kind of sadness about him which Marian always interpreted as moral depth, so she cautiously agreed. But nine sittings later the finished portrait appalled Lewes by the tense and melancholic version of Marian it revealed. Refusing to have the picture in Blandford Square, Lewes even put a ban on it leaving Laurence's studio. A compromise was reached only when an admiring John Blackwood bought the painting to hang in a back room at his Edinburgh office, well away from public view.[36]

Marian's own work also reveals her struggling with the new factors in her life. During their stay in Italy Lewes had suggested that her next subject might be Savonarola, the fifteenth-century Florentine priest who had died trying to reform the Church. Determined to protect Marian from the red, swollen eyes which had accompanied the writing of *The Mill*, Lewes had been casting around for a relatively impersonal subject that she might try. Less of an admirer of Scott than Marian, he had always thought that historical romance was a relatively easy genre to master, requiring one only to cram background information about the costume, speech and political events of one's chosen period.

Although initially fired by Lewes's suggestion, once home Marian found it impossible to begin. Despite spending hours researching the historical background to Savonarola, the only writing she achieved that summer was a different kind of thing altogether. Set in her familiar turn-of-the-century Midlands landscape, 'Brother Jacob' is a novella written in the form of a dry, wry fable. The aptly named David Faux is an unscrupulous, ambitious confectioner who steals his mother's savings and runs away to the West Indies. Returning a few years later, with the polish of foreign travel upon him, the renamed Edward Freely sets up a fancy pastry shop and becomes a favourite with the local women. Just as he is about to make a highly desirable match to the local squire's daughter Penny Palfrey, Faux's idiot brother Jacob arrives and unwittingly unmasks him. Far from being a wealthy gentleman-merchant, Edward Freely is revealed as a local working lad, a swindler and a thief.

Generations of critics have remarked on the negative, cynical tone of the piece. No one is nice, not even silly Penny Palfrey, whose only dream is to make a goodish marriage and keep up with her sisters. David Faux feels no remorse as he strips his mother of her carefully hoarded golden guineas. Is this how Marian felt about the three careless young men who were spending her capital on their education, without feeling the need to repay her with hard work or success? And when Jacob arrives to remind David of his family obligations, in the process scuppering the advantageous match to Penny, was Marian thinking of Charlie, whose well-meaning, blundering presence had spoiled her 'dual solitude'?

Deep processes within Marian's psyche were being stirred. Although she returned to preparatory work on what would eventually become *Romola*, her imagination remained deep in the Midlands landscape. At the end of August she was telling Blackwood that although she planned to write a 'historical romance' set in Florence, she intended first to produce 'another English story'.[37] Two months later she noted in her journal that she had started on that story, which had 'thrust itself between me and the other book I was meditating. It is "Silas Marner, the Weaver of Raveloe"'.[38] Only five days after the dreaded move to central London she had escaped in her imagination to 'the rich central plain of what we are pleased to call Merry England'.[39]

The idea of *Silas Marner* forcing itself upon Marian – cutting across the sluggish, elusive *Romola* – suggests something of its immediacy and power. Less than half the length of *Adam Bede* and *The Mill*, it tells its story with economy and pace. Mindful of the way in which the first part of *The Mill* had run away with her, Marian kept her characters and plot under close control, at one point even considering telling the tale in verse. Each element of the story is disciplined and integrated. Romance is balanced by realism, allegory is conveyed through naturalistic detail, individual characters carry symbolic weight.

The 'millet-seed of thought' around which the book grew had its roots deep in Marian's memory.[40] She told Blackwood that she had always retained a 'childish recollection of a man with a stoop and expression of face that led her to think that he was an alien from his fellows'.[41] Marner is indeed alienated, both from his original community, a religious sect in an unnamed northern city, and from the village of Raveloe where he has since settled. Tolerated because he is a hard and necessary worker, Marner makes no effort to integrate with his new neighbours: 'he invited no comer to step across his door-sill, and he never strolled into the village to drink a pint at the Rainbow, or to gossip at the wheelwright's.'[42] Memories of the false accusation of theft which led to his expulsion from the Lantern Yard religious community mean that he is unwilling to trust again. Instead, he devotes his energy to his work, sitting at his cottage loom for hours on end. His only pleasure comes from counting the golden coins amassed through years of labour and saving.

Silas's story begs to be read in terms of Marian's own situation. Ostracised by her family, remote from her neighbours, she believed herself to be the victim of just that kind of unfair accusation which had ended with Marner being driven out of Lantern Yard. Like the weaver, she too had spent the last five years bent close over her work, earning good money for hard, skilled labour. During the very week that she started the novel she recorded with obvious satisfaction in her journal that she had 'invested £2000 in East Indies Stock, and expect shortly to invest another £2000, so that with my other money, we have enough in any case to keep us from beggary'.[43]

Marner is devastated when his little store of gold disappears – stolen by Dunstan Cass, the Squire's reprobate younger son. But within a few weeks a substitute magically appears in his cottage in the form of a baby girl whose hair is so golden that for a moment the short-sighted Marner thinks that his money has been restored to him. In time he learns to care for the child and, as a mark of the way in which she has revived his atrophied affections, he gives her the name 'Eppie' in memory of his long-dead sister and mother. The daily duties of father/motherhood draw Marner towards his Raveloe neighbours who, after a sceptical start, are happy to help him raise the child as his own. Marian links Wordsworth's insistence on the importance of childhood memory with Feuerbach's stress on the human divine to rehabilitate Marner as a good, feeling man.

Like Marner, Marian had been obliged to take on the rearing of someone else's children at the age of forty. She too had exchanged some of her hard-earned and carefully managed money for the gamble of parenthood. Now she too was being drawn back towards the 'family' community. At the end of 1860 she met Lewes's mother for the first time.[44] The reason for the long stand-off is not clear: although Mrs Willim remained on affectionate terms with Agnes, there is nothing to suggest that she disapproved of her son's new partner. Her own 'marriage', to Lewes's father John Lee Lewes, had never been legalised and from the little we know of her she was an intelligent, tolerant woman. Perhaps the permanently angry Captain Willim, with whom she was once again living, had refused until now to let the infamous George Eliot into his house.[45] Whatever the reason for the delay, the initial meeting with Mrs Willim seems to have gone well, and the two women began to build a relationship based on liking and respect. When *Silas Marner* was published in the spring of 1861 the only presentation copy Marian requested from Blackwoods went to Mrs Willim.[46]

If Marian's experience of early family expulsion followed by acceptance in middle age suggested Silas's story, other aspects of her life show through in other strands. Nancy Lammeter, who is married to Eppie's natural father Godfrey Cass, remains involuntarily childless. At the symbolic level, this is Cass's punishment for denying that he has previously been married and fathered a child. As Marian moved beyond her fertile years was she also pondering the fact that she had been denied her own child because of Lewes's messy married life? And was it of her own tortured, self-critical nature she was thinking when she described the effect of childlessness on Nancy?

> This excessive rumination and self-questioning is perhaps a morbid habit inevitable to a mind of much moral sensibility when shut out from its share of outward activity and of practical claims on its affections – inevitable to a noble-hearted, childless woman, when her lot is narrow. 'I can do so little – have I done it well?' is the perpetually recurring

thought; and there are no voices calling her away from that soliloquy, no peremptory demands to divert energy from vain regret or superfluous scruple.[47]

It comes as no surprise that it was now that both Marian and Lewes began the practice of referring to George Eliot's novels as babies. In July 1859 Lewes told Blackwood that Mrs Lewes is about 'to rock the cradle of the new "little stranger" with fresh maternal vigour'. A month after becoming a full-time stepmother Marian reported to the publisher that she was 'naturally jealous for "The Mill" which is my youngest child'.[48]

Blackwood's aversion to the darkness in Marian's work was amplified by the knowledge that his brother, the Major, was dying. Certainly he found the first 100 pages of *Silas Marner* 'very sad, almost oppressive'.[49] Marian responded with reassurances that the tale was not meant to be gloomy 'since it sets – or is intended to set – in a strong light the remedial influences of pure, natural human relations. The Nemesis is a very mild one.'[50] The next instalment of the manuscript went some way towards mollifying Blackwood, although he joked that he had been hoping for the appearance of a good-hearted clergyman 'but I suppose you had not a good one at hand as *sometimes* happens in this life'.[51] The critics liked it too. The scenes in the Rainbow Inn where the villagers bicker and gossip in broad dialect drew praise from those who hoped that this marked a return to the high days of Mrs Poyser. Several flattering comparisons were made with Shakespeare's crowd scenes. Mudie took 3000 copies, and the twelve-shilling edition sold 8000 copies in all, bringing Marian a very handsome £1600.

Once the proofs were read, the Leweses set off again for Italy. The Blandford Square house was left in the capable hands of Charlie, who proved to be a natural housekeeper, supervising the hanging of curtains and the washing of Marian's favourite summer frock, as well as worrying about the welfare of the servants Amelia and Grace. *Silas Marner* had been the most trouble-free of all her books, and this time Marian had no need to rest and recuperate. She was returning to Florence to continue the research for her historical romance begun the previous summer. The Leweses travelled via Paris, Avignon and Pisa to Florence, where they set to work in the libraries, museums and galleries gathering material about the life and times of Savonarola. Lewes's help was invaluable, not just as an enthusiastic sketcher of historical costumes, but as a note-taker in those places where women were not admitted, such as parts of the San Marco monastery. They made contact again with Tom Trollope, the Florence-based British historian and novelist who had been a knowledgeable guide to local history and culture during their fortnight's visit the previous year. It was his idea that they should stay on into early June to travel to the hillside monasteries at La Vernia and Camaldoli. During the journey an incident occurred which shows how far Marian had moved emotionally since her overwrought early womanhood. At one point her horse fell on the edge of a precipice, turning Lewes 'very sick and faint from the shock', but leaving her 'neither hurt nor shaken'.[52] It was only fifteen years earlier that she had crossed the Alps screaming with terror, convinced that her mount was about to pitch her into oblivion.

Unfortunately, this new-found equanimity did not extend to her writing. Returning to London on 14 June, having first visited Bertie at Hofwyl, Marian and Lewes were plunged into the most agonising period of what had become their joint career. Swamped by the heavy fruits of the Florentine research, Marian could not find the imaginative spark which would turn a mountain of documentary detail into a living, breathing world. In desperation she read historical novels by Scott and Bulwer-Lytton to see how they had managed it, but her only conclusion was that she still did not know enough. Instead of beginning to write, she waded through Gibbon, Michelet, Montalembert, Machiavelli, Petrarch and Boccaccio. Finding the faithful London Library inadequate for her purposes, she now applied for a ticket at the British Museum, trudging up to Bloomsbury to check the last detail on Florentine dress.[53] There was a false start to the writing on 7 October, followed by several sets of revised outlines and schedules. By Christmas there was still no opening chapter, only constant journal references to the 'depression on the probability or improbability of my achieving the work I wish to do'. Plagued by headaches, she paced with Lewes every day around Regent's Park 'brooding, producing little'. On one occasion things were so bad that she 'almost resolved to give up my Italian novel'.[54]

For once, Lewes's understanding of what Marian needed to hear had deserted him. In Florence he had tried to cheer her up with the odd suggestion that Savonarola was a topic no more distant to her than the late eighteenth-century Midlands of *Adam Bede* or *Silas Marner*. Missing the intense connection between her and Marner, he confided to Blackwood that 'she knows infinitely more about Savonarola than she knew of Silas, besides having deep personal sympathies with the old reforming priest which she had not with the miser'.[55]

If Lewes was unable to find the right thing to say, he at least grasped that John Blackwood might do better. The publisher had come to visit them immediately on their return to London and had sent his wife a report of Marian's struggles. 'Her great difficulty seems to be that she, as she describes it, hears her characters talking, and there is a weight upon her mind as if Savonarola and friends ought to be speaking Italian instead of English.'[56] While Marian had been able to imagine Lisbeth Bede's speech by thinking back to the way her father spoke when he got together with his northerly brothers, she had no point of reference for the priests, scholars and merchants of Renaissance Florence.

By Christmas 1861 Lewes sensed that Marian's paralysis was now unprecedented, and he persuaded Blackwood to make several visits over the holiday period in order to 'discountenance the idea of a Romance being the product of an Encyclopaedia' and get her to begin.[57] Blackwood responded to the challenge creatively, grasping that the roots of the block went deep into the most troubled layers of Marian's psyche. On one of the three visits he made during this fortnight he brought his wife Julia with him, a sign of social accept-ance which may actually have annoyed Marian by its heavy-handedness, since she barely mentions it in her journal. A more welcome gesture was the china dog which he produced as a reminder of beloved Pug, whose name suddenly disappears from the Leweses' letters and journals after their move to central London in September 1860.[58] Equally gratifying was a letter which he produced from the great French author Montalembert, praising *Silas Marner*. One or more of these tactics worked because, on New Year's Day, Marian was able to record in her journal that she had begun 'my novel of Romola'.[59]

Unfortunately, the fresh start petered out quickly, despite Blackwood appear-ing for another visit on the 12th. By the end of the month Marian was already recording her 'malaise and despair' in her journal. Although Lewes gallantly expressed himself delighted with the Proem and opening scene, she was still not able to take flight: by the middle of February she had managed only two chapters, held back by 'an oppressive sense of the far-stretching task before me'.[60] This mood of despair was to last for another miserable eighteen months until the novel lurched to a finish. It was a time of headache, depression, sparse journal entries and only minimal correspondence with friends. Years later Marian was to confide to John Cross: 'I began . . . [*Romola*] a young woman – I finished it an old woman.'[61]

It is hardly surprising that *Romola* turned out to be lengthy, laboured and dull. There is much to admire in it, but admiration is not what keeps readers going. The historical detail is as bright and particular as the background of a Pre-Raphaelite painting. The door-knockers, head-dresses, friars, barbers, and carnivals are, according to Anthony Trollope, 'wonderful in their energy and their accuracy'.[62] Where textual sources proved mute, Marian had relied on the encyclopaedic knowledge of the Florence-raised artist Frederic Leighton, who had been engaged to draw the illustration, as well as the helpful Tom Trollope. But no amount of documentary detail could disguise the fact that the novel was dead at its centre. Marian's early worry that she could not hear her charac-ters speak turned out to be an indication of major problems to come. Instead of using a supple, colloquial English, her Florentines speak in a literal transla-tion of classical Italian. A phrase like 'A bad Easter and a bad year to you, and may you die by the sword!' comes straight from *Decameron* and has none of the immediate liveliness which, in her essay on von Riehl, Marian had argued was the mark of spoken idiom.[63] Compared with the Raveloe villagers, the Dodson aunts or Mrs Poyser, the characters in *Romola* speak a creaky, made-up kind of language which, according to the review in the *Spectator*, is 'a blank to us'.

The plot and the characters work better. Our way into the city is through Tito Melema, an educated young Greek who has recently been shipwrecked off the Tuscan coast. He finds the place in an uproar following the death of Lorenzo de Medici. On the one side are the scholars keen to continue Medici's programme of intellectual and scientific revival. On the other is Savonarola, the Dominican monk intent on reforming the Church by emphasising its mystical and miraculous origins.

Tito has all the qualities needed to succeed in this fluctuating, treacherous environment. His good looks, learning and charm allow him to move easily between the two camps, exchanging information and disinformation with calculating ease. His lack of fixed principles, suggests the narrator, comes from denying the obligations of his own past. Unlike Silas Marner, whose dormant good nature can be revived by an appeal to the emotional and moral learning of childhood, Tito remains a stranger to the family piety which, for every Eliot narrator, is the root of adult integrity. Tito's crime is that he has abandoned his adoptive father to slavery and sold his jewels. Just like Arthur Donnithorne and *Middlemarch*'s banker Bulstrode, his past now pursues him in the form of the very person whom he has wronged. Crazed with grief and a hunger for vengeance, the old man Baldassarre has tracked his adopted son down to Florence, where he publicly confronts him with his crime.

Tito's easy manner and accommodating conscience allow him to brush off the embarrassment. Like Bulstrode and Donnithorne before him, he is not a vicious man, simply one used to equivocation. 'Our lives make a moral tradition for our individual selves . . . Tito was feeling the effect of an opposite tradition: he had won no memories of self-conquest and perfect faithfulness from which he could have a sense of falling.'[64] Years of deceit have impaired the young man's ability to act properly in the present. As well as exploiting the factionalism in Florence for his own purposes, he is a callous husband to his new wife, the virtuous and beautiful Romola Bardi.

Romola is the daughter of a blind scholar who is one of the main opponents of the increasingly fundamentalist Savonarola. She is as clever as the son whom her father never had. But like all Eliot's educated heroines, she is not permitted a life of significant endeavour. Just as the young Marian Evans sat day after day reading to the ungrateful Robert Evans, so Romola is content to be her cantankerous father's eyes, translating the ancient texts that he is no longer able to read for himself. Essentially naïve, she is attracted to Tito by his plausible kindness to her father. It is only once they are married that she begins to realise his capacity for deception, in particular his relationship with Tessa, a servant girl by whom he has several children.

Romola's gradual disillusionment with Tito is wonderfully done, and anticipates those other terrible marriages – of Rosamond and Lydgate, and Grandcourt and Gwendolen. The sweetness of his manner when he wooed her now reveals itself as moral emptiness. Tito, for his part, begins to hate Romola because her palpable integrity is a silent reproach to his shoddiness. The marriage unravels as Romola comes increasingly under the influence of the charismatic Savonarola. She ends the book as an unlikely Madonna, tending to the needs of the inhabitants of a plague village and helping Tessa to look after her children by Tito.

It is possible that Marian might have abandoned a novel which so obviously wasn't working were it not for the fact that by the time she was half-way through, the first chapters were already appearing in print. After floating the idea with *Adam Bede*, and considering it seriously for *The Mill*, she was finally bringing out a novel in instalments. But *Romola* did not appear in the form of Lewes's old scheme of shilling parts, nor was it serialised in *Maga*. Instead it was published over twelve months in one of *Maga*'s newest rivals, the *Cornhill Magazine*. The Leweses' relationship with the Blackwoods, viewed as one of the most successful in the publishing industry, had foundered.

In the months leading up to the rupture John Blackwood had been his usual thoughtful self. While dealing with the illness and death of his brother and business partner at the age of only forty-eight, he had helped find Thornie somewhere to live, sent consistently encouraging news about *The Mill* and had answered repeated summonses to Blandford Square to try to shake Marian out of her creative block. In addition he had encouraged two senior members of his staff, Simpson and Langford, to do the Leweses a great many little services, from befriending the 'amiable and troublesome' Thornie to hunting down references for the interminable *Romola*. He was generous with money too. He offered to bring forward one of the payments on *The Mill* to help with the moving costs to Harewood Square and had even allowed Marian to keep a bit of extra money which had been incorrectly calculated as profit on the twelve-shilling edition of *The Mill*.

But still this was not enough for Marian, who could not forgive John Blackwood for seeming to undervalue her work during those tense negotiations over *The Mill*. Although he was probably unaware that anything was wrong, there are signs that by the end of 1860 Marian was once again feeling aggrieved. In early October 1860 she turned down an offer from Blackwood of £3000 for the remaining copyright on all her books from *Scenes* to *Silas Marner*. The reason isn't clear, but the fact that in her journal she links her decision to a letter from Bradbury and Evans, the publishers who had courted her over *The Mill*, suggests that Blackwood's offer struck her as below the market price. She expressed her dissatisfaction in her usual way, by finding the tiniest flaws in Blackwood's immaculate dealing. In January 1862, having read rejection into something he had said during one of his morale-boosting visits to Blandford Square, she wrote a complaining letter about the arrangements for a new cheap edition of her work.[65] A few weeks later she was gripped by the sudden certainty that Simpson was not bothering to publicise this new edition. It was only when she was presented with an exhaustive list of the advertisements which had been placed that she was forced to admit that her accusations of indifference were misplaced.[66]

It was during these anguished first few weeks of 1862 when *Romola* would not catch fire and nothing Blackwood did was right, that George Smith reappeared in the Leweses' life. He had been circling ever since those difficult days of negotiation over *The Mill*. Buoyed up by a remarkable overseas investment income, his company of Smith and Elder not only published novels, but the previous year had set up the *Cornhill Magazine*, edited by William Thackeray. With plenty of money in his pocket, Smith was exactly that kind of high-spending, head-hunting publisher with whom John Blackwood had made it clear that he could and would not compete.

But Smith did not initially receive a warm welcome when he appeared at

Blandford Square. The previous year he had cancelled a series in the *Cornhill* by Lewes on 'Animal Life' because of a worry that its evolutionary assumptions might offend orthodox readers. Since then the magazine had been floundering, much to the satisfaction of Lewes, who had pointedly refused to make any further contributions. However, the terms of the original agreement for the 'Animal Life' pieces meant that Smith and Elder had the right to publish them in book form, and this was what Smith now came on 23 January 1862 to discuss. During his visit Smith sounded out Lewes as to whether Marian was open to a magnificent offer for her new work, and a month later returned to propose the extraordinary sum of £10,000 which, as Lewes recorded in his journal, would be the largest sum ever paid for a novel.[67] But timing was the problem, just as it had been two years earlier when Dickens tried to get Marian to serialise a novel in *All the Year Round*. Smith would need to start publishing *Romola* in the April or May issue, so that Marian would be writing only a few weeks ahead of each deadline. Both she and Lewes agreed that it would impose too great a strain on a process which was already painful enough. Marian then suggested that the unpublished 'Brother Jacob' might do as a three-month filler until she was ready to start publishing *Romola* in the autumn, but Smith was not keen. Naturally Lewes was disappointed to lose such a magnificent deal, but recorded that he was 'just as well pleased that Polly should not be hurried or flurried, by being bound to appear at an earlier date than she would like'.[68]

Smith was a man of business, not books. He had not yet read a word of *Romola*, but he knew the value of the name 'George Eliot'. Marian could not but be flattered by this contrast with the attitude of John Blackwood, who had always seemed to find her name such an embarrassment. But Smith's designs on the Leweses went further. On 8 April he arrived at Blandford Square to propose that Lewes should take over the editorship of the *Cornhill*, which had been left vacant by the hurried departure of Thackeray. Lewes had no desire for a job that would not leave him enough time for his scientific work, but he did agree to the very congenial role of consulting editor.[69] For £600 a year he would suggest topics and select articles while a hard-working sub-editor of his own choosing managed the daily grind.

Having Lewes at the head of the *Cornhill* gave Smith a persuasive ally in his campaign to get George Eliot on board. By the beginning of May she was coming round to the idea of letting him publish *Romola* in weekly sixpenny parts of twenty-four pages. However, first she insisted on reading him some of what she had already written so that he should be absolutely aware of the uncommercial nature of the novel for which he was bidding. Having heard it, Smith decided that the story would not work in such small segments, and said that he would prefer to publish it in the *Cornhill* in twelve instalments of forty to forty-five pages, starting in July. For this he would pay £7000.[70] The Leweses accepted, but it was an odd, botched deal, which did not work properly for anyone. Smith did not get the strong successor he had wanted to Trollope's *Framley Parsonage*, which finished its *Cornhill* run in April. And Marian was still left having to write a book against horrendous deadlines.

The next task was to tell Blackwood, who was still under the impression that he was George Eliot's publisher. On 19 May, the day she struck a deal with Smith, Marian wrote to Edinburgh. She started by apologising that 'this letter will seem rather abrupt to you, but the abruptness is unavoidable', then explained that she had recently received an offer which she supposed 'was handsomer than almost any terms ever offered to a writer of Fiction'. Then, in a barbed reference to the way in which she had always felt undervalued by John Blackwood, she continued, 'I felt that, as I was not at liberty to mention the terms to you, and as they were hopelessly beyond your usual estimate of the value of my books to you, there would be an indelicacy in my making an appeal to you before decision.'[71]

Blackwood replied the next day with superhuman restraint. He was sorry that the new novel was not to come out 'under the old colours', but was quite aware of the vast sums which were being offered to 'writers of much inferior mark to you'. He concluded with a flattering reference, which may or may not have been sarcastic, to her lack of greed and high-minded loyalty. Marian certainly took him at face value, for in her journal three days later she recorded complacently that although there had been 'regret' in leaving Blackwood, he 'has written me a letter in the most perfect spirit of gentlemanliness and good-feeling'.[72]

In fact John Blackwood was feeling anything but gentlemanly. Three days later, Langford wrote with the news that Smith and Elder had had the cheek to send an advertisement for insertion in *Maga* in which George Eliot's new story was announced in the next number of the *Cornhill Magazine*. Langford, who had long disapproved of Marian, pointedly referred to her as 'Miss Evans' and branded the whole business a 'disgusting transaction, which certainly does not surprise me on her part, but does rather on the part of Mr Smith'. Faced with Langford's 'attempt to sour my stomach', Blackwood retreated to his usual defence of trying to convince himself that it was Lewes rather than Marian who was the prime mover in this bit of treachery. He blamed Lewes's 'voracity' for making her act 'against her inclination' in 'going over to the enemy'. He consoled himself with the thought that *Romola* was unlikely to go down well with the readers of the *Cornhill* and stuck to the moral high ground by refusing to quarrel since 'quarrels especially literary ones are vulgar'.[73]

No sooner had Marian accepted Smith's offer than she regretted it. The writing of *Romola* was not going well and the realisation that she was about to produce her first flop must have seemed like a punishment for her disloyalty and greed. On 17 June she invited Blackwood to visit Blandford Square and took advantage of a few moments alone together to tell him 'that she could never feel to another publisher as she felt towards me – that pleasure to her was gone in the matter and she did not feel sure now whether she had acted right'. Blackwood reported with righteous satisfaction to his nephew Willie, who had taken his late father's place in the business, that on this occasion he 'merely looked her full in the face and shaking hands said, "I'm fully satisfied that it must have been a very sharp pang to you."'[74]

No one could have blamed Blackwood for feeling smug. Although a critical success, *Romola* did not come near to reimbursing Smith for his tremendous outlay. It did nothing to halt the decline in the sales of the *Cornhill* and as a three-decker it was slow to sell. Painfully aware that she had not delivered her side of the bargain, Marian gave Smith 'Brother Jacob', for which he had been prepared to pay 250 guineas, absolutely free. It eventually appeared in the July 1864 edition of the magazine.

The obligation to write to order brought extra strain to what was already a difficult experience. Time was sometimes perilously tight: at the end of September 1862 Marian had still not finished the instalment due to be published in December.[75] For writers like Dickens and Trollope who were used to working in this way, the pressure of serialisation was offset by certain advantages. Allowed to gauge reaction to a character or storyline as they went along, they could be sure of satisfying popular taste. Because Marian took care not to read or listen to criticism, she was unable to profit by this time lag. In any case, the organic construction of her books meant that, even if she had heard a whisper of criticism or praise, she would have been incapable of changing her work in response.

Much has been written about the damaging effects of Marian's refusal to confront and absorb reactions to her work. Her morbid sensitivity had worsened as she grew more successful. Lewes had stretched himself into what amounted to a cordon of steel, allowing no adverse comment to reach her. In September 1862 Sara Hennell, who had still not got the point that her response to Marian's work was not wanted, had sent a letter in which she repeated some critical remarks she had heard about *Romola*. Lewes made sure that Marian didn't see these comments by pretending to lose the letter before she could read it for herself. The moment he was on his own, he sat down and wrote sternly to 'My dear Miss Hennell', explaining that after the horrors of the public gossip about *Adam Bede*, they had decided that Marian should pay no attention to anyone's comments about her books: 'No one speaks about her books to her, but me; she sees no criticisms.' As for the remarks about *Romola* which Sara had repeated, Lewes explains loftily that Marian had always been aware that the book would not be popular. Then, in a swipe at the provincial company which Sara kept, he continued: 'If you only knew the wonderful eulogies which have reached her from learned Florentines, and Englishmen of high culture (F. Maurice, Bulwer, Anthony Trollope etc.) you would be surprised that she should be made miserable by doubts as to whether the book will be a success.' Lewes finished with an emphatic and confused warning to Sara.

> The principle is this: *never tell her anything that other people say about her books, for good or evil*; unless of course it should be something exceptionally gratifying to her – something you know would please her apart from its being praise . . . You can tell me any details (I'm a glutton in all that concerns her, though I never look after what is said about myself [not true]) favorable or unfavorable; but for her let her mind be as much as possible fixed on her art and not on the public.[76]

Perhaps it would have been better if Marian had read the offending paragraph in Sara's letter. By closing her ears to popular opinion she lost touch during these middle years of her career with the springs of her own talent. Instead of the creamy dairy and the pithy sayings, the green fields and the Christmas dance of an England only just disappeared, there was the history-lesson tedium of a culture far removed from anyone's experience. Anthony Trollope had tactfully warned her after the first instalment of *Romola* not to 'fire too much over the heads of your readers', but she had stubbornly insisted that if her readers were not able to follow her into new territory, then it was no concern of hers.[77] Her next endeavour, the prose poem *The Spanish Gypsy*, was likewise to baffle and bore all but her most devoted fans. Other critics pointed to the complicated scientific metaphors in *Middlemarch*, which they assumed must have been the result of Lewes's overbearing influence.

Posterity blamed Lewes for keeping Marian in a 'mental greenhouse', but those who knew her personally were adamant that if it had not been for this constant protection, self-doubt would have stopped her from writing.[78] What is sometimes missed is that while Marian invited Lewes's total protection, Lewes had a corresponding need to control Marian. As a couple they were by now in a situation unique in mid-Victorian England. Marian's huge earnings not only supported Lewes in his unprofitable scientific work, but paid for his mother, his children, his wife, her children, as well as his widowed sister-in-law and her child. In the unlikely event that Marian were to leave him or to die, Lewes would have found himself in severe financial difficulties. His income for 1862 was £639 14s, handsome enough for a self-employed writer, but hardly sufficient to keep all those impecunious Leweses out of the workhouse. No wonder that his anxiety about Marian's career tipped over into an exaggerated fussiness. No surprise, either, that he felt the need to maintain his influence over her by making sure that no one else had access.

It is a shame that Marian was kept away from helpful criticism, because on the rare occasions she heard it she was able to respond creatively. When Richard Hutton, the *Spectator* critic, wrote thoughtfully to her about *Romola*, she neither crumbled nor resorted to lofty dismissals of his fitness to comment. Instead, she wrote back agreeing with and even amplifying some of his points. She reassured him that there was nothing in his *Spectator* review which struck her as wrong and was delighted that he had grasped the way in which she had tried to show the impact of Florentine political life on the development of Tito's nature. She went on to stress what critics (both then and now) have failed to grasp, that while the subject matter of *Romola* represented a new departure, the treatment remained the same.

> It is the habit of my imagination to strive after as full a vision of the medium in which a character moves as of the character itself. The psychological causes which prompted me to give such details of Florentine life and history as I have given, are precisely the same as those which determined me in giving the details of English village life in 'Silas Marner', or the 'Dodson' life, out of which were developed the destinies of poor Tom and Maggie. But you have correctly pointed out the reason why my tendency to excess in this effort after artistic vision makes the

impression of a fault in 'Romola' much more perceptibly than in my previous books.[79]

Marian probably found it easier to admit that there were important things wrong with *Romola* precisely because it was proving to be such a big critical hit. Lewes had not been exaggerating when he boasted to Sara Hennell that men of the calibre of F. D. Maurice and Anthony Trollope revered the book. Italy was in the process of fighting its way to freedom and unity, and Marian's careful consideration of its history and culture provided a useful background to the current debate among the British intellectual establishment as to the legitimacy of the revolutionary cause. So there was something entirely fitting about the fact that when on 18 April 1864 the Leweses went to see Garibaldi fêted at the Crystal Palace, none other than F. D. Maurice stepped forward in person to be introduced to the author of *Romola*.[80]

During the years 1859 to 1862 the Leweses were nearly always ill. Marian's letters and journal entries are full of headaches, some of them lasting days. In part this was a response to the difficulties with *Romola*, but it was also the result of feeling choked and trapped in the city. As Marian told Barbara Bodichon, 'The wide sky, the *not*-London, makes a new creature of me in half an hour.'[81] Whenever possible Lewes would take Marian for a break down to Surrey or Sussex. While it is hard today to imagine Dorking or Littlehampton representing some kind of rural idyll, in the 1860s they were sufficiently quiet to give Marian the glimpse of the country she needed, complete with foxhounds and stag meets. They were near enough to London, too, to allow Lewes to travel up to town to take care of business whenever necessary. Taking her Florentines with her, Marian managed to get through a significant amount of work in anonymous hotel rooms, a skill which she had enjoyed ever since her earliest days with Lewes.

The Lewes boys – their noise and chaos and failure to excel – hardly helped her spirits. Although Thornie was safely away in Edinburgh, there were still the occasional and disruptive weeks when he had to be in Blandford Square, usually *en route* for a summer break in Hofwyl. Although Marian tried manfully not to mind, she could not help her true feelings leaking out in letters. To Willie Blackwood, who had befriended Thornie in Edinburgh, she wrote that she hoped the boy was not being a nuisance: 'Young gentlemen of seventeen have often immense resources for boring their elders.'[82] Once Thornie had failed his exams and refused to re-sit them, there was the worry of designing a new future for him. At one time the worry became too much for Marian and she departed for a fortnight to Wandsworth, leaving Lewes and Thornie to thrash it out between them. This time, with the advice and practical help of Barbara Bodichon, it was decided that he should try Africa. In October 1863 Thornton Lewes set off with a rifle, a revolver, a bit of Dutch and Zulu, and his usual high spirits.

Bertie was a bigger problem. When the unpromising boy arrived home for good in July 1863 Marian admitted that she felt 'up to the ears in Boydom and imperious parental duties'.[83] Once it was decided that he should be a farmer, he was dispatched as a pupil to Scotland, where he stayed for two years before being brought down to a farm in, of all places, Warwickshire. Marian must have found it hard to imagine how this childish, spoiled young man would succeed in a way of life which had stretched her canny, hard-working father to the limit, especially now that farming needed 'great skill to render it otherwise than hazardous'.[84]

But the roots of Marian's depression and physical ill-health went deeper than noisy teenagers and smoky skies. Although the relationship with Lewes brought joy to both sides, it also locked the two protagonists into a strange romance of sickness. Caring for each other's aching heads, numb feet, agitated livers, weight loss and dizzy spells bound them together in a way that even literature never could. Perhaps this was because at some level they knew that these endless symptoms – which did not bring death for another fifteen years – were the price of their felicity. 'We have so much happiness in our love and uninterrupted companionship', wrote Marian, 'that we must accept our miserable bodies as our share of mortal ill.'[85]

That it was psychological conflict which lay behind Lewes's alarming fainting spells and loss of weight is suggested by two separate incidents. When Anthony Trollope announced that Charlie was not doing well at the Post Office the anxious father had an immediate bilious attack. John Blackwood's first visit to Blandford Square after the defection to George Smith disturbed Lewes so much that he had to go upstairs and lie down.[86] Yet during those endless night journeys and bad hotel rooms, which had been a part of Lewes's hectic travelling schedule over so many years, we seldom hear of him being less than perfectly fit.

Lewes, the pioneering writer on psychology, had some insight into the effect of his mental state on his physical well-being. In particular, he recognised the appalling strain which came with constantly having to appear cheerful and encouraging in the face of Marian's black moods. As he confided to Blackwood on 6 March 1861, 'I cannot help *occasionally* being made anxious by her persistent depreciation of what she writes.'[87] Unable to express his true feelings about Marian's work except to his private journal, Lewes was left with no option but to get sick. And at times he got very sick indeed. Weight loss, dyspepsia and headaches meant that he could on occasion write for only a few hours a day, although within those constraints he remained prolific. He became almost a professional invalid, canvassing friends for the best or latest cures. Riding was tried and rejected because it shook up his liver. Walking tours with Spencer went better. Spa towns in Britain and abroad were sampled for their bracingly cold and salty regimes.

The dynamic which allowed the Leweses to catch their unhappiness and ill-health from one another had been forged in the dual solitude they had enjoyed for so many years. Yet intriguingly it was just as that solitude began to break down that these symptoms became most severe. Arriving in central London in November 1863, among the writers, artists and politicians who made up their natural social circle, meant renegotiating Marian's situation and status. Tucked away in the suburbs, there had been no problem. Marian stayed *persona non grata* in Wandsworth, while Lewes popped to London. The situation had been painful, but it was stable. But now, installed in an elegant house in central London where anyone might make a call, the whole issue of Mrs Lewes's position in society was once again under review. While Marian had to face the old problem of dodging snubs, Lewes was obliged to confront his responsibility for ruining the life of the woman he loved. It was no wonder they both got headaches.

Moving to central London meant Marian seeing much less of her passionate Wandsworth friend Maria Congreve, who could manage only occasional overnight visits up in town. The Coventry trio were now so preoccupied with their own house moves, the result of dwindling fortunes, that they did not often have the time or the money to venture to town. Barbara Bodichon had a house in the same square, but for half the year she was in Algeria with her new, odd husband. One possible new friend was Mrs Clementia Taylor, wife of the Liberal MP Peter Taylor, a feminist who had been one of the few people to write to Marian expressing her support during the early days with Lewes. On 4 April 1861 Mrs Taylor had called at Blandford Square and invited the Leweses to her home. A couple of days later Marian wrote explaining to her new friend that 'I have found it a necessity of my London life to make the rule of *never* paying visits': instead she preferred people to come to her.[88] She gave her reasons as bad health and lack of time, but this was simply to protect herself from situations where she might be humiliated by a freezing glance from a fellow guest.

It was now, when Marian was about to re-enter London literary life, that Lewes made serious enquiries as to whether it would be possible to divorce Agnes in Europe. Changes to English divorce law in 1857 had still not brought the Leweses' strange case – where the man had condoned his wife's adultery – within its scope. The fact that Charlie was living under their roof was another reason for trying to regularise the relationship: no one wanted the boy to face sniggers, stares or snubs every time he left the house. But the legal situation remained intractable and Marian's attitude one of studied indifference: 'I am not sorry. I think the boys will not suffer, and for myself I prefer excommunication.'[89] Turning the situation on its head, she used her status as stepmother to buttress her claim to be considered a proper wife. As she explained to Mrs Taylor, who had followed her other feminist friends in referring to her by her maiden name:

For the last six years I have ceased to be 'Miss Evans' for anyone who has personal relations with me – having held myself under all the responsibilities of a married woman. I wish this to be distinctly understood; and when I tell you that we have a great boy of eighteen at home who calls me 'mother', as well as two other boys, almost as tall, who write to me under the same name, you will understand that the point is not one of mere egoism or personal dignity, when I request that any one who has a regard for me will cease to speak of me by my maiden name.[90]

At first the Leweses' new social life revolved around men. By that curious Victorian double standard, there was no impropriety in a respectable man spending time with a 'fallen woman', although for his wife it was a very different matter. In June 1861 when Blackwood arranged a whitebait dinner in Greenwich in Marian's honour, she had been the only woman present.[91] At Blandford Square, too, the atmosphere was heavily masculine. At the first dinner party held there, on 20 November 1860, Arthur Helps, now Clerk to the Privy Council, arrived with the news that Queen Victoria had told him how much she admired George Eliot's books. But Helps did not bring his wife to dine, nor did fellow guest Anthony Trollope, despite the fact that Marian had stayed in the Florentine house of his brother Tom.

The arrival in October 1861 of a grand piano – always a symbol of luxury in the mid-Victorian household – meant that social life in Blandford Square increasingly revolved around music. Charles was taken to all the concerts he could possibly want. Musical 'at homes' on Saturday evenings became a fixture, with Herbert Spencer's and Edward Pigott's singing accompanied by Charles or Marian on the piano. Other less tuneful guests included the poet Robert Browning and the painter Frederic Burton. A new kind of expansiveness, previously only seen on holiday, gradually settled over the Leweses' living arrangements. A dinner on 27 May 1862 in honour of Tom Trollope had Marian as well as Lewes bustling out to buy some new claret glasses for the occasion.

With women it remained trickier. Bessie Rayner Parkes, who was now absorbed in running the feminist *English Woman's Journal*, was obliged to duck invitations to Blandford Square because, even though she was over thirty, she worried about upsetting her parents. In this case it was not so much her beloved Marian she felt she could not visit as Lewes, whom she persisted in seeing as a libertine. In a letter to Barbara in which she explained her difficulty she finished with the key question: 'Anthony Trollope goes there next week; but will he take his wife?'[92]

The answer was no. The occasion to which both Bessie and Trollope had been invited was a combined house-warming and twenty-first birthday party. In November 1863 the Leweses had moved into the Priory, on the edge of Regent's Park. This was the first house they had bought and it cost £2000. Aware of the significance of such a step, they decided to have it renovated and redecorated by their friend Owen Jones, the country's foremost designer who had been responsible for parts of the Crystal Palace. Owen Jones looked after every detail, from the drawing-room chairs to the hanging of their engravings. The result was a 'very exquisite thing', the kind of place where Britain's most successful author might hold court. Despite a few local difficulties, including the piano tuner being sick on the specially commissioned wallpaper and Marian getting her purse stolen by the removal men, the move went well.[93] Owen Jones stayed until 2 a.m. on two nights to check that everything was ready for the party.

But there was one thing which was not quite right, apart from the conspicuous absence of Mrs Anthony Trollope, Mrs Owen Jones and a great many other ladies. Marian's dowdy looks did not match her splendid setting. While Lewes had a dandyish touch, Marian still lacked elegance. Determined that his aesthetic vision should not be spoiled, Owen Jones gave her a stern sermon on 'her general neglect of personal adornment' and insisted that she should at least try to look pretty for the evening. He bossed her into a silver-grey dress, bought specially for the occasion, creating an image which appalled and secretly delighted her.[94] She had just turned forty-four and although several men had told her that she was plain, none had ever suggested what she might do about it. It was extraordinary what a difference success made.

CHAPTER 12

'The Bent of My Mind Is Conservative'

_____

Felix Holt and The Spanish Gypsy
1864–8

DURING HER MIDDLE forties Marian achieved something approaching peace of mind. The self-criticism, despair and morbid sensitivity which had continued to haunt even the commercial success of *The Mill* and the critical buzz of *Romola* now began to melt. The letters she wrote to friends during the mid-1860s have lost their characteristic defensive, combative tone. There are not so many swipes at 'frivolous women', fewer proud references to her lack of friends, less posing as an intellectual Olympian, unconcerned with what the masses think about her work. For the first time in Marian's correspondence, there is something like an unguarded heart. A week after her forty-third birthday, in November 1862, she had written to M. D'Albert Durade: 'I think this year's end finds me enjoying existence more than I ever did before, in spite of the loss of youth. Study is a keener delight to me than ever, and I think the affections, instead of being dulled by age, have acquired a stronger activity – or at least their activity seems stronger for being less perturbed by the egoism of young cravings.'[1] Viewed from outside there was no obvious reason for this softening. The two pieces of work which she produced during these years, *Felix Holt, The Radical* and *The Spanish Gypsy*, hardly marked a return to the glory days of *Adam Bede* and *The Mill*. Profits were down and praise muted, especially in the case of *The Spanish Gypsy*, a dramatic poem woefully lacking in drama. Thornton and Bertie continued to be a worry, especially as the time drew near when they would have to stand alone. And Lewes's health seemed to get, if anything, more precarious.

The secret of Marian's growing happiness lay in her new ability to absorb and transform these unsought factors in her life. The death of friends and family, the coolish response to her work, even Lewes's gaunt face, no longer had the power to plunge her into headachy despair from which it took days to emerge. Her new serenity may have followed the menopause, leaving her free from monthly swings of mood and vitality. Then again, her successful re-integration into London literary society may have given her the confidence to brush off the kind of imagined slight which had once filled her mind for days. Whatever the reason, it was during these years that Marian began to acquire her reputation for an emotional serenity to sit alongside her undisputed intellectual and creative powers. The intense young men and women who wrote adoring letters from around the world, together with the lucky few who were invited to the Priory, were drawn not by Mrs Poyser's country sayings or Maggie Tulliver's stubborn curls, but by the voice of George Eliot herself. It was this voice – wise, tolerant, all-seeing – which seemed to understand their greatest joys and deepest fears. In an age of increasing unbelief George Eliot's ability to point the way to a meaningful life bestowed on Marian Lewes the status of secular saint.

Reactions to a new portrait reflect this shift in the way Marian was perceived. Frederic Burton's painting, which was finished in 1865, was no more flattering than the one by Laurence five years earlier, yet this time Lewes was delighted and gave permission for it to be shown at the Royal Academy. Where once commentators stressed Marian's plainness, sniggeringly implying that she was most unlikely mistress material, these days they rushed to see nobility in her heavy features. The general and often-repeated impression that she looked like a horse was now fleshed out by more careful and kindly detail. A young Henry James agreed on meeting Marian that her face was 'equine', but added that it had 'a delightful expression'.[2] Others preferred to make comparisons with Dante, Savonarola and Locke who, while men, were at least wise ones. From this point the myth grew that there was something magically transformative about Marian Lewes's face. Visitors who arrived at the Priory expecting long, lumpy features reported that they were introduced to a woman whose inner light recast her face so that she looked 'both good and loving and gentle'.[3] Appropriately for a woman named Marian, it was like hearing that a stony-faced Virgin had produced real tears.

Death was everywhere now. In November 1861 it came to the poet Arthur Hugh Clough, who had been born the same year as Marian. It was not the passing of a youngish man she pondered so much as the effect on his poor widow.[4] Queen Victoria's intense and protracted mourning following the death of the Consort the following month was likewise to draw her sympathy on the grounds that 'I am a woman of about the same age, and also have my personal happiness bound up in a dear husband whose loss would render my life simply a series of social duties and private memories'.[5] The idea that she might one day have to live without Lewes pressed heavily. He was now in his late forties, and his face had grown thin and shockingly old. Even on holiday, where he had always rallied, he was now sometimes sick and faint. One doctor advised giving up naturalising because it entailed too much hanging of the head over rock pools and microscope. Mostly, though, it was a question of paying another visit to one more foul-tasting spa where, sociable as ever, the little man usually managed to bump into some equally frail literary friend. Although Marian was herself enjoying better health during these post-menopausal years, she was reluctant to leave Lewes behind in the land of invalids. She liked the idea that they were a 'rickety old couple', perhaps because its image of mutual dependence and old age suggested that they were long-time married.[6] 'We hardly know now what it is to be free from bodily malaise,' she regularly intoned to her correspondents.[7]

Other deaths came nearer. In May 1866 the appalling Dr Brabant finally succumbed at the age of eighty-five. Marian must still have felt embarrassed at the memory of their awkward affair twenty years before, because her letter of condolence to his daughter Rufa Call skillfully avoids mentioning the old man's name or, indeed, a single thing about him.[8]

News of another loss stirred up more positive attachments to the past. In early 1864 Robert Evans, the eldest son of her father by his first wife, had died. The news came in a courteous letter from Evans's son, also Robert Evans. Apart from a little contact with her schoolgirl niece Emily, it was the first time Marian had heard from her family in seven years. She replied promptly to 'My dear Nephew', thanking Evans for his 'kind attention' towards her and recalling the 'unbroken kindness and generous brotherliness' of his father.[9] In a fuller letter of condolence to her sister-in-law Marian expanded on her memories of Robert's kindness – so different from Isaac's coldness – and repeated her hope that if ever Mrs Evans were in town, she might pay a visit to the Priory. It was the kind of message which routinely closed letters between female relatives who lived at a distance, but in this case the meaning was momentous. By saying 'To see you again or to hear from you . . . would be a very sweet renewal of the past',[10] Marian was asking Jane to break Isaac Evans's boycott.

Once her grief had settled, Jane would probably have made the gesture Marian was hoping for: in her reply of 18 March she told her sister-in-law that the last book Robert Evans held in his hand had been *Adam Bede*.[11] But death intervened again, this time making things more difficult. Six weeks later another letter came from Robert Evans announcing that Henry Houghton, Fanny's husband, had died.[12] Marian was in Scotland when it arrived, a point she emphasised to her nephew to explain a slight delay in responding. Now that a precious link had been made to her family, she was determined to protect it from misunderstanding: 'my silence was not a neglectful one,' she assured Robert Evans and, to make certain the letter reached him, she gave it 'a double address'.[13]

Having sent her condolences to 'my affectionately remembered Sister' via Robert, Marian does not seem to have written directly to Fanny. Perhaps she was waiting for a sign that her half-sister was ready to break the ban on communication imposed by Isaac. If so, none was forthcoming. Fanny had moved from a sceptical youth into an orthodox middle age. Since complying with the boycott she had spent her time stalking Marian through the pages of her novels. She was sharp enough to note that the 'marvellously clever' *Felix Holt* was likely to be 'much more to the taste of the ordinary novel reader than *Romola* was' and even spotted that Marian had written a couple of articles in the first issue of a new periodical, the *Fortnightly*. None the less, when it came to the vexed question of her half-sister's domestic arrangements, Fanny was as bigoted as any provincial farmer's wife. On tracking down a photograph of Lewes in a Leamington bookstore she wrote with delighted disgust to Isaac that there was something positively inhuman about the face of the man who had ruined their sister's life.[14]

Fanny's bereavement stopped any further bridge-building between Marian and the Evanses. On the death of Henry Houghton Fanny moved to Nottingham to live with Robert's widow Jane. Now any overtures made by Jane towards Marian would have to take place under the disapproving eye of Fanny. With this new pressure, the pace of reconciliation slowed. There seems to have been no communication between the Priory and Nottingham until two years later in August 1866, when Marian received a letter from her nephew inviting herself and Lewes to visit. This put her in a difficult position. While she was assured of a warm welcome from Robert, his wife and his mother, would she be forced to endure Fanny's pointed absence? Rather than risk that painful possibility, she used the strategy she always adopted when faced with invitations to homes where she could not be sure she would not meet some snub from a fellow guest. She wrote back warmly to Robert thanking him and his wife for their 'attention' but excusing herself on the grounds that she had only just returned from two months on the Continent.[15]

But it was the death of twenty-year-old Nelly Bray which hit hardest. On 1 March 1865 the Brays' adopted daughter finally succumbed to the consumption she had been fighting for several years.[16] In her letter of condolence to Cara Marian's thoughts turned inevitably to the subject she had discussed so many times with the Hennell sisters: the possibility of a future life.

> I don't know whether you strongly share, as I do, the old belief that made men say the gods loved those who died young. It seems to me truer than ever, now life has become more complex and more and more difficult problems have to be worked out. Life, though a good to men on the whole, is a doubtful good to many, and to some not a good at all. To my thought, it is a source of constant mental distortion to make the denial of this a part of religion, to go on pretending things are better than they are ... So to me, early death takes the aspect of salvation – though I feel too that those who live and suffer may sometimes have the greater blessedness of *being* a salvation.[17]

The problem of what happened to the soul after death tormented the mid-century agnostic mind. If there was no God, did that mean there was no heaven? The new and growing craze for drawing-room seances sprang directly from the powerful hope that, even if God had gone, something of the human spirit remained after death. The Leweses were sceptical. During their second visit to the Villino Trollope in Florence in 1861 Lewes had argued vigorously against the whole nonsense of table tapping. Much later, in 1874, he and Marian were to storm out of a seance at Erasmus Darwin's house 'in disgust' because the medium insisted on complete darkness.[18] In an article which Marian wrote for the first issue of the *Fortnightly* in 1865 she pointed out that the human need for an afterlife was so strong that intelligent men and women

By the time William Thackeray sketched George Henry Lewes, Agnes
Lewes and Thornton Hunt in 1848, the affair between Mrs Lewes and
Hunt was probably under way.

George Henry Lewes with Pug, a present from her publisher John Blackwood to George Eliot. Both Eliot and Lewes adored dogs.

Holly Lodge, Wandsworth, oppressed Eliot with a sense of suburban claustrophobia. It was during their two years here that she wrote *The Mill on the Floss*, published in 1860.

The old mill at Arbury, a probable model for the mill in *The Mill on the Floss*.

'The best of publishers' is how Eliot described John Blackwood, the man who brought out all but one of her novels. His tact and encouragement went a long way to offsetting her morbid sensitivity and self-doubt.

Generally maintained to be the ugliest man in London, Lewes's nickname was 'Ape'. In the course of his lifetime he was variously described as resembling a French dancing-master, a mercurial little showman and a satyr.

In 1863 the Leweses paid £2000 for the Priory, Regent's Park, the first house they had ever owned. The leading designer of the day, Owen Jones, was in charge of the decoration.

Below: On Sunday afternoons the Leweses were 'at home'. Twenty or so men and a few women would gather in the Priory drawing-room, hoping for the chance of a brief conversation with George Eliot.

Barbara Leigh Smith, later Bodichon, was the only woman with whom Eliot had something approaching a relationship of equals, with Smith neither hero-worshipping nor envying Eliot.

Described as tall and with beautiful hair, Romola, the heroine of Eliot's 1863 novel, illustrated here by Frederic Leighton, was based on Barbara Leigh Smith.

The Heights at Witley, the country retreat in Surrey which the Leweses bought towards the end of their lives. They loved the 'small paradise' and even took up lawn tennis at the suggestion of John Cross. During the last summer of his life, Lewes would walk with Eliot at dawn through their patch of woodland in an attempt to relieve the pain of what was probably bowel cancer.

Catching sight of Eliot in the audience of a concert in 1877, Princess Louise, Queen Victoria's daughter, drew a hasty sketch on the back of her programme.

John Walter Cross, the thirty-nine-year-old banker, whom Eliot married eight months before her death at the age of sixty-one (Cross is seated on the right).

swore blind that they had seen the fashionable medium Daniel Home float through the air.[19]

Unlike Lewes, Marian did not characterise this credulity as craven weakness. Again and again she returned to the sharedness of all human yearning, regardless of the doctrine in which it came clothed. Cardinal Newman's *Apologia Pro Vita Sua*, in which he charts his journey from Oxford High Anglicanism to Roman Catholicism, drew her 'as the revelation of a life – how different in form from one's own, yet with how close a fellowship in its [spiritual] needs and burthens'.[20] But she did not take refuge in a hazy theism made up of the most appealing bits of other people's religions. Ever the natural historian, she understood that each way of worship was the product of a particular moment in man's historic and social development. It would always be her native Church of England which spoke directly to her 'as a portion of my earliest associations and most poetic memories', rather than the dissenting traditions about which she had written so convincingly, and was to do so again in *Felix Holt*.[21]

But if Marian understood the human attachment to religious forms, she still believed that the best and highest thing was to live without them. The driving force behind her writing, she told Dr Clifford Allbutt, one of the earnest young men who became a friend and correspondent in the late 1860s, was to show readers 'those vital elements which bind men together and give a higher worthiness to their existence', while trying to wean them off their dependency on 'an outworn teaching' based on 'transient forms'.[22]

It was this determination to live without the man-made props of faith which made Marian steer clear of Comte's ersatz 'Religion of Humanity', a sort of secularised Catholicism. She had already made her feelings tactfully clear to the Congreves, but her obvious sympathy for Comte's sociological writings meant that she would always find herself under pressure from those who wanted to recruit her to the cause. In 1866 she became friends with a young radical barrister called Frederic Harrison who had been influenced by Richard Congreve at Wadham and was an enthusiastic follower of Comtism in its cultist aspects. Initially Marian had asked Harrison to help her with the complicated legal plot which formed the background to *Felix Holt*. His enthusiasm for the task, together with his obvious moral earnestness – he was heavily involved in the trade union movement and the Working Men's College – warmed her to him. Gradually their conversations began to roam over every aspect of human experience. Hopeful that Marian might put her talents in the service of Comte, Harrison wrote her a long letter on 19 July 1866 suggesting that her next book should show the Religion of Humanity in action. Helpfully, he even provided the sketch of a plot.[23]

Marian was gentle with Harrison, whom she had grown to like and respect. Whereas a few years earlier the young pup would have got a fierce letter from Lewes warning him not to be so impertinent, now Marian replied herself at length. She thanked Harrison for his suggestion and assured him that she was always interested to hear his ideas. She explains, though, that writing about Utopias does not make for good novels. Although she believes that fiction can deliver 'the highest of all teaching because it deals with life in its highest complexity', it is crucial that it should never become crudely didactic. For years she has strained to ensure that her novels present philosophical ideas in a 'thoroughly incarnate' form 'as if they had revealed themselves to me first in the flesh and not in the spirit'. If at any point the writing should lapse 'from the picture to the diagram' then it becomes offensively preachy. In an unconscious recognition that *Romola*'s final chapters might well have had something of the diagram about them – and a Comtist one at that – Marian emphasises to Harrison the 'unspeakable pains' she took in the book to repro-duce the texture of a living, breathing past.[24]

Having spent so long detaching herself and then revaluing the teachings of the Church of England, Marian was not about to sign up for another set of doctrines. She was happy to help the Positivists with a donation which never went higher than five pounds a year, just as she did for other causes whose energy she admired but whose aims she could not whole-heartedly endorse. Her personal friendship with the Congreves drew her to the first few public lectures which Richard Congreve gave on Positivism in the late spring of 1867. All the same, she was powerless to prevent the Positivists from hijacking her work for their own ends. Her poem 'O May I Join the Choir Invisible', pub-lished in 1874, was a case in point. Its expressed hope that a well-spent life would endure in the hearts and minds of those left behind made it into a kind of unofficial anthem for the Religion of Humanity. Yet as Congreve himself was careful to point out to a private correspondent in 1880, Marian Lewes 'is not nor ever has been more than by her acceptance of the general idea of Humanity a Positivist'.[25]

Until now Marian had very seldom mentioned politics or public events in her letters and journal. It was not that she had no interest in these matters, simply that she had always been more concerned with the social and psychological organisation of mankind. Her belief that human development was necessarily slow and organic meant that the quick cut and thrust of politics seemed not so much wrong as irrelevant. Intellectual fervour was a poor social glue com-pared with the feelings, associations and memories which bound communities together. It was for this reason that on 1 August 1865 Marian refused Mrs Taylor's request that she and Lewes contribute to the Mazzini fund, set up in support of Giuseppe Mazzini, the Italian patriot. While she admired the man himself, she worried that his followers might resort 'to acts which are more unsocial in their character than the very wrong they are directed to extinguish'.[26]

But from the mid-1860s Marian showed signs of a growing engagement with the political process. This was partly due to the influence of Lewes, whose work was once again taking him to the heart of public life. In October 1864 he had given up the *Cornhill*, keen to be master of his own time. But now Trollope was trying to entice him back into harness with the editorship of the *Fortnightly*, which was intended to map the new Britain as it emerged from the now inevitable Second Reform Act. According to the Prospectus, written by Lewes, the *Fortnightly*'s aim would be 'that of aiding Progress in all directions', including science, politics and literature.[27] But there was to be nothing prescriptive about it. For the first time in publishing history contributors would sign their articles, so making it clear that the review's liberalism consisted in its willingness to listen to a wide range of different opinions.

Lewes eventually agreed to take on the editorship for £600 a year, as long as he could have a hard-working sub-editor – the kind of person Marian had once been at the *Westminster* – to carry the burden of routine. He achieved the same deal, too, at the *Pall Mall Gazette*, another periodical run by George Smith. Quite why Lewes had decided to take on so much work, especially when he was not well, is a puzzle. It may have been money. Marian had not had a commercial hit for four years, and her new project, the dramatic poem called *The Spanish Gypsy*, was unlikely to make much. In a letter to Cara, Marian mentioned proudly how lucky she was to have a husband who did not pressure her to churn out one best-seller after another.[28] Perhaps Lewes now felt morally bound to take up some of the financial strain which had rested exclusively on Marian for the past eight years. But did he also relish being seen as a powerful person in his own right? Certainly the first thing he did on getting to the *Fortnightly* was to ask Marian to contribute an article for the opening issue of May 1865. Signed 'George Eliot', it flagged to the world that there was only one man in London who had the influence to entice the nation's greatest novelist back into journalism. This piece – the one sharp-eyed Fanny had spotted – was followed by two rather plodding articles for the *Pall Mall*.

Whatever the reason for his return to editing, Lewes's new jobs drew him back to the heart of the nation's business. He was out all the time now, meeting politicians and peers, as well as the more usual writers and artists. After the relative quiet of the early 1860s, the public mood had darkened. Economic depression meant industrial unrest, which in turn was fuelling demands for an extention of the franchise. Middle-class women, too, no longer confined themselves to campaigns for improving education and employment opportunities. Bessie, Barbara and Clementia had their eye on nothing less than the vote for women.

Lewes was not Marian's only source of information. In February 1862 she had received a circular from James Quirk, a kind-hearted curate at Attleborough who had made a nuisance of himself during the Liggins business. In it he explained how local ribbon weavers were suffering from the effects of a strike among the Coventry workers.[29] At the end of the year Marian sent a pound to the Coventry men via Charles Bray, keenly aware that the parallel plight of the Lancashire cotton factories was diverting attention away from the Midlands.[30]

Friends were in trouble too. Since 1860 when a trade treaty had been signed with France, the Coventry silk industry had been in decline. The Brays and Hennells, whose fortunes depended on it, had been obliged to move away from Rosehill altogether and settle at Barr's Hill Terrace on the outskirts of Coventry. They struggled constantly to find tenants for their house at Sydenham, too. 'Dear Sara,' wrote Marian to Cara Bray on 16 July 1867, 'I think a great deal, though she may not, of her income being reduced.' She may implicitly have meant the Brays too, for she goes on to beg Cara to let her know if she can give them any financial help.[31] But the unhappiness did not stop there. Arthur Helps, Lewes's old friend and the bearer of several kind messages from the Queen to Marian, had recently lost everything when he tried to produce a profit from the clay deposits at Vernon Hill.[32]

It was against this backdrop of distress that demands to extend the franchise had been growing. The Great Reform Bill of 1832 might have seemed like a huge symbolic victory for progress, but it had done little to change the balance of power in Britain. Well-to-do middle-class men could now vote, Birmingham had been given an MP and the most blatant examples of corruption had been tackled. But that still left the vast majority of men and all women unrepresented. Thirty years on it became clear that a second instalment of electoral reform was inevitable. Although the first attempt foundered on 12 April 1866, a bill enfranchising skilled working-class urban men was passed the following year.

Marian, as always, took a cautious view of political change. The heady days when she had sung out to John Sibree about the European revolutions of 1848 were long gone. These days, the bent of her mind was, she explained to Clifford Allbutt, 'conservative rather than destructive', and she remained convinced that political change which ran ahead of social and psychological development was at best useless and at worst dangerous.[33] The hopes riding on the secret ballot – for so long a key demand of radical campaigners – struck her as absurd.[34] Likewise, she thought the giving of the vote to urban working-class men a mixed blessing. Without the moral and social education that would make them cherish the best of the *status quo*, there was a danger that they would cut loose from their roots and degenerate into a selfish mob.

The same thing went for the vexed issue of what had become known as 'The Woman Question'. Ever since Marian had gone to live with Lewes, her feminist friends had been trying to harness the prestige of her name to their various causes. Clementia Taylor, Bessie Parkes (now Belloc) and Barbara Bodichon had all at one time insisted on calling her 'Miss Evans', under the assumption that her living arrangement represented a refusal of the married state. And even now that they had finally got the point that Marian would have preferred to be legally married, they still assumed that she must be a natural supporter of votes for women. In fact, Marian felt about the question exactly as she did about working-class men: until women were properly educated, female suffrage would remain 'an extremely doubtful good'.[35] For this reason she was deliberately vague when Clementia Taylor tried to get her to back John Stuart Mill's amendment to the Reform Bill, which proposed enfranchising women on the same terms as men. To Sara Hennell she was more candid: 'I love and honour my friend Mrs Taylor, but it is impossible that she can judge beforehand of the proportionate toil and interruption such labours cause to women whose habits and duties differ so much from her own.'[36]

Those habits and duties which Marian was thinking of included child-rearing, housekeeping, looking after the elderly – all chores that women without Mrs Taylor's large income were obliged to carry out themselves. Although Marian had no desire to keep middle-class women confined to simpering, ignorant 'angels in the house', she worried that too much education would lead them to turn their backs on 'the great amount of social unproductive labour' which they currently undertook.[37] While she agreed that women needed equal access to education if they were to have 'the possibilities of free development', she wanted that development to keep women securely attached to the family and the home rather than in paid employment.[38] Instead of a new generation of mediocre women novelists, painters and doctors, she wanted intelligent wives and thoughtful mothers. 'The highest work' – the creative work which she did – must always be reserved for the special few.

It was what she saw as her unique position – both domestic and professional – which made Marian reluctant to be quoted on anything to do with women. Behind the scenes, though, she was ready to listen and learn. In November 1867 she asked Barbara Bodichon's friend Emily Davies to tea in order to hear her plans for a women's college attached to Cambridge University.[39] As cautious towards Girton as she was towards the Positivists, Marian donated a modest fifty pounds in March 1868 and asked it to be tagged 'From the author of *Romola*'. If any of the girls entering the college in 1869 got round to reading their benefactor's book, they may have wondered at the fate of her stupendously learned heroine and by extension their own. Romola ends up not as a scholar, doctor or teacher, but as a nurse-cum-mother-cum-saint.

On 29 March 1865, *The Spanish Gypsy* having ground to a halt, Marian began a new novel. In *Felix Holt, The Radical*, she returned once again to 'that central plain, watered at one extremity by the Avon, at the other by the Trent'.[40] The year is 1831, just before the passing of the Great Reform Act which its advocates believed would bring the electoral system into line with modern conditions once and for all. With the benefit of hindsight, Marian was able to show that 1832 was actually the thin edge of the wedge, the first step in a process that was moving into its second phase even as she wrote. By concentrating on the role of the unenfranchised urban mob in the 1832 election she was implicitly asking whether these men were ready for the vote in 1867.

Naturally, Marian drew on her own terrifying memories of the December 1832 general election. As a girl in Nuneaton she had watched from a school window while the poll descended into chaotic fighting between the Tories and Radicals. The magistrate read the Riot Act, while a detachment of Scots Greys was ordered to break up the angry mob. Many were trampled, one man died, and Robert Evans's scare stories about the French Revolution had never seemed so real.[41] As always, Marian buttressed personal knowledge by careful reading: as she prepared for *Felix Holt* she worked her way through *The Times* and the Annual Register for 1832–3, read Macaulay and copied out long excerpts from Samuel Bamford's *Passages in the Life of a Radical*.

Marian's mature position on franchise reform steered a middle way between her father's die-hard resistance and the lunge towards universal suffrage which was favoured by many of her progressive friends. In her masterly Introduction to *Felix Holt* she shows that while there was much that needed changing about the Midlands on the eve of the 1832 Reform Act, 'there were some pleasant things too, which have also departed'.[42] Pocket boroughs, an unrepresented

Birmingham, the Corn Laws and widespread pauperism might all have vanished under the new regimes, but so had a way of life which was gentle, rhythmic and self-sustaining. She shows how the community of pre-industrial Britain is being threatened by the hurrying pace of modern life – of stage-coaches which can race from one end of the country to another in only a few days, bringing change and creating a bland homogeneity. Returning to her old distinction, rooted in Riehl, between change which presses slowly from below and that which is imposed speedily from above, Eliot makes the point that progress is a mixed blessing, creating new problems even as it attempts to tackle old ones.

This conservative sensibility is shared by the novel's hero, Felix Holt, a radical of the most unusual kind. For while he identifies himself with the working classes, Holt remains pessimistic about what would happen if they got the vote. The way in which the local miners form an encouraging mob around any candidate who 'treats' them with ale suggests that once enfranchised they would throw their weight unthinkingly behind any politician who played on their immediate self-interest. For Felix, as for Marian, working men needed to be taught to cherish the *status quo* before they were fit to change it.

In a series of set-piece speeches to groups of local workers Holt lays out his idiosyncratic stall. He maintains that the standard demands of the radical programme – for annual parliaments, universal male suffrage and reformed electoral districts – are nothing but 'engines'. These engines work well or badly according to the 'passions, feelings, desires' which power them.[43] And given the ignorant state of most working men, these passions, feelings and desires are likely to be self-serving and short-term, easily exploited by the parliamentary candidate with the biggest pocket. In a confusing jump, Felix suggests that working men will gain more power by forgetting about the vote and going soberly about their everyday business, lifting their heads only occasionally to exert moral pressure on their lords and masters.

Felix is a prig. Built on an even more massive scale than Adam Bede, he shares the carpenter's idealisation of the 'working-day world' over the abstractions of religious or political ideology. Like Adam, he has a good basic education, which he prefers to put in the service of his fellows rather than use as a stepping stone into the middle class. 'That's how the working men are left to foolish devices and keep worsening themselves,' he explains to Rufus Lyon, the Independent minister, 'the best heads among them forsake their born comrades, and go in for a house with a high door-step and a brass knocker.'[44] Instead of straining for 'clerkly gentility', Felix divides his time between watchmaking, trying to stop his widowed mother selling patent medicines and playing self-appointed moral guardian to the masses.

The upright, oak-like Felix Holt is thematically pitted against the fat, pragmatic Harold Transome. Transome, heir to a dwindling fortune, has recently returned to the Midlands after fifteen years in the Near East. While he is expected to run for Parliament, his mother and clergyman uncle are mortified when he announces that far from being a Tory, he will stand as a Radical. But he is just the kind of Radical that Felix is not – unprincipled, ego-bound,

loving to hurt. In the end, Transome loses the election and damages his reputation by his association with the violent, looting mob. He redeems himself
only by speaking in court on behalf of Felix Holt who has been unfairly accused
of leading the riot and killing a policeman.

Transome's careless egotism, his inability to see or care for others, originates
in the self-enclosed hell of Transome Court. A careful chronological reading
of Marian's notebooks suggests that she had always seen the drama of the
Transome family as the main thread of the book, with the political story grafted
on later. The fact that she was reading Aeschylus at the time implies that she
was still interested in themes that had engaged her in *The Mill* – the fall of a
once solid family. Certainly the descriptions of Mrs Transome's bitter, withered
life among the heavy sunlight and shabby drapes of a house she can barely
afford to run are more vivid than anything we ever learn about the tiresomely
upright Felix. The reason for Mrs Transome's misery lies deep in the past.
As a handsome young married woman she had had an affair with the sleek,
self-serving family lawyer by whom she had a son, Harold. Saddled with a
feeble husband, she has spent the last thirty-five years running the estate and
trying to contain the greedy damage done by the lawyer Jermyn. Only the
thought that the handsome Harold might one day return from Smyrna and
restore Transome Court to its glory has kept a tiny light flickering inside her.

But Harold's arrival is a disappointment. He is accompanied by a small son
and no wife: the implication is that the boy's mother was a local courtesan
whose meek manner perfectly suited the despotic Harold. And although
blandly attentive to Mrs Transome, Harold takes no notice of her real needs.
Instead of listening to her worries about the estate, he makes carelessly flattering
remarks about her dress and figure. His will, though sheathed in silk, strikes
Mrs Transome as unassailable: 'Harold's rapidity, decision, and indifference
to any impressions in others which did not further or impede his own purposes,
had made themselves felt by her as much as she would have felt the unmanageable strength of a great bird which had alighted near her, and allowed her to
stroke its wing for a moment because food lay near her.'[45]

The mechanism by which Marian brings the political and the Transome
strands of her story together is a tangled legal plot which makes the Newdigate–
Newdegate case of her youth look simple. With the expert legal help of Frederic
Harrison she wended her careful way through the impenetrable business of
entail and settlement. Her ultimate aim was to have the Independent minister's
daughter Esther Lyon shown to be the rightful inheritor of Transome Court,
and to do this Marian had to add swapped identities and unknown parentage
to the already rich mix. Her need for absolute realism means that this part of
the plot takes up far too much of the book. All that really matters is getting
Esther to a point where she is obliged to make a decision between fulfilling
her dearest fantasy of becoming a lady, or marrying the resolutely proletarian
Felix Holt.

In the end, of course, Esther chooses Felix, drawn by what seems to be the
properly moral choice. Her previous life of surface and studied refinement has
been replaced by a deep attachment to his stringent, difficult way of life. It is

a decision which brings her into line with the values of the man who has raised her as his own, the Independent minister Rufus Lyon, whose quaint virtue is modelled on Francis Franklin, the father of Marian's old Baptist schoolteachers.

The fiendishly tricky legal plot made Marian's imaginative return to the Midlands countryside less of a pleasure than it might otherwise have been. Even a month away in France during the summer of 1865 could not raise her spirits. By Christmas she was 'sticking in the mud' and 'miserable'.[46] But the next month a saviour came in the shape of Frederic Harrison, who was only too delighted to have the honour of being the first person, apart from Lewes, to read a George Eliot manuscript before it went to the publishers. His expert help boosted her confidence and the writing speeded up until on 1 June 1866 Lewes was able to record in his journal: 'Yesterday Polly finished *Felix Holt*. The sense of relief was very great and all day long suffused itself over our thoughts. The continual ill health of the last months, and her dreadful nervousness and depression, made the writing a serious matter. Blackwood . . . thinks the book superior to *Adam Bede*. I cannot share that opinion; but the book is a noble book and will I think be more popular than the *Mill*.'[47]

If conserving the best of the past was what *Felix Holt* was all about, then it fits nicely that it was the occasion on which 'old relations' were now restored with Blackwoods.[48] Marian's feelings for George Smith had never been as warm as the ones she retained for 'the best of publishers'. At first she may have relished the fact that, unlike Blackwood, Smith never presumed to comment or interfere with his authors' work. He had been content to pay Marian a big fee for *Romola*, send her occasional boxes of chocolates and custom-made luggage, then quietly assess in his own time whether or not he had profited by their arrangement. By contrast, Blackwood tended to fuss and flap along the way and his payments were modest, but there could be no doubting his engagement with Marian's work.

Smith claimed in his memoirs that Marian and Lewes came to him first with *Felix Holt* and that he turned them down. They wanted £5000 for the book and he wasn't convinced that it was 'a profitable venture'.[49] It's not absolutely clear whether this is retrospective embroidery on Smith's part: it must have been hard to go down in history as the man to whom George Eliot offered her only duff novel. Whatever the case, Blackwood certainly believed that Marian had returned voluntarily to the fold. Gratifying though this might be, he was not about to override his customary caution. Lewes had asked him to make an offer for the book without seeing it, which Blackwood pleasantly but firmly refused to do. If it should turn out to be another *Romola*, he wanted time to think. Marian agreed to send the first two volumes to Edinburgh, but was so anxious about their reception, on every level, that she insisted Blackwood telegraph the moment he got them.[50] In the event she need not have worried: three days later Blackwood was able to write to Lewes that he was 'lost in wonder and admiration of Mrs Lewes' powers. It is not like a Novel and there may be a complaint of want of the ordinary Novel interest, but it is like looking on at a series of panoramas where human beings speak and act before us.' The same day William Blackwood made an offer of £5000, and the correspondence with Marian, which in recent years had dwindled to a few notes about royalties, was now restored to its former fullness.[51] Before very long she was back leaning on John Blackwood as she had never done with Smith: asking him to track down historical references to add documentary authority to the background of the book.

Blackwood genuinely loved *Felix Holt*. After the turgid strangeness of *Romola* – which he had been lucky enough not to publish – it was wonderful to be back in a Midlands landscape teeming with vivid, particular characters. The gossip in the saddler's, the smell of feather and leather in the golf ball maker's shop, the chat of the town worthies all enchanted him. And, of course, the political conservatism of the piece was exactly what he liked too. 'I had nearly forgot to say how good your politics are,' he said in a postscript to his first full response to the book on 26 April. 'As far as I see yet, I suspect I am a radical of the Felix Holt breed, and so was my father before me.'[52]

So impressed was Blackwood by *Felix Holt* that shortly after the Reform Act was passed he asked Marian to write an 'Address to Working Men, by Felix Holt' along the lines of the speech made by Disraeli to the working men of Edinburgh. It is hard to imagine that many of the 'artisans, and factory hands, and miners, and labourers' whom Holt addressed were likely readers of the January 1868 issue of *Blackwood's*. Still, his earnest appeal that they should use their new vote carefully to preserve the 'treasure of knowledge, science, poetry, refinement of thought, feeling, and manners' must have played well with the predominantly Tory-voting middle-class readership of *Maga*.[53] At this point it became clear that, despite the precedent of Disraeli speaking to the men in Edinburgh, Holt was not a Tory democrat. His position was more like that of Matthew Arnold, who believed that culture should be guarded by 'the remnant' or, looking further back, by Coleridge's notion of 'the clerisy'.

Certainly most of the reviewers approved of *Felix Holt*. Dallas gave his usual praise in *The Times* and John Morley, Lewes's successor at the *Fortnightly*, was equally enthusiastic in the crucial *Saturday Review*.[54] A very young Henry James was more muted in the *Nation* and some of the more stuffy critics found Eliot's return yet again to illicit sexual relationships distasteful.[55] A few voices were raised in criticism of the wearisome legal details, but as Bulwer-Lytton put it, 'it has the excellence of good writing.'[56] One critic, trying to be clever, even thought he had found an error in the legal plot. Frederic Harrison rushed to reassure Marian that no such mistake had been made, and on another occasion declared that he knew 'whole families where the three volumes [of *Felix Holt*] have been read chapter by chapter and line by line and reread and recited as are the stanzas of In Memoriam.'[57] In truth this was unlikely, but Harrison had by now worked out that this was exactly what Marian needed to hear.

By the time *Felix Holt* was published, Marian's celebrity had become a phenomenon in itself, standing between herself and new friendships, as well as transforming those which lingered from the past. Things had not been easy with Sara Hennell since the embarrassment of *Thoughts in Aid of Faith* of 1860 which both Marian and Lewes had found pretentious and dull. Sara's inscription on Marian's copy – 'in grateful remembrance of how much I owed to her during the season of happy intercourse which formed the "German" period of our lives' – suggests that at one level she accepted that their intimacy belonged to the past. But in other ways she clearly felt that she had the right to comment on Marian's work as if they were still both struggling writers together. Her remarks on *The Mill* may have been perceptive, but they were not wanted, especially the part where she urged, 'Go on! – write once more, and give us something . . . better.'[58] Likewise, although she was quite right when she said of Romola's character that she was 'pure idealism . . . you have painted a goddess, and not a woman', the point was that no one had asked her.[59] Most annoying of all was the moment in spring 1862 when Sara mistakenly assumed that a second-rate tale appearing in *Blackwood's* was Marian's work. 'Salem Chapel', the latest in a series called 'The Chronicles of Carlingford', certainly covered familiar George Eliot territory, dealing with the conflicts between Evangelicals, dissenters and High Churchmen in a country town. But it was written by the hackish churchwoman Mrs Oliphant, whose hazy understanding of dissent showed up in the false tone and many inaccuracies of the piece.

A week after sending off a snappy note to Coventry denying she was the author of 'Salem Chapel', Marian repented and wrote a softer letter to Sara, admitting that she could see how the mistake might have been made.[60] She had talked so often about the piety of memory and the unimportance of intellectual agreement compared with emotional affiliation that she was determined not to be riled by Sara's increasingly difficult ways. Rather than sulkily withdrawing from the older woman, Marian merely mildly reminded herself, by means of a letter to Cara, to be patient with Sara's self-absorption. And while she continued to find Sara's writing impenetrable – volume one of the new *Present Religion: As a Faith Owing Fellowship with Thought* (1865) was virtually unreadable – Marian had reached the point in her life where she was able quite genuinely to offer tactful support.[61]

The new faces which found their way into Marian's life were still mainly male. Usually they had been scooped up by Lewes during one of the many breakfasts, lunches and dinners which he now attended in his role as editor. Robert Browning, the poet and politician Richard Monckton Milnes, the constitutionalist Walter Bagehot and the scientist Huxley now supplemented the old circle of Spencer, Pigott and the Congreves. The intimate Saturday evenings had been replaced with Sunday afternoon At Homes, the amateur, musical entertainment with wide-ranging conversation. In time these gatherings became so large that it was impossible for Marian to meet more than a lucky handful of her guests: by 1868 Frederic Harrison was noting wistfully that 'talking is impossible in your Sunday conversazione'.[62]

Clearly the little difficulty of the Leweses not being married no longer mattered. Success had a magic effect on people's moral scruples. The most blatant change of heart involved the sculptor Thomas Woolner who in 1854 had written an unpleasant letter implying that Marian was a whore. But on bumping into her with Lewes at the Louvre in 1867 he became a fan and a friend, and a regular visitor to the Priory.[63] And W. B. Scott, the man to whom the nasty letter had been written, also renewed his relationship with Lewes and was happy to report that Marian was 'the most bland and amiable of plain women, and most excellent in conversation'.[64]

The experience of living and socialising almost exclusively with men meant that Marian developed an interested understanding of their lives, especially those of the young whom she identified as 'just the class I care most to influence'.[65] Clifford Allbutt, for instance, was a young doctor with whom she stayed in touch even when he moved to his appointment at the Leeds Infirmary. From there he wrote to Marian about his religious doubts and his frustratingly long engagement, and asked her to come with Lewes to see round his hospital.[66] The two-day trip in September 1868 suggested many details that would find their way into Lydgate's story in *Middlemarch*.

Then there was Emanuel Deutsch, a prodigiously clever young German working at the British Museum whose expertise in Jewish history and culture sustained Marian's growing interest in the subject. He was to give Marian lessons in Hebrew and his tragically short life suggested some of the details for Mordecai, the scholar-saint in *Daniel Deronda*, Marian's last novel.

Another young man who played a part in shaping George Eliot's legacy was Oscar Browning, fellow of King's College Cambridge and a master at Eton until he was dismissed for making sexual advances to the boys. Chatty and adoring, he invited Lewes and Marian to the school in June 1867 to row on the river and watch a cricket match.[67] When Marian remarked how much she liked one of his chairs, he arranged to have a copy made and sent to her. His gossipy biography of George Eliot in 1890 was one of the major sources of the rumour about Lewes's infidelity.

Naturally there were times when Marian missed women. One day in 1864 when Bessie Rayner Parkes took a friend along to the Priory, she had found Marian marooned in a sea of masculinity: 'It *was* so sad to see Marian sitting alone with four men when we entered the room. Isa and I brought in quite a wholesome atmosphere of womanhood and I read in Marian's expressive face that she felt it.'[68] Gradually, though, brave women were beginning to make overtures. In May 1867 Lewes had introduced Marian to Lady Amberley at the first of the Positivist lectures given by Richard Congreve. Lady Amberley had immediately issued an invitation to lunch, but was told that this was 'against rules'.[69] Instead, she visited the Priory soon afterwards, slightly panicky as to what the correct 'etiquette' might turn out to be.[70] After a slow start, Marian came to like the young woman and in time two of Lady Amberley's sisters, equally lively and well-married, also became regular callers at the Priory.

Although these three Stanley girls all invited Marian to their homes, she continued in her old practice of turning them down. With other women, though, she was learning to be more flexible. It was around now that she met two young people who were to become, in time, her keenest disciples. At this stage they were simply restless young married women drawn to Mrs Lewes's wise and empathic manner. There was Nina Lehmann, daughter of Lewes's old Edinburgh friend Robert Chambers. Marian sometimes visited the

Highgate home which Nina shared with her cultured industrialist German husband, Frederick, for an evening of music and well-informed talk. When Nina was sent to Pau for her health in 1867, the Leweses stopped off for two days on their way to Spain. Nina was in seventh heaven, writing rapturously to her husband, 'I think she loves me – we are sworn friends. What a sweet, mild, womanly presence hers is – so soothing, too, and *elevating* above all.'[71] Another young woman who had the distinction of home visits from George Eliot was Georgiana Burne-Jones, wife of the painter, Edward. Marian was so enchanted with Georgie's knowledge of art and allied matters that she and Lewes frequently arrived at the young couple's house in Fulham, bearing gifts for their children like doting grandparents.

As Marian's celebrity grew it was not snubbing but mobbing which posed the greater threat. Even in obscure corners of the Continent there was no guarantee that earnest fans might not suddenly descend. During a stay in Granada in February 1867 where they had gone after seeing Nina Lehmann in Pau, Lewes had abandoned his usual precaution of scribbling his name illegibly in the hotel register with the result that 'it was whispered round at once who we were, and the attention of the guests was flattering but boring'. One enthusiastic American lady in the throng, whom Lewes could not help noticing was 'very pretty', claimed that she regarded *Romola* as her Bible, and begged for an autograph.[72] For Marian, who even in her unknown years had chosen to eat hotel dinners in her own room to avoid strangers' glances, it was all becoming an ordeal.

This new expansiveness in Marian's private life sent echoes through her work. The hermit years at Richmond, Wandsworth and even Blandford Square had produced novels which sprang from the deepest parts of her memory and psyche, untouched by anything happening around her. But with the opening up of the Priory years, Marian's work became more susceptible to immediate influence. *Felix Holt*, as we have seen, was written partly in response to the events leading up to the 1867 Second Reform Act. Its successor, *The Spanish Gypsy*, owed its genesis to two of the many new friendships which were breaking in upon the Leweses' dual solitude.

The poem had a laborious gestation and, just like *Romola*, was at one point put aside for an English novel, *Felix Holt*. The twisted turn of events started in February 1863 when an old friend of Lewes, Theodore Martin, brought his wife to the Priory. Marian was delighted with Helen Faucit, whom fifteen years earlier Lewes had tagged 'the finest tragic actress on our stage', and decided that she would like to write a play for her.[73] The Martins, in turn, showed Marian a charming portrait of Helen by Frederic Burton which, in a round-about way, led to Burton both painting Marian and accompanying the Leweses on holiday to Italy in May 1864. It was while the trio was visiting the Scuola di San Rocco in Venice that Marian was struck by an Annunciation, possibly by Titian, which gave her the idea of writing about a young woman chosen from the ranks of ordinary womanhood to 'fulfil a great destiny'.[74] Once home she became convinced that the only setting which would do was that of Spain in the 1490s when the struggle between the ruling Catholics and the Moors was at its height.

From the start the omens were not good. Just as with *Romola*, Marian over-researched herself into imaginative paralysis. Reading up on Gibbon's *Decline and Fall* did not provide that important spark, not even with Lewes plugging away in parallel on *Don Quixote*. The journal entries make depressing reading. After an agonising few months on the first two acts, Marian started 'sticking in the mud continuously' and found herself plunging in 'a swamp of miseries'. Act Three was disrupted by Christmas 1864, Act Four could not be resuscitated even by a ten-day trip to Paris and by the middle of February even the usually upbeat Lewes had to admit that the play wasn't working. On the 21st of the month Marian recorded in her journal that he had 'taken my drama away from me'.[75]

The next two years were taken up with *Felix Holt*, which appeared in June 1866. Marian and Lewes did their usual thing of escaping immediately to the Continent to avoid having to confront the book's fate directly. While they toured Germany and the Low Countries, John Blackwood oversaw slow sales (another effect of the difficult economic situation) and came to terms with the idea that for the first time he was going to lose money on a George Eliot novel. The reviews, though, were sufficiently positive to make everyone involved feel that Marian Lewes's return to her original publishers had been a success: 'I do not know that I ever saw a Novel received with a more universal acclaim,' wrote Blackwood in his old, admiring way.[76] At the end of the year he offered Marian £1000 for the copyright of all the novels, with the intention of bringing them out in a sixpenny series complete with illustrations.[77]

Six days later, on 27 December, the Leweses set off on another trip, this time to the South of France. Inevitably Lewes had found the *Fortnightly* commitment too draining and had asked Trollope to release him. Ostensibly the trip was for the sake of his health, but during a walk on the beach at Biarritz Marian confided that she hoped they might press on to Spain where she could research the background for her abandoned play which she was now considering recasting as a poem. For two frail middle-aged people they did very well, travelling by rackety diligence and cold trains through San Sebastian, Barcelona, Granada and Seville. This was the pleasurable part of research, the drinking in of random sights, sounds and impressions which would eventually have to be worked up into a picture of a life very different from anything Marian had written about before. Having decided that her heroine's 'great destiny' would be to lead the gypsies in their fight against the Moors, Marian was keen to spend time absorbing the gypsy culture, carefully observing one family troop as they danced and sang. She also occupied herself with the more usual examples of high Western culture, viewing the paintings in the Prado in Madrid, and wandering through the magnificent cathedral in Seville.[78]

Having been told that her new work was connected with Spain, Blackwood was naturally hungry for details: 'is it a Romance?' he asked.[79] Her reply from Granada can hardly have thrilled him: 'The work connected with Spain is not a Romance. It is – prepare your fortitude – it is – a poem.'[80] As it turned out,

Blackwood did indeed need fortitude, because the poem was not completed for another year, on 29 April 1868. The usual mix of depression and headache stopped Marian pushing ahead on her return to London in the middle of March 1867. This time it was not just a question of getting the historical detail right, or bringing the characters to life, but of turning what had started off as a prose drama into a dramatic poem. The end result was, inevitably, an odd mix of narrative and dialogue, mainly blank verse but with some linking passages of prose and lyric.

Just as with *Romola*, Marian knew there was something fundamentally wrong with the piece. Lewes's renewed dyspepsia – he had fattened up wonderfully in Spain, despite worries about the food – also suggested that he was far from easy. By the beginning of July they were off again in search of health, this time for a fortnight at the Isle of Wight. When that failed to work, they decided to try to recover the happiness of their honeymoon days by returning to Weimar, where they had first lived together in 1854. They repeated walks, re-inhabited lodgings, recreated schedules all in the hope that some of that easy flow would return. But by the time they were back in London on 1 October it was clear that Marian was once again facing the kind of paralysis which had preceded *Romola*. When she struggled to the close of part one by the end of the month, Blackwood suggested setting it in print, complete with possible variations, so that she might get a realistic sense of how it might read.[81] It was a kind gesture, particularly since he obviously did not like it. For the first time ever he avoided making a direct comment about Marian's work and offered her only £300, a fraction of the £5000 he had given for *Felix Holt*.

If *The Spanish Gypsy* had been written by anyone else, Blackwood would not have published it. The poem is strained and plodding, clever and dull. The influence of the Leweses' new friend Robert Browning is clear, especially his dramatic monologues 'Fra Lippo Lippi' and 'Andrea del Sarto'. But Marian's vision did not lend itself to verse. Although she could manage metre as well as the next man, the compressed form did not allow her to build character or create landscape with the fullness she had achieved in her novels. Instead of intricate descriptions of inner worlds and psychological states, there are only rough approximations of mood and type. Even the heroine, Fedalma, feels like a pencil sketch. And, just as in *Romola*, far too much energy has gone into re-creating a world which, despite Marian's best endeavours, remains distant and dead.

Still, *The Spanish Gypsy* makes interesting reading because of the way it both develops and anticipates typical George Eliot themes.[82] Fedalma is made to choose between duty and desire. She may either marry her beloved Duke Silva or take up her hereditary role as a gypsy princess, destined to lead her people to a better life in Africa. Fedalma's decision to honour the obligations of family and race recall Eppie's renunciation of life at the Red House and Esther's rejection of the ease of Transome Court. Both girls, like Fedalma, choose to put their duties as daughters, fathers' daughters, over social status. Fedalma's renunciation of an ordinary woman's satisfactions in favour of an exceptional destiny – just like Titian's Virgin she will not experience mortal childbirth – anticipates Alcharisi in *Daniel Deronda*, who sacrifices motherhood to her singer's vocation. And the position of the gypsies as a disinherited and despised race points the way to Marian's growing interest in the Jews as the inheritors of true culture.

Publicly people said they liked the poem, in private they were not so sure. Frederic Harrison, who had gushed over *Felix Holt* and urged Marian to try poetry, thought that it was a mess. Professional critics like Henry James and Richard Holt Hutton realised that verse simply was not her medium and looked forward to the time when she would return to what she did best.[83] But by some fluke of a capricious market, *The Spanish Gypsy* actually sold well and brought Marian a modest profit. People wrote suggesting that she turn it into a play, or asking permission to set the minstrel songs to music.[84]

With hindsight, these mediocre middle years, which saw the publication of *Romola*, *Felix Holt* and *The Spanish Gypsy*, are redeemed by what came after, the magnificent *Middlemarch*. But what would have happened if Marian had simply stopped writing in 1868, silenced by death or despair? She would be remembered for the great trio of English provincial novels, *Adam Bede*, *The Mill* and *Silas Marner*, and perhaps for the minor triumph that is *Felix Holt*. But she would have been set down as a medium talent, to stand alongside Elizabeth Gaskell. As it was, she continued to write, producing a few more so-so poems until at the beginning of 1869 she began to plan the book which would elevate her to the rank of the Immortals.

Marian's increasingly public life was buttressed by a domestic happiness which grew more secure as the years passed. So it is odd that this was the time when London gossip was busy putting Lewes down as unfaithful. It is possible to see how the rumour started. The little man was out on his own virtually every evening, flirting, chatting, always managing to end up next to the prettiest woman. The fact that he had not divorced Agnes and married Marian, despite having the money to explore and exploit any legal loophole, suggested to some that he liked the situation the way it was. Clearly Marian and Lewes were both aware of the rumours, because on one occasion when Lewes was away Marian explained her decision not to attend a lecture by Richard Congreve on the grounds that people might jump to false conclusions about her 'husband's' absence.[85]

We don't know if any of Lewes's flirtations ever ended in sex, but they certainly never developed into relationships. Lewes was as staunch as ever in his love and admiration for the woman he called 'Polly', always delighted when the dinner conversation turned to the subject of her genius. Whenever he came across an interesting new face, he immediately issued an invitation to the Priory so that she could share his discovery. The Sunday At Homes increasingly came to resemble a cross between a court and a church service, in which the best minds in London paid homage to George Eliot. It was now that Lewes was dubbed the 'mercurial little showman' by George Meredith as he bobbed and weaved around the room, making sure that Marian was neither bored nor overwhelmed by the people he ushered to her side. If he occasionally had sex with other women – and there is no direct evidence that he did – it never came close to threatening his relationship with 'the best of women'. Marian's dedication at the front of the manuscript of *Felix Holt* suggests her sense of absolute security: 'From George Eliot (otherwise Polly) to her dear husband, this thirteenth year of their united life, in which the deepening sense of her own imperfectness has the consolation of their deepening love.'[86]

Aside from their undimmed affection for one another, joint responsibility for young and old strengthened Marian's and Lewes's commitment to one another. Early in 1864 Captain Willim had died, bringing to an end a painful marriage of over thirty years. For Lewes's mother it was a relief to be free of this angry man who had tried to control every aspect of her existence. For her son and his partner it meant extra work. The Captain's tangled business affairs were sorted out by the end of March, but that didn't resolve the problem of how and where the old lady was to live. In the end Mrs Willim seems to have continued in Kensington, but she made an increasing number of visits to the Priory. Sometimes she joined Lewes and Marian on their daily walks round Regent's Park Zoo, once taking fright when Lewes got a couple of bear cubs out of their cage.[87] During the remaining six years of her life she put pressure on her son not to spend too much time away from her on the Continent. This, maintained Marian, was the reason why they never made their planned trip to the East.

Charlie was as easy as ever. His close relationship with Marian and Agnes, together with his obvious love of domestic life, made him a candidate for early marriage. When his parents returned from their trip to Italy in 1864 he told them that he had become engaged to Gertrude Hill, granddaughter of the public health reformer Dr Southwood Smith. Gertrude was four years older than Charlie, pretty and with an excellent contralto voice – all factors which made Lewes and Marian unflatteringly surprised that she would want to marry 'our amiable bit of crudity'.[88] Marian, as always, lost no time in playing the part of concerned mother and expert moral voice: 'One never knows what to wish about marriage,' she intoned to D'Albert Durade, 'the evils of an early choice may be easily counterbalanced by the vitiation that often comes from long bachelorhood.'[89]

The two aunts who had raised Gertrude seem to have had no worries about her marrying into one of the most notorious households in the land. The one bit of curiosity came from Gertrude's sister Octavia Hill, later well known for her work in public housing, who asked about Mrs Lewes's religious beliefs. By now Marian had had enough practice to play the role of concerned moral matriarch to perfection. Although on 21 September 1866 she admitted in a letter to François D'Albert Durade that she and Lewes 'enjoy our tete a tete too much' to be looking forward to becoming grandparents, by the time Gertrude had lost her first baby a week later she was writing with all the grief of a concerned mother-in-law.[90]

Thornie and Bertie were off their hands, too. Thornie had left for Durban on 16 October 1863 in his usual bouncy way. During the three-month journey he scandalised his fellow passengers by dressing up as the devil, and editing a robust and saucy ship's newspaper.[91] His first couple of years in Africa were spent getting into scrapes and sniffing at different possibilities, until he decided finally on farming. On 9 September 1866 Bertie was removed from his pupillage in Warwickshire and shipped out to join his elder brother.

We do not know much about the next two years except that by the end of them all the money was gone. In October 1868 a pathetic letter arrived at the Priory from Thornie asking for a loan. In the first instance he wanted a modest £200 to cover his losses on a wild scheme to trade blankets for ivory with the local tribesmen. But then he went on to more serious matters. He was, he told his father, 'gradually wasting away. I eat almost nothing, nothing but delicacies tempt me, and those we can't afford.' He described the fearsome pain which racked his back and chest, making him shout out in agony. Were he fifty instead of twenty-four, he said, he would have walked over the nearest waterfall by now. His only hope was to return to Britain and consult the best doctors. 'I know this trip, seeing physicians etc, perhaps undergoing some operation will cost a great deal of money, but – que voulez vous. It is my last chance in life, and you are the only person I can apply to, so I don't hesitate to make the application.'[92]

Of course Lewes sent the money immediately, haunted by the vision of his jaunty boy crushed by pain. But nothing had prepared him for his first sight of Thornie eight months later. For once, the boy had not exaggerated: he had lost four stone and was barely able to stand, let alone walk. The day after his arrival his condition suddenly deteriorated to the point where all he could do was lie on the ground and scream. But this was Sunday and guests were due. Into the crisis walked two American women, Grace Norton and Sara Sedgwick, accompanied by their friend, the young writer Henry James, who had already written three reviews of George Eliot and was all agog to meet the literary mother whom he had come to kill. Marian tried bravely to carry on something approaching ordinary conversation, chatting about their recent trip abroad. But soon all pretence at normality was given up and James knelt on the floor trying to soothe Thornie, while Lewes rushed to the chemist for some morphine.[93]

It was the lack of a clear diagnosis which made Thornie's decline so difficult to deal with. Perhaps it was only a kidney stone, in which case something might be done. Even the best doctors, including the Queen's physician Sir James Paget, admitted they were stumped. 'We feel utterly in the dark as to the probabilities of his case,' Marian wrote to Cara on 21 August, 'and must resignedly accept what each day brings.'[94] When Charlie arrived back from a holiday in June, unaware of his brother's condition, the sight of the skeletal Thornie shocked him into a faint. One afternoon Agnes came to visit, at which point Marian tactfully went out, leaving the legal Mrs Lewes alone with her child. Pigott came in to play cards. Barbara Bodichon, who had done so much to set Thornie up in Africa with letters of introduction, also popped in twice a week to distract him.[95]

By the end of August it was clear that Thornie was dying. This was no kidney stone but tuberculosis of the spine, a horrible condition in which the backbone gradually crumbled away. Marian already knew something of the terrible devastation it could wreak on a merry disposition: the January 1856 edition of the *Westminster* had carried her essay on Heinrich Heine, the German wit and philosopher who was tortured by this 'terrible nervous disease'.[96] Mercifully Thornie did not follow Heine's example and linger agonizingly for a decade. He died, in *Mutter*'s arms, on 19 October.

Although Thornie resembled his father, Marian had never liked the boy. It is possible that once his noise and bluster had been tempered by life she would have learned to love him, but at this point he was still an annoying, disruptive pup. And yet there can be no doubt about her grief when he was gone, 'still a boy' at only twenty-five. This time she had no need to think herself into the role of pious mother; the words and feelings came easily. 'This death', she wrote in her journal, 'seems to me the beginning of our own.'[97]

CHAPTER 13

'Wise, Witty and Tender Sayings'

Middlemarch
1869–72

THE DAY AFTER Thornie's funeral – at Rosslyn Hill Unitarian chapel, the parish church for unbelievers – Lewes and Marian left London for the country. For three weeks they hid themselves and their grief away at a farmhouse in Limpsfield, Surrey. Lewes told Blackwood that Marian had taken the loss hardest, having 'lavished almost a mother's love on my dear boy, and felt almost a mother's grief. I was better prepared, having never from the first held much hope of his recovery.'[1]

The next few months were scrappy and bleak. Christmas was subdued – dinner with Charles and Gertrude in Hampstead and a walk over the Heath to visit Thornie's grave in Highgate Cemetery. In March they decided to try the cure of a trip to Germany, still their special place. But the magic was running out: 'wandering to and fro upon the earth', in Marian's disenchanted phrase, no longer answered.[2] The lionising was gratifying but wearing: in Berlin Marian was mobbed by a mass of women each wanting to have 'a peck' at her.[3] Princes begged to be introduced, scientists threw open their laboratories and ambassadors queued up for an audience. By now, Lewes's researches had moved to the fledgling discipline of psychiatry and he spent much time closeted with mad doctors, a preoccupation which struck Marian as macabre. Perhaps it was the dull ache of Thornie's death, or maybe, as Marian maintained, Europe had become a tourist hell-hole, but these weeks away failed to take off. Tried and tested comforts, like a trip to the concert hall to tackle Wagner once again, resulted only in 'hours of noise and weariness'.[4]

Marian's writing life was likewise fitful. Ever since the publication of *The Spanish Gypsy* in the summer of 1868 she had been pottering on minor projects while cogitating big ones. The entry for 1 January 1869 laid out a confident new programme for the year ahead, comprising 'A Novel called Middlemarch, a long poem on Timoleon, and several minor poems'.[5] But although Marian did a lot of background reading in Greek history through the first half of 1869,

Timoleon never materialised. This is lucky, because the subject and form threatened to produce another *Spanish Gypsy* – long, learned and dull.

But despite Marian's declaration to Blackwood in February 1869 that 'I mean to begin my novel at once, having already sketched the plan', she stayed mainly with verse.[6] In the first months of the year she produced two short poems, 'Agatha' and 'How Lisa Loved the King'. The American publisher James Fields paid an extravagant £300 for the first, John Blackwood a more temperate £50 for the second. Returning from their Italian trip on 5 May, Marian again tried to settle to *Middlemarch*, but the usual despair about her capabilities was this time capped by agonies about Thornie. The experience of watching and waiting by a sickbed took her back to Griff, or maybe it was the meditations preliminary to *Middlemarch* that were stirring up memories. Whatever their precise reason for coming now, the eleven 'Brother and Sister' sonnets which Marian wrote during July show her still 'yearning in divorce' for reconciliation with her brother.[7]

The intensity and compression of verse suited a writing life fragmented by nursing duties. As Thornie withered away, Marian started another poem, 'The Legend of Jubal'.[8] Less obviously autobiographical than the 'Brother and Sister' sequence, 'Jubal' none the less resonates with Marian's increasing anxiety about her status as an artist. Jubal is an old man who returns to his people expecting their thanks for his great gift to them – the lyre. But while his memory is cherished, Jubal's physical presence goes unrecognised to the point where he himself begins to wonder whether he exists at all. Marian, too, was struggling with the fact that while George Eliot's stock had never been higher, her own creativity was at an all-time low. She was failing to make headway on *Middlemarch* and was haunted by the usual terror that her previous books had all been flukes. Like Jubal, she sometimes wondered whether she existed at all. Clearly *Macmillan's* thought she did, for they paid a handsome £200 for the piece, while the *Atlantic Monthly* in America managed £50.

The next and final poem written during this creatively scrappy time was 'Armgart', put together during another break at Limpsfield in the late summer of 1870. Like 'Jubal', it deals with the subject of the musician whose music has fled, but this time Eliot turns to the particular problem of the female artist.[9] Armgart is a supremely talented opera singer who has dedicated herself to public performance. Count Dornberg wants to marry her on condition that she gives up her vocation, since he believes that a woman is 'royal' only when she expresses 'the fulness of her womanhood'.[10] Armgart is not prepared to compromise – 'I am an artist by my birth' – and insists that 'The man who marries me must wed my Art/Honour and cherish it, not tolerate'.[11] When Armgart loses her voice permanently, her friends suggest that there is nothing now to stop her marrying. She, however, insists that she is still worth more than ' "The Woman's Lot": a Tale of Everyday'.[12] It is only through her (female) cousin's urging that she agrees eventually to follow the example of her old singing master and dedicate herself to a life of service, teaching others.

Armgart's renunciation of a woman's life in favour of that of the professional singer anticipates the choice made by Alcharisi in *Daniel Deronda*. But Marian was also considering her own situation as an artist who has been struck dumb. For two years now, she had been struggling with *Middlemarch* in one form or another and the result was still nothing more than a few chapters. If something did not change soon, then she too would be obliged to settle for 'a Tale of Everyday', a companionable life of financial ease but creative deadness. Unlike Armgart, she had not had to face the agonising choice between her man and her art, but that did not mean that she relished returning full circle to those Griff years when she had longed to write but could not. Was her life to be confined once again to housekeeping, sick-nursing and attendance on a much-loved man?

The death of a young person is the ultimate test for all shades of faith and Marian was no exception in finding it difficult. Although it would have been a comfort now to believe that there was a benevolent being who had planned Thornie's end for some higher purpose, she refused to take refuge in that consoling delusion. Nor did she, like so many Victorian agnostics, try to fill the void by turning to spiritualism. As she made clear to a new correspondent, the American novelist Harriet Beecher Stowe, the whole business of table rapping struck her as nothing but 'the lowest charlatanerie'.[13] Mrs Stowe, though, remained firmly convinced of the value of talking to the spirits and even suggested to Marian in June 1872 that she had managed to have a conversation with the long-dead Charlotte Brontë.

Marian was tactfully non-committal about Miss Brontë's chatty ghost. She understood that in its most well-meaning form spiritualism offered as great a comfort to human yearning as any other variety of belief. She continued to attend Unitarian chapels in Hampstead and in Little Portland Street from time to time, went to hear the celebrated preacher Charles Haddon Spurgeon (concluding that he was even more awful than she had anticipated) and followed with interest Barbara Bodichon's increasing attachment to Catholicism, on one occasion even accompanying her to High Anglican mass.

But still Marian's greatest wish was to move beyond the easy consolations of orthodox faith. What was needed now, she told Mrs Stowe, was a religion which would inculcate 'a more deeply-awing sense of responsibility to man, springing from sympathy with . . . the difficulty of the human lot'.[14] This was a restatement of the principles she had set before Clifford Allbutt the previous year, when she had urged upon him the need 'Never to beat and bruise one's wings against the inevitable but to throw the whole force of one's soul towards the achievement of some possible better'.[15] Agonising over the meaning of Thornie's death would, in Marian's stringent terms, be to give in to the endless demands of the ego. Her job now was to love more fully those who were left behind.

Marian's posing and partial answering of the question 'how shall we live now?' brought her a status somewhere between savante and saint. Hundreds of people wrote to her with their religious difficulties; the lucky few got to pose their questions face to face. Always she told them the same thing: resign yourself to suffering, wean yourself off the hope of a future life and nourish your fellow feeling towards the men and women you encounter every day. Ever since *Romola* her work had been viewed as deeply moral: early disgust at Hetty's bastard and Maggie's flight with Stephen Guest had long dissolved. Improvement Societies put George Eliot on the syllabus and one enterprising lady suggested that extracts from her books should be displayed prominently in railway waiting-rooms instead of the usual Bible texts.[16] Likewise, the whiff of infidelity, which had followed Marian ever since her translation of Strauss, no longer seemed to bother even the most orthodox. Clergymen were known to quote George Eliot from the pulpit and one pious visitor to the Priory confided that she had copied passages from *Romola* into her New Testament.

In part, this devotional atmosphere was created by Lewes, who was delighted to see Marian treated with reverence after years of ostracism. He increasingly called her 'Madonna', liked the conceit that they lived at the 'Priory' and enjoyed Charles Dickens's joke that the regular Sunday gathering was nothing less than a 'service'.[17] But no amount of stage management by 'the mercurial little showman' could have sustained an image based only on word play. There was something about Marian's combination of rigorous intellectual analysis and warm empathy that drew men and women to confide the state of their troubled souls. On her first meeting with Marian at the Priory in March 1873, the Hon. Mrs Henry Frederick Ponsonby, wife of Queen Victoria's Private Secretary, found herself compelled first to drop a deep curtsy (a style of greeting which was going out of fashion) and then to confide 'all that was lying deepest in one's heart and mind without reserve'. Listened to in the 'kindest and most sympathetic way', Mrs Ponsonby followed up her audience with a twenty-four-page letter to Marian detailing her religious difficulties. The courtier's wife was convinced that the farmer's daughter was 'in possession of some secret' about how to live a good life at a time when science was reducing humanity to a bundle of selfish impulses.[18] It was the beginning of a correspondence which lasted until Marian's death.

Marian's status as the Sage of Unbelief was further boosted by the publication of a volume of her *Wise, Witty and Tender Sayings* in 1871. The idea for the book came from her newest and most adoring fan, a young Scotsman called Alexander Main. Main had written to her in the summer asking for confirmation that the proper way to pronounce *Romola* was with the stress on the first syllable. Marian was delighted with his detailed and thoughtful response to this most difficult of her novels, and quickly wrote back to tell him so, falling naturally into the role of confessor: 'I shall always be glad to hear from you when you have anything in your mind which it will be a solace to you to say to me.'[19] Main did not need to be told twice and immediately sent off two long letters on *The Spanish Gypsy*, which Marian said made her cry because: 'You have thoroughly understood me ... you have put your finger on the true key.'[20] Two weeks later Main sent a sample of extracts from Marian's work suggesting that they would make a good separate publication, along the lines of a commonplace book. If it had been left to Marian she probably would not have agreed: her novels grew organically out of her moral vision and to reduce them to a series of platitudes, even striking ones, ran counter to the way she wanted her work to be understood. But Lewes could see the boost that Main's adoration was giving to Marian's tottering confidence as she struggled with *Middlemarch*. So he asked Blackwood to meet the young man and see if he could consent to let the book go ahead. For several reasons Blackwood was not keen. First there was the matter of the copyrights, which still belonged to the firm. Then there was Main's fervent devotion to Marian. Meeting Main in person at the Edinburgh office did nothing to dispel the impression that there was something repellent about him: the young man revealed that he was thirty years old, lived with his mother and liked to walk the sea shore reading aloud from the works of George Eliot.[21] In private, Blackwood dubbed Main 'the Gusher', but agreed to bring out the book in time for Christmas 1871. Marian declared herself delighted with the selected texts which Main forwarded for her approval, but secretly disliked the oleaginous Preface which went through without either her or Lewes having the chance to veto it.

It was probably lucky that the Gusher never got South to meet Marian – he would probably have bubbled over with the excitement. The Sunday At Homes had begun again on the Leweses' return from the Continent in May 1870. As befitted a household frequented by the great and the good, the Priory was currently being upgraded under the discriminating eye of Owen Jones. The interior was to be repainted and a new bathroom installed. Not only did this cost the Leweses a massive £500, it also involved them moving into a cottage in the country for several months while the work was being completed. But this wasn't the only change. In September 1871 the old servants, Amelia and Grace, gave notice. Although Marian had always counted on them seeing out their days with her, their departure was a great relief.[22] The grumpy sisters had refused to let her hire a much-needed third servant and had made life very difficult for the woman employed to nurse Thornie. Now they were gone, Marian was able to start again from scratch, hiring three excellent employees of Mrs Call, the former Rufa Hennell. Later an extra parlourmaid was added, bringing the indoor staff to a highly prosperous four.

Luckily callers at the Priory were grand enough to justify the magnificent new lavatory. 'Lords and Ladies, poets and cabinet ministers, artists and men of science, crowd upon us,' crowed Lewes to Main.[23] And these days they were bringing their wives with them. Marian and Lewes had been together for so long now that it was an effort to remember that they were not married. In fact, even they often seemed confused: when writing to Alexander Main in January 1873 Lewes maintained that he had lived with his mother until he had 'married' Marian, with absolutely no mention of Agnes and the children.[24] Marian continued in her usual and, for those in the know embarrassing, custom of referring to Lewes as 'my husband'. No wonder, then, that it was often rumoured that there had been a quiet divorce and remarriage on the Continent. When Arthur Stanley, Dean of Westminster, and his wife Lady Augusta met Marian at dinner at the Lockers in 1871 they were blithely unaware that 'Mrs

Lewes' was still legally 'Miss Evans'.[25] And even though the Stanleys were later upset to learn the true state of affairs, it is unlikely that they dissolved in a froth of righteous indignation. The times were changing and just as a reluctance to believe in God no longer constituted a bar to good society, long-term cohabitation was no longer exactly the scandal it used to be. Even Queen Victoria, writing to her daughter Vicky in Germany in 1870, conceded that in those cases where it was too expensive or difficult to divorce, long-term unmarried partnership must surely be 'holy and right'.[26]

There was still the occasional priggish objection, but this usually came from someone with a personal axe to grind, like Charles Norton. The Bostonian and his wife visited the Priory in the early weeks of 1869 having, so he maintained, been begged to attend by Lewes. Just like his friend Henry James, Norton seems to have been engaged in an Oedipal struggle with these representatives of an older intellectual generation. In a letter home, Norton assured his correspondent that no decent woman ever went near the Priory: while Mrs Lewes was generally agreed to be 'a good woman in her present life', society still looked askance at the bad example she had set. Indeed, Norton maintained that he knew of one infamous case where a 'poor weak woman' went to live with her lover, taking Marian Lewes as her precedent.

More spiteful altogether was Norton's contempt for the Leweses' aesthetic taste. He described the Priory as hideously vulgar, stuffed with bad paintings, including the portrait of Marian by Burton. Lewes, in a phrase much repeated down the years, was 'like an old-fashioned French barber or dancing master' while Marian was extraordinarily plain, of 'dull complexion, dull eye, heavy features'. Moreover, she had an unpleasantly self-conscious manner, as if accustomed 'to the adoring flattery of a coterie of not undistinguished admirers'. This, said Norton, showed up in her theatrical adoption of a 'very low and eager' speaking voice, which required her to lean over 'till her face is close to yours'.[27] Although Norton loftily maintained that he and his wife had no intention of extending their friendship with the Leweses, a few weeks later they invited both of them to lunch at the house they had taken in Queen's Gate Terrace. Shortly afterwards Mrs Norton brought her young children to the Priory, which suggests that she hardly saw it as the haunt of the demimonde which her husband's letter had blusteringly implied.

The question remains why Marian and Lewes went through the strain of hosting a party for twenty or so people every single week. They were both in fragile health and Marian was always fretting about her failure to push ahead with work. For Lewes the reason was simple: socialising with congenial people always had a magically reviving effect. There was hardly any headache or bilious attack which could not be improved by companionable chat over dinner (the food was not important, his tastes were plain). But Marian had always had more ambivalent feelings about the clatter of forced conversation, finding it an emotional and physical drain. What made the Priory At Homes different was that she was rarely subjected to unwanted chat. Lewes picked the lucky ones who were to have an audience and there was a tacit understanding that no one was there to talk about the weather. Conversation was carefully channelled into areas preselected by Marian: religion, painting, literature, her most recent trip abroad. When she grew tired, bored or offended, a hovering Lewes was at hand to whisk the tedious or impertinent guest away.

But the single most important reason why the Leweses continued their weekly entertainment of the great and the good was to show that they could. After years of Marian dining at home alone, it was sweet to watch while the most famous names in the country and on the Continent – Turgenev was a new guest – hovered in the hope of a few minutes' conversation with Mrs Lewes.

While the Leweses' contradictory feelings about other people were contained by the strict format of Priory Sundays, once they stepped outside the door their ambivalence led to some baffling behaviour. In April 1869 they were visiting Florence when they were asked to dine by the American ambassador and his wife. They accepted on condition that no one except Isa Blagdon, an old friend of Robert Browning's, should be asked as well. So when the American poet Longfellow heard that they were in town and begged for an invitation he was turned down. Confusingly, when the Leweses heard about this they announced themselves disappointed, whereupon their hostess sent a note to the poet's lodgings asking him to present himself immediately. But he was out.[28]

The fact was that although they insisted that they despised celebrity friendships, whenever a famous face hove into view the Leweses could not resist adding it to their collection. In the summer of 1871 when they were staying for a few months at the little village of Shottermill in Surrey, they were clearly intrigued by the fact that the Tennysons lived at nearby Aldworth. On 14 July Lewes bumped into the Laureate on the train from London and lost no time in bringing him home to meet Marian. Formal visits were duly exchanged and by the end of August the two households were on sufficiently familiar terms for Tennyson to round off a neighbourly evening by reading from his work. Both sides, however, indulged in a little *post hoc* tweaking to make it seem as though the other household had made all the running. Marian affected a world-weary tone when she mentioned to John Blackwood that it was Tennyson who had hunted her down, rather than the other way round.[29] Meanwhile Mrs, later Lady, Tennyson was careful to make sure that posterity did not know just how hard she had pushed to meet the notorious George Eliot. Although a few copies of Alfred Lord Tennyson's memoir contain an entry from his wife's diary which makes it clear that she had received and called on Mrs Lewes, in most copies the incriminating passage has been reworked to imply that the poet visited Shottermill alone.[30]

In the ancient cities of Oxford and Cambridge there was no such suburban squeamishness. Lewes had long been building links with the scientific men at the universities and Marian had taken great interest in the many young men she knew who had been obliged to give up their fellowships when they lost their faith. In May 1870 the Leweses spent three days with Mark Pattison, the Rector of Lincoln College, and his wife Emilia. For two entirely self-taught people, it was gratifying to be treated as honoured guests by the most obviously educated people in Britain. Distinguished scientists opened their laboratories and Benjamin Jowett, the next Master of Balliol, came to dinner. The Leweses also went to hear Emanuel Deutsch deliver his fearsomely learned paper on the Moabite Stone at the Sheldonian.[31]

On their first evening in Oxford the Leweses dined at Lincoln College, where among the guests was the eighteen-year-old Mary Arnold, niece of Matthew Arnold. The young girl was naturally agog to meet George Eliot, especially since she had literary aspirations, in later life becoming the novelist Mrs Humphrey Ward. Mary's first reaction was one of disappointment at Mrs Lewes's quietness, which amounted almost to silence. But with her usual perception Marian spotted the girl's hunger and sought her out for special attention. Knowing that Mary was interested in Spain, Marian started to talk about her recent stay there, 'with perfect ease and finish, without misplacing a word or dropping a sentence,' remembered Mrs Ward much later, 'and I realised at last that I was in the presence of a great writer.'[32]

Cambridge was equally welcoming. In February 1868 Oscar Browning and William Clark, fellows of Kings and Trinity respectively, invited the Leweses to see round the place. There was something about the aura of moral seriousness combined with the pedagogic tradition which always brought out the prig in Marian. Browning recalled how during dinner at Trinity 'she talked to me solemnly about the duties of life, about the shallow immorality of believing that all things would turn out for the best, and the danger of fixing our attention too much on the life to come, as likely to distract us from doing our duty in this world'.[33] On another visit to Cambridge, by now revelling in her status as sage, Marian returned to her favourite subjects as she walked round the Fellows' Garden at Trinity with Frederic Myers: 'she, stirred somewhat beyond her wont, and taking as her text the three words which have been used so often as the inspiriting trumpet-calls of men, – the words, *God, Immortality, Duty*, – pronounced, with terrible earnestness, how inconceivable was the *first*, how unbelievable the *second*, and yet how peremptory and absolute the *third*.'[34] The staginess of this often repeated anecdote is partly explained by the fact that Myers was writing years later and well after Marian's death. Elsewhere in his essay he refers to her as a 'Sibyl', a tag which unfortunately caught on and contributed to the doomy image of a massive, mythic figurehead, given to spouting riddles. But Marian also contributed to this impression herself when, in 1878, she published a ponderous poem called 'The College Breakfast-Party', probably based on an actual conversation at Trinity, which discusses the conflict between duty to others and the desire for self-fulfilment.[35]

During these years Marian had increasingly engineered her life so that she was always speaking to a rapt and sympathetic audience. Spontaneous utterance in front of neutral and unknown people was to be avoided at all costs. In 1871 she was invited to Edinburgh to take part in the celebration of the centenary of Scott's birth.[36] Although she was destined to sit on the top table alongside other worthies, including John Blackwood, the prospect of unscripted conversation and public scrutiny terrified her. After initially agreeing to attend out of gratitude for the comfort which Scott had brought to her dying father,

Marian panicked and got Lewes to write and withdraw her name using her usual excuse of ill-health.

Beneath the public image of sage and sibyl there remained a woman intensely involved with the details of domestic life. Gertrude Lewes's delivery of a baby girl in 1872 after two miscarriages was greeted with delight. When two more girls followed in 1874 and 1877, Marian allowed herself the luxury of joining in with Lewes's moan that they had wanted a grandson. She remained as interested as she ever had been in Bertie, who had stayed on in Africa after Thornie's death. In August 1870 Lewes and Marian had received a letter from the twenty-three-year-old in Natal announcing that he had become engaged to a 'well-educated young lady, Eliza Stevenson Harrison', the daughter of a long-time settler.[37] But there was a hitch: the girl's father objected to the match, on the grounds that the boy's father did not have a penny. Luckily, a substantial injection of cash into the equation seems to have made the difference, for the couple were married in August 1871. In gratitude for the help they had received from the Leweses, Bertie and Eliza named their first child Marian and the second George.

Nor, despite her wealth and status, did Marian lose her grasp on the daily details of housekeeping. Moving into rented accommodation at Shottermill in the summer of 1871 prompted her to write detailed letters to the landlady about blinds, keys and the failure of the butcher to deliver meat. The experience of running Griff, particularly the hiring and managing of the servants, had never left her. As mistress of the Priory she drew up an exact schedule of the housemaid's daily and weekly duties, including the when and where of carpet-beating and brass-polishing.[38] On 11 November 1872 she wrote to Frederic Harrison's new young wife recommending the daughter of the Priory's cook as a housemaid. She assures Mrs Harrison that Mary Dowling left her last post only because she was not quick enough at some of the fancier aspects of the job. Marian also believes that the rest of the servants took against the girl because 'her underclothing was thought arrogantly good' and her attitude towards the male staff 'had a little too much dignity'. It is hard to imagine Dickens, Thackeray or Trollope taking such a detailed interest in their footmen's underpants.[39]

Marian was aware that her need to watch over others sometimes gushed out of control. On 10 August 1869 she wrote to Emilia Pattison apologising for her effusiveness during the latter's visit to the Priory, which was not 'warranted by the short time we had known each other'. Touchingly, she put this down to the fact that she had never given birth and was therefore 'conscious of having an unused stock of motherly tenderness, which sometimes overflows'.[40] Perhaps watching her stepson's life slip away had also added to Marian's need to reach out to young people. Between now and the end of her life all the new relationships she formed were with people of an age to be her children. She adopted the Greek model of friendship for her own purposes, talking often of how much she valued the idea that 'the most satisfactory of all ties is this effective invisible intercourse of an elder mind with a younger.'[41] But beneath the rationalisation there was something far more powerful at work. Until she was thirty Marian had spent her time falling in love with teachers of either sex. Now that she was of an age to inhabit that role herself, she found it natural to draw adoring acolytes towards her.

Marian was particularly drawn to young people who were already involved in a family structure into which she could be incorporated as an honorary senior member. She enjoyed the idea that she and Lewes were 'grandparents' to a host of her friends' children, especially Philip and Margaret Burne-Jones. Another household where she fitted in easily belonged to the Cross family. Lewes had first been introduced to the widow Mrs William Cross by Herbert Spencer when they stopped off at Weybridge during a walking tour in October 1867. Eighteen months later the Leweses were in Rome when they bumped into Mrs Cross, her eldest daughter Mrs Bullock and her son, the twenty-nine-year-old banker John Walter Cross. Back in Britain the friendship flourished, partly because both the Leweses and the Crosses spent a lot of time in Surrey and partly because the Cross clan fulfilled the crucial criterion that it 'worshipped' the work of George Eliot. Marian and Lewes spent New Year's Day 1872 in Weybridge being made a fuss of by their new friends, and the following September they celebrated Marian's finishing of *Middlemarch* by visiting the family on the country estate, Six Mile Bottom, near Newmarket, recently inherited by Mrs Cross's son-in-law, Henry Bullock-Hall. Exhausted by the past year's tight writing schedule, which, Marian confided to Mrs Cross, was 'a sort of nightmare in which I have been scrambling on the slippery bank of a pool, just keeping my head above water', she plunged into reviving country conversations about livestock and crops.[42] Tantalisingly, John Cross was present during this weekend, along with several of his sisters, but there is no suggestion that he had caught Mrs Lewes's eye as a future lover. At this point she was more entranced with the family as a whole, and it was now that she started to call Johnny 'nephew'.

In any case Marian's interest in young men was in the process of being superseded by her involvement with young women. Much has been written and even more hinted about Marian's friendships with the group of girls who hung around her during the last decade of her life. These relationships were certainly intense, but to pronounce on whether or not they were 'lesbian' is to impose a sensibility which belongs to the late twentieth century. Certainly some Victorian women had physical relationships with other women, even more organised their emotional lives around best friends and sisters, while others combined marriage to a man they loved with enduring friendships with other women. But it would be anachronistic to describe any of these situations as 'lesbian' (or not) because lesbianism had not been defined in the way we understand it today. Certainly Harriet Martineau lived lovingly and jealously with her niece, Henry James's sister Alice had what was described as a 'Boston marriage' with a woman friend, and Barbara Bodichon's sister Annie, also known as Nanny, set up home in Rome with a fellow female artist.

Likewise, the conventions of language and tone which Victorian women observed in their friendships with one another might suggest to us meanings that were never intended. Women frequently used the language of love – calling each other 'darling' and 'dearest' and swearing undying loyalty – without wishing to express more than warm affection. On other occasions they used phrases which hinted at an attachment which perhaps neither fully understood. For instance, how are we to read those professions of love between Sara Hennell and her 'unfaithful husband' Mary Ann Evans during the 1840s? As a submerged 'lesbian' enchantment or as a metaphor for the strength of the platonic love between them? The impossibility of knowing suggests the futility of trying to guess.

It is certainly true that those young women who developed a passion for Marian were either enduringly single or stuck in a disappointing marriage. Just like Marian herself, they had an 'unused stock' of feelings which were looking for expression. For instance, Georgiana Burne-Jones's feelings for Marian Lewes grew more intense as her husband's interest in her waned, reaching a climax when he started an affair with another woman. In June 1870 Georgie arranged to take the children to Whitby to coincide with the Leweses' arrival in the resort following a tour of health-giving Cromer and Harrogate. Over the two weeks of sandy walks and dinner discussions that followed, Georgie, minus Edward, developed a passionate attachment to Marian. Her first letter to the Priory on Marian's return to town suggests how profoundly she had been moved:

Dearest Mrs Lewes,
    Don't laugh if I say that my impulse is to address you as 'Honoured Madame' – I wish you wouldn't think it ludicrous and would allow me to do so – it so exactly says what I mean . . .
    I think much of you, and of your kindness to me during this past fortnight, and my heart smites me that I have somewhat resembled those friends who talk only of themselves to you . . . Forgive me if it has been so, and reflect upon what a trap for egotism your unselfishness and tender thought for others is. The only atonement I can make is a resolve that what you have said to me in advice and warning shall not be lost.[43]

Another of Marian's honorary daughters was Emilia Pattison, the much younger wife of the Rector of Lincoln College, Oxford. Like Georgie, Emilia was unhappy with her husband, a man whose vast learning and advanced years made many think that he must be the model for Edward Casaubon. There were certain details about Emilia's intense Anglo-Catholic adolescence which found their way into the description of the Evangelical Dorothea Brooke, including a propensity to fast and to pray spontaneously for the souls of the astonished poor. Following the successful visit to Lincoln College in 1870, the friendship deepened and Marian started to fall naturally into calling Emilia 'Daughter', and signing herself '*Madre*'.

But Georgie's and Emilia's sentimental devotion was nothing compared with that of Elma Stuart, a soldier's widow living in Dinan, France, with her small son. She initially wrote to Marian in January 1872, enclosing an oak book-slide which she had carved herself. It was the first of a stream of presents which arrived at the Priory over the years. There were other examples of the dextrous Elma's craft – an elaborately carved table, mirror and writing board – as well as the more conventional sweets and photographs. Mrs Stuart was obsessed with Marian's physical comfort – as was Marian – and put a great deal of time and energy into designing knickers, shirts and slippers which might suit her beloved's increasingly fragile body. But it was the accompanying letters which capped anything that had gone before. The first one set the tone: 'What for years, you have been to me, how you have comforted my sorrows, peopled my loneliness, added to my happiness, and bettered in every way my whole nature, you can never know.'[44] Over the next few years Mrs Stuart offered, among many other things, to be Marian's servant and kiss the hem of her garment. On Marian's death she booked the plot next to her beloved's grave in Highgate so that she could be sure of lying alongside her. The headstone, erected in 1903, was boastfully devoted, describing Mrs Stuart as one 'whom for 8½ blessed years George Eliot called by the sweet name of "Daughter"'.[45]

Lewes was not threatened by these intense attachments between Marian and other, younger women. He saw the effect which their adoration had on her shaky confidence and was happy to encourage them to keep writing and visiting. This, of course, ran counter to his declared strategy of not allowing Marian to see or hear anything about her work. In practice, he increasingly allowed anyone whose reaction Marian found pleasing to have controlled access to her. Undiscriminating gush still offended her by its failure to see the difference between her own work and the run-of-the-mill pot-boiler. But these new young female fans gave her the kind of response she wanted, an intensely personal testimony to the way their own lives had been morally uplifted by their encounters with Romola, Fedalma or Esther Lyon.

Women were drawn to Marian for the same reasons as men. Just as Mrs Ponsonby said, George Eliot seemed to understand how to live a good life in a godless universe. And then there was her famous empathy which, as Georgie Burne-Jones had discovered in Whitby, encouraged people to give up their most intimate secrets. It would be naïve to suggest that as Marian leaned eagerly towards some young man or woman, drawing out their inner life, she was consciously trawling material for her next set of characters. By now she was far beyond lifting people from real life and transplanting them into her books. But the understanding of human frailty which at this very moment was feeding her construction of Dorothea, Lydgate and Rosamond was also at work in the drawing-room of the Priory. Her great skill, as young Mary Arnold had noted, was to listen intently to what she was being told, leaving the speaker feeling that, for once, she had been properly heard. A decade before Freud and a century before the counselling boom, Marian Lewes had stumbled upon the power of attentive listening.

There were other things which Marian offered specifically to women who found themselves both excited and confused by the intensifying debate around 'The Woman Question'. Barbara Bodichon, Emily Davies, Emily Faithful, Bessie Rayner Parkes and their many friends were beginning to see results for their years of dedicated work. Throughout the fifties and sixties they had campaigned for better schools and jobs for women, and set up a whole range of initiatives, from Girton College to the *English Woman's Journal* and an all-women printing business. Now others were beginning to listen: in 1869, following his failure to get women included in the franchise, the mighty John Stuart Mill published his influential *The Subjection of Women*; the following year Barbara's dream was realised when the Married Women's Property Act went through. For the group known as the 'Langham Place Ladies', after their headquarters, these were triumphs. But for many other middle-class women the issues were less clear. They might feel restricted in their marriages and frustrated by their lack of publicly recognised achievements, but that did not mean they necessarily wanted to go down the path laid out by liberal trail blazers like Barbara Bodichon. For these women Marian Lewes offered an alternative model of educated, effective womanhood. Unlike Barbara and Bessie, she had not been raised in the tradition of Bentham and the Mills. She did not trust the free market to deliver solutions to cultural and historic tangles. In January 1871, with obvious approbation she quoted the story of a woman who had taken back her drunken husband again and again 'and at last nursed and watched him into penitence and decency'. This for Marian was not 'mere animal constancy. It is duty and human pity.'[46] While Barbara had worked hard for nearly twenty years to ensure that such a woman need not be shackled to her husband, Marian saw something admirable in the fact that she had stayed.

When Marian started to write *Middlemarch* at the beginning of 1869 she was already steeped in the medical history which feeds the background to the book. From her recollections of Chrissey's husband Edward Clarke, she knew all about the difficulties faced by a 'gentleman' entering what was still as much a trade as a profession. From Lewes's ward-walking days as a medical student in the 1830s she got information about basic anatomy, the pathologies of prevalent illnesses including typhoid and cholera, not to mention the scare stories about the infamous Burke and Hare. For the details he was not able to supply she had a host of other sources close at hand. Gertrude Lewes had material about her grandfather, the illustrious medical reformer Thomas Southwood Smith, which fitted nicely with the profile Marian wanted for her hero Tertius Lydgate. Dr Clifford Allbutt was able to answer questions about the organisation and practice of provincial hospitals, which Maria Congreve, daughter of a doctor, supplemented with more research. In addition, Marian did her usual detailed reading on all aspects of the development of medicine.

More than any of Marian's previous books *Middlemarch* was concerned with national political and economic life. While in *Adam Bede, The Mill on the Floss* and *Silas Marner* Eliot mentions high grain prices, the far-away French War and the Emancipation of Catholics, the communities she writes about remain aloof from wider political and commercial pressures. In *Felix Holt* we take a step towards the larger world, as the conflicts surrounding the Great Reform Bill are explored through their impact on one provincial community. But while Eliot had famously maintained in *Felix Holt* that there is no individual life which is not shaped by wider circumstance, it is in *Middlemarch* that she shows this process fully at work.

This wider grasp of the relationship between town and country, province and metropolis, country and state was fed by Marian's continued growing interest in politics and political history. The very week after finishing *Felix Holt* she had gone to the Houses of Parliament to hear the debate over Abyssinia – something which it would be hard to imagine her doing five years earlier.[47] The outbreak of the Franco-Prussian War in July 1870 had her devouring *The Times* and the *Daily News* in a way which, given her previous indifference to newspapers, even she found strange.[48] Marian had started out on the side of the Prussians, warrior guardians of that German culture which had fed and shaped so much of her life. But as the extent of Junker cruelty became clear, especially during the siege of Paris in December 1870, she began to feel increasing sympathy with the French and a general abhorrence of the brutalising effects of the war. Never noted for her political insight, Marian made an extraordinarily prophetic remark to Sara Hennell on 12 August 1870 when she declared, 'We have entered into the period which will be marked in future historical charts as "The period of German ascendency".'[49]

Middlemarch, of course, is not concerned with the Franco-Prussian War. The novel begins in the late 1820s, and its main political focus is the agitation leading up to the 1832 Great Reform Act. This material was already familiar to Marian from her work on *Felix Holt*. But her new and wider understanding of economic and social history allowed her to deal in detail with such matters as the coming of the railway to Middlemarch, Ladislaw's Polish heritage as well as her more expected analysis of the state of agriculture during the post-war depression.

The opening chapters of *Middlemarch* were not the first which Marian actually wrote. During that scrappy, painful year of 1869 she started work on the story of the young doctor, Lydgate, who arrives in the provincial town of Middlemarch ambitious for himself and for his profession. But only a few weeks into the New Year Marian acknowledged to Blackwood that the work was not going fast: 'between the beginning and the middle of a book I am like the lazy Scheldt; between the middle and end I am like the arrowy Rhône.'[50] Thornie's illness throughout the summer was a further drag on her work, making her even more doubtful about the novel's progress: on 11 September she wrote, 'I do not feel very confident that I can make anything satisfactory of Middlemarch.'[51] By the end of the year she had completed fifty pages, but Thornie's death made further progress impossible. The next we hear of the book is in March 1870 when Marian tells Blackwood despondingly, 'My novel, I suppose, will be finished some day.'[52] But by May she was feeling sufficiently positive to give him a sketch of the book, which left him feeling that 'It promises to be something wonderful – English provincial life'.[53] Then at the beginning of December she paused again and started on a different story altogether. This was called 'Miss Brooke' and, according to her journal, 'is a subject which has been recorded among my possible themes ever since I began to write fiction'.[54] Quite possibly this was the germ for 'The Clerical Tutor', which had once been mentioned as a possible addition to *Scenes of Clerical Life*. By the end of the month she had managed a brisk and promising one hundred pages. But it was only at the beginning of the third year, 1871, that she had the idea of joining the Lydgate and Dorothea fragments together to produce the book which we know now as *Middlemarch*.

It would be strange if from this point Marian had charged ahead. By March 1871 she was already tormented by the fact that languor and illness had produced a disappointing total of only 236 (print equivalent) pages. Typically, too, she despaired of the book's structure, believing that she had 'too much matter, too many "momenti"'.[55]

By May, however, she was feeling sufficiently positive to let Lewes start making provisional arrangements with Blackwood for publication. Both men had good reasons for wanting to depart from the usual way of doing things. Blackwood's profits had long suffered from the hold which Mudie and the other circulating libraries had on the reading public: people were reluctant to buy a book which, if they waited a few weeks, they could borrow. The Leweses were shocked to note how even the wealthy Mary Cash, formerly Sibree, refused to part with her money if she thought there was a good chance of getting a book from the library. If there was a way of publishing which weakened the grip of Mudie and W. H. Smith on the market, Blackwood was keen to consider it. Lewes, for his part, had always been intrigued by the idea that bringing out Marian's books in instalments would make her fortune. On 7 May he sketched out a plan for *Middlemarch* to Blackwood, based on the precedent of Victor Hugo's massive *Les Misérables*. *Middlemarch* was already heading for four volumes instead of the more usual three, so it made sense to divide the material up in a completely new way. Lewes proposed that the book should appear in eight instalments published every two months. Each would cost five shillings and Marian was to get a royalty of two shillings on every copy sold. The high royalty reflected the fact that Marian was gambling on the success of her work, having waived her claim to the more usual lump sum.[56]

Blackwood did not jump immediately. Years before, he had rejected a similar plan for Bulwer-Lytton's monumental *My Novel*. He knew that this kind of bold scheme would only be profitable if the book was a huge popular success. And in his usual tactless way Lewes had already made the proposal less attractive by concluding a parallel arrangement with the American publisher Osgood & Co. to bring out the book there in weekly instalments. Despite the fact that Marian hated to be read in such small parts, the price of £1200 was too good to let pass. Blackwood was naturally worried that advance extracts might cross the Atlantic and reach London in time to spoil the full impact of *Middlemarch*. But if he was tempted to make a fuss, his first taste of the manuscript on 31 May made him determined not to scare the Leweses into the arms of another George Smith. To Marian, Blackwood wrote that Book One was 'filled to overflowing with touches of nature and character that could not be surpassed', while to his clerk George Simpson he confided that he 'would willingly be content with a moderate gain to ourselves rather than let it go past us'.[57]

Both the Leweses and the Blackwoods were acutely aware of what was at stake and moved softly to avoid conflict. At the dinner celebrating Scott which

Marian should have attended on 15 August, Blackwood gave a speech in which he emphasised that he had always delighted in making friends of his authors. Lewes, in turn, made a point of letting Edinburgh know how moved Marian had been when she had reached this part of the transcript, remarking that she was sure that any author who was not friends with Blackwood had only him- or herself to blame.[58]

In the end *Middlemarch* came out in eight parts, the last three appearing at monthly intervals instead of every two months. Lewes's hunch that this method of publication would extend the swell of interest in the novel proved correct. People felt more intensely involved with *Middlemarch* than they had with any of the previous books. Marian, too, liked the idea that readers were more likely to give each instalment greater attention than if they had swallowed the book whole. The only unhappy effect of this new arrangement was the paper wrapper designed for each section. It was fussy, very green, and appalled those like Owen Jones or Barbara Bodichon who had an eye for these things.

As it turned out, *Middlemarch* marked a return to the high-water days of Marian's relationship with Blackwood. Not since *Adam Bede* had she brought out a book with such large profits and so little fuss. This was all the luckier because her attitude to money was as confused as it had been at the beginning of her writing career. She was as haughty as ever about people who wrote 'trash' for money, maintaining that she felt 'quite oppressed with the quantity of second rate art everywhere about'.[59] To the many correspondents, from schoolgirls to published authors, who asked for advice about their writing, she was nearly always coolly discouraging, suggesting they try something else. This went even for Anthony Trollope, about whom she commented that it was a bad idea for him to give up the Post Office because he had written quite enough novels already.[60]

Yet more than any of her books, *Middlemarch* was written for money. Marian had not had a really significant income from a new work since *Felix Holt*, five years before. Her outgoings were continuing to rise. The Priory gobbled cash and both the Leweses had been poor for long enough to believe that charity began at home. There were Mrs Willim, Agnes Lewes, Emily Clarke and Nursie to support, not to mention Bertie and Charlie, and the growing brood of grandchildren. Lewes was not bringing in much money, so the whole burden fell on Marian. It is no coincidence that it was now that she decided to return to the provincial English landscape, which had always proved most popular with her readers. And despite the extra pressure which came with serialisation – including having to rejig her narrative so that the books came out in equal parts – she was happy to fall in with an arrangement that promised to make her absolutely secure for the rest of her life.

Much of Book Two of *Middlemarch* – 'Old and Young' – was written down in Shottermill, a little village near Haslemere, Surrey. The Leweses moved there temporarily in May 1871 while the Priory was being refitted. They were, as always, picky about their surroundings, rejecting at least five cottages suggested by helpful friends before they found Brookbank. They stayed there from 2 May until 1 August, when they were obliged to move out for another tenant. Luckily the cottage opposite was free and they took Cherrimans for a further month before returning to London on 1 September.

In the quiet of the country Marian wrote fluently and well. Disturbed only by an occasional visit from Barbara Bodichon, the Calls and the Tennysons, she spent her mornings working and her afternoons walking with Lewes. Blackwood was increasingly enthusiastic about the instalments which were arriving in Edinburgh, remarking after reading Book Two, 'You are like a great giant walking about among us.'[61]

Once Book One of *Middlemarch* appeared in print in December, new voices were raised in admiration. James Paget refused to believe that Mrs Lewes had never known a doctor intimately, since her portrayal of Lydgate was so exact. Lawyers expressed surprise that a layperson could get the details about Featherstone's will so right. 'And all of us', concluded a triumphant Lewes writing to Main, 'wonder at the insight into Soul!'[62]

By this time Marian needed to hear every little bit of praise which Lewes could soak up. A week after her return to the Priory on 1 September she had suddenly become 'depressed in spirits and in liver'. Lewes had no doubt that this was linked to the creative process, writing hopefully to Blackwood that 'perhaps gestation is more favourable when so much emotion accompanies it'.[63] But a week later Marian took a turn for the worse, falling seriously ill for five days with gastric fever which left her, she told Sara, 'as thin as a mediaeval Christ'.[64] Sensing that he had a full-scale crisis on his hands, Lewes now urged Blackwood to sanction Alexander Main's tribute of a commonplace-style selection from Eliot's published work in the hope that good Christmas sales and some nice reviews would boost Marian's tottering confidence.

Over 1872, which saw the publication of the remaining seven parts of *Middlemarch*, Marian's spirits rose and fell almost daily. She held a small party at the Priory on 30 November 1871 to celebrate the publication of Book One and enjoyed the fun of sending out presentation copies to very close friends, among whom she now counted 'the Gusher'. Two months later, on 27 January, the Leweses held a large dinner party and musical evening at the Priory, the biggest of its kind since the death of Thornie. But even in the midst of this returning buoyancy Marian could not help focusing on the dark side, writing gloomily to Blackwood, 'I am thoroughly comforted as to the half of the work which is already written – but there remains the terror about the *un*written.'[65] Only a few weeks later she was back in deep despair. Rereading her previous book, *Felix Holt*, she declared to Lewes that she 'could never write like that again and that what is now in hand is rinsings of the cask!'[66]

From this low point Marian's health and spirits gradually began to rise. In order to give her a chance to work concentratedly on Book Six of *Middlemarch*, in May 1872 the Leweses tried the trick of moving once again to the country, this time choosing Redhill. They kept their address secret even from close friends and were rewarded with nothing more disruptive than the occasional noisy hen or dog. The magic did not work straight away, for Marian found herself in severe agony from aching teeth and sore gums – a trouble spot with her which would get worse over the years. But the combination of attention from the dentist and visits from James Paget – who presumably was given the address – gradually eased the problem and Book Six was finished in a record five weeks. Encouraged by Marian's characteristic late burst of speed, Lewes now suggested to Blackwood that he bring out Books Seven and Eight at monthly intervals. By 17 September 1872 Marian had finished correcting the proofs of Book Eight, and the very next day she and Lewes set out for Germany.

'Why always Dorothea?' asks Eliot famously at the beginning of chapter 29 of *Middlemarch*, making the point that while her heroine might be one of the principal centres of consciousness in the novel, her elderly, unappealing husband Casaubon also has an internal life, as vivid to him as Dorothea's is to her. One could say the same of Marian and Lewes. For all the time that Marian was battling with fading inspiration, depressed liver and grief over Thornie, Lewes was tackling parallel pressures in his own life.

The letter from Thornie in October 1868 telling of his terrible health had rattled Lewes dreadfully. Although there was nothing which could be done immediately, aside from sending off the money the boy had asked for, he felt restless with responsibility. He was committed to spending the spring in Italy with Marian, but appeared distracted and tetchy throughout the holiday. This time it was sciatica which made things difficult, although never enough to stop him visiting the people he wanted to see. In Florence, staying once again at the Villino Trollope, Lewes made an excursion to Professor Schiff's laboratory to see a machine which, it was claimed, could measure the speed of thought.

Naples turned out to be wet and Rome unpleasantly crowded. Normally the cheeriest of souls, Lewes seemed perpetually irritated by those things that he usually found charming: lazy trains, tricky cabbies and other people. He could not be bothered to remember his fifty-second birthday on 18 April, and fretted constantly to be home and 'at work again'. When he did finally get back to the Priory on 5 May, he was shocked to find a skeletal Thornie waiting for him.

Despite Lewes's suggestion to Blackwood that he had never held out any hope of recovery for Thornie, the death hit him very hard. Usually able to work through anything, he was forced to put aside his monumental *Problems of Life and Mind*, in which he was trying to find a physiological basis for human psychology. His constant companions of headache and ringing in the ears now intensified and on one frightening evening in February 1870 he fainted in bed, waking the next morning to find his hands and feet numb and tingling. If this was a minor stroke, it remained undiagnosed and a couple of weeks later Lewes was just able to drag himself off to the Isle of Wight for a convalescent break with the hypochondriacal but supremely robust Herbert Spencer.[67]

The trip to Germany the following month, in March 1870, did a fair amount for Lewes's ego, if nothing for his health. In Europe he had long been treated as a great man of both Science and Letters, rather than a versatile hack. In Berlin he talked as an equal with leading researchers in neurology and attended a University Festival in honour of the King's birthday, where he was 'seated apart from the public among the Princes, Professors, Ambassadors, and persons covered with stars and decorations'.[68] Invited to dinner by the American ambassador, he was delighted to meet the distinguished chemist Robert Wilhelm Bunsen. Prince Frederick VIII, the Duke of Schleswig-Holstein, spotted him in a bookshop and 'begged to be introduced'.[69] This was the kind of thing Lewes loved. Unlike Marian, who genuinely preferred not to be recognised by the public, Lewes had been known to drop hints about his identity to fellow hotel guests, especially if they were female, young and pretty.

With progress on *Problems* still stalled, Lewes consulted yet another doctor. Following Dr Reynolds' advice on phosphates, cod liver oil and plenty of rest by the sea, the Leweses duly set out for a tour of east-coast health spots in June 1870, taking in Cromer and Harrogate before meeting up with Georgie Burne-Jones in Whitby. From this low point Lewes's health gradually improved. It may have been the happy news of Bertie's engagement, or the peaceful death of Mrs Willim on 10 December 1870, which allowed him to release a little of the heavy responsibility he always carried for his clan. On the other hand it is possible that Marian's descent into nausea and toothache while writing *Middlemarch* required him to vacate the role of invalid. In the ceaseless dance of sickness that the Leweses performed down the years, the jobs of nurse and patient were swapped several times. Now it was Lewes's turn to fuss around Marian, summoning Paget from town and making sure there was a steady supply of pain-relieving quinine. Marian reported that Lewes was now 'in an altogether flourishing condition, enjoying all things from his breakfast to the highest problems in statics and dynamics'.[70] She had not seen him so well for many years.

The Leweses' continued devotion to one another sometimes baffled onlookers. On the last day of 1870 Marian wrote in her journal: 'In my private lot I am unspeakably happy, loving and beloved,' while Lewes maintained to a friend that the experience of being Marian's partner 'is a perpetual Banquet to which that of Plato would present but a flat rival'.[71] What puzzled people who met the Leweses at dinner or who came to the Priory was how this vulgar, obnoxious little man could enthral a woman as morally refined as Marian. Even the unsophisticated and prepared-to-be-impressed Mary Arnold had taken 'a prompt and active dislike' when she met Lewes at Lincoln College and had wondered how the great George Eliot could bear to fall silent in order to hang on every word that issued from the big, wet lips of her companion.[72] Charles Norton was more specific about his dislike. Although he grudgingly conceded that Lewes's talents 'seem equal to anything', he went on to point out that 'his moral perceptions are not acute and he consequently often fails in social tact and taste'.[73]

Norton had a point. Over Christmas 1870 the Leweses went to stay at a High Church parsonage on the Isle of Wight with Barbara Bodichon. Lewes was highly amused to find a scourge hanging in the priest's study and organised a little trick which, mindful of Barbara's growing interest in Roman Catholicism, seems extremely tasteless. He arranged with the parlour maid that she would present the scourge on a covered plate during dinner. When Barbara removed the lid the thongs of the scourge gave a little jump 'as if a live eel or so were there'.[74] Reporting the incident to Charlie and Gertrude, Lewes maintained that there was 'Immense laughter!' from the assembled company. Did Marian, with her great empathy for other people's religious faith, really find this funny? If so, it means that her love and need for Lewes were powerful enough to send her carefully calibrated moral compass swinging wildly off course.

Middlemarch represents George Eliot's most comprehensive and finely rendered view of human experience. It is a vast, inclusive 'Study of Provincial Life', setting out her beliefs about how society works, how it supports and thwarts the individuals who compose it, and how an accommodation can be made between the two. It is, in effect, an answer to all those correspondents and callers who entreated Marian Lewes: 'how must I live now?'

Middlemarch represents that literal and metaphoric middling part of Britain. In 1829, when the book opens, it is a thriving market town with some light industry, of which Mr Vincy's silk factory is the prominent example, and enduring connections to the surrounding agricultural estates, owned by county families like the Brookes and the Chettams. Eliot uses the image of the web over and over to reinforce the idea that all parts of the community are intimately interwoven, and becoming more so as the time of political reform approaches. In chapter 10 the landowner Brooke invites the professional and manufacturing men of Middlemarch to dinner, already half aware that in the coming years his interests will increasingly be meshed with theirs.[75] These 'fresh threads of connection' between the agricultural and urban communities call the hitherto unstoppable Brooke to a new kind of account.[76] During his campaign to be returned as a reforming MP, the Middlemarch mob taunt him with his record as a stingy, careless landlord who allows his tenants to languish in unnecessary poverty. In embarrassment and confusion Brooke withdraws from the election.

In her handling of Brooke's changing relationship with the men of Middle-march, Eliot's determination to show the 'stealthy convergence of human lots' is perfectly grounded in the changes in social and political power which took place in Britain from the late twenties. Other attempts to show this shifting interconnectedness between one life and another result in some fantastic coincidences of plot, which seem to go against everything Eliot once sketched out as vital to her kind of realism. The narrative thread which reveals that Will Ladislaw, already in the neighbourhood to visit his second cousin Casaubon, is also the grandson of the banker Bulstrode's first wife, would not be out of place in a novel by Scott or Dickens. It is in these dense, stringy corners of the plot that Henry James's comment that *Middlemarch* 'sets a limit, we think to the development of the old-fashioned English novel' starts to seem less of a competitive barb by the Young Pretender and more of a valid assessment of the limits to literary realism.[77]

In other respects, though, Eliot manages her material magnificently. When Blackwood made the remark about her being a giant he was referring not so much to her status in the literary world as to her ability to stride through her fictional landscape, eavesdropping on every kind of life. In the earliest days of

'Amos Barton' Blackwood had wondered at his new author's ability to describe the conversation of a group of clerics; twenty-five years later he was marvelling at the way she managed to get the slangy talk of 'those horsy men' who fleece Fred Vincy exactly right.[78]

There seemed no end to the lives Eliot was able to inhabit. Drawing on her own priggish adolescence she could imagine the Evangelical banker Bulstrode, rigid with spiritual pride. Her schoolgirl pleasure 'On Being Called a Saint' was transferred to the late-middle-aged man whose overweening ambition is to be seen to be good. When revelations made by the scurrilous stranger Raffles mean that Bulstrode is about to be unmasked as a swindler, the banker's refusal to admit the full extent of his sin to himself or to God captures exactly the agony of the narcissistic soul. It is an agony which the adolescent Mary Ann Evans, caught in her own relationship with an unforgiving Deity, knew only too well.

'She never forgets anything which comes within the curl of her eyelash,' Lewes had said to Mary Cash, formerly Sibree, in answer to her reverential query in 1873 about the source of George Eliot's power.[79] The political infighting on Middlemarch's Board of Health over the new fever hospital was probably suggested by some story Robert Evans carried home from one of the committees that increasingly occupied him during the last decade at Griff. Fred Vincy's listless assumption that he will go into the Church is possibly based on what Marian had picked up about her nephew, Fred Evans. Just like Mr Vincy, Isaac Evans had educated his children with an eye to social advancement. His son Fred had been sent to Exeter College, Oxford, where he managed a lacklustre third before becoming ordained and taking up a post in the parish of Bedworth, the little industrial village where Mary Ann had once busied herself providing second-hand clothing for the coal-miners. Here is a fine example of what Marian hated most: young men and women aiming for 'the highest work' without any regard to talent or calling. Luckily Fred Vincy is redeemed by his childhood sweetheart, Mary Garth, who refuses to marry him unless he finds a career for which he is more honestly suited.

There are more marvels in *Middlemarch*. Although she had not been born into the gentry, young Mary Anne's ladylike ways had elevated her from agent's daughter to the favourite of Mrs Maria Newdegate, mistress of Arbury Hall. And Robert Evans's increasing reputation as a clever land agent not only now provided the model for Caleb Garth, but had given the adolescent Mary Ann some access to the local county families. Whatever her exact sources, Eliot was able to write about the gentry as if she knew them intimately. There is Sir James Chettam, a well-meaning, slightly stupid baronet who wants to marry Dorothea Brooke, but ends up as her protective brother-in-law. Unlike his blustery neighbour Brooke, Chettam treats his tenants well, engaging Caleb Garth to make sure the land is farmed along the most modern and effective lines. There is Mrs Cadwallader, an impoverished gentlewoman and rector's wife, whose snobbish adherence to the old country ways is saved by a sharp wit and her loathing of the dusty Casaubon. And finally there is Mr Brooke, a pompous, windy old fool who likes the idea of being at the cutting edge of art, music and politics, but lives in horror of 'going too far' in anything. His promiscuous activities, which include becoming proprietor of the local newspaper in order to influence local politics, recall Charles Bray's ubiquitous presence in the public life of Coventry.

While the town and county families in *Middlemarch* muddle through, being ordinarily kind and cutting to one another, there are two young people, one from each side, who are resolved to do better. Mr Brooke's nineteen-year-old niece Dorothea is impatient with the privileges of her position, and spends her time designing cottages for the poor and praying enthusiastically for them when they fall ill. Noble-hearted and 'ardent', she longs for a great cause to shape her life. Unimpressed by Sir James Chettam's courtship, which promises to turn her into nothing more special than a liberal baronet's wife, she insists upon marrying the middle-aged scholar and cleric Edward Casaubon. By becoming her husband's amanuensis and helpmate on his monumental life-work, the 'Key to All Mythologies', Dorothea hopes to find the key which will unlock the meaning of her own life.

The twenty-seven-year-old Tertius Lydgate shares Dorothea's hunger to improve the lot of the people around him. Unlike her, he has a clear arena in which to realise his ambitions. Although a gentleman by birth, he has qualified in medicine from the prestigious universities of Edinburgh and Paris. Armed with the new tools of stethoscope and microscope, he plans to combine an effective modern practice with a continued interest in pure scientific research, 'to do good small work for Middlemarch, and great work for the world'.[80]

Lydgate's first step is to practise a general medicine which is rigorous and effective. This means refusing to follow what family doctors have been doing for centuries – making money by sending out drugs which would be better obtained from the apothecary or the dispensary. Although willing to attend anyone who asks to see him, Lydgate has a horror of appearing to court favour and wears his independence with more than a hint of pride. He believes his energies will be best used introducing up-to-date procedures at the fever hospital or persuading bereaved relatives to allow him to carry out the novel procedure of an autopsy.

Eliot uses one of her stunning scientific metaphors to explain the disabling egotism of her major characters. She imagines a lighted candle held against a piece of polished steel and points out that the random scratches on the surface will appear to fall 'in a fine series of concentric circles round that little sun'. These things, she tells us, are a parable. The scratches are events and the candle is the powerfully distorting centre of an individual consciousness.[81]

Dorothea is so short-sighted that she falls over small dogs and bumps into furniture. Her need to see Casaubon as a great and subtle thinker requires her to ignore all the evidence that he is actually a frigid pedant, paralysed by a fear of failure and unable to start on what will certainly be a second-rate work. Lydgate is likewise flawed by his 'spots of commonness', which means that he is unable to perceive that the delightfully mild and pretty Rosamond Vincy will not make the docile wife of his lazy dreams. Miss Vincy, a manufacturer's daughter, wants to marry a gentlemanly doctor, not an ardent reformer. Her ambitions are the natural ones of a girl who has been given the most pretentious of provincial educations. She thinks about houses, dresses and the fact that Lydgate's uncle is a baronet, while Lydgate's own mind runs on the improvements he can make to the practice of general medicine. The result is a 'total missing of each other's mental track, which is too evidently possible even between persons who are continually thinking of each other'.[82]

These two dreadful marriages – of the Casaubons and the Lydgates – are among the best of the many wonderful things Eliot ever did. Given that her own partnership with Lewes was mutually sustaining, it is a testimony to her art that she was able to portray the excruciating pain of an incompatible marriage. The confidences of Emilia Pattison and Georgie Burne-Jones about their difficult relationships may have provided the kind of intimate detail that she could not get elsewhere. In the same way, the letters she had received from two idealistic young men, Frederic Harrison and Clifford Allbutt, about the expectations of marriage they had forged during long engagements, gave her an insight into the impact which Lydgate's alliance with a narrow-minded woman might have on his desire to dedicate himself to the service of mankind.

Eliot makes the point repeatedly that both Lydgate and Dorothea are trapped in hells of their own making. While their respective spouses fail to understand them, they too have failed to see that Rosamond and Casaubon have wishes, fears and desires which exist quite independently of them. Having asked at the beginning of chapter 29 why Dorothea's consciousness should dominate the account of her marriage, Eliot makes us see Casaubon in all his sad completeness. Despite his thin calves, white moles and noisy soup-eating, he is 'spiritually a-hungered like the rest of us', disappointed that the marriage he has entered in good faith is dissolving into the dull ache of mutual misunderstanding.[83] Having picked Dorothea for her ignorance and assumed pliability, Casaubon is confronted by an intelligent woman who in a matter of months has stumbled upon the fact that his life's work is misconceived and redundant. Dorothea's gentle questioning chimes with the critical voices already installed in his head to produce a drowning chorus of accusation and mockery. In the circumstances Casaubon does the only thing he knows how to: withdraws to the library.

Harriet Peirce, gushy wife of a Harvard philosophy lecturer, implored Marian after *The Spanish Gypsy*: 'the poetry was so beautiful, but must noble women always fail? Is there no sumptious [sic] flower of happiness for us?'[84] It is a question which women were to ask even more wistfully about Dorothea Brooke. From the first page of the Preface to *Middlemarch*, Eliot sets up the ardent girl to fail in her yearning to find an 'epic life'. Unlike St Teresa of Avila who lived at a time which could use and sanction her extraordinary spirit, Dorothea is destined to flounder around in a society which allows her only the diminished scope of small, private acts. She ends the book as we have been promised that she will, not as a great social reformer or inspiring religious figure, but as the wife of a forward-looking MP. Her young adult life has been a painful education in the limits of self-determination. Claiming Casaubon as her ticket to a great destiny has resulted only in suffering. Now she must submit to the less than perfect circumstances in which she finds herself. But the very last paragraph of the book makes it clear that Dorothea's fine spirit will never be completely buried. In the tiny 'unhistoric acts' of goodness which she performs within her limited circle a ripple of influence has been set in motion which may eventually lap the edge of the world.[85]

Lydgate is given an even less heroic ending. In his keenness to reform the standards of medical practice in Middlemarch he fails to understand the strength of attachment to the old ways of doing things. While some patients pronounce themselves delighted with his work, there are others who remain suspicious of his refusal to send out medicine and his indecent desire to cut up the bodies of the dead. These are the ones who renew their loyalty to Messrs Minchin and Sprague, two old-time practitioners who display none of Lydgate's gentlemanly indifference to profit.

Sucked into debt by Rosamond's refusal to honour his principled ambition, Lydgate ends up by becoming what he always most despised, a society doctor supported by a pack of rich patients. Instead of the paper he had longed to write on the structures of the origins of tissue, he produces only a treatise on gout. He dies early, a broken man, regarding himself as a failure because 'he had not done what he once meant to do'.[86] Starting out with the fire and spirit of Dorothea, he ends with the choked despair of Casaubon.

Critical reaction to *Middlemarch* came in several waves and different registers, from Henry James's concern about where it stood in the development of the English novel, to Oscar Browning's unlikely boast that he was the model for Lydgate. The leading papers and periodicals loved it, with the *Telegraph* declaring that it was 'almost profane to speak of ordinary novels in the same breath with George Eliot's'.[87] Edith Simcox, who was to become the last and most intense of George Eliot's women fans, pointed out in her review in the *Academy* that what made *Middlemarch* so different was the way it drew its drama from the inner psychological life of its characters.[88]

Marian and Lewes, as usual, played that odd game in which he filtered through to her a few of the best reviews, while she pretended not to be bothered about them at all. She was disappointed with the little she read, believing that no critic had offered her 'the word which is the refle[ction] of one's own aim and delight in writing'.[89] Private readers, however, fell over themselves to supply this lack. Even Harriet Martineau, who always did her best to think of something nasty to say about the Leweses, had to admit that 'The Casaubons set me dreaming all night', although she added pointedly to her correspondent, 'Do you ever hear *anything* of Lewes and Miss Evans?' Emily Dickinson, part of that New England circle which had claimed Eliot as spiritually one of its own, said, 'What do I think of *Middlemarch*? What do I think of glory?' while Barbara Bodichon thought it 'a beautiful book', though unbearably sad.[90]

There were, as usual, the oddly determined people who loved to point out little mistakes. The good thing about serialisation was that, if the complaint arrived in time, Marian could try to accommodate it in the next instalment. This happened over an inevitable querying of the legal procedure by which Featherstone tries to revive his first will by destroying the second. Other mistakes had to wait until the revised one-volume edition which came out in 1874. These included the exact appearance of Lydgate's eyes during his brief experience with opium and the Finale's assertion that society had smiled on Dorothea's engagement to Casaubon, when in fact it had done no such thing.

It was this 1874 edition which made Marian her fortune. Sales of each of the eight instalments had been a little disappointing, around 5000 copies instead of the 8000 Lewes had hoped for. The lending libraries of Mudie and W. H. Smith were obliged to take between 1000 and 1500 copies of each part. The four-volume edition of 1873 accounted for another 3000 copies, but it was the one-volume edition which followed in 1874 which really took off. By 1879 nearly 30,000 copies of the book had been sold world-wide, bringing Marian a profit of about £9000.[91]

Some of the most intense excitement generated by *Middlemarch* concerned that intriguing issue of real-life models. People queued up either to claim that they were the original Lydgate, or to point to someone who they felt sure was the model for Casaubon (no one, unsurprisingly, nominated himself for this honour). Robert Chambers, a fussy bachelor from the *Westminster Review* days who had made the mistake of marrying at the age of forty-eight, was one candidate for the ageing scholar. The futile, flapping Dr Brabant, whose much-vaunted preliminary work on the Strauss translation turned out to be nothing more than a few notes, was the theory put forward by Eliza Lynn. This would certainly tie in with the young Mary Ann's desire to dedicate herself to helping him in his work. But the most talked-about option was Mark Pattison, Rector of Lincoln College, who had married the much younger Emilia Strong when he was middle-aged. The fact that in the early 1870s Pattison was working on a *Life of Isaac Casaubon*, the French scholar, seemed to fit, as did the fact that the marriage was obviously ill-fated. However, both the Pattisons continued to be cheerful friends of Eliot, talking unselfconsciously about the Rector's book on Casaubon, which suggests that they, at least, could not see the similarities.

Where once upon a time the sport of matching real people to characters in her books appalled Marian, these days she was able to take it lightly. This was partly the freedom of a clear conscience since, unlike with *Adam Bede* and *Scenes*, she had no buried half-awareness of her guilt as a plagiarist. What she had said in those early days was now actually true – her characters were creations of her own imagining. So when Harriet Beecher Stowe wrote and asked her if Dorothea's marriage was based on her relationship with Lewes, Marian replied, 'Impossible to conceive of any creature less like Mr Casaubon than my warm, enthusiastic husband,' before admitting that 'I fear that the Casaubon-tints are not quite foreign to my own mental complexion'.[92] In truth, she knew all about the clamourings of what she had earlier described to Maria Congreve as 'a fastidious yet hungry ambition', which had condemned her until the age of nearly forty to an endless loop of journalism, translation and editing.[93] No surprise that when on another occasion someone asked her from what source she had drawn Casaubon, she pointed silently to her own heart.[94]

But Lewes would have none of it. He told Blackwood that if Marian was like anyone, it was Dorothea. By this he presumably meant that she too had learned to bring her ardent nature in line with petty circumstance, to concentrate on the small good instead of the great deed. But perhaps what he also half recognised is that there is a kind of ambitious fantasy here too. Dorothea Brooke was the strikingly beautiful daughter of a gentleman, in possession of an independent fortune of £700 a year and the inheritor of a country estate. Marian Evans Lewes was the notoriously plain daughter of a land agent, who had ninety pounds a year and no other assets. While it is often remarked that George Eliot would not allow Dorothea the social freedoms she claimed for herself, it is less frequently noticed that by identifying with Dorothea she created just that fantasy of social advancement which she had always been so quick to condemn in others.

CHAPTER 14

'Full of the World'

Daniel Deronda
1873–6

WITH DICKENS AND Thackeray gone and Trollope past his peak, George Eliot was now the country's greatest living novelist. Even in their prime none of this august trio had inspired feelings as intense, personal and reverential as the ones that surged towards the Priory now. Flowers were left anonymously at the door. Adoring fan mail arrived daily. When Marian ventured out strangers pressed forward, wanting to pat, touch and kiss their idol's hand. On one occasion, at the theatre, a young woman helped Marian on with her cloak before embracing her. When Marian inquired politely, 'Forgive me, but I do not recollect you,' the girl replied, 'Oh! it is good of you to let me. If you speak to me I shall cry.'[1]

It was because George Eliot wrote with such intensity about interior life that people felt they knew her or, more accurately, that she knew them. One of the compliments most commonly paid to her was that the reader felt as if she must have had access to his or her innermost emotions. Her characters grappled with the problems that beset thoughtful Victorians, especially how to balance the rights of the individual with the needs of others, and her wise narrative voice seemed to offer at least partial answers. From all over the world came letters bearing testimony to the way in which she had helped people lead moral lives. Feckless young men swore they had given up their foolish ways and wives said they had tried to love their husbands better. Although publicly Marian stressed that she was no teacher, religious or otherwise, she did little to stop others seeing her that way. For thousands of readers her words had become knitted into the fabric of their daily lives. One man was so panicked when he dreamed that George Eliot was seriously ill that he wrote to Lewes begging him to return the pre-addressed card on which was written 'DREAM WRONG'.[2]

Lewes lapped it up. He was calling Polly 'Madonna' all the time now and asking the Crosses to accept 'fervent blessings' from 'this Religious House' in a way which she would surely have found offensive had she known.[3] He loved the fact that members of Europe's numerous royal clans were pressing for introductions, although he was always careful to pretend not to care. In July 1875 Lady Airlie, one of the Stanley sisters, invited Marian and Lewes to a garden party. Lewes went alone and found himself whisked away to meet the Queen of Holland. In a letter to Mary Cross, Lewes gives a mocking account of what happened next, describing how the plain old lady barked *non sequiturs* while he tried to make his escape.[4] A year later, in May 1876, the indefatigable people-collector, Lord Houghton, invited Marian and Lewes to meet the rapturous King of the Belgians. When Marian refused to go because she needed all her strength to tackle the last few pages of *Daniel Deronda*, Houghton sulked, while King Leopold made the best of it by asking to meet Lewes. Lewes later reported grandly to William Blackwood that he had found the young king 'amiable and uninteresting' and 'was glad enough to be released and give place to others who were so eager to bask in the royal smile'.[5]

The British royal family were equally intrigued by George Eliot. Queen Victoria had made a point of letting her know, via her Clerk to the Privy Council Arthur Helps, how much she enjoyed her books. When Helps's daughter Alice showed the Queen the condolence letter she had received from the Leweses on the death of her father, the Queen asked if she might tear off the double autograph to keep.[6] One of the royal daughters, Princess Louise, was so intrigued by the sight of Marian among the audience at a concert in March 1877, that she drew a profile of her massive head on the back of the programme.[7] A few months later the Princess asked the banker and Liberal politician Goschen to make sure the Leweses were invited to a dinner she was scheduled to attend. The moment the Princess arrived she broke with protocol by asking to be introduced to Marian, whom she proceeded to engage in long and earnest talk.[8]

There were less exalted people who were also thinking about Marian. In April 1874 the Priory had received a visit from Isaac Evans's eldest daughter. Now married – to a Birmingham clergyman – Edith Griffiths presumably felt sufficiently sure of herself to defy her father's ban on communication with her wayward aunt, just as her cousin Emily Clarke had always done. A couple of weeks after the meeting Edith thoughtfully sent her Aunt Pollie some photographs of Griff House, where her father still lived.[9]

Mary Cash, née Sibree, had also re-established contact and now kept Marian informed of Coventry news by letter. As Marian became increasingly aware of her own frailty, and that of her Warwickshire contemporaries, she began to think kindly about the people towards whom she had nourished grudges down the years. When John Sibree senior died, Marian wrote to Mary saying kind things about a man to whom she had been exceedingly catty when she had last seen him in Geneva in 1849. Through Cara Bray she sent her love to Mrs Pears, the neighbour who had done so much to help her during the difficult holy war and towards whom she had afterwards become cool.[10] In June 1873 the news about the long senility and death of Rebecca Franklin, the Coventry schoolmistress whose learning and refinement had once seemed like a benchmark of civilisation, made Marian mindful of long-standing obligations.[11] The following summer she sent Cara to track down Maria Lewis, her old teacher and correspondent, to whom she sent the first of several much-needed gifts of ten pounds.[12]

But not all contacts with the past were so eagerly sought or met. In September 1874 Marian received a letter from Robert Evans junior suggesting that the elderly Fanny Houghton might now be prepared for a meeting with her half-sister. Marian wrote back saying that it was 'too late' for a rapprochement since 'some (perhaps eight or ten) years ago, she spoke of me with dislike and unkindness'.[13] How much Fanny knew about her nephew's overtures and Marian's rejection of them is not entirely clear, but she certainly stayed bitter to the end. When Marian died in 1880 Fanny wrote Isaac an angry letter, returning yet again to the scandal which their sister's domestic arrangements had brought the family. There was no shred of doubt in Fanny's mind that George Henry Lewes had 'spoiled' Marian's life.[14]

Perhaps Marian was still waiting for that letter which never came, the one from Isaac asking for forgiveness, a meeting, anything. Relations between brothers and sisters, always a precious subject, now flooded her thoughts. In the summer of 1874 she rushed to comfort her on-off American correspondent, Harriet Beecher Stowe, when the latter's clergyman brother was publicly accused of adultery. Mrs Stowe was already strongly associated in Marian's mind with the tangled business of erotic relations between siblings, since in 1869 she had published a notorious essay in the *Atlantic*, in which she dragged up the old allegation of Lord Byron's incest with his half-sister. Marian maintained that she cared little about the rights and wrongs of the case, but deeply disliked the fact that such an unpleasant subject should have been given another public airing. One critic has suggested that this is why Marian did not publish her 'Brother and Sister' sonnets immediately they were written in 1869: she was aware of their ambiguity in the light of the reheated Byron scandal. Whether or not this is exactly true, Marian had clearly made the connection, because in the 1873 letter in which she told Blackwood about the existence of the sonnets, she immediately weighed in with 'And I was proportionately enraged about that execrable discussion raised in relation to Byron', setting out instead her own vision of the brother–sister bond: 'life might be so enriched if that relation were made the most of, as one of the highest forms of friendship'.[15]

This was not the only brother-and-sister drama engaging her now. Harriet Martineau's autobiography, written in the early 1860s, was finally published in the year following her death in 1876. Marian was appalled by the way in which Harriet had taken this chance to settle scores with her brother James who, she maintained, had always been eaten by envy of her success. It is true that James Martineau's public humiliation of his sister in 1851 via a cutting book review had been spiteful. But Marian was repelled by Harriet Martineau's 'ignoble desire to perpetuate personal animosities', by laying them out in print. In a confused and emotional letter written on 15 May 1877 in which Marian moves from Harriet Martineau to Harriet Beecher Stowe and back again, she maintains, 'To write a cruel letter in a rage is very pardonable ... But I have no pity to spare for the rancour that corrects its proofs and revises and lays it by, chuckling with the sense of its future publicity.'[16] No matter how hurt she was by her own brother's cruel behaviour, 'the root of piety' demanded that Marian Lewes would never speak publicly about Isaac Evans.[17]

If real blood relatives continued to disappoint, make-believe ones were behaving better than ever. The Leweses continued to grow close to the Cross family, often spending Christmases at their Weybridge home. Johnny Cross was a particular favourite and by now they were both calling the tall, bearded young man 'nephew'. After a successful stint working as a banker in New York, Cross was doing equally well in London and had taken over the management of the Leweses' business affairs. Marian's feelings for Johnny were fed, in a way which Lewes's probably were not, by her continued idealisation of friendships between older and younger people. She also grasped the erotic current which might be at play when the situation involved a man and a woman. On hearing that Thackeray's daughter Anne was to be married to a man seventeen years younger than herself, Marian wrote to Barbara Bodichon with an odd precognisance, 'This is one of several instances that I have known of lately, showing that young men with even brilliant advantages will often choose as their life's companion a woman whose attractions are wholly of the spiritual order.'[18] All the same, she could not help sometimes being shocked by Cross's puppyish ignorance. Despite having received a gentleman's education at Rugby, he seemed to be labouring under the impression that Jesus Christ spoke Greek.

Luckily lapses like these did not affect Cross's ability to make money for the Leweses. He invested their capital wisely and well, concentrating on the emerging American markets, which he knew at first hand. It was thanks to him that over half of Marian's 1873 income – £5000 in all – was made up of interest payments. The Leweses were now financially secure for the rest of their lives and they celebrated with another surge of spending. Marian started investing in expensive clothes, depending on her team of 'spiritual daughters' for advice about the latest fashions. Where once upon a time she had worn whatever came to hand, now she started to worry about what kind of dress would be suitable for a morning visit at Oxford or Cambridge. Emilia Pattison and Jane Senior took her round the shops and guided her towards the best fabric and design, while Lady Castletown and Alice Helps helped her choose furs – a subject with which both the Leweses were obsessed, perhaps because they felt the cold. It was now that Marian adopted a lace mantilla as her signature indoor wear.[19] Yet there remained something incongruous about her excursions into high fashion, as the writer Edmund Gosse noticed on the several occasions he passed her in the street around 1876. He was struck by the contrast between her 'massive features, somewhat grim' and the flouncy hat 'always in the height of the Paris fashion', which framed them. 'The contrast between the solemnity of the face and the frivolity of the headgear', said Gosse, 'had something pathetic and provincial about it.'[20]

More magnificent than any fancy headgear was the splendid carriage in which Gosse often glimpsed Marian and Lewes as they trotted slowly homewards to north-west London. After consulting with Johnny Cross, they had finally invested in a custom-made landau by Morgan, the equivalent of buying their first Rolls-Royce.[21]

Despite the earnestness with which she pursued high style, Marian knew she did not look right. To the many correspondents, famous or otherwise, who sent their photographs to the Priory and demanded one in return, she always said that she had never had her picture taken. In 1859 she made the Brays promise to remove her portrait from their dining-room, well away from prying eyes.[22] Unlike every other famous or half-famous writer, she did not allow photographs of herself to slip into circulation, which explains why Fanny Houghton was unable to find one when she went looking in the Leamington bookshop in 1866. In fact, there had been a photograph taken in 1858, but Marian did not like it, with good reason: the conventionally coy pose made her features look even heavier than usual.[23] That it was self-consciousness about her looks which stopped her submitting to the camera is suggested by her warning to Elma Stuart just before they met face to face in September 1873 that she looked nothing like the Burton portrait of 1865. Instead, Elma should prepare herself for 'a first cousin of the old Dante's – rather smoke-dried – a face with lines in it that seem a map of sorrows'.[24]

Sadly, not all the money that Johnny Cross made for Marian was available for new hats and fancy carriages. At the end of July the news came from Natal that Bertie had followed his brother Thornie into tubercular decline and an early grave. He died on 29 June, aged twenty-nine, leaving behind two children, a little Marian and one-month old George, as well as their mother Eliza. Big Marian would now be responsible for their support, as well as the continuing burden of the rest of the Lewes clan. Even though Thornton Hunt's death in 1873 had left Agnes Lewes slightly more secure, she still received a regular income from the Priory. In addition there were occasional money gifts for her children by Hunt, including £101 3s in 1875 for Edmund, which may have gone towards setting him up as a dentist.[25]

Another charitable cause close to home was the Brays. By now their financial situation was dire. Marian pressed Cara to accept a series of payments of fifty pounds or so as private advances for various children's books she planned to write. Well aware that this was charity by another name, Cara had to be bullied into cashing any of the cheques. Charles Bray, once so robust, was now wheezing into old age, as annoying as ever. Naturally he misunderstood the thrust of Lewes's thesis in the second volume of *Problems of Life and Mind* and was not backward in saying so. Just like his despised sister-in-law Sara Hennell, Bray continued to publish diffuse and lengthy philosophic works, which managed to miss the point: *Illusion and Delusion* (1873) baffled everyone.[26]

While Marian was generous towards those she considered her own, it has often been hinted that she was mean towards everyone else. This is not fair. Like her father, she kept track of money, once writing a note to Barbara Bodichon to remind her that she had forgotten to repay a shilling borrowed from one of the Priory servants. She was quick to support anyone whom she felt was kith and kin, but suspicious of claims from people she did not know and whose motives she did not exactly understand. For this reason Marian remained conspicuously aloof from her friend Jane Senior's work in educating pauper girls. Admiring her energy and commitment, she none the less believed that: 'Do what one will with a pauper system it remains a huge system of vitiation, introducing the principle of communistic provision instead of provision through individual, personal responsibility and activity.'[27] In the same way, while Marian was notoriously cautious about giving money to charitable causes such as Mrs Garrett Anderson's Hospital for Women, she was happy to donate £200 towards raising an annuity for Octavia Hill, so that she might give up teaching and concentrate on her work in housing the poor. The difference here was that while Marian had only met Mrs Anderson once, Miss Hill and her work were well known to the Leweses through her sister, Charlie's wife Gertrude.

This way of thinking determined the Leweses' contributions to charity giving in these last years of their life. There were tiny donations – sometimes for as little as five pounds – to causes like the Positivists or the Working Women's College, but generous and continued support for family members such as Emily Clarke, who was battling with deafness while continuing to work as a governess in Brighton. On one occasion Marian wrote explaining to Barbara that she could not send the £100 needed for new rooms at Girton because she had just heard that she would now be responsible for Bertie's widow and children.[28] Here was a perfect illustration of George Eliot's meliorist philosophy in action: unobtrusive good done to those close at hand was more valuable than heroic efforts in the name of an abstract cause.

Priory life was not much disrupted by Bertie's death. The event itself, and the life which preceded it, quickly took on an air of unreality. Lewes did not bother to announce the passing in the paper, or even tell his friends about it. Marian first mentioned the fact to Blackwood nearly eighteen months later, explaining that Lewes had not said anything at the time because he 'dreaded letters of condolence'.[29] To a few of her own friends, though, she indulged in a little *post hoc* romanticising about the boy whom she had not seen for nearly ten years. Bertie, she explains to correspondents, had been 'not clever, but diligent and well-judging about the things of daily life' while his marriage to Eliza was 'peculiarly united', their 'being all in all to each other'.[30] In death, Marian had made the most unpromising of her stepsons into someone of whom she finally found it possible to approve.

Spiritual daughters were altogether easier to love. By 1873 Elma Stuart's tentative early correspondence had turned into a fulsome flood. She wrote all the time from Dinan now, gradually weaving herself into Lewes family life. Apart from the stream of hand-crafted gifts to Marian, she sent toys to Charlie's and Gertrude's girls, as well as enclosing photographs of her son Roland and her two adored dogs, to stand on the Priory sideboard. She finally got to meet her idol when she came to lunch at Blackbrook, the house in Kent where the Leweses spent the autumn of 1873. The interview went well, with Marian writing to Elma the very next day, 'I love you the better for having seen you in the flesh' and enclosing a lock of hair, while Lewes reassured her, 'you left behind you a very sweet and lovable image'.[31]

Elma's largely epistolary romance with Marian, and with her proxy Lewes, was a tender, intimate one. It did not, like the letters from Mrs Frederick Ponsonby, cover the great issues of belief and unbelief, but concerned itself more often with the question of underwear. Elma was tireless in her search for the perfect pair of drawers and often wrote to both the Leweses with her suggestions, to which they were happy to respond. She also corralled her only child, Roland, into this imaginary family life, getting him to send headache-soothing eau de cologne to his 'honorary grandmother'. Although an educated, intelligent woman, Elma was less a disciple than the attentive daughter whom Marian never had.

But there was someone whose feelings for George Eliot exceeded even Elma's steady devotion. Edith Simcox, a tiny, clever twenty-eight-year-old, had first visited the Priory late in 1872. Although she came on the strength of reviewing *Middlemarch* for the *Academy*, literature was only one of her many interests. Combining a first-rate mind with a strong, reforming zeal, she crammed a dizzying amount into her days. Not only did she produce a stream of articles and three books on everything from folklore to suffrage, she also set up a shirt-making business in Soho, which guaranteed its female employees reasonable working conditions and good wages. A committed trade unionist, she represented the movement abroad and was elected, too, to the London School Board, which oversaw the provision of compulsory elementary schooling following the 1870 Education Act.[32]

Tramping round London in all weathers, the bird-like Edith often called in at the Priory on her way to somewhere else. With Elma in France, Emilia in Oxford and Alexander Main in Aberdeen, Lewes was on the look-out for a morale-boosting fan who might be wheeled in whenever Polly's spirits were low. Edith fitted the bill exactly. There could be no doubting her devotion, which was suffused with both sexual and religious ardour. Marian was 'the Madonna' in all seriousness now, a female Deity who was to be worshipped with a full range of hem-kissing and feet-hugging. At night, home alone, Edith poured out her devotion to her journal, the only surviving record of this one-sided love affair: 'Day by day let me begin and end by looking to Her for guidance and rebuke, ... every night what has been done ill or left undone shall be confessed on my knees to my Darling and my God.'[33]

While Lewes thought Edith's ardour was funny, Marian could find it off-putting. Sometimes she shuffled her legs round, to get them out of feet-kissing range. When Edith gave her a copy of her book, *Natural Law*, inscribed 'with idolatrous love', Marian maintained a pointed silence.[34] Edith, arriving unasked at the door of the Leweses' 1875 summer hideaway in Rickmansworth, was greeted with cold astonishment.

All this only inflamed Edith's passion, which continued to feed morbidly upon itself. As long as Lewes was there to act as a buffer Marian was able to tolerate and even draw strength from Edith's engagement with her work, which was as thoughtful as it was passionate. But in 1878, with Lewes gone, Marian became edgy about the implications of what was clearly a sexual crush. On Boxing Day 1879 Edith arrived at the Priory to find Marian cool and distracted.

Unwilling to return her kiss, Marian then asked her to give up calling her 'Mother' since 'her feeling for me was *not* at all of a mother's'.[35] A couple of months later Marian went further. After an intense afternoon during which the conversation touched on Edith's reluctance to marry, Marian emphasised to her young admirer that 'the love of men and women for each other must always be more and better than any other'. Edith responded with anguished strokes and pats, whereupon Marian told her sharply that 'she had never all her life cared very much for women'. This was then hastily qualified by the statement that while 'she cared for the womanly ideal, sympathised with women and liked them to come to her in their troubles . . . the friendship and intimacy of men was more to her'. Naturally this only stirred Edith's passion further. Before she left the Priory that afternoon, 'I asked her to kiss me – let a trembling lover tell of the intense consciousness of the first deliberate touch of the dear one's lips. I returned the kiss to the lips that gave it and started to go – she waved me farewell.'[36]

Whether there was competition between George Eliot's spiritual daughters for her love and attention is hard to say. Edith certainly kept a weather-eye out for who had received most letters from Madonna. However, she was happy to co-operate with Elma over the design and making-up of shirts for both the Leweses. And by the time Marian was dead Edith and Maria Congreve seem to have gained strength from meeting and becoming friends, happy to fill the void by sharing memories. Any feelings of jealousy were offset by the relief of discovering that there were other women who, in Edith's words, had 'loved my Darling lover-wise too'.[37]

After years of constant but vague ill-health, it now seemed as if there might actually be something wrong with Lewes and Marian. The fact that three out of four of the Lewes boys had died before reaching thirty, while Agnes's second family by Hunt continued to flourish, suggests that Lewes's system was inherently weak. Scurrilous rumours put this down to venereal disease, picked up in early life. But the fact that both Lewes's brothers had died young points to a family pathology which had a more respectable, or at least more enduring, origin.

From 1875 Lewes was never well. The problem for us is knowing why. He was often diagnosed as having 'a relaxed mucous membrane', which means little in the late twentieth century. Sometimes the severest of his symptoms turned out to have the most innocent causes: shooting pains and deafness were on one occasion relieved simply by having his ear wax cleaned out. But underlying the constant headaches, dizzy turns and nausea there was clearly something seriously wrong. On 14 December 1875, for instance, he recorded a frightening incident in which 'After dinner while dozing in my chair [I] felt a strange pressure inside the ears accompanied by inability to move or speak. Thought paralysis had come on or Death. But it passed away, leaving only a sense of Indigestion behind.'[38] There were other, more humiliating, infirmities. For several weeks in 1877 the usually nimble man was reduced to shuffling along on two sticks as a result of a bad attack of 'rheumatic gout'.[39]

Marian was not well either. Writing *Daniel Deronda* brought the inevitable headachy depression – 'I had hardly a day of good health while it was in progress', although she had the insight to admit to Elma that this might be caused less by 'bodily feebleness' than 'mental anxiety'.[40] But by the summer of 1876 she was passing blood in her urine, a symptom of the kidney disease which had killed her father and was to kill her. The following February she was diagnosed as having a stone, following a terrifying incident which Lewes recorded in his journal for 23 February. He had been about to take an after-dinner nap, when: 'I was alarmed by [Polly's] . . . violent screams in the drawing room and rushing in found her hysterically screaming and sobbing – *not* from pain but strange and excessive irritation in the kidneys.'[41]

Marian's other recurring problem was her mouth. Her teeth had never been good and they got worse as she grew older. Throughout the seventies she had several removed, latterly under gas, and tried to calm her gums by rubbing them with a lotion supplied by Elma. Both Marian's and Lewes's correspondence with Dinan now concentrated on ill-health, theirs and hers. Elma, in turn, sent a stream of gadgets and potions designed to ease their discomfort, from a writing board to help the strain on Marian's back to a design for drawers intended to take the weight off her hips.

This growing ricketiness meant that travel was increasingly brief. The Leweses had long promised themselves a trip to the East when Mrs Willim died and there was even talk of going to America. But in the end they stayed put, hiring a series of houses in a ring around London, from Rickmansworth in the north to Redhill in the south. To modern ears these places sound an odd choice, suburban and dull. But in the 1870s they still passed as the country-side, albeit within a convenient hour's journey of London. There was enough green for Marian to ramble through in the afternoons and a train station nearby to whisk Lewes up to London for any unmissable parties. Most important of all, they were too far away for casual callers. The only people who found their way to this series of secluded country cottages were those who had been issued with an invitation.

That it took the Leweses so long to buy a country house of their own is testament to their fussiness as to what would and wouldn't do. They wanted a perfect little house with 'the cab-stand before and the desert behind', close to every amenity but far away from other people.[42] Friends recommended properties in Weybridge, Reigate, Dorking, Croydon, but none was quite right. Instead, the Leweses muddled through with a series of short-term lets which caused more bother than many would have thought worth it. Thus in June 1873 they signed a twelve-month lease on a house called Blackbrook near Bickley, Kent. Since it was let until September, they filled the intervening weeks with a tour of French and German spas. But when the time came to take possession on 5 September, Marian and Lewes found that the furniture, which they thought came with the house, actually belonged to the previous tenants. All that remained was a few broken bits and pieces.[43] They lasted seven weeks before breaking their contract, leaving on the last day of October.

The next summer they went south, this time to Redhill, Surrey. As was usual in those days, they took the whole Priory household with them, including the three servants and the carriage. During the morning writing hours Marian made progress on *Daniel Deronda*, while Lewes worked at the second volume of *Problems of Life and Mind*. In the afternoon they walked or drove through the surrounding countryside.

The following year, 1875, they went north to a house at Rickmansworth. While this may not sound very rural, the beautiful countryside around Denham and Harefield was easily accessible by carriage. But there was no avoiding the usual inconveniences that come from splitting one's life between two places. Returning home to the Priory on 23 September they found it in a dreadful mess. The decorating they had commissioned was not finished, there was a dreadful smell of paint and the gardener had stolen Lewes's cigars.[44] Leaving the servants behind to stand guard, they set off for two weeks in Wales.

It was not until the very end of 1876, after years of renting, that the Leweses finally found a permanent country home.[45] Or rather, John Cross found it. The Heights at Witley was not far from Mrs Cross's house at Weybridge, deep in the Surrey countryside, which had become so familiar to the Leweses from their visits over the last few years. It was made from the local red stone, covered in vines, and came attached to nine acres of land. The railway station, with its fast link to London, was only five minutes away.

Careful in so many things, the Leweses were strangely hasty when it came to property. Having paid £5000 for the Heights, they announced themselves disappointed to discover that the kitchen was poky and the plumbing bad. When their architect gave them an estimate of £640 for bringing the place up to scratch or £375 for making it barely adequate, they immediately considered selling. In the end they agreed to make the minimum changes and see how they managed during the coming summer. As it turned out, they did very well. Having moved into so many temporary new homes in the past few years, they were used to negotiating an unreliable water supply, infrequent grocery deliveries and not enough furniture. Within months they had decided that it was 'ravishing' and worked to accommodate themselves to its inconveniences.[46] Twice a week they got the fishmonger at Waterloo station to send down something for their dinner on the train.

The grand and the good who hung around the Priory were now replaced by more modest callers, like the local vicar. Those who made calls from further afield had been specifically invited. John Blackwood travelled down from town, the Frederic Harrisons came over from his family home near Guildford and Benjamin Jowett, now Master of Balliol, popped in several times during his stay with the Leweses' neighbours, the Hollands. Even Lewes, with his insatiable weakness for the rich and famous, enjoyed this new and discriminating way of living – 'so much better than Society! (with a big S),' he crowed to Cross.[47]

Most remarkable of all, the Leweses took up lawn tennis. Johnny Cross was a great fan of the game, had taken them to a match in London and now rigged up a net in the garden at the Heights. Once they'd learned the rules, the rickety sixty-year-olds ran around the court, sweating and laughing. Marian said she had not felt this well for years. Back at the Priory they tried to go on playing, but the garden was not big enough for a court. So Johnny Cross suggested badminton, which had the advantage that on windy days they could play in the drawing-room.

Although she would never take a big trip again, Marian still continued to feed from the new scenes and landscapes which came her way. Immediately after Marian corrected the proofs of Book Eight of *Middlemarch* the Leweses set out for Homburg, a fashionable German spa resort. They arrived on 21 September 1872 and proceeded to drink the waters and take the baths. Refreshed and rested, Marian wrote the Finale to *Middlemarch* and sent it off to Edinburgh.

This stay in Homburg is famous for the incident which inspired the powerful opening scene of Marian's next book, *Daniel Deronda*. In between sipping and splashing, trotting through pine forests and listening to music, the Leweses made several trips to the casino and found themselves unnerved by scenes of feverish play. In particular, Marian noticed a beautiful English girl, Byron's great-niece, hanging compulsively around the gaming table. Marian told Blackwood, 'It made me cry to see her young fresh face among the hags and brutally stupid men around her.'[48] It is this contrast which Daniel Deronda observes as he watches the cool and dazzling Gwendolen Harleth play the tables at Leubronn, surrounded by the puckered faces of casino *habitués*.

Staying at Homburg gave Marian the chance to absorb a new kind of speedy cash-culture which she had not encountered before. Buzzing around the casino and the concert hall, the hotel lounges and the elaborate carriages was a promiscuous mix of Irish aristocracy, German public men, English manufacturers and retired stage people. They were everything that virtuous characters from an Eliot novel should not be: rootless, restless, detached from 'the piety of memory' which would have kept them anchored to a stable set of values.

Homburg clearly fascinated Marian, for the next summer she returned to gather more material for *Daniel Deronda*. By this time her focus had shifted from the casino to the synagogue. She was researching the Jewish part of her story now and wanted to find locations where Daniel Deronda could excavate his family origins. In Frankfurt the Leweses made a point of staying until Friday evening so that they could attend the service at the synagogue, just like Deronda. In Mainz, too, they went to the service, where Lewes recorded that they were 'delighted with the singing'.[49]

As a young woman Marian had displayed the casual anti-semitism of her time and class, making the usual nasty remarks about Disraeli. Over time, though, her interest in the history of Christianity had gradually educated her about Judaism too. But the idea of Jewish nationalism – specifically the idea of a Jewish homeland – was something which she had encountered only recently, through her young friend and Hebrew teacher, Emanuel Deutsch. Impressed by his impassioned scholarship, Marian was carried along by Deutsch's ecstatic reaction to his first visit to Palestine in the spring of 1869. So it was sad to learn shortly afterwards that Deutsch had begun to suffer from the cancer that would kill him four years later. As he lay dying, Marian visited him several times in his lodgings and wrote to him – addressing him as 'My Dear Rabbi'

– urging him not to commit suicide: 'Remember,' she warned, 'it has happened to many to be glad they did not commit suicide, though they once ran for the final leap, or as Mary Wollstonecraft did, wetted their garments well in the rain hoping to sink better when they plunged.'[50] It was this cloak-wetting device which Marian was to give to the character of Mirah Lapidoth, who is rescued from her intended plunge into the Thames by the passing Daniel Deronda. News of Deutsch's death – during a second trip to the East – came in May 1873, just as Marian was planning her book in detail. Much of Deutsch's circumstances, especially his combination of learning, poverty and ill-health, found its way into the character of Mordecai.

Marian had supplemented Deutsch's informative talks with her usual detailed reading. 'In the mornings', she wrote to Emilia Pattison, 'my dwelling is among the tombs, farther back than the times of the Medici.'[51] Frederic Harrison was consulted about the legal implications of the plot and Leslie Stephen provided details about the Cambridge scholarship for which Deronda competes.

But there was another kind of research to be done. Marian had decided to set the English strand of the book in a part of the countryside unfamiliar to her, in that county which Thomas Hardy had recently designated 'Wessex'. In October 1874 she and Lewes set off for Salisbury to try to find exactly the right location for Offendene and Topping Abbey, the homes of Gwendolen Harleth and Sir Hugo Mallinger. The villages around the city failed to catch her imagination, so a few days later they made a second trip, this time to Wiltshire. A tour around the great country estates and a trip through Savernake Forest provided Marian with exactly what she was looking for and she returned home with a clear visual sense of the great estates of this affluent landscape, so different from the small manor farms of her native Warwickshire.

It did not follow that the writing came easily. Marian's despair with *Daniel Deronda* was as great as it had been with any of her other books. Indeed, this point of comparison became a comfort, for on Christmas Day 1875 she wrote in her journal, 'I see on looking back . . . that I really was in worse health and suffered equal depression about Romola – and so far as I have recorded, the same thing seems to be true of Middlemarch.'[52] She became obsessed with the idea that the world was over-flowing with pointless books to which she had no wish to add. She was still engaged with public events through her daily reading of *The Times*, and the idea of writing an unnecessary novel came to seem like a kind of sin. She spoke constantly of the need for writers to recognise when they had nothing more to say. Continuing to publish indiscriminately was, she maintained, 'like an eminent clergyman's spoiling his reputation by lapses and neutralizing all the good he did before'.[53] She told Clifford Allbutt that she relied on Lewes to tell her whenever her writing was not up to scratch and should be thrown away.[54] This is odd, because never once in twenty-five years did Lewes tell Marian that her work was anything other than brilliant. If he had said what he really felt on many occasions, she would never have written a word of fiction.

Even with Lewes's constant encouragement and Blackwood's background murmurings, the progress on *Daniel Deronda* was tortuous. When William Blackwood visited on 21 April 1875, he made the reasonable blunder of asking if he might take away the first part of the manuscript, and was shocked by Marian's response. He told his uncle, 'if you had seen her face of horror and fright and meek expression you would have been startled. It was one of the most striking scenes I have ever seen and for a minute or two she would not speak. She seemed just to tremble at the idea of the M.S. being taken from her as if it were her baby.'[55] Over the months that followed, both the Leweses became fixated with the physical safety of the new manuscript. Lewes was reluctant to trust it to the post and together they made the Blackwoods promise that it would be kept in a fire-proof safe in Edinburgh. These worries were not unreasonable in a time before carbon copies, photo-copiers or floppy discs. But the possibility of losing a manuscript had never struck them quite so acutely before. One explanation is that there was a part of Marian which did indeed believe that *Deronda* did not deserve to be published, that it was one of the many 'heap of books' which should never have seen the light of day.

There is a curious coda to all this. In 1878 Marian gave Alexander Main permission to publish *The George Eliot Birthday Book*.[56] This consisted of a diary illustrated by quotations from Eliot's work in which one entered the birthdays of friends and relatives. It was kitsch and crass and, unlike *Witty, Wise and Tender Sayings*, did not come at a time when Marian's spirits needed particular boosting. Given her horror of 'literary trash', it was an odd thing to do.

In March 1874 Marian broke off her preparatory reading for *Daniel Deronda*, which she had originally conceived as a play, to prepare a volume of collected poetry. Most of the pieces had been published previously in magazines but others, like the 'Brother and Sister' sonnets and 'O May I Join the Choir Invisible', now appeared in print for the first time. It went without saying that Blackwood would be the publisher, although this sort of ponderous material was not to his taste. Enclosed with the proofs he sent a note, entirely without irony, asking 'if you have any lighter pieces written before the sense of what a great author should do for mankind came so strongly upon you'.[57] But she did not, and *The Legend of Jubal, and Other Poems*, which appeared that May, was her one and only collection of verse.

Blackwood was also far from keen on Lewes's new work, *Problems of Life and Mind*. Back in January 1873 he had said that he had 'no hesitation in agreeing to publish the work' and waved away Lewes's uncharacteristically delicate doubts about whether its atheistic underpinnings would prove person-ally offensive to him.[58] But when Blackwood actually read the manuscript the following May he changed his mind. On the 24th he wrote to Lewes: 'I am sorry to say your book grates upon me more than I expected . . . I knew quite well that I should not agree with you but I did not expect that the difference between us would have been very wide.'[59] Fifteen years previously, when dealing with the vacillating publisher Bohn over Marian's translation of Spi-noza's *Ethics*, Lewes had flown into a rage. Now he knew better. Although irritated by the waste of time, he sent a polite note to Blackwood telling him not to worry and briskly arranged to have the book published by Trubner & Co.

This was an uncharacteristically jerky movement by Blackwood, who usually managed to avoid these kinds of scrapes. But he too was ageing and ailing, and his touch may have been deserting him. Still, he valiantly tried to play the part expected of him when it became clear in the spring of 1875 that Marian was jumpy about her new 'big book', *Daniel Deronda*. On 22 April he wrote to tell her gently: 'I have seen that depression on you before at periods when other authors would have been crowing and flapping their wings without the solid reason which I am sure you have for doing so.'[60] He then reminded her of that day years before when he took away the manuscript of *Adam Bede* and started reading it greedily on the way home to Edinburgh. By tactfully recalling a former triumph, Blackwood nudged Marian into giving him the first part of *Daniel Deronda* when he called for lunch on 18 May.

That very evening at half past eight Blackwood sat down and devoured the manuscript at one sitting, staying up until three o'clock in the morning. He loved what he read and dashed off a note to say so. Five days later he wrote a fuller response and, at Lewes's prompting, made it even more appreciative than usual. Gwendolen was 'a fascinating witch', Grandcourt 'a most original character', the Meyricks' domestic virtue delightful. All in all, said Blackwood, 'I beg to congratulate you on this most auspicious opening of another immortal work.'[61]

Despite being primed by Lewes, Blackwood was genuinely delighted with the first part of *Daniel Deronda* and probably believed he was speaking the truth when he told Marian on 10 November that she was 'fairly outdoing *Middlemarch*'.[62] The English country setting, the affable but lax clergyman, the minxy heroine, the hopeless boy, were all familiar ingredients. At first he was happy with the Jewish part too, probably assuming that the effect would be the same as with the Methodists in *Adam Bede* – a revelation of their common humanity. But as he read subsequent parts of the book and observed the narrative concentrating increasingly on Mordecai, Blackwood found it hard to see how ordinary readers would stay engaged. On 24 February 1876, having finished Book Six, Blackwood backed off from making any comment, maintaining that 'it would be presumptuous to speak until one has read more'.[63] Marian was quick to pick up on his ambivalence about the Jewish part of the book, having already anticipated that it would not be popular. Called to his senses, and with who-knows-what prompting, Blackwood wrote another letter on 2 March, ostensibly to Lewes, in which he sang his 'unbounded congratulations' to Mrs Lewes. 'She is *A Magician*. It is a Poem, a Drama, and a Grand Novel.' Touching specifically on her fears about the Jewish plot, he continued, 'There is no doubt about the marvellous Mordecai and oh that Cohen family! The whole tribe of Israel should fall down and worship her.'[64]

Although in truth Blackwood remained doubtful about the Jewish strand of the book, he set about doing the best he could for *Daniel Deronda*. It was decided to publish in eight monthly instalments, starting in February 1876.

The financial deal was the same as with *Middlemarch*: a two-shilling payment on every part sold. Blackwood was as careful as ever not to make any mention of the reviews in front of Marian, although for the first time ever he privately questioned just how consistent and useful this policy was: 'I think Lewes fidgets her in his anxiety both about her and her work and himself,' he confided in William. 'She says she never reads any review, but she certainly hears plentifully all that is said or written in London on the subject of Deronda.'[65]

Blackwood's consistently kind treatment of Marian continued to be tested by annoying twitches of bad behaviour. From time to time she would get picky about advertising, convinced that George Simpson was not doing enough to publicise her books. In early 1876 when Blackwoods was slow to send proofs of *Deronda* to the book's American publisher, the Leweses panicked that they were going to lose the contract (and the money) and snapped nastily at Blackwood himself.[66] Despite these pettish interludes, Marian remained at some level aware that she had been exceedingly lucky in falling in with what she called 'the best of publishers'. In October 1876 she was rereading some of Blackwood's old letters when she felt compelled to write and tell him how grateful she was for his nearly twenty years of support. Although her letter has been lost, the depth of Blackwood's response suggests that it was touchingly frank. He tells her that 'Tears came into my eyes, and I read the passage at once to my wife' and promises to keep her letter for his children 'as a memorial that their father was good for something in his day'.[67]

A week later Blackwood wrote again to say that the copyright on George Eliot's books was almost up and that he was anxious to renegotiate, 'as I am bent upon continuing your publisher as well as friend through life'. He then goes on: 'We have a long career of successive triumphs to look back upon and I hope there is much yet before us.'[68] Although his offer was generous – £4000 for another ten years – the Leweses decided to go for a royalty instead. It wasn't that £4000 was not enough, but they would rather carry the risk themselves, as well as retaining a say over editions and prices. It was, as Gordon Haight points out, a wise decision: the next edition of Eliot's work, the Cabinet Edition, brought £4330 in royalties over the following eight years.[69]

In the lost letter to Blackwood of October 1876, Marian had touched on her fear that after her death she would become the subject of gossipy biography. Obliquely she was telling him not to co-operate with anyone who came asking for access to their correspondence. Blackwood wrote back reassuring Marian that he considered the public's desire for this kind of information 'depraved' and, paraphrasing something which she had said repeatedly during the Liggins scandal, asked, 'why are great authors not to enjoy the privacy of common life?'[70]

It was an issue which had been worrying Marian as far back as 1861, when she told Sara Hennell, 'I have destroyed almost all my friends' letters to me, simply . . . because they were only intended for my eyes, and could only fall into the hands of persons who knew little of the writers, if I allowed them to remain till after my death.'[71] And only a month before that death, she was writing to Cara Bray, 'I think you are quite right to look over your old letters and papers and decide for yourself what should be burned. Burning is the most reverential destination one can give to relics which will not interest any one after we are gone. I hate the thought that what we have looked at with eyes full of living memory should be tossed about and made lumber of, or (if it be writing) read with hard curiosity.'[72]

Although Blackwood and the Hennell sisters proved staunch, Marian had reason to be worried. As her celebrity travelled around the world, there was growing opportunity for inaccuracies to get grafted on to her reputation. One American correspondent casually referred to her having sat at the feet of Herbert Spencer, while the biographical dictionary *Men of the Time* spun a fanciful line about her being born the daughter of a poor clergyman who was subsequently adopted by a rich one.[73] In other places a long-time myth about her being born into nonconformity was constantly rehashed. But if inaccuracy was annoying, revelation was mortifying. Marian had hated the third volume of John Forster's *Life of Dickens* because it revealed a loud, flashy character quite unlike the thoughtful dinner guest she had known.[74] In a frenzy of righteous anger, she asked Blackwood whether he did not think that it was 'odious that as soon as a man is dead his desk is raked, and every insignificant memorandum which he never meant for the public, is printed for the gossiping amusement of people too idle to re-read his books?'[75] As Marian moved towards her own death she worried about the versions of her life which might soon be released into general circulation.

Other people's autobiographies also brought a threat of exposure. Herbert Spencer had for some time been working away on his odd, self-justifying autobiography and made sure that Marian knew it was in progress. Would he be revealing the details of their one-sided love affair? In 1877 the example of Harriet Martineau's autobiography, which had nothing nice to say about anyone, had set a worrying precedent. Marian, for her part, had long made up her mind that she would not be adding to the genre. On her fifty-first birthday, Lewes had given her 'a Lock-up book for her Autobiog[raphy]'. It has never been found.[76]

Daniel Deronda is, in Henry James's famous comment, 'full of the world'. It has a geographical and social stretch unseen in any other George Eliot novel. Instead of the Casaubons' single epoch-making stay in Rome, the characters in *Daniel Deronda* whisk from Wessex to the Midlands to Germany to Genoa, pausing only for an occasionally tricky train connection. They plan trips to the East and take sailing holidays in the Mediterranean. The small-town merchants of *Middlemarch* have been replaced by second-generation business people whose large estates and ambitious marriages make them indistinguishable from the gentry. Sir James Chettam and Mr Brooke look like local squires compared with the grandees who own Wessex. Instead of sitting as a JP or worrying about a tenant's broken gates, a wealthy landowner like Henleigh Grandcourt flits around the Continent, occasionally coming to roost at one of his several magnificent homes.

Daniel Deronda is George Eliot's only novel to be set in the near-present, around 1875. There is no galloping coachman or historian-narrator taking us back to the England of the 1820s or beyond. This landscape is not caught in the moment of transition between the old agricultural ways and the new mechanised age. That process has already been completed, and life is self-consciously modern, fast and hard. Any change still to come is of an unambiguously bad kind. In February 1874 Marian Lewes had spoken of the contemporary 'eager scrambling after wealth and show' and in *Daniel Deronda* she shows this process at work.[77] An enervated ruling class, detached from its historic ties and duties, spends its days in pointless ritual and empty display. In the endless round of country balls and London dinners the main topic of conversation is money – who has it, might have it or could get it. Matches are plotted between heiresses and penniless aristocrats; fortunes are lost in the city and gained at the roulette table. In this febrile world, men profit from their neighbours' debts.

Henleigh Grandcourt stands at the exhausted heart of this busy world. Although he is wealthy, landed, heir to a baronetcy and perhaps one day to a peerage, his inner life has atrophied to the point where nothing can rouse him from a despairing cynicism. His pulse is slow, his blood cold, his skin drained of colour. Flooded with ennui, he can barely bother to acknowledge the people who stumble across his world. If a conversation bores him, he simply walks away. If his surroundings grow stale, he moves to another estate, city or country. His sole excitement comes from the slow breaking and taming of spirited creatures. Once women and men, but chiefly women, have submitted to his power, he feels only a spasm of pleasure at their broken-backed subjection.

When the book opens Grandcourt's chief victims are Lush, his secretary, and Lydia Glasher, his mistress. Fifteen years ago Lush gave up a college fellowship and the possibility of ordination in order to work for the young Henleigh Mallinger Grandcourt. The intervening time has been spent looking after Grandcourt's business interests, organising his social life and sorting out his women. Lush's 'departed learning' has been put to pragmatic use and his reward is a life of magnificent luxury, hovering on the edge of the best circles. But Grandcourt treats this 'half-caste among gentlemen' like one of the many pet dogs which swarm around him, alternately claiming Lush's attention before dismissing him with a well-aimed kick.[78]

The scenes between Grandcourt and Lush are heavy with a disgusted sexual attraction. It is Lush's job to pimp for Grandcourt, to manage his erotic life. He makes sure that Lydia Glasher, mistress and mother of Grandcourt's children, does not make trouble, and looks out for likely marriage prospects for his thirty-five-year-old master. Now that Grandcourt has taken up residence at Diplow, his Wessex estate, there is a new group of young women for Lush to trawl. One bridal candidate is Catherine Arrowpoint, the intelligent, straightforward heiress to a million-pound fortune. Wessex gossip has, in its mercenary way, speculated on a match between Miss Arrowpoint's promised cash and Mr Grandcourt's prospective land and title. However, after only a brief introduction to the local marriage pool, Grandcourt perversely decides that it is not Miss Arrowpoint but the beautiful, comparatively poor Gwendolen Harleth whom he will have as his wife.

In the character of Gwendolen, Eliot combines two strands of her writing about women. Gwendolen starts the book with all the heedless narcissism of Hetty Sorrel or Rosamond Vincy. While Hetty and Rosamond pat their hair in front of the mirror, Gwendolen literally kisses her own reflection. While Hetty has been transplanted from her own birthplace, Gwendolen has spent her youth rattling round the country, never spending long in any one place. Emotionally rootless, she is incapable of acting on anything beyond her own desire. She believes that her beauty, wit and refinement 'well equipped [her] for the mastery of life'.[79] Her four clumsy half-sisters flutter round, their governess scurries to do her errands and her mother lives in terror of her daughter's rage if she does not get her way. Gwendolen is 'the princess in exile', waiting for the world to shape itself according to her wish.[80]

All Gwendolen's dreams of love are actually about power. With no spontaneous interest in men or sex, she sees marriage as a kind of game in which she can gain the upper hand. She will 'manage' her husband, using his protection to carve herself an expanded circle of influence, gathering more admirers as she goes. Gwendolen pays little attention to the infatuated courtship of either her cousin or her uncle's curate, for neither can offer the enlarged court of which she dreams. Her eye is on the highest prize, the newly arrived bachelor, Henleigh Mallinger Grandcourt. Even before they meet she knows the outcome: 'He will declare himself my slave.'[81]

But in the end it is Gwendolen who is forced to submit to Grandcourt. A sudden change in family fortunes means that her glittering maidenhood is set to end in the ignominy of a position as governess in a bishop's family. Instead of facing that terrible duty, Gwendolen accepts Grandcourt's proposal of marriage despite knowing that there is another woman he has promised to marry, the mother of his illegitimate son. In becoming Grandcourt's wife, Gwendolen is able to secure financial independence for her mother and half-sisters, the first truly selfless act she has ever done.

But unlike Hetty or Rosamond, Gwendolen achieves moral growth. She follows Dorothea in moving beyond her own narcissism to learn about 'that unmanageable world which was independent of her wishes'.[82] As with Dorothea, her lessons come through the discipline of a dreadful marriage and the inspiring friendship of a man nearer her own age. Even before the wedding, Grandcourt's cold mastery begins to pinch. He takes particular pleasure in Gwendolen's humiliating knowledge that he already has a mistress and a family. Outwardly passive, he brings the full weight of his terrible will to bear, crushing her spirit while leaving her brilliant exterior intact.

Gwendolen is a magnificent creation, quite possibly the best character Eliot ever drew. Deepening and refining her portrayal of Esther Lyon in *Felix Holt*, another pretty, selfish girl who learns there is more to life than the admiration of others, Eliot shows the full range of a contradictory personality constantly in flux. Gwendolen is heartless, frightened and disengaged; but she is also capable of becoming loving, engaged and real. Although she fantasises constantly about Grandcourt dying, when the moment comes during a sailing accident she is racked with remorse. She longs to see him drown, yet is anguished by the thought that she could have done something to save him. Like Bulstrode in *Middlemarch*, she must constantly weigh up her culpability for a death that would pass in the wider world as an accident.

Gwendolen confesses her 'crime' to Daniel Deronda, the man whom she has made her saviour. The enigmatic young Englishman has been brought up as the ward of Sir Hugo Mallinger, the baronet from whom Grandcourt will inherit most of his land and his title. Handsome and good, Deronda takes it upon himself to disapprove of Gwendolen the moment he first sets eyes on her, gambling feverishly at the roulette table in a German casino. He is, in truth, as restless as she, unable to settle to any profession or course of action. As the story unfolds, the reason for this dilatoriness becomes clear: Deronda has been kept in ignorance of his Jewish parentage. In the terms of Eliot's moral world the consequences are clear: a man who does not know where he comes from is unable to lead a morally integrated life. It is only once Deronda discovers the truth about his birth that he can commit himself to love and to work. He marries the Jewess Mirah Lapidoth and sets off to found a Jewish homeland in Palestine.

While the character of Gwendolen Harleth is magnificently concrete, Deronda's remains unsatisfyingly vague. Like Will Ladislaw in *Middlemarch*, he is a man waiting to happen, whose life will begin only when the book has ended. Yet he has none of Ladislaw's charm or Lydgate's moral mix. Like that other prig Felix Holt, his flaws are of the kind that would be a virtue in anyone else: unflinching honesty and a need to put others first.

The other Jewish characters are even harder to like. Working against a prevailing anti-semitism, which labelled the entire race tricky and coarse, George Eliot created a couple of saints in Mirah Lapidoth and her brother Mordecai. Mirah is humble and good, loyal to a father who has treated her badly, sexually chaste despite a degrading upbringing. Mordecai is a scholar and a seer, a man whose whole life is devoted to the Jewish cause. Physically feeble and soon to die, he charges Daniel Deronda with the task of travelling to the Near East to found a Jewish homeland. Readers followed Blackwood in remaining unmoved by Deronda's attachment to this displaced couple and the gradual discovery of the truth about his birth. This strand of the novel had all the hallmarks of being, in Eliot's famous distinction, a diagram rather than a picture: abstract, didactic and dull. The 'English' chapters involving Grandcourt and Gwendolen were, by contrast, full of the vigorous oddness of real life.

Eliot's decision to put Judaism at the heart of a novel was a brave one, anticipated only by Disraeli back in the 1840s with the hugely sentimental *Coningsby*. She was motivated partly by the anti-semitism she saw all around her. 'Can anything be more disgusting', she asked Mrs Beecher Stowe, author of *Uncle Tom's Cabin*, 'than to hear people called "educated" making small jokes about eating ham, and showing themselves empty of any real knowledge as to the relation of their own social and religious life to the history of the people they think themselves witty in insulting?'[83] But she was also interested in the model which a new Jewish state might offer a degenerated Christian Britain. She is careful to make it clear that Mordecai and Deronda are not anticipating the fierce exclusiveness of Zionism, but look forward instead to a blend of 'separateness and communication'.[84] Only once it is secure in its location and national identity will the Jewish race be able to leave behind the unpalatable defences it has developed in scattered exile.

If British audiences were bored by the Jewish part of *Daniel Deronda*, Jewish readers were delighted with it. Rabbis, scholars, cultural leaders and politicians wrote to thank Eliot for a version of themselves that went far beyond the cringing shopkeeper or vulgar banker. Her vision of an independent Jewish nation was heady stuff: it would be another twenty years before Theodor Herzl set out the arguments clearly in his hugely influential *The Jewish State*.

The weaknesses in Eliot's vision have long been pointed out. Jewish history is as bloody and shameful as Christianity's. There is no reason to believe that a Jewish nation would run its affairs any better than Catholic Spain or Protestant Sweden. Eliot was herself famously agnostic, so it is hard to see why anyone should take her endorsement of the religiously committed life seriously. Finally, and most important, why can nothing be done to regenerate society from within? Are the Philistine British doomed to tear each other to pieces at the roulette table? Why has Eliot's long line of doctrinally lax but morally engaged clergy ended up in the worldly figure of Mr Gascoigne, a rector whose main concern is how to get his niece Gwendolen married off to a rich man whom he knows to be a libertine? Always before, Eliot has offered us a hopeful ending in which the small kindnesses of a Dorothea or a Dinah gently tip the scales towards the greater good. But while Gwendolen has made an internal moral shift, she ends the book barely able to hold her fragile psyche together. 'I shall live,' she tells her mother, 'I shall be better.'[85] But it will be a long time before she is fit to work for others.

Running alongside the idealisation of the Jew as a man of culture, faith and purpose is Eliot's equal veneration of the artist. Dedication to music, and especially singing, come to stand as a metaphor for all kinds of vocation. The centrepoint of this equation is Herr Klesmer, the professional musician who is currently in residence at Quetcham, the Arrowpoints' cultured and magnificent home. Based on Anton Rubinstein, whom the Leweses had met in Weimar in 1854 and later in London, Klesmer is both a Jew and a dedicated artist. Heedless of social rank and convention, he is an abrupt, aloof man who venerates only talent. It is for this reason – and not her fortune – that Klesmer falls in love and proposes to his pupil Catherine Arrowpoint. Equally committed to music, she accepts, much to the horror of her parents, who condemn Klesmer as 'a gypsy, a Jew, a mere bubble of the earth'.[86]

Catherine Arrowpoint's humble dedication to art, in her case the piano, is made to contrast with Gwendolen's shallow, exploitative approach. Indifferently taught and only amateurishly competent, Gwendolen fondly believes that she can support her family by becoming a professional singer. Appealing to Klesmer for advice, Gwendolen is shocked to hear that ladylike manners and a charming warble are not enough. He tells her sternly that she lacks both the talent and the 'inward vocation' to achieve anything 'more than mediocrity'. In desperation, she accepts Grandcourt's proposal of marriage.[87]

Mirah Lapidoth, by contrast, has the singer's true vocation. Trained from an early age, she has only to audition for Herr Klesmer for him to announce, 'Let us shake hands: you are a musician.'[88] Unlike Gwendolen, Mirah loathes the idea of scrutiny during public performance and would prefer to make her living either by teaching or giving drawing-room recitals in front of a few people she already knows. Her motive for singing professionally is to save herself from destitution and there is no question of her continuing after her marriage to Daniel. In this respect she ends the book like all Eliot's heroines, with her sphere of action much diminished. From now on her job will be to love Daniel and raise his children, while he dedicates himself to founding the Jewish state.

Should Mirah ever consider putting her vocation before her marriage, there is a terrible warning on hand in the shape of the book's third female singer, Daniel's mother. The Princess Halm-Eberstein summons the son she has not seen for twenty-five years to hear the story of her – and his – life. She reveals that as a young woman she was the renowned singer and actress Alcharisi: 'All the rest were poor beside me. Men followed me from one country to another.' Dedicated to her art, Alcharisi married her husband on condition that he would 'put no hindrance in the way of my being an artist'.[89] When a baby is born – Daniel – she gives the child away to one of her greatest admirers, Sir Hugo Mallinger, to be raised as an English gentleman. Free of all ties, she spends the next nine years living entirely for her art. It is only once her voice begins to fade that she seriously considers domestic duties. Rather than endure the humiliation of a dwindling career, she marries a Russian prince by whom she has five children. Now dying, she reveals to Daniel that he is fully Jewish.

Women are given difficult lives in *Daniel Deronda*. Reprising 'Armgart', Eliot explores the sacrifices a woman must make if she wishes to be an artist: 'you can never imagine what it is to have a man's force of genius in you,' Daniel's mother tells him fiercely, 'and yet to suffer the slavery of being a girl.'[90] When Lydia Glasher likewise gives up her husband and child – in this case to be with Grandcourt – she is condemned to a ghastly wilderness of waiting and wondering. 'I am a woman's life,' her pinched face and hard figure seem to say to a terrified Gwendolen.[91] Only Mirah, with her face turned towards a new beginning in the East, seems to have any kind of viable future.

As always, Marian wrote the final pages of her book in a frenzy of speed and tears. She would not even break for lunch when Blackwood and his son visited the Priory on 6 June. Emotions were running high, with both Marian and Lewes inclined to cry at the final interview between Gwendolen and Daniel, and the death of Mordecai. Two days later the book was finished and they set off for a recuperative trip to Switzerland. For the first few days both were sluggish and ill, but by the time they got to Ragatz they were having fun, with Marian trying to teach Lewes Hebrew.

They reached home on 1 September 1876, 'both the better for our journey,'

Marian told Blackwood, though accepting that no amount of nasty-tasting water and mountain air was going to make them young again.[92] Their illnesses were nagging all the time now and Marian was conscious of a pain in her side, which never went away. Five days after their return she wrote in sombre mood to Barbara Bodichon, 'Death is the only physician, the shadow of his valley the only journeying that will cure us of age and the gathering fatigue of years.'[93]

CHAPTER 15

'A Deep Sense of Change Within'

Death, Love, Death
1876–80

THE LEWESES SPARED no expense in fitting out the Heights, certain that this was the last home they would ever be called upon to furnish. Although Marian declared herself bored and fidgeted by the details, especially when they interfered with work on her new book, she enjoyed the game of creating the perfect country house environment. There was even going to be a billiard table, for any guests who found themselves at a loose end on a rainy day.

So it was a pity that Lewes was dying. His guts and bowels were in spasm all the time now. The only relief came at dawn, when he threw off the bed covers, woke Polly and set out for a ramble through the patch of woodland attached to the house. Visitors were shocked by how gaunt he looked, while London gossips who caught an occasional glimpse of him speculated about whether, this time, he was actually dying. The man himself was as jaunty as ever, joking and telling stories, and on one occasion singing his way through *The Barber of Seville* to the astonishment of a visiting Johnny Cross.[1] If all this pluck was for Marian's benefit it worked: the letters she wrote that summer of 1878 reported him as suffering from nothing more ominous than 'gout'. Domestic life went on almost as usual: literary neighbours and nuisances continued to call, and on one occasion Lewes found himself at Tennyson's house, trying to be kind about the Laureate's latest venture, a plodding drama on the life of Thomas à Becket.[2]

Beyond Witley it was another matter. The annual trip to Oxford during Whitsun had been spoiled by Lewes's poor health. Ordinary irritations like jostling tourists and vanishing luggage had become intolerable to the crampy invalid and his increasingly anxious partner. In July they accepted Blackwood's invitation to visit his estate in Scotland, then thought better of it. 'You do not realize my state,' Lewes explained to his disappointed host. 'If I could even read an amusing book for three hours I should consider myself strong enough to come. But I can't work at all, and can't read for more than an hour.'[3] In the end, the furthest the Leweses got that year was to Newmarket, where they spent a few days during October with the Bullock-Halls.

They were drawn there by Turgenev, an old friend and admirer, who was to be among the house party at Six Mile Bottom. Newer faces, no matter how talented, did not have the same power to break through their increasing self-absorption. On 1 November Henry James paid a dismal call to the Heights. Instead of the warm and admiring reception he was expecting – *The Europeans* was just out – he found two chilly, elderly people sunk in misery. Sitting in a 'queer, bleak way', one on each side of the fireplace, the Leweses barely greeted him, failed to offer tea and clearly could not wait for him to leave.[4]

On 11 November the Leweses left Witley for the last time to spend a week in Brighton. They saw Marian's niece Emily Clarke, treating her to dinner and a trip to the Aquarium. Emily had always adored Lewes and he, genuinely thoughtful, had recently provided her with an ear trumpet to help with her deafness. Despite breezy walks along the sea front, Lewes was in worse pain than ever, though in his journal he put it down to nothing more sinister than 'piles'. Back in London, Sir James Paget diagnosed that old and vague friend, 'a thickening of the mucous membrane'.

Despite increasing incapacity, it was business as usual at the Priory. Lewes intervened in a crisis over his nephew Vivian, whose proposal to a girl called Constance had been turned down by her father. Lewes sent an encouraging letter to the doubtful paterfamilias, which must have worked, for the couple married soon afterwards. Then, on 21 November, Lewes wrote to Blackwood, enclosing the manuscript of Marian's new book, *Impressions of Theophrastus Such*, sketching arrangements for its publication.[5]

After another week of excruciating pain, Lewes acknowledged that he was dying. On the 29th Johnny Cross was summoned for a final summit about Marian's investments and business affairs. As a parting gift Lewes handed the younger man his stock of prized cigars to pass on to Willie Cross, an enthusiastic smoker.

Marian also recognised that Lewes was on his way out. On 25 November she wrote to Blackwood asking him to postpone the publication of the new book. She had a horror of the public assuming that she had been busily working away on her manuscript all the while that Lewes was dying. Later that evening she wrote to Barbara Bodichon of her 'deep sense of change within, and of a permanently closer companionship with death'.[6]

On 30 November, just before six in the evening George Henry Lewes died. He was sixty-one. The certificate gave the cause as enteritis, but Paget told Charles that his father had been suffering from cancer, which 'would have carried him off within six months'.[7] Charles kept news of the death and the funeral quiet, perhaps at Marian's request. As a result only a dozen people turned up at Highgate Cemetery Chapel for the funeral on 4 December. Old friends – and there were many – were naturally upset to discover that they had been deprived of the chance to pay their last respects. The service, a kind of watered-down Anglican one, was conducted by Dr Sadler of the Rosslyn Hill Unitarian Chapel. The Harrisons and the Burne-Joneses were there. Herbert

Spencer broke the habit of a lifetime and attended. Marian did not go and nor, probably, did Agnes. The chief mourners were Charles Lewes and Johnny Cross. John Blackwood, heading for death himself, was represented by Joseph Langford.

Without George Henry Lewes there could have been no George Eliot. Lewes gave Eliot his Christian name, introduced him to a publisher and managed his career shrewdly over twenty years. He got the best financial and distribution deals for Eliot, yet never once put him under pressure to write for money. He understood *The Spanish Gypsy*, as well as *Adam Bede*, and delighted in them equally. In short, Lewes provided just that kind of committed, discriminating, selfless support which authors dream of.

But none of this would have counted for anything without the corresponding caretaking which Lewes performed in Marian Evans's private life. It was his encouragement which enabled her to make the break from poorly paid periodical journalism to highly profitable fiction writing. His deep understanding of her contradictory emotional needs allowed him to provide exactly what she required to continue working in the face of self-distrust and despair. Observing that his early comment on her lack of dramatic power unsettled her, Lewes was careful to keep all such further thoughts to himself. His doubts about *The Mill*, *Romola* and *The Spanish Gypsy* went straight into his journal, while he drip-fed Marian a diet of sunshiny approval. When that was not enough he chivied Blackwood into boosting the message with a stream of detailed and fulsome letters.

Lewes has been criticised for the way he kept Marian aloof from the professional and lay criticism which might have steered her away from the eccentric detours of her mid-career. Although he maintained that he never showed or told her anything, he was always careful to communicate any bits and pieces that he knew would keep her buoyant. A nice comment from a clever man or news of a peak in sales always found its way back to Marian. What detractors from this method missed was that if Lewes had ceased to wrap Marian in cotton wool she would have stopped writing completely. Without his mothering there would have been no *Spanish Gypsy*, but there would have been no *Middlemarch* either.

Lewes's professional life, away from Marian's, was something extraordinary. The early years of journalistic ducking and diving showed an intellectual range that few could equal. If some of his editors, Marian included, found him slipshod, this was because he was under pressure to publish and move on quickly. None the less, his best work from this period was to become hugely influential. His biography of Goethe remained the standard work for decades and his enthusiastic, fluent writings on science, especially *The Physiology of Common Life*, nudged hundreds of young men, including Pavlov, towards careers which would have been unthinkable a few decades earlier.

Once Lewes was relieved from the need to make money by Marian's growing wealth, he showed himself quite able to settle down and specialise. Even those who disliked him had to admit that by the 1860s he had become much more than a versatile hack. 'I have heard both Darwin and Sir Charles Lyell speak very highly of the thoroughness of his knowledge in their departments,' admitted Charles Norton through clenched teeth.[8] And those who liked Lewes found it easier to go further. According to William Bell Scott, the old intellectual sparring partner of his youth, Lewes was 'nearly the only man among all my friends who has never ceased to advance'.[9] The project he was working on when he died, *Problems of Life and Mind*, was to set out an agenda which shaped research in the physiological and psychological sciences for the first two decades of the next century.

It was this classic tale of the clever outsider who penetrates the Establishment that gave rise to rumours that Lewes was Jewish. These reached a climax with the publication of *Daniel Deronda*, which had American biographers making facile connections between the subject matter and the racial origins of George Eliot's partner. It was more than the fact that Lewes had not gone to university – practising Jews could not attend Oxford or Cambridge – that made people think this way. There was also the fact that in 1866 he had written a piece in the *Fortnightly* about his student days at the Philosophers Club in Red Lion Square, where he had learned about Spinoza from the watchmaker Cohn. And finally there was his dark, grubby appearance, which chimed with popular racial stereotypes. Far from improving with age, Lewes looked more unwholesome than ever. Catching sight of him in the street in the mid-seventies, Edmund Gosse described a 'hirsute, rugged, satyr-like' little man.[10] An enduring dandiness in the form of fancy waistcoats only added to the impression that he must surely be a cousin of Disraeli.

Then there was Lewes's behaviour, which continued to be the antithesis of the English gentleman's. Wealth and success had not left its usual polish. Right up to his death he was chatting away in French, noticing pretty girls and cracking *risqué* jokes. He seemed always, metaphorically, to be winking and poking you in the ribs. Observers found it odd and often resented that such a rake should be the partner of the earnest, moral George Eliot: Mrs Gaskell wondered how such a wholesome woman could be attracted to such a 'soiled' man.[11] But closer friends, Eliot's as well as Lewes's, understood that he provided the crucial airy counter-balance to her marshy gloom.

Lewes and Marian admired, as well as loved, one another. He honoured her genius without resenting it, while she saw that behind the flippant mask was a man of enormous personal integrity. Lewes's conduct as a family man was irreproachable. When the experiment in Shelleyan living broke down in the mess of Agnes's affair with Thornton Hunt, Lewes accepted his part in the whole unhappy business. He continued to support his wayward wife who, as the daughter of a landowning MP, might be expected to find resources of her own. He worked himself into chronic ill-health to provide not just for his own sons, but for the batch of children Hunt had sired on Agnes. And despite the latter's hopelessness with money, Lewes never went beyond the odd snappy comment, even helping her get her affairs in order when Hunt died having long since left her. In addition, Lewes kept a watching financial brief over his mother, and his brother's widow and son. As a father he was loving and involved, and his decision to send his three sons to school in Switzerland, well away from gossipy London, was a logical one, even if it also allowed him to concentrate on his new relationship with Marian.

These were the qualities which Marian turned over in her mind as she sank deep in mourning. For a week she kept to her room, poring over Tennyson's 'In Memoriam' and other verse of consolation. Meanwhile, hundreds of letters of condolence arrived at the Priory, to be intercepted and sifted by Charles. In his note of 5 December Herbert Spencer tried his best to get beyond his own self-involvement by assuring Marian, 'I grieve with you.'[12] Turgenev, writing from Paris two days earlier, said that he hoped that Marian would 'find in your own great mind the necessary fortitude to sustain such a loss! All your friends, all learned Europe mourn with you.'[13] Anthony Trollope wrote a touching obituary – one of many – in the *Fortnightly Review*.

What eventually got Marian out of her bedroom was her determination to finish the fourth volume of Lewes's *Problems of Life and Mind*. Although it was still at note stage, this was not the frozen pedantry of a 'Key to All Mythologies' waiting for the organisational skills of a widowed Dorothea. Lewes's intentions were advanced and reasonably clear, and Marian was familiar enough with the subject to be able to assemble and order the material. Despite offers of fact-checking from Lewes's old scientist friends, Marian was beset with the fear that she might misrepresent him in some way. Or worse still, that some textual error of hers might be ascribed to him. Although *Problems* I and II came together relatively quickly, *Problem* III proved to be trickier, and much of February was spent in headachy despair. In the end Marian decided to publish *Problem* I separately in May, under the title *The Study of Psychology*, with the rest of the work following a few months later.

Gratified by the way that so many of the tributes from academic and professional scientists had emphasised Lewes's influence on younger scholars, Marian resolved that the best way to perpetuate his name was to set up a scholarship. After taking soundings mainly from Cambridge men, she designated £5000 to fund the George Henry Lewes Studentship, designed to support a young physiologist at an early stage in his research career. The Studentship was to be held for three years at Cambridge and would provide the kind of access to first-class facilities of which the young Lewes, with his borrowed microscope, had only dreamed. The first appointee, chosen by trustees who included T. H. Huxley and Henry Sidgwick, went on to become a professor and over the decades some of the country's finest physiologists held the Studentship. With Barbara's nudging Marian opened the award to female candidates. However, it was not until after the Great War that the first woman was appointed to the George Henry Lewes Studentship.

If coming up with the idea of the Studentship had been a comfort and a kind of pleasure, getting hold of the £5000 to fund it was a painful business. All Marian's assets, cash as well as bricks and mortar, were in Lewes's name. To claim them back again she had to go through a complicated and humiliating two-stage process. Lewes's will of 1859 left the copyright of his work to his sons and everything else to 'Mary Ann Evans, Spinster', who was also the executrix. Beady-eyed Fanny Houghton spotted the will in the paper and was not impressed, first by the tiny amount which Lewes himself left – under £1000 – and then by the fact that the name of Evans was yet again publicly associated with that nasty man: 'his poor legacy was a farce,' Fanny wrote to Isaac on 28 January 1881, 'besides, her name ought not to have been mentioned. The sons should have been made executors.'[14] On 16 December 1878 Marian went to court to prove the will, an ordeal which even the usually snipy George Simpson thought she should have been spared.[15] But before she could get possession of her own property she had first to change her name by deed to Lewes. In January 1879, witnessed by Charles Lewes and John Cross, Marian legally took the surname she had been using since 1857, but this time combined it with her childhood Christian names. Thus by a long and strange detour she had become, at the age of fifty-eight, 'Mary Ann Evans Lewes'.

Restarting her personal life took longer. Marian hid away over Christmas and New Year, refusing to see any of the old friends who arrived at the Priory with tender enquiries and thoughtful gifts. She shrank even from the sight of Charles as he worked softly to acknowledge the hundreds of letters which were pouring in.[16] Luckily the young man had the sense and sensitivity to understand his stepmother's need for solitude. In a series of notes and conversations he begged her close friends to be patient and to let her 'choose her own way and her own time of struggling back to life'.[17]

Not until she had finished a complete second reading of the fourth volume of *Problems* on 5 January did Marian communicate with the outside world in the form of a letter to Barbara Bodichon. 'Dearest Barbara,' she said, 'I bless you for all your goodness to me, but I am a bruised creature and shrink even from the tenderest touch. As soon as I feel able to see anybody I will see *you*.'[18] A month later, and with the Priory pipes burst by the vicious cold, Marian wrote to Georgie Burne-Jones to say that 'my everlasting winter has set in. You know that, and will be patient with me.'[19] Johnny Cross was also told not to pester. He had taken Marian's comment of 22 January that she would see him 'some time' to mean that she would see him soon. On 30 January she wrote back telling him that she had meant a 'distant time'.[20] At the moment all her energy must be dedicated to finishing Lewes's work.

But only a week later there were signs that Marian was beginning to thaw. One day she ordered the carriage to be got ready for a drive along the Kilburn Road. Over the next few weeks she gradually ventured further, past the hideous suburbs to something approaching the countryside. There she stopped the carriage, got down and walked alone through the fields.[21]

On 7 February Marian wrote again to Cross telling him: 'In a week or two I think I shall want to see you. Sometimes even now I have a longing, but it is immediately counteracted by a fear.' That fear was the feeling that she might bore him with a 'grief that can never be healed'.[22] But Cross knew all about that terror too, for only nine days after Lewes's death he had lost his own beloved mother. It was this shared experience of loss which meant that on Sunday, 23 February, John Cross was the first person since Lewes's death to make a personal call on Marian. Even Herbert Spencer, who presented himself the same day, was turned away.[23] This was the breakthrough which Charles

Lewes had assured her friends would come. By the end of the following month Marian had seen Spencer, Georgie Burne-Jones and Elma Stuart.

Throughout the whole sad winter of 1878–9 Edith Simcox had been hovering in the wings. Her diary shows her making almost daily visits to the Priory, oblivious to the dreadful weather. She was not, of course, allowed to see Marian, but she became on increasingly good terms with the servants who clucked over her wet clothes and wondered at her devotion. In the closing days of Lewes's life she had sent little notes of enquiry up to the house, only to be told by Brett, the parlourmaid, that there was no change and little hope. On the last day, the 30th, Edith paced up and down in front of the gates. At one point she saw 'a carriage like a doctor's' draw up and two men get out. For twenty minutes she stood in a dream, struck by the way in which passers-by continued their ordinary lives while she waited, trembling, for the fateful news. When the doctors eventually reappeared she rushed towards them and asked if there was no hope. 'A tall man, probably Sir James Paget, answered kindly: "None: he is dying – dying quickly." '[24]

If Edith fantasised that grief would tear down Marian's defences and allow her to rush in and comfort her beloved, she was disappointed. Until the momentous 12 April when she was finally admitted to the Priory drawing-room, she had to make do with briefings on her beloved's progress from Gertrude Lewes in Hampstead and Eleanor Cross in Weybridge. The Priory servants were also useful sources of information, happy to let Edith hang around and pick up scraps of gossip. On one occasion she bumped into Johnny Cross doing the same thing and hoped that Brett would pass on to Marian news of 'our meeting as friends'.[25] Yet despite her over-identification with the Lewes household, Edith retained some of the good sense and brisk authority that belonged to her other, active life. When she heard that the Priory cook had been gossiping to the neighbours about Mrs Lewes's howls of grief, she hinted to Brett that it would be a good idea if everyone tried 'not to be too communicative' in future.[26]

Aside from working steadily on *Problems of Life and Mind* throughout the first half of 1879, Marian found other ways of staying close to Lewes. She went through his papers, reread Goethe and visited the grave in Highgate where she discussed plans with the gardener for planting ivy and jessamine. On at least two occasions she became so lost in mental conversations with 'my lost darling' that, despite her scepticism about all things supernatural, she really believed she saw his ghost.[27]

Back in some kind of circulation, Marian began to discover just how much of her life had previously been screened and sorted by Lewes. The business side of things continued to be taken care of by Johnny, who advised her efficiently and unobtrusively on her investments. But when it came to the small change of friends and family, she found herself besieged by requests to which she was not sure how to respond. On 21 April Lewes's nephew Vivian came and asked for £100. She gave him fifty pounds, but he returned it the next morning with a covering letter 'confessing his error'. Bessie Belloc, personally wealthy, wanted £500, probably for a pet feminist cause.[28] Unprotected by

Lewes's twinkly but firm shield, there was a danger that Marian could be seen as a soft touch. On 22 April she dashed off a panicky note to John Cross at his city office begging him to come at once and advise her.[29] He arrived that same evening and a letter turning down Bessie's request was sent shortly afterwards.

But the greatest impertinence came from a new source. Until now Bertie Lewes's widow, Eliza, had been happy to stay in Natal with her two children, living off the £200 which Lewes sent annually. But Eliza was a calculating woman and her father-in-law's death panicked her into wanting to strengthen her connection with Marian who, after all, was the source of the crucial £200. So without waiting to be asked she bundled little Marian and George on to a boat and headed for Britain, arriving on 28 April. They were collected by Charles and taken to stay in Hampstead. Marian visited them the next day and brought them back to the Priory for lunch. Tensions emerged immediately. The 'little Africans' were rude and rough, especially in contrast to their small Lewes cousins. Eliza missed the deference of colonial life and launched into a tirade against the rudeness of the British working class. More alarming still, she clearly thought that she was going to be invited to live at the Priory. Marian quickly put her right in a 'painful letter' written on the 29th.[30] Despite constantly threatening to return home to Natal, Eliza never did. Supported by Marian's money and great name she stayed in Britain, moving from place to place until she found some kind of tetchy stability in Brighton.

John Blackwood had been so struck by the beauty of the Heights, when he first saw it in June 1877, that he told Marian that 'something should be born here'.[31] A couple of surviving fragments of projected novels from this time suggest that Marian thought so too. One scrap is nothing more than a list of names for characters drawing heavily on her stay in Geneva in 1849. The second is a sketch for a novel set in Midlands England during the time of the Napoleonic War. Neither plan came to anything.[32] Now nearing sixty, Marian did not have the emotional or physical strength to embark on another big novel. Her journal review for the year shows her doubtful about whether she should attempt any more writing at all. 'Many conceptions of works to be carried out present themselves,' she wrote, 'but confidence in my own fitness to complete them worthily is all the more wanting because it is reasonable to argue that I must have already done my best.'[33]

As it turned out, Marian did think it worthwhile pushing on, although not along the lines that Blackwood had imagined for her. Over that last difficult summer when Lewes was dying she wrote the sixteen essays that make up *Impressions of Theophrastus Such*. The last piece of business Lewes carried out at the end of November had been to send the manuscript off to Edinburgh.[34]

Certainly not a novel, *Impressions* purports to be a series of essays and character sketches by Theophrastus Such, a Herbert Spencer-ish kind of bachelor who declares, 'the person I love best has never loved me, or known that I love her'.[35] They form an immensely dense, intricate piece of work, which literary scholars find fascinating because it seems to show Eliot anticipating many of the themes and debates of literary Modernism. The allusive title, *Impressions of Theophrastus Such*, for instance, points to the impossibility of defining intellectual origins or charting the point where an artistic influence becomes a borrowing. The first essay, 'Looking Inward', explores the shifting nature of consciousness and the fictionality of autobiography.[36] As this suggests, these are not easy essays to read. Their punning references to other, earlier texts meant that they were unlikely to be understood, let alone enjoyed, by any but a highly educated élite.

George Eliot's turning away from her usual broad readership excited dismay among the newspaper critics. *The Times*, for instance, admitted that *Impressions* was 'emphatically a work of genius', but worried that it put a 'serious strain on the facilities' of the reader.[37] The tendency which had been there in the 'Jewish' half of *Daniel Deronda* to ignore the likely interests of the British reading public was seen again in the final essay of *Impressions*, 'The Modern Hep! Hep! Hep!' This piece returns to the question of how the Jews can develop an identity in exile that honours the inherited traditions that sustain cultural difference, without falling into sectarianism and bigotry.[38]

As Theophrastus's discussion develops, it becomes clear that he is talking about other kinds of exile too, including his own. In the second essay of the collection, 'Looking Backwards', he has described his rural Midlands childhood in rapturous detail. Biographers of George Eliot have long used this lyrical description of 'the tiled roof of cottage and homestead', 'the long cow-shed' and 'the broad-shouldered barns' to pad out the scanty details of Mary Anne Evans's childhood. According to Theophrastus, the memories of these 'childish loves' have become vital to him over the intervening years during which he has lived the urban, disconnected life of the modern intellectual, eventually settling in a fretful London 'half sleepless with eager thought and strife'.[39]

As Marian sat in the garden of the Heights in a county far removed from her own, she too pondered the power of early memory to give her a continuing sense of belonging to a particular community, while still leaving her free to experience the complexity and anonymous freedoms of the modern world. In all her seven novels she had never suggested that the way forward was to return to an imaginary past. Indeed, she makes it clear that this would not be possible. Her Midlands landscapes are always developing, albeit slowly. *Middlemarch* has the railway, Hayslope its Methodists. Or, as Theophrastus puts it in 'Looking Backwards': 'our midland plains have never lost their familiar expression and conservative spirit for me; yet at every other mile, since I first looked on them, some sign of worldwide change, some new direction of human labour has wrought itself into what one may call the speech of the landscape.'[40]

Marian Lewes was never a romantic conservative of the unthinking kind. The Young England movement of the 1840s, which clung to an imagined feudal past and suggested turnip growing as the answer to the social ills caused by industrialisation, struck her as ludicrous. She was a modern woman who, pushed along by Lewes, was interested in the technological developments unfolding around her. Shortly before his death they had both attended a demonstration of the prototype of the telephone. Marian's concern, echoed in Theophrastus's wordy essays, was how to find a way of preserving the best of the past while embracing the benefits of the future.

Marian was diffident about publishing *Theophrastus Such*, tormented by the usual worries that it was not good enough, together with a new concern that it might be disrespectful to Lewes's memory. In the end she made Blackwood affix the cumbersome notice, 'The Manuscript of this Work was put into our hands towards the close of last year, but the publication has been delayed owing to the domestic affliction of the Author.' Blackwood extended her every kindness, not fussing too much over the fact that she was holding up the type and letting her read the proofs in her own time. In the end, his assessment of the book was nearer the mark than hers: when it was published in July it quickly ran into three editions and sold 6000 copies in the first four months.

Around the time that *Theophrastus Such* was published Blackwood had a heart attack. Although he recovered sufficiently to spend the summer at St Andrews, even the gentlest round of golf was now out of the question. At the end of September he had another attack and Marian wrote sweetly to him, ordering him to 'be a good, good patient and cherish your life wisely' for the sake of Mrs Blackwood.[41] She wrote to her old friend again on 28 October, but he died before he could read her letter. For Marian it was the second bereavement within a year – the third if you count the passing of her 'Maman', Madame D'Albert Durade. 'He will be a heavy loss to me,' she told Charles Lewes of John Blackwood. 'He has been bound up with what I most cared for in my life for more than twenty years and his good qualities have made many things easy to me that without him would often have been difficult.'[42]

Once Marian had done her duty by lunching Eliza and the 'little Africans' on 28 April 1879, she was free to leave town for Witley. Sir James Paget arranged for her to be looked after by a local GP and sent her off to the country with the jolly prescription of a pint of champagne a day. Marian arrived at the Heights at the sunny end of May, opening up the house for the first time since she and Lewes had left the previous sad autumn. Once or twice a week Johnny Cross came over by train from Weybridge. Although she seldom mentions his visits in her diary, Marian dropped hints to her correspondents about the 'devoted friend' who looked after her every need, just as she had at the beginning of her love affairs with Herbert Spencer and George Henry Lewes.

Cross's comforting presence soothed Marian into something approaching a normal life. On 27 May he persuaded her to open the piano again and she played for the first time in months.[43] But it was over Dante that they fell in love. To distract himself from his mother's death, Cross had started to struggle through the *Divine Comedy* in the original, with Carlyle's translation as his only guide. When Marian heard she offered to help. Throughout that spring and summer of 1879 she sat with Cross in the summer-house at the Heights, patiently taking him through line by line. For Cross it was a revelation: 'The divine poet took us into a new world. It was a renovation of life.'[44]

This was not a meeting of minds of the kind that had made Marian's relationship with Lewes so rich. She was the teacher and Cross, educated but not agile, stumbled along behind her as best he could. Later he was to describe their relationship to Henry James as being like 'a carthorse yoked to a racer'.[45] Letters from this time have been lost and Cross is inevitably reticent in his *Life*, so we do not know exactly how companionship deepened into love. It looks, though, as if Cross confided his feelings for Marian some time in August, only to have them embarrassedly pushed away. There followed a couple of difficult months in which Marian withdrew emotionally, plunged into panic by this unexpected declaration. By October, however, she had resolved to meet Cross's request for emotional intimacy. On the 16th she sent him a love letter – written on black-bordered mourning paper – which still startles by its intensity. We have to go back to the summer of 1852 and those anguished outpourings to Herbert Spencer to find anything similar, although who knows what her correspondence with Lewes, which went to the grave with her, might have revealed.

The letter starts, 'Best loved and loving one – the sun it shines so cold, so cold, when there are no eyes to look love on me.' But although Marian uses the lovers' rapturously intimate 'thou', she is sufficiently clear-sighted to refer to the differences between them, starting with the intellectual. 'Thou dost not know anything of verbs in Hiphil and Hophal or the history of metaphysics or the position of Kepler in science, but thou knowest best things of another sort, such as belong to the manly heart – secrets of lovingness and rectitude'. Marian then proceeds to acknowledge the twenty-year age gap – 'Consider what thou wast a little time ago in pantaloons and back hair' – before signing off as 'thy tender Beatrice', Dante's heroine.[46]

To those who were to ask themselves over the next year 'how could Marian Evans Lewes fall in love with John Cross?' one might answer, 'how could she not?' From her earliest years she had needed to feel deeply attached to another person, male or female. Before she joined her life to Lewes's at the age of thirty-four she had charged recklessly after love with Robert Brabant, Herbert Spencer and John Chapman. She had stuck with Lewes because he was the first person able to respond to her demands for an all-consuming, symbiotic attachment. Now that he was gone she felt even more than most bereaved lovers that she was only half a person. It was inevitable that the need to bind herself to another human soul would quickly reassert itself. Some biographers have suggested that the discovery of an old infidelity by Lewes tipped Marian towards accepting Cross as her new lover.[47] Even if this is the meaning behind that single-word diary entry 'Crisis' for 16 May 1879, Marian needed no such disenchantment with the past before she could love again.

John Cross struck Marian's friends as unsuitable, but then so had Lewes. By the time the little man had died it was hard to remember just how horrified liberal spirits like Barbara and Bessie had been by the idea of their Marian shackled to a shady rake. Cross's private life, by contrast, was unimpeachable. He was that rare thing, a forty-year-old bachelor without a 'past'. There were no former wives or illegitimate children waiting to ambush this new relationship. While he was not especially clever, he had a gentleman's education and a genuine interest in music and literature. He might not be able to jump from Hiphil to Kepler, but nor did he crack *risqué* jokes or elbow himself to the front of your attention. Tall, with a neatly trimmed beard, Cross was exactly that kind of dignified, eligible presence which Marian's friends had longed for her to find twenty-five years ago.

More baffling altogether is why Cross fell in love with Marian. As far as we know, he had not loved any other woman in this way before. He was not a man driven by strong sexual needs: apart from (and possibly as well as) the eight months of his marriage to Marian, he remained celibate until the end of his long life in 1924. Nor did he need her money, having both capital and income of his own. The obvious answer is that he had just lost his adored mother and was looking for a replacement. Marian was twenty years older, had long called him 'nephew', and by her own admission delighted in playing mother–teacher to young men.

Just because Marian and Cross came together out of pressing emotional needs does not mean that the relationship was not productive for both of them. Knowing that Cross loved her allowed Marian to begin to move through the stages of bereavement. By the time the first anniversary of Lewes's death came round she was able to write, 'I spent the day in the room where I passed through the first three months. I read his letters, and packed them together, to be buried with me.'[48]

At this point Marian was still poised between wanting to move ahead and guilt about being able to do so: she goes on to speculate whether she will be dead by the time the second anniversary comes round. This worry that she might be dishonouring Lewes's memory by becoming attached to someone else is there, too, in the poem on 'Remembrance' by Emily Brontë, which she copied into her diary a couple of weeks later.

> Sweet love of youth, forgive, if I forget thee
>   while the world's tide is bearing me along;
> Other desires and other hopes beset me,
>   Hopes which obscure but cannot do thee wrong!

That Christmas, 1879, Marian stayed alone at the Priory. The letter she wrote on Christmas Eve to Cross, who was visiting his sister in Lincolnshire, shows how much she had come to depend on him. She asks whether he will be back in time to have dinner with her on Tuesday and, if not, Wednesday, then shares an intimate joke by signing herself 'Your obliged ex-shareholder of A and C Gaslight and Coke' in reference to some shares he had recently sold for her.[49]

Publicly Marian was not so keen to acknowledge Cross as her lover. Although Sundays at the Priory restarted in a small way, it was Charles and not Cross who took on Lewes's old duties as master of ceremonies. The new couple steered clear of concert halls, too, preferring art galleries where there were no sharp-eyed audience members waiting with a sketch pad.

By now, Cross was pressing Marian to become his wife. Initially reluctant, she was gradually coming round to the idea. After years of not being married and wanting it badly, it felt sweet to have the choice. There is a story that once the engagement had been agreed Marian took a young girl's delight in preparing her trousseau. She was spotted in the swankiest shops being measured and fitted for the elaborate new wardrobe which every bride was assumed to need. Nothing could be more unlike the furtive rush for Germany in 1854 when she and Lewes left with little more than the clothes they stood up in. Nasty-minded gossips, naturally, thought the results of her shopping spree pathetic. According to Mrs Lionel Tennyson, who met the couple at dinner shortly after their return from honeymoon, Marian's new clothes were obviously designed 'to show her slenderness, yet hiding the squareness of age'. No amount of high fashion, sneered the young Mrs Tennyson, could disguise the fact that a rickety woman of sixty was marrying a sporty man of forty.[50]

Having turned down Cross's proposal twice, by March 1880 Marian was again considering the situation. What may finally have tipped her in his favour was a weekend spent in Weybridge at the end of the month. Marian had always loved families, or at least the idea of them, and the thought of becoming part of Cross's close clan was a great inducement. Writing to Eleanor Cross a few days after the marriage had been agreed, Marian said sweetly that she was longing to be called 'sister' again, a name she had not heard 'for so many, many years'.[51] On 9 April Marian called in Sir James Paget to ask whether her health could stand the excitement of such a dramatic change of regime. He must have dealt with her worries optimistically, for that night she wrote in her diary, 'My marriage decided'.[52]

In her letter to Eleanor Cross of 13 April Marian admitted, 'I quail a little in facing what has to be gone through – the hurting of many whom I care for.'[53] She was perfectly aware that many of the people who had an investment in the George Eliot story would be angry and disappointed if it turned out to have a different ending from the one they had imagined. That story involved a woman of integrity enduring social ostracisim for the sake of a moral principle. Different groups had filled in the details in different ways. Feminists like Clementia Taylor and Bessie Belloc were keen to see in Marian's decision to live with Lewes a rejection of legal marriage on the grounds that it was oppressive to women. Positivists like the Harrisons and the Congreves subscribed to the idea of perpetual widowhood, and wanted to see Marian spending the rest of her days dedicated to the memory of Lewes. Sentimental romantics, meanwhile, liked the idea of a love affair, which had started so scandalously, enduring exclusively beyond the grave. For all three groups the thought that Marian Lewes might get married within eighteen months of her beloved's death ran counter to everything they wanted for her and for themselves.

So it was hardly surprising that for the second time in her life Marian chose to start her new partnership with an unannounced dash to the Continent. She was particularly worried about the reaction of those devoted women friends who had been able to accept and honour Lewes as the very first worshipper, but might have a problem with a Johnny-come-lately like Cross. Thus she resorted to the strategy she had used when she was frightened of telling the Brays about her plan to go off with Lewes – she dropped hints. In a letter to

Elma Stuart on 23 April she asked 'whether your love and trust in me will suffice to satisfy you that, when I act in a way which is thoroughly unexpected there are reasons which justify my action, though the reasons may not be evident to you'?[54] Georgie Burne-Jones likewise got an oblique nudge. When Marian called upon her that same day she seemed, remembered Georgie, 'loth to go, and as if there was something that she would have said, yet did not'. With what must surely be *post hoc* insight, Georgie adds that Marian sighed wearily on that occasion: 'I am so tired of being set on a pedestal and expected to vent wisdom.'[55]

Even telling Charlie Lewes was an ordeal. It looks as if Marian sent Cross over to Hampstead to break the news. As it turned out, she need not have worried. Charlie was as generous a man as his late father. He rushed over to St John's Wood for a long interview with his stepmother and pronounced himself delighted with the new arrangement. He had no doubt that his father would have wanted her to be happy and he was probably relieved at the prospect of being able to shift more of the responsibility for the old lady on to Cross. His own life was busier than ever, with a recent promotion at the Post Office, a growing sideline in journalism and a family of three to juggle. Even the most conscientious of young men must have longed for more time of his own.

On the eve of the wedding Marian wrote to Cara, Barbara, Georgie and William Blackwood breaking the news. In all four letters she stressed many of the same points. First, that Lewes had known and loved Cross for years. Second, that Cross had money of his own and so, by implication, was no fortune-hunter. Third, that she would continue to support the Lewes clan. To Georgie Burne-Jones in particular Marian sounded like a wise Eliot narrator when she added, 'Explanations for these crises, which seem sudden though they are slowly dimly prepared, are impossible. I can only ask you and your husband to imagine and interpret according to your deep experience and loving kindness.'[56]

There remains a puzzle about what happened to these difficult letters. From her honeymoon in Venice Marian writes to Charles about the 'inexplicable failure of the letter I wrote to some of my friends, letters intended to reach them on the morning of my marriage'. She wonders if the coachman Burkin forgot them, but given that the letter to Barbara Bodichon turned up in a drawer at the Priory seven weeks later, it may be that Marian had unconsciously sabotaged the communication herself.[57]

On 6 May at 10.15, Marian Evans Lewes was led up the aisle by Charles Lewes to marry John Walter Cross in front of a tiny congregation made up of the groom's family. There was still one more surprise for those who read about it later in the papers. The service was held not at the Leweses' unofficial parish church of Rosslyn Hill Unitarian Chapel, but at the Anglican church of St George's Hanover Square, in the heart of the West End. Here was another blow for those who had always seen Marian Lewes as incapable of hypocrisy. For an agnostic to get married in church was, said Dr Richard Congreve as tactfully as he knew how, 'rather a queer step'.[58] If she could not subscribe to the Thirty-nine Articles, then how could she repeat words which she did not believe in front of witnesses?

By the time London got the chance to argue these points the new Mr and Mrs Cross were safely on their honeymoon journey through France and Italy. As the letters of congratulation poured into the Priory, Charles sifted, bundled and forwarded the most important ones to the appropriate Poste Restante. Cara, in contrast to her angrily muted response of twenty-five years ago, was careful to write immediately and say that she was delighted: 'it is a comfort to know that you have now one to protect and cherish you.'[59] Charles Bray, whose differences with Lewes over phrenology had made friendship impossible, saw the chance to make a new beginning. At the end of the year he wrote asking Marian for details about her new husband's skull, to which she was able to respond lightly, 'I think you would be satisfied with his coronal arch which finishes a figure six feet high. If his head does not indicate fine moral qualities, it must be phrenology that is in fault.'[60]

Georgie Burne-Jones dashed off a letter the moment she received Marian's, but did not send it for six weeks. Instead she ruminated, hoping, she explained subsequently, to find 'more and brighter words' to send.[61] But those words did not come, buried under a blanket of resentment that Marian had not confided in her. So Georgie decided to send the original note, together with a plea to 'Give me time – this was the one "change" I was unprepared for – but that is my own fault – I have no right to impute to my friends what they do not claim'.[62]

Barbara typically was not offended by the non-arrival of Marian's news-bearing letter. She had in the meantime read about the marriage in the papers and dashed off a generous response:

> My dear I hope and I think you will [be] happy.
>
> Tell Johnny Cross I should have done exactly what he has done if you would have let me and I had been a man.
>
> You see I know all love is so different that I do not see it unnatural to love in new ways – not to be unfaithful to any memory.
>
> If I knew Mr. Lewes he would be glad as I am that you have [a] new friend.[63]

Both Edith Simcox and Clementia Taylor took the news, broken by Charles in person, surprisingly well. Since both loved Marian unconditionally, they wanted whatever made her happy. Edith, in any case, had recently become 'much mellowed' as a result of finding a focus for her passionate energy on the London School Board.[64] She enclosed a thoughtful note for John Cross in her longer letter of congratulations to her Madonna.

It was, in the end, only Maria Congreve who found it hard to be happy. This may have been because she followed her husband in upholding the importance of 'perpetual widowhood', but also because of all Marian's circle her devotion went back the furthest, to the Coventry where they had both been girls forty years before. On the eve of the marriage Marian had written to tell her that Charles Lewes would soon be calling with some remarkable news. Charles's reluctance to report back to his stepmother suggests that the subsequent interview was emotional and difficult.[65] Three weeks later Maria finally managed a 'loving though brief' letter, which was forwarded to an anxious Marian in Milan. On 10 June, by now writing from Venice, Marian attempted to explain to Maria why she had not confided the news sooner and in person. She said what she had said to other friends, that the marriage had only been decided a fortnight before it happened. This was technically true, although it had been a real possibility for well over six months. While to various people Marian had given the excuse that a bout of flu had stopped her spreading the news, to Maria she maintained that it was sensitivity to the fact that the Congreves' niece Emily had recently been widowed that stopped her being fully frank.[66]

All the same, this was not the most important correspondence which Marian embarked upon now. She had received a letter, dated 17 May, from Griff House:

> My dear Sister
> I have much pleasure in availing myself of the present opportunity to break the long silence which has existed between us, by offering our united and sincere congratulations to you and Mr Cross.

The letter was signed 'Your affectionate brother Isaac P Evans'.[67]

Marian wrote back delightedly, 'it was a great joy to me to have your kind words of sympathy, for our long silence has never broken the affection for you which began when we were little ones.'[68] In fact, Isaac's letter was not unprompted. Marian, made optimistic by the brief note of condolence she had received on Lewes's death from Isaac's wife Sarah, had made a point of asking Vincent Holbeche, the family solicitor, to let her brother know the news about her marriage. She could justify this to herself on the grounds that Isaac was still in charge of sending her income from their father's estate and so needed to know her change of name and legal status. In practice, though, this was a way of making a cautious overture, while reminding Isaac that it was he who had first chosen to communicate by solicitor. She signed her letter 'Always your affectionate Sister, Mary Ann Cross'.

Letters which the Crosses wrote as they travelled through Paris, Lyons, Grenoble, Milan and Verona suggest that the honeymoon was going well. Marian clearly enjoyed the novelty of having 'Sisters' to correspond with and felt no awkwardness in telling Charles about the good time she was having in places she had previously visited with his father. Being married, and being married to Cross, delighted her: 'we seem to love each other better than we did when we set out,' she told Florence Cross from Milan on 25 May.[69] Back in October 1879, just as she was deciding to accept Cross as a lover, she had told Elma that after a year of celibacy she feared her heart was drying up, 'so that one has to act by rule without the tide of love to carry one'. Now she was able to write to Maria Congreve touchingly, 'I seem to have recovered the loving sympathy that I was in danger of losing.'[70]

The only sign that something might be wrong comes in a letter of 6 June when Marian mentions that Cross had lost so much weight that his clothes were hanging off him. While she liked his new appearance, she told his youngest brother ominously, 'I hope it will not turn out to be disadvantageous in any other way.'[71] Later Cross's sisters revealed to Edith Simcox that Johnny had set out on the honeymoon utterly 'worn and ill'. They put this down to the fact that Marian had badgered him into continuing his ordinary business until the very eve of the marriage, in order not to arouse suspicion.[72]

Several years later, rumours of Cross's depressive nature began to trickle out. Some said that one of his brothers was mad and that it ran in the family. Barbara Bodichon told Edith Simcox that by the time Cross met Marian he had already had at least one breakdown. His sisters, talking also to the rapt Edith, hinted that Johnny had always had a tendency to get het up under pressure.[73] Whatever the exact strains which were playing on him now, the fact is that on 16 June John Cross jumped from the hotel bedroom which he and Marian were sharing on Venice's Grand Canal. The gondoliers, who had spent the last two weeks ferrying the honeymoon couple around churches, palaces and art galleries, now rushed to fish the English signor out of the water.

Writing up the incident two years later in *George Eliot's Life*, on a page defensively headed 'Dangers of Venice', Cross put his unspecified 'illness' – no mention of the desperate leap – down to an unlikely combination of bad drains, the heat and a lack of regular physical exercise, presumably lawn tennis.[74] Marian's contemporary diary, meanwhile, reflects the seriousness of the incident by falling into virtual silence. During the days following the 16th her entries become terse and businesslike, recording the arrival of doctors, the prescribing of chloral and the sending of a telegram to Willie Cross asking him to come at once.

The sniggering explanation, and the one that naturally endured in the *Athe- naeum* and the *Garrick*, was that Cross was so overwhelmed by having to make physical love to an ugly old woman that he preferred death to intercourse. It was a line of reasoning which reprised all those old jokes from 1854 about Marian being a nymphomaniac whose incontinent lusts broke through every legal and social constraint. In the original 1854 rumour Lewes had been viewed as Marian's partner in crime, a man whose urge to sexual misconduct was matched only by her own. In the 1880 version Cross was cast as the naïve virgin, and perhaps even unacknowledged homosexual, chased around the bed by a hideous, lascivious woman demanding sex. There may have been a grain of truth in this. Marian's marriage with Lewes had been fully sexual. Her writing demonstrates a deep understanding of the power of sex in relations between men and women. It was a subject which interested her. At the age of sixty and in fragile health, she was unlikely to have anticipated a huge amount of sexual activity with her new husband, but with the rigours of the honeymoon journey perhaps she assumed that a little gentle love-making might ensue.

Why was Cross so horrified at this prospect? Perhaps he had always taken it for granted that the marriage was to be celibate. Or maybe he thought the exact opposite but found, when it came to it, that he could not bear to have sex with a woman whom he thought of as his aunt or his mother. Or perhaps it was the fact that he described his wife as 'my ideal', which made sex with her impossible.[75]

We shall never know the answers to these questions. Two days after the fateful leap Willie Cross arrived in Venice to try to calm his agitated brother. Five days on and John Cross was deemed well enough to travel. The honeymoon trio set off by gentle stages to Verona, Innsbruck, Munich and Wildbad. By now it was 8 July and Cross had rallied sufficiently in the brisk German climate for it to seem safe for Willie Cross to set out for home. The bride and groom spent a further two weeks on the Continent before travelling slowly back to Britain.

They went straight to Witley where they began a summer of gentle entertaining as if nothing had happened. Marian relished all the little rituals attached to being newly married. Having spent twenty years telling everyone how much she hated making social calls, she threw herself into visiting her husband's three married sisters who lived at some distance. Sharp-eyed and sour-tongued observers noted that she was not always at ease on these occasions. According to Mrs (later Lady) Jebb, who met her at dinner at Six Mile Bottom:

> There was not a person in the drawing-room, Mr Cross included, whose mother she might not have been, and I thought she herself felt depressed at the knowledge that nothing could make her young again . . . She adores her husband, and it seemed to me it hurt her a little to have him talk so much to me. It made her, in her pain, slightly irritated and snappish, which I did not mind, feeling that what troubled her was beyond remedy. He may forget the twenty years' difference between them, but she never can.[76]

A few weeks later Marian had more to worry about than younger women chatting to her husband. In mid-September she was again suffering from kidney trouble. A trip to Brighton did not produce much improvement and by the third week of October she was in enough pain to justify calling down Dr Andrew Clark from London. By the end of November she had returned to town. But she did not go to the Priory. Before the marriage it had been arranged that she and Cross would share a new home at 4 Cheyne Walk, on Chelsea Embankment. Ever since their return to Witley in July Cross had been up to town at least once a week to supervise refurbishments and make arrangements for the transfer of furniture and books from the Priory. The fact that the temporary housekeeper installed at Cheyne Walk turned out to have a fondness for gin had not made the whole business any smoother. After four bridging days in a hotel in the Gloucester Road, the Crosses finally moved into their new home on 3 December.[77]

The next day, a Saturday, they went to a concert at St James Hall. It was the first public appearance of George Eliot and her new husband, and doubtless there was some nudging and surreptitious sketching. The following week seems to have been a happy one, although Cross responded to the stress of moving house with that common protest, a cold. The next Saturday the new couple went again to St James and in the evening Marian played some of the music they had heard on the piano. The following day, the 19th, Herbert Spencer and Edith Simcox both called by appointment. Spencer thought Marian looked tired; Edith cut her visit short when her beloved confessed that she had the beginnings of a sore throat.[78]

Over the next three days Marian's condition deteriorated rapidly. Fighting off the throat infection put pressure on a system already weakened by kidney disease. By Wednesday lunch-time the situation was grave. Marian spent the afternoon slipping in and out of consciousness: 'I listened to her breathing, hoping it was curing sleep,' explained John Cross in a letter the next day to Elma Stuart, 'but it was death coming on.' When Dr Clark arrived at 6 p.m. he listened to the patient's chest with a stethoscope and told Cross that her heart was giving way. Just at that moment Marian confirmed the diagnosis by whispering to Cross that she had a 'great pain in the left side'. These were the last words she ever spoke. By 10 p.m. George Eliot was dead. Cross, battered by the 'frightful suddenness', could only mutter, 'And I am left alone in this new House we meant to be so happy in.'[79]

At George Eliot's funeral on 29 December at Highgate Cemetery there was a face among the chief mourners that no one could quite place. It belonged to a tall man past sixty, with strong, stern features and a slight stoop. Isaac Evans had come to pay his respects to the sister whom he so physically resembled and had not seen for nearly thirty years. Without any apparent embarrassment he took his place in the coaches that collected at Cheyne Walk, ready to follow the hearse across London to Highgate Cemetery. One wonders what on earth he had to say to his fellow chief mourners John Cross and Charles Lewes. Did he mention or explain his long estrangement from the woman they had come to bury? Or did he confine himself to a few bland, grave remarks? Did he still feel ashamed to be associated with the sister who had brought their shared surname into such disrepute? Or was he flushed with pride as he watched the great, the good and the adoring ordinary surge forward to mourn the little girl with whom he had once fished in the brown canal?

The service was once again conducted by Dr Thomas Sadler along Unitarian lines. 'O May I Join the Choir Invisible' was, inevitably, quoted during the sermon. At the end of it the coffin, covered with white flowers, was carried out to the cemetery and buried in a grave touching upon Lewes's. The birth date on the coffin was given as 1820, not 1819. Since her thirties and possibly before, Marian had knocked a year off her age. Cross and Charles seem to have been unaware of the little deception and Isaac, presumably, was too gallant to say anything.

The delay between George Eliot's death and funeral is not explained simply by Christmas intervening. John Cross, elevated now to Chief Worshipper, wanted his wife buried in Poets' Corner at Westminster Abbey. In the general run of things there would have been no problem about her joining Shakespeare, Dr Johnson and Dickens, all of whom are remembered there. But right from the start it was clear that Dean Stanley, although a personal friend of the Leweses, would find it difficult to sanction a place for a woman who for so long had ignored the sanctity of marriage and expressed doubts about the literal truth of Christianity. It was a position which various friends and admirers of the Leweses, including T. H. Huxley, understood. Others like Herbert Spencer, Edward Burne-Jones and Henry Sidgwick felt that George Eliot should take her rightful place among the great men of English letters and wrote to tell the Dean so.

One of this latter group, John Tyndall, informed Stanley in a letter written on Christmas Day that he had been told – by Cross, presumably – that it was 'the expressed wish of George Eliot to be buried in Westminster Abbey'.[80] If this is true, then it is yet another twist in the tale of the oddly principled yet pragmatic life of Marian Lewes. Ever since she had been cast off for going to live with Lewes, she had proudly rejected any attempts to re-integrate her back into the heart of society. Princesses had been made to wait their turn; peeresses had their invitations to dinner rejected; foreigners heavy with decorations were told that a meeting was impossible. But now, after death, Marian Lewes was hinting that she was not immune to the pleasures of celebrity after all.

But society turned her down. A few days after Christmas it was clear that permission was not going to be granted for burial at the Abbey and Cross quietly dropped the campaign. This was Marian's worst nightmare come to life. She had dared, as she had never done before, to reach out to the Establishment and ask to be given her rightful place. And the Establishment had snubbed her, just as she had always been terrified that a fellow dinner guest or knowing shopkeeper might turn his or her back and walk away.

In the end, it seems fitting that Marian Evans Lewes should have been buried next to George Henry Lewes, the man who had made her life possible. The great and the good might not have wanted her in their midst, but there was one man, a little ridiculous but totally loving, who contrived to reach out to her in death as he had always done in life.

Epilogue

WITHIN TEN YEARS of her death no one was reading George Eliot. Or no one who mattered. Sales of her work continued steadily in the cheaper editions, but the intellectual élite, the opinion formers, had already moved on. As the nineteenth century spun to a close, new and more apt chroniclers stepped forward to capture the particular combination of despair, ennui and hectic pleasure which marked the 1890s. Hardy and Wilde between them – there was no one whose vision could arc the whole – charted a society that was already dancing on the grave of Victorianism.

The 1919 centenary of Eliot's birth failed to reverse the decline in her reputation. Now that all her oldest and staunchest friends had died – Cara in 1905, Sara in 1899, Edith in 1901, Elma in 1903 – there was no one to agitate for a proper memorial. An attempt to raise money for a commemorative corner in Coventry library failed, despite the Newdigates stepping in with the gift – appropriate for the daughter of their one-time forester – of some oak panels. But the truth was that by now Joseph Conrad and Henry James had used their un-English eyes and ears to produce a new kind of novel, which expressed doubts about the ability of language to represent the social world that had stood at the heart of Eliot's work. Before long, D. H. Lawrence, James Joyce and Virginia Woolf would take the novel even further away from the certain world of *Middlemarch*.

John Cross could have done something about the centenary. He did not die until 1924 and there was no new marriage to distract him from his job as Chief Worshipper. Ironically, though, it had been his attempt in 1885 to honour his wife in the three-volume *Life* which had led to her falling so spectacularly out of favour. The version of George Eliot that Cross presents in his well-meaning work is heavy with Victorian righteousness. *His* Eliot is the Sibyl, the Sage, the earnest talking head who urges the world to try harder. Cross's method of presentation was to quote extensively from his late wife's letters, linking them with small contextualising comments from himself. The rationale, he boasted, was to let Eliot tell her story in her own words. But these are not her words. Or rather they are only some of them. Cross pruned everything from Eliot's letters that might sit badly with his authorised version. Anything catty, sexy or funny has disappeared completely. 'It is not a Life at all,' exclaimed Gladstone when he read it. 'It is a Reticence in three volumes.'[1] People who had known Eliot felt cheated. William Hale White, the novelist who had worked with her during the early Strand days, felt obliged to write to the *Athenaeum* and say: 'I do hope that in some future edition, or in some future work, the salt and spice will be restored to the records of George Eliot's entirely unconventional life. As the matter now stands she has not had full justice done to her, and she has been removed from the class – the great and noble church, if I may so call it – of the Insurgents, to one more genteel, but certainly not so interesting.'[2]

It was an extraordinary paradox. The woman whose private life had been too scandalous – and too sexually scandalous at that – for the High Victorian age now seemed too staid and dreary for the naughty nineties. George Eliot had become like an old aunt at a youngsters' party whose current reputation for a rebellious youth was confined to the occasional daring cigarette.

And so Eliot languished until the 1940s. It was then that F. R. Leavis picked her off the back shelf, dusted her down and gave her a place in his Canon, that oddly authorised version of literary history. Now she sat alongside Dickens and Shakespeare as a maker of the English essence. But just as had been the case with Cross, Leavis's attempt to rehabilitate Eliot led to her being buried even deeper. By the 1970s a new generation of critics had arrived to do battle with Leavis's phallic pretensions. Women writers who had been excluded from the feast, such as the Brontës, were reread with attention and claims made for their absolute significance. Others who were all but unknown were brought back into print by the new feminist printing presses. And even classic texts which had stood proudly down the central spine of English literature were given a new, unfamiliar look. Armed with the sharp bright tools of psychoanalytic and post-structuralist theory, critics now worked to find unauthorised meanings in novels which had previously seemed as closed as a cobwebby chest.

Eliot did not suit this new intellectual mood. Critics favour texts that serve their purpose. Post-structuralists found Dickens very much to their taste. The loose tags in his writing offered them an easy entry point from where they could start their meticulous burrowing: feminists liked the Brontës, Emily Dickinson and even Jane Austen, all of whom could be made to talk thrillingly of psychic and social rebellion. But George Eliot, who clung to a male pseudonym, was invited to dine at Oxford and wrote from the centre of high culture, seemed to be exactly the kind of dead white male in whom seventies people could have no interest.

The snub was unfair. Critics accused Eliot of dogmatism when it was they who wrote out of totalitarianising systems. For instance, Eliot had never rejected feminism, but she shied away from a single reading of it, always insisting that the issues were more complex than her friends like Bessie and Barbara, with their arguments grounded in economic liberalism, liked to believe. She knew from her own, often painful, experiences that it was possible to be deeply dependent on male attention and yet enjoy a career which involved beating the best of them. To combine a belief in marriage with an approval of divorce. To want the best for women, yet insist that 'the best' did not necessarily mean qualifying as a doctor. And despite what her critics said,

George Eliot had never clung, Canute-like, to the literary programme of High Victorianism. Her last published book, *Theophrastus Such*, was a dazzling calling-card for Modernism. Here was a narrator who fibbed, a text made up of allusions to other kinds of writing, the whole thing wrapped up with a bitter glee.

Yet all the signs point to the fact that, had she lived and written longer, Eliot's next book would have represented a turning away from the worldly exhaustion of *Theophrastus Such*. Some time in 1877 she had written a fragment for a new work, which suggests a return to the time and landscape of her first novel, *Adam Bede*. The book was to be set among a group of families living in the Midlands at the beginning of the nineteenth century. One of the main characters is the suggestively named Richard Forrest, yet another version of her father, who is described as being 'not an ordinary tenant farmer' but 'a man of weight in his district'.[3]

From the time of beginning *The Mill on the Floss* in 1859 it had been Eliot's habit to plan a book, then put it aside for another piece of work. Thus 'The Lifted Veil' had cut across *The Mill*, *Silas Marner* across *Romola*, *Felix Holt* across *The Spanish Gypsy*. Assuming this pattern continued, it seems likely that George Eliot would have turned back from the precipice represented by *Theophrastus Such* and moved once again to the middle ground, 'the rich Central plain' of Richard Forrest. This was not a retreat, but a reclaiming of the social and moral centre as the only place from where the future could properly be grasped. She had done it during the holy war, giving up her early refusal to go to church in favour of the other less glamorous calls on her integrity. She had done it again during her relationship with Lewes when, to the embarrassment of feminist friends, she insisted on claiming the identity of a conventionally married woman. It was not cowardice, although it could sometimes look like that. Eliot was showing in her private life, as she demanded in her fiction, that our relationship to the future is like that of medieval stonemasons working on a great cathedral. While we may work painfully and hard, we are always working blind. The results of our labour will not be seen until many years after our death.

If all this sounds familiar, that is because the dilemmas in which Eliot and her readers found themselves resemble our own. Two hundred years of industrialisation have fragmented the landscape before sticking it back together in virtual terms, via the modem. 'Community' has been hooked out of an imagined village pump past and pressed into service to describe something as culturally variegated as the entire black population of Great Britain. Nationalism is increasingly disrupted and made bloody by claims based on ethnicity. Calls for devolution criss-cross with demands for a single European currency. Town and country dwellers declare themselves abandoned by each other. After decades of agnosticism, the flourishing Evangelical wing of the Anglican church competes with the biggest surge of interest in Buddhism, not to mention psychotherapy, since the seventies. Feminism, which once seemed such a simple good, reveals itself as a set of conflicting agendas.

George Eliot was the last Victorian who believed that it was possible to face these kinds of crises without shattering into shards. She would have understood where Post-Modernism came from, recognised the seductive call to retreat from the centre, to take refuge in partial narratives and solutions, to despair of 'the real'. But she would have hated its defeatedness. For Eliot believed that it was possible for society to move forward from the centre. The pace would be slow, certainly, the mood both sceptical and humble. But there would also be value, purpose, a sense that this was *right*. Eliot despaired of Progress, with its crude 'Victorian' triumphalism and lack of doubt. In its place she proposed Meliorism, a slow, consensual grasping towards something better. It is Meliorism which we need now.

Notes

CHAPTER 1 'Dear Old Griff'

1. J. W. Cross, *George Eliot's Life as Related in Her Letters and Journals*, 3 vols. (Edinburgh and London, 1885), I, 1. In 1886 Cross published a new version of his work incorporating some important new material, in particular an account of Mary Anne during her early twenties from her Coventry friend Mary Sibree. This revised edition will be noted as Cross, *Life* (1886).

2. *The George Eliot Letters*, ed. Gordon S. Haight, 9 vols. (New Haven, 1954–78), I, 254.

3. Ibid., VI, 129n.

4. Ibid., VI, 374.

5. *Daniel Deronda* (1876), ed. Barbara Hardy (Harmondsworth, 1967), p. 50, Bk.1, ch.3.

6. *Felix Holt, The Radical* (1866), ed. Peter Coveney (Harmondsworth, 1972), p. 79, Author's Introduction.

7. *Silas Marner* (1861), ed. Q. D. Leavis (Harmondsworth, 1967), p. 147, ch.11.

8. *Scenes of Clerical Life* (1858), ed. David Lodge (Harmondsworth, 1973), 'The Sad Fortunes of the Revd Amos Barton,' pp. 59–60, ch.2.

9. 'Occurrences at Nuneaton' 1810–45, MS Nuneaton Library.

10. *Adam Bede* (1859), ed. Stephen Gill (Harmondsworth, 1980), p. 324, ch.25.

11. *The Mill on the Floss* (1860), ed. A. S. Byatt (Harmondsworth 1979), p. 197, Bk.1, ch.13.

12. See, for example, Robert Evans to Francis Newdigate, 1 January 1838, MS Warwickshire County Record Office.

13. Robert Evans to Francis Newdigate, 29 December 1835–23 January 1836, MSs WCRO.

14. *Letters*, III, 174.

15. *Middlemarch* (1871–2), ed. Rosemary Ashton (Harmondsworth, 1994), p. 326, Bk.4, ch.34.

16. *The Mill on the Floss*, p. 96, Bk.1, ch.6.

17. *Letters*, VI, 45–46.

18. See illustration no.1, an engraving taken from this 1842 miniature by Carlisle.

19. Cross, *Life*, I, 12–13.

20. On one occasion Evans enthusiastically supplied the Arbury tenants with copies of *Chemistry Made Easy for the Use of the Agriculturalist*, Robert Evans to Francis Newdigate, 2 Sept. 1843, MS WCRO.

21. Robert Evans to Francis Newdigate, 8 July 1839, MS WCRO.

22. 'Occurrences,' MS Nuneaton.
23. Robert Evans to Francis Newdigate, 6 July 1834, MS WCRO.
24. *Letters*, III, 168.
25. 'Occurrences', MS Nuneaton.
26. Robert Evans to Francis Newdigate, 31 July 1837, MS WCRO.
27. Cross, *Life*, I, 13.
28. Robert Evans, Journal, 2 August 1832, MS Nuneaton.
29. Cross, *Life*, I, 10.
30. *The Mill on the Floss*, p. 60, Bk. 1, ch.2.
31. 'Self and Life', reprinted *George Eliot Collected Poems*, ed. Lucien Jenkins (London, 1989), pp. 189–91. The date of composition is unclear. The poem first appeared in the Cabinet Edition of GE's works, 1878.
32. *The Mill on the Floss*, p. 120, Bk. 1, ch.7.
33. Ibid., p. 79, Bk. 1, ch.4.
34. *Letters*, 1, 173.
35. 'Brother and Sister' sonnets (1874), reprinted *Collected Poems*, pp. 84–90.
36. Quoted Gordon S. Haight, *George Eliot: A Biography* (1968), (Harmondsworth, 1992), p. 5.
37. 'Brother and Sister' sonnets, p. 90.
38. Cross, *Life*, I, 17.
39. Ibid., I, 15.
40. Ibid.
41. My understanding of the dynamics and tensions in the Evans household is indebted to Ruby Redinger's discussion in *George Eliot: The Emergent Self* (London, 1976).
42. Cross, *Life*, I, 16.
43. Ibid.
44. *Letters*, I, 41n.
45. Ibid., I, 22.
46. This copy of *The Linnet's Life* can be seen at the Beinecke Rare Book and Manuscript Library, Yale University.
47. Cross, *Life*, I, 19–20.

CHAPTER 2 'On Being Called a Saint'
1. Edith Simcox, Autobiography, 9 March 1880, K. A. McKenzie, *Edith Simcox and George Eliot* (Oxford, 1961), p. 97.
2. Ibid., 12 June 1885, p. 129.
3. Ibid.
4. *Scenes of Clerical Life*, p. 320, 'Janet's Repentance', ch.10.
5. *Silas Marner*, p. 137, ch.10.
6. *Scenes of Clerical Life*, p. 121, 'Mr Gilfil's Love Story', ch.1.
7. Simcox, *Autobiography*, 12 June 1885, McKenzie, p. 129.
8. Cross, *Life* I, 25.
9. Ibid., I, 26.
10. Ibid.
11. Quoted Haight, *George Eliot*, p. 20.
12. Mathilde Blind, *George Eliot* (London, 1883), p. 19.
13. Reproduced Haight, *George Eliot*, pp. 553–4, Appendix 1.
14. *Letters*, I, 298.
15. Ibid., IV, 116.
16. Blind, *George Eliot*, p. 18.
17. Quoted Haight, *George Eliot*, pp. 13–14.
18. *Letters*, I, 3.
19. Robert Evans to Francis Newdigate, 22 February 1836, MS WCRO.
20. Cross, *Life*, I, 24.
21. Ibid., I, 39–40; *Letters*, 1, 6–7.
22. Cross, *Life*, 157.
23. *Letters*, I, 42.
24. Cross, *Life*, I, 30–31.
25. Ibid., I, 35.
26. *Letters*, I, 8.
27. Ibid., I, 284.
28. Ibid., I, 6.

29. Ibid., I, 31, 24.
30. Ibid., III, 175.
31. Ibid., I, 19.
32. Cross, *Life*, I, 156.
33. *Letters*, I, 40–1.
34. Quoted Cross, *Life*, I, 36.
35. Marghanita Laski, *George Eliot and Her World* (London, 1978) p. 36.
36. *Letters*, I, 25.
37. Ibid., I, 23.
38. Ibid., I, 12.
39. Ibid., I, 23.
40. Ibid., I, 64.
41. Ibid., I, 51.
42. Ibid., I, 107–8.
43. See Rosemarie Bodenheimer's excellent discussion of GE's correspondence in *The Real Life of Mary Ann Evans: George Eliot, Her Letters and Fiction* (Ithaca, 1994), pp. 23–56.
44. *Scenes of Clerical Life*, p. 121, 'Mr Gilfil's Love Story', ch.1.
45. *Letters*, I, 36.
46. Ibid., I, 60.
47. Ibid., I, 47–8.
48. Ibid., I, 64.
49. Ibid., I, 11.
50. Ibid., I, 59.
51. Ibid., I, 29.
52. Cross, *Life*, I, 27.
53. Ibid., I, 21–3.
54. Reproduced in Haight, *George Eliot*, pp. 554–62, Appendix 1.
55. *Letters*, I, 13.
56. Ibid., I, 41.

CHAPTER 3 'The Holy War'
1. *Letters*, I, 22.
2. Ibid., I, 34.
3. Ibid., I, 45–6.
4. Ibid., I, 34.
5. Ibid., I, 84.
6. Ibid., I, 90.
7. Ibid., I, 91.

8. Ibid., I, 90–1.
9. Ibid., I, 102.
10. Ibid., I, 103.
11. Ibid., I, 108.
12. Ibid., I, 111–12.
13. Ibid., I, 116.
14. Ibid., I, 116.
15. Ibid., I, 119.
16. Ibid., I, 120–1.
17. Ibid., I, 50.
18. Ibid., I, 60.
19. Ibid., I, 68.
20. Cross, *Life*, I, 44.
21. *Letters*, I, 46–7.
22. Ibid., I, 51.
23. Ibid., I, 70.
24. Robert Evans, Journal, 19 March 1841, quoted Haight, *George Eliot*, p. 30.
25. *Letters*, I, 86.
26. Ibid., I, 93.
27. Ibid., I, 91.
28. Cross, *Life* (1886), I, 403.
29. *Letters*, I, 90.
30. Cross, *Life* (1886), I, 126.
31. Charles Bray, *Phases of Opinion and Experience during a Long Life* (London, 1884), p. 82.
32. Ibid., p. 48.
33. Charles Christian Hennell, *An Inquiry Concerning the Origin of Christianity* (London, 1838, 2nd edition 1841), pp. 476, 489.
34. Cross, *Life*, I, 158.
35. Bray, *Phases*, p. 76.
36. *Letters*, I, 120.
37. Bray, *Phases*, p. 76.
38. Robert Evans, Journal, 2 January 1842, *Letters*, I, 124.
39. *Letters*, I, 125, 127.
40. Ibid., I, 157.
41. Ibid., I, 156–7.
42. Ibid., I, 128–30.
43. Ibid., I, 131.
44. Ibid., I, 132.
45. Ibid., I, 132.

46. Ibid., I, 134.
47. Ibid., I, 138.
48. Ibid., I, 132.
49. Cross, *Life* (1886), I, 397.
50. Cross, *Life*, I, 157–8.
51. Cross, *Life* (1886), I, 397.
52. Ibid., I, 398.
53. Robert Evans, Journal, 15 May 1842, *Letters*, I, 138n.
54. *Letters*, I, 127.
55. Ibid., I, 134.
56. Cross, *Life*, I, 113.
57. *Letters*, I, 162–3.
58. Ibid., I, 140.
59. Ibid., I, 230n.
60. Simcox, *Autobiography*, 12 June 1885, McKenzie, p. 131.
61. Ibid., 12 June 1885, p. 130.
62. *Letters*, I, lxxiii.
63. Ibid., I, xlix-l.
64. Ibid., III, 176.
65. Ibid., I, 113.
66. Cross, *Life* (1886), I, 403–4.
67. Laski, *George Eliot*, pp. 24–5. For an account of how GE's 'northerly' relatives continued to view her right into the twentieth century, see William Mottram, *The True Story of George Eliot* (London, 1905).

CHAPTER 4 'I Fall Not In Love With Everyone'
1. Bray, *Phases*, p. 70.
2. Quoted Gordon S. Haight, 'George Eliot's Bastards', *George Eliot: A Centenary Tribute*, ed. Gordon S. Haight and Rosemary T. VanArsdel (London, 1982), p. 5.
3. *Letters*, I, 193.
4. Ibid., I, 194.
5. Kathleen Adams, *Those of Us Who Loved Her: The Men in George Eliot's Life* (Warwick, 1980), pp. 52–6.
6. John Chapman, Diary, 27 June 1851, Gordon S. Haight, *George Eliot and John Chapman* (London, 1940), pp. 184–5.
7. Bray, *Phases*, p. 125.
8. Simcox, *Autobiography*, 12 June 1885, McKenzie, p. 131.
9. Quoted Laski, *George Eliot*, p. 95.
10. Cross, *Life*, I, 160.
11. Cross, *Life* (1886), I, 399.
12. See illustration no. 10.
13. Bray, *Phases*, p. 75.
14. Ibid., p. 73.
15. Cross, *Life*, I, 160; Cross, *Life* (1886), I, 402.
16. *Letters*, I, 144.
17. Cross, *Life* (1886), I, 406.
18. Ibid., I, 407.
19. Ibid., I, 406.
20. Ibid., I, 412.
21. *Letters*, I, 150.
22. Ibid., I, 164.
23. Ibid., I, 165.
24. Ibid., I, 167.
25. Chapman, Diary, 27 June 1851, *George Eliot and John Chapman*, p. 186.
26. Anna Kitchel, *George Lewes and George Eliot* (New York, 1933), p. 314.
27. Cross, *Life* (1886), I, 398.
28. *Letters*, I, 136.
29. Ibid., I, 142.
30. Ibid., I, 154.
31. Ibid., I, 158.
32. Ibid., I, 158n.
33. Ibid., I, 167–8.
34. Ibid., I, 225.
35. Ibid., I, 231.
36. Ibid., I, 236n.
37. Ibid., I, 363.
38. Ibid., I, 364.
39. Laski, *George Eliot*, p. 94.
40. Cross, *Life*, I, 36.
41. *Letters*, I, 194.
42. Ibid., I, 205–6.

43. Ibid., I, 176.
44. Ibid., I, 208.
45. Ibid., I, 185.
46. David Friedrich Strauss, *The Life of Jesus, Critically Examined*, tr. from the 4th German Edition (1846), (New York, 1855), p. 69.
47. *Letters*, I, 203.
48. Strauss, *The Life of Jesus*, p. 636.
49. *Letters*, I, 206.
50. Ibid., I, 218.
51. Ibid., I, 190–1.
52. 'accurate and perceptive'.
53. *Letters*, II, 171.
54. Ibid., I, 191.
55. Ibid., VIII, 384.
56. Quoted Cross, *Life*, I, 151.
57. *Letters*, I, 214–15.
58. Ibid., I, 147.
59. Ibid., I, 240–1.
60. Ibid., I, 279.
61. Simcox, *Autobiography*, 12 June 1885, McKenzie, p. 131.
62. *Letters*, I, 277.
63. Ibid., I, 277–8.
64. Ibid., I, 184.
65. Ibid., I, 184.
66. Ibid., I, 186.
67. Ibid., I, 188.
68. Ibid., I, 186.
69. Ibid., I, 179.
70. Ibid., I, 178n.
71. Ibid., I, 180.
72. Ibid., I, 180n.
73. Ibid., I, 271n.
74. Ibid., I, 245.
75. Ibid., I, 254.
76. Ibid., I, 251, 255.
77. Cross, *Life* (1886), I, 412.
78. *Letters*, I, 260–1.
79. Ibid., I, 306.
80. Ibid., I, 309.
81. Ibid., I, 315.
82. Ibid., VIII, 12–14.

CHAPTER 5 'The Land of Duty and Affection'

1. *Letters*, I, 141 and n.
2. Ibid., II, 97.
3. *The Mill on the Floss*, p. 139, Bk. 1, ch.8.
4. Cross, *Life* (1886), I, 409–10.
5. *Letters*, I, 268.
6. Ibid., I, 188.
7. See p. 154.
8. The five sketches appeared between December 1846 and February 1847 and are reprinted in *The Essays of George Eliot*, ed. Thomas Pinney (New York, 1963).
9. 'Brothers in Opinion: Edgar Quinet and Jules Michelet', reprinted *George Eliot: Selected Essays, Poems and Other Writings*, ed. A. S. Byatt and Nicholas Warren (Harmondsworth, 1990), pp. 261–4.
10. *Letters*, I, 200n.
11. Ibid., I, 263.
12. Ibid., I, 266.
13. Ibid., I, 265.
14. Ibid., I, 264.
15. Cross, *Life*, I, 204.
16. *Letters*, I, 264.
17. Ibid., I, 280n.
18. Ibid., I, 276.
19. Ibid., I, 283–4.
20. Ibid., I, 272.
21. Ibid., I, 284.
22. 'J. A. Froude's *The Nemesis of Faith*', *Coventry Herald*, 16 March 1849, reprinted *George Eliot: Selected Essays*, p. 265.
23. *Letters*, I, 279n.
24. Ibid., I, 280.
25. Bray, *Phases*, p. 75.
26. *Letters*, III, 321.
27. Ibid., I, 261.
28. Ibid., I, 289.
29. Cross, *Life*, I, 208.

30. *Letters*, I, 308.
31. Ibid., I, 297.
32. Ibid., I, 298.
33. Ibid., I, 290–1.
34. Ibid., I, 298.
35. Ibid., I, 308.
36. Ibid., I, 301.
37. Ibid., I, 292.
38. Ibid., I, 308.
39. Ibid., I, 301–2.
40. Ibid., I, 309.
41. Ibid., I, 314–15.
42. Ibid., I, 294.
43. Ibid., I, 289.
44. Ibid., I, 303–4.
45. Ibid., I, 327.
46. Ibid., I, 302.
47. Ibid., I, 307.
48. Ibid., I, 320.
49. Ibid., I, 324.
50. Ibid., I, 307.
51. Ibid., I, 328.
52. Ibid., I, 317.
53. Ibid.
54. Ibid., I, 316.
55. Ibid., I, 322, 318.
56. Ibid., I, 316–17.
57. Ibid., I, 330.
58. Ibid., I, 328.
59. Ibid., I, 330.
60. Ibid., I, lxiv.
61. Blind, *George Eliot*, p. 53.
62. Cross, *Life*, I, 231.
63. *Letters*, I, 321.
64. Ibid., I, 322.
65. Ibid., I, 335.
66. Ibid., I, 336.
67. Ibid., I, 334.
68. Ibid., I, 335.
69. Ibid., I, 335n.
70. Ibid., I, 225n.
71. For an account of Chapman's early life see Haight, *George Eliot and John Chapman*.
72. *Letters*, I, 231.
73. 'R. W. Mackay's *The Progress of the Intellect*', *Westminster Review*, January 1851, reprinted *George Eliot: Selected Essays*, pp. 268–85.
74. *Letters*, I, 337.
75. Chapman, Diary, 10 August 1851, *George Eliot and John Chapman*, p. 200.
76. Ibid., 24 July 1860, p. 246.
77. Ibid.
78. Ibid., 30 July 1851, p. 196.
79. Ibid., 8 January 1851, p. 129.
80. Ibid., 9 January 1851, p. 129.

CHAPTER 6 'The Most Important Means of Enlightenment'
1. Haight, *George Eliot and John Chapman*, p. 114.
2. Ibid., pp. 87–92.
3. For an account of Chapman's 1851 Diary, see Haight, *George Eliot and John Chapman*, pp. 123–220.
4. Ibid., 8 January 1851, *George Eliot and John Chapman*, p. 129.
5. Ibid., 12 January 1851, p. 131.
6. Ibid., 18–19 January 1851, pp. 133–4.
7. Ibid., 22 January 1851, pp. 135–6.
8. Ibid., 18 February 1851, pp. 140–1.
9. Ibid., 11 January 1851, p. 130.
10. Ibid., 12 January 1851, p. 131.
11. *Letters*, I, 346.
12. It has always been assumed that Marian failed to get any commissions during this trial period at The Strand. But recently Rosemary Ashton has argued that the *Leader* published two pieces from her on Harriet Martineau's new book. See Rosemary Ashton, *George Eliot: A Life* (London, 1996), pp. 81–2.
13. Chapman, Diary, 21 February 1851, *George Eliot and John Chapman*, p. 143.

14. Ibid., 19–23 March 1851, pp. 146–7.
15. Ibid., 24 March 1851, p. 147.
16. Ibid., 25 March 1851, p. 148.
17. *Letters*, I, 348.
18. Chapman, Diary, 21 April 1851, *George Eliot and John Chapman*, p. 157.
19. Ibid., 28 April 1851, p. 160.
20. Ibid., 27 May 1851, p. 171.
21. Ibid., 30 May 1851, p. 172.
22. Ibid., 10 October 1851, p. 218.
23. Ibid., 31 May 1851, p. 173.
24. Ibid., 5 June 1851, p. 175.
25. Ibid., 2 June 1851, p. 174.
26. Ibid., 15 June 1851, p. 179.
27. Ibid., 16 June 1851, p. 179.
28. Ibid., 21 June 1851, p. 182.
29. Ibid., 15 August 1851, pp. 201–2.
30. The Prospectus is reprinted in *George Eliot: Selected Essays*, pp. 3–7.
31. *Letters*, VIII, 23.
32. Chapman, Diary, 10 June 1851, *George Eliot and John Chapman*, pp. 176–7.
33. Ibid., 7 June 1851, p. 176.
34. Ibid., 21–22 August 1851, p. 204.
35. Ibid., 21 September 1851, p. 213.
36. *Letters*, II, 206.
37. Ibid., II, 208.
38. Chapman, Diary, 23 September 1851, *George Eliot and John Chapman*, p. 213.
39. *Letters*, I, 371.
40. Ibid., I, 377.
41. Ibid., I, 378.
42. Ibid., II, 33.
43. Ibid., II, 55n.
44. William Hale White, *Athenaeum*, No. 3031 (28 November 1885), 702.
45. *Letters*, II, 47–9.
46. Ibid., II, 23–5 and n.
47. Ibid., II, 15.
48. Ibid., I, 365–6.
49. Ibid., II, 4.
50. Ibid., II, 45.
51. Ibid., II, 44.
52. Ibid., II, 87.
53. For the life of Barbara Bodichon see Pam Hirsch, *Barbara Leigh Smith Bodichon* (London, 1998).
54. *Letters*, II, 138.
55. Quoted Haight, *George Eliot*, p. 103.
56. Herbert Spencer, *An Autobiography*, 2 vols. (London, 1904), I, 360–2.
57. Ibid., I, 394–5.
58. *Letters*, VIII, 42–3n.
59. Ibid., VIII, 42.
60. Ibid., II, 16.
61. Ibid., II, 22.
62. Ibid., II, 40.
63. Ibid., II, 35.
64. Spencer, *Autobiography*, II, 445.
65. Haight, *George Eliot*, p. 115.
66. Quoted Haight, *George Eliot*, pp. 102–3.
67. *Letters*, II, 22–3.
68. Ibid., II, 38, 25.
69. Ibid., VIII, 50–1.
70. Ibid., II, 42.
71. Ibid., VIII, 56–7.
72. Ibid., VIII, 61.
73. Spencer, *Autobiography*, I, 467.
74. Ibid., I, 478–9.
75. Ibid., II, 131.
76. Haight, *George Eliot*, p. 120; Spencer, *Autobiography*, I, 398.
77. This correspondence is quoted in Haight, *George Eliot*, pp. 121–2.

Chapter 7 'A Man of Heart and Conscience'

1. *Letters*, II, 54.
2. George Combe, Journal, 29 August 1851, *Letters*, VIII, 27–8.
3. *Letters*, VIII, 33.
4. Ibid., II, 59.
5. Quoted Haight, *George Eliot*, p. 124.

6. *Letters*, II, 62.
7. Ibid., II, 65.
8. Ibid., II, 74.
9. Ibid., II, 75.
10. Haight, *George Eliot*, p. 126.
11. *Letters*, II, 97.
12. Ibid., II, 97.
13. Ibid., II, 163.
14. Ibid., VIII, 115n.
15. Ibid., II, 83.
16. Ibid., II, 93.
17. Ibid., II, 127.
18. Ibid., VIII, 104.
19. Haight, *George Eliot and John Chapman*, p. 71.
20. *Letters*, II, 130–1.
21. Chapman, Diary, 6 October 1851, *George Eliot and John Chapman*, p. 217.
22. *Letters*, I, 367.
23. Chapman, Diary, 20 August 1851, *George Eliot and John Chapman*, p. 203; *Letters*, II, 49.
24. Rosemary Ashton, *G. H. Lewes: A Life* (Oxford, 1991), pp. 58–9.
25. GHL to F. O. Ward (Spring 1853), *The Letters of George Henry Lewes*, ed. William Baker, 2 vols (Victoria, British Columbia, 1995), I, 227.
26. *Letters*, II, 68.
27. Ibid., III, 49n.
28. Ibid., II, 94.
29. Ibid., II, 97.
30. Ibid., II, 98.
31. For an account of G. H. Lewes's early life, see Ashton, *G. H. Lewes*.
32. GHL, Journal, 16 April 1861, quoted Haight, *George Eliot*, p. 337.
33. *Letters*, IV, 154n.
34. Kitchel, *George Lewes and George Eliot* (New York, 1933), pp. 61–2.
35. Ashton, *G. H. Lewes*, pp. 11–12.
36. G. H. Lewes, 'Spinoza', *Fort-nightly Review* 4 (April 1866), 385.
37. W. B. Scott, *Autobiographical Notes*, ed. W. Minto, 2 vols. (London, 1950), I, 130.
38. G. H. Lewes, 'Percy Bysshe Shelley', *Westminster Review* 35 (April 1841), 303–4.
39. Quoted Kitchel, *George Lewes and George Eliot*, pp. 12–13.
40. Scott, *Autobiographical Notes*, I, 130.
41. Quoted Ashton, *G. H. Lewes*, p. 25.
42. Scott, *Autobiographical Notes*, I, 134; Jane Welsh Carlyle, *Letters to Her Family 1839–63*, ed. Leonard Huxley (London, 1924), p. 320.
43. Quoted Haight, *George Eliot*, pp. 129–30.
44. Quoted Ashton, *G. H. Lewes*, p. 40.
45. *Letters*, 11, 126.
46. Kitchel, *George Lewes and George Eliot*, p. 46.
47. Ibid., pp. 312–13.
48. See illustration no. 21.
49. Jane Welsh Carlyle, *Letters*, p. 329.
50. *Leader*, 3 July 1852, pp. 639–40.
51. *Leader*, 12 November 1853, p. 1099.
52. GHL, Journal, 28 January 1859, Haight, *George Eliot*, p. 133.
53. Oscar Browning was the source of this rumour, spreading it to Henry James and Eliza Lynn. He also managed to drop several hints in his *Life of George Eliot* (London, 1890), especially over his treatment of Romola's discovery of Tito's infidelity.
54. GHL, Journal, 28 January 1859, quoted Haight, *George Eliot*, p. 271.
55. Thomas Trollope, *What I*

Remember, 2 vols (London, 1887), II, 299.

56. Spencer, *Autobiography*, I, 377.

57. Elizabeth Haldane, *George Eliot and Her Times* (New York, 1927), p. 92n.

58. *Letters*, II, 112.

59. Ibid., II, 178.

60. Ibid., II, 134n.

61. Ludwig Feuerbach, *The Essence of Christianity*, tr. Marian Evans (London, 1854), p. 47.

62. Ibid., p. 268.

63. *Letters*, II, 165.

64. Ibid., II, 154–5.

65. Ibid., II, 156.

66. Ibid., II, 157.

67. George Eliot to John Chapman, December 1853, Rosemary Ashton, 'New George Eliot Letters at the Huntington', *Huntington Library Quarterly* LIV, (Spring 1991), 120.

68. *Letters*, II, 158.

69. Quoted Laski, *George Eliot*, p. 44.

70. *Letters*, II, 166.

CHAPTER 8 'I Don't Think She Is Mad'

1. GE, Journal, 20 July 1854, MS Yale.

2. *Letters*, II, 171.

3. Ibid.

4. Ibid., II, 174.

5. Ibid., II, 170–2.

6. Sara Hennell to GE, 20 October 1854, quoted Ashton, *George Eliot: A Life*, p. 116.

7. *Letters*, II, 179.

8. Sara Hennell to GE, quoted Ashton, *George Eliot: A Life*, p. 116.

9. *Letters*, II, 19–20.

10. Ibid., II, 186.

11. Ibid., VIII, 122–3, 126.

12. Ibid., VIII, 129–30.

13. Ibid., VIII, 131.

14. Ibid., VIII, 124–5.

15. Ibid., VIII, 125–6.

16. Ibid., VIII, 129.

17. Haight, *George Eliot*, p. 166.

18. R. K. Webb, *Harriet Martineau, A Radical Victorian* (London, 1960), p. 14.

19. *Letters*, II, 176n.

20. Ibid., II, 176–7.

21. Ibid., II, 178.

22. One of these, 'Liszt, Wagner and Weimar', *Fraser's Magazine* (July 1855), is reprinted in *George Eliot, Selected Critical Writings*, ed. Rosemary Ashton (Oxford, 1992), pp. 82–109.

23. 'Recollections of Weimar, 1854', written at the back of GE's Journal, MS Yale.

24. *Letters*, II, 171, 173.

25. GE, Journal, 10 August 1854, MS Yale.

26. *Letters*, II, 173.

27. Ibid., II, 169.

28. Ibid., II, 173.

29. GE, 'Recollections of Weimar, 1854', MS Yale.

30. Ibid.

31. *Letters*, VIII, 134.

32. Ibid., II, 190.

33. Ibid., II, 184.

34. 'The Future of German Philosophy', *Leader* (28 July 1855), reprinted *George Eliot, Selected Critical Writings*, p. 133.

35. *Letters*, II, 192n.

36. 'Recollections of Weimar, 1854', MS Yale.

37. George Henry Lewes, *The Life and Works of Goethe*, 2 vols. (London, 1855), I, 144.

38. 'The Morality of *Wilhelm Meister*', *Leader* (21 July 1855), reprinted *George Eliot, Selected Critical Writings*, pp. 129–32.

39. *Letters*, II, 156.
40. 'Woman in France: Madame de Sablé' (*Westminster Review*, October 1854), reprinted *George Eliot: Selected Essays*, pp. 8–37.
41. Ibid., p. 11.
42. *Letters*, II, 189.
43. Ibid., VIII, 133.
44. Ibid., II, 189.
45. 'Recollections of Berlin, 1855', written at the back of GE's Journal, MS Yale.
46. *Letters*, II, 197.
47. Quoted Ashton, *George Eliot: A Life*, p. 125.
48. GE, Journal, 9–14 April 1855, MS Yale.
49. A remark from Cara Bray to Edith Simcox in 1885, quoted Haight, *George Eliot*, p. 179.
50. *Letters*, II, 194, 196.
51. Ibid., II, 197.
52. Quoted Ashton, *George Eliot: A Life*, p. 124.
53. *Letters*, II, 200, 232.
54. This is a paraphrase, given to Gordon Haight by Bessie's daughter. Haight, *George Eliot*, p. 205.
55. *Letters*, II, 199–200.
56. Ibid., II, 199.
57. Ibid., II, 209.
58. Ibid., II, 217.
59. Ibid., II, 214–18.
60. Ibid., II, 224.
61. 'Charles Kingsley's *Westward Ho!*,' *Westminster Review* (July 1855), reprinted *George Eliot: Selected Essays*, p. 312.
62. 'Geraldine Jewsbury's *Constance Herbert*', *Westminster Review* (July 1855), reprinted *George Eliot: Selected Essays*, pp. 321–22.
63. 'The Morality of *Wilhelm Meister*', *Leader* (21 July 1855), reprinted *George Eliot, Selected Critical Writings*, p. 131.
64. *Letters*, II, 221.
65. 'Evangelical Teaching: Dr Cumming', *Westminster Review* (October 1855), reprinted *George Eliot: Selected Essays*, pp. 36–68.
66. Ibid., p. 52.
67. Cross, I, 384.
68. Quoted Ashton, *George Eliot: A Life*, p. 146.
69. *Letters*, II, 233.
70. Ibid., VIII, 159.
71. Ibid., VIII, 120.
72. Ibid., II, 235.
73. Ibid., II, 233.
74. Ibid., II, 251.
75. Ibid., II, 184.
76. Ibid., II, 197.
77. Ibid., II, 184.
78. Ibid., II, 204.
79. Ibid., II, 202.
80. 'Recollections of Ilfracombe 1856' in GE, Journal, MS Yale.
81. Ibid.
82. Ibid.
83. Ibid.
84. Ibid.
85. 'The Natural History of German Life', *Westminster Review* (July 1856), reprinted *George Eliot: Selected Essays*, pp. 107–39.
86. Ibid., p. 127.
87. Ibid., p. 131.
88. Ibid., p. 111.
89. 'Recollections of Ilfracombe, 1856', MS Yale.
90. John Chapman to Barbara Leigh Smith, 17 September 1855, quoted Haight, *George Eliot and John Chapman*, p. 91.
91. GE, Journal, 20 July 1856, MS Yale.
92. *Letters*, I, 223n.
93. 'How I Came to Write Fiction', GE, Journal, 6 December 1857, MS Yale.
94. Ibid.

95. Ibid.
96. Ibid.
97. Ibid.

CHAPTER 9 'The Breath of Cows and the Scent of Hay'

1. *Letters*, II, 261.
2. 'Silly Novels by Lady Novelists', *Westminster Review* (October 1856), reprinted *George Eliot: Selected Essays*, pp. 140–63.
3. Ibid., p. 141.
4. Ibid., p. 148.
5. Ibid., p. 149.
6. Ibid., p. 156.
7. Ibid., p. 162.
8. GE, Journal, 22 September 1857, MS Yale. Haight points out that GE was probably referring to 23 September, *Letters*, II, 407n.
9. 'How I Came to Write Fiction', GE, Journal, 6 December 1857, MS Yale.
10. *Scenes of Clerical Life*, p. 41, 'Amos Barton', ch.1.
11. Ibid., p. 85, ch.5.
12. Ibid., p. 81, ch.5.
13. Ibid., p. 80, ch.5.
14. Ibid., p. 44, ch.1.
15. Ibid., p. 48, ch.1.
16. Ibid., p. 49, ch.1.
17. See p. 154.
18. *Scenes of Clerical Life*, pp. 102–3, 'Amos Barton', ch.7.
19. Ibid., p. 111, ch.9.
20. Ibid., p. 112, ch.9.
21. Ibid., p. 113, ch.10.
22. *Letters*, III, 377n.
23. Ibid., II, 269.
24. Ibid.
25. Ibid., II, 270.
26. Ibid., II, 272.
27. Ibid., II, 274.
28. 'Worldliness and Other-Worldliness: The Poet Young', *Westminster Review* (January 1857), reprinted *George Eliot: Selected Essays*, pp. 164–213.
29. *Letters*, II, 290–91.
30. Ibid., II, 291, 293.
31. Ibid., II, 292.
32. Ibid., II, 297.
33. Ibid., II, 299.
34. Ibid., II, 308.
35. Ibid., II, 309.
36. Ibid., II, 347.
37. *Scenes of Clerical Life*, p. 322, 'Jane's Repentance', ch.10.
38. *Letters*, II, 347–8.
39. Ibid., II, 352–3.
40. Ibid., II, 353.
41. Ibid., II, 292.
42. Cross, *Life*, I, 431.
43. *Letters*, II, 309–10.
44. 'Silly Novels', *George Eliot: Selected Essays*, p. 161.
45. *Letters*, II, 436.
46. Simcox, 'George Eliot, a Valedictory Article', *The Nineteenth Century* (May 1881), McKenzie, p. 120.
47. *Letters*, II, 273–4.
48. Ibid., II, 275.
49. Ibid., II, 277.
50. Ibid., II, 298n.
51. Ibid., II, 294.
52. Ibid., II, 410n.
53. Ibid., II, 435.
54. Samuel Lucas, unsigned review, *The Times*, 2 January 1858, p. 9. David Carroll, ed., *The Critical Heritage* (London 1977), p. 61.
55. Unsigned review, *Saturday Review*, 29 May 1858, v, 566, Carroll, *Critical Heritage*, p. 70.
56. *Letters*, II, 424.
57. Ibid., II, 426.
58. GE, Journal, 17 March 1857, MS Yale.
59. Haight, *George Eliot*, p. 226.
60. *Letters*, II, 314.
61. Ibid., II, 317.

62. GE, Journal, 2 May 1857, MS Yale.
63. *Letters*, II, 331.
64. Ibid., II, 333.
65. Ibid., II, 336–7.
66. Ibid., II, 346.
67. Ibid., II, 350.
68. Ibid., II, 350.
69. Ibid., II, 364.
70. Ibid., II, 342; ibid., III, 26.
71. 'The *Antigone* and Its Moral', *Leader* (29 March 1856), reprinted *George Eliot: Selected Essays*, pp. 363–6.
72. GE, Journal, 31 December 1857, MS Yale.
73. *Letters*, II, 387.
74. GE, Journal, 28 February–5 March 1858, MS Yale. *Letters*, II, 439n.
75. *Letters*, II, 452.
76. GE, Journal, 14 April 1858, MS Yale.
77. *Letters*, II, 454.
78. GE, Journal, 17–24 June 1858, MS Yale.
79. *Letters*, II, 451.
80. *Adam Bede*, pp. 223–4, Bk.2, ch. 17.
81. *Letters*, II, 474.
82. Ibid., II, 445–6.
83. Ibid., II, 504.
84. Ibid., II, 484.
85. Ibid., II, 492.
86. 'The History of *Adam Bede*', GE, Journal, 30 November 1858, MS Yale.
87. *Adam Bede*, p. 50, Bk.1, ch.1.
88. Ibid., pp. 53–4, Bk.1, ch.1.
89. Ibid., pp. 258–9, Bk.2, ch.19.
90. *Letters*, III, 25.
91. 'The History of *Adam Bede*', MS Yale.
92. *Adam Bede*, p. 359, Bk.4, ch.29.
93. Ibid., p. 170, Bk.1, ch.12.
94. Ibid., p. 199, Bk.1, ch.15.

95. Ibid., p. 293, Bk.3, ch.22.
96. Ibid., p. 324, Bk.3, ch.25.
97. See p. 29.
98. 'The History of *Adam Bede*', MS Yale.
99. *Letters*, II, 324.

CHAPTER 10 'A Companion Picture of Provincial Life'
1. *Letters*, III, 55.
2. Ibid., II, 505.
3. Ibid., II, 509.
4. Ibid., II, 513.
5. *The Times*, 12 April 1859, Carroll, *Critical Heritage*, p. 77.
6. *Letters*, III, 148.
7. Ibid., III, 18.
8. J. A. Froude to GE, 13 March 1859, quoted Haight, *George Eliot*, p. 275.
9. *Letters*, III, 9.
10. Quoted Haight, *George Eliot*, p. 273.
11. These paintings are still in the possession of the Queen and hang at Buckingham Palace.
12. *Letters*, III, 44.
13. GHL, Journal, 12 February 1859, *Letters*, III, 12.
14. *Letters*, III, 25.
15. Ibid., III, 7.
16. Ibid., III, 33.
17. Ibid., III, 89.
18. Ibid., III, 152.
19. Ibid., III, 41.
20. Redinger, *George Eliot*, p. 393.
21. *Letters*, II, 461.
22. Ibid., III, 44.
23. Ibid., III, 50.
24. Ibid., III, 68, 73.
25. Ibid., III, 77.
26. Ibid., III, 93.
27. Ibid., III, 103.
28. Ibid., III, 109n.
29. Ibid., III, 109.
30. Ibid., III, 94.

31. Ibid., III, 151.
32. Ibid., III, 160.
33. Ibid., III, 161.
34. Ibid., III, 161–2.
35. Ibid., III, 183.
36. Ibid., III, 188, 184–5.
37. Ibid., III, 190.
38. Ibid., III, 191–2.
39. Ibid., III, 192.
40. Ibid., III, 194.
41. Ibid., III, 204–5.
42. Ibid., III, 208.
43. Ibid., III, 115.
44. Ibid., III, 43.
45. Ibid., III, 204.
46. Ibid., III, 173.
47. Ibid., III, 215.
48. Ibid., III, 216.
49. Ibid., III, 217.
50. Ibid., III, 217.
51. Ibid., III, 218.
52. Ibid., III, 236.
53. Ibid., II, 337.
54. Ibid., III, 98.
55. Fanny Houghton to Isaac Evans, 13 June 1866, quoted Haight, *George Eliot*, p. 394.
56. *Letters*, II, 457.
57. Ibid., II, 458.
58. Ibid., II, 459–60.
59. Ibid., II, 375.
60. Ibid., II, 376.
61. Ibid., III, 83–5.
62. Ibid., III, 85–6.
63. Ibid., III, 110n.
64. Ibid., III, 179.
65. Ibid., III, 155–7.
66. Ibid., III, 174–7.
67. Ibid., II, 486.
68. Ibid., II, 443.
69. GHL, Journal, 23 June 1859, *Letters*, III, 90.
70. *Letters*, III, 945.
71. Ibid., III, 90.
72. Ibid., III, 95–6.
73. Ibid., II, 494n.
74. Spencer, *Autobiography*, I, 38.
75. *Letters*, III, 124.
76. Ibid., II, 494.
77. Ibid., III, 3.
78. Ibid., III, 13.
79. Haight, *George Eliot*, p. 278.
80. *Letters*, VIII, 257n.
81. GHL, Journal, 24 March 1859, *Letters*, III, 49n.
82. *Letters*, III, 170n.
83. Ibid., III, 56.
84. Ibid., III, 65.
85. Ibid., III, 106.
86. Ibid., III, 41.
87. Ibid., III, 124.
88. Ibid., III, 112.
89. Ibid., III, 118.
90. GE, Journal, 31 December 1858, MS Yale.
91. *Letters*, III, 91.
92. Ibid., III, 103.
93. Ibid., III, 62n.
94. Quoted Haight, *George Eliot*, p. 299.
95. *Letters*, III, 79.
96. Ibid., III, 116.
97. Ibid., VIII, 142n.
98. Ibid., VIII, 250.
99. Ibid., III, 33n.
100. *The Mill on the Floss*, p. 54, Bk.1, ch.1.
101. Ibid., p. 55, Bk.1, ch.1.
102. Ibid., p. 362, Bk.4, ch.1.
103. Ibid., p. 363, Bk.4, ch.1.
104. Ibid.
105. Ibid., p. 405, Bk.5, ch.2.
106. Ibid., p. 60, Bk.1, ch.2.
107. Ibid., p. 655, Bk.7, ch.5.
108. *Letters*, III, 269.
109. Ibid., III, 285.
110. *The Mill on the Floss*, p. 91, Bk.1, ch.5.
111. Ibid., p. 628, Bk.7, ch.2.
112. Ibid., p. 612, Bk.7, ch.1.
113. Ibid., pp. 613–14, Bk.7, ch.1.
114. Ibid., p. 621, Bk.7, ch.2.

CHAPTER II 'Pure, Natural Human Relations'

1. *Letters*, III, 244.
2. Ibid., III, 245.
3. Ibid., III, 256, 259n.
4. *The Mill on the Floss*, p. 113, Bk.1, ch.7.
5. *Letters*, III, 277, 276.
6. Ibid., III, 289.
7. Ibid., III, 290.
8. Ibid., III, 292.
9. *The Times*, 19 May 1860, Carroll, *Critical Heritage*, p. 131; *Letters*, III, 299.
10. *Macmillan's*, 3 April 1861, *Letters*, III, 397.
11. *Letters*, III, 296.
12. Ibid., III, 297.
13. GHL, Journal, 7 April 1860, quoted Haight, *George Eliot*, pp. 323–4.
14. *Letters*, III, 288.
15. 'Recollections of Italy, 1860', GE, Journal, MS Yale.
16. *Middlemarch*, p. 194, Bk.2, ch.20.
17. *Letters*, III, 231.
18. Ibid., III, 366n.
19. *Silas Marner*, pp. 135–6, ch.10.
20. *Letters*, III, 366.
21. Ibid., VIII, 259–60.
22. Ibid., III, 327.
23. Ibid., III, 474.
24. Ibid., VIII, 295.
25. Ibid., IV, 117.
26. GE, Journal, 17 December 1860, MS Yale.
27. *Letters*, III, 363.
28. Quoted Bodenheimer, *The Real Life of Mary Ann Evans*, p. 190.
29. My discussion of GE's relationship with her stepsons is indebted to Bodenheimer, ch.7, pp. 189–231.
30. GHL, Journal, 26–8 June 1860, *Letters*, III, 309.
31. *Letters*, III, 421.
32. Ibid., III, 324.
33. Ibid., III, 448.
34. Ibid., IV, 34.
35. Quoted Bodenheimer, *The Real Life of Mary Ann Evans*, p. 199.
36. *Letters*, III, 343; see illustration no. 18.
37. *Letters*, III, 339.
38. GE, Journal, 28 November 1860, MS Yale.
39. *Silas Marner*, p. 53, ch.1.
40. *Letters*, III, 371.
41. Ibid., III, 427.
42. *Silas Marner*, p. 54, ch.1.
43. GE, Journal, 28 November 1860, MS Yale.
44. *Letters*, III, 372n.
45. See Redinger, *George Eliot*, p. 235.
46. *Letters*, III, 393.
47. *Silas Marner*, pp. 214–15, ch.17.
48. *Letters*, III, 117, 335.
49. Ibid., III, 379.
50. Ibid., III, 382.
51. Ibid., III, 386.
52. GHL, Journal, 3–6 June 1861, *Letters*, III, 424.
53. *Letters*, III, 394n.
54. GE, Journal, quoted Haight, *George Eliot*, pp. 350–1.
55. *Letters*, III, 420.
56. Ibid., III, 427.
57. Ibid., III, 474.
58. Ibid., IV, 3.
59. GHL, Journal, November 1859, *Letters*, IX, 345.
60. GE, Journal, 31 January, 17 February 1862, MS Yale.
61. Cross, *Life*, II, 255.
62. *Letters*, VIII, 303.
63. *Romola* (1863), ed. Andrew Sanders (Harmondsworth, 1980), pp. 58–9, Bk.1, ch.1.
64. Ibid., p. 420, Bk.2, ch.39.
65. *Letters*, IV, 6–7.
66. Ibid., IV, 15–16, 18.

67. GHL, Journal, 27 February 1862, *Letters*, IV, 17–18.
68. GHL, Journal, 1 March 1862, *Letters*, IV, 20.
69. GHL, Journal, 8 May, 8 April 1862, *Letters*, IV, 29, 24.
70. GHL, Journal, 17 May 1862, *Letters*, IV, 33–4.
71. *Letters*, IV, 34–5.
72. Ibid., IV, 36n.
73. Ibid., IV, 38 and n.
74. Ibid., IV, 44.
75. GE, Journal, 30 September 1862, MS Yale.
76. *Letters*, IV, 58–9.
77. Ibid., VIII, 304.
78. The phrase comes from Margaret Oliphant, another Blackwood writer, who had no choice but to write for the market. Margaret Oliphant, *Autobiography and Letters* (Edinburgh, 1899), p. 5.
79. *Letters*, IV, 97.
80. GHL, Journal, 18 April 1862, Haight, *George Eliot*, p. 395.
81. *Letters*, IV, 102.
82. Ibid., III, 462.
83. Ibid., IV, 84.
84. Ibid., IV, 212.
85. Ibid., IV, 233.
86. Ibid., IV, 34, 48.
87. Ibid., III, 387.
88. Ibid., III, 398.
89. Ibid., III, 366.
90. Ibid., III, 396.
91. GE, Journal, 19 June 1861, *Letters*, III, 427–8.
92. Quoted Ashton, *George Eliot: A Life*, p. 268.
93. GHL, Journal, 1–13 November 1863, *Letters*, IV, 111–12.
94. *Letters*, IV, 116.

CHAPTER 12 'The Bent of My Mind Is Conservative'

1. *Letters*, IV, 68.
2. Henry James to William James, 1 May 1878, *Letters of Henry James*, ed. Leon Edel, 4 vols (London 1974–84), II, p. 72.
3. Lady Amberley, quoted Haight, *George Eliot*, p. 391.
4. *Letters*, IV, 17.
5. Ibid., IV, 417.
6. Ibid., IV, p. 175.
7. Ibid., IV, 232.
8. Ibid., IV, 268–9.
9. Ibid., IV, 130–1.
10. Ibid., IV, 134.
11. Ibid., VIII, 316–17.
12. Ibid., IV, 140.
13. Ibid.
14. Fanny Houghton to Isaac Evans, 11 December, and 13 June 1866, quoted Haight, *George Eliot*, pp. 393–4.
15. *Letters*, IV, 299.
16. Ibid., IV, 179.
17. Ibid., IV, 183.
18. GHL, Diary, 16 January 1874, *Letters*, VI, 6n.
19. 'The Influence of Rationalism', *Fortnightly Review* (15 May 1865), reprinted *George Eliot: Selected Essays*, pp. 389–404.
20. *Letters*, IV, 159.
21. Ibid., IV, 214.
22. Ibid., IV, 472.
23. Ibid., IV, 284–9.
24. Ibid., IV, 300–1.
25. Richard Congreve to Sophie Edger, 10 May 1880, quoted Haight, *George Eliot*, p. 302.
26. *Letters*, IV, 200.
27. G. H. Lewes, Prospectus for the *Fortnightly Review*, March 1865, *Letters*, VIII, 336.
28. *Letters*, IV, 438.
29. Ibid., IV, 16.

30. Ibid., IV, 72.
31. Ibid., IV, 374–5.
32. Ibid., IV, 375n.
33. Ibid., IV, 472.
34. Ibid., IV, 496.
35. Ibid., IV, 390.
36. Ibid., IV, 390.
37. Ibid., IV, 425.
38. Ibid., VIII, 402.
39. Ibid., IV, 399.
40. *Felix Holt, The Radical*, p. 76, Author's Introduction.
41. 'Occurrences at Nuneaton', MS Nuneaton.
42. *Felix Holt*, p. 75, Author's Introduction.
43. Ibid., p. 400, ch.30.
44. Ibid., p. 145, ch.5.
45. Ibid., p. 101, ch.1.
46. GE, Journal, 24 December 1865, MS Yale.
47. GHL, Journal, 1 June 1866, *Letters*, IV, 265.
48. *Letters*, IV, 244.
49. Ibid., IV, 240n.
50. Ibid., IV, 241.
51. Ibid., IV, 243.
52. Ibid., IV, 246.
53. 'Address to Working Men, by Felix Holt', *Westminster Review* (January 1868), reprinted *George Eliot, Selected Critical Writings*, pp. 338–54.
54. John Morley, unsigned review, *Saturday Review*, 16 June 1866, XXI, 722–4, Carroll, *Critical Heritage*, pp. 251–7.
55. Henry James, *Nation*, August 1866, Carroll, *Critical Heritage*, pp. 273–5.
56. *Letters*, VIII, 378.
57. Ibid., IV, 285.
58. Quoted Haight, *George Eliot*, pp. 334–5.
59. *Letters*, IV, 103–4n.
60. Ibid., IV, 28–9.
61. Ibid., IV, 193.
62. Ibid., IV, 447.
63. Haight, *George Eliot*, p. 398.
64. Scott, *Autobiographical Notes*, II, 271.
65. *Letters*, IV, 397.
66. Ibid., IV, 473.
67. Oscar Browning, *Life of George Eliot* (London, 1890), pp. 96–7.
68. Quoted Ashton, *George Eliot: A Life*, p. 271.
69. GHL, Journal, 5 May 1867, *Letters*, IV, 360.
70. Lady Amberley, Diary, 5 May 1867, *Letters*, VIII, 399n.
71. *Letters*, IV, 336.
72. Ibid., IV, 346.
73. *Leader* (31 January 1852), p. 580.
74. Cross, *Life*, III, p. 42.
75. GE, Journal, 5 December 1864–21 February 1865, MS Yale.
76. *Letters*, IV, 289.
77. Ibid., IV, 320–3.
78. For an account of this trip see GE's and GHL's letters home, *Letters*, IV, 343–9.
79. Ibid., IV, 353.
80. Ibid., IV, 354.
81. Ibid., IV, 394–8.
82. *The Spanish Gypsy*, in *Collected Poems*, pp. 201–456.
83. For a summary of critical reactions, see Haight, *George Eliot*, pp. 404–5.
84. *Letters*, IV, 486.
85. Ibid., IV, 413.
86. *Felix Holt*, Dedication.
87. *Letters*, IV, 34.
88. Ibid., IV, 154.
89. Ibid., IV, 155.
90. Ibid., IV, 311–12.
91. Ibid., IV, 140.
92. Ibid., VIII, 431–4.
93. Henry James to his father, *Henry James Letters*, I, 116–17.
94. *Letters*, V, 53.

95. Ibid., V, 41.
96. 'German Wit: Heinrich Heine', *Westminster Review* (January 1856), reprinted *George Eliot, Selected Critical Writings*, 193–233.
97. GE, Journal, 19 October 1869, MS Yale.

CHAPTER 13 'Wise, Witty and Tender Sayings'
1. *Letters*, V, 66.
2. Ibid., V, 93.
3. Ibid., V, 84.
4. GHL, Journal, 25 March 1870, *Letters*, V, 85n.
5. GE, Journal, 1 January 1869, MS Yale.
6. *Letters*, V, 16.
7. Ibid., V, 403; 'Brother and Sister' sonnets, *Collected Poems*, pp. 84–90.
8. 'The Legend of Jubal', *Collected Poems*, pp. 91–114.
9. 'Armgart', *Collected Poems*, pp. 115–51.
10. Ibid., p. 128.
11. Ibid., p. 129, 133.
12. Ibid., p. 143.
13. *Letters*, V, 253.
14. Ibid., V, 31.
15. Ibid., IV, 499.
16. Ibid., V, 192.
17. Haight, *George Eliot*, p. 454.
18. Ibid.
19. *Letters*, V, 175.
20. Ibid., V, 185.
21. Ibid., V, 207.
22. Ibid., V, 197.
23. Ibid., V, 275.
24. Ibid., V, 361.
25. Haight, *George Eliot*, pp. 452–3.
26. Quoted Laski, *George Eliot*, p. 98.
27. *Letters*, V, 7–9.
28. Ibid., V, 37.
29. Ibid., V, 170.
30. Ibid., V, 180–1n.
31. GE, Journal, 25–8 May 1870, MS Yale.
32. Haight, *George Eliot*, p. 426.
33. Oscar Browning, *George Eliot*, p. 99.
34. F. W. H. Myers, *Century Magazine* 23 (November 1881), 62.
35. 'A College Breakfast-Party', *Collected Poems*, pp. 160–84.
36. *Letters*, V, 144.
37. GE, Journal, 27 October 1870, MS Yale.
38. Quoted Haight, *George Eliot*, p. 440n.
39. *Letters*, V, 341.
40. Ibid., V, 52.
41. Ibid., V, 367.
42. Ibid., V, 301.
43. Ibid., VIII, 482–3.
44. Haight, *George Eliot*, p. 451.
45. *Letters*, I, lxxvii.
46. Ibid., V, 132–3.
47. Ibid., IV, 404.
48. Ibid., V, 117.
49. Ibid., V, 112.
50. Ibid., V, 16.
51. GE to John Blackwood, 11 September 1869, quoted Haight, *George Eliot*, p. 420.
52. *Letters*, V, 81.
53. GE, Journal, 2 December 1870, MS Yale.
54. *Letters*, V, 124.
55. GE, Journal, 19 March 1871, MS Yale.
56. *Letters*, V, 145–6.
57. Ibid., V, 148; letter from John Blackwood to George Simpson, 4 June 1871, quoted Haight, *George Eliot*, p. 434.
58. *Letters*, V, 182.
59. Ibid., VIII, 466.
60. Ibid., IV, 392.
61. Ibid., V, 167.
62. Ibid., V, 337–8.
63. Ibid., V, 184.

64. Ibid., V, 197.
65. Ibid., V, 237.
66. Ibid., V, 246.
67. GHL, Diary, 17 February–3 March 1870, *Letters*, V, 79n.
68. *Letters*, V, 83.
69. Ibid., V, 84.
70. Ibid., V, 157.
71. GE, Journal, 31 December 1870, MS Yale; *Letters*, VIII, 482.
72. Quoted Haight, *George Eliot*, pp. 426–28.
73. *Letters*, V, 7.
74. Ibid., V, 127.
75. *Middlemarch*, Bk.1, ch.10.
76. Ibid., p. 95, Bk.1, ch.11.
77. Henry James, *Galaxy*, March 1873, *Critical Heritage*, p. 359.
78. *Letters*, V, 167.
79. Cross, *Life* (1886), I, 412.
80. *Middlemarch*, p. 149, Bk.2, ch.15.
81. Ibid., p. 264, Bk.3, ch.27.
82. Ibid., p. 587, Bk.6, ch.58.
83. Ibid., p. 278, Bk.3, ch.29.
84. *Letters*, VIII, 463.
85. *Middlemarch*, p. 838, Finale.
86. Ibid., p. 835, Finale.
87. *Daily Telegraph*, 18 June 1872, quoted Haight, *George Eliot*, p. 444.
88. Simcox, *Academy* (1 January 1873), McKenzie, p. 84.
89. *Letters*, V, 374.
90. Quoted Haight, *George Eliot*, p. 445; *Letters*, IX, 33.
91. Haight, *George Eliot*, p. 443.
92. *Letters*, V, 322.
93. Ibid., V, 125.
94. F. W. H. Myers, 'George Eliot', *Century Magazine* 23 (November 1881), p. 60.

CHAPTER 14 'Full of the World'
1. GHL, Diary, 20 March 1878. *Letters*, VII, 16.
2. *Letters*, VI, 413n.
3. Ibid., VI, 436.
4. Ibid., VI, 154–5.
5. Ibid., VI, 257–8.
6. Ibid., VI, 129n.
7. See illustration no. 32.
8. *Letters*, VI, 374.
9. Ibid., VI, 45–6.
10. Ibid., VI, 321.
11. Ibid., V, 418.
12. Ibid., VI, 192 and n.
13. Ibid., IX, 134.
14. Fanny Houghton to Isaac Evans, 28 January 1881, quoted Ashton, *George Eliot: A Life*, p. 339.
15. *Letters*, V, 403.
16. Ibid., VI, 372.
17. 'Brother and Sister' sonnets, *Collected Poems*, p. 87.
18. *Letters*, VI, 398.
19. See, for instance, the sketch of Princess Louise in which GE is wearing a mantilla, illustration no.32.
20. Quoted Laski, *George Eliot*, p. 97.
21. *Letters*, V, 469.
22. Ibid., VIII, 245.
23. See illustration no. 20.
24. *Letters*, V, 437.
25. Haight, *George Eliot*, p. 461.
26. *Letters*, V, 400n.
27. Ibid., VI, 47.
28. Ibid., VI, 161.
29. Ibid., VI, 304.
30. Ibid., VI, 165, 174.
31. Ibid., V, 442, 462.
32. For Edith Simcox's life, see K. A. McKenzie, *Edith Simcox and George Eliot* (London, 1961).
33. Simcox, *Autobiography*, 24 April 1881, quoted Haight, *George Eliot*, p. 495.
34. Ibid., 5 June 1880, quoted Haight, *George Eliot*, p. 495.
35. Ibid., 26 December 1879, *Letters*, IX, 283.

36. Ibid., 9 March 1880, McKenzie, p. 97.
37. Ibid., 18 January 1881, McKenzie, p. 102.
38. GHL, Diary, 14 December 1875, *Letters*, VI, 197–8n.
39. *Letters*, VI, 342.
40. Ibid., VI, 277, 168.
41. GHL, Diary, 23 February 1877, *Letters*, VI, 345n.
42. *Letters*, V, 461.
43. GHL, Diary, 5 September 1873, *Letters*, V, 433.
44. *Letters*, VI, 171n, Haight, *George Eliot*, p. 480.
45. GE, Journal, 11 December 1876, MS Yale.
46. *Letters*, VI, 386.
47. Ibid.
48. Ibid., V, 314.
49. Ibid., V, 427n.
50. Ibid., V, 160–1.
51. Ibid., V, 461.
52. GE, Journal, 25 December 1875, MS Yale.
53. *Letters*, VI, 76.
54. Ibid., V, 451.
55. Ibid., VI, 136.
56. Ibid., VI, 433–4.
57. Ibid., VI, 37.
58. Ibid., V, 369.
59. Ibid., V, 410–11.
60. Ibid., VI, 137.
61. Ibid., VI, 144–5.
62. Ibid., VI, 183.
63. Ibid., VI, 221–2.
64. Ibid., VI, 227.
65. Ibid., VI, 253.
66. Ibid., VI, 211–14.
67. Ibid., VI, 294.
68. Ibid., VI, 297.
69. Haight, *George Eliot*, p. 498.
70. *Letters*, VI, 295.
71. Ibid., III, 376.
72. Ibid., VII, 340–1.
73. Ibid., VI, 56n, 68n.
74. Ibid., VI, 23.
75. Ibid.
76. Ibid., V, 123n.
77. Ibid., VI, 17.
78. *Daniel Deronda*, p. 618, Bk.6, ch.45.
79. Ibid., p. 69, Bk.1, ch.4.
80. Ibid., p. 71, Bk.1, ch.4.
81. Ibid., p. 127, Bk.1, ch.9.
82. Ibid., pp. 294–5, Bk.3, ch.23.
83. *Letters*, VI, 302.
84. *Daniel Deronda.*, p. 791, Bk.8, ch.60.
85. Ibid., p. 879, Bk.8, ch.69.
86. Ibid., p. 289, Bk.3, ch.22.
87. Ibid., p. 298, Bk.3, ch.23; p. 303, Bk.3, ch.23.
88. Ibid., p. 541, Bk.5, ch.39.
89. Ibid., p. 695, Bk.7, ch.51.
90. Ibid., p. 694, Bk.7, ch.51.
91. Ibid., p. 190, Bk.2, ch.14.
92. *Letters*, VI, 275.
93. Ibid., VI, 280.

CHAPTER 15 'A Deep Sense of Change Within'

1. Cross, *Life*, III, 334.
2. GHL, Journal, 12 August 1878, *Letters*, VII, 57.
3. *Letters*, VII, 50.
4. Quoted Haight, *George Eliot*, p. 514.
5. *Letters*, VII, 78–9.
6. Ibid., VII, 84.
7. Ibid., IX, 244.
8. Ibid., V, 8.
9. Scott, *Autobiographical Notes*, II, 244.
10. Quoted Laski, *George Eliot*, p. 97.
11. Elizabeth Gaskell to George Smith, 2 November 1857, *The Letters of Mrs Gaskell*, ed. J. A. V. Chapple and Arthur Pollard (Manchester, 1966), p. 587.
12. *Letters*, VII, 87.
13. Ibid., IX, 247.

14. Quoted Haight, *George Eliot*, p. 523.
15. *Letters*, IX, 346.
16. Simcox, *Autobiography*, 12 April 1879, McKenzie, p. 96.
17. Ibid., 13 January 1879, quoted Haight, *George Eliot*, p. 516.
18. *Letters*, VII, 93.
19. Ibid., VII, 101.
20. Ibid., VII, 99.
21. Ibid., VII, 131.
22. Ibid., VII, 101–2.
23. GE, Diary, 23 February 1879, MS New York Public Library.
24. Simcox, *Autobiography*, 30 November 1878, *Letters*, IX, 243.
25. Ibid., 6 January 1878, *Letters*, IX, 256.
26. Haight, *George Eliot*, p. 516.
27. GE, Diary, 28 May 1879, MS New York Public Library.
28. *Letters*, VII, 138n.
29. Ibid., VII, 138.
30. Ibid., VII, 143n.
31. Ibid., VI, 390.
32. See William Baker, 'A New George Eliot Manuscript' in *George Eliot: Centenary Essays and an Unpublished Fragment*, ed. Anne Smith (London, 1980), pp. 11, 13.
33. *Letters*, VI, 440.
34. Ibid., VII, 78–9.
35. *Impressions of Theophrastus Such* (1879), ed. Nancy Henry (London, 1994), p. 6, I.
36. *Impressions of Theophrastus Such*, pp. 3–13, I.
37. *The Times*, 5 June 1879, p. 4d.
38. *Theophrastus Such*, pp. 143–66, XVIII.
39. Ibid., pp. 14–27, II
40. Ibid., p. 24, II.
41. *Letters*, VII, 207.
42. Ibid., VII, 217.
43. Cross, *Life*, III, 360.
44. Ibid., III, 359.
45. Henry James to Alice James, 30 January 1881, *Henry James Letters*, II, 337.
46. *Letters*, VII, 212.
47. See Laski, *George Eliot*, p. 112.
48. GE, Diary, 29 November 1879, MS New York Public Library.
49. *Letters*, VII, 235.
50. Lady Jebb, *With Dearest Love To All* (London, 1960), p. 163.
51. GE, Diary, 9 April 1880, MS Yale.
52. Ibid.
53. *Letters*, VII, 259.
54. Ibid., VII, 262–3.
55. Quoted Haight, *George Eliot*, p. 537.
56. *Letters*, VII, 269.
57. Ibid., VII, 293.
58. Quoted Haight, *George Eliot*, p. 543.
59. *Letters*, VII, 275.
60. Ibid., VII, 342.
61. Ibid., VII, 299.
62. Ibid., VII, 299.
63. Ibid., VII, 273.
64. Ibid., VII, 233.
65. Ibid., VII, 289.
66. Ibid., VII, 295–6.
67. Ibid., VII, 280.
68. Ibid., VII, 287.
69. Ibid., VII, 286.
70. Ibid., VII, 210, 296.
71. Ibid., VII, 292.
72. Simcox, *Autobiography*, 12 July 1880, *Letters*, IX, 314.
73. Ibid., 16 April 1882, McKenzie, p. 122.
74. Cross, *Life*, III, 407–8.
75. *Letters*, VII, 276.
76. Lady Jebb, *With Dearest Love To All*, pp. 163–4.
77. *Letters*, VII, 341–2.
78. Simcox, *Autobiography*, 23 December 1880, *Letters*, IX, 321.

79. *Letters*, VI, 351.
80. Quoted Haight, *George Eliot*, p. 548.

Epilogue
1. *Letters*, I, xiv.
2. *Athenaeum*, No. 3031, 28 November 1885, 702.
3. Baker, 'A New George Eliot Manuscript', pp. 11–13.

Select Bibliography

1. Manuscript Sources

The main manuscript sources for George Eliot (GE) and G. H. Lewes (GHL) are held at the Beinecke Rare Book and Manuscript Library of Yale University. In addition, GE's 1879 Diary is held at the New York Public Library. However, nearly all the letters have now appeared in print, either in *The George Eliot Letters*, 9 vols, ed. Gordon S. Haight (New Haven, 1954–78), or have been extensively quoted in the secondary literature which has appeared subsequently. Likewise the manuscript diaries and journals have been heavily extracted in Haight's *George Eliot Letters*.

Robert Evans's correspondence with his employer, Francis Newdigate, is held at the Warwickshire County Record Office (WCRO). The MS diary 'Occurrences at Nuneaton' 1810–45, writer unknown, is held at Nuneaton Public Library.

2. Works by George Eliot

Adam Bede (1859), ed. Stephen Gill (Harmondsworth, 1980).
Brother Jacob (1864), ed. Peter Mudford (London, 1996).
Collected Poems, ed. Lucien Jenkins (London, 1989).
Daniel Deronda (1876), ed. Barbara Hardy (Harmondsworth, 1967).
Essays of George Eliot, ed. Thomas Pinney (New York, 1963).
Essays and Leaves from a Note-Book By George Eliot (London, 1883).
(trans.) *The Essence of Christianity* by Ludwig Feuerbach (London, 1854).
(trans.) *Ethics* by Benedict de Spinoza, ed. Thomas Deegan (Salzburg, 1981).
Felix Holt, The Radical (1866), ed. Peter Coveney (Harmondsworth, 1972).
George Eliot: A Writer's Notebook 1854–79, and Uncollected Writings, ed. Joseph Wiesenfarth (Charlottesville, Virginia, 1981).
George Eliot, Selected Critical Writings, ed. Rosemary Ashton (Oxford, 1992).
George Eliot: Selected Essays, Poems and Other Writings, ed. A. S. Byatt and Nicholas Warren (Harmondsworth, 1990).
Impressions of Theophrastus Such (1879), ed. Nancy Henry (London, 1994).
(trans.) *The Life of Jesus, Critically Examined* by David Friedrich Strauss, 3 vols. (London, 1846).
The Lifted Veil (1859), ed. Peter Mudford (London, 1996).

Middlemarch (1871–2), ed. Rosemary Ashton (Harmondsworth, 1994).
The Mill on the Floss (1860), ed. A. S. Byatt (Harmondsworth, 1979).
Romola (1863), ed. Andrew Sanders (Harmondsworth, 1980).
Scenes of Clerical Life (1858), ed. David Lodge (Harmondsworth, 1973).
Silas Marner (1861), ed. Q. D. Leavis (Harmondsworth, 1967).

The most reliable collected edition of GE's works is the Cabinet Edition, published by William Blackwood and Sons, 20 vols, 1878–80, which she corrected herself before her death.

3. Books and Articles
Acton, Lord, 'George Eliot's "Life"', *Nineteenth Century* 17 (March 1885).
Adams, Ian, *This Particular Web* (Toronto, 1975).
Adams, Kathleen, *Those of Us Who Loved Her: The Men in George Eliot's Life* (Warwick, 1980).
Anderson, Nancy Fix, *Women Against Women in Victorian England: A Life of Eliza Lynn Linton* (Bloomington, Indiana, 1987).
Ashton, Rosemary, *G. H. Lewes: A Life* (Oxford, 1991).
——*George Eliot: A Life* (London, 1996).
——*George Eliot* (Oxford, 1983).
——'New George Eliot Letters at the Huntington', *Huntington Library Quarterly*, LIV (Spring 1991).
Baker, William, *George Eliot and Judaism* (Salzburg, 1975).
——*The George Eliot–George Henry Lewes Library: An Annotated Catalogue of Their Books at Dr Williams's Library, London* (London, 1977).
——'A New George Eliot Manuscript', *George Eliot: Centenary Essays and an Unpublished Fragment*, ed. Anne Smith (London, 1980).
Barrett, Dorothea, *Vocation and Desire, George Eliot's Heroines* (London, 1989).
Beer, Gillian, *Darwin's Plots: Evolutionary Narrative in Darwin, George Eliot and Nineteenth-Century Fiction* (London, 1983).
——*George Eliot* (Brighton, 1986).
Belloc, Bessie Rayner Parkes, *In a Walled Garden* (London, 1895).
Blind, Mathilde, *George Eliot* (London, 1883).
Bodenheimer, Rosemarie, *The Real Life of Mary Ann Evans: George Eliot, Her Letters and Fiction* (Ithaca, 1994).
Bonaparte, Felicia, *The Triptych and the Cross* (Brighton, 1979).
Brady, Kristin, *George Eliot* (London, 1992).
Bray, Charles, *Phases of Opinion and Experience during a Long Life* (London, 1884).
——*The Philosophy of Necessity*, 2 vols (London, 1841).
Browning, Oscar, *Life of George Eliot* (London, 1890).
Carlyle, Jane Welsh, *Letters to Her Family, 1839–63*, ed. Leonard Huxley (London, 1924).
Carroll, David, *George Eliot and the Conflict of Interpretations* (Cambridge, 1992).

——(ed.), *George Eliot: The Critical Heritage* (London, 1977).

Cross, J. W., *George Eliot's Life as Related in Her Letters and Journals*, 3 vols (Edinburgh and London, 1885; reprinted with additions, 1886).

Darwin, Charles, *Origin of Species* (London, 1859).

David, Deidre, *Intellectual Women and Victorian Patriarchy: Harriet Martineau, Elizabeth Barrett Browning, George Eliot* (London, 1987).

Dentith, Simon, *George Eliot* (Brighton, 1986).

Dodd, Valerie A., *George Eliot: An Intellectual Life* (London, 1990).

Faderman, Lillian, *Surpassing the Love of Men: Romantic Friendship and Love Between Women from the Renaissance to the Present* (New York, 1981).

Fisher, Philip, *Making Up Society: The Novels of George Eliot* (London, 1981).

Froude, J. A., *The Nemesis of Faith* (London, 1849, reprinted with an introduction by Rosemary Ashton, 1988).

Gaskell, Elizabeth, *The Letters of Mrs Gaskell*, ed. J. A. V. Chapple and Arthur Pollard (Manchester, 1966).

Graver, Suzanne, *George Eliot and Community: A Study in Social Theory and Fictional Form* (Berkeley, 1984).

Haight, Gordon S. (ed.), *A Century of George Eliot Criticism* (London, 1966).

——*George Eliot: A Biography* (Oxford, 1968; Harmondsworth, 1992).

——*George Eliot and John Chapman* (London, 1940).

——'George Eliot's Bastards', *George Eliot: A Centenary Tribute*, ed. Gordon S. Haight and Rosemary T. VanArsdel (London, 1982).

Handley, Graham, *George Eliot: A Guide through the Critical Maze* (Bristol, 1990).

Hands, Timothy, *A George Eliot Chronology* (London, 1989).

Hardy, Barbara (ed.), *Critical Essays on George Eliot* (London, 1970).

——*The Novels of George Eliot: A Study in Form* (London, 1959).

——*Particularities* (London, 1982).

Hennell, Charles C., *An Inquiry Concerning the Origin of Christianity* (London, 1838, 2nd edition 1841).

Hirsch, Pam, *Barbara Leigh Smith Bodichon* (London, 1998).

Hutchinson, Stuart (ed.), *George Eliot: Critical Assessments* (London, 1996).

James, Henry, *Letters of Henry James*, ed. Leon Edel, 4 vols (London 1974–84).

Jay, Elisabeth, *Mrs Oliphant: A Fiction to Herself* (Oxford, 1995).

Karl, Frederick, *George Eliot: A Biography* (London, 1995).

Kitchel, Anna, *George Lewes and George Eliot* (New York, 1933).

Knoepflmacher, U. C., *George Eliot's Early Novels: The Limits of Realism* (Berkeley, 1968).

Laski, Marghanita, *George Eliot and Her World* (London, 1973, reprinted 1978).

Layard, George Somes, *The Life of Mrs Lynn Linton* (London, 1901).

Leavis, F. R., *The Great Tradition* (London, 1948).

Levine, George, with the assistance of Patricia O'Hara, *An Annotated Critical Bibliography of George Eliot* (Brighton, 1988).

Lewes, George Henry, *A Biographical History of Philosophy*, 4 vols (London, 1845–6).

——*The Letters of George Henry Lewes*, ed. William Baker, 2 vols (Victoria, British Columbia, 1995).

——*The Life and Works of Goethe*, 2 vols (London, 1855).

——*The Physiology of Common Life*, 2 vols (London, 1859–60).

——*Problems of Life and Mind*, 5 vols (London, 1874–9).

Linton, Eliza Lynn, *The Autobiography of Christopher Kirkland*, 3 vols (London, 1885).

——*My Literary Life* (London, 1899).

Lowndes, Susan (ed.), *Diaries and Letters of Marie Belloc Lowndes 1911–1947* (London, 1971).

——*I, Too, Have Lived in Arcadia* (London, 1941).

McKenzie, K. A., *Edith Simcox and George Eliot* (Oxford, 1961).

McSweeney, Kerry, *George Eliot: A Literary Life* (London, 1991).

Martin, Carol A., *George Eliot's Serial Fiction* (Columbus, Ohio, 1994).

Martineau, Harriet, *Autobiography*, 2 vols. (London, 1877).

Mintz, Alan, *George Eliot & the Novel of Vocation* (London, 1978).

Mottram, William, *The True Story of George Eliot in Relation to 'Adam Bede'* (London, 1905).

Myers, F. W. H., *Essays*, 2 vols. (London, 1883).

Myers, William, *The Teaching of George Eliot* (Leicester, 1984).

Nestor, Pauline, *Female Friendships and Communities* (London, 1985).

Newdigate–Newdegate, Lady, *The Cheverels of Cheverel Manor* (London, 1898).

Newton, K. M., *George Eliot, Romantic Humanist: A Study of the Philosophical Structure of Her Novels* (1981).

Oliphant, Margaret, *Autobiography and Letters*, ed. Mrs Haley Coghill (Edinburgh, 1899).

Parkinson, S., *Scenes from the 'George Eliot' Country* (Leeds, 1888).

Paxton, Nancy L., *George Eliot and Herbert Spencer: Feminism, Evolutionism, and the Reconstruction of Gender* (Oxford, 1991).

Purkis, John, *A Preface to George Eliot* (London, 1985).

Redinger, Ruby, *George Eliot: The Emergent Self* (London, 1976).

Rose, Phyllis, *Parallel Lives: Five Victorian Marriages* (London, 1984).

Scott, William Bell, *Autobiographical Notes*, ed. W. Minto, 2 vols. (London, 1892).

Shuttleworth, Sally, *George Eliot and Nineteenth-Century Science* (Cambridge, 1984).

Smith, Anne, ed., *George Eliot: Centenary Essays and an Unpublished Fragment*, ed. Anne Smith (London, 1980).

Spencer, Herbert, *An Autobiography*, 2 vols. (London, 1904).

——*The Life and Letters of Herbert Spencer*, ed. David Duncan (London, 1908).

Spittles, Brian, *George Eliot: Godless Woman* (London, 1993).

Stephen, Leslie, *George Eliot* (London, 1902).

Sutherland, John, *Victorian Fiction: Writers, Publishers, Readers* (London, 1995).

Taylor, Ina, *George Eliot: Woman of Contradictions* (London, 1989).

Trollope, Thomas Adolphus, *What I Remember*, 2 vols. (London, 1887).

Uglow, Jennifer, *George Eliot* (London, 1987).

Ward, Mrs Humphrey, *A Writer's Recollections*, 2 vols. (London, 1918).

Webb, R. K., *Harriet Martineau: A Radical Victorian* (London, 1960).

White, William Hale, *The Autobiography of Mark Rutherford* (London, 1881, reprinted 1988).

Witemeyer, Hugh, *George Eliot and the Visual Arts* (London, 1979).

Wright, T. R., *The Religion of Humanity: The Impact of Comtean Positivism on Victorian Britain* (Cambridge 1986).

Index